Practical C#

Charts and Graphics

Advanced Chart and Graphics Programming
for Real-World .NET Applications

Practical C#
Charts and Graphics

Advanced Chart and Graphics Programming
for Real-World .NET Applications

Jack Xu, Ph.D

UniCAD Publishing

Practical C# Charts and Graphics

Editor: Anna Y. Hsu

The author and publisher have made every effort in the preparation of this book to ensure the accuracy of the information, however this book is sold without warranty, either express or implied. No liability is assumed for incidental or consequential damages in connection with or arising out of the use of the information or programs contained in the book.

The publisher offers excellent discounts on this book when ordered in quantity for bulk purchases or special sales, which may include electronic versions and /or custom covers and content particular to your business, training goals, marketing focus, and branding interests. For more information, please contact:

sales.publishing@unicadinc.com
Visit us on the Website: http://publishing.unicadinc.com

Published by UniCAD Publishing.
Phoenix, USA
ISBN 978-0-9793725-0-6

Publisher's Cataloging-in-Publication Data

Xu, Jack.
Practical C# Charts and Graphics – Advanced Chart and Graphics Programming for Real-World .NET Applications / Jack Xu.
– 1st ed.
p.cm.
ISBN 978-0-9793725-0-6

1. C# programming. 2. Charts and Graphics. 3. .NET Application
I. Title. II. Title III Title: Practical C# Charts and Graphics

Contents

6 3D Charts..279

Introduction

Overview

Welcome to *Practical C# Charts and Graphics*. This book is intended for C# .NET developers who want to add professional graphics and charts to their applications. My hope is to write the ultimate C# chart and graphics programming guide that would be useful to C# application programmers of all skill levels.

We've all heard the saying "a picture's worth a thousand words". Creating charts and graphics plays a very important role in every Windows application. Charts and graphics can make data easier to understand, can make a report more interesting to read, and can have wide applications in our daily life. For instance, in the scientific, engineering, and mathematics community, there is always a need for presenting data and results graphically. Microsoft's visual C# programming language is one of the few and best development tools available for providing both the computational capabilities of generating data as a simulation engine and displaying it in a variety of graphical representations based on its Graphical Device Interface (GDI+).

The power of the C# programming language, combined with the simplicity of implementing Windows Form applications in Visual Studio .NET, makes real-world Windows program development faster and easier than ever before. Visual C# is a versatile and flexible tool which allows users with even the most elementary programming abilities to produce sophisticated charts, graphics, and graphical user interfaces (GUIs). The level of complexity and sophistication of the graphics and charting applications is limited only by your needs, curiosity, and imagination.

As you may have already noticed, most bookstores offer hundreds of C# programming books. The vast majority of these books are general-purpose user guides and tutorials that explain the basics of the C# tool and how to use it to implement simple C# applications. Some of these books contain a chapter or two that cover graphics and charts. None, however, provide the level of detail that you will find in this book.

This book is written with the intent of providing you with a complete and comprehensive explanation about the C# graphics and chart capability, and pays special attention on how to create various charts that can be directly used in your real world C# Applications. Much of this book contains original work based on my own programming experience while developing commercial Computer Aided Design (CAD) packages. Without C# and .NET framework, development of advanced graphics and charts is a difficult and time-consuming task. To add even simple charts or graphs to your applications, you have to waste effort creating a chart program, or buy commercial graphics and chart add-on packages.

Using third-party graphics and chart add-on products in your applications has several drawbacks, however:

- It isn't cost effective – it might cost hundreds or thousands of dollars for a sophisticated graphics and chart package.

- Compatibility is an issue – these third-party graphics and chart add-on tools are usually provided as DLL or COM components, which often leads to unexpected interface exceptions and unstable operations.

- There is little flexibility – from users' point of view, these packages seem to be black boxes because the source code was not provided usually, making hard for users to add or modify any functionality to them. You may often find that these third-party products lack the special features that you want to use in your applications, even though these products usually provide mamy other functionalities that you will never use.

- The coding is inefficient – these third-party add-on tools are often very large packages that contain far more functionalities than you need in your applications. Even for a simple program, the final release tends to be huge due to the use of third party add-ons. This is very inefficient for both coding management and distribution.

- License royalty is another issue – some third-party add-ons require not only the developing license, but also the distributed license royalty, resulting in an unnecessary increase of the development cost.

- Finally, maintenance is a problem – in most cases, third-party tools use different programming language than the one you use in developing your applications, so you have to maintain the codes in an unmanaged manner.

Visual C# and its powerful GDI+ class make it possible to easily implement your own professional graphics and chart package entirely using managed C# codes. However, Visual C# provides no tools for creating three-dimensional (3D) graphics objects. Even a 3D point, the simplest 3D graphics object, must be defined first in a suitable 3D coordinate system before it can be used as a 3D graphics object.

Practical C# Charts and Graphics provides everything you need to create advanced charts and graphics in your .NET applications. In this book I will show you how to create a variety of graphics and charts that range from simple two-dimensional (2D) X-Y plots to complicated three-dimensional (3D) surface graphs using managed C# code. I try my best to introduce readers to the C# graphics program in a simple way – simple enough to be easily followed by C# beginners who have never had experience in developing C# graphics and chart applications. You can learn from this book how to create a full range of color graphics applications and how to use C# controls to create impressive graphic and chart effects without having to buy expensive third-party add-on products.

Practical C# Charts and Graphics is not just a book, but a powerful 2D and 3D chart and graphics package. You may find that some of the examples in this book can be immediately used in your real-world problems, and that some may give you inspiration to add advanced graphical and sophisticated chart capabilities to your applications.

What this Book includes

This book and and its sample code listings, which are available for download from our website at www.publishing.unicadinc.com, provide you with:

- A complete, in-depth instruction to practical chart and graphics programming in visual C# and GDI+. After reading this book and running the example programs, you will be able to create various sophisticated charts and graphics in your C# applications.

- Ready-to-run example programs that allow you to explore the chart and graphics techniques described in the book. You can use these examples to get a better understanding of how the chart and graphics algorithms work. You can also modify the code or add new features to them to form the basis of your own programs. Some of the example code listings provided with this book are already sophisticated chart and graphics packages, and can be directly used in your own real-world applications.

- Many C# classes in the sample code listings that you will find useful in your chart and graphics programming. These classes contain matrix manipulation, coordinate transformation, color maps, 2D and 3D chart user controls, as well as the other useful utility classes. You can extract these classes and plug them into your applications.

- A chapter that contains a detailed discussion on how to integrate Microsoft Excel chart functionality into C# applications. This chapter is designed specifically for readers who prefer not to create C# chart programs from scratch, and would like to take advantage of Microsoft Excel's wide selection of chart types.

Is This Book for You?

You don't have to be an experienced C# developer or expert to use this book. I designed this book to be useful to people of all levels of C# programming experience. In fact, I believe if you have some experience with programming languages other than C#, you will be able to sit down in front of your computer, start up Microsoft Visual Studio .NET and C#, follow the examples that are provided with this book, and quickly become familiar with C# graphics programming. For those of you who are already experienced C# developers, I believe this book has a lot to offer you as well. There is much information in this book about graphics and chart programming that is not available in any other C# tutorial and reference book. In addition, most of the example programs provided with this book can be directly used in your real-world application development. This book will provide you with a level of detail, explanation, instruction, and sample program code that will enable you to do just about anything that is graphics and charts related using visual C#.

Perhaps you are a scientist, engineer, mathematician, student, or teacher instead of a professional programmer, this book is still a good bet for you. In fact, my own background is in theoretical physics, a field involving extensive numerical calculations, as well as graphical and charting representations of calculated data. I had dedicated my effort to this field for many years, starting from undergraduate up to Ph.D. My first computer experience was with FORTRAN. Later on, I had programming experience with Basic, C, C++, and MATLAB. I still remember how hard it was in the early days to present computational results graphically. I often spent hours creating a publication-quality chart by hand, using a ruler, graph paper, and rub-off lettering. A year later, our group bought a graphics and chart package. However, I still needed to prepare my data in a proper format in order to process the data with this package. During that time, I started paying attention to various development tools that could be used to create integrated applications. I tried to find an ideal development tool that would allow me not only to easily generate data (computation capability) but also to easily represent data graphically (graphics and chart power). The C# and Microsoft Visual Studio .NET development environment made it possible to develop such integrated applications. Ever since Microsoft .NET 1.0 came out, I have been in love with the C# language, and have been able to use this tool to successfully create powerful graphics and chart applications, including commercial CAD packages.

The majority of the example programs in this book can be routinely used by C# developers and technical professionals. Throughout this book, I will emphasize the *usefulness* of C# chart and graphics programming to real-world applications. If you follow this book closely, you will be able to easily develop various practical graphics and chart applications from simple 2D x-y plots to sophisticated 4D slice graphs. At the same time, I will not spend too much time discussing program style, execution speed, and code optimization, because there is a plethora of books out there already dealing with those topics. Most of the example programs in this book omit error handlings. This makes the code easier to understand by focusing on the key concepts.

What Do You Need to Use This Book?

To make the best use of this book and understand the algorithm, you will need no special equipment. To run and modify the sample programs, you need a computer that is capable of running Windows 2000 or Windows XP operating system. The software installed on your computer should include Visual Studio .NET (or Visual C# .NET) standard edition or higher. If you want to run the samples included in Chapter 9, you also need Microsoft Excel installed on your computer.

All of the example programs in this book were created and tested in the professional version of Visual Studio .NET 2005 and Microsoft Excel 2002 (which is part of Microsoft Office XP) under Windows XP. They should run something with little or no modification in other operating systems and with other versions of Visual Studio .NET and Excel.

How This Book Is Organized

This book is organized into nine chapters, each of which focuses on a different topic about creating C# graphics and chart solutions. The following summaries of each chapter will give you an overview of this book's contents:

Chapter 1, *C# Graphics Basics*

This chapter reviews some of the fundamental aspects of C# graphics programming. If you are an experienced C# programmer, some of this material may already be familiar to you. It includes discussions of various coordinate systems; basic graphics shapes in the GDI+ class, the color system, and advanced custom color maps used in C# applications.

Chapter 2, 2D *Matrices and Transformations*

This chapter covers mathematical basics for 2D graphics programming. 2D matrices and transformations in homogeneous space are discussed, including translation, scaling, reflection, and rotation. These 2D matrices and transformations allow a C# application to perform a wide variety of graphical operations on graphics objects in a simple and consistent manner.

Chapter 3, *2D Line Charts*

This chapter contains instructions on how to create elementary 2D X-Y line charts. It introduces basic chart elements including chart area, plot area, axes, title, labels, ticks, symbols, legend, etc. These basic chart elements are common in the other types of charts, as well.

Chapter 4, *Specialized 2D Charts*

This chapter covers the specialized charts that are often found in commercial chart packages and spreadsheet applications. These specialized charts include bar charts, stair-step charts, stem charts, charts with error bars, pie charts, area charts, polar charts, as well as stock charts.

Chapter 5, 3D *Matrices and Transformations*

This chapter extends the concepts described in Chapter 2 into the third dimension. It explains how to define 3D graphics objects, and how to translate, scale, reflect, and rotate these 3D objects. It also describes the transformation matrices that represent projections and transformations that allow you to view 3D graphics objects on a 2D screen. Unlike 2D, there is no 3D matrix class defined in C# and GDI+. This chapter includes instructions on how to create these 3D transformation matrices with C#.

Chapter 6, *3D Charts*

This extensive chapter begins with a description of the coordinate system that is used in 3D charts and graphics, and shows you how to create the 3D coordinate axes, tick marks, axis labels, and grid lines. It then explains techniques on how to create a wide variety of 3D charts that include 3D line charts, 3D mesh and surface charts, contour charts, 3D bar charts, 4D slice charts, and 3D combination charts. In creating these charts, a few specialized techniques, including Z-order, are used to manipulate the data displayed on your 2D computer screen.

Chapter 7, *Charts and User Controls*

This chapter shows you how to put 2D and 3D chart applications into a custom user control, and how to use such a control in your C# applications. It begins by explaining the basics of the custom user controls in a C# Windows application, including how to provide the design-time support to the controls. Then, it describes the detailed procedure for creating the custom user controls for 2D and 3D chart applications, and demonstrates how to use these controls in real-world C# applications.

Chapter 8, *DataGridView and Chart User Controls*

This chapter consists of a discussion on the basics of the `DataGridView` and the possibility of combining it with the chart controls to create spreadsheet-like chart applications. It shows how to implement spreadsheet-like interface in which the data is displayed in the `DataGridView` control; the displayed data in the `DataGridView` is plotted in the chart user controls; and the direct interaction is allowed between the `DataGridView` and the Chart controls.

Chapter 9, *Excel Charts in C# Applications*

This chapter explains how a Microsoft Excel chart can be embedded into a C# application. It shows how to implement charts and graphics in C# projects by taking advantage of the Excel's chart and graphics features.

What Is Left Out

This book provides an in-depth description of C# chart and graphics programming for real-world .NET applications. The background material about the C# graphics was selected for inclusion in the book specifically according to the need for creating C# chart applications. It does not cover image processing, such as the technique for manipulating bitmapped images and image animation. Advanced ray traced images that display reflective, shadowed, transparent, and textured objects are beyond the scope of this book and are not addressed.

Conventions

This book uses a number of different styles of text and layout to help differentiate between different kinds of information. These conventions include

Italic: used for names of directories and files, options, emphasis, and names of examples.

`Constant width`: used for code listings and code items such as commands, options, variables, attributes, functions, types, classes, namespaces, methods, properties, parameters, values, objects, event handlers, contents of files, and the output from commands.

Using Code Examples

You may use the code in this book in your applications and documentation. You do not need to contact me or the publisher for permission unless you are reproducing a significant portion of the code. For example, writing a program that uses several chunks of code from this book does not require permission. Selling or distributing the example code listings does require permission. Incorporating a significant amount of example code from this book into your applications and documentation does require permission. Integrating the example code from this book into your commercial products is not allowed without the written permission from the author and publisher.

Customer Support

I am always interested in hearing from readers, and want to know what you think about this book. You can send me your comments by e-mail to support.publishing@unicadinc.com. I also provide updates, bug fixes, and ongoing support through the publisher's web site:

> http://publishing.unicadinc.com

You can obtain the source code for all of the examples in this book from this web site.

1

C# Graphics Basics

Visual C# provides all of the tools you need to create any type of graphics and charts. It supplies a GDI+ class library interface that allows users to draw various graphics objects, including text, lines, rectangles, circles, ellipses, polygons, and a host of other graphical shapes. This chapter begins by describing graphics coordinate systems used in Visual C#, and shows you several different coordinate systems you can use to make graphics programming easier. Then it will discuss two basic drawing objects, *Pen* and *Brush,* that are used to draw basic graphics shapes and fill enclosed surface with patterns, colors, or bitmaps. It will show you how to use `Pen` and `Brush` to create basic graphics shapes. Finally, it will explain the color system used in C# and discuss how to define the custom color map and shading.

Coordinate Systems

When creating a graphic object, you must determine where the graphic object or drawing will be displayed. To do that, you need to understand how Visual C# measures graphic object coordinates. Each point on a Window Form or a control has an X and a Y coordinate. In the following sections, we will discuss various coordinate systems and their relationships.

Default Coordinates

Visual C# and GDI+ graphics library have three default coordinate systems in 2D space: world, page, and device. World coordinates are the coordinates used to model a particular graphic world and are the coordinates you pass to methods in C#. Page coordinates refer to the coordinate system used by a drawing surface, such as a form or control. Device coordinates are the coordinates used by the physical device being drawn on, such as a screen or sheet of paper. When you ask C# to draw a line from point (`x1, y1`) to point (`x2, y2`), this points are in the world coordinate system. The unit used to measure the distance in the world coordinate system can be defined according to your applications.

It should be noted that you can not directly draw the graphics object in world coordinate system on you computer screen. Before drawing a graphics object on the screen, the coordinates must go through a sequence of transformations. One transformation, called the world transformation, converts world coordinates to page coordinates, and another transformation, called the page transformation, converts page coordinates to device coordinates.

By default, the origin of all three coordinate systems is at point (0, 0), which is located at the upper left corner of the drawing area. The X coordinate represents the distance from the left edge of the drawing area to the point, and the Y coordinate represents the distance from the top edge of the drawing area to the point. Figure 1-1 shows how the X and Y coordinates of a point relate to the drawing area.

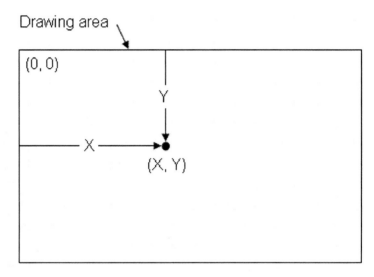

Figure 1-1 Default C# coordinate system.

The default unit for all three of these coordinate systems is pixels. The coordinate system can be customized by shifting the origin to another location in the client area, and by setting a different unit of measure.

Let's look at an example to see how this can be achieved. Start with Microsoft Visual Studio .NET 2005 and select **File | New | Project** to create a new Windows Application under C# projects. Name the project *Example1_1*. Now a Windows Form called Form1 is created within the Visual Studio .NET Integrated Development Environment (IDE). We want Form1 to have a redraw function, which can be achieved by overriding Form1's OnPaint method. We will first draw a line from Point (0, 0) to Point (1, 1), with units of inches. The following is the Form1.cs code listing that will accomlish this:

```
using System;
using System.Drawing;
using System.Windows.Forms;
```

```
namespace Example1_1
{
    public partial class Form1 : Form
    {
        public Form1()
        {
            InitializeComponent();
            this.SetStyle(ControlStyles.ResizeRedraw, true);
            this.BackColor = Color.White;
        }

        protected override void OnPaint(PaintEventArgs e)
        {
            Graphics g = e.Graphics;
            // Following codes draw a line from (0, 0) to (1, 1) in unit of inch:
            g.PageUnit = GraphicsUnit.Inch;
            Pen blackPen = new Pen(Color.Black, 1 / g.DpiX);
            g.DrawLine(blackPen, 0, 0, 1, 1);
        }
    }
}
```

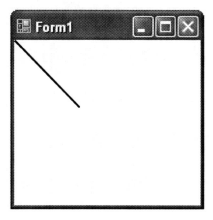

Figure 1-2 Draw a line from (0, 0) to (1, 1).

The resulting graphics is shown in Figure 1-2. From the code listing of the Form1 class, it can be seen that the PageUnit property was set to GraphicsUnit.Inch, specifying that the unit of measure is an inch. Then a Pen object was created and its width set to 1 / g.Dpix. The DpiX property of the Graphics class indicates a value, in dots per inch, for the horizontal resolution supported by this Graphics object. This is necessary because the current PageUnit settings will affect the way a pen draws so that a pen of unit width will draw a one pixel, one millimeter, one point, one inch, or one 1300th of an inch thick line, depending on the way the Graphics object is set up. So, if the pen width is not set like this, a one inck thick line would be drawn. Next, we drew a line with one unit measure, which in this case is one inch long. Also note that we have set ControlStyles.ResizeRedraw to true inside Form1 constructor, making sure everything in the Form1 gets redrawn when the form is resized.

Ensuring that the Pen draws a line with a specific thickness is not always straightforward. One trick that you can use is to set the line width to any negative value that works for single pixel lines. However, to get lines with a specific thickness (say 5 pixels), the only reliable method is to scale the pen by DpiX.

Let's now move the origin to the centre of the client area and draw the line again. This can be done by changing the OnPaint method of *Example1_1* to the following:

```
protected override void OnPaint(PaintEventArgs e)
{
    Graphics g = e.Graphics;
    // Following codes shift the origin to the center of the client area, and
    // then draw a line from (0,0) to (1,1):
    g.PageUnit = GraphicsUnit.Inch;
    g.TranslateTransform((ClientRectangle.Width / g.DpiX) / 2,
        (ClientRectangle.Height / g.DpiY) / 2);
    Pen greenPen = new Pen(Color.Green, 1 / g.DpiX);
    g.DrawLine(greenPen, 0, 0, 1, 1);
}
```

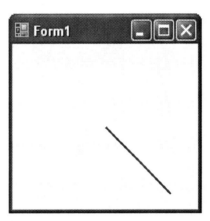

Figure 1-3 Draw a line from point (0, 0) to point (1, 1) with origin at the
center of the client area.

This produces results of Figure 1-3. Here, after setting the unit to inches using the PageUnit property, the TranslateTransform method was called to shift the origin to the centre of the client area. Because this method maps the world coordinates to page coordinates, the transformation is called a world transformation. The X and Y values in the world coordinate system passed to the TranslateTransform method get added to every X and Y value we pass to the Graphics methods. The units of world coordinates are the same as that of the page coordinates, but the origin of both the page and device coordinate systems is still at the upper-left corner of the drawing area. The line coordinates in these two coordinate systems depends on the size of the ClientRectangle size (in this case, the Form1's client area). In this example, the size of the ClientRectangle is (292, 266). The end points of the line in three coordinate systems are as follows:

World	(0,0) to (1, 1)	Unit: inch
Device	(146, 133) to (242, 229)	Unit: pixel
Page	(1.52, 1.39) to (2.52, 2.25)	Unit: inch

You can see the difference between page and device coordinate systems. Device coordinates determine what you actually see on your screen and usually in unit of pixels. The PageUnit property of the Graphics class is a type of GraphicsUnit enumeration. You can easily specify a page-unit setting of inches, millimeters, or points, but this setting applies to everything, including Pen and Brush objects. This means that if you don't pay attention to the scaling, the graphics you created might end up looking weird.

To draw a shape or fill an area specified in a real-world measuring system with a Pen or Brush of the desired appearance is simply a matter of scaling the Pen or Brush to the reciprocal of the page settings. For inches, this is simple enough and can be accomplished with the DpiX and DpiY properties, namely 1/g.DpiX for the X direction and 1/g.DpiY for the Y direction. In this way, you can draw a line with a pixel width of one unit. To draw a line with arbitrary width, such as 5 pixels, you just specify a Pen with a width of 5/g.DpiX.

However, things become complicated for other measuring units such as millimeters or points. In this case, you must know the relationship between the unit of measure you are using and inches, because the Graphics class only provides DpiX and DpiY properties to convent inches to pixels. For example, there are 25.40 millimeters in an inch and 72 points in an inch. Other more abstract units such as Display and Document can be catered to easily as well. The following method can be used to calculate the reciprocal ratios for all standard PageUnit settings given a specific Graphics object g:

```
public Pen UnitScaling(Graphics g)
{
    switch (g.PageUnit)
    {
        case GraphicsUnit.Pixel:
            return new Pen(Color.Black, 1f);
        case GraphicsUnit.Inch:
            return new Pen(Color.Black, 1f/g.DpiX);
        case GraphicsUnit.Millimeter:
            return new Pen(Color.Black, 25.4f / g.DpiX);
        case GraphicsUnit.Point:
            return new Pen(72f / g.DpiX);
        case GraphicsUnit.Display:
            return new Pen(75f / g.DpiX);
        case GraphicsUnit.Document:
            return new Pen(300f / g.DpiX);
    }
}
```

You can use the above code to specify a Pen with a width of one pixel in any page unit.

Custom Coordinates

In addition to the standard coordinate systems discussed in the previous section, an application can define its own coordinate system. In this book, we will use a custom coordinate system for 2D chart and graphics applications. This coordinate system is independent of the unit of your real-world graphics objects, and its Y-axis points from bottom to top as it does in most chart applications. In this system, the page coordinate system is identical to the device system, and the unit for both systems is in pixels. This customized coordinate system is illustrated in Figure 1-4.

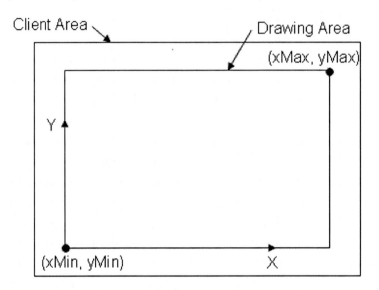

Figure 1-4 Custom coordinate system to be used in this book.

Inside the Client Area, a drawing area is defined with an offset margin. The conventional X-Y coordinate system can be defined within the drawing area. Here we will demonstrate how to achieve this with C#.

Create a new Visual C# Windows Application project, and name it *Example1-2*. The following is the code listing of Form1.cs:

```
using System;
using System.Drawing;
using System.Windows.Forms;

namespace Example1_2
{
    public partial class Form1 : Form
    {
        // Define the drawing area
        private Rectangle PlotArea;
        // Unit defined in world coordinate system:
        private float xMin = 0f;
        private float xMax = 10f;
```

```csharp
            private float yMin = 0f;
            private float yMax = 10f;

            // Define the offset in pixel:
            private int offset = 30;

            public Form1()
            {
                InitializeComponent();
                this.SetStyle(ControlStyles.ResizeRedraw, true);
                this.BackColor = Color.White;
            }

            protected override void OnPaint(PaintEventArgs e)
            {
                Graphics g = e.Graphics;

                // Calculate the location and size of the drawing area
                // within which we want to draw the graphics:
                Rectangle rect = ClientRectangle;
                PlotArea = new Rectangle(rect.Location, rect.Size);
                PlotArea.Inflate(-offset, -offset);
                //Draw ClientRectangle and PlotArea using Pen:
                g.DrawRectangle(Pens.Red, rect);
                g.DrawRectangle(Pens.Black, PlotArea);
                // Draw a line from point (3,2) to Point (6, 7)
                // using a Pen with a width of 3 pixels:
                Pen aPen = new Pen(Color.Green, 3);
                g.DrawLine(aPen, Point2D(new PointF(3, 2)), Point2D(new PointF(6, 7)));
                aPen.Dispose();
                g.Dispose();
            }

            private PointF Point2D(PointF ptf)
            {
                PointF aPoint = new PointF();
                aPoint.X = PlotArea.X + (ptf.X - xMin) *
                    PlotArea.Width / (xMax - xMin);
                aPoint.Y = PlotArea.Bottom - (ptf.Y - yMin) *
                    PlotArea.Height / (yMax - yMin);
                return aPoint;
            }
        }
    }
```

In this example, we begin by creating member fields to hold the minimum and maximum values of the custom coordinate axes, as well as a PlotArea member that represents the size of the drawing area. Please note that by changing the values of xMin, xMax, yMin, and yMax, you can define any size of the drawing area you like depending on the requirement of your applications. Make sure that the units of xMin, xMax, yMin, and yMax must be in the real world units defined in the world coordinate system.

Next, we initially define the PlotArea to be the same size as the client area of Form1. Since we don't want the graphics to take up the whole area of Form1, we use the Inflate method to shrink the drawing area with an offset margin. Here we simply use an arbitrary offset, however, in later applications we will use a more efficient way to derive this offset when adding labels for X and Y axes. Then we draw the outlines of both the client and drawing rectangles using `DrawRectangle` method.

You may notice that there is an issue on how to draw graphics objects inside the drawing area, which should be independent of the units of the world coordinate system. Here we use the `Point2D` method to convert the points in the world coordinate system to the device coordinate system. After this conversion, the unit for all graphics objects is in pixels, including `Pen` and `Brush`. We simply pass the points of any unit in the world coordinate system to the method `Point2D`, which performs the unit conversion automatically and always returns the points with a unit of pixels in the device coordinate system. In this process, we never touch the page coordinate system. If you change any thing in the page coordinate system, such as the `PageScale` or `PageUnit` property, you will get unexpected results. For this reason, you should not change anything in page coordinate system when using these customized coordinates.

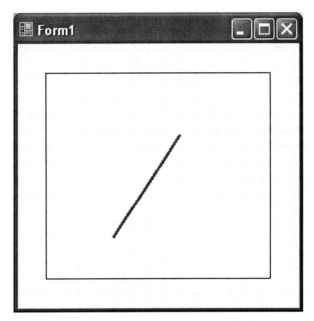

Figure 1-5 Draw a line from point (3, 2) to point (6, 7) in the custom coordinate system.

Let's examine what we did inside the `Point2D` method. First, we convert the X-component of a point in the world coordinate system using the following formula:

```
aPoint.X = PlotArea.X + (ptf.X - xMin) * PlotArea.Width / (xMax - xMin);
```

An offset, `PlotArea.X` with a unit of pixels, is added to the X-component of the `aPoint`, which is necessary in order to place the origin's X-component of our custom coordinates in the right position in the device coordinate system. Then we perform the scaling operation. Both `(ptf.X - xMin)` and `(xMax - xMin)` have the same unit in the world coordinate system, which is cancelled out by division. So the unit of this scaling term is determined solely by the term of `PlotArea.Width`, whose unit is in pixels. You can easily check that the above conversion indeed provides not only the correct unit, but also the correct position in the device coordinate system.

For the Y-component conversion, the situation is a bit different. You need to not only perform the scaling operation, but also reverse the Y axes in the device coordinate system. The following formula is used for the Y-component conversion:

```
aPoint.Y = PlotArea.Bottom - (ptf.Y - yMin) * PlotArea.Height / (yMax - yMin);
```

As shown in Figure 1-5, we draw a line from Point (3, 2) to Point (6, 7) in the drawing area. The end points of this line are in the unit (which can be any unit!) defined in the world coordinate system. These points are not directly used in drawing the line, but the points converted through `Point2D` method are used instead. This line was drawn using a green `Pen` with a width of three pixels:

```
Pen aPen = new Pen(Color.Green, 3);
g.DrawLine(aPen, Point2D(new PointF(3, 2)), Point2D(new PointF(6, 7)));
```

It is apparent that the unit of the pen's width is always in pixels, and that there is no need to perform any transformation of the `Pen` and `Brush` regardless of the unit used in world coordinate system.

Window and Viewport

A graphics object can be considered to be defined in its own coordinate system, which is some abstract place with boundaries. For example, suppose that you want to create a simple X-Y chart that plots Y-values from 50 to 100 over an X-data range from 0 to 10. You can work in a coordinate system space with 0<= X <=10 and 50<=Y<=100. This space is called the world coordinate system.

In practice, you usually are not interested in the entire graphics, but only a portion of it. Thus, you can define the portion of interest as a specific area in the world coordinate system. This area of interest is called the "Window". In order to draw graphics objects on the screen, you need to map this "Window" to the device coordinate system. This mapped "Window" in the device coordinate system is called a Viewport.

In the previous section, we defined the limits for the X and Y axes in the custom coordinate system. For example:

```
private float xMin = 0f;
private float xMax = 10f;
private float yMin = 0f;
private float yMax = 10f;
```

This defines a portion of interest in our custom coordinate system, and this area of interest is called "Window". Once you know what you want to display, you need to decide where on the computer screen to display it. In *Example1_2*, we defined the `PlotArea` in the device coordinate system to create a screen area to display the graphics object. This `PlotArea` is called the ViewPort.

You can use this Viewport to change the apparent size and location of the graphics objects on the screen. Changing the viewport affects the display of the graphics objects on the screen. These effects are called "*Zooming*" and "*Panning*".

Zooming

The size and position of the "Window" determine which part of the graphics object is drawn. The relative size of the Window and viewport determine the scale at which the graphics object is displayed on the screen. For a given viewport or `PlotArea`, a relatively large Window produces a small graphics object, because you are drawing a large piece of the custom coordinate space into a small viewport (`PlotArea`). On the other hand, a relatively small Window produces a large graphics object. Therefore, you can increase the size of the Window (specified by the X and Y axis limits) to see the "zooming out" effect by changing the parameters: `xMin`, `xMax`, `yMin`, and `yMax` in *Example1_2*, discussed in the previous section:

```
private float xMin = -10f;
private float xMax = 20f;
private float yMin = 0f;
private float yMax = 20f;
```

Executing the application generates the output results shown in Figure 1-6.

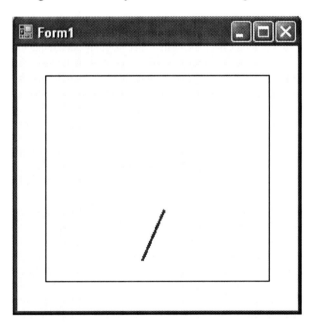

Figure 1-6 Both the size and location of the line are changed by
increasing the size of the Window: "Zoom Out".

On the other hand, if you decrease the Window size, the line appears larger on the screen; basically, you have a "zoom in" effect. Change the parameters in *Example1_2* to the following:

```
private float xMin = 2f;
```

```
private float xMax = 7f;
private float yMin = 2f;
private float yMax = 8f;
```

You will get the following results by running the program, as shown in Figure 1-7.

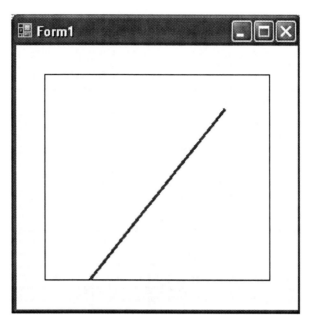

Figure 1-7 Both the size and location of the lines are changed by
decreasing the size of the Window: "Zoom in".

Panning

Panning is defined as the moving of all graphics objects in the scene by shifting the Window. In a panning process, the Window size is kept unchanged. For example, you can move the Window to the left by changing the code in *Example1_2*.

```
// Moving original window left 3 units:
private float xMin = -3f ;
private float xMax = 7;
private float yMin = 0f;
private float yMax = 10f;
```

This produces the result shown in Figure 1-8 which is equivalent to moving the line toward the right side of the drawing area. On the other hand, if we move the Window to the right by use of the following code:

```
// Moving original Window right in 3 units:
private float xMin = 3f ;
private float xMax = 13;
private float yMin = 0f;
private float yMax = 10f;
```

The results are shown in Figure 1-9.

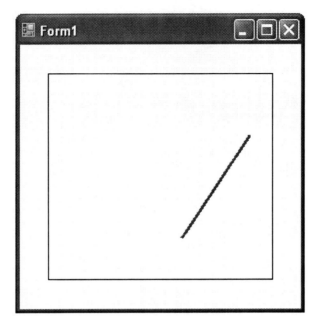

Figure 1-8 Move Window toward left.

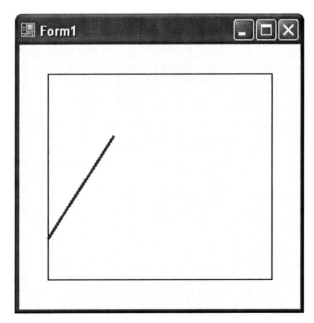

Figure 1-9 Move Window to the right.

Be careful about the "zooming in" effect when using the code in *Example1_2*. An issue occurs when you zoom in too far. For example, if you want to zoom in with the code:

```
private float xMin = 4f;
```

```
private float xMax = 6;
private float yMin = 3f;
private float yMax = 6f;
```

An unexpected result is obtained, as shown in Figure 1-10. Namely, the line is drawn outside of the drawing area.

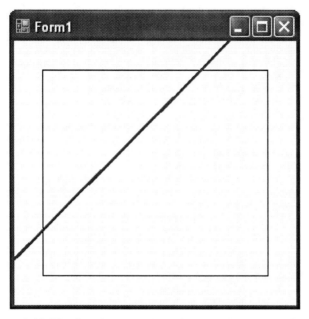

Figure 1-10 The line drawn outside of the drawing area by further zooming in.

In order to avoid this problem, you can use a user control to replace the current drawing area. Here we will use a `Panel` control to achieve this goal. Let's start off by creating a new C# Windows Application project and calling it *Example1_3*. Select a `Panel` control from the `Toolbox`, drag it over the empty `Form1`, and rename the panel control to `drawingPanel`. The following is the code listing of `Form1.cs`:

```
using System;
using System.Drawing;
using System.Windows.Forms;

namespace Example1_3
{
    public partial class Form1 : Form
    {
        // Unit defined in world coordinate system:
        private float xMin = 0f;
        private float xMax = 10f;
        private float yMin = 0f;
        private float yMax = 10f;
        // Unit in pixel:
        private int offset = 30;
```

```
public Form1()
{
    InitializeComponent();
    this.SetStyle(ControlStyles.ResizeRedraw, true);
    this.BackColor = Color.White;
    // Subscribing to a paint eventhandler to drawingPanel:
    drawingPanel.Paint += new PaintEventHandler(drawingPanelPaint);
    drawingPanel.BorderStyle = BorderStyle.FixedSingle;
    drawingPanel.Anchor = AnchorStyles.Bottom;
    drawingPanel.Anchor = AnchorStyles.Left;
    drawingPanel.Anchor = AnchorStyles.Right;
    drawingPanel.Anchor = AnchorStyles.Top;
}

private void drawingPanelPaint(object sender, PaintEventArgs e)
{
    drawingPanel.Left = offset;
    drawingPanel.Top = offset;
    drawingPanel.Width = ClientRectangle.Width - 2 * offset;
    drawingPanel.Height = ClientRectangle.Height - 2 * offset;
    Graphics g = e.Graphics;
    Pen aPen = new Pen(Color.Green, 3);
    g.DrawLine(aPen, Point2D(new PointF(2, 3)),
            Point2D(new PointF(6, 7)));
    aPen.Dispose();
    g.Dispose();
}

private PointF Point2D(PointF ptf)
{
    PointF aPoint = new PointF();
    aPoint.X = (ptf.X - xMin) * drawingPanel.Width / (xMax - xMin);
    aPoint.Y = drawingPanel.Height - (ptf.Y - yMin) *
            drawingPanel.Height / (yMax - yMin);
    return aPoint;
}
    }
}
```

It should be noted that in order to be able to draw something inside the Paint event handler of the panel control, you need to tell Windows that it should notify you every time the Paint event is called. You can do this by subscribing to the event, or in case you inherit from a control, by overriding the paint event. The paint event is subscribed using the following syntax inside Form1's constructor:

```
drawingPanel.Paint += new PaintEventHandler(drawingPanelPaint);
```

This way, a method drawingPanelPaint with the same name specified in the subscription is implemented. Another point we want to make here is that the Point scaling method, Point2D, is slightly different from that in *Example1_2*. The reason is that the origin of the Panel control is always located at the upper-left corner of this control. If we run the program, the same results as shown in Figure 1-5 should be obtained, as expected. Now if you change parameters in the above code listing as follows:

```
private float xMin = 4f;
private float xMax = 6;
private float yMin = 3f;
private float yMax = 6f;
```

You will get the results of Figure 1-11.

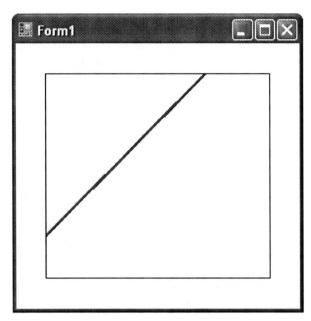

Figure 1-11 The line is always drawn inside of the drawingPanel even
when zooming in further.

You can clearly see the difference between Figure 1-10 and Figure 1-11. In this book, both viewports will be used depending on the application being discussed. For simple 2D line chart applications, we will employ the viewport defined using `PlotArea` because this viewport is easily implemented and allows us to create both chart styles (such tick labels, axis labels, and title) and data curves. On the other hand, for complicated 2D and 3D graphics drawing applications, we will use the viewport based on the `drawingPanel`.

Pen and Brush

`Graphics` objects provide an interface between the application program and the display device (the computer screen). After creating a `Graphics` object, you can use it to draw lines and fill shapes. However, even though the `Graphics` class provides the platform to draw on, you still need a tool to draw with. Two basic tools you will often use are the `Pen` and `Brush`. The GDI+ library provides the `Pen` and `Brush` through the `Pen` and `Brush` classes respectively. You use the `Pen` class to draw lines, curves, and outlines of shapes. You use the `Brush` class to fill shapes with colors and patterns. If you've read the previous section, you've already seen the `Pen` class used to demonstrate the coordinate systems.

Pen Class

You use the Pen class to create custom pens with specified color and width properties. The line drawn by a Pen object can be filled in a variety of fill styles, including solid colors and textures. The fill style depends on the brush or texture that is used as the fill object.

There are four different types of constructors for the Pen class: two constructors allow you to specify a Brush object instead of color, and two constructors give you the option of specifying the pen's width. These four constructors are as follows:

Creates a new instance of the Pen class with the specified Color:

```
public Pen(color);
```

Creates a new instance of the Pen class with the specified Brush:

```
public Pen(brush);
```

Creates a new instance of the Pen class with the specified Brush and width:

```
public Pen(brush, float);
```

Creates a new instance of the Pen class with the specified Color and width:

```
public Pen(color, float);
```

In these constructors, color represents a Color object, float is a value of Float type for the width, and brush is a Brush object. You'll see examples of these constructors as we progress through this book. The Pen class has a number of properties, offering you a large amount of control over how your Pen object draws graphics elements. The most commonly used properties include:

- Alignment – Gets or sets the alignment for the Pen object.
- Brush – Gets or sets the Brush object that determines the attributes of the Pen object.
- Color – Gets or sets the color of the Pen object.
- DashStyle – Gets or sets the style used for dashed lines drawn with the Pen object.
- Width – Gets or sets the width of the Pen object.

Brush Class

The brushes are used to fill shapes with colors, patterns, and images. The Brush class is an abstract base class and cannot be instantiated. In order to create a Brush object, you must use its derived classes, which include:

- SolidBrush – This class defines a brush made of a single color.
- TextureBrush – This class defines a brush that uses an image to fill the interior of a shape.
- HatchBrush – This class defines a rectangle brush with a hatch style, a foreground color, and a background color.
- LinearGradientBrush – This class encapsulates both two-color gradients and custom multi-color gradients.

- PathGradientBrush – This class encapsulates a `Brush` object that fills the interior of a `GraphicsPath` object with a gradient.

The following code snippet creates various brush objects:

```
// Create a SolidBrush with red color:
SolidBrush sb = new SolidBrush(Color.Red);

// Create a TextureBrush with an image file (myImage.gif):
Bitmap bmp = new Bitmap("myImage.gif");
TextureBrush tb = new TextureBrush(bmp);

// Create a HatchBrush with a Cross pattern:
HatchBrush hb = new HatchBrush(HatchStyle.Cross,
                   Color.Black, Color.White);

// Create a LinearGradientBrush with a Gradient described by two points:
LinearGradientBrush lgb = new LinearGradientBrush(New Point(10, 10),
                   new Point(100, 30), Color.Red, Color.Black);

// Create a PathGradientBrush for a Graphics path:
PathGradientBrush pgb = new PathGradientBrush(graphicsPath);
pgb.CenterColor = Color.Red;
pgb.SurroundColors = new Color[] {Color.Black};
```

The above code creates various brushes that are ready to fill graphics shapes. For the `PathGradientBrush`, we pass a `GraphicsPath` object to the constructor. Then we set the `pgb.CenterColor` property with a red color. Pay special attention to next statement:

```
pgb.SurroundColors = new Color[] {Color.Black};
```

Here we pass an array of colors for the `SurroundColors` property. In this case, we create an array with only one color, so this brush paints black at the edge of the graphics path, transitioning to red at the center.

Basic Graphics Shapes

The Windows Forms in C# are the largest unit in a typical user interface of an application. You can draw graphics shapes directly on a Form. The Form can also contain other controls. As shown in *Example1_1* and *Example1_2*, the line was drawn directly on `Form1`. As with the Form, you can also draw graphics objects directly onto controls, as shown in *Example1_3* where the graphics objects are drawn on a panel control. If you want to move a drawing to another part of the Form, you can simply move the panel to a new position. In contrast, to move a graphics drawing that you have created directly on a Form, you need to modify the drawing source code.

Next, we will discuss some basic graphics shapes in the C# and GDI+ graphics library. Understanding these basic objects is very important, as they are used often throughout this book.

Points

In C# and GDI+, there are two point structures: `Point` and `PointF`. The `Point` structure represents an ordered pair of integer X- and Y- coordinates that define a point in a 2D plane. The

`Point` constructor includes three overloaded methods that allow you to create a `Point` object from an integer, a size object, or two integers as follows:

- Point() – Creates a `Point` object and initializes the X- and Y-data members to zeros. This is the default constructor.

- Point(Size) – Creates a `Point` object using a `Size` object to initialize the X- and Y-data members.

- Point(int, int) – Creates a `Point` object using two integers to initialize the X- and Y-data members.

The following code snippet creates `Point` objects using all three types of the constructors:

```
Point pt1 = new Point();
Point pt2 = new Point(new Size(10, 100));
Point pt3 = new Point(20, 200);
```

The `PointF` structure is similar to the `Point` structure, but uses floating-point values instead of integers. Unlike the `Point` structure, `PointF` cannot take a `Size` or `SizeF` object. `PointF` has only two constructors `PointF()` and `PointF(float, float)`.

Both the `Point` and `PointF` defines three properties: `IsEmpty`, `X`, and `Y`. The `IsEmpty` property returns true if a point is empty, which means that both X and Y values are zero; otherwise it returns false. The constructors, `Point()` and `PointF()` create an empty field with X and Y values set to zero.

Lines and Curves

Line objects include straight lines and curves. A straight line can be created using the `DrawLine` method, which connects two points specified by coordinate pairs. The following code snippet creates a straight line:

```
Graphics g = new Graphics();
g.DrawLine(Pens.Black, x1, y1, x2, y2 );
g.DrawLine(Pens.Black, point1, point2);
```

where (x1, y1) is the starting point of the line and (x2, y2) is the endpoint of the line. It is also possible to directly specify the start- and end-points using `point1` and `point2`. The coordinates or the points can be integers or float values.

The `DrawCurve` method creates a `spline` that passes through each point in a point array, and connects all points in a smooth way:

```
Graphics g = new Graphics();
g.DrawCurve(Pens.Black, new Point[]);
```

In these cases, only solid lines and curves are drawn. However, lines and curves can have many different styles. For example, you can draw a dash-line with a diamond starting cap and an arrow ending cap, as illustrated in Figure 1-12. This shows that a line can have three parts: the line body, starting cap, and ending cap.

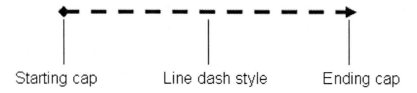

Figure 1-12 A line with starting cap, ending cap, and dash style.

There is no direct way to apply line caps and styles to a line. These caps and styles need to be specified by the Pen class. As discussed in the previous sections, to draw a line you have to use a Pen object with a specified color and width. The Pen object also provides members for associating line caps and dash styles. By specifying these members, you can use the pen to draw different styles of lines.

We will use an example to show you how to draw lines and curves with different styles. Create a new C# Windows Application. We call it *Example1_4*. The following code listing of Form1 of this project creates a Pen object with a specified color and width. It then set the line caps using the StartCap and EndCap properties of the Pen class, followed by the DashStyle and dashOffset properties. Finally it calls the DrawLine and DrawCurve methods to draw lines and curves.

```
using System;
using System.Drawing;
using System.Drawing.Drawing2D;
using System.Windows.Forms;

namespace Example1_4
{
    public partial class Form1 : Form
    {
        public Form1()
        {
            InitializeComponent();
            This.BackColor = Color.White;
        }

        protected override void OnPaint(PaintEventArgs e)
        {
            Graphics g = e.Graphics;
            // Create a pen object:
            Pen aPen = new Pen(Color.Blue, 4);
            // Set line caps and dash style:
            aPen.StartCap = LineCap.DiamondAnchor;
            aPen.EndCap = LineCap.ArrowAnchor;
            aPen.DashStyle = DashStyle.DashDot;
            aPen.DashOffset = 50;
            //draw straight line:
            g.DrawLine(aPen, 50, 30, 200, 30);
            // define point array to draw a curve:
            Point point1 = new Point(50, 200);
            Point point2 = new Point(100, 75);
            Point point3 = new Point(150, 60);
```

```
            Point point4 = new Point(200, 160);
            Point point5 = new Point(250, 250);
            Point[] Points ={ point1, point2, point3, point4, point5};
            g.DrawCurve(aPen, Points);
            aPen.Dispose();
            g.Dispose();
        }
    }
}
```

Building and running the project will obtain the results shown in Figure 1-13.

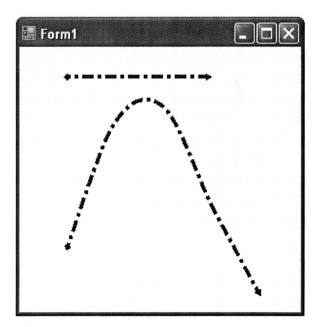

Figure 1-13 Line and curve with dash styles and caps.

Rectangles, Ellipses, and Arcs

The Rectangle and RectangleF structures represent a rectangle in C# and GDI+. A Rectangle structure stores the top-left corner as well as the width and height of a rectangle region. You can create a Rectangle object from the Point and Size objects or by using four integers or float values as the coordinates of the rectangle.

The Rectangle and RectangleF structures also provide properties which can be used to obtain the width, height, and position of the rectangle.

An ellipse is a circular shape defined by its bounding rectangle. The DrawEllipse method will draw an empty ellipse within the bounding rectangle.

While DrawEllipse method draws a closed curve around the whole boundary of the ellipse, the DrawArc method draws part of the ellipse. Which part is drawn is specified by a StartAngle and a SweepAngle.

The method `DrawPie` is also closely related to the ellipse. You specify an ellipse by supplying the enclosing rectangle. In addition, you specify a `StartAngle` and a `SweepAngle` to define where the pie starts, and how large of a section of the ellipse it spans.

You can easily create these basic graphics shapes in Visual C#. Take a look at this new example project, *Example1_5*. Rectangles, ellipses, arcs, and pies can be created using the following code:

```
using System;
using System.Drawing;
using System.Windows.Forms;

namespace Example1_5
{
    public partial class Form1 : Form
    {
        public Form1()
        {
            InitializeComponent();
            SetStyle(ControlStyles.ResizeRedraw, true);
        }

        protected override void OnPaint(PaintEventArgs e)
        {
            Graphics g = e.Graphics;
            // Create a pen object:
            Pen aPen = new Pen(Color.Blue, 2);
            // Create a brush object with a transparent red color:
            SolidBrush aBrush = new SolidBrush(Color.Red);

            // Draw a rectangle:
            g.DrawRectangle(aPen, 20, 20, 100, 50);
            // Draw a filled rectangle:
            g.FillRectangle(aBrush, 20, 90, 100, 50);
            // Draw ellipse:
            g.DrawEllipse(aPen, new Rectangle(20, 160, 100, 50));
            // Draw filled ellipse:
            g.FillEllipse(aBrush, new Rectangle(170, 20, 100, 50));
            // Draw arc:
            g.DrawArc(aPen, new Rectangle(170, 90, 100, 50),
                    -90, 180);
            g.FillPie(aBrush, new Rectangle(170, 160, 100, 100),
                    -90, 90);
            g.FillPie(Brushes.Green,
                    new Rectangle(170, 160, 100, 100), -90, -90);
        }
    }
}
```

This project produces the results of Figure 1-14.

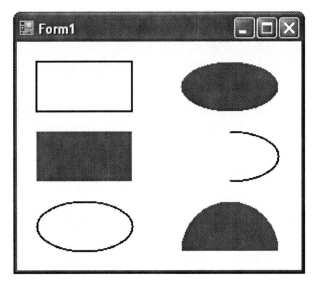

Figure 1-14 Basic graphics shapes created from project Example1_5.

Polygons

The polygon is one of the most important graphics objects we deal with when we render 2D and 3D graphics or process computational geometry. The Graphics.DrawPolygon method draws a polygon defined by an array of point structures. Every pair of two consecutive points in the array specifies a side of the polygon. In addition, if the last point and the first point of the array do not coincide, it specifies the last side of the polygon.

The Graphics.FillPolygon method fills the interior of a polygon defined by an array of points specified by point structures.

In the following example, we will create a US flag object that contains fifty star polygons. First we need to define the coordinates of a star. As illustrated in Figure 1-15, we will assume that the center coordinates of the star are at (xc, yc), r1 is the radius of the inner circle, and r is the radius of the outer circle. The angles $\alpha = 72$ degrees and $\beta = 36$ degrees. From this figure, we can easily determine the coordinates of points 0 to 9:

Points	x coordinates	y coordinates
0	xc	yc − r
1	xc + r1 sinβ	yc − r1 cosβ
2	xc + r sinα	yc − r cosα
3	xc + r1 sinα	yc + r1 cosα
4	xc + r sinβ	yc + r cosβ
5	xc	yc + r1
6	xc − r sinβ	yc + r cosβ

7	xc − r1 sinα	yc + r1 cosα
8	xc − r sinα	yc − r cosα
9	xc − r1 sinβ	yc − r1 cosβ

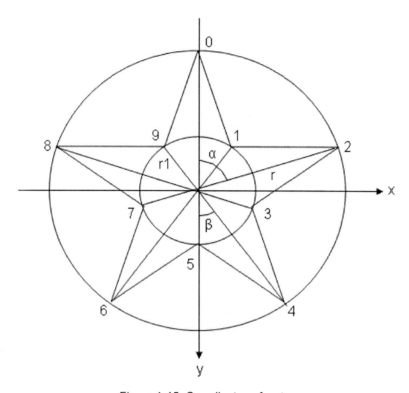

Figure 1-15 Coordinates of a star.

Now, start off with a new C# Windows Application project named *Example1_6*. The following is the code listing of the Form1 class:

```
using System;
using System.Drawing;
using System.Drawing.Drawing2D;
using System.Windows.Forms;

namespace Example1_6
{
    public partial class Form1 : Form
    {
        public Form1()
        {
            InitializeComponent();
            SetStyle(ControlStyles.ResizeRedraw, true);
            this.Width = 500;
```

```
        this.Height = 310;
        this.BackColor = Color.LightGreen;
    }

protected override void OnPaint(PaintEventArgs e)
{
    Graphics g = e.Graphics;
    g.SmoothingMode = SmoothingMode.AntiAlias;
    DrawFlag(g, 20, 20, this.Width - 50);
    g.Dispose();
}

private void DrawFlag(Graphics g, float x0, float y0, float width)
{
    SolidBrush whiteBrush = new SolidBrush(Color.White);
    SolidBrush blueBrush = new SolidBrush(Color.FromArgb(0, 0, 128));
    SolidBrush redBrush = new SolidBrush(Color.Red);

    float height = 10 * width / 19;

    // Draw white rectangle background:
    g.FillRectangle(whiteBrush, x0, y0, width, height);

    // Draw seven red stripes.
    for (int i = 0; i < 7; i++)
    {
        g.FillRectangle(redBrush, x0,
            y0 + 2 * i * height / 13, width, height / 13);
    }

    // Draw blue box.
    // Size it so that it covers two fifths of the flag width
    // and the top four red stripes vertically.
    RectangleF blueBox = new RectangleF(x0, y0,
            2 * width / 5, 7 * height / 13);
    g.FillRectangle(blueBrush, blueBox);

    // Draw fifty stars in the blue box.
    // Divide the blue box into a grid of 11 x 9 squares and
    // place a star in every other square.
    float offset = blueBox.Width / 40;
    float dx = (blueBox.Width - 2 * offset) / 11;
    float dy = (blueBox.Height - 2 * offset) / 9;

    for (int j = 0; j < 9; j++)
    {
        float yc = y0 + offset + j * dy + dy / 2;
        for (int i = 0; i < 11; i++)
        {
            float xc = x0 + offset + i * dx + dx / 2;
            if ((i + j) % 2 == 0)
            {
                DrawStar(g, this.Width/55, xc, yc);
            }
```

```
                }
            }
            whiteBrush.Dispose();
            blueBrush.Dispose();
            redBrush.Dispose();
        }

        private void DrawStar(Graphics g, float r, float xc, float yc)
        {
            // r: determines the size of the star.
            // xc, yc: determine the location of the star.
            float sin36 = (float)Math.Sin(36.0 * Math.PI / 180.0);
            float sin72 = (float)Math.Sin(72.0 * Math.PI / 180.0);
            float cos36 = (float)Math.Cos(36.0 * Math.PI / 180.0);
            float cos72 = (float)Math.Cos(72.0 * Math.PI / 180.0);
            float r1 = r * cos72 / cos36;
            // Fill the star:
            PointF[] pts = new PointF[10];
            pts[0] = new PointF(xc, yc - r);
            pts[1] = new PointF(xc + r1 * sin36, yc - r1 * cos36);
            pts[2] = new PointF(xc + r * sin72, yc - r * cos72);
            pts[3] = new PointF(xc + r1 * sin72, yc + r1 * cos72);
            pts[4] = new PointF(xc + r * sin36, yc + r * cos36);
            pts[5] = new PointF(xc, yc + r1);
            pts[6] = new PointF(xc - r * sin36, yc + r * cos36);
            pts[7] = new PointF(xc - r1 * sin72, yc + r1 * cos72);
            pts[8] = new PointF(xc - r * sin72, yc - r * cos72);
            pts[9] = new PointF(xc - r1 * sin36, yc - r1 * cos36);
            g.FillPolygon(Brushes.White, pts);
        }
    }
}
```

This project produces the output of Figure 1-16. Here the method DrawStar draws a single star polygon at the center position (xc, yc) with a size control parameter r (the radius of the outer circle, as shown in Figure 1-15). The coordinates of the point array are defined as in Figure 1-15. We use a white brush to draw the star with a g.FillPolygon method.

Inside the DrawFlag method, we first draw seven red stripes on a white rectangle background. Note that the aspect ratio of the flag is maintained by setting

```
            float height = 10 * width / 19;
```

Then we can draw the blue rectangle with the proper size. Finally we put fifty stars on the blue rectangle uniformly by calling the DrawStar method to finish the project.

Something that you might notice is that we set the SmoothingMode of the graphics object to AntiAlias inside the OnPaint method. This enhances the rendering quality of the flag greatly. If you don't use AntiAlias, you will get a flag with a lower-quality rendering and jagged edges.

Figure 1-16 US flag created from project Example1_6.

Color

In C# and GDI+, color is specified as `Color` structures from the `System.Drawing` namespace. It is easy to create a color object using these color structures. There are several different ways of creating color in C#, including:

- An ARGB (alpha, red, green, blue) color value. You specify each value as an integer in the range [0, 255].

- An environment setting from the current color scheme. You choose the correspondingly named property from the system Color class.

- A predefined .NET color name. You choose the correspondingly named property from the Color class.

- An HTML color name. You specify this value as a string using the ColorTranslator class.

- A Win32 color code. You specify this value as an integer (representing a hexadecimal value) using the ColorTranslator class.

- An OLE color code. You specify this value as an integer (representing a hexadecimal value) using the ColorTranslator class.

- A ColorDialog. You pick a color from the color palette.

System Colors

In C#, a color is represented by a 32-bit structure made up of four components: alpha (A), red (R), green (G), and blue (B), referred to as ARGB mode. The components' values range from 0 to 255. The alpha component of the color represents transparency, which determines how such a color is blended with the background. A zero alpha value represents a fully transparent color, while a value of 255 represents a fully opaque color.

The following code snippet shows several ways of specifying the background color of a `Form` using the `Color`, `ColorTranslator`, and `SystemColors` types. In order to use this code as written, you must import the `System.Drawing` namespace.

```
// Create a color from an ARGB value
int alpha = 100;
int red = 255;
int green = 0;
int blue = 0;
this.BackColor = Color.FromARGB(alpha, red, green, blue);

// Create a color from an environment setting:
this.BackColor = SystemColors.HighlightText;

// Create a Color using a .NET name
this.BackColor = Color.LightGray;

// Create a color from an HTML code:
this.BackColor = ColorTranslator.FromHTML("Red");

// Create a color from a Win32 color code:
this.BackColor = ColorTranslator.FromWin32(0xA000);

// Create a color from an OLE color code:
this.BackColor = ColorTranslator.FromOle(0xFF00);

// Create a color from a ColorDialog():
ColorDialog cd1 = new ColorDialog();
cd1.ShowDialog();
this.BackColor = cd1.Color;
```

The next code snippet will show you how to transform the `KnownColors` enumeration into an array of strings that represent color names. This is useful when you need to display a list of valid colors by name in your applications.

```
String[] colorName = Enum.GetNames(typeOf(KnownColor));
```

You can also use a few useful methods on any `Color` structure to retrieve color information. For example, you can use a `GetBrightness`, `GetHue`, `GetSaturation`, or `ToArgb` method to obtain corresponding color information.

Let's take a look at a new C# Windows Application example, *Example1_7* which puts all of these techniques to work. This example creates a form which gives you two ways to select a color: by clicking the "Color Dialog" button to bring up the Color Palette, or by selecting a color from a list box loaded with all of the known colors. When you select an item from this list box or a color from the `ColorDialog`, the background color of the `panel1` is changed accordingly.

Here is the code listing of *Example1_7*:

```
using System;
using System.Drawing;
using System.Windows.Forms;

namespace Example1_7
{
    public partial class Form1 : Form
    {
        ColorDialog cdl = new ColorDialog();

        public Form1()
        {
            InitializeComponent();
        }

        private void Form1_Load(object sender, EventArgs e)
        {
            string[] colorNames = Enum.GetNames(typeof(KnownColor));
            listBox1.Items.AddRange(colorNames);

        }

        private void listBox1_SelectedIndexChanged(object sender,
                EventArgs e)
        {
            KnownColor selectedColor =
                (KnownColor)Enum.Parse(typeof(KnownColor), listBox1.Text);
            panel1.BackColor = Color.FromKnownColor(selectedColor);
            ColorInfo();
        }

        private void button1_Click(object sender, EventArgs e)
        {
            cdl.ShowDialog();
            panel1.BackColor = cdl.Color;
            ColorInfo();
        }

        private void ColorInfo()
        {
            // Show color information on the labels:
            // Brightness info:
            lblBrightness.Text = "Brightness = " +
                panel1.BackColor.GetBrightness().ToString();
            lblHue.Text = "Hue = " +
                    panel1.BackColor.GetHue().ToString();
            // HUE Info:
            lblSaturation.Text = "Saturation = " +
                panel1.BackColor.GetSaturation().ToString();
            // RGB Hex info:
            string strRGBHex = string.Format("0x{0:X8}",
                panel1.BackColor.ToArgb());
```

```
        strRGBHex = "RGB = #" + strRGBHex.Substring(
            strRGBHex.Length - 6, 6);
        lblRGBHex.Text = strRGBHex;
        // ARGB value info:
        string strRGBValue = "ARGB = [" +
            panel1.BackColor.A.ToString() + ", " +
            panel1.BackColor.R.ToString() + ", " +
            panel1.BackColor.G.ToString() + ", " +
            panel1.BackColor.B.ToString() + "]";
        lblRGBValue.Text = strRGBValue;
    }
  }
}
```

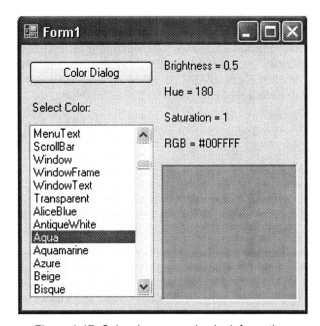

Figure 1-17 Color changes and color information.

Figure 1-17 shows the output from this example. It can be seen from this figure that when you select a color, the background color of panel1 is changed. At the same time, the information about the color is displayed on the screen, including the color's brightness, HUE value, saturation, and RGB hex number.

The KnownColor enumeration contains 174 colors, and each represented by name. For example, the names of Black and White names the colors of black and white, respectively. You can also find the system colors such as Control, ControlText, Highlight, or ActiveCaption, using the IsSystemColor enumeration.

Custom Color Map

In C#, there is a default `ColorMap` class, defined in the `System.Drawing.Imaging` namespace. This class defines a mapping between existing colors and the new colors to which they are to be converted. When the map is applied, any pixel of the old color is converted to the new color. This class is useful for image processing applications.

However, in some graphics and chart applications, you may need the custom color maps to achieve specific visual effects. These color maps are simply tables or lists of colors that are organized in some desired fashion. The surface, patch, and image objects can be associated with a custom color map. You can easily create a color map with an m x 4 color map matrix. Each row of this matrix represents ARGB values. The row index can represent the y data of a 2D chart or the height (the z data) of a 3D surface plot. For a given color map matrix with m rows, the color data values can be linearly scaled to the color map.

For example, if you want to use the color map to represent the y coordinates of a 2D graphics object, you can use the `YMin` and `YMax` to linearly transform the y data values to indices where each index identifies an ARGB row (i.e., a color) in the color map matrix. The mathematical transformation of the color index values is described by the formula:

$$Color\ Index = \begin{cases} 1 & y < Y\min \\ (\text{int})\left(\dfrac{(y - Y\min)m}{Y\max - Y\min} \right) & Y\min \le y < Y\max \\ m & y \ge Y\max \end{cases}$$

Here y is the individual value of Y data and m is the length of the color map matrix. This allows you to use the entire range of colors in the color map over the plotted data. For 3D graphics objects and 3D surface charts, the y data should be replaced with the z data.

Let's use an example to illustrate how to create custom color map matrices and how to use these matrices. Start off with a new C# Windows Application project, *Example1_8*. Add a new class called `ColorMap` to the project. In this class, we create eight color map matrices, each one with a special name. These color map matrices are commonly used in graphics and chart applications. Here is the code listing of the `ColorMap` class:

```
using System;
using System.Drawing;
using System.Drawing.Drawing2D;

namespace Example1_8
{
    public class ColorMap
    {
        private int colormapLength = 64;
        private int alphaValue = 255;

        public ColorMap()
        {
        }

        public ColorMap(int colorLength)
        {
```

```
        colormapLength = colorLength;
    }

    public ColorMap(int colorLength, int alpha)
    {
        colormapLength = colorLength;
        alphaValue = alpha;
    }

    public int[,] Spring()
    {
        int[,] cmap = new int[colormapLength, 4];
        float[] spring = new float[colormapLength];
        for (int i = 0; i < colormapLength; i++)
        {
            spring[i] = 1.0f * i / (colormapLength - 1);
            cmap[i, 0] = alphaValue;
            cmap[i, 1] = 255;
            cmap[i, 2] = (int)(255 * spring[i]);
            cmap[i, 3] = 255 - cmap[i, 1];
        }
        return cmap;
    }

    public int[,] Summer()
    {
        int[,] cmap = new int[colormapLength, 4];
        float[] summer = new float[colormapLength];
        for (int i = 0; i < colormapLength; i++)
        {
            summer[i] = 1.0f * i / (colormapLength - 1);
            cmap[i, 0] = alphaValue;
            cmap[i, 1] = (int)(255 * summer[i]);
            cmap[i, 2] = (int)(255 * 0.5f * (1 + summer[i]));
            cmap[i, 3] = (int)(255 * 0.4f);
        }
        return cmap;
    }

    public int[,] Autumn()
    {
        int[,] cmap = new int[colormapLength, 4];
        float[] autumn = new float[colormapLength];
        for (int i = 0; i < colormapLength; i++)
        {
            autumn[i] = 1.0f * i / (colormapLength - 1);
            cmap[i, 0] = alphaValue;
            cmap[i, 1] = 255;
            cmap[i, 2] = (int)(255 * autumn[i]);
            cmap[i, 3] = 0;
        }
        return cmap;
    }
```

```csharp
public int[,] Winter()
{
    int[,] cmap = new int[colormapLength, 4];
    float[] winter = new float[colormapLength];
    for (int i = 0; i < colormapLength; i++)
    {
        winter[i] = 1.0f * i / (colormapLength - 1);
        cmap[i, 0] = alphaValue;
        cmap[i, 1] = 0;
        cmap[i, 2] = (int)(255 * winter[i]);
        cmap[i, 3] = (int)(255 * (1.0f - 0.5f * winter[i]));
    }
    return cmap;
}

public int[,] Gray()
{
    int[,] cmap = new int[colormapLength, 4];
    float[] gray = new float[colormapLength];
    for (int i = 0; i < colormapLength; i++)
    {
        gray[i] = 1.0f * i / (colormapLength - 1);
        cmap[i, 0] = alphaValue;
        cmap[i, 1] = (int)(255 * gray[i]);
        cmap[i, 2] = (int)(255 * gray[i]);
        cmap[i, 3] = (int)(255 * gray[i]);
    }
    return cmap;
}

public int[,] Jet()
{
    int[,] cmap = new int[colormapLength, 4];
    float[,] cMatrix = new float[colormapLength, 3];
    int n = (int)Math.Ceiling(colormapLength / 4.0f);
    int nMod = 0;
    float[] fArray = new float[3 * n - 1];
    int[] red = new int[fArray.Length];
    int[] green = new int[fArray.Length];
    int[] blue = new int[fArray.Length];

    if (colormapLength % 4 == 1)
    {
        nMod = 1;
    }

    for (int i = 0; i <fArray.Length; i++)
    {
        if (i < n)
            fArray[i] = (float)(i + 1) / n;
        else if (i >= n && i < 2 * n - 1)
            fArray[i] = 1.0f;
        else if (i >= 2 * n - 1)
            fArray[i] = (float)(3 * n - 1 - i) / n;
```

```
            green[i] = (int)Math.Ceiling(n / 2.0f) - nMod + i;
            red[i] = green[i] + n;
            blue[i] = green[i] - n;
        }

        int nb = 0;
        for (int i = 0; i < blue.Length; i++)
        {
            if (blue[i] > 0)
                nb++;
        }

        for (int i = 0; i < colormapLength; i++)
        {
            for (int j = 0; j < red.Length; j++)
            {
                if (i == red[j] && red[j] < colormapLength)
                {
                    cMatrix[i, 0] = fArray[i - red[0]];
                }
            }
            for (int j = 0; j < green.Length; j++)
            {
                if (i == green[j] && green[j] < colormapLength)
                    cMatrix[i, 1] = fArray[i - (int)green[0]];
            }
            for (int j = 0; j < blue.Length; j++)
            {
                if (i == blue[j] && blue[j] >= 0)
                    cMatrix[i, 2] = fArray[fArray.Length - 1 - nb + i];
            }
        }

        for (int i = 0; i < colormapLength; i++)
        {
            cmap[i, 0] = alphaValue;
            for (int j = 0; j < 3; j++)
            {
                cmap[i, j+1] = (int)(cMatrix[i, j] * 255);
            }
        }
        return cmap;
    }

    public int[,] Hot()
    {
        int[,] cmap = new int[colormapLength, 4];
        int n = 3 * colormapLength / 8;
        float[] red = new float[colormapLength];
        float[] green = new float[colormapLength];
        float[] blue = new float[colormapLength];
        for (int i = 0; i < colormapLength; i++)
        {
            if (i < n)
```

```
                        red[i] = 1.0f*(i+1) / n;
                 else
                        red[i] = 1.0f;
                 if (i < n)
                        green[i] = 0f;
                 else if (i >= n && i < 2 * n)
                        green[i] = 1.0f * (i+1 - n) / n;
                 else
                        green[i] = 1f;
                 if (i < 2 * n)
                        blue[i] = 0f;
                 else
                        blue[i] = 1.0f * (i + 1 - 2 * n) / (colormapLength - 2 * n);
                 cmap[i, 0] = alphaValue;
                 cmap[i, 1] = (int)(255 * red[i]);
                 cmap[i, 2] = (int)(255 * green[i]);
                 cmap[i, 3] = (int)(255 * blue[i]);
             }
             return cmap;
         }

         public int[,] Cool()
         {
             int[,] cmap = new int[colormapLength, 4];
             float[] cool = new float[colormapLength];
             for (int i = 0; i < colormapLength; i++)
             {
                 cool[i] = 1.0f * i / (colormapLength - 1);
                 cmap[i, 0] = alphaValue;
                 cmap[i, 1] = (int)(255 * cool[i]);
                 cmap[i, 2] = (int)(255 * (1 - cool[i]));
                 cmap[i, 3] = 255;
             }
             return cmap;
         }
     }
 }
```

In this class, there are three constructors. If you use

```
ColorMap cm = new ColorMap();
```

to create a new ColorMap object, the default parameters colormapLength = 64 and alphaValue = 255 will be used. Here colormapLength is the length of the color map matrix and the alphaValue is the color transparency parameter. The default alphaValue of 255 represents an opaque color. The following constructor

```
ColorMap cm = new ColorMap(32);
```

overrides the colormapLength with the input parameter 32, and the alphaValue remains the default value of 255. You can override both parameters by calling the ColorMap class with the following code snippet:

```
COlorMap cm = new ColorMap(32, 100);
```

This sets colormapLength = 32 and alphaValue = 100. The class Form1 draws various color bars using the ColorMap class. The following is the code listing of the Form1 class:

```
using System;
using System.Drawing;
using System.Windows.Forms;

namespace Example1_8
{
    public partial class Form1 : Form
    {
        public Form1()
        {
            InitializeComponent();
            SetStyle(ControlStyles.ResizeRedraw, true);
            This.BackColor = Color.White;
            this.Width = 340;
            this.Height = 340;
        }

        protected override void OnPaint(PaintEventArgs e)
        {
            Graphics g = e.Graphics;

            int width = 30;
            int height = 128;
            int y = 10;
            // Create opaque color maps with alpha = 255:
            ColorMap cm = new ColorMap();
            Font aFont = new Font("Arial", 20, FontStyle.Bold);
            g.DrawString("OPAQUE COLOR", aFont, Brushes.Black, 10, 60);
            DrawColorBar(g, 10, y, width, height, cm, "Spring");
            DrawColorBar(g, 10 + 40, y, width, height, cm, "Summer");
            DrawColorBar(g, 10 + 2 * 40, y, width, height, cm, "Autumn");
            DrawColorBar(g, 10 + 3 * 40, y, width, height, cm, "Winter");
            DrawColorBar(g, 10 + 4 * 40, y, width, height, cm, "Jet");
            DrawColorBar(g, 10 + 5 * 40, y, width, height, cm, "Gray");
            DrawColorBar(g, 10 + 6 * 40, y, width, height, cm, "Hot");
            DrawColorBar(g, 10 + 7 * 40, y, width, height, cm, "Cool");

            y = y + 150;
            // Create transparent color maps with alpha = 150:
            ColorMap cm1 = new ColorMap(64, 150);
            g.DrawString("TRANSPARENT COLOR", aFont, Brushes.Black, 10, 210);
            DrawColorBar(g, 10, y, width, height, cm1, "Spring");
            DrawColorBar(g, 10 + 40, y, width, height, cm1, "Summer");
            DrawColorBar(g, 10 + 2 * 40, y, width, height, cm1, "Autumn");
            DrawColorBar(g, 10 + 3 * 40, y, width, height, cm1, "Winter");
            DrawColorBar(g, 10 + 4 * 40, y, width, height, cm1, "Jet");
            DrawColorBar(g, 10 + 5 * 40, y, width, height, cm1, "Gray");
            DrawColorBar(g, 10 + 6 * 40, y, width, height, cm1, "Hot");
            DrawColorBar(g, 10 + 7 * 40, y, width, height, cm1, "Cool");
        }
```

```csharp
private void DrawColorBar(Graphics g, int x, int y,
    int width, int height, ColorMap map, string str)
{
    int[,] cmap = new int[64, 4];
    switch(str)
    {
        case "Jet":
            cmap = map.Jet();
            break;
        case "Hot":
            cmap = map.Hot();
            break;
        case "Gray":
            cmap = map.Gray();
            break;
        case "Cool":
            cmap = map.Cool();
            break;
        case "Summer":
            cmap = map.Summer();
            break;
        case "Autumn":
            cmap = map.Autumn();
            break;
        case "Spring":
            cmap = map.Spring();
            break;
        case "Winter":
            cmap = map.Winter();
            break;
    }

    int ymin = 0;
    int ymax = 32;
    int dy = height / (ymax - ymin);
    int m = 64;
    for (int i = 0; i < 32; i++)
    {
        int colorIndex = (int)((i - ymin) *
            m / (ymax - ymin));
        SolidBrush aBrush = new SolidBrush(Color.FromArgb(
            cmap[colorIndex, 0], cmap[colorIndex, 1],
            cmap[colorIndex, 2], cmap[colorIndex, 3]));
        g.FillRectangle(aBrush, x, y + i * dy, width, dy);
    }
}
```

Inside the DrawColorBar method, we draw a color bar by dividing it into 32 sub-rectangles. We then assign the y data from 0 to 31. The switch statement selects a specified color map matrix. The following code snippet

```csharp
int colorIndex = (int)((i - ymin) * m / (ymax - ymin));
```

computes the index of the color map matrix using the Y data. Then we create a `SolidBrush` object using this color map matrix.

Inside the `OnPaint` method, we create two `ColorMap` objects, cm and cm1. cm uses the default parameters: `colormapLength` = 64 and `alphaValue` = 255; i.e. the opaque color. The parameters of cm1 are reassigned to `colormapLength` = 64 and `alphaValue` = 150, indicating that the color becomes transparent.

This project produces the output displayed Figure 1-18, which shows eight different color maps defined in the `ColorMap` class.

Figure 1-18 Color map from Example1_8.

Color Shading

In the previous subsection, we drew color bars by associating the y data with the indices of the color map matrix. In some graphics applications, you may want to directly map the color of a surface object according to a given set of color data. Consider a situation involving the color map matrix with the name "Jet", as defined in the previous project *Example1_8*, with the default color map length = 64. Suppose we have a 3-by-3 color data matrix

$$Color\ Data = \begin{pmatrix} 3 & 0 & 4 \\ -2 & 3 & 1 \\ -1 & 2 & -3 \end{pmatrix}$$

In this case, the maximum and minimum of the color data are 4 and -3 respectively. We can easily determine the color map index numbers using the formula given in the previous subsection to be

$$Color\ Index = \begin{pmatrix} 54 & 27 & 63 \\ 9 & 54 & 36 \\ 18 & 45 & 0 \end{pmatrix}$$

Up to this point, we have not been supplying the x- and y- coordinate data. We believe that the color data values along the row (x data) and column (y data) specify 9 vertices where each neighboring set of four elements is connected by means of a quadrilateral. As shown in Figure 1-19, in terms of the elements within the color data matrix, there are four quadrilaterals. You might wonder why we need nine indices in the color map when there are only four quadrilaterals. With surface objects, each vertex can be assigned a color. This allows you to perform a bilinear interpolation among four vertex colors to determine the color at any point within the quadrilateral.

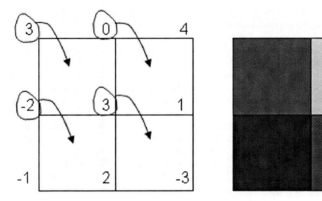

Figure 1-19 Color matrix and color map.

If you do not want to use color interpolation, the color data can also be a 2-by-2 matrix, as shown in Figure 1-19 with the circled elements. Basically, you can take the top-left vertex color data to fill the corresponding quadrilateral. Combining this with the color indices, you obtain the direct color map for these four quadrilaterals, as shown in Figure 1-19.

You can see from Figure 1-19 that the color changes very dramatically from one quadrilateral to another. To obtain a better color shading effect, you need to perform a bilinear color interpolation. Bilinear interpolation uses the four vertex values surrounding each quadrilateral to obtain any value inside the quadrilateral. Suppose you want to get the value at (x, y), and the vertices of the quadrilateral are located at (x0, y0), (x1, y0), (x0, y1), and (x1, y1), where they have the color data values C00, C10, C01, and C11, respectively, as show in Figure 1-20.

Linear interpolation on the top row of neighbors, between (x0, y0) and (x1, y0), estimates the value C0 at (x, y0) as

$$C0 = \frac{x1-x}{x1-x0}C00 + \frac{x-x0}{x1-x0}C10$$

Likewise, linear interpolation on the bottom row of neighbors, between (x0, y1) and (x1, y1), estimates the value C1 at (x, y1) as

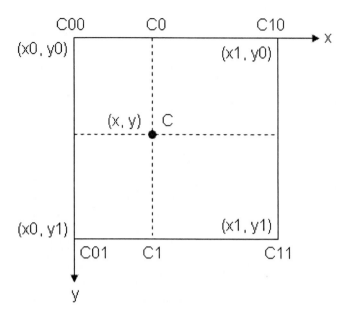

Figure 1-20 Coordinates used for bilinear interpolation.

$$C1 = \frac{x1 - x}{x1 - x0}C01 + \frac{x - x0}{x1 - x0}C11$$

Finally, linear interpolation between C0 and C1 estimates the value C at (x, y) as

$$C = \frac{y1 - y}{y1 - y0}C0 + \frac{y - y0}{y1 - y0}C1$$

By substituting the expressions for C0 and C1 into the above equation, you obtain:

$$C = \frac{y1 - y}{y1 - y0}\left(\frac{x1 - x}{x1 - x0}C00 + \frac{x - x0}{x1 - x0}C10\right) + \frac{y - y0}{y1 - y0}\left(\frac{x1 - x}{x1 - x0}C01 + \frac{x - x0}{x1 - x0}C11\right)$$

You can see that the equation for C is a polynomial involving powers of x and y no greater than 1, and with four coefficients: C = a1+ a2*x + a3*y + a4*x*y. Because these four coefficients were determined by four values (C00, C01, C10, and C11), they are usually uniquely determined by the data. This immediately implies that the comparable procedure of first interpolating along columns (in the y-direction) and then interpolating the results in the x-direction will give the same result, because it, too, will have a similar formula with a unique solution.

Note that the term "bilinear" derives from the process of linear interpolation (twice in one direction, then once in the perpendicular direction), *not* from the formula for C. The formula involves a term with x * y, which is not linear.

Now, start off with a new C# Windows Application example, and call it *Example1-9*. Add the ColorMap class from the previous project *Example1_8* to this project and change its namespace to *Example1_9*. In this project, we implement the bilinear interpolation for the color map to get a better shading effect than the direct map in Figure 1-19. You also need to add a new point class,

PointC, with a color data and a color ARGB array. Here is the code listing for the PointC class:

```
using System;
using System.Drawing;
using System.Drawing.Drawing2D;

namespace Example1_9
{
    public class PointC
    {
        public PointF pointf = new PointF();
        public float C = 0;
        public int[] ARGBArray = new int[4];

        public PointC()
        {
        }

        public PointC(PointF ptf, float c)
        {
            pointf = ptf;
            C = c;
        }

        public PointC(PointF ptf, float c, int[] argbArray)
        {
            pointf = ptf;
            C = c;
            ARGBArray = argbArray;
        }
    }
}
```

This class is very simple; we just associate the color data and the ARGB array with the point. The following is the code listing of the Form1 class:

```
using System;
using System.Drawing;
using System.Drawing.Drawing2D;
using System.Windows.Forms;

namespace Example1_9
{
    public partial class Form1 : Form
    {
        public Form1()
        {
            InitializeComponent();
            this.Width = 400;
            this.Height = 250;
        }

        protected override void OnPaint(PaintEventArgs e)
        {
```

```csharp
        Graphics g = e.Graphics;
        DrawObjects(g);
        g.Dispose();
}

private void DrawObjects(Graphics g)
{
    ColorMap cm = new ColorMap();
    int[,] cmap = cm.Jet();
    int x0 = 10;
    int y0 = 10;
    int width = 85;
    int height = 85;
    PointC[,] pts = new PointC[3, 3];
    pts[0, 0] = new PointC(new PointF(x0, y0), 3);
    pts[0, 1] = new PointC(new PointF(x0 + width, y0), 0);
    pts[0, 2] = new PointC(new PointF(x0 + 2 * width, y0), 4);
    pts[1, 0] = new PointC(new PointF(x0, y0 + height), -2);
    pts[1, 1] = new PointC(new PointF(x0 + width,
                          y0 + height), 3);
    pts[1, 2] = new PointC(new PointF(x0 + 2 * width,
                          y0 + height), 1);
    pts[2, 0] = new PointC(new PointF(x0,
                          y0 + 2* height), -1);
    pts[2, 1] = new PointC(new PointF(x0 + width,
                          y0 + 2* height), 2);
    pts[2, 2] = new PointC(new PointF(x0 + 2 * width,
                          y0 + 2 * height), -3);
    float cmin = -3;
    float cmax = 4;
    int colorLength = cmap.GetLength(0);

    // Original color map:
    for (int i = 0; i < 3; i++)
    {
        for (int j = 0; j < 3; j++)
        {
            int cindex = (int)Math.Round((
                colorLength * (pts[i, j].C - cmin) +
                (cmax - pts[i, j].C)) / (cmax - cmin));
            if (cindex < 1)
                cindex = 1;
            if (cindex >  colorLength)
                cindex = colorLength;
            for (int k = 0; k < 4; k++)
            {
                pts[i, j].ARGBArray[k] = cmap[cindex - 1, k];
            }
        }
    }

    for (int i = 0; i < 2; i++)
    {
        for (int j = 0; j < 2; j++)
```

```csharp
                {
                    SolidBrush aBrush = new SolidBrush(
                        Color.FromArgb(pts[i, j].ARGBArray[0],
                        pts[i, j].ARGBArray[1], pts[i, j].ARGBArray[2],
                        pts[i, j].ARGBArray[3]));
                    PointF[] pta = new PointF[4]{pts[i,j].pointf,
                        pts[i+1,j].pointf,pts[i+1,j+1].pointf,
                        pts[i,j+1].pointf};
                    g.FillPolygon(aBrush, pta);
                    aBrush.Dispose();
                }
            }
            g.DrawString("Direct Color Map", this.Font,
                    Brushes.Black, 50, 190);

            // Bilinear interpolation:
            x0 = x0 + 200;
            pts[0, 0] = new PointC(new PointF(x0, y0), 3);
            pts[0, 1] = new PointC(new PointF(x0 + width, y0), 0);
            pts[0, 2] = new PointC(new PointF(x0 + 2 * width, y0), 4);
            pts[1, 0] = new PointC(new PointF(x0, y0 + height), -2);
            pts[1, 1] = new PointC(new PointF(x0 + width,
                                    y0 + height), 3);
            pts[1, 2] = new PointC(new PointF(x0 + 2 * width,
                                    y0 + height), 1);
            pts[2, 0] = new PointC(new PointF(x0,
                                    y0 + 2 * height), -1);
            pts[2, 1] = new PointC(new PointF(x0 + width,
                                    y0 + 2 * height), 2);
            pts[2, 2] = new PointC(new PointF(x0 + 2 * width,
                                    y0 + 2 * height), -3);

            for (int i = 0; i < 2; i++)
            {
                for (int j = 0; j < 2; j++)
                {
                    PointF[] pta = new PointF[4]{pts[i,j].pointf,
                        pts[i+1,j].pointf,
                        pts[i+1,j+1].pointf, pts[i,j+1].pointf};
                    float[] cdata = new float[4]{pts[i,j].C,
                        pts[i+1,j].C, pts[i+1,j+1].C,pts[i,j+1].C};
                    Interp(g, pta, cdata, 50);
                }
            }
            g.DrawString("Interpolated Color Map", this.Font,
                    Brushes.Black, 240, 190);
        }

        private void Interp(Graphics g, PointF[] pta,
                        float[] cData, int npoints)
        {
            PointC[,] pts = new PointC[npoints + 1, npoints + 1];
            float x0 = pta[0].X;
            float x1 = pta[3].X;
```

```
float y0 = pta[0].Y;
float y1 = pta[1].Y;
float dx = (x1 - x0) / npoints;
float dy = (y1 - y0) / npoints;
float C00 = cData[0];
float C10 = cData[1];
float C11 = cData[2];
float C01 = cData[3];

for (int i = 0; i <= npoints; i++)
{
    float x = x0 + i * dx;
    for (int j = 0; j <= npoints; j++)
    {
        float y = y0 + j * dy;
        float C = (y1 - y) * ((x1 - x) * C00 +
            (x - x0) * C10) / (x1 - x0) / (y1 - y0) +
            (y - y0) * ((x1 - x) * C01 +
            (x - x0) * C11) / (x1 - x0) / (y1 - y0);
        pts[j, i] = new PointC(new PointF(x, y),C);
    }
}

ColorMap cm = new ColorMap();
int[,] cmap = cm.Jet();
float cmin = -3;
float cmax = 4;
int colorLength = cmap.GetLength(0);
for (int i = 0; i <= npoints; i++)
{
    for (int j = 0; j <= npoints; j++)
    {
        int cindex = (int)Math.Round((
            colorLength * (pts[i, j].C - cmin) +
            (cmax - pts[i, j].C)) / (cmax - cmin));
        if (cindex < 1)
            cindex = 1;
        if (cindex > colorLength)
            cindex = colorLength;
        for (int k = 0; k < 4; k++)
        {
            pts[j, i].ARGBArray[k] = cmap[cindex - 1, k];
        }
    }
}

for (int i = 0; i < npoints; i++)
{
    for (int j = 0; j < npoints; j++)
    {
        SolidBrush aBrush = new SolidBrush(
            Color.FromArgb(pts[i, j].ARGBArray[0],
            pts[i, j].ARGBArray[1],
            pts[i, j].ARGBArray[2],
```

```
                            pts[i, j].ARGBArray[3]));
                    PointF[] points = new PointF[4]{pts[i,j].pointf,
                        pts[i+1,j].pointf,
                        pts[i+1,j+1].pointf, pts[i,j+1].pointf};
                    g.FillPolygon(aBrush, points);
                    aBrush.Dispose();
                }
            }
        }
    }
}
```

This project produces the output of Figure 1-21. You can see that the interpolated color map gives a much better shading effect indeed.

Let's examine how the program works. The method `Interp` in the `Form1` class takes four vertex points and the corresponding color data values of a given quadrilateral as inputs, and interpolates the color data values within the quadrilateral using the bilinear interpolation approach. The color shading quality is controlled by the number of the interpolation points: `npoints`.

In the `DrawObjects` method, we first draw the objects using the direct map approach, and then using the bilinear interpolation by calling the `Interp` method. The bilinear interpolated color map has found wide applications in image processing and 3D surface chart applications.

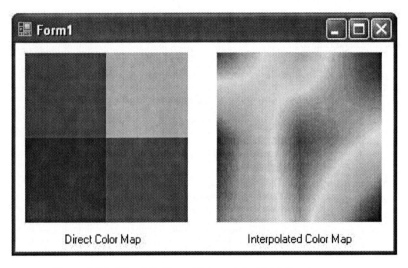

Figure 1-21 Direct (left) and interpolated (right) color maps.

2

2D Matrices and Transformations

In a graphics application, operations can be performed in different coordinate systems. Moving from one coordinate space to another requires the use of transformation matrices. In this chapter, we review the mathematic basis about matrices and transformation in 2D space. Here we acknowledge the importance of matrices and transformation in graphics and chart programming by presenting you with a more formal exposition of their properties. We concern ourselves with linear transformation among different coordinate systems. Such transformations include simple scaling, reflection, and translation, as well as rotations. More complicated transformations in 3D will be the topic of Chapter 5.

Basics of Matrices and Transformations

Matrices play an important role in the transformation process. A matrix is a multi-dimensional array. This section explains the basics of 2D matrices and transformations. As we discussed in the previous chapter, by changing the coordinates of a graphics object in the world coordinate system, such as zooming and panning, you can easily move the graphics object to another part of a viewport. However, if the graphics contains more than one object, you may want to move one of the objects without moving the others. In this case, you cannot use simple zooming and panning to move the object because these approaches would move the other objects as well.

Instead, you can apply a transformation to the object you want to move. Here we discuss the transformations that scale, rotate, and translate an object.

Scaling

To scale or stretch an object in the X direction, you simply need to multiply the X coordinates of each of the object's points by the scaling factor s_X. Similarly, you can scale an object in the Y direction:

$$\begin{pmatrix} x_1 \\ y_1 \end{pmatrix} = \begin{pmatrix} s_x & 0 \\ 0 & s_y \end{pmatrix} \begin{pmatrix} x \\ y \end{pmatrix} = \begin{pmatrix} s_x x \\ s_y y \end{pmatrix} \tag{2.1}$$

For example, the scaling matrix that shrink x and y uniformly by a factor of two, as well as a matrix that halves in the y direction and increases to three-halves in the x direction, are given below respectively:

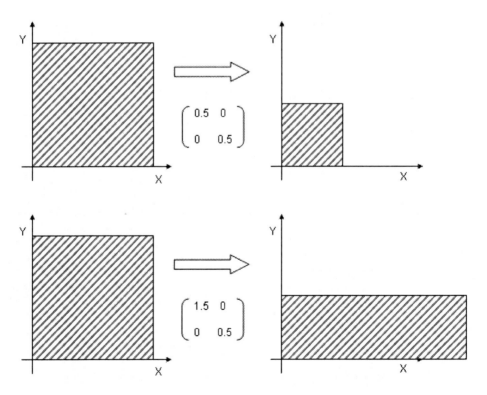

Figure 2-1 Uniform scaling by half for the x and y directions (top) and non-uniform scaling in x and y directions (bottom).

$$\begin{pmatrix} 0.5 & 0 \\ 0 & 0.5 \end{pmatrix} \text{ and } \begin{pmatrix} 1.5 & 0 \\ 0 & 0.5 \end{pmatrix}$$

The above two scaling matrix operations have very different effects on objects (see Figure 2-1).

Reflection

By reflecting an object across the X and Y axis, you can create a mirror image of the object. In fact, reflecting an object across an axis is equivalent to scaling it with a negative scaling factor. The transformation matrices across either of the coordinate axes can be written in the following forms:

Reflect across the x axis: $\begin{pmatrix} -1 & 0 \\ 0 & 1 \end{pmatrix}$

Reflect across the y axis: $\begin{pmatrix} 1 & 0 \\ 0 & -1 \end{pmatrix}$

As you might expect, a matrix with -1 in both elements of the diagonal is a reflection that is just a rotation by 180 degrees.

Rotation

Suppose we want to rotate an object by an angle θ counter-clockwise. First, suppose you have a point $(x1, y1)$ that you want to rotate by an angle θ to get to the point $(x2, y2)$, as shown in Figure 2-2.

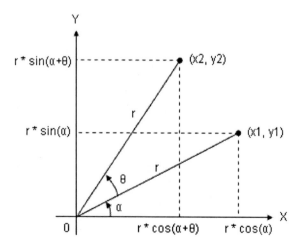

Figure 2-2 Rotation from point (x1, y1) to point (x2, y2).

Suppose that the distance from the point to the origin r, meaning you have the following relations:

$$x1 = r \cos \alpha$$
$$y1 = r \sin \alpha$$

The point $(x2, y2)$ is the same point rotated by an additional angle of θ. Since this point also has a distance r from the origin, its coordinates are given by:

$$x2 = r \cos(\alpha + \theta) = r \cos \alpha \cos \theta - r \sin \alpha \sin \theta$$
$$y2 = r \sin(\alpha + \theta) = r \sin \alpha \cos \theta + r \cos \alpha \sin \theta$$

Substituting the components of $x1 = r \cos\alpha$ and $y1 = r \sin\alpha$ into the above equations gives

$$x2 = x1 \cos \theta - y1 \sin \theta$$
$$y2 = x1 \sin \theta + y1 \cos \theta$$

In matrix form, the equivalent rotation transformation that takes point $(x1, y1)$ to $(x2, y2)$ is

$$R(\theta) = \begin{pmatrix} \cos \theta & -\sin \theta \\ \sin \theta & \cos \theta \end{pmatrix} \tag{2.2}$$

Translation

To translate an object, you simply add an offset to the original X and Y coordinates of the points that make up the object

$$x1 = x + dx$$
$$y1 = y + dy \tag{2.3}$$

Although translations look very simple, they cannot be expressed in terms of transformation matrices. It would be feasible to keep track of scales, reflections, and rotations as a matrix, while keeping track of translations separately, but doing so would involve fairly painful bookkeeping, particularly the application includes many different transformations. Instead, you can use a technique to move the computation into a higher dimension. This technique allows you to treat the different transformations in a uniform or homogeneous way. This approach, called homogeneous coordinates, has become standard in almost every graphiccs program. In the following section, we will introduce homogeneous coordinates that allow you to manipulate all of these transformations with matrices.

Homogeneous Coordinates

We expect that all transformations in 2D space, including scaling, reflection, rotation, and translation, can be treated equally, if points are expressed in homogeneous coordinates. Homogeneous coordinates were first introduced in geometry and have been applied subsequently to graphics.

In homogeneous coordinates, you add a third coordinate to a point. Instead of being represented by a pair of (X, Y) numbers, each point is represented by a triple (X, Y, W). If the W coordinate is nonzero, you can divide through by it: (X, Y, W) represents the same point as (X/W, Y/W, 1).

When W is nonzero, you normally perform this division, and the numbers X/W and Y/W are usually called the point coordinates in the homogeneous coordinate system. The points where W = 0 are called points at infinity.

Because points in 2D space are now three-element column vectors, transformation matrices, which multiply a point vector to produce another point vector, should be 3x3.

Translation in Homogeneous Coordinates

In homogeneous coordinates, a translation can be expressed in the form:

$$\begin{pmatrix} x1 \\ y1 \\ 1 \end{pmatrix} = \begin{pmatrix} 1 & 0 & dx \\ 0 & 1 & dy \\ 0 & 0 & 1 \end{pmatrix} \begin{pmatrix} x \\ y \\ 1 \end{pmatrix} \tag{2.4}$$

The above transformation can be expressed differently as

$$P_1 = T(dx, dy)P \tag{2.5}$$

Here P and P_1 represent point (x, y) and point (x1, y1) respectively, and T(dx, dy) is the translation matrix:

$$T(dx, dy) = \begin{pmatrix} 1 & 0 & dx \\ 0 & 1 & dy \\ 0 & 0 & 1 \end{pmatrix} \tag{2.6}$$

What happens if a point P is translated by T(dx1, dy1) to P_1 and then translated by T(dx2, dy2) to P_2? The result, we intuitively expect, is a net translation of T(dx1 + dx2, dy1+ dy2). This can be confirmed by the definitions:

$$P_1 = T(dx1, dy1)P$$
$$P_2 = T(dx2, dy2)P_1$$

From the above equations we have:

$$P_2 = T(dx2, dy2)T(dx1, dy1)P$$

The matrix product T(dx1, dy1) T(dx2, dy2) is

$$\begin{pmatrix} 1 & 0 & dx2 \\ 0 & 1 & dy2 \\ 0 & 0 & 1 \end{pmatrix} \begin{pmatrix} 1 & 0 & dx1 \\ 0 & 1 & dy1 \\ 0 & 0 & 1 \end{pmatrix} = \begin{pmatrix} 1 & 0 & dx1 + dx2 \\ 0 & 1 & dy1 + dy2 \\ 0 & 0 & 1 \end{pmatrix} \tag{2.7}$$

The net translation is indeed T(dx1 + dx2, dy1 + dy2).

Scaling in Homogeneous Coordinates

Similarly, the scaling equation (2.1) can be represented in matrix form in homogeneous coordinates as:

$$\begin{pmatrix} x1 \\ y1 \\ 1 \end{pmatrix} = \begin{pmatrix} s_x & 0 & 0 \\ 0 & s_y & 0 \\ 0 & 0 & 1 \end{pmatrix} \begin{pmatrix} x \\ y \\ 1 \end{pmatrix}$$ (2.8)

It can also be expressed in the form as:

$$P_1 = S(s_x, s_y)P$$ (2.9)

Just as successive translations are additive, we expect that successive scalings should be multiplicative. Given

$$P_1 = S(s_{x1}, s_{y1})P$$ (2.10)

$$P_2 = S(s_{x2}, s_{y2})P_1$$ (2.11)

Substituting Eq.(2.10) into Eq.(2.11) obtains

$$P_2 = S(s_{x2}, s_{y2}) \cdot (S(s_{x1}, s_{y1}) \cdot P) = (S(s_{x2}, s_{y2}) \cdot S(s_{x1}, s_{y1})) \cdot P$$

The matrix product in the above equation is

$$\begin{pmatrix} s_{x2} & 0 & 0 \\ 0 & s_{y2} & 0 \\ 0 & 0 & 1 \end{pmatrix} \begin{pmatrix} s_{x1} & 0 & 0 \\ 0 & s_{y1} & 0 \\ 0 & 0 & 1 \end{pmatrix} = \begin{pmatrix} s_{x1}s_{x2} & 0 & 0 \\ 0 & s_{y1}s_{y2} & 0 \\ 0 & 0 & 1 \end{pmatrix}$$

Thus, the scalings are indeed multiplicative.

Reflection is a special case of scaling with a scaling factor of -1. You can represent a reflection in the same way as scaling.

Rotation in Homogeneous Coordinates

A rotation in homogeneous coordinates can be represented as

$$\begin{pmatrix} x1 \\ y1 \\ 1 \end{pmatrix} = \begin{pmatrix} \cos\theta & -\sin\theta & 0 \\ \sin\theta & \cos\theta & 0 \\ 0 & 0 & 1 \end{pmatrix} \begin{pmatrix} x \\ y \\ 1 \end{pmatrix}$$ (2.12)

It can be also written as

$$P_1 = R(\theta)P$$

Where R(θ) is the rotation matrix in homogeneous coordinates. We expect that two successive rotations should be additive. Given

$$P_1 = R(\theta_1)P$$ (2.13)

$$P_2 = R(\theta_2)P_1$$ (2.14)

Substituting Eq. (2.13) into Eq. (2.14) gets

$$P_2 = R(\theta_2) \cdot (R(\theta_1) \cdot P) = (R(\theta_2) \cdot R(\theta_1)) \cdot P$$

The matrix product $R(\theta_1)\, R(\theta_2)$ is

$$\begin{pmatrix} \cos\theta_2 & -\sin\theta_2 & 0 \\ \sin\theta_2 & \cos\theta_2 & 0 \\ 0 & 0 & 1 \end{pmatrix} \begin{pmatrix} \cos\theta_1 & -\sin\theta_1 & 0 \\ \sin\theta_1 & \cos\theta_1 & 0 \\ 0 & 0 & 1 \end{pmatrix}$$

$$= \begin{pmatrix} \cos\theta_2\cos\theta_1 - \sin\theta_2\sin\theta_1 & -\cos\theta_2\sin\theta 1 - \sin\theta_2\cos\theta_1 & 0 \\ \sin\theta_2\cos\theta_1 + \cos\theta_2\sin\theta_1 & \cos\theta_2\cos\theta_1 - \sin\theta_2\sin\theta_1 & 0 \\ 0 & 0 & 1 \end{pmatrix}$$

$$= \begin{pmatrix} \cos(\theta_1 + \theta_2) & -\sin(\theta_1 + \theta_2) & 0 \\ \sin(\theta_1 + \theta_2) & \cos(\theta_1 + \theta_2) & 0 \\ 0 & 0 & 1 \end{pmatrix}$$

Thus, the rotations are indeed additive.

Combining Transformations

It is common for graphics applications to apply more than one transformation to a graphics object. For example, you might want to first apply a scaling transformation S, and then a rotation transformation R. You can combine the fundamental S, T, and R matrices to produce desired general results. The basic purpose of combining transformations is to gain efficiency by applying a single composed transformation to a point, rather than applying a series of transformations, one after another.

Consider the rotation of an object about some arbitrary point P1. Since you only know how to rotate about the origin, you need to convert the original problem into several separate problems. Thus, to rotate about P1, you need to perform a sequence of several fundamental transformations:

- Translate it so that the point is at the origin
- Rotate it to the desired angle
- Translate so that the point at the origin returns back to P1.

This sequence is illustrated in Figure 2-3, in which a rectangle is rotated about P1 (x1, y1). The first translation is by (-x1,-y1), whereas the later translation is by the inverse (x1, y1). The result is quite different from that of applying just the rotation. The net transformation is

$$T(x1, y1) \cdot R(\theta) \cdot T(-x1, -y1) = \begin{pmatrix} 1 & 0 & x1 \\ 0 & 1 & y1 \\ 0 & 0 & 1 \end{pmatrix} \begin{pmatrix} \cos\theta & -\sin\theta & 0 \\ \sin\theta & \cos\theta & 0 \\ 0 & 0 & 1 \end{pmatrix} \begin{pmatrix} 1 & 0 & -x1 \\ 0 & 1 & -y1 \\ 0 & 0 & 1 \end{pmatrix}$$

$$= \begin{pmatrix} \cos\theta & -\sin\theta & x1(1-\cos\theta) + y1\sin\theta \\ \sin\theta & \cos\theta & y1(1-\cos\theta) - x1\sin\theta \\ 0 & 0 & 1 \end{pmatrix}$$

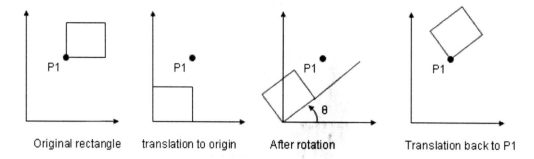

Figure 2-3 Rotation of a rectangle about the point P1 by an angle θ.

Matrix Class and Transformation in C#

Visual C# and GDI+ have implemented a matrix class in homogeneous coordinates for 2D space. Note that C# uses a convention of pre-multiplying matrices by row vectors, rather then post-multiplying by column vectors. In this case, the transformation matrices must be transposed to go from one convention to the other. For your reference, I will list here the fundamental transformation matrices for a point expressed using a row vector.

Translation:

$$\begin{pmatrix} x1 & y1 & 1 \end{pmatrix} = \begin{pmatrix} x & y & 1 \end{pmatrix} \begin{pmatrix} 1 & 0 & 0 \\ 0 & 1 & 0 \\ dx & dy & 1 \end{pmatrix} \tag{2.15}$$

Scaling:

$$\begin{pmatrix} x1 & y1 & 1 \end{pmatrix} = \begin{pmatrix} x & y & 1 \end{pmatrix} \begin{pmatrix} s_x & 0 & 0 \\ 0 & s_y & 0 \\ 0 & 0 & 1 \end{pmatrix} \tag{2.16}$$

Rotation:

$$\begin{pmatrix} x1 & y1 & 1 \end{pmatrix} = \begin{pmatrix} x & y & 1 \end{pmatrix} \begin{pmatrix} \cos\theta & \sin\theta & 0 \\ -\sin\theta & \cos\theta & 0 \\ 0 & 0 & 1 \end{pmatrix} \tag{2.17}$$

Matrix Definition in C#

You might notice that the transformation matrices always have a last column of (0 0 1). It can be shown that any combined transformation matrix based on these fundamental transformations has the same last column. Based on this fact, C# defines the transformation in terms of a 3x2 matrix. Namely, the matrix class in C# takes 6 elements arranged in 3 rows by 2 columns.

For example, the default identity matrix constructed by the default constructor has a value of $(1, 0, 0, 1, 0, 0)$. In matrix representation, this means:

$$\begin{pmatrix} 1 & 0 \\ 0 & 1 \\ 0 & 0 \end{pmatrix}$$. This is a simplification of $$\begin{pmatrix} 1 & 0 & 0 \\ 0 & 1 & 0 \\ 0 & 0 & 1 \end{pmatrix}$$. The last column is always $$\begin{pmatrix} 0 \\ 0 \\ 1 \end{pmatrix}$$.

Thus a translation transformation of a movement of 3 in the x-axis and 2 in the y-axis would be represented as $(1, 0, 0, 1, 3, 2)$. In matrix form, we have:

$$\begin{pmatrix} 1 & 0 \\ 0 & 1 \\ 3 & 2 \end{pmatrix}$$. This is a simplification of $$\begin{pmatrix} 1 & 0 & 0 \\ 0 & 1 & 0 \\ 3 & 2 & 1 \end{pmatrix}$$.

You can create a matrix object in C# by using its overloaded constructors, which take an array of points (which hold the matrix items) as arguments. Please note that before using the matrix class in your applications, you need to add a reference to the System.Drawing.Drawing2D namespace. The following code snippet creates three matrix objects for translation, scaling, and rotation:

```
float dx = 3f;
float dy = 2f;
float sx = 0.5f;
float sy = 1.5f;
float theta = (float)Math.PI / 4;
float sin = (float)Math.Sin(theta);
float cos = (float)Math.Cos(theta);
Matrix tm = new Matrix(1, 0, 0, 1, dx, dy);
Matrix sm = new Matrix(sx, 0, 0, sy, 0, 0);
Matrix rm = new Matrix(cos, sin, -sin, cos, 0, 0);
```

The matrix tm is a translation matrix that translates an object by 3 units in the x direction and by 2 units in the y direction. The scaling matrix sm scales an object by a factor of 0.5 in the x direction and by a factor of 1.5 in the y direction. The other matrix rm is a rotation matrix that rotates an object by 45 degrees about the origin.

The matrix class in C# provides public properties for accessing and setting its member values. These properties include:

- Elements: Returns an array containing matrix elements.
- IsIdentity: Returns true if the matrix is an identity matrix.
- IsInvertible: Returns true if the matrix is invertible.
- OffsetX: Returns the x translation value of the matrix.
- OffsetY: Returns the y translation value of the matrix.

Matrix Operation in C#

The matrix class in C# provides methods to rotate, scale, and translation. It also implements several methods to perform the matrix operations. For example, the Reset method resets a matrix to the identity matrix. If you call the Reset method and then apply a matrix to transform an object, the result will be the original object.

The Invert method is used to reverse a matrix if it is invertible. This method takes no parameters. The Multiply method multiplies a new matrix against an existing matrix and stores the result in the first matrix. Multiply takes two arguments. The first is the new matrix by which you want to multiply the existing matrix, and the second is an optional MatrixOrder argument that indicates the order of multiplication.

The MatrixOrder enumeration has two values: Append and Prepend. Append specifies that the new operation is applied after the preceding operation; Prepend specifies that the new operation is applied before the preceding operation during cumulative operations.

Let's examine an example of how you can perform matrix operations in C#. Start off with a C# Windows Application project, and call it *Exampe2_1*. The following is the code listing of Form1 class:

```csharp
using System;
using System.Drawing;
using System.Drawing.Drawing2D;
using System.Windows.Forms;

namespace Example2_1
{
    public partial class Form1 : Form
    {
        public Form1()
        {
            InitializeComponent();
            This.BackColor = Color.White;
        }

        protected override void OnPaint(PaintEventArgs e)
        {
            Graphics g = e.Graphics;
            int offset = 20;

            // Invert matrix:
            Matrix m = new Matrix(1, 2, 3, 4, 0, 0);
            g.DrawString("Original Matrix:", this.Font,
                        Brushes.Black, 10, 10);
            DrawMatrix(m, g, 10, 10 + offset);
            g.DrawString("Inverted Matrix:", this.Font,
                        Brushes.Black, 10, 10 + 2*offset);
            m.Invert();
            DrawMatrix(m, g, 10, 10 + 3 * offset);

            // Matrix multiplication - MatrixOrder.Append:
            Matrix m1 = new Matrix(1, 2, 3, 4, 0, 1);
```

```
        Matrix m2 = new Matrix(0, 1, 2, 1, 0, 1);
        g.DrawString("Original Matrices:", this.Font,
                    Brushes.Black, 10, 10 + 4 * offset);
        DrawMatrix(m1, g, 10, 10 + 5 * offset);
        DrawMatrix(m2, g, 10 + 100, 10 + 5 * offset);
        m1.Multiply(m2, MatrixOrder.Append);
        g.DrawString("Resultant Matrix - Append:", this.Font,
                    Brushes.Black, 10, 10 + 6 * offset);
        DrawMatrix(m1, g, 10, 10 + 7 * offset);

        // Matrix multiplication - MatrixOrder.Prepend:
        m1 = new Matrix(1, 2, 3, 4, 0, 1);
        m1.Multiply(m2, MatrixOrder.Prepend);
        g.DrawString("Resultant Matrix - Prepend:", this.Font,
                    Brushes.Black, 10, 10 + 8 * offset);
        DrawMatrix(m1, g, 10, 10 + 9 * offset);
    }

    private void DrawMatrix(Matrix m, Graphics g, int x, int y)
    {
        string str = null;
        for (int i = 0; i < m.Elements.Length; i++)
        {
            str += m.Elements[i].ToString();
            str += ", ";
        }
        g.DrawString(str, this.Font, Brushes.Black, x, y);
    }
    }
}
```

This project produces the results shown in Figure 2-4.

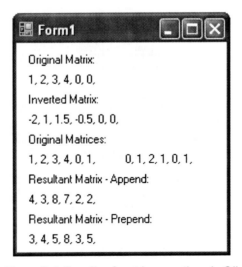

Figure 2-4 Results of matrix operations in C#.

In this example, we implement a private method `DrawMatrix`, which draws the matrix elements at a point (x, y) on the screen. First we examine the matrix invert method that inverts a matrix (1, 2, 3, 4, 0, 0). The `Matrix.Invert()` method gives the result (-2, 1, 1.5, -0.5, 0, 0). This can be easily confirmed by considering the matrix operation: matrix (1, 2, 3, 4, 0, 0) multiplied by (-2, 1, 1.5, -0.5, 0, 0) should be an identity matrix (1, 0, 0, 1, 0, 0). In fact:

$$\begin{pmatrix} 1 & 2 & 0 \\ 3 & 4 & 0 \\ 0 & 0 & 1 \end{pmatrix} \begin{pmatrix} -2 & 1 & 0 \\ 1.5 & -0.5 & 0 \\ 0 & 0 & 1 \end{pmatrix} = \begin{pmatrix} -2+2\times1.5 & 1-2\times0.5 & 0 \\ -2\times3+4\times1.5 & 3-4\times0.5 & 0 \\ 0 & 0 & 1 \end{pmatrix} = \begin{pmatrix} 1 & 0 & 0 \\ 0 & 1 & 0 \\ 0 & 0 & 1 \end{pmatrix}$$

which is indeed an identity matrix, as expected.

Next, we consider the matrix multiplication. We create two matrices `m1` = (1, 2, 3, 4, 0, 1) and `m2` = (0, 1, 2, 1, 0, 1). Please note that the result is stored in `m1` if the matrix `m1` is multiplied by `m2`. We first set the `MatrixOrder` to `Append`, indicating that the new operation is applied after the preceding operation. We see from Figure 2-4 that the resultant matrix is (4, 3, 8, 7, 2, 2). In fact:

$$\begin{pmatrix} 1 & 2 & 0 \\ 3 & 4 & 0 \\ 0 & 1 & 1 \end{pmatrix} \begin{pmatrix} 0 & 1 & 0 \\ 2 & 1 & 0 \\ 0 & 1 & 1 \end{pmatrix} = \begin{pmatrix} 4 & 3 & 0 \\ 8 & 7 & 0 \\ 2 & 2 & 1 \end{pmatrix}$$

Then we set the `MatrixOrder` as `Prepend`, and expect the following result:

$$\begin{pmatrix} 0 & 1 & 0 \\ 2 & 1 & 0 \\ 0 & 1 & 1 \end{pmatrix} \begin{pmatrix} 1 & 2 & 0 \\ 3 & 4 & 0 \\ 0 & 1 & 1 \end{pmatrix} = \begin{pmatrix} 3 & 4 & 0 \\ 5 & 8 & 0 \\ 3 & 5 & 1 \end{pmatrix}$$

which is consistent with (3, 4, 5, 8, 3, 5).

Basic Matrix Transformations in C#

The matrix class in C# also provides methods to `rotate`, `scale`, and `translate` the matrices.

The `Rotate` and `RotateAt` methods are used to rotate a matrix. The `Rotate` method rotates a matrix at a specified angle. This method takes two arguments: a floating point value specifying the angle, and (optionally) the matrix order. The `RotateAt` method is useful when you need to change the center of the rotation. Its first parameter is the angle; the second parameter (of type float) specifies the center of rotation. The third (optional) parameter is the matrix order.

Let's illustrate the basic matrix transformations (translation, scaling, rotation, and shear) in C# through an example. Start off with a new C# Windows Application project and call it *Example2_2*. This project is very similar to the previous example. Here is its code listing:

```
using System;
using System.Drawing;
using System.Drawing.Drawing2D;
using System.Windows.Forms;
```

```
namespace Example2_2
{
    public partial class Form1 : Form
    {
        public Form1()
        {
            InitializeComponent();
            This.BackColor = Color.White;
            this.Width = 300;
            this.Height = 500;
        }

        protected override void OnPaint(PaintEventArgs e)
        {
            Graphics g = e.Graphics;
            int offset = 20;

            // Scale:
            Matrix m = new Matrix(1, 2, 3, 4, 0, 1);
            g.DrawString("Original Matrix:", this.Font,
                Brushes.Black, 10, 10);
            DrawMatrix(m, g, 10, 10 + offset);
            g.DrawString("Scale - Prepend:", this.Font,
                Brushes.Black, 10, 10 + 2 * offset);
            m.Scale(1, 0.5f, MatrixOrder.Prepend);
            DrawMatrix(m, g, 10, 10 + 3 * offset);
            g.DrawString("Scale - Append:", this.Font,
                Brushes.Black, 10, 10 + 4 * offset);
            // Reset m to the original matrix:
            m = new Matrix(1, 2, 3, 4, 0, 1);
            m.Scale(1, 0.5f, MatrixOrder.Append);
            DrawMatrix(m, g, 10, 10 + 5 * offset);

            // Translation:
            m = new Matrix(1, 2, 3, 4, 0, 1);
            g.DrawString("Translation - Prepend:", this.Font,
                Brushes.Black, 10, 10 + 6 * offset);
            m.Translate(1, 0.5f, MatrixOrder.Prepend);
            DrawMatrix(m, g, 10, 10 + 7 * offset);
            g.DrawString("Translation - Append:", this.Font,
                Brushes.Black, 10, 10 + 8 * offset);
            // Reset m to the original matrix:
            m = new Matrix(1, 2, 3, 4, 0, 1);
            m.Translate(1, 0.5f, MatrixOrder.Append);
            DrawMatrix(m, g, 10, 10 + 9 * offset);

            // Rotation:
            m = new Matrix(1, 2, 3, 4, 0, 1);
            g.DrawString("Rotation - Prepend:", this.Font,
                Brushes.Black, 10, 10 + 10 * offset);
            m.Rotate(45, MatrixOrder.Prepend);
            DrawMatrix(m, g, 10, 10 + 11 * offset);
            g.DrawString("Rotation - Append:", this.Font,
                Brushes.Black, 10, 10 + 12 * offset);
```

```
                      // Reset m to the original matrix:
                      m = new Matrix(1, 2, 3, 4, 0, 1);
                      m.Rotate(45, MatrixOrder.Append);
                      DrawMatrix(m, g, 10, 10 + 13 * offset);

                      // Rotation at (x = 1, y = 2):
                      m = new Matrix(1, 2, 3, 4, 0, 1);
                      g.DrawString("Rotation at - Prepend:", this.Font,
                          Brushes.Black, 10, 10 + 14 * offset);
                      m.RotateAt(45, new PointF(1, 2), MatrixOrder.Prepend);
                      DrawMatrix(m, g, 10, 10 + 15 * offset);
                      g.DrawString("Rotation At - Append:", this.Font,
                          Brushes.Black, 10, 10 + 16 * offset);
                      // Reset m to the original matrix:
                      m = new Matrix(1, 2, 3, 4, 0, 1);
                      m.RotateAt(45, new PointF(1, 2), MatrixOrder.Append);
                      DrawMatrix(m, g, 10, 10 + 17 * offset);

                      // Shear:
                      m = new Matrix(1, 2, 3, 4, 0, 1);
                      g.DrawString("Shear - Prepend:", this.Font,
                          Brushes.Black, 10, 10 + 18 * offset);
                      m.Shear(1, 2, MatrixOrder.Prepend);
                      DrawMatrix(m, g, 10, 10 + 19 * offset);
                      g.DrawString("Shear - Append:", this.Font,
                          Brushes.Black, 10, 10 + 20 * offset);
                      // Reset m to the original matrix:
                      m = new Matrix(1, 2, 3, 4, 0, 1);
                      m.Shear(1, 2, MatrixOrder.Append);
                      DrawMatrix(m, g, 10, 10 + 21 * offset);
                  }

          private void DrawMatrix(Matrix m, Graphics g, int x, int y)
          {
              string str = null;
              for (int i = 0; i < m.Elements.Length; i++)
              {
                  double dd = Math.Round(m.Elements[i], 3);
                  str += dd.ToString();
                  str += ",   ";
              }
              g.DrawString(str, this.Font, Brushes.Black, x, y);
          }
      }
  }
```

Building and running this project generates the output in Figure 2-5. The original matrix m = (1, 2, 3, 4, 0, 1) is operated on by various transformations. First, we examine the scale transformation that sets the scaling factor to be 1 in the x direction, and 0.5 in the y direction. For the Prepend scaling (the default setting), we have:

$$\begin{pmatrix} 1 & 0 & 0 \\ 0 & 0.5 & 0 \\ 0 & 0 & 1 \end{pmatrix} \begin{pmatrix} 1 & 2 & 0 \\ 3 & 4 & 0 \\ 0 & 1 & 1 \end{pmatrix} = \begin{pmatrix} 1 & 2 & 0 \\ 1.5 & 2 & 0 \\ 0 & 1 & 1 \end{pmatrix}$$

This confirms the output result (1, 2, 1.5, 2, 0, 1) of Figure 2-5. On the other hand, for the Append scaling, we have:

$$\begin{pmatrix} 1 & 2 & 0 \\ 3 & 4 & 0 \\ 0 & 1 & 1 \end{pmatrix} \begin{pmatrix} 1 & 0 & 0 \\ 0 & 0.5 & 0 \\ 0 & 0 & 1 \end{pmatrix} = \begin{pmatrix} 1 & 1 & 0 \\ 3 & 2 & 0 \\ 0 & 0.5 & 1 \end{pmatrix}$$

This gives the same result (1, 1, 3, 2, 0, 0.5) as in Figure 2-5.

Then, we translate the matrix m in the x direction by one unit, and in the y direction by a half unit. For the Prepend translation, this means the following transformation:

$$\begin{pmatrix} 1 & 0 & 0 \\ 0 & 1 & 0 \\ 1 & 0.5 & 1 \end{pmatrix} \begin{pmatrix} 1 & 2 & 0 \\ 3 & 4 & 0 \\ 0 & 1 & 1 \end{pmatrix} = \begin{pmatrix} 1 & 2 & 0 \\ 3 & 4 & 0 \\ 2.5 & 5 & 1 \end{pmatrix}$$

This confirms the result (1, 2, 3, 4, 2.5, 5) listed in Figure 2-5. For the Append translation, we have:

$$\begin{pmatrix} 1 & 2 & 0 \\ 3 & 4 & 0 \\ 0 & 1 & 1 \end{pmatrix} \begin{pmatrix} 1 & 0 & 0 \\ 0 & 1 & 0 \\ 1 & 0.5 & 1 \end{pmatrix} = \begin{pmatrix} 1 & 2 & 0 \\ 3 & 4 & 0 \\ 1 & 1.5 & 1 \end{pmatrix}$$

This is consistent with the result (1, 2, 3, 4, 1, 1.5) of Figure 2-5.

For rotation transformation, we rotate the original m matrix by 45 degrees. In the case of the Prepend rotation, we have:

$$\begin{pmatrix} \cos(\pi/4) & \sin(\pi/4) & 0 \\ -\sin(\pi/4) & \cos(\pi/4) & 0 \\ 0 & 0 & 1 \end{pmatrix} \begin{pmatrix} 1 & 2 & 0 \\ 3 & 4 & 0 \\ 0 & 1 & 1 \end{pmatrix} = \begin{pmatrix} 2.828 & 4.243 & 0 \\ 1.414 & 1.414 & 0 \\ 0 & 1 & 1 \end{pmatrix}$$

Note that in the above calculation, we have used the fact of $\cos(\pi/4) = \sin(\pi/4) = 0.707$. This result is also the same as (2.828, 4.243, 1.414, 1.414, 0, 1) of Figure 2-5. While for the Append rotation, we have:

$$\begin{pmatrix} 1 & 2 & 0 \\ 3 & 4 & 0 \\ 0 & 1 & 1 \end{pmatrix} \begin{pmatrix} \cos(\pi/4) & \sin(\pi/4) & 0 \\ -\sin(\pi/4) & \cos(\pi/4) & 0 \\ 0 & 0 & 1 \end{pmatrix} = \begin{pmatrix} -0.707 & 2.121 & 0 \\ -0.707 & 4.949 & 0 \\ -0.707 & 0.707 & 1 \end{pmatrix}$$

This is the same result (-0.707, 2.121, -0.707, 4.95, -0.707, 0.707) that is given in Figure 2-5.

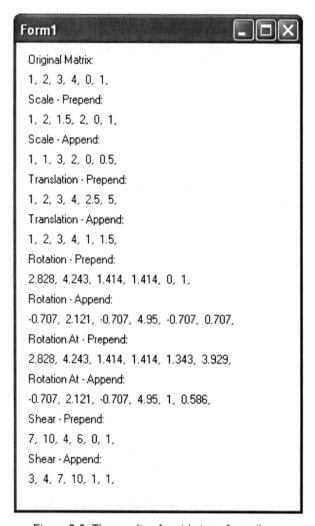

Figure 2-5 The results of matrix transformations.

The `RotateAt` method is designed for cases in which you need to change the center of rotation. In fact, the `Rotate` method is a special case of `RotateAt` with the rotation center at (0, 0). In our example, we rotate the matrix m by 45 degrees at the point (1, 2). As we discussed in the previous "Combining Transformations" subsection of this Chapter, the rotation of an object about some arbitrary point P1 must be performed according to the following procedures:

- Translate P1 to the origin.

- Rotate it to the desired angle.

- Translate so that the point at the origin returns back to P1.

Considering the matrix transformation definition in C#, the rotation matrix at point (1, 2) should be expressed in the following form:

$$T(-dx,-dy) \cdot R(\theta) \cdot T(dx, dy)$$

$$= \begin{pmatrix} 1 & 0 & 0 \\ 0 & 1 & 0 \\ -1 & -2 & 1 \end{pmatrix} \begin{pmatrix} \cos(\pi/4) & \sin(\pi/4) & 0 \\ -\sin(\pi/4) & \cos(\pi/4) & 0 \\ 0 & 0 & 1 \end{pmatrix} \begin{pmatrix} 1 & 0 & 0 \\ 0 & 1 & 0 \\ 1 & 2 & 1 \end{pmatrix} = \begin{pmatrix} 0.707 & 0.707 & 0 \\ -0.707 & 0.707 & 0 \\ 1.707 & -0.121 & 1 \end{pmatrix}$$

Thus, the Prepend rotation of matrix m by 45 degrees at point (1, 2) becomes:

$$\begin{pmatrix} 0.707 & 0.707 & 0 \\ -0.707 & 0.707 & 0 \\ 1.707 & -0.121 & 1 \end{pmatrix} \begin{pmatrix} 1 & 2 & 0 \\ 3 & 4 & 0 \\ 0 & 0 & 1 \end{pmatrix} = \begin{pmatrix} 2.828 & 4.242 & 0 \\ 1.414 & 1.414 & 0 \\ 1.344 & 3.93 & 1 \end{pmatrix}$$

This gives the same result (2.828, 4.242, 1.414, 1.414, 1.343, 3.929) of Figure 2-5. The minor difference is due to the decimal rounding.

Similarly, for the Append rotation of matrix m by 45 degrees at point (1, 2) should be:

$$\begin{pmatrix} 1 & 2 & 0 \\ 3 & 4 & 0 \\ 0 & 1 & 1 \end{pmatrix} \begin{pmatrix} 0.707 & 0.707 & 0 \\ -0.707 & 0.707 & 0 \\ 1.707 & -0.121 & 1 \end{pmatrix} = \begin{pmatrix} -0.707 & 2.121 & 0 \\ -0.707 & 4.949 & 0 \\ 1 & 0.586 & 1 \end{pmatrix}$$

Again, the result is the same as the one shown in Figure 2-5.

Finally, we discuss the Shear method that provides a shearing transformation and takes two floating point arguments, which represent the horizontal and vertical shear factors. The shear transformation in homogeneous coordinates can be expressed in the form:

$$(x1 \quad y1 \quad 1) = (x \quad y \quad 1) \begin{pmatrix} 1 & \beta & 0 \\ \alpha & 1 & 0 \\ 0 & 0 & 1 \end{pmatrix} = (x + \alpha y \quad y + \beta x \quad 1)$$

Where α and β are the shear transformation factors in the x and y directions, respectively. Return to the shear transformation in our example. The shear factors we use in the example are 1 in the x direction and 2 in the y direction. For the Prepend shear transformation, we have:

$$\begin{pmatrix} 1 & 2 & 0 \\ 1 & 1 & 0 \\ 0 & 0 & 1 \end{pmatrix} \begin{pmatrix} 1 & 2 & 0 \\ 3 & 4 & 0 \\ 0 & 1 & 1 \end{pmatrix} = \begin{pmatrix} 7 & 10 & 0 \\ 4 & 6 & 0 \\ 0 & 1 & 1 \end{pmatrix}$$

This confirms the result shown in Figure 2-5. For the Append shear transformation, we have:

$$\begin{pmatrix} 1 & 2 & 0 \\ 3 & 4 & 0 \\ 0 & 1 & 1 \end{pmatrix} \begin{pmatrix} 1 & 2 & 0 \\ 1 & 1 & 0 \\ 0 & 0 & 1 \end{pmatrix} = \begin{pmatrix} 3 & 4 & 0 \\ 7 & 10 & 0 \\ 1 & 1 & 1 \end{pmatrix}$$

This result is the same as the one given in Figure 2-5.

Here, we have presented detailed explanations of the matrix transformations in C#. This information is useful in understanding the definitions and internal representations of matrices in C# and to apply them to your applications correctly.

Object Transformations in C#

Once you have created the matrix transformations in C#, you will want to apply them to real-world graphics objects. For each graphics object, you can apply various transformations separately.

Basic Transformations

Let's start off with a new C# Windows Application project, *Example2_3*. The following code listing of the Form1 class applies basic transformations (scale, translation, rotation, and shear) to a house object:

```csharp
using System;
using System.Drawing;
using System.Drawing.Drawing2D;
using System.Windows.Forms;

namespace Example2_3
{
    public partial class Form1 : Form
    {
        public Form1()
        {
            InitializeComponent();
            this.BackColor = Color.White;
            // Subscribing to a paint eventhandler to drawingPanel:
            panel1.Paint += new PaintEventHandler(panel1Paint);
        }

        private void panel1Paint(object sender, PaintEventArgs e)
        {
            Graphics g = e.Graphics;
            DrawAxes(g);
            ApplyTransformation(g);
        }

        private void ApplyTransformation(Graphics g)
        {
            // Create a new transform matrix:
            Matrix m = new Matrix();
            // Bring origin to the center:
            m.Translate(panel1.Width/2, panel1.Height/2);

            if (rbTranslation.Checked)
            {
                // Translation:
                int dx = Convert.ToInt16(tbTranslationX.Text);
```

```
                int dy = - Convert.ToInt16(tbTranslationY.Text);
                m.Translate(dx, dy);
        }
        else if (rbScale.Checked)
        {
            // Scaling:
            float sx = Convert.ToSingle(tbScaleX.Text);
            float sy = Convert.ToSingle(tbScaleY.Text);
            m.Scale(sx, sy);
        }
        else if (rbRotation.Checked)
        {
            // Rotation:
            float angle = Convert.ToSingle(tbRotaionAngle.Text);
            float x = Convert.ToSingle(tbRotateAtX.Text);
            float y = - Convert.ToSingle(tbRotateAtY.Text);
            g.FillEllipse(Brushes.Black, x - 4, y - 4, 8, 8);
            m.RotateAt(angle, new PointF(x, y));
        }
        else if (rbShear.Checked)
        {
            // Shear:
            float alpha = Convert.ToSingle(tbShearX.Text);
            float beta = Convert.ToSingle(tbShearY.Text);
            m.Shear(alpha, beta);
        }
        g.Transform = m;
        DrawHouse(g, Color.Black);
}

private void DrawHouse(Graphics g, Color color)
{
    HatchBrush hb = new HatchBrush(HatchStyle.HorizontalBrick,
                        color, Color.White);
    Pen aPen = new Pen(color, 2);
    Point[] pta = new Point[5];
    pta[0] = new Point(-40, 40);
    pta[1] = new Point(40, 40);
    pta[2] = new Point(40, -40);
    pta[3] = new Point(0, -80);
    pta[4] = new Point(-40, -40);
    g.FillPolygon(hb, pta);
    g.DrawPolygon(aPen, pta);
    hb.Dispose();
    aPen.Dispose();
}

private void DrawAxes(Graphics g)
{
    Matrix m = new Matrix();

    // Define the translation matrix:
    m.Translate(panel1.Width/2, panel1.Height/2);
    // Apply the transformation matrix to graphics object:
```

```
        g.Transform = m;

        // Draw x and y axes:
        g.DrawLine(Pens.Blue, -panel1.Width / 2, 0,
                    panel1.Width / 2, 0);
        g.DrawLine(Pens.Blue, 0, -panel1.Height / 2,
                    0, panel1.Height / 2);
        // Add labels to the X and Y axes:
        g.DrawString("X", this.Font, Brushes.Blue,
                    panel1.Width / 2 - 20, -20);
        g.DrawString("Y", this.Font, Brushes.Blue, 5,
                    -panel1.Height / 2+5);

        // Draw Ticks:
        int tick = 40;
        StringFormat sf = new StringFormat();
        sf.Alignment = StringAlignment.Far;
        for (int i = -200; i <= 200; i += tick)
        {
            g.DrawLine(Pens.Blue, i, -3, i, 3);
            g.DrawLine(Pens.Blue, -3, i, 3, i);

            SizeF sizeXTick = g.MeasureString(i.ToString(),
                    this.Font);
            if (i != 0)
            {
                g.DrawString(i.ToString(), this.Font, Brushes.Blue,
                    i + sizeXTick.Width / 2, 4f, sf);
                g.DrawString((-i).ToString(), this.Font, Brushes.Blue,
                    -3f, i - sizeXTick.Height / 2, sf);
            }
            else
            {
                g.DrawString("0", this.Font, Brushes.Blue,
                    new PointF(i - sizeXTick.Width / 3, 4f), sf);
            }
        }
    }
}

private void btnReset_Click(object sender, EventArgs e)
{
    // Reset parameters to default values:
    tbTranslationX.Text = "0";
    tbTranslationY.Text = "0";
    tbScaleX.Text = "1";
    tbScaleY.Text = "1";
    tbRotaionAngle.Text = "0";
    tbRotateAtX.Text = "0";
    tbRotateAtY.Text = "0";
    tbShearX.Text = "0";
    tbShearY.Text = "0";
    panel1.Invalidate();
}
```

```
            private void btnShow_Click(object sender, EventArgs e)
            {
                panel1.Invalidate();
            }
        }
    }
```

In this example, we draw the graphics object on a panel control, panel1. For simplicity, a unit of pixels is used in both the world and device coordinate systems. The DrawAxes method creates the X and Y coordinate axes in the world coordinate system with the origin located at the center of the panel1. We first define the translation matrix m using the Translate method:

```
    m.Translate(panel1.Width/2, panel1.Height/2);
```

This is equivalent to the following statement:

```
    Matrix m = new Matrix(1, 0, 0, 1, panel1.Width/2, panel1.Height/2);
```

Then we perform a transformation on the Graphics object using the translation matrix through the g.Transform method:

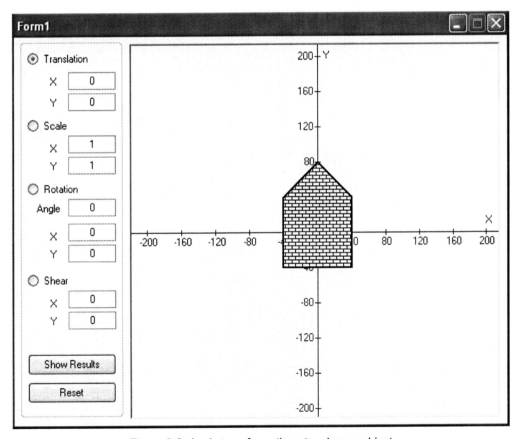

Figure 2-6 Apply transformations to a house object.

```
g.Transform = m;
```

This shifts the origin of the coordinate system to the center of panel1. Next, we draw the X- and Y-axes relative to the origin (i.e. the center of the panel1 control), and add labels to the axes using the DrawString method. We also add code to create ticks and to label tick marks along the axes with numbers. Notice how we pass a StringFormat object to the DrawString method, setting its Alignment property to far so that the text is aligned to the right.

The DrawHouse method creates a house object at the origin. We first define a HatchBrush and a Pen object that are to be used to draw the house. We then create a point array that constructs the house object by calling the FillPolygon and DrawPolygon methods.

We perform all transformations and operations on the house object inside the ApplyTransformation method. In this method, we first define an identity matrix, and then translate it to the center of the panel1 control so that the following transformations are performed relative to the origin of the coordinate system. Next, we create various transformation matrices, including translation, scaling, rotation, and shearing. Finally, we associate the transformation matrix m with the Graphics object, and draw the transformed house object by calling the DrawHouse method:

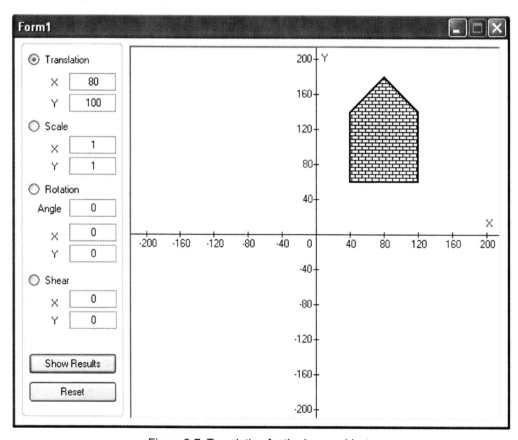

Figure 2-7 Translation for the house object.

```
g.Transform = m;
DrawHouse(g, Color.Black);
```

Building and executing this project generates the results shown in Figure 2-6.

You can then select different transformations by clicking on the corresponding radio buttons, and enter proper values into the corresponding textboxes. Finally, you click on the "Show Results" button in order for your selection to take effect.

Please note that there is only one line code inside the "Show Results" button click event handler:

```
panel1.Invalidate();
```

This forces the `panel1` to refresh, reflecting your changes in transformation on the house object. `Invalidate` is a very useful method when you think something needs to be repainted. Basically, it marks an area of the client window as invalid, and therefore, in need of repainting, then makes sure that a `Paint` event is raised. There are a couple of overrides to Invalidate(): you can pass it a rectangle that specifies precisely which area of the window needs repainting, or you can pass no parameters at all and it will just mark the entire client area as invalid.

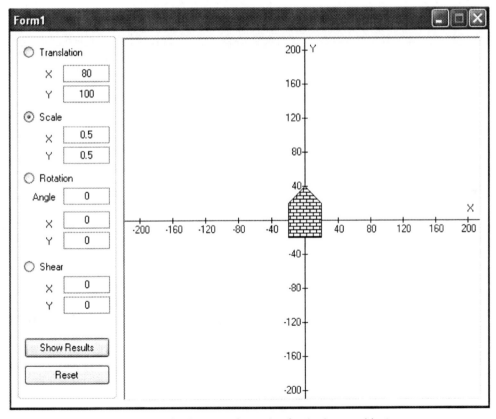

Figure 2-8 Scaling transformation for the house object.

Inside the `ApplyTransformation` method, we first translate the origin to the center of the `panel1`, and then flip the y axis (by changing the sign for all y values). This is necessary because we want the Y axis to be bottom-up. Now, let's examine the various transformations. First, select translation, and set x = 80, y = 100. Figure 2-7 shows the output. In this case, the house object moves 80 units in the X-direction and 100 units in the Y-direction from the origin.

The scale transformation scales the objects at the origin by setting proper scaling factors. Click on the Scale radio button, enter 0.5 into both the x and y textboxes, and click on "Show Results" button. You should obtain the new output shown in Figure 2-8. You can see that the house is reduced by a factor of 2 in both the x and y directions.

Now, let's rotate the house object. Click on the "Rotation" radio button, and set angle = 30 degrees, x = 40, and y = -40. Namely, we want to rotate the house object by 30 degrees at the point (40, - 40). The new output result is shown in Figure 2-9. The rotation center is marked by a black dot.

Finally, let's examine the shear transformation. The shear transformation is performed at the origin. Select the shear option by clicking on the "Shear" radio button, and enter 1 in the X shear and 0 in the Y shear. You should obtain the result shown in Figure 2-10.

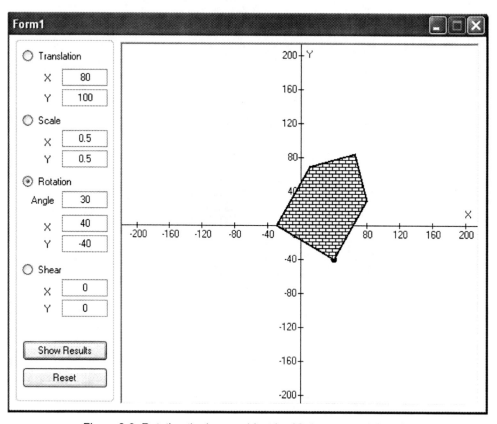

Figure 2-9 Rotating the house object by 30 degrees at (40, -40).

You can examine the effect of various transformations with different parameters on the house object based on *Example2_3*. I would like to point out here that the parameters you specify must be valid values. For example, in a shear transformation, if you set α = β = 1, you will get the "argument unhandled exception", because this setting is unphysical.

Combining Transformation in C#

It is convenient to represent the basic transformations, including translation, scaling, rotation, and shearing, in unified matrix forms based on homogeneous coordinates. However, the real value of the homogeneous coordinate system comes when you combine several different transformations together.

Suppose you want to rotate the house object by applying a rotation matrix R(θ), and then translate the object by applying a translation matrix T(dx, dy). You can write the transformation equation for this operation as (PH * R(θ)) * T(dx, dy), where PH stands for the points constructing the house.

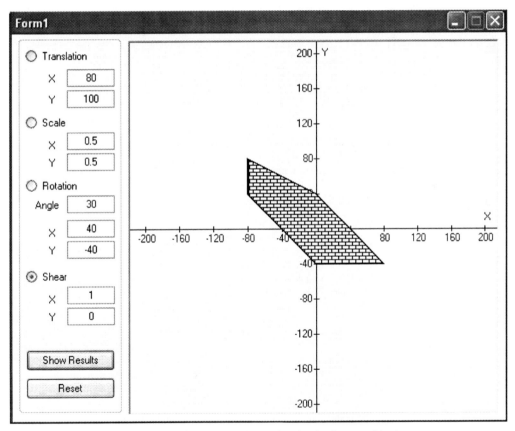

Figure 2-10 Shear transformation for the house object.

Please note that the multiplication of points (vectors) and matrices is associative. This means that it does not matter whether you multiply PH by R(θ) first or not. This allows you to rewrite the operation as PH * (R(θ) * T(dx, dy)), indicating that you can compute the matrix R(θ) * T(dx, dy) first and then multiply this new matrix by the point PH. This means that instead of multiplying the point PH by two matrices, you only need to multiply it by one matrix that combines both transformations.

Another aspect I will emphasize is that the order of the transformations is very important. The operation PH * (R(θ) * T(dx, dy)) ≠ PH * (T(dx, dy) * R(θ)). This can be demonstrated by a new C# Windows Application example: *Example2_4*. Here is the code listing of the Form1 class:

```csharp
using System;
using System.Drawing;
using System.Drawing.Drawing2D;
using System.Windows.Forms;

namespace Example2_4
{
    public partial class Form1 : Form
    {
        public Form1()
        {
            InitializeComponent();
            This.BackColor = Color.White;
            // Subscribing to a paint eventhandler to drawingPanel:
            panel1.Paint += new PaintEventHandler(panel1Paint);
        }

        private void panel1Paint(object sender, PaintEventArgs e)
        {
            Graphics g = e.Graphics;
            DrawAxes(g);
            ApplyTransformation(g);
        }

        private void ApplyTransformation(Graphics g)
        {
            // Create a new transform matrix:
            Matrix m = new Matrix();
            // Bring origin to the center:
            m.Translate(panel1.Width/2, panel1.Height/2);

            if (rbTranslationFirst.Checked)
            {
                // Translation:
                int dx = Convert.ToInt16(tbTranslationX.Text);
                int dy = - Convert.ToInt16(tbTranslationY.Text);
                m.Translate(dx, dy,MatrixOrder.Append);
                // Rotation:
                float angle = Convert.ToSingle(tbRotaionAngle.Text);
                m.RotateAt(angle, new PointF(panel1.Width/2,
                    panel1.Height/2), MatrixOrder.Append);
            }
            else if (rbRotationFirst.Checked)
```

```
    {
        // Rotation:
        float angle = Convert.ToSingle(tbRotaionAngle.Text);
        m.RotateAt(angle, new PointF(panel1.Width/2,
            panel1.Height/2), MatrixOrder.Append);
        // Translation:
        int dx = Convert.ToInt16(tbTranslationX.Text);
        int dy = - Convert.ToInt16(tbTranslationY.Text);
        m.Translate(dx, dy, MatrixOrder.Append);
    }
    g.Transform = m;
    DrawHouse(g, Color.Black);
}

private void DrawHouse(Graphics g, Color color)
{
    HatchBrush hb = new HatchBrush(HatchStyle.HorizontalBrick,
                        color, Color.White);
    Pen aPen = new Pen(color, 2);
    Point[] pta = new Point[5];
    pta[0] = new Point(-40, 40);
    pta[1] = new Point(40, 40);
    pta[2] = new Point(40, -40);
    pta[3] = new Point(0, -80);
    pta[4] = new Point(-40, -40);
    g.FillPolygon(hb, pta);
    g.DrawPolygon(aPen, pta);
    hb.Dispose();
    aPen.Dispose();
}

private void DrawAxes(Graphics g)
{
    Matrix m = new Matrix();
    // Move the origin to center of panel1:
    m.Translate(panel1.Width/2, panel1.Height/2);
    // Apply the transformation
    g.Transform = m;

    // Draw x and y axes:
    g.DrawLine(Pens.Blue, -panel1.Width / 2, 0,
        panel1.Width / 2, 0);
    g.DrawLine(Pens.Blue, 0, -panel1.Height / 2, 0,
        panel1.Height / 2);
    g.DrawString("X", this.Font, Brushes.Blue,
        panel1.Width / 2 - 20, -20);
    g.DrawString("Y", this.Font, Brushes.Blue, 5,
        -panel1.Height / 2+5);

    // Draw Ticks:
    int tick = 40;
    StringFormat sf = new StringFormat();
    sf.Alignment = StringAlignment.Far;
    for (int i = -160; i <= 160; i += tick)
```

```
                {
                    g.DrawLine(Pens.Blue, i, -3, i, 3);
                    g.DrawLine(Pens.Blue, -3, i, 3, i);

                    SizeF sizeXTick = g.MeasureString(i.ToString(),
                        this.Font);
                    if (i != 0)
                    {
                        g.DrawString(i.ToString(), this.Font,
                            Brushes.Blue,
                            i + sizeXTick.Width / 2, 4f, sf);
                        g.DrawString((-i).ToString(), this.Font,
                            Brushes.Blue,
                            -3f, i - sizeXTick.Height / 2, sf);
                    }
                    else
                    {
                        g.DrawString("0", this.Font, Brushes.Blue,
                            new PointF(i - sizeXTick.Width / 3, 4f), sf);
                    }
                }
            }

            private void btnReset_Click(object sender, EventArgs e)
            {
                // Reset parameters to default values:
                tbTranslationX.Text = "0";
                tbTranslationY.Text = "0";
                tbRotaionAngle.Text = "0";
                panel1.Invalidate();
            }

            private void btnShow_Click(object sender, EventArgs e)
            {
                panel1.Invalidate();
            }
        }
    }
```

In this example, we consider the combination of two transformations: translation and rotation. Within the ApplyTransformation method, we first bring the origin of the world coordinate system to the center of the panel1, and then perform the successive transformations: either the translation first or rotation first depending on your selection. We set the MatrixOrder property to Append, making sure that the order of transformations is correct.

As mentioned before, in transformation operations on a graphics object, the order of operations is very important. A translation followed by a rotation is different from a rotation followed by a translation, as illustrated in Figure 2-11 and Figure 2-12. In Figure 2-11, we first translate the house object 100 pixels in the y direction, and then perform a rotation by 45 degrees (clockwise). Please note that the rotation is always performed about the origin. That is why we get the result shown in Figure 2-11.

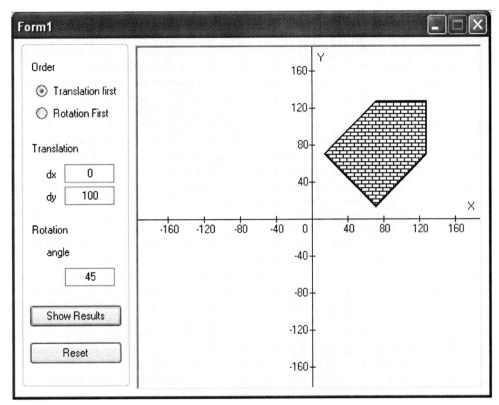

Figure 2-11 Transformation on the house object: translation followed by rotation.

On the other hand, in Figure 2-12, we first rotate the house by 45 degrees (also clockwise) about the origin, and then translate the house object in the y direction by 100 pixels. It is clear that the final location of the house is very different from that in Figure 2-11. You can practice composite transformations with different parameters by running this example.

Transformation of Multiple Objects in C#

As mentioned in Chapter 1, you can easily move objects to another position of the viewport by zooming and panning. However, in this way, you will move all objects inside the viewport. If you want to move a specific object without moving the others, you cannot use this method.

Instead you can apply transformations to the object you want to move. Here I will show you how to perform operations on different objects separately. Let's start with a new C# Windows Application project, and call it *Example2_5*. In this project, we create two house objects, and then apply different transformations on each one. This example is basically similar to the previous *Example2_4*. The only difference is the ApplyTransformation and DrawHouse methods. Here is the code listing of the ApplyTransformation and DrawHouse methods:

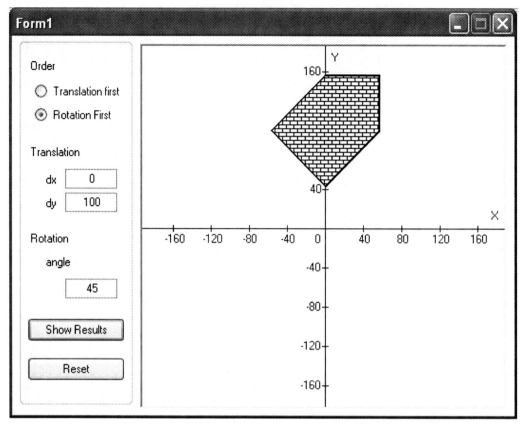

Figure 2-12 Transformation on the house object: rotation followed by translation.

```
private void ApplyTransformation(Graphics g)
{
    // Define a Pen and a HatchBrush objects used to draw house object:
    Pen aPen = new Pen(Color.Black, 2);
    HatchBrush hb;

    // Transformation on a horizontal-brick house:
    if (cbHBrickHouse.Checked)
    {
        // Create a new transform matrix:
        Matrix m = new Matrix();
        // Bring origin to the center:
        m.Translate(panel1.Width / 2, panel1.Height / 2);

        // Translation:
        int dx = Convert.ToInt16(tbRedTranslationX.Text);
        int dy = - Convert.ToInt16(tbRedTranslationY.Text);
        m.Translate(dx, dy,MatrixOrder.Append);

        // Rotation:
```

```
        float angle = Convert.ToSingle(tbRedRotaionAngle.Text);
        m.RotateAt(angle, new PointF(panel1.Width/2,
            panel1.Height/2), MatrixOrder.Append);
        g.Transform = m;

        // Define horizontalbrick brush:
        hb = new HatchBrush(HatchStyle.HorizontalBrick,
            Color.Black, Color.White);

        // Draw house object by calling DrawHouse method:
        DrawHouse(g, hb, aPen);
    }

    // Transformation on a diagonal-brick house:
    if (cbDBrickHouse.Checked)
    {
        // Create a new transform matrix:
        Matrix m1 = new Matrix();
        // Bring origin to the center:
        m1.Translate(panel1.Width / 2, panel1.Height / 2);

        // Rotation:
        float angle = Convert.ToSingle(tbGreenRotationAngle.Text);
        m1.RotateAt(angle, new PointF(panel1.Width/2,
            panel1.Height/2), MatrixOrder.Append);

        // Translation:
        int dx = Convert.ToInt16(tbGreenTranslationX.Text);
        int dy = - Convert.ToInt16(tbGreenTranslationY.Text);
        m1.Translate(dx, dy, MatrixOrder.Append);
        g.Transform = m1;

        // Define diagonal-brick brush:
        hb = new HatchBrush(HatchStyle.DiagonalBrick,
            Color.Black, Color.White);

        // Draw house obect by calling DrawHouse method:
        DrawHouse(g, hb, aPen);
    }
}

private void DrawHouse(Graphics g, HatchBrush hb, Pen aPen)
{
    Point[] pta = new Point[5];
    pta[0] = new Point(-40, 40);
    pta[1] = new Point(40, 40);
    pta[2] = new Point(40, -40);
    pta[3] = new Point(0, -80);
    pta[4] = new Point(-40, -40);
    g.FillPolygon(hb, pta);
    g.DrawPolygon(aPen, pta);
}
```

Inside the `ApplyTransformation` method, we define a `Pen` and a `HatchBrush` object that will be passed to the `DrawHouse` method to draw the house object. We then create two new matrices, m and m1, operatng on the horizontal-brick house and diagonal-brick house respectively. For the horizontal-brick house object, we first apply the translation and then the rotation, while for the diagonal-brick house, we reverse the transformation order: i.e., a rotation followed by a translation. You can specify different sets of parameters for these two house objects, and see how they move independently. You can view either both the house objects on the screen at the same time, or just look at one house object by un-checking the other.

Figure 2-13 shows a sample output by setting a translation of 100 pixels in the x direction and a rotation of 90 degrees for both house objects. You can see that their positions on the screen are very different because the transformation was performed in different orders.

Using the procedure described in this example, you can create an unlimited number of graphics objects inside a viewport, and move (by translation, rotation, scaling, and shearing) any specific objects among them, according to requirements of your applications. You simply create a transformation matrix and apply it to each object that you want to move.

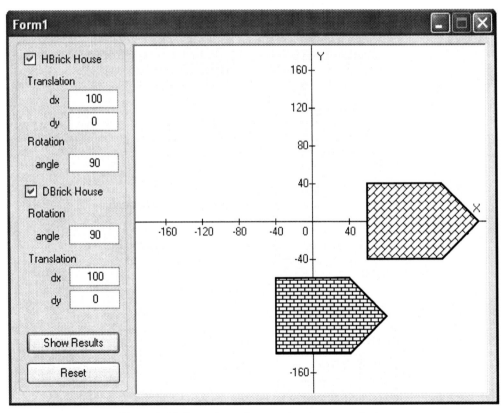

Figure 2-13 Transformations on two house projects.

Text Transformation

Placing a simple text string on the screen is easy with visual C#. You can use labels to display text, and text boxes to allow users to change text. Using Form or controls' ForeColor and BackColor properties, you can specify the color of the text. The Form and controls also have a Font property that determines the appearance of the text.

You can draw text directly on Form and controls using the Graphics.DrawString method. You can also apply various transformations to the text string. Transforming a text string is very useful. For example, you might need a vertical text string for the y axis label of a 2D charting program. Annotating charts with text and other explanatory material can improve the ability of charts to convey information. In these cases, you need to place the text string in the right position with the proper rotation angle.

As an example, we will create a new C# Windows Application project, *Example2_6*, based on the previous project *Example2_5*. In this example, I will show you how to translate, rotate, scale, and shear a text string. The main difference between the current project and *Example2_5* lies in the ApplyTransformation and DrawText methods:

```
private void ApplyTransformation(Graphics g)
{
    // Text Transformation:
    // Create a new transform matrix:
    Matrix m = new Matrix();
    // Bring origin to the center:
    m.Translate(panel1.Width / 2, panel1.Height / 2);

    // Translation:
    int dx = Convert.ToInt16(tbTranslationX.Text);
    int dy = - Convert.ToInt16(tbTranslationY.Text);
    m.Translate(dx, dy, MatrixOrder.Append);

    // Rotation:
    float angle = Convert.ToSingle(tbRotaionAngle.Text);
    m.RotateAt(angle, new PointF(panel1.Width / 2,
        panel1.Height / 2), MatrixOrder.Append);

    // Scaling:
    float sx = Convert.ToSingle(tbScaleX.Text);
    float sy = Convert.ToSingle(tbScaleY.Text);
    m.Scale(sx, sy);

    //Shearing:
    float shearx = Convert.ToSingle(tbShearX.Text);
    float sheary = Convert.ToSingle(tbShearY.Text);
    m.Shear(shearx, sheary);

    // Apply transformation matrix m to graphics object:
    g.Transform = m;
    DrawText(g, Color.Red);
}

private void DrawText(Graphics g, Color color)
```

```
    {
        string str = tbString.Text;
        Font aFont = new Font("Arial", 12, FontStyle.Bold);
        StringFormat sf = new StringFormat();
        sf.Alignment = StringAlignment.Center;
        SolidBrush aBrush = new SolidBrush(color);
        g.DrawString(str, aFont, aBrush, new PointF(0, 0), sf);
        aFont.Dispose();
        aBrush.Dispose();
    }
```

In this example, you enter a text string into the corresponding textbox, and specify various parameters for transformations of this text string. Building and running the project will obtain the results shown in Figure 2-14. In this example, we translate the text string 150 pixels in the y direction, then rotate it by 45 degrees (clockwise), followed by scaling and shearing as specified in the figure. From this example you can see how to place, rotate, stretch, and shear a text string anywhere on your screen.

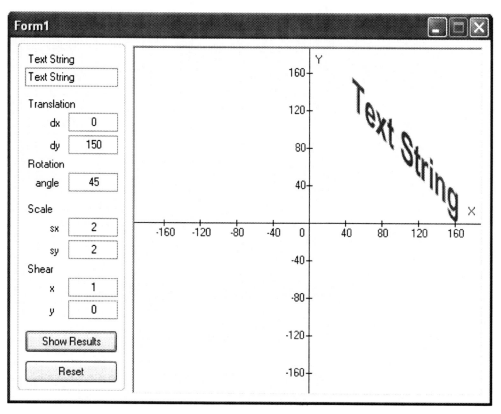

Figure 2-14 Transformations on a text string.

Transformations in Graphics Class

In the above several subsections, we discussed the transformations in the Matrix class. In fact, the Graphics class of C# and GDI+ also defines transformation functionalities. The transformations in the Graphics class take place in the world coordinate system. The members that specify the world transformation are stored in a matrix object. Graphics class has several methods for setting the members in the world transformation matrix. These members in the Graphics class are similar to those in the Matrix class as discussed previously. Here we list the transformation members in the Graphics class:

- TranslateTransform: a method that prepends the specified translation to the transformation matrix of a Graphics object.

- TranslateClip: a method that translates the clipping region of a Graphics object by specified amount in the horizontal and vertical directions.

- RotateTransform: a method that applies a specified rotation to the transformation matrix of a Graphics object.

- ScaleTransform: a method that applies a specified scaling operation to the transformation matrix of a Graphics object by prepending it to the object's transformation matrix.

- MultiplyTransform: a method that multiplies the world transformation of a Graphics object and a matrix object.

- Transform: a property that represents the world transformation for a Graphics object.

Thus, in your graphics applications, you have the option to use either the transformations in the Matrix class, as discussed in the previous sections, or the transformations in the Graphics class. Please note that there is no method for shearing transformation in the Graphics class. You have to use the Matrix class to perform shearing transformations.

Generally, for simple graphics transformations, it is convenient to use transformations in the Graphics class, while for complicated transformations, you should use transformations in the Matrix class.

For comparison, we will start with a new C# Windows Application project, *Example2_7*, that uses the transformations defined in the Graphics class. This project is similar to the previous project *Example2_3*. The following is its code listing:

```
using System;
using System.Drawing;
using System.Drawing.Drawing2D;
using System.Windows.Forms;

namespace Example2_7
{
    public partial class Form1 : Form
    {
        public Form1()
        {
            InitializeComponent();
            // Subscribing to a paint eventhandler to drawingPanel:
```

```
        panel1.Paint += new PaintEventHandler(panel1Paint);
}

private void panel1Paint(object sender, PaintEventArgs e)
{
    Graphics g = e.Graphics;
    DrawAxes(g);
    ApplyTransformation(g);
}

private void ApplyTransformation(Graphics g)
{
    // Reset graphics matrix to identity matrx:
    g.ResetTransform();
    // Bring origin to the center of the panel1:
    g.TranslateTransform(panel1.Width / 2, panel1.Height / 2);

    if (rbTranslation.Checked)
    {
        // Translation:
        int dx = Convert.ToInt16(tbTranslationX.Text);
        int dy = - Convert.ToInt16(tbTranslationY.Text);
        g.TranslateTransform(dx, dy);
    }
    else if (rbScale.Checked)
    {
        // Scaling:
        float sx = Convert.ToSingle(tbScaleX.Text);
        float sy = Convert.ToSingle(tbScaleY.Text);
        g.ScaleTransform(sy, sy);
    }
    else if (rbRotation.Checked)
    {
        // Rotation:
        float angle = Convert.ToSingle(tbRotaionAngle.Text);
        float x =  Convert.ToSingle(tbRotateAtX.Text);
        float y =  - Convert.ToSingle(tbRotateAtY.Text);
        g.FillEllipse(Brushes.Black, x - 4, y - 4, 8, 8);
        g.RotateTransform(angle);
    }
    else if (rbShear.Checked)
    {
        // Shear:
        Matrix m = new Matrix();
        float alpha = Convert.ToSingle(tbShearX.Text);
        float beta = Convert.ToSingle(tbShearY.Text);
        m.Shear(alpha, beta);
        g.MultiplyTransform(m);
    }
    DrawHouse(g, Color.Black);
}

private void DrawHouse(Graphics g, Color color)
{
```

```
        HatchBrush hb = new HatchBrush(HatchStyle.HorizontalBrick,
                         color, Color.White);
        Pen aPen = new Pen(color, 2);
        Point[] pta = new Point[5];
        pta[0] = new Point(-40, 40);
        pta[1] = new Point(40, 40);
        pta[2] = new Point(40, -40);
        pta[3] = new Point(0, -80);
        pta[4] = new Point(-40, -40);
        g.FillPolygon(hb, pta);
        g.DrawPolygon(aPen, pta);
        aPen.Dispose();
        hb.Dispose();
}

private void DrawAxes(Graphics g)
{
        // Move the origin to center of panel1:
        g.ResetTransform();
        g.TranslateTransform(panel1.Width / 2, panel1.Height / 2);

        // Draw x and y axes:
        g.DrawLine(Pens.Blue, -panel1.Width / 2, 0,
                panel1.Width / 2, 0);
        g.DrawLine(Pens.Blue, 0, -panel1.Height / 2, 0,
                panel1.Height / 2);
        g.DrawString("X", this.Font, Brushes.Blue,
                panel1.Width / 2 - 20, -20);
        g.DrawString("Y", this.Font, Brushes.Blue, 5,
                -panel1.Height / 2+5);

        // Draw Ticks:
        int tick = 40;
        StringFormat sf = new StringFormat();
        sf.Alignment = StringAlignment.Far;
        for (int i = -200; i <= 200; i += tick)
        {
            g.DrawLine(Pens.Blue, i, -3, i, 3);
            g.DrawLine(Pens.Blue, -3, i, 3, i);

            SizeF sizeXTick = g.MeasureString(i.ToString(), this.Font);
            if (i != 0)
            {
                g.DrawString(i.ToString(), this.Font, Brushes.Blue,
                    i + sizeXTick.Width / 2, 4f, sf);
                g.DrawString((-i).ToString(), this.Font, Brushes.Blue,
                    -3f, i - sizeXTick.Height / 2, sf);

            }
            else
            {
                g.DrawString("0", this.Font, Brushes.Blue,
                    new PointF(i - sizeXTick.Width / 3, 4f), sf);
            }
```

```
            }
        }

        private void btnReset_Click(object sender, EventArgs e)
        {
            // Reset parameters to default values:
            tbTranslationX.Text = "0";
            tbTranslationY.Text = "0";
            tbScaleX.Text = "1";
            tbScaleY.Text = "1";
            tbRotaionAngle.Text = "0";
            tbRotateAtX.Text = "0";
            tbRotateAtY.Text = "0";
            tbShearX.Text = "0";
            tbShearY.Text = "0";
            panel1.Invalidate();
        }

        private void btnShow_Click(object sender, EventArgs e)
        {
            panel1.Invalidate();
        }

    }
}
```

Running this project will obtain the same results shown in *Example2_3*. Please note that the shearing transformation has to be performed using a matrix transformation because there is no shearing transformation in the Graphics class.

3

2D Line Charts

In the previous two chapters, we discussed graphics basics and matrix transformations in C#. This chapter will show you how to apply the knowledge and approaches from these two chapters to create a real-world charting application. We will discuss the common charting elements and their implementation in a simple 2D X-Y line plot.

Your First Simple Line Chart

The most basic and useful type of chart that you may wish to create with C# is the simple 2D line chart of numerical data. Visual C# and its graphics class library GDI+ provide a set of commands and methods that can be used to create these charts. Even the most elementary 2D chart consists of several basic elements, including the lines, symbols, axes, tick markers, labels, title, and legend that make up the chart. The following list gives a quick overview of some of the most basic chart elements without getting into details. These elements will often be referred to in this book:

- Axes - a graphics object that defines a region of the chart in which the chart is drawn.
- Line - a graphics object that represents the data you have plotted.
- Text - a graphics object that is comprised of a string of characters.
- Title - the text string object that is located directly above an axis object.
- XLabel - the text string object associated with the X-axis.

- YLabel - the text string object associated with the Y-axis.
- Legend - the string array object that represents the color and values of the lines.

In the next few sections, we will discuss how to create various line charts using C#.

Basic Elements of 2D Line Charts

The X-Y line chart is probably the most basic, yet most useful plot you may want to create. It uses two values to represent each data point. It is very useful describing relationships between data, and is often used in statistical analysis of data. This type of chart has found wide applications in the scientific, mathematic, engineering, and finance communities, as well as our daily lives.

Figure 3-1 shows the basic terms used to describe 2D X-Y chart elements. It can be seen from this figure that the chart area element represents the area of the chart that contains data as well as title, labels, tick markers, legend, and axes. Most line charts have two axes, X and Y. The title element is used to display descriptive information about the chart. Sometimes, it is often omitted. The legend element displays information about each data series of the chart, including line color, symbol, and a text description about each data series. When creating a legend for a chart, you should allow users to change its position, font, and background color.

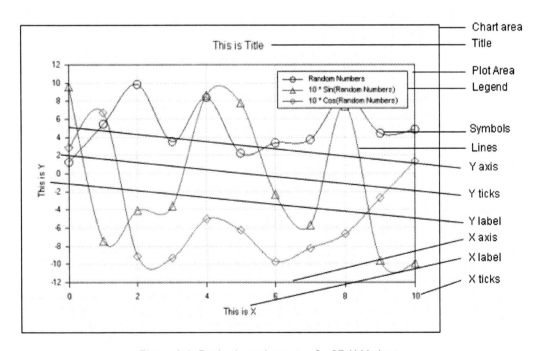

Figure 3-1 Basic chart elements of a 2D X-Y chart.

Sometimes a chart can have a secondary Y axis, called Y2. In this case, the chart is said to have three axes: X, Y, and Y2. The plot area element represents the part of the chart area that is used to display the data series, which is similar to the viewport discussed in Chapter 1. The lines and symbols used to represent the data series cannot be drawn outside this plot area. The tick markers, X- and Y- labels, lines, and symbols are all self-explanatory.

Creating a Simple 2D Line Chart Using C#

It's easy to create a 2D X-Y chart using C#. Let's use an example to illustrate the procedure. Start off with a new C# Windows Application project and call it *Example3_1*. The following is the code listing of `Form1` class that generates a simple X-Y chart with two lines, representing `Sine` and `Cosine` functions respectively:

```csharp
using System;
using System.Drawing;
using System.Windows.Forms;

namespace Example3_1
{
    public partial class Form1 : Form
    {
        // Define the drawing area
        private Rectangle PlotArea;
        // Unit defined in world coordinate system:
        private float xMin = 0f;
        private float xMax = 6;
        private float yMin = -1.1f;
        private float yMax = 1.1f;
        private int nPoints = 61;
        // Unit in pixel:
        private int offset = 30;

        public Form1()
        {
            InitializeComponent();
            This.BackColor = Color.White;
            this.SetStyle(ControlStyles.ResizeRedraw, true);
        }

        protected override void OnPaint(PaintEventArgs e)
        {
            Graphics g = e.Graphics;

            // Calculate the location and size of the plot area
            // within which we want to draw the graphics:
            Rectangle ChartArea = ClientRectangle;
            PlotArea = new Rectangle(ChartArea.Location,
                        ChartArea.Size);
            PlotArea.Inflate(-offset, -offset);

            //Draw PlotArea:
            g.DrawRectangle(Pens.Black, PlotArea);

            // Generate Sine and Cosine data points to plot:
            PointF[] pt1 = new PointF[nPoints];
            PointF[] pt2 = new PointF[nPoints];
```

```
                for (int i = 0; i < nPoints; i++)
                {
                    pt1[i] = new PointF(i / 5.0f, (float)Math.Sin(i/5.0f));
                    pt2[i] = new PointF(i / 5.0f, (float)Math.Cos(i/5.0f));
                }

                // Draw Sine and Cosine lines:
                for (int i = 1; i < nPoints; i++)
                {
                    g.DrawLine(Pens.Blue, Point2D(pt1[i - 1]),
                                          Point2D(pt1[i]));
                    g.DrawLine(Pens.Red, Point2D(pt2[i - 1]),
                                          Point2D(pt2[i]));
                }
                g.Dispose();
            }

            private PointF Point2D(PointF ptf)
            {
                PointF aPoint = new PointF();
                if (ptf.X < xMin || ptf.X > xMax ||
                    ptf.Y < yMin || ptf.Y > yMax)
                {
                    ptf.X = Single.NaN;
                    ptf.Y = Single.NaN;
                }
                aPoint.X = PlotArea.X + (ptf.X - xMin) *
                    PlotArea.Width / (xMax - xMin);
                aPoint.Y = PlotArea.Bottom - (ptf.Y - yMin) *
                    PlotArea.Height / (yMax - yMin);
                return aPoint;
            }
        }
    }
```

Building and executing the program produces the results shown in Figure 3-2.

How It Works

You might notice that most of the *Example3_1* program is the same as *Example1_2*, except that
we define two PointF arrays that represent Sine and Cosine functions. We move sequentially
through these arrays of values in Sine and Cosine functions, drawing lines from one data point
to the next:

```
        for (int i = 1; i < nPoints; i++)
        {
            g.DrawLine(Pens.Blue, Point2D(pt1[i - 1]), Point2D(pt1[i]));
            g.DrawLine(Pens.Red, Point2D(pt2[i - 1]),Point2D(pt2[i]));
        }
```

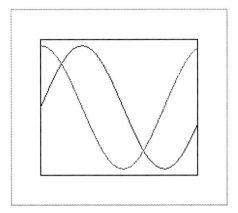

Figure 3-2 2D chart for Sine and Cosine functions.

Again, we transform the original data points in the world coordinate system into points in the device coordinate system using the Point2D method. Also note that we limited the lines to be drawn only inside the plot area using an if-statement in the Point2D method:

```
if (ptf.X < xMin || ptf.X > xMax || ptf.Y < yMin || ptf.Y > yMax)
{
    ptf.X = Single.NaN;
    ptf.Y = Single.NaN;
}
```

Here, when a point is located outside of the plot area, we set its X- and Y-components to be the Single.NaN, meaning that they are not a number or not defined. Be careful with confining the drawings inside the plot area using this approach. This method is only applicable in two situations: a line has many data points (for example, at least 10), and there are points defined at or close to the boundary of the plot area. Otherwise, some line segments may not be drawn. For example, suppose that you are defining a line with three points, and that two end points are outside of the plot area. In this case, when you call the g.DrawLine method, nothing will be drawn inside the plot area because there is only one valid point. In this situation, you need to use the viewport based on the drawingPanel, as discussed in Chapter 1.

Changing Chart Position

Another point I like to make here is that we define the Chart Area as the ClientRectangle, i.e., the entire area of Form1. In some cases, you may want the chart to occupy only a portion of Form1, while in some other situations, you may want to move the chart to a particular position in Form1. This can be achieved by redefining the Chart Area without touching the rest of the code. For example, replace the following code in *Example3_1*:

```
Rectangle ChartArea = ClientRectangle;
```

with the following code snippet:

```
Rectangle ChartArea = new Rectangle(50, 50,
    ClientRectangle.Width - 70, ClientRectangle.Height-70);
```

```
g.DrawRectangle(Pens.LightCoral, ChartArea);
```

In this case, the chart area is reduced compared to Form1 and moved to the bottom-right corner. By redefining the chart area, you can place your chart anywhere you like.

Creating Line Charts Using ArrayList

In the above example, we demonstrated how easy it is to create a simple line plot in C#, but didn't pay much attention to the program structure. We used a 1D point array to represent the data points. A problem with this method is that you must predetermine the number of points in order to use this point array. This is not very convenient if the number of points in your applications grow dynamically, such as in real-time stock charts. A way to avoid this problem is to use the ArrayList instead of a 1D point array. For the program to be more object-oriented and easily extend to add new features, we will define four new classes, including DataCollection, DataSeries, ChartStyle, and LineStyle. The ChartStyle class includes all chart-layout-related information. The DataCollection class holds the DataSeries, with each DataSeries representing one curve on the chart. The DataSeries class holds the chart data and line styles. The LineStyle class is used to specify the line color, thickness, dash style, etc.

Chart Style

Let's create a new C# Windows Application project, and call it *Example3_2*. Right click on the *Example3_2* project in the solution explorer, choose Add|Class... and change the class name to ChartStyle.cs. Add the other three classes, DataCollection.cs, DataSeries.cs, and LineStyle.cs, to the project in the same manner. We will first examine the ChartStyle class. The following is its code listing:

```
using System;
using System.Drawing;
using System.Drawing.Drawing2D;

namespace Example3_2
{
    public class ChartStyle
    {
        private Form1 form1;
        private Rectangle chartArea;
        private Rectangle plotArea;
        private Color chartBackColor;
        private Color chartBorderColor;
        private Color plotBackColor = Color.White;
        private Color plotBorderColor = Color.Black;
        private float xLimMin = 0f;
        private float xLimMax = 10f;
        private float yLimMin = 0f;
        private float yLimMax = 10f;

        public ChartStyle(Form1 fm1)
        {
            form1 = fm1;
```

```
            chartArea = form1.ClientRectangle;
            chartBackColor = fm1.BackColor;
            chartBorderColor = fm1.BackColor;
            PlotArea = chartArea;
        }

        public Color ChartBackColor
        {
            get { return chartBackColor; }
            set { chartBackColor = value; }
        }

        public Color ChartBorderColor
        {
            get { return chartBorderColor; }
            set { chartBorderColor = value; }
        }

        public Color PlotBackColor
        {
            get { return plotBackColor; }
            set { plotBackColor = value; }
        }

        public Color PlotBorderColor
        {
            get { return plotBorderColor; }
            set { plotBorderColor = value; }
        }

        public Rectangle ChartArea
        {
            get { return chartArea; }
            set { chartArea = value; }
        }

        public Rectangle PlotArea
        {
            get { return plotArea; }
            set { plotArea = value; }
        }

        public float XLimMax
        {
            get { return xLimMax; }
            set { xLimMax = value; }
        }

        public float XLimMin
        {
            get { return xLimMin; }
            set { xLimMin = value; }
        }
```

```
        public float YLimMax
        {
            get { return yLimMax; }
            set { yLimMax = value; }
        }

        public float YLimMin
        {
            get { return yLimMin; }
            set { yLimMin = value; }
        }

        public void AddChartStyle(Graphics g)
        {
            // Draw ChartArea and PlotArea:
            Pen aPen = new Pen(ChartBorderColor);
            SolidBrush aBrush = new SolidBrush(ChartBackColor);
            g.FillRectangle(aBrush, ChartArea);
            g.DrawRectangle(aPen, ChartArea);
            aPen = new Pen(PlotBorderColor, 1f);
            aBrush = new SolidBrush(PlotBackColor);
            g.FillRectangle(aBrush, PlotArea);
            g.DrawRectangle(aPen, PlotArea);
            aPen.Dispose();
            aBrush.Dispose();
        }

        public PointF Point2D(PointF pt)
        {
            PointF aPoint = new PointF();
            if (pt.X < XLimMin || pt.X > XLimMax ||
                pt.Y < YLimMin || pt.Y > YLimMax)
            {
                pt.X = Single.NaN;
                pt.Y = Single.NaN;
            }
            aPoint.X = PlotArea.X + (pt.X - XLimMin) *
                PlotArea.Width / (XLimMax - XLimMin);
            aPoint.Y = PlotArea.Bottom - (pt.Y - YLimMin) *
                PlotArea.Height / (YLimMax - YLimMin);
            return aPoint;
        }
    }
}
```

We first pass Form1 to this class because we need to use the ClientRectangle of Form1 as the default value of the ChartArea. Then we create various member fields that can be used to manipulate the chart layout, including PlotArea, ChartArea, the background color of the chart, and the limits of the axes. Next, we define corresponding public properties for these fields using the Get and Set statements. The default values of these public properties can be overridden according to your application requirements. The real action happens inside the public method AddChartStyle, which places the specified chart layout to your chart. We also move the

Point2D method from the original Form1 class to the ChartStyle class, making the codes clearer and more readable.

Data Collection

The following is the code listing of the DataCollection class:

```
using System;
using System.Collections;
using System.Drawing;
using System.Drawing.Drawing2D;

namespace Example3_2
{
    public class DataCollection
    {
        private ArrayList dataSeriesList;
        private int dataSeriesIndex = 0;

        public DataCollection()
        {
            dataSeriesList = new ArrayList();
        }

        public ArrayList DataSeriesList
        {
            get { return dataSeriesList; }
            set { dataSeriesList = value; }
        }

        public int DataSeriesIndex
        {
            get { return dataSeriesIndex; }
            set { dataSeriesIndex = value; }
        }

        public void Add(DataSeries ds)
        {
            dataSeriesList.Add(ds);
            if (ds.SeriesName == "Default Name")
            {
                ds.SeriesName = "DataSeries" +
                  dataSeriesList.Count.ToString();
            }
        }

        public void Insert(int dataSeriesIndex, DataSeries ds)
        {
            dataSeriesList.Insert(dataSeriesIndex, ds);
            if (ds.SeriesName == "Default Name")
            {
                dataSeriesIndex = dataSeriesIndex + 1;
                ds.SeriesName = "DataSeries" +
```

```
                    dataSeriesIndex.ToString();
            }
        }

        public void Remove(string dataSeriesName)
        {
            if (dataSeriesList != null)
            {
                for (int i = 0; i < dataSeriesList.Count; i++)
                {
                    DataSeries ds = (DataSeries)dataSeriesList[i];
                    if (ds.SeriesName == dataSeriesName)
                    {
                        dataSeriesList.RemoveAt(i);
                    }
                }
            }
        }

        public void RemoveAll()
        {
            dataSeriesList.Clear();
        }

        public void AddLines(Graphics g, ChartStyle cs)
        {
            // Plot lines:
            foreach (DataSeries ds in DataSeriesList)
            {
                if (ds.LineStyle.IsVisible == true)
                {
                    Pen aPen = new Pen(ds.LineStyle.LineColor,
                        ds.LineStyle.Thickness);
                    aPen.DashStyle = ds.LineStyle.Pattern;
                    for (int i = 1; i < ds.PointList.Count; i++)
                    {
                        g.DrawLine(aPen,
                            cs.Point2D((PointF)ds.PointList[i - 1]),
                            cs.Point2D((PointF)ds.PointList[i]));
                    }
                    aPen.Dispose();
                }
            }
        }
    }
}
```

The DataCollection class is used to hold the DataSeries. We start off by introducing two member fields: dataSeriesList and dataSeriesIndex. The dataSeriesList field holds the DataSeries, and the dataSeriesIndex represents the index of a particular DataSeries object in the dataSeriesList. Then, we create properties for these two fields using the Get and Set statements. Next we define several methods, including Add, Insert,

Romove, and RemoveAll. These methods allow us to add, insert, and remove DataSeries to or from the dataSeriesList. The RemoveAll method removes all DataSeries in the dataSeriesList.

There is an important method in this class, AddLines, which was originally defined in Form1 in *Example3_1*. This method draws lines using the DataSeries objects in the DataCollection class. For each data series, we create a new Pen using different LineStyle properties. Then we move sequentially through the PointList in each DataSeries, and draw a line from one data point to the next using a-for loop. Also note how we finish by disposing of the Pen and the Graphics object.

Data Series

The following is the code listing of the DataSeries class:

```
using System;
using System.Collections;
using System.Drawing;

namespace Example3_2
{
    public class DataSeries
    {
        private ArrayList pointList;
        private LineStyle lineStyle;
        private string seriesName = "Default Name";

        public DataSeries()
        {
            lineStyle = new LineStyle();
            pointList = new ArrayList();
        }

        public LineStyle LineStyle
        {
            get { return lineStyle; }
            set { lineStyle = value; }
        }

        public string SeriesName
        {
            get { return seriesName; }
            set { seriesName = value; }
        }

        public ArrayList PointList
        {
            get { return pointList ; }
            set { pointList = value; }
        }

        public void AddPoint(PointF pt)
```

```
        {
            pointList.Add(pt);
        }
    }
}
```

In this class, we start off by creating three member fields: `pointList`, `lineStyle`, and `seriesName`. The `pointList` field is an `ArrayList` object that holds the data points to be plotted on the chart, and the `lineStyle` field is an object of the `LineStyle` class that specifies the line color, thickness, and dash style. The `seriesName` field allows you to assign a name to the `DataSeries`, which will be used later in the chart legend. We also create corresponding public properties to get and set these fields. In this way, we can access various line style properties from the `DataSeries` class. Finally, an `AddPoint` method in the `DataSeries` class is implemented, enabling you to add the data points to the `PointList`.

Line Style

The code of `LineStyle` class is listed in the following:

```
using System;
using System.Drawing;
using System.Drawing.Drawing2D;

namespace Example3_2
{
    public class LineStyle
    {
        private DashStyle linePattern = DashStyle.Solid;
        private Color lineColor = Color.Black;
        private float LineThickness = 1.0f;
        private bool isVisible = true;

        public LineStyle()
        {
        }

        public bool IsVisible
        {
            get { return isVisible; }
            set { isVisible = value; }
        }

        virtual public DashStyle Pattern
        {
            get { return linePattern; }
            set { linePattern = value; }
        }

        public float Thickness
        {
            get { return LineThickness; }
            set { LineThickness = value; }
```

```
        }

        virtual public Color LineColor
        {
            get { return lineColor; }
            set { lineColor = value; }
        }
    }
}
```

The LineStyle class is straightforward. The first three member fields are standard line styles: color, thickness, and dash style. The fourth field is the isVisible which allows you to selectively turn the line's visibility on or off. The rest of the class consists of definitions of corresponding properties for these fields using the Get and Set statements.

Form1 class

The following is the code listing of the Form1 class:

```
using System;
using System.Drawing;
using System.Drawing.Drawing2D;
using System.Collections;
using System.Windows.Forms;

namespace Example3_2
{
    public partial class Form1 : Form
    {
        private DataCollection dc;
        private ChartStyle cs;

        public Form1()
        {
            InitializeComponent();
            this.SetStyle(ControlStyles.ResizeRedraw, true);
            dc = new DataCollection();
            cs = new ChartStyle(this);
            cs.XLimMin = 0f;
            cs.XLimMax = 6f;
            cs.YLimMin = -1.1f;
            cs.YLimMax = 1.1f;
        }

        protected override void OnPaint(PaintEventArgs e)
        {
            Graphics g = e.Graphics;
            cs.ChartArea = this.ClientRectangle;
            AddData();
            SetPlotArea(g);
            cs.AddChartStyle(g);
            dc.AddLines(g, cs);
            g.Dispose();
```

```
        }

        public void AddData()
        {
            dc.DataSeriesList.Clear();
            // Add Sine data with 20 data points:
            DataSeries ds1 = new DataSeries();
            ds1.LineStyle.LineColor = Color.Red;
            ds1.LineStyle.Thickness = 2f;
            ds1.LineStyle.Pattern = DashStyle.Dash;
            for (int i = 0; i < 20; i++)
            {
                ds1.AddPoint(new PointF(i / 5.0f,
                    (float)Math.Sin(i / 5.0f)));
            }
            dc.Add(ds1);

            // Add Cosine data with 40 data points:
            DataSeries ds2 = new DataSeries();
            ds2.LineStyle.LineColor = Color.Blue;
            ds2.LineStyle.Thickness = 1f;
            ds2.LineStyle.Pattern = DashStyle.Solid;
            for (int i = 0; i < 40; i++)
            {
                ds2.AddPoint(new PointF(i / 5.0f,
                    (float)Math.Cos(i / 5.0f)));
            }
            dc.Add(ds2);
        }

        private void SetPlotArea(Graphics g)
        {
            // Set PlotArea:
            int xOffset = cs.ChartArea.Width / 10;
            int yOffset = cs.ChartArea.Height / 10;
            // Define the plot area:
            int plotX = cs.ChartArea.X + xOffset;
            int plotY = cs.ChartArea.Y + yOffset;
            int plotWidth = cs.ChartArea.Width - 2 * xOffset;
            int plotHeight = cs.ChartArea.Height - 2 * yOffset;
            cs.PlotArea = new Rectangle(plotX, plotY, plotWidth, plotHeight);
        }
    }
}
```

In this class, we begin by creating instances for ChartStyle and DataCollection. Inside
Form1's instructor, we override the axis limit properties which have been originally defined in
ChartStyle class, to meet the requirements of the current application. We implement three
methods in this class: OnPaint, AddData, and SetPlotArea. We override the PlotArea
property by redefining its size in the SetPlotArea method using the code snippet:

```
    cs.PlotArea = new Rectangle(plotX, plotY, plotWidth, plotHeight);
```

If you do not override this property, the default value will be used, which is the ChartArea defined in ChartStyle class. In real-world applications, you should set the PlotArea property carefully in the SetPlotArea method. Generally, the users of your programs should not have to define this property so that they can concentrate on their data processing, instead of the chart layout.

The real action happens inside the AddData method. Please pay attention to how we add DataSeries objects to the DataCollection class:

```
dc.DataSeriesList.Clear();
// Add Sine data with 20 data point:
DataSeries ds1 = new DataSeries();
ds1.LineStyle.LineColor = Color.Red;
ds1.LineStyle.Thickness = 2f;
ds1.LineStyle.Pattern = DashStyle.Dash;
for (int i = 0; i < 20; i++)
{
    ds1.AddPoint(new PointF(i / 5.0f,
            (float)Math.Sin(i / 5.0f)));
}
dc.Add(ds1);
```

We first clear up the DataSeriesList, an object of the DataCollection class, to make sure there are no old DataSeries objects left. Then, we create a DataSeries object, ds1, and define its LineStyle properties. We add data points to the ds1.PointList using the ds1.AddPoint method. Finally, we add the data series ds1 to the DataCollection class using the dc.Add method. This way, you can add any number of DataSeries objects to the DataCollection. The AddLines method in the DataCollection class draws curves on the chart for all the DataSeries objects inside the DataCollection using a foreach loop:

```
foreach (DataSeries ds in DataSeriesList)
{
    .....
}
```

Inside the OnPaint method, we plot the Sine and Cosine data by calling various methods. Please note that we redeclare the ChartArea:

```
cs.ChartArea = this.ClientRectangle;
```

This is just the default value for the ChartArea property, as defined in the ChartStyle class, so why do we redefine it here? The reason is to give your chart the capability to resize when Form1 gets resized. Otherwise, the size of your chart is fixed regardless if Form1 is resized or not.

Testing Project

Building and running the project *Example4_2* produces the result shown in Figure 3-3.

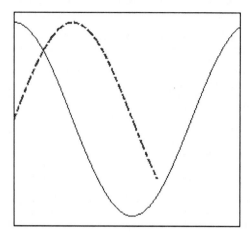

Figure 3-3 Sine and Cosine chart generated from Example3_2.

Gridlines and Labels

In the above subsection, only the lines for the Sine and Cosine functions were drawn on the chart. In this section, we will add more elements to the 2D line chart, including gridlines, a title, tick marks, and labels for axes. Let's start with a new example project *Example3_3*, that is based on the previous example, *Example3_2*. We will modify some codes in the ChartStyle and Form1 classes. The other classes, DataCollection, DataSeries, and LineStyle, will be kept the same as in *Example3_2*.

Modifying Form1 Class

There are two places in the Form1 class that need to be modified. First, change the constructor of Form1 to the following:

```
public Form1()
{
    InitializeComponent();
    SetStyle(ControlStyles.ResizeRedraw, true);
    // Set Form1 size:
    this.Width = 350;
    this.Height = 300;
    dc = new DataCollection();
    cs = new ChartStyle(this);
    cs.XLimMin = 0f;
    cs.XLimMax = 6f;
    cs.YLimMin = -1.5f;
    cs.YLimMax = 1.5f;
    cs.XTick = 1f;
    cs.YTick = 0.5f;
    cs.TickFont = new Font("Arial", 7, FontStyle.Regular);
    cs.XLabel = "X Axis";
```

```
        cs.YLabel = "Y Axis";
        cs.Title = "Sine & Cosine Plot";
        cs.TitleFont = new Font("Arial", 10, FontStyle.Regular);
    }
```

Here, we change the size of Form1 to 350x300 to display the chart on screen more clearly. Then we override the tick font, labels, and title properties. There are more features in the ChartStyle class that you can play with, this example simply shows you how to set some of these properties.

Another area you need to modify is the SetPlotArea method. Since the labels of the axes, title, and tick markers all have an effect on the size of the PlotArea, the implementation of this method becomes more complicated than that of the previous project. Here is the code snippet of this method:

```
    private void SetPlotArea(Graphics g)
    {
        // Set PlotArea:
        float xOffset = cs.ChartArea.Width / 30.0f;
        float yOffset = cs.ChartArea.Height / 30.0f;
        SizeF labelFontSize = g.MeasureString("A", cs.LabelFont);
        SizeF titleFontSize = g.MeasureString("A", cs.TitleFont);
        if (cs.Title.ToUpper() == "NO TITLE")
        {
            titleFontSize.Width = 8f;
            titleFontSize.Height = 8f;
        }
        float xSpacing = xOffset / 3.0f;
        float ySpacing = yOffset / 3.0f;
        SizeF tickFontSize = g.MeasureString("A", cs.TickFont);
        float tickSpacing = 2f;
        SizeF yTickSize = g.MeasureString(
                cs.YLimMin.ToString(), cs.TickFont);
        for (float yTick = cs.YLimMin;
                yTick <= cs.YLimMax; yTick += cs.YTick)
        {
            SizeF tempSize = g.MeasureString(
                    yTick.ToString(), cs.TickFont);
            if (yTickSize.Width < tempSize.Width)
            {
                yTickSize = tempSize;
            }
        }
        float leftMargin = xOffset + labelFontSize.Width +
                xSpacing + yTickSize.Width + tickSpacing;
        float rightMargin = 2 * xOffset;
        float topMargin = yOffset + titleFontSize.Height + ySpacing;
        float bottomMargin = yOffset + labelFontSize.Height +
                ySpacing + tickSpacing + tickFontSize.Height;

        // Define the plot area with one Y axis:
        int plotX = cs.ChartArea.X + (int)leftMargin;
        int plotY = cs.ChartArea.Y + (int)topMargin;
        int plotWidth = cs.ChartArea.Width -
```

```
                    (int)leftMargin - (int)rightMargin;
        int plotHeight = cs.ChartArea.Height -
                    (int)topMargin - (int)bottomMargin;
        cs.PlotArea = new Rectangle(plotX, plotY, plotWidth, plotHeight);
}
```

Please note how we take the font size of the label, title, and ticks into consideration when determining the `PlotArea` size. We measure the font size using the `g.MeasureString` method:

```
SizeF labelFontSize = g.MeasureString("A", cs.LabelFont);
SizeF titleFontSize = g.MeasureString("A", cs.TitleFont);
SizeF tickFontSize = g.MeasureString("A", cs.TickFont);
```

We also find the maximum string size of the tick markers, making sure that there is enough room for the axis labels:

```
SizeF yTickSize = g.MeasureString(
    cs.YLimMin.ToString(), cs.TickFont);
for (float yTick = cs.YLimMin;
    yTick <= cs.YLimMax; yTick += cs.YTick)
{
    SizeF tempSize = g.MeasureString(
        yTick.ToString(), cs.TickFont);
    if (yTickSize.Width < tempSize.Width)
    {
        yTickSize = tempSize;
    }
}
```

Taking all these factors into account, we determine the margins of the `PlotArea` relative to the `ChartArea`, and we are finally able to create the `Rectangle` of `PlotArea`.

Modifying Chart Style

Compared to the previous project, here we add more features to the `ChartStyle` class. The following is the code listing of this class:

```
using System;
using System.Collections;
using System.Drawing;
using System.Drawing.Drawing2D;

namespace Example3_3
{
    public class ChartStyle
    {
        private Form1 form1;
        private Rectangle chartArea;
        private Rectangle plotArea;
        private Color chartBackColor;
        private Color chartBorderColor;
        private Color plotBackColor = Color.White;
        private Color plotBorderColor = Color.Black;
```

```csharp
private float xLimMin = 0f;
private float xLimMax = 10f;
private float yLimMin = 0f;
private float yLimMax = 10f;
private DashStyle gridPattern = DashStyle.Solid;
private Color gridColor = Color.LightGray;
private float gridLineThickness = 1.0f;
private bool isXGrid = true;
private bool isYGrid = true;
private string xLabel = "X Axis";
private string yLabel = "Y Axis";
private string sTitle = "Title";
private Font labelFont = new Font("Arial", 10,
        FontStyle.Regular);
private Color labelFontColor = Color.Black;
private Font titleFont = new Font("Arial", 12,
 FontStyle.Regular);
private Color titleFontColor = Color.Black;
private float xTick = 1f;
private float yTick = 2f;
private Font tickFont;
private Color tickFontColor = Color.Black;

public ChartStyle(Form1 fm1)
{
    form1 = fm1;
    chartArea = form1.ClientRectangle;
    chartBackColor = fm1.BackColor;
    chartBorderColor = fm1.BackColor;
    PlotArea = chartArea;
    tickFont = form1.Font;
}

public Font TickFont
{
    get { return tickFont; }
    set { tickFont = value; }
}

public Color TickFontColor
{
    get { return tickFontColor; }
    set { tickFontColor = value; }
}

public Color ChartBackColor
{
    get { return chartBackColor; }
    set { chartBackColor = value; }
}

public Color ChartBorderColor
{
    get { return chartBorderColor; }
```

```csharp
        set { chartBorderColor = value; }
    }

    public Color PlotBackColor
    {
        get { return plotBackColor; }
        set { plotBackColor = value; }
    }

    public Color PlotBorderColor
    {
        get { return plotBorderColor; }
        set { plotBorderColor = value; }
    }

    public Rectangle ChartArea
    {
        get { return chartArea; }
        set { chartArea = value; }
    }

    public Rectangle PlotArea
    {
        get { return plotArea; }
        set { plotArea = value; }
    }

    public bool IsXGrid
    {
        get { return isXGrid; }
        set { isXGrid = value; }
    }

    public bool IsYGrid
    {
        get { return isYGrid; }
        set { isYGrid = value; }
    }

    public string Title
    {
        get { return sTitle; }
        set { sTitle = value; }
    }

    public string Label
    {
        get { return xLabel; }
        set { xLabel = value; }
    }

    public string YLabel
    {
        get { return yLabel; }
```

```
        set { yLabel = value; }
    }

    public Font LabelFont
    {
        get { return labelFont; }
        set { labelFont = value; }
    }

    public Color LabelFontColor
    {
        get { return labelFontColor; }
        set { labelFontColor = value; }
    }

    public Font TitleFont
    {
        get { return titleFont; }
        set { titleFont = value; }
    }

    public Color TitleFontColor
    {
        get { return titleFontColor; }
        set { titleFontColor = value; }
    }

    public float XLimMax
    {
        get { return xLimMax; }
        set { xLimMax = value; }
    }

    public float XLimMin
    {
        get { return xLimMin; }
        set { xLimMin = value; }
    }

    public float YLimMax
    {
        get { return yLimMax; }
        set { yLimMax = value; }
    }

    public float YLimMin
    {
        get { return yLimMin; }
        set { yLimMin = value; }
    }

    public float XTick
    {
        get { return xTick; }
```

```csharp
        set { xTick = value; }
    }

    public float YTick
    {
        get { return yTick; }
        set { yTick = value; }
    }

    virtual public DashStyle GridPattern
    {
        get { return gridPattern; }
        set { gridPattern = value; }
    }

    public float GridThickness
    {
        get { return gridLineThickness; }
        set { gridLineThickness = value; }
    }

    virtual public Color GridColor
    {
        get { return gridColor; }
        set { gridColor = value; }
    }

    public void AddChartStyle(Graphics g)
    {
        // Draw ChartArea and PlotArea:
        Pen aPen = new Pen(ChartBorderColor, 1f);
        SolidBrush aBrush = new SolidBrush(ChartBackColor);
        g.FillRectangle(aBrush, ChartArea);
        g.DrawRectangle(aPen, ChartArea);
        aPen = new Pen(PlotBorderColor, 1f);
        aBrush = new SolidBrush(PlotBackColor);
        g.FillRectangle(aBrush, PlotArea);
        g.DrawRectangle(aPen, PlotArea);
        SizeF tickFontSize = g.MeasureString("A", TickFont);

        // Create vertical gridlines:
        float fX, fY;
        if (IsYGrid == true)
        {
            aPen = new Pen(GridColor, 1f);
            aPen.DashStyle = GridPattern;
            for (fX = XLimMin + XTick; fX < XLimMax; fX += XTick)
            {
                g.DrawLine(aPen, Point2D(new PointF(fX, YLimMin)),
                    Point2D(new PointF(fX, YLimMax)));
            }
        }

        // Create horizontal gridlines:
```

```
    if (IsXGrid == true)
    {
        aPen = new Pen(GridColor, 1f);
        aPen.DashStyle = GridPattern;
        for (fY = YLimMin + YTick; fY < YLimMax; fY += YTick)
        {
            g.DrawLine(aPen, Point2D(new PointF(XLimMin, fY)),
                Point2D(new PointF(XLimMax, fY)));
        }
    }

    // Create the x-axis tick marks:
    aBrush = new SolidBrush(TickFontColor);
    for (fX = XLimMin; fX <= XLimMax; fX += XTick)
    {
        PointF yAxisPoint = Point2D(new PointF(fX, YLimMin));
        g.DrawLine(Pens.Black, yAxisPoint,
            new PointF(yAxisPoint.X, yAxisPoint.Y - 5f));
        StringFormat sFormat = new StringFormat();
        sFormat.Alignment = StringAlignment.Far;
        SizeF sizeXTick = g.MeasureString(fX.ToString(),
                TickFont);
        g.DrawString(fX.ToString(), TickFont, aBrush,
            new PointF(yAxisPoint.X + sizeXTick.Width / 2,
            yAxisPoint.Y + 4f), sFormat);
    }

    // Create the y-axis tick marks:
    for (fY = YLimMin; fY <= YLimMax; fY += YTick)
    {
        PointF xAxisPoint = Point2D(new PointF(XLimMin, fY));
        g.DrawLine(Pens.Black, xAxisPoint,
            new PointF(xAxisPoint.X + 5f, xAxisPoint.Y));
        StringFormat sFormat = new StringFormat();
        sFormat.Alignment = StringAlignment.Far;
        g.DrawString(fY.ToString(), TickFont, aBrush,
            new PointF(xAxisPoint.X - 3f,
            xAxisPoint.Y - tickFontSize.Height / 2), sFormat);
    }
    aPen.Dispose();
    aBrush.Dispose();
    AddLabels(g);
}

private void AddLabels(Graphics g)
{
    float xOffset = chartArea.Width / 30.0f;
    float yOffset = chartArea.Height / 30.0f;
    SizeF labelFontSize = g.MeasureString("A", LabelFont);
    SizeF titleFontSize = g.MeasureString("A", TitleFont);

    // Add horizontal axis label:
    SolidBrush aBrush = new SolidBrush(LabelFontColor);
    SizeF stringSize = g.MeasureString(XLabel, LabelFont);
```

```
            g.DrawString(XLabel, LabelFont, aBrush,
                new Point(PlotArea.Left + PlotArea.Width / 2 -
                (int)stringSize.Width / 2, ChartArea.Bottom -
                (int)yOffset - (int)labelFontSize.Height));

            // Add y-axis label:
            StringFormat sFormat = new StringFormat();
            sFormat.Alignment = StringAlignment.Center;
            stringSize = g.MeasureString(YLabel, LabelFont);
            // Save the state of the current Graphics object
            GraphicsState gState = g.Save();
            g.TranslateTransform(xOffset,
                    yOffset + titleFontSize.Height
                    + yOffset / 3 + PlotArea.Height / 2);
            g.RotateTransform(-90);
            g.DrawString(YLabel, LabelFont, aBrush, 0, 0, sFormat);
            // Restore it:
            g.Restore(gState);

            // Add title:
            aBrush = new SolidBrush(TitleFontColor);
            stringSize = g.MeasureString(Title, TitleFont);
            if (Title.ToUpper() != "NO TITLE")
            {
                g.DrawString(Title, TitleFont, aBrush,
                    new Point(PlotArea.Left + PlotArea.Width / 2 -
                    (int)stringSize.Width / 2,
                    ChartArea.Top + (int)yOffset));
            }
            aBrush.Dispose();
        }

        public PointF Point2D(PointF pt)
        {
            PointF aPoint = new PointF();
            if (pt.X < XLimMin || pt.X > XLimMax ||
                pt.Y < YLimMin || pt.Y > YLimMax)
            {
                pt.X = Single.NaN;
                pt.Y = Single.NaN;
            }
            aPoint.X = PlotArea.X + (pt.X - XLimMin) *
                PlotArea.Width / (XLimMax - XLimMin);
            aPoint.Y = PlotArea.Bottom - (pt.Y - YLimMin) *
                PlotArea.Height / (YLimMax - YLimMin);
            return aPoint;
        }
    }
}
```

To this class, we add more member fields and corresponding properties, which can be used to manipulate the chart layout and appearance. You can easily understand the meaning of each field and property from its name. We also add the following member fields to define the chart gridlines

```
        private DashStyle gridPattern = DashStyle.Solid;
```

```
private Color gridColor = Color.LightGray;
private float gridLineThickness = 1.0f;
private bool isXGrid = true;
private bool isYGrid = true;
```

These fields and corresponding properties provide a great deal of flexibility when customizing the look of the gridlines. The `gridPattern` field allows you to choose various line dash styles, including solid, dash, dot, dash-dot, etc. You can change the gridlines' color and line thickness using the `gridColor` and `gridLineThickness` fields. In addition, we implement two `bool` fields, `isXGrid` and `isYGrid`, that allow you to turn horizontal or vertical grids on or off.

We then define member fields for the X- and Y-Labels, title, and the ticks:

```
private string xLabel = "X Axis";
private string yLabel = "Y Axis";
private string sTitle = "Title";
private Font labelFont = new Font("Arial", 10,
    FontStyle.Regular);
private Color labelFontColor = Color.Black;
private Font titleFont = new Font("Arial", 12,
    FontStyle.Regular);
private Color titleFontColor = Color.Black;
private float xTick = 1f;
private float yTick = 2f;
private Font tickFont;
private Color tickFontColor = Color.Black;
```

These fields and their corresponding properties let you change the labels, title, and tick marks, as well as their font and text color. If you set the `Title` property to "No Title", there will be no title displayed on the chart.

Gridlines and Ticks

The `AddChartStyle` method seems quite complicated in this class; however, it is actually reasonably easy to follow what is happening. First we draw the `ChartArea` and `PlotArea` with specified background color and borders, as we did in the previous project. Next, we create a `Pen` object with the `GridColor` and the dash style specified by the `GridPattern` property, and use the `DrawLine` method to draw the gridlines. Please note that all the end points of the gridlines have been transformed from the world coordinate system to the device coordinate system through the `Point2D` method.

We then draw the tick marks for the X- and Y-axes of the chart. For each tick mark, we find the points in the device coordinate system where the tick mark joins the axes and draw a black line, 5 pixels long, from this point toward inside the `PlotArea`. You can also place these tick marks outside of the `PlotArea` using −5f.

Both `g.DrawLine` and `g.DrawString` use `yAxisPoint` (or `xAxisPoint`) to create ticks and tick labels. We also use `g.MeasureString` method to measure the size of the tick label string, which is necessary if you want to put the labels in the center of the tickers. Notice how we pass a `StringFormat` object to the `g.DrawString` method, setting its `Alignment` property to `StringAlignment.Far` so that the text is aligned to the right.

Labels and Title

The `AddLabels` method creates labels for the X- and Y-axes as well as the title of the chart. It is easy to place the X-axis label and title, and make sure that they are at the bottom-center, and top-center respectively. However, the Y-axis label is more complicated because we need to rotate this label `-90` degrees. There is a default vertical rotated text string in C#, defined through the `StringFormatFlags`:

```
StringFormat sf = new StringFormat(StringFormatFlags.DirectionVertical);
```

But this command gives a vertical text string read from top to bottom. Conventionally, we use a string that reads from bottom to top, which can be achieved using the following code snippet:

```
// Add y-axis label:
StringFormat sFormat = new StringFormat();
sFormat.Alignment = StringAlignment.Center;
stringSize = g.MeasureString(YLabel, LabelFont);

// Save the state of the current Graphics object
GraphicsState gState = g.Save();
g.TranslateTransform(xOffset, yOffset +
    titleFontSize.Height + yOffset / 3 + PlotArea.Height / 2);
g.RotateTransform(-90);
g.DrawString(YLabel, LabelFont, aBrush, 0, 0, sFormat);

// Restore it:
g.Restore(gState);
```

Here we define a `StringFormat` object that aligns the text string in the center. Then we save the current Graphics state using the `g.Save` method. Next we make two transformations to the Graphics object g: one is a translation and the other a rotation by `-90` degrees. After drawing the text string using `g.DrawString` method, we restore the previous saved Graphics state. In order to put the Y-axis label in the right position in a real-world application, you need to do some try-and-error iterations. The above code snippet provides you with a reference and a starting point.

Testing Project

Building and executing the project generates the chart with the gridlines, X- and Y-axis labels, title, ticks, and tick labels shown in Figure 3-4. Obviously, there is still no chart legend yet. We will show you how to add legend in the next subsection.

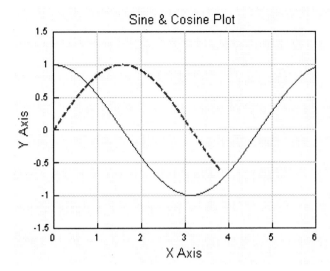

Figure 3-4 Sine and Cosine plot generated from project Example3_3.

Legends

For a 2D X-Y chart with multiple lines, you may want to use a legend to identify each line plotted on the chart. This legend shows a sample of the line type, marker symbol, color, and text label you specify. Let's start with a new project *Example3_4*, and see how we can create such a legend. This project is based on the previous project *Example3_3*.

Legend Class

We add one new class to this project, `Legend`. The following is its code listing:

```
using System;
using System.Drawing;
using System.Drawing.Drawing2D;
using System.Collections;

namespace Example3_4
{
    public class Legend
    {
        private bool isLegendVisible;
        private Color textColor;
        private LegendPositionEnum legendPosition;
        private bool isBorderVisible;
        private Color legendBackColor;
        private Color legendBorderColor;
        private Font legendFont;

        public Legend()
        {
```

```csharp
        legendPosition = LegendPositionEnum.NorthEast;
        textColor = Color.Black;
        isLegendVisible = false;
        isBorderVisible = true;
        legendBackColor = Color.White;
        legendBorderColor = Color.Black;
        legendFont = new Font("Arial", 8, FontStyle.Regular);
    }

    public Font LegendFont
    {
        get { return legendFont; }
        set { legendFont = value; }
    }

    public Color LegendBackColor
    {
        get { return legendBackColor; }
        set { legendBackColor = value; }
    }

    public Color LegendBorderColor
    {
        get { return legendBorderColor; }
        set { legendBorderColor = value; }
    }

    public bool IsBorderVisible
    {
        get { return isBorderVisible; }
        set { isBorderVisible = value; }
    }

    public LegendPositionEnum LegendPosition
    {
        get { return legendPosition; }
        set { legendPosition = value; }
    }

    public Color TextColor
    {
        get { return textColor; }
        set { textColor = value; }
    }

    public bool IsLegendVisible
    {
        get { return isLegendVisible; }
        set { isLegendVisible = value; }
    }

    public enum LegendPositionEnum
    {
        North,
```

```csharp
        NorthWest,
        West,
        SouthWest,
        South,
        SouthEast,
        East,
        NorthEast
}

public void AddLegend(Graphics g,
            DataCollection dc, ChartStyle cs)
{
    if (dc.DataSeriesList.Count < 1)
    {
        return;
    }
    if (!IsLegendVisible)
    {
        return;
    }
    int numberOfDataSeries = dc.DataSeriesList.Count;
    string[] legendLabels = new string[dc.DataSeriesList.Count];
    int n = 0;
    foreach (DataSeries ds in dc.DataSeriesList)
    {
        legendLabels[n] = ds.SeriesName;
        n++;
    }
    float offSet = 10;
    float xc = 0f;
    float yc = 0f;
    SizeF size = g.MeasureString(legendLabels[0], LegendFont);
    float legendWidth = size.Width;
    for (int i = 0; i < legendLabels.Length; i++)
    {
        size = g.MeasureString(legendLabels[i], LegendFont);
        float tempWidth = size.Width;
        if (legendWidth < tempWidth)
            legendWidth = tempWidth;
    }
    legendWidth = legendWidth + 50.0f;
    float hWidth = legendWidth / 2;
    float legendHeight = 18.0f * numberOfDataSeries;
    float hHeight = legendHeight / 2;

    switch (LegendPosition)
    {
        case LegendPositionEnum.East:
            xc = cs.PlotArea.X + cs.PlotArea.Width -
                offSet - hWidth;
            yc = cs.PlotArea.Y + cs.PlotArea.Height / 2;
            break;
        case LegendPositionEnum.North:
            xc = cs.PlotArea.X + cs.PlotArea.Width / 2;
```

```
                    yc = cs.PlotArea.Y + offSet + hHeight;
                    break;
                case LegendPositionEnum.NorthEast:
                    xc = cs.PlotArea.X + cs.PlotArea.Width -
                        offSet - hWidth;
                    yc = cs.PlotArea.Y + offSet + hHeight;
                    break;
                case LegendPositionEnum.NorthWest:
                    xc = cs.PlotArea.X + offSet + hWidth;
                    yc = cs.PlotArea.Y + offSet + hHeight;
                    break;
                case LegendPositionEnum.South:
                    xc = cs.PlotArea.X + cs.PlotArea.Width / 2;
                    yc = cs.PlotArea.Y + cs.PlotArea.Height -
                        offSet - hHeight;
                    break;
                case LegendPositionEnum.SouthEast:
                    xc = cs.PlotArea.X + cs.PlotArea.Width -
                        offSet - hWidth;
                    yc = cs.PlotArea.Y + cs.PlotArea.Height -
                        offSet - hHeight;
                    break;
                case LegendPositionEnum.SouthWest:
                    xc = cs.PlotArea.X + offSet + hWidth;
                    yc = cs.PlotArea.Y + cs.PlotArea.Height -
                        offSet - hHeight;
                    break;
                case LegendPositionEnum.West:
                    xc = cs.PlotArea.X + offSet + hWidth;
                    yc = cs.PlotArea.Y + cs.PlotArea.Height / 2;
                    break;
            }
            DrawLegend(g, xc, yc, hWidth, hHeight, dc, cs);
        }

        private void DrawLegend(Graphics g, float xCenter,
                float yCenter, float hWidth, float hHeight,
                DataCollection dc, ChartStyle cs)
        {
            float spacing = 8.0f;
            float textHeight = 8.0f;
            float htextHeight = textHeight / 2.0f;
            float lineLength = 30.0f;
            float hlineLength = lineLength / 2.0f;
            Rectangle legendRectangle;
            Pen aPen = new Pen(LegendBorderColor, 1f);
            SolidBrush aBrush = new SolidBrush(LegendBackColor);

            if (isLegendVisible)
            {
                legendRectangle = new Rectangle((int)xCenter -
                    (int)hWidth, (int)yCenter - (int)hHeight,
                    (int)(2.0f * hWidth), (int)(2.0f * hHeight));
                g.FillRectangle(aBrush, legendRectangle);
```

```
            if (IsBorderVisible)
            {
                g.DrawRectangle(aPen, legendRectangle);
            }

            int n = 1;
            foreach (DataSeries ds in dc.DataSeriesList)
            {
                // Draw lines and symbols:
                float xSymbol = legendRectangle.X +
                    spacing + hlineLength;
                float xText = legendRectangle.X +
                    2 * spacing + lineLength;
                float yText = legendRectangle.Y + n * spacing +
                    (2 * n - 1) * htextHeight;
                aPen = new Pen(ds.LineStyle.LineColor,
                    ds.LineStyle.Thickness);
                aPen.DashStyle = ds.LineStyle.Pattern;
                PointF ptStart = new PointF(legendRectangle.X +
                    spacing, yText);
                PointF ptEnd = new PointF(legendRectangle.X +
                    spacing + lineLength, yText);
                g.DrawLine(aPen, ptStart, ptEnd);
                // Draw text:
                StringFormat sFormat = new StringFormat();
                sFormat.Alignment = StringAlignment.Near;
                g.DrawString(ds.SeriesName, LegendFont,
                    new SolidBrush(textColor),
                    new PointF(xText, yText - 8), sFormat);
                n++;
            }
        }
        aPen.Dispose();
        aBrush.Dispose();
    }
  }
}
```

The Legend class looks quite complicated. However, if you read through it carefully, you will find that it is actually quite easy to follow what is happening. We start off by creating member fields to describe the legend behavior:

```
            private bool isLegendVisible;
            private Color textColor;
            private Font legendFont;
            private LegendPositionEnum legendPosition;
            private bool isBorderVisible;
            private Color legendBackColor;
            private Color legendBorderColor;
```

The isLegendVisible allows you to turn the legend on or off. The default setting of this field is false. Therefore, you need to change this default value to true if you want to display the legend on the chart. You can change legend's text color and font using the textColor and legendFont fields.

Legend Layout

In this example, we use the legend layout shown in Figure 3-5. The placement of the legend in a chart is controlled by the `legendPosition` field that is specified by the enumeration `LegendPositionEnum`. There are eight positions you can choose from. These positions defined in `LegendPositionEnum` include North, South, West, East, NorthWest, NorthEast, SouthWest, and SouthWest. The default setting is NorthEast, corresponding to the upper-right corner of a chart.

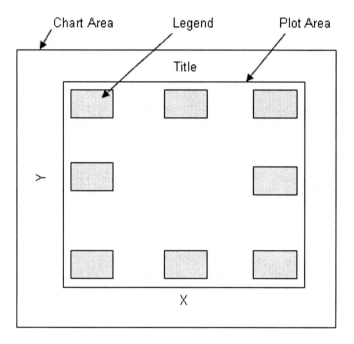

Figure 3-5 Legend layout on the chart.

You can also add more positions to the `LegendPositionEnum`. For example, you may add the position at the right side or bottom of the chart. The `isBorderVisible` field allows you to turn the Legend rectangle border on or off. The `legendBackColor` and `legendFont` fields let you set Legend's background color and text font, respectively. Next we implement the properties for all of these member fields using the `Get` and `Set` statements.

Finally, the two methods `AddLegend` and `DrawLegend` are used to create the Legend. The `DrawLegend` method defines the contents of a single legend, including the line type, marker symbol, color, and text label, while the `AddLegend` method places the Legend in the suitable position through a `switch` statement by calling the `DrawLegend` method.

Modifying Form1 Class

In order to have the legend on your chart, you need to call the AddLegend method from Form1 class. First, add a new member field to the Form1 class:

```
private Legend lg;
```

Then create the corresponding instances for this field, and set Legend parameters inside the Form1's instructor

```
lg = new Legend();
lg.IsLegendVisible = true;
```

Note that we specify one Legend property, IsLegendVisible. The default values are used for all of the other Legend parameters, such as its position, text font, and background color. Since the default value of IsLegendVisible is false, you must set its property to true in order to show the Legend on your chart.

Next, add the AddLegend method to the OnPaint method:

```
lg.AddLegend(g, dc, cs);
```

Testing Project

If you build and run the project, you will obtain the chart with the simple but a nice looking Legend, as shown in Figure 3-6.

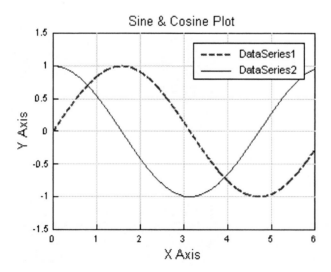

Figure 3-6 Sine and Cosine chart with legend generated from
Example3_4.

Symbols

Sometimes, you might want a chart to display not only lines but the symbols as well at the data points. Sometimes you might want a chart with only symbols and no lines. In this section, we show you how to create such a chart with symbols using C#.

Defining Symbols

Let's look at two symbols, Diamond and Triangle, as shown in Figure 3-7. The surrounding dot-line square outlines the size of the symbol, and (xc, yc) represent the center coordinates of the symbol in the device coordinate system. Suppose the length of each side of the dot-line square is size, and we define halfsize = size/2. Then we can easily determine the coordinates of the points at the vertices of each symbol.

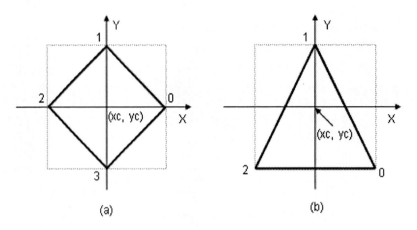

(a)   (b)

Figure 3-7 Definitions of Diamond (a) and Triangle (b) symbols.

For the Diamond symbol, we have the following coordinates:

```
Point0: (xc + halfsize, yc)
Point1: (xc, yc + halfsize)
Point2: (xc - halfsize, yc)
Point3: (xc, yc - halfsize)
```

We can then create the Open-Diamond symbol by drawing lines from point0 to point1 to point2 to point3 to point0. We can also create the Solid-Diamond symbol in this manner, constructing a PointArray with these four points and drawing a polygon with this PointArray using the g.FillPolygon(aBrush, PointArray) method.

For the Triangle symbol, the corresponding point coordinates are:

```
Point0: (xc + halfsize, yc - halfsize)
Point1: (xc, yc + halfsize)
Point2: (xc - halfsize, yc - halfsize)
```

We can then easily create the Open-Triangle symbol and the Solid-Triangle symbol using the similar approach as that used in creating Diamond symbol. Following this discussion, we can create any symbols that can be used in a chart application.

Symbol Style Class

Now, it is time to create a real-world application, *Example3_5*, that produces a chart with symbols. This example can be regarded as a complete 2D line chart project. It is based on the previous project, *Example3_4*. We need to add a new class, SymbolStyle, to the project. The symbols in this SymbolStyle class are created using the approach we discussed in the previous subsection. The following is the code listing of the SymbolStyle class:

```
using System;
using System.Drawing;
using System.Drawing.Drawing2D;

namespace Example3_5
{
    public class SymbolStyle
    {
        private SymbolTypeEnum symbolType;
        private float symbolSize;
        private Color borderColor;
        private Color fillColor;
        private float borderThickness;

        public SymbolStyle()
        {
            symbolType = SymbolTypeEnum.None;
            symbolSize = 8.0f;
            borderColor = Color.Black;
            fillColor = Color.Black;
            borderThickness = 1f;
        }

        public float BorderThickness
        {
            get { return borderThickness; }
            set { borderThickness = value; }
        }

        public Color BorderColor
        {
            get { return borderColor; }
            set { borderColor = value; }
        }

        public Color FillColor
        {
            get { return fillColor; }
            set { fillColor = value; }
        }
```

```csharp
public float SymbolSize
{
    get { return symbolSize; }
    set { symbolSize = value; }
}

public SymbolTypeEnum SymbolType
{
    get { return symbolType; }
    set { symbolType = value; }
}

public enum SymbolTypeEnum
{
    Box = 0,
    Circle = 1,
    Cross = 2,
    Diamond = 3,
    Dot = 4,
    InvertedTriangle = 5,
    None = 6,
    OpenDiamond = 7,
    OpenInvertedTriangle = 8,
    OpenTriangle = 9,
    Square = 10,
    Star = 11,
    Triangle = 12,
    Plus = 13
}

public void DrawSymbol(Graphics g, PointF pt)
{
    Pen aPen = new Pen(BorderColor, BorderThickness);
    SolidBrush aBrush = new SolidBrush(FillColor);
    float x = pt.X;
    float y = pt.Y;
    float size = SymbolSize;
    float halfSize = size / 2.0f;
    RectangleF aRectangle = new RectangleF(x - halfSize,
                y - halfSize, size, size);

    switch (SymbolType)
    {
        case SymbolTypeEnum.Square:
            g.DrawLine(aPen, x - halfSize, y - halfSize,
                x + halfSize, y - halfSize);
            g.DrawLine(aPen, x + halfSize, y - halfSize,
                x + halfSize, y + halfSize);
            g.DrawLine(aPen, x + halfSize, y + halfSize,
                x - halfSize, y + halfSize);
            g.DrawLine(aPen, x - halfSize, y + halfSize,
                x - halfSize, y - halfSize);
            break;
```

```
case SymbolTypeEnum.OpenDiamond:
    g.DrawLine(aPen, x, y - halfSize, x + halfSize, y);
    g.DrawLine(aPen, x + halfSize, y, x, y + halfSize);
    g.DrawLine(aPen, x, y + halfSize, x - halfSize, y);
    g.DrawLine(aPen, x - halfSize, y, x, y - halfSize);
    break;

case SymbolTypeEnum.Circle:
    g.DrawEllipse(aPen,x-halfSize,y-halfSize,size,size);
    break;

case SymbolTypeEnum.OpenTriangle:
    g.DrawLine(aPen, x, y - halfSize, x + halfSize,
        y + halfSize);
    g.DrawLine(aPen, x + halfSize, y + halfSize,
        x - halfSize, y + halfSize);
    g.DrawLine(aPen, x - halfSize, y + halfSize, x,
        y - halfSize);
    break;

case SymbolTypeEnum.None:
    break;

case SymbolTypeEnum.Cross:
    g.DrawLine(aPen, x - halfSize, y - halfSize,
        x + halfSize, y + halfSize);
    g.DrawLine(aPen, x + halfSize, y - halfSize,
        x - halfSize, y + halfSize);
    break;

case SymbolTypeEnum.Star:
    g.DrawLine(aPen, x, y - halfSize, x, y + halfSize);
    g.DrawLine(aPen, x - halfSize, y, x + halfSize, y);
    g.DrawLine(aPen, x - halfSize, y - halfSize,
        x + halfSize, y + halfSize);
    g.DrawLine(aPen, x + halfSize, y - halfSize,
        x - halfSize, y + halfSize);
    break;

case SymbolTypeEnum.OpenInvertedTriangle:
    g.DrawLine(aPen, x - halfSize, y - halfSize,
        x + halfSize, y - halfSize);
    g.DrawLine(aPen, x + halfSize, y - halfSize, x,
        y + halfSize);
    g.DrawLine(aPen, x, y + halfSize, x - halfSize,
        y - halfSize);
    break;

case SymbolTypeEnum.Plus:
    g.DrawLine(aPen, x, y - halfSize, x, y + halfSize);
    g.DrawLine(aPen, x - halfSize, y, x + halfSize, y);
    break;
```

```
case SymbolTypeEnum.Dot:
    g.FillEllipse(aBrush, aRectangle);
    g.DrawEllipse(aPen, aRectangle);
    break;

case SymbolTypeEnum.Box:
    g.FillRectangle(aBrush, aRectangle);
    g.DrawLine(aPen, x - halfSize, y - halfSize,
        x + halfSize, y - halfSize);
    g.DrawLine(aPen, x + halfSize, y - halfSize,
        x + halfSize, y + halfSize);
    g.DrawLine(aPen, x + halfSize, y + halfSize,
        x - halfSize, y + halfSize);
    g.DrawLine(aPen, x - halfSize, y + halfSize,
        x - halfSize, y - halfSize);
    break;

case SymbolTypeEnum.Diamond:
    PointF[] pta = new PointF[4];
    pta[0].X = x;
    pta[0].Y = y - halfSize;
    pta[1].X = x + halfSize;
    pta[1].Y = y;
    pta[2].X = x;
    pta[2].Y = y + halfSize;
    pta[3].X = x - halfSize;
    pta[3].Y = y;
    g.FillPolygon(aBrush, pta);
    g.DrawPolygon(aPen, pta);
    break;

case SymbolTypeEnum.InvertedTriangle:
    PointF[] ptb = new PointF[3];
    ptb[0].X = x-halfSize;
    ptb[0].Y = y - halfSize;
    ptb[1].X = x + halfSize;
    ptb[1].Y = y - halfSize;
    ptb[2].X = x;
    ptb[2].Y = y + halfSize;
    g.FillPolygon(aBrush, ptb);
    g.DrawPolygon(aPen, ptb);
    break;

case SymbolTypeEnum.Triangle:
    PointF[] ptc = new PointF[3];
    ptc[0].X = x;
    ptc[0].Y = y - halfSize;
    ptc[1].X = x + halfSize;
    ptc[1].Y = y + halfSize;
    ptc[2].X = x - halfSize;
    ptc[2].Y = y + halfSize;
    g.FillPolygon(aBrush, ptc);
    g.DrawPolygon(aPen, ptc);
    break;
```

```
                }
            }
        }
    }
```

In this class, we define five private fields and their corresponding public properties. You can select the type of symbol from the SymbolTypeEnum enumeration using the SymbolType property. The SymbolTypeEnum contains thirteen different symbols, as well as a None type, which results in no symbols being drawn on your chart. This type is the default value, this means you must choose a symbol type other than None if you want to draw symbols on your chart application. You can easily add your own symbols to this enumeration as you like.

The BorderColor property allows you to specify the border color of a symbol. For the Star, Plus, and open-symbols, you only need to define this BorderColor property. The default color for this property is black. The FillColor property with a default color of white is for solid symbols, such as the diamond, triangle, box, dot, etc. This means that it is possible for a solid symbol to have a border with a different color than fill by specifying different colors for the BorderColor and FillColor properties.

The BorderThickess property allows you to specify the border line thickness for a symbol. The default value of this property is one pixel. The symbol size is controlled by the SymbolSize property, which has a default value of 8 pixels.

There is a public method in this class called DrawSymbol, which takes a PointF object as input. This input Point is the center location of the symbol. Note that this input Point must be defined in the device coordinate system. Namely, a Point in the world coordinate system must go through a transformation from the world to device system using the Point2D method.

Modifying Form1 Class

Now we turn our attention to the Form1 class. The fields and constructor of Form1 are the same as they are in the previous example. The methods of SetPlotArea and OnPaint are also identical to those in *Example3_4*. We need only to modify the method AddData to include the symbols on the chart. The following code snippet is for the AddData method:

```
private void AddData(Graphics g)
{
    // Override ChartStyle properties:
    cs.XLimMin = 0f;
    cs.XLimMax = 6f;
    cs.YLimMin = -1.5f;
    cs.YLimMax = 1.5f;
    cs.XTick = 1.0f;
    cs.YTick = 0.5f;
    cs.XLabel = "This is X axis";
    cs.YLabel = "This is Y axis";
    cs.Title = "Sine and Cosine Chart";

    dc.DataSeriesList.Clear();
    // Add Sine data with 7 data points:
    DataSeries ds1 = new DataSeries();
```

```
        ds1.LineStyle.LineColor = Color.Red;
        ds1.LineStyle.Thickness = 2f;
        ds1.LineStyle.Pattern = DashStyle.Dash;
        ds1.LineStyle.PlotMethod =
                LineStyle.PlotLinesMethodEnum.Lines;
        ds1.SeriesName = "Sine";
        ds1.SymbolStyle.SymbolType =
                SymbolStyle.SymbolTypeEnum.Diamond;
        ds1.SymbolStyle.BorderColor = Color.Red;
        ds1.SymbolStyle.FillColor = Color.Yellow;
        ds1.SymbolStyle.BorderThickness = 1f;
        for (int i = 0; i < 7; i++)
        {
            ds1.AddPoint(new PointF(i / 1.0f,
                (float)Math.Sin(i / 1.0f)));
        }
        dc.Add(ds1);

        // Add Cosine data with 7 data points:
        DataSeries ds2 = new DataSeries();
        ds2.LineStyle.LineColor = Color.Blue;
        ds2.LineStyle.Thickness = 1f;
        ds2.LineStyle.Pattern = DashStyle.Solid;
        ds2.LineStyle.PlotMethod =
                LineStyle.PlotLinesMethodEnum.Splines;
        ds2.SeriesName = "Cosine";
        ds2.SymbolStyle.SymbolType =
                SymbolStyle.SymbolTypeEnum.Triangle;
        ds2.SymbolStyle.BorderColor = Color.Blue;
        for (int i = 0; i < 7; i++)
        {
            ds2.AddPoint(new PointF(i / 1.0f,
                (float)Math.Cos(i / 1.0f)));
        }
        dc.Add(ds2);
    }
```

Please note how both the `LineStyle` and `SymbolStyle` are associated with the
`DataSeries` instances, `ds1` and `ds2`.

Modifying Data Collection

Another area you need to modify is the `AddLines` method in the `DataCollection` class.
This method must now be extended to include drawing symbols and drawing lines. The following
is the code listing of `AddLines` method in the `DataCollection` class:

```
        public void AddLines(Graphics g, ChartStyle cs)
        {
            // Plot lines:
            foreach (DataSeries ds in DataSeriesList)
            {
                if (ds.LineStyle.IsVisible == true)
                {
```

```
                Pen aPen = new Pen(ds.LineStyle.LineColor,
                 ds.LineStyle.Thickness);
                aPen.DashStyle = ds.LineStyle.Pattern;
                if (ds.LineStyle.PlotMethod ==
                LineStyle.PlotLinesMethodEnum.Lines)
                {
                    for (int i = 1; i < ds.PointList.Count; i++)
                    {
                        g.DrawLine(aPen,
                cs.Point2D((PointF)ds.PointList[i - 1]),
                        cs.Point2D((PointF)ds.PointList[i]));
                    }
                }
                else if (ds.LineStyle.PlotMethod ==
                LineStyle.PlotLinesMethodEnum.Splines)
                {
                    ArrayList al = new ArrayList();
                    for (int i = 0; i < ds.PointList.Count; i++)
                    {
                        PointF pt = (PointF)ds.PointList[i];
                        if (pt.X >= cs.XLimMin &&
                            pt.X <= cs.XLimMax &&
                            pt.Y >= cs.YLimMin &&
                            pt.Y <= cs.YLimMax)
                        {
                            al.Add(pt);
                        }
                    }
                    PointF[] pts = new PointF[al.Count];
                    for (int i = 0; i < pts.Length; i++)
                    {
                        pts[i] = cs.Point2D((PointF)(al[i]));
                    }
                    g.DrawCurve(aPen, pts);
                }
                aPen.Dispose();
            }
        }


    // Plot Symbols:
    foreach (DataSeries ds in DataSeriesList)
    {
        for (int i = 0; i < ds.PointList.Count; i++)
        {
            PointF pt = (PointF)ds.PointList[i];
            if (pt.X >= cs.XLimMin && pt.X <= cs.XLimMax &&
                pt.Y >= cs.YLimMin && pt.Y <= cs.YLimMax)
            {
                ds.SymbolStyle.DrawSymbol(g,
                    cs.Point2D((PointF)ds.PointList[i]));
            }
        }
    }
}
```

Note that we can have two different approaches of drawing lines by specifying the PlotMethodEnum property, Lines and Splines. A line is a standard straight line connecting two points. On the other hand, a spline is a curve that passes smoothly through a given set of points. To draw a spline, you create a Graphics object and pass the address of an array of points to the g.DrawCurve method. You can clearly see the difference between lines and splines from Figure 3-8, where the Sine curve is drawn using lines while the Cosine is drawn using splines.

You may also notice that we add an if-statement when we draw splines:

```
if (pt.X >= cs.XLimMin && pt.X <= cs.XLimMax &&
    pt.Y >= cs.YLimMin && pt.Y <= cs.YLimMax)
```

This statement is necessary for drawing splines. In some cases, your data points might be outside of the limits of the axes. The points outside the limits of the axes are reassigned the values of NaN after a transformation through the Point2D method. Drawing splines with points of NaN will throw an overflow exception. Here, the if-statement removes any NaN points before drawing splines.

Similarly, we draw the symbols using the same if-statement. The reason is also similar: to avoid the overflow exception and to make sure there are no any NaN points in the point array used by the g.FillPolygon method in the SymbolStyle class.

Modifying Line Style

We add the following code snippet to the LineStyle class:

```
private PlotLinesMethodEnum pltLineMethod =
    PlotLinesMethodEnum.Lines;

public PlotLinesMethodEnum PlotMethod
{
    get { return pltLineMethod; }
    set { pltLineMethod = value; }
}

public enum PlotLinesMethodEnum
{
    Lines = 0,
    Splines = 1
}
```

You can see that we create the PlotMethod as an object of the PlotLinesMethodEnum enumeration, so that you can represent your data on the chart using either Lines or Splines by specifying PlotMethod.

The rest of classes in the current project are identical to those used in the previous example, which you can consult to find the code listings of these classes.

Testing Project

If you build and run the program, you will obtain the following chart, as shown in Figure 3-8.

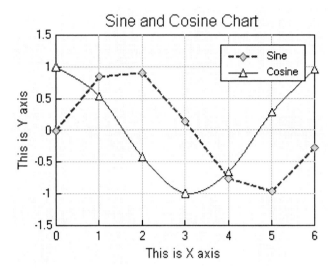

Figure 3-8 Sine and Cosine plot generated from project Example3_5.

Line Charts with Two Y Axes

In the previous sections, we implemented a powerful 2D line chart program. In *Example3_5*, there are no restriction on the number of lines or curves that you would like to create in a single chart. In this section, we will add another feature, that is another Y-axis, to the 2D line charts.

Why Two Y Axes

In some instances, you have data sets that you want to display on the same chart. However, the Y-axis data values are not within the same range. Let's say you have implemented the following code for the AddData method inside the Form1 class of *Example4_5*:

```
private void AddData(Graphics g)
{
    cs.XLimMin = 0f;
    cs.XLimMax = 30f;
    cs.YLimMin = -100f;
    cs.YLimMax = 700f;
    cs.XTick = 5.0f;
    cs.YTick = 100f;
    cs.XLabel = "X";
    cs.YLabel = "Y";
    cs.Title = "x1 * cos(x1) & 100 + 20 * x2";

    dc.DataSeriesList.Clear();
```

```
// Add data points to ds1:
DataSeries ds1 = new DataSeries();
ds1.LineStyle.LineColor = Color.Red;
ds1.LineStyle.Thickness = 2f;
ds1.LineStyle.Pattern = DashStyle.Dash;
ds1.SeriesName = "x1*cos(x1)";
for (int i = 0; i < 20; i++)
{
    float x1 = 1.0f * i;
    float y1 = x1 * (float)Math.Cos(x1);
    ds1.AddPoint(new PointF(x1, y1));
}
dc.Add(ds1);
// Add data points to ds2:
DataSeries ds2 = new DataSeries();
ds2.LineStyle.LineColor = Color.Blue;
ds2.LineStyle.Thickness = 2f;
ds2.SeriesName = "100 + 20*x2";
for (int i = 5; i < 30; i++)
{
    float x2 = 1.0f * i;
    float y2 = 100.0f + 20.0f*x2;
    ds2.AddPoint(new PointF(x2, y2));
}
dc.Add(ds2);
}
```

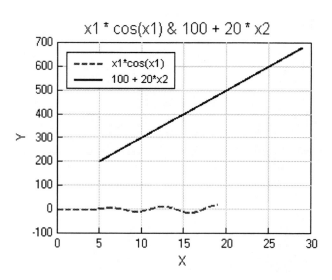

Figure 3-9 Chart for `y1` and `y2` whose data values in different ranges.

This will produce the results of Figure 3-9. It is clear from the figure that it is very hard to see the y1 values because you have defined the Y-axis limits to display all of the data points on the same chart, but the y1 and y2 values have different data ranges. This problem can be solved by adding another Y2 axis to the chart program.

Modifying Chart Style

There are many ways to implement the Y2 axis. Here we use the codes of the previous project, *Example3_5*, as a basis and try to change as little as possible in the program. First, create a new C# Windows Application, and name it *Example3_6*. Add the classes (Form1.cs ChartStyle.cs, LineStyle.cs, SymbolStyle.cs, Legend.cs, DataCollection.cs, and DataSeries.cs) in *Example3_5* to the current project by right clicking on the project in the solution explorer and selecting Add|Existing item... Change the namespace for all of the classes from *Example3_5* to *Example3_6*. Then, add five member fields and corresponding public properties to the ChartStyle class:

```
// Define Y2 axis:
private bool isY2Axis = false;
private float y2LimMin = 0f;
private float y2LimMax = 10f;
private float y2Tick = 2f;
private string y2Label = "Y2 Axis";

public ChartStyle(Form1 fm1)
{
    form1 = fm1;
    chartArea = form1.ClientRectangle;
    chartBackColor = fm1.BackColor;
    chartBorderColor = fm1.BackColor;
    plotArea = chartArea;
}

public bool IsY2Axis
{
    get { return isY2Axis; }
    set { isY2Axis = value; }
}

public string Y2Label
{
    get { return y2Label; }
    set { y2Label = value; }
}

public float Y2Tick
{
    get { return y2Tick; }
    set { y2Tick = value; }
}

public float Y2LimMin
{
    get { return y2LimMax; }
    set { y2LimMax = value; }
}

public float Y2LimMin
{
```

```
        get { return y2LimMin; }
        set { y2LimMin = value; }
    }
```

The `bool` property `IsY2Axis` tells the program whether or not a Y2 axis needs to be created. Its default value is `false`. You also need to add the following code fragment to the `AddChartStyle` method:

```
// Create the y2-axis tick marks:
if (IsY2Axis)
{
    for (fY = Y2LimMin; fY <= Y2LimMax; fY += Y2Tick)
    {
        PointF x2AxisPoint = Point2DY2(
            new PointF(XLimMax, fY));
        g.DrawLine(Pens.Black, x2AxisPoint,
            new PointF(x2AxisPoint.X - 5f, x2AxisPoint.Y));
        StringFormat sFormat = new StringFormat();
        sFormat.Alignment = StringAlignment.Near;
        g.DrawString(fY.ToString(), TickFont, aBrush,
            new PointF(x2AxisPoint.X + 3f,
            x2AxisPoint.Y - tickFontSize.Height / 2),
        sFormat);
    }
}
```

The above code creates the ticks and tick labels for the Y2 axis. Pay special attention to how we transform the points in the world coordinate system to points in device coordinate system:

```
PointF x2AxisPoint = Point2DY2(new PointF(XLimMax, fY));
```

Here, the method `Point2DY2` is used. This method is added to this class in the same manner as `Point2D`:

```
public PointF Point2DY2(PointF pt)
{
    PointF aPoint = new PointF();
    if (pt.X < XLimMin || pt.X > XLimMax ||
        pt.Y < Y2LimMin || pt.Y > Y2LimMax)
    {
        pt.X = Single.NaN;
        pt.Y = Single.NaN;
    }
    aPoint.X = PlotArea.X + (pt.X - XLimMin) *
        PlotArea.Width / (XLimMax - XLimMin);
    aPoint.Y = PlotArea.Bottom - (pt.Y - Y2LimMin) *
        PlotArea.Height / (Y2LimMax - Y2LimMin);
    return aPoint;
}
```

The only difference between `Point2D` and `Point2DY2` is that the `YLimMin` and `YLimMax` in `Point2D` are replaced by `Y2LimMin` and `Y2LimMax` in `Point2DY2`.

Modifying Form1 Class

We change the code for `Form1` as well. Here is the code listing of the modified `Form1` class:

```
using System;
using System.Drawing;
using System.Drawing.Drawing2D;
using System.Collections;
using System.Windows.Forms;

namespace Example3_6
{
    public partial class Form1 : Form
    {
        private DataCollection dc;
        private ChartStyle cs;
        private Legend lg;

        public Form1()
        {
            InitializeComponent();
            SetStyle(ControlStyles.ResizeRedraw, true);
            This.BackColor = Color.White;

            // Set Form1 size:
            this.Width = 350;
            this.Height = 300;
            dc = new DataCollection();
            cs = new ChartStyle(this);
            lg = new Legend();
            lg.IsLegendVisible = true;
            lg.LegendPosition = Legend.LegendPositionEnum.NorthWest;
            cs.IsY2Axis = true;
            cs.IsXGrid = false;
            cs.IsYGrid = false;
            cs.TickFont = new Font("Arial", 7, FontStyle.Regular);
            cs.TitleFont = new Font("Arial", 10, FontStyle.Regular);
            cs.XLimMin = 0f;
            cs.XLimMax = 30f;
            cs.YLimMin = -20f;
            cs.YLimMax = 20f;
            cs.XTick = 5.0f;
            cs.YTick = 5f;
            cs.Y2LimMin = 100f;
            cs.Y2LimMax = 700f;
            cs.Y2Tick = 100f;
            cs.XLabel = "X Axis";
            cs.YLabel = "Y Axis";
            cs.Y2Label = "Y2 Axis";
            cs.Title = "With Y2 Axis";
        }

        private void AddData(Graphics g)
        {
```

```csharp
        dc.DataSeriesList.Clear();
        // Add data points to ds1:
        DataSeries ds1 = new DataSeries();
        ds1.LineStyle.LineColor = Color.Red;
        ds1.LineStyle.Thickness = 2f;
        ds1.LineStyle.Pattern = DashStyle.Dash;
        ds1.SeriesName = "x1*cos(x1)";
        for (int i = 0; i < 20; i++)
        {
            float x1 = 1.0f * i;
            float y1 = x1 * (float)Math.Cos(x1);
            ds1.AddPoint(new PointF(x1, y1));
        }
        dc.Add(ds1);
        // Add data points to ds2:
        DataSeries ds2 = new DataSeries();
        ds2.LineStyle.LineColor = Color.Blue;
        ds2.LineStyle.Thickness = 2f;
        ds2.SeriesName = "100 + 20*x2";
        ds2.IsY2Data = true;
        for (int i = 5; i < 30; i++)
        {
            float x2 = 1.0f * i;
            float y2 = 100.0f + 20.0f*x2;
            ds2.AddPoint(new PointF(x2, y2));
        }
        dc.Add(ds2);
    }

    protected override void OnPaint(PaintEventArgs e)
    {
        Graphics g = e.Graphics;
        cs.ChartArea = this.ClientRectangle;
        AddData(g);
        SetPlotArea(g);
        cs.AddChartStyle(g);
        dc.AddLines(g, cs);
        lg.AddLegend(g, dc, cs);
        g.Dispose();
    }

    private void SetPlotArea(Graphics g)
    {
        // Set PlotArea:
        float xOffset = cs.ChartArea.Width / 30.0f;
        float yOffset = cs.ChartArea.Height / 30.0f;
        SizeF labelFontSize = g.MeasureString("A", cs.LabelFont);
        SizeF titleFontSize = g.MeasureString("A", cs.TitleFont);
        if (cs.Title.ToUpper() == "NO TITLE")
        {
            titleFontSize.Width = 8f;
            titleFontSize.Height = 8f;
        }
        float xSpacing = xOffset / 3.0f;
```

```
float ySpacing = yOffset / 3.0f;
SizeF tickFontSize = g.MeasureString("A", cs.TickFont);
float tickSpacing = 2f;
SizeF yTickSize = g.MeasureString(
        cs.YLimMin.ToString(), cs.TickFont);
for (float yTick = cs.YLimMin; yTick <= cs.YLimMax;
        yTick += cs.YTick)
{
    SizeF tempSize = g.MeasureString(
        yTick.ToString(), cs.TickFont);
    if (yTickSize.Width < tempSize.Width)
    {
        yTickSize = tempSize;
    }
}
float leftMargin = xOffset + labelFontSize.Width +
        xSpacing + yTickSize.Width + tickSpacing;
float rightMargin = xOffset;
float topMargin = yOffset + titleFontSize.Height + ySpacing;
float bottomMargin = yOffset + labelFontSize.Height +
        ySpacing + tickSpacing + tickFontSize.Height;

if (!cs.IsY2Axis)
{
    // Define the plot area with one Y axis:
    int plotX = cs.ChartArea.X + (int)leftMargin;
    int plotY = cs.ChartArea.Y + (int)topMargin;
    int plotWidth = cs.ChartArea.Width -
            (int)leftMargin - (int)rightMargin;
    int plotHeight = cs.ChartArea.Height -
            (int)topMargin - (int)bottomMargin;
    cs.PlotArea = new Rectangle(plotX, plotY,
            plotWidth, plotHeight);
}
else
{
    // Define the plot area with Y and Y2 axes:
    SizeF y2TickSize = g.MeasureString(
            cs.Y2LimMin.ToString(), cs.TickFont);
    for (float y2Tick = cs.Y2LimMin;
            y2Tick <= cs.Y2LimMax; y2Tick += cs.Y2Tick)
    {
        SizeF tempSize2 = g.MeasureString(
            y2Tick.ToString(), cs.TickFont);
        if (y2TickSize.Width < tempSize2.Width)
        {
            y2TickSize = tempSize2;
        }
    }

    rightMargin = xOffset + labelFontSize.Width +
            xSpacing + y2TickSize.Width + tickSpacing;
    int plotX = cs.ChartArea.X + (int)leftMargin;
    int plotY = cs.ChartArea.Y + (int)topMargin;
```

```
            int plotWidth = cs.ChartArea.Width -
                    (int)leftMargin - (int)rightMargin;
            int plotHeight = cs.ChartArea.Height -
                    (int)topMargin - (int)bottomMargin;
            cs.PlotArea = new Rectangle(plotX, plotY,
                    plotWidth, plotHeight);
            }
        }
    }
}
```

We have highlighted the change we made to include the Y2 axis. First, we set different limits for the Y and Y2 axes. Also note how we associate the y2 DataSeries object with the IsY2Data. A DataSeries object with an IsY2Data = true property tells the program that this DataSeries object should be drawn on the chart using the Y2 axis. Inside the SetPlotArea method, you can see how the existence of Y2 affects the PlotArea.

Modifying Data Series

We add just one member field and its public property to the DataSeries class:

```
        private bool isY2Data = false;

        public bool IsY2Data
        {
            get { return isY2Data; }
            set { isY2Data = value; }
        }
```

As discussed above, this property allows you to associate a DataSeries object with the Y2 axis.

Modifying Data Collection

The big change occurs in the AddLines method inside the DataCollection class because this method must be able to add lines for the Y2 axis. The following is the code listing of the Addlines method:

```
        public void AddLines(Graphics g, ChartStyle cs)
        {
            // Plot lines:
            foreach (DataSeries ds in DataSeriesList)
            {
                if (ds.LineStyle.IsVisible == true)
                {
                    Pen aPen = new Pen(ds.LineStyle.LineColor,
                        ds.LineStyle.Thickness);
                    aPen.DashStyle = ds.LineStyle.Pattern;
                    if (ds.LineStyle.PlotMethod ==
                            LineStyle.PlotLinesMethodEnum.Lines)
                    {
                        for (int i = 1; i < ds.PointList.Count; i++)
```

```
                {
                    if (!ds.IsY2Data)
                    {
                        g.DrawLine(aPen,
                            cs.Point2D((PointF)ds.PointList[i - 1]),
                            cs.Point2D((PointF)ds.PointList[i]));
                    }
                    else
                    {
                        g.DrawLine(aPen,
                            cs.Point2DY2((PointF)ds.PointList[i - 1]),
                            cs.Point2DY2((PointF)ds.PointList[i]));
                    }
                }
            }
            else if (ds.LineStyle.PlotMethod ==
                    LineStyle.PlotLinesMethodEnum.Splines)
            {
                ArrayList al = new ArrayList();
                for (int i = 0; i < ds.PointList.Count; i++)
                {
                    PointF pt = (PointF)ds.PointList[i];
                    if (!ds.IsY2Data)
                    {
                        if (pt.X >= cs.XLimMin &&
                            pt.X <= cs.XLimMax &&
                            pt.Y >= cs.YLimMin &&
                            pt.Y <= cs.YLimMax)
                        {
                            al.Add(pt);
                        }
                    }
                    else
                    {
                        if (pt.X >= cs.XLimMin &&
                            pt.X <= cs.XLimMax &&
                            pt.Y >= cs.Y2LimMin &&
                            pt.Y <= cs.Y2LimMax)
                        {
                            al.Add(pt);
                        }
                    }

                }
                PointF[] pts = new PointF[al.Count];
                for (int i = 0; i < pts.Length; i++)
                {
                    if (!ds.IsY2Data)
                    {
                        pts[i] = cs.Point2D((PointF)(al[i]));
                    }
                    else
                    {
                        pts[i] = cs.Point2DY2((PointF)(al[i]));
```

```
                        }
                    }
                    g.DrawCurve(aPen, pts);
                }
                aPen.Dispose();
            }
        }

        // Plot Symbols:
        foreach (DataSeries ds in DataSeriesList)
        {
            for (int i = 0; i < ds.PointList.Count; i++)
            {
                PointF pt = (PointF)ds.PointList[i];
                if (!ds.IsY2Data)
                {
                    if (pt.X >= cs.XLimMin && pt.X <= cs.XLimMax &&
                        pt.Y >= cs.YLimMin && pt.Y <= cs.YLimMax)
                    {
                        ds.SymbolStyle.DrawSymbol(g,
                            cs.Point2D((PointF)ds.PointList[i]));
                    }
                }
                else
                {
                    if (pt.X >= cs.XLimMin && pt.X <= cs.XLimMax &&
                        pt.Y >= cs.Y2LimMin && pt.Y <= cs.Y2LimMax)
                    {
                        ds.SymbolStyle.DrawSymbol(g,
                            cs.Point2DY2((PointF)ds.PointList[i]));
                    }
                }
            }
        }
    }
}
```

This method is easy to follow. Just note that all of the data points for the Y2 axis must go through a coordinate transformation using the `Point2DY2` method.

Testing Project

By building and running this example, you should obtain the result of Figure 3-10. Comparing this result with the one shown in Figure 3-9, you can see that the two sets of data are clearly displayed in Figure 3-10, even through these two sets of data have drastically different data ranges.

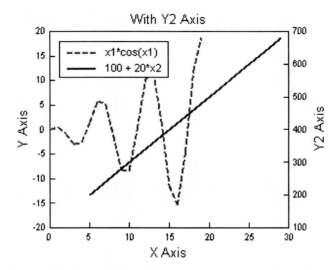

Figure 3-10 Chart with two Y- axes generated from Example3_6.

Sub-Charts

In the previous section, you learned how to create a chart with two Y axes (Y and Y2). Here we will show you that you are not limited to only one chart in a `Form` or a `Control`. The way to create multiple charts in a `Form` or a `Control` is a sub-chart approach. This approach breaks the `Form`'s or `Control`'s space into sub-regions or panes. After creating a chart in one of these sub-regions, you can then use any chart commands you want for these sub-charts. The charts generated in the sub-regions can be treated in the same way as the ones created when no sub-regions are specified. In the next few sections, we will demonstrate how to create such sub-charts using C#.

Layout of Sub-charts

Figure 3-11 shows the sub-chart layout. First, we define a total chart area that holds all of the sub-charts. We will implement a mechanism that allows us to move this total chart area around the `Form` or `Control` and specify its background color. We also define a margin space around the total chart area. This margin space makes the chart more visually appealing. Each sub-chart in the sub-regions behaves like an independent chart. A given sub-chart can be identified by a pair of integers of `Rows` and `Cols`.

Sub-Chart Class

Start off with a new C# Windows Application project, and name it *Example3_7*. This project is based on the previous example, you will need to add all existing classes except for `Form1` of *Example3_6* into the current project and change their `namespace` to *Example3_7*. Then, add a new class called `SubChart` to the project. The following is the code listing of the `SubChart` class:

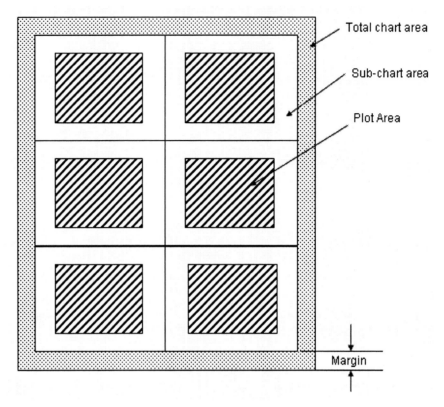

Figure 3-11 Sub-chart layout.

```
using System;
using System.Drawing;
using System.Collections;

namespace Example3_7
{
    public class SubChart
    {
        private int rows = 1;
        private int cols = 1;
        private int margin = 0;
        private Rectangle totalChartArea;
        private Color totalChartBackColor;
        private Color totalChartBorderColor;
        private Form1 form1;

        public SubChart(Form1 fm1)
        {
            form1 = fm1;
            TotalChartArea = form1.ClientRectangle;
            totalChartBackColor = fm1.BackColor;
            totalChartBorderColor = fm1.BackColor;
```

```
    }

    public int Rows
    {
        get { return rows; }
        set { rows = value; }
    }

    public int Cols
    {
        get { return cols; }
        set { cols = value; }
    }

    public int Margin
    {
        get { return margin; }
        set { margin = value; }
    }

    public Rectangle TotalChartArea
    {
        get { return totalChartArea; }
        set { totalChartArea = value; }
    }

    public Color TotalChartBackColor
    {
        get { return totalChartBackColor; }
        set { totalChartBackColor = value; }
    }

    public Color TotalChartBorderColor
    {
        get { return totalChartBorderColor; }
        set { totalChartBorderColor = value; }
    }

    public Rectangle[,] SetSubChart(Graphics g)
    {
        Rectangle[,] subRectangle = new Rectangle[Rows, Cols];
        int subWidth = (TotalChartArea.Width - 2 * Margin) / Cols;
        int subHeight = (TotalChartArea.Height - 2*Margin) / Rows;
        for (int i = 0; i < Rows; i++)
        {
            for (int j = 0; j < Cols; j++)
            {
                int x = TotalChartArea.X + Margin + j * subWidth;
                int y = TotalChartArea.Y + Margin + i * subHeight;
                subRectangle[i, j] = new Rectangle(x, y,
                    subWidth, subHeight);
            }
        }
        // Draw total chart area:
```

```
            Pen aPen = new Pen(TotalChartBorderColor, 1f);
            SolidBrush aBrush = new SolidBrush(TotalChartBackColor);
            g.FillRectangle(aBrush, TotalChartArea);
            g.DrawRectangle(aPen, TotalChartArea);
            return subRectangle;
        }
    }
}
```

You should use the `rows` and `cols` fields and their properties to specify your sub-chart layout. For example, in order to create a sub-chart like the one shown in Figure 3-11, you should set:

```
        Rows = 3;
        Cols = 2;
```

The default value of these fields is one, meaning that there is only one chart in a `form` or `control` which gives you the standard one chart layout. The `Margin` property allows you to set margin space around the total chart area. Its default value is zero. The other three fields, `totalChartArea`, `totalChartBackColor`, and `totalChartBorderColor` allow you to define the total chart area and set its background and border colors. We also pass the `Form1` object to this class because we set the default size of the total chart area to `Form1`'s `ClientRectangle`. We also set the default color of the total chart area using `Form1`'s background color.

The public method `SetSubChart` in this class creates the sub-chart layout. It returns a 2D `Rectangle` array that holds the sizes and positions for every sub-chart inside the `TotalChartArea`.

Modifying Chart Style

To concentrate on the sub-chart implementation and make the code more readable, we move the `SetPlotArea` method from the `Form1` class to `ChartStyle` class. In doing so, we need to make corresponding changes. Here we give the code listing of this method after modification:

```
        private void SetPlotArea(Graphics g)
        {
            // Set PlotArea:
            float xOffset = ChartArea.Width / 30.0f;
            float yOffset = ChartArea.Height / 30.0f;
            SizeF labelFontSize = g.MeasureString("A", LabelFont);
            SizeF titleFontSize = g.MeasureString("A", TitleFont);

            if (Title.ToUpper() == "NO TITLE")
            {
                titleFontSize.Width = 8f;
                titleFontSize.Height = 8f;
            }

            float xSpacing = xOffset / 3.0f;
            float ySpacing = yOffset / 3.0f;
            SizeF tickFontSize = g.MeasureString("A", TickFont);
            float tickSpacing = 2f;
```

```
SizeF yTickSize = g.MeasureString(YLimMin.ToString(), TickFont);

for (float yTick = YLimMin; yTick <= YLimMax; yTick += YTick)
{
    SizeF tempSize = g.MeasureString(yTick.ToString(), TickFont);
    if (yTickSize.Width < tempSize.Width)
    {
        yTickSize = tempSize;
    }
}

float leftMargin = xOffset + labelFontSize.Width +
        xSpacing + yTickSize.Width + tickSpacing;
float rightMargin = xOffset;
float topMargin = yOffset + titleFontSize.Height + ySpacing;
float bottomMargin = yOffset + labelFontSize.Height +
        ySpacing + tickSpacing + tickFontSize.Height;

if (!IsY2Axis)
{
    // Define the plot area with one Y axis:
    int plotX = ChartArea.X + (int)leftMargin;
    int plotY = ChartArea.Y + (int)topMargin;
    int plotWidth = ChartArea.Width - (int)leftMargin -
            2 * (int)rightMargin;
    int plotHeight = ChartArea.Height -
            (int)topMargin - (int)bottomMargin;
    PlotArea = new Rectangle(plotX, plotY,
            plotWidth, plotHeight);
}
else
{
    // Define the plot area with Y and Y2 axes:
    SizeF y2TickSize = g.MeasureString(
            Y2LimMin.ToString(), TickFont);
    for (float y2Tick = Y2LimMin;
            y2Tick <= Y2LimMax; y2Tick += Y2Tick)
    {
        SizeF tempSize2 = g.MeasureString(
            y2Tick.ToString(), TickFont);
        if (y2TickSize.Width < tempSize2.Width)
        {
            y2TickSize = tempSize2;
        }
    }

    rightMargin = xOffset + labelFontSize.Width +
            xSpacing + y2TickSize.Width + tickSpacing;
    int plotX = ChartArea.X + (int)leftMargin;
    int plotY = ChartArea.Y + (int)topMargin;
    int plotWidth = ChartArea.Width -
            (int)leftMargin - (int)rightMargin;
    int plotHeight = ChartArea.Height -
            (int)topMargin - (int)bottomMargin;
```

```
                    PlotArea = new Rectangle(plotX, plotY,
                            plotWidth, plotHeight);
                }
            }
```

Then, add this method to the `AddChartStyle` method:

```
        public void AddChartStyle(Graphics g)
        {
            SetPlotArea(g);

            // Draw TotalChartArea, ChartArea, and PlotArea:
            Pen aPen = new Pen(ChartBorderColor, 1f);
            SolidBrush aBrush = new SolidBrush(ChartBackColor);
            g.FillRectangle(aBrush, ChartArea);
            g.DrawRectangle(aPen, ChartArea);
            aPen = new Pen(PlotBorderColor, 1f);
            aBrush = new SolidBrush(PlotBackColor);
            g.FillRectangle(aBrush, PlotArea);
            g.DrawRectangle(aPen, PlotArea);
            ......
            ......
        }
```

This way, you no longer need to set the plot area inside `Form1`, making the program more readable.

Modifying Form1 Class

Suppose we want to create a `2x2` sub-chart layout. Each sub-chart has its own chart styles. The following is the sample code of the `Form1` class that creates such `2x2` sub-charts:

```
using System;
using System.Drawing;
using System.Drawing.Drawing2D;
using System.Collections;
using System.Windows.Forms;

namespace Example3_7
{
    public partial class Form1 : Form
    {
        private SubChart sc;
        private DataCollection dc1;
        private DataCollection dc2;
        private DataCollection dc3;
        private DataCollection dc4;
        private ChartStyle cs1;
        private ChartStyle cs2;
        private ChartStyle cs3;
        private ChartStyle cs4;
        private Legend lg;

        public Form1()
```

```csharp
{
    InitializeComponent();
    SetStyle(ControlStyles.ResizeRedraw, true);
    This.BackColor = Color.White;

    // Set Form1 size:
    this.Width = 650;
    this.Height = 600;

    // Sub Chart parameters:
    sc = new SubChart(this);
    sc.TotalChartBackColor = Color.White;
    sc.Margin = 20;
    sc.Rows = 2;
    sc.Cols = 2;

    // Parameters for sub-chart 1 (0, 0):
    dc1 = new DataCollection();
    cs1 = new ChartStyle(this);
    cs1.TickFont = new Font("Arial", 7, FontStyle.Regular);
    cs1.TitleFont = new Font("Arial", 10, FontStyle.Regular);
    cs1.XLimMin = 0f;
    cs1.XLimMax = 7f;
    cs1.YLimMin = -1.5f;
    cs1.YLimMax = 1.5f;
    cs1.XTick = 1.0f;
    cs1.YTick = 0.5f;
    cs1.Title = "Sin(x)";

    // Parameters for sub-chart 2 (0, 1):
    dc2 = new DataCollection();
    cs2 = new ChartStyle(this);
    cs2.TickFont = new Font("Arial", 7, FontStyle.Regular);
    cs2.TitleFont = new Font("Arial", 10, FontStyle.Regular);
    cs2.XLimMin = 0f;
    cs2.XLimMax = 7f;
    cs2.YLimMin = -1.5f;
    cs2.YLimMax = 1.5f;
    cs2.XTick = 1.0f;
    cs2.YTick = 0.5f;
    cs2.Title = "Cos(x)";

    // Parameters for sub-chart 3 (1, 0):
    dc3 = new DataCollection();
    cs3 = new ChartStyle(this);
    cs3.TickFont = new Font("Arial", 7, FontStyle.Regular);
    cs3.TitleFont = new Font("Arial", 10, FontStyle.Regular);
    cs3.XLimMin = 0f;
    cs3.XLimMax = 7f;
    cs3.YLimMin = -0.5f;
    cs3.YLimMax = 1.5f;
    cs3.XTick = 1.0f;
    cs3.YTick = 0.5f;
    cs3.Title = "Sin(x)^2";
```

```csharp
        // Parameters for sub-chart 4 (1, 1):
        dc4 = new DataCollection();
        cs4 = new ChartStyle(this);
        cs4.IsY2Axis = true;
        cs4.IsXGrid = false;
        cs4.IsYGrid = false;
        cs4.TickFont = new Font("Arial", 7, FontStyle.Regular);
        cs4.TitleFont = new Font("Arial", 10, FontStyle.Regular);
        cs4.XLimMin = 0f;
        cs4.XLimMax = 30f;
        cs4.YLimMin = -20f;
        cs4.YLimMax = 20f;
        cs4.XTick = 5.0f;
        cs4.YTick = 5f;
        cs4.Y2LimMin = 100f;
        cs4.Y2LimMax = 700f;
        cs4.Y2Tick = 100f;
        cs4.XLabel = "X Axis";
        cs4.YLabel = "Y Axis";
        cs4.Y2Label = "Y2 Axis";
        cs4.Title = "With Y2 Axis";
        lg = new Legend();
        lg.IsLegendVisible = true;
        lg.LegendPosition = Legend.LegendPositionEnum.SouthEast;
    }

    private void AddData(Graphics g)
    {
        float x = 0f;
        float y = 0f;

        // Add Sin(x) data to sub-chart 1:
        dc1.DataSeriesList.Clear();
        DataSeries ds = new DataSeries();
        ds.LineStyle.LineColor = Color.Red;
        ds.LineStyle.Thickness = 2f;
        ds.LineStyle.Pattern = DashStyle.Dash;
        for (int i = 0; i < 50; i++)
        {
            x = i / 5.0f;
            y = (float)Math.Sin(x);
            ds.AddPoint(new PointF(x, y));
        }
        dc1.Add(ds);

        // Add Cos(x) data sub-chart 2:
        dc2.DataSeriesList.Clear();
        ds = new DataSeries();
        ds.LineStyle.LineColor = Color.Blue;
        ds.LineStyle.Thickness = 1f;
        ds.SymbolStyle.SymbolType =
         SymbolStyle.SymbolTypeEnum.OpenDiamond;
        for (int i = 0; i < 50; i++)
```

```
    {
        x = i / 5.0f;
        y = (float)Math.Cos(x);
        ds.AddPoint(new PointF(x, y));
    }
    dc2.Add(ds);

    // Add Sin(x)^2 data to sub-chart 3:
    dc3.DataSeriesList.Clear();
    ds = new DataSeries();
    ds.LineStyle.IsVisible = false;
    ds.SymbolStyle.SymbolType = SymbolStyle.SymbolTypeEnum.Dot;
    ds.SymbolStyle.FillColor = Color.Yellow;
    ds.SymbolStyle.BorderColor = Color.DarkCyan;
    for (int i = 0; i < 50; i++)
    {
        x = i / 5.0f;
        y = (float)Math.Sin(x);
        ds.AddPoint(new PointF(x, y * y));
    }
    dc3.Add(ds);

    // Add y1 and y2 data to sub-chart 4:
    dc4.DataSeriesList.Clear();
    // Add y1 data:
    ds = new DataSeries();
    ds.LineStyle.LineColor = Color.Red;
    ds.LineStyle.Thickness = 2f;
    ds.LineStyle.Pattern = DashStyle.Dash;
    ds.SeriesName = "x1*cos(x1)";
    for (int i = 0; i < 20; i++)
    {
        float x1 = 1.0f * i;
        float y1 = x1 * (float)Math.Cos(x1);
        ds.AddPoint(new PointF(x1, y1));
    }
    dc4.Add(ds);
    // Add y2 data:
    ds = new DataSeries();
    ds.LineStyle.LineColor = Color.Blue;
    ds.LineStyle.Thickness = 2f;
    ds.SeriesName = "100 + 20*x2";
    ds.IsY2Data = true;
    for (int i = 5; i < 30; i++)
    {
        float x2 = 1.0f * i;
        float y2 = 100.0f + 20.0f * x2;
        ds.AddPoint(new PointF(x2, y2));
    }
    dc4.Add(ds);
}

protected override void OnPaint(PaintEventArgs e)
{
```

```
            Graphics g = e.Graphics;

            // Re-define TotalChartArea for resizing:
            sc.TotalChartArea = this.ClientRectangle;

            // Add data for all sub-charts:
            AddData(g);

            // Create sub-chart layout:
            Rectangle[,] subchart = sc.SetSubChart(g);

            // Create sub-chart 1:
            cs1.ChartArea = subchart[0, 0];
            cs1.AddChartStyle(g);
            dc1.AddLines(g, cs1);

            // Create sub-chart 2:
            cs2.ChartArea = subchart[0, 1];
            cs2.AddChartStyle(g);
            dc2.AddLines(g, cs2);

            // Create sub-chart 3:
            cs3.ChartArea = subchart[1, 0];
            cs3.AddChartStyle(g);
            dc3.AddLines(g, cs3);

            // Create sub-chart 4:
            cs4.ChartArea = subchart[1, 1];
            cs4.AddChartStyle(g);
            dc4.AddLines(g, cs4);
            lg.AddLegend(g, dc4, cs4);
            g.Dispose();
        }
    }
}
```

It is apparent that the current Form1 class looks more like an application program. All of the chart styles, symbols, line styles, etc. are encapsulated in the other classes. In the Form1 class, you simply create various instances, set parameters, and add your data to the chart.

Let's look at how the program works. First we create a SubChart object sc. Then we define four DataCollect objects and four ChartStyle objects, because we want to create a sub-chart plot with four sub-charts, each using different DataCollection and ChartStyle. We also create a legend object which can be used in any sub-chart. Inside Form1's constructor, we create the instance for the SubChart object and define the corresponding parameters. Here we set cs.Row = 2 and cs.Cols = 2 to create a 2X2 sub-chart layout. The code that follows is standard parameter settings for each sub-chart, such as those of the single chart program we created in the previous sections. In particular, sub-chart 4 has a Y2 axis, which demonstrates that each sub-chart can have its own chart style, and can even have two Y axes.

Inside the AddData method, we add various DataSeries object, ds, to the different data collections, dc1, dc2, dc3, and dc4. Each dc has a different line and symbol style. Please note that we re-create the `ds` instance when we add it to the different `DataCollection` objects with the following code:

```
ds = new DataSeries();
```

This is necessary because, otherwise, some of the previously defined parameters in `ds` will affect the new `DataCollection` object.

Then we turn our attention to the `OnPaint` method. We redefine the `TotalChartArea` property because we want our chart to have resize and repaint capability. Then we create the sub-chart layout:

```
Rectangle[,] subchart = sc.SetSubChart(g);
```

The `subchart` in this example is a `2x2 Rectangle` array. Next, we put the sub-charts in their proper positions by assigning the `ChartArea` to the element of the subchart. For example:

```
cs3.ChartArea = subchart[1, 0];
```

This places the sub-chart 3 to at `subchart[1, 0]`, i.e., the bottom-left corner of the total chart area.

Testing Project

By building and running the project, you should obtain the results shown in Figure 3-12. Here we break up `Form1` into four panes configured in a 2-by-2 fashion. It can be seen that each chart has its own chart style. Please note that the total chart area is surrounded by a white color due to the following commands:

```
sc.TotalChartBackColor = Color.White;
sc.Margin = 20;
```

We set the background color of the total chart area to white (it can be any color), and its margin to 20 pixels. If you set the margin = 0 (the default value), you will not see the background color because the sub-charts will occupy the entire chart area.

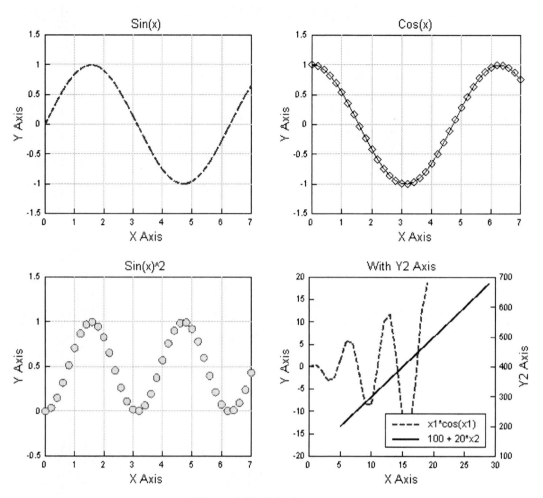

Figure 3-12 Sub-charts

Specialized 2D Charts

In this chapter, we show you how to create certain special or application-specific charts using Visual C#. Some of these charts are typically found in commercial charting packages or spreadsheet applications. We will discuss a variety of special charts that help display statistical distributions of data or discrete data, including bar, stair-step, error bar, area, and stock charts. You will also learn how to create charts in other coordinate systems, such as pie and polar charts.

Creating Bar Charts

The bar chart is useful for comparing classes or groups of data. In a bar chart, a class or group can have a single category of data, or can be broken down further into multiple categories for a greater depth of analysis. A bar chart is often used in exploratory data analysis to illustrate the major features of the distribution of the data in a convenient form. It displays the data using a number of rectangles of the same width, each of which represents a particular category. The length (and hence area) of each rectangle is proportional to the number of cases in the category it represents, such as, age group, religious affiliation, etc.

Implementation

You might remember that in Chapter 1, we discussed two kinds of viewports: one based on the plot rectangle, such as the one used in developing the 2D line charts in the previous chapter, and one based on the drawing panel. The advantage of the first viewport is that it is simple, allowing you to draw both the chart style (tick labels, axis labels, and title) and the data curves on the same `control` (including `form`). Its drawback is that you have to deal with the possibility of drawing outside of the viewport when you change the limits of the axes. If your application involves drawing graphics objects (for example, simple shapes such as rectangles and polygons), this viewport is not convenient.

For the second kind of viewport, you can draw anything inside it. You don't need to worry about drawing outside of this viewport. Since bar charts involve drawing rectangles or polygons, this viewport will be a natural choice. Before using it for your bar charts, you need to answer a question first: how can you put the title, tick labels, and axis labels on your charts if this viewport doesn't allow you to draw on the outside? The solution is to draw the bar chart data (various rectangles) on the viewport (a panel `control`), while placing the title, tick labels, and axis labels on another control (a `form`). Be careful when you create charts on different controls; sometimes, the `Graphics` objects used to draw on these two separate controls might conflict with each other (synchronization issues), and you may get unexpected results when you resize and repaint your controls.

Let's look at an example that shows how to create a bar chart with C#. Start off with a new C# Windows Application project and call it *Example4_1*. Add a panel control to `Form1`, naming it `PlotPanel` using the designer. Set this panel's anchor property to anchor all four of its sides, `left`, `right`, `top`, and `bottom`. Open `Form.Designer.cs` and change the panel's private property to public:

```
public System.Windows.Forms.Panel PlotPanel;
```

This way, you can access this `PlotPanel` from classes other than `Form1`.

Add four new classes to the project, `DataCollection`, `DataSeries`, `ChartStyle`, and `BarStyle`. We have used first three classes extensively in the previous chapter. You can copy them from previous projects (such as *Example3_7*), and modify them to fit the current project. The `BarStyle` class is new and specific to this project. The following is its code listing:

```
using System;
using System.Drawing;
using System.Drawing.Drawing2D;

namespace Example4_1
{
    public class BarStyle
    {
        private Color fillColor = Color.Black;
        private Color borderColor = Color.Black;
        private float borderThickness = 1.0f;
        private float barWidth = 0.8f;
        private DashStyle borderPattern = DashStyle.Solid;

        public float BarWidth
        {
            get { return barWidth; }
            set { barWidth = value; }
        }
```

```
    virtual public DashStyle BorderPattern
    {
        get { return borderPattern; }
        set { borderPattern = value; }
    }

    public float BorderThickness
    {
        get { return borderThickness; }
        set { borderThickness = value; }
    }

    virtual public Color FillColor
    {
        get { return fillColor; }
        set { fillColor = value; }
    }

    virtual public Color BorderColor
    {
        get { return borderColor; }
        set { borderColor = value; }
    }
  }
}
```

This class is very simple. We define several member fields and their corresponding properties that allow you to specify the bar width, fill color, and border style.

You also need to modify the ChartStyle class. First we add a bar chart type field and its property:

```
    private BarTypeEnum barType = BarTypeEnum.Vertical;

    public BarTypeEnum BarType
    {
        get { return barType; }
        set { barType = value; }
    }

    public enum BarTypeEnum
    {
        Vertical = 0,
        Horizontal = 1,
        VerticalStack = 2,
        HorizontalStack = 3,
        VerticalOverlay = 4,
        HorizontalOverlay = 5
    }
```

Here, we define the barType as a BarTyleEnum object. From this enumeration, you can choose different bar chart types, including vertical, horizontal, etc. We also remove the PlotArea field and its property from the class because we use PlotPanel instead of PlotArea in this project. We don't define PlotPanel as a member field, so its property is defined internally and encapsulated by users. The other fields and properties in this class are the same as before, so we don't need to list them here. You can look at the complete source code in Example4_1 on your computer.

There are three public methods in this class. The Point2D method, which is used to transform the points from the world coordinates to the device coordinates, is the same as in project *Example1_3*,. The PlotPanelStyle method defines the styles for the PlotPanel, including gridlines and ticks (here, we put the ticks inside the PlotPanel). This method is basically similar to the previous projects in Chapter 3, but a minor modification is necessary to reflect the bar chart's specifics. The following is the code snippet of the PlotPanelStyle method:

```
public void PlotPanelStyle(Graphics g)
{
    Pen aPen = new Pen(ChartBorderColor, 1f);
    SolidBrush aBrush = new SolidBrush(ChartBackColor);
    SizeF tickFontSize = g.MeasureString("A", TickFont);

    // Create vertical gridlines:
    float fX, fY, xm, ym;

    aPen = new Pen(GridColor, 1f);
    aPen.DashStyle = GridPattern;
    xm = XLimMin + XTickOffset;
    if (BarType == BarTypeEnum.Vertical ||
        BarType == BarTypeEnum.VerticalOverlay ||
        BarType == BarTypeEnum.VerticalStack)
    {
        xm = XTickOffset + XLimMin + XTick / 2;
    }

    // Create vertical gridelines:
    if (IsYGrid == true)
    {

        for (fX = xm; fX < XLimMax; fX += XTick)
        {
            g.DrawLine(aPen, Point2D(new PointF(fX, YLimMin)),
                Point2D(new PointF(fX, YLimMax)));
        }
    }

    // Create the x-axis tick marks:
    for (fX = xm; fX < XLimMax; fX += XTick)
    {
        PointF yAxisPoint = Point2D(new PointF(fX, YLimMin));
        g.DrawLine(Pens.Black, yAxisPoint,
                new PointF(yAxisPoint.X, yAxisPoint.Y - 8f));
    }

    // Create horizontal gridlines:
    aPen = new Pen(GridColor, 1f);
    aPen.DashStyle = GridPattern;
    ym = YLimMin + YTickOffset;
    if (BarType == BarTypeEnum.Horizontal ||
```

```
            BarType == BarTypeEnum.HorizontalOverlay ||
            BarType == BarTypeEnum.HorizontalStack)
        {
            ym = YTickOffset + YLimMin + YTick / 2;
        }

        if (IsXGrid == true)
        {
            for (fY = ym; fY < YLimMax; fY += YTick)
            {
                g.DrawLine(aPen, Point2D(new PointF(XLimMin, fY)),
                    Point2D(new PointF(XLimMax, fY)));
            }
        }

        // Create the y-axis tick marks:
        for (fY = ym; fY < YLimMax; fY += YTick)
        {
            PointF xAxisPoint = Point2D(new PointF(XLimMin, fY));
            g.DrawLine(Pens.Black, xAxisPoint,
                new PointF(xAxisPoint.X + 5f, xAxisPoint.Y));
        }
        aPen.Dispose();
        aBrush.Dispose();
    }
```

Please note how the method takes care of both vertical and horizontal bar charts. In this method, we create a `SolidBrush` object to fill the bar charts with different colors. If you like, you can use other Brush objects, such as TextureBrush, HatchBrush, and LinearGradientBrush, to fill the bar charts with images, patterns, or gradient colors.

Another public method is `SetChartArea`. This method is used to specify the ticks, labels, etc. It also contains two private methods: `SetPlotPanel` and `AddLabels`. The `SetPlotPanel` method is used to set the size and position of the `PlotPanel`. The `AddLabels` method creates the title and labels of the axes for the bar chart. The following is the code listing of these classes:

```
public void SetChartArea(Graphics g)
{
    // Define PlotPanel:
    SetPlotPanel(g);

    // Draw chart area:
    Pen aPen = new Pen(ChartBorderColor, 1f);
    SolidBrush aBrush = new SolidBrush(ChartBackColor);
    SizeF tickFontSize = g.MeasureString("A", TickFont);
    g.FillRectangle(aBrush, ChartArea);
    g.DrawRectangle(aPen, ChartArea);

    // Create the x-axis tick labels:
    aBrush = new SolidBrush(TickFontColor);
    float xm = XLimMin + XTickOffset;
    float xticklabel = 0f;
    if (BarType == BarTypeEnum.Vertical ||
        BarType == BarTypeEnum.VerticalOverlay ||
```

```csharp
              BarType == BarTypeEnum.VerticalStack)
        {

            xm = XTickOffset + XLimMin + XTick / 2;
            xticklabel = XTick / 2;

        }

        for (float fX =  xm; fX <= XLimMax; fX += XTick)
        {
            PointF yAxisPoint = Point2D(new PointF(fX, YLimMin));
            StringFormat sFormat = new StringFormat();
            sFormat.Alignment = StringAlignment.Center;
            g.DrawString((fX + xticklabel).ToString(),
                TickFont, aBrush,
                new PointF(form1.PlotPanel.Left + yAxisPoint.X,
                form1.PlotPanel.Top + yAxisPoint.Y + 4f), sFormat);
        }

        // Create the y-axis tick labels:
        float ym = YLimMin + YTickOffset;
        float yticklabel = 0f;
        if (BarType == BarTypeEnum.Horizontal ||
            BarType == BarTypeEnum.HorizontalOverlay ||
            BarType == BarTypeEnum.HorizontalStack)
        {
            ym = YTickOffset + YLimMin + YTick / 2;
            yticklabel = YTick / 2;
        }
        for (float fY = ym; fY <= YLimMax; fY += YTick)
        {
            PointF xAxisPoint = Point2D(new PointF(XLimMin, fY));
            StringFormat sFormat = new StringFormat();
            sFormat.Alignment = StringAlignment.Far;
            g.DrawString((fY + yticklabel).ToString(),
                TickFont, aBrush,
                new PointF(form1.PlotPanel.Left + xAxisPoint.X - 3f,
                form1.PlotPanel.Top + xAxisPoint.Y
                - tickFontSize.Height / 2), sFormat);
        }

        AddLabels(g);
    }

    private void SetPlotPanel(Graphics g)
    {
        // Set form1.PlotPanel:
        float xOffset = ChartArea.Width / 30.0f;
        float yOffset = ChartArea.Height / 30.0f;
        SizeF labelFontSize = g.MeasureString("A", LabelFont);
        SizeF titleFontSize = g.MeasureString("A", TitleFont);
        if (Title.ToUpper() == "NO TITLE")
        {
            titleFontSize.Width = 8f;
            titleFontSize.Height = 8f;
```

```
    }
    float xSpacing = xOffset / 3.0f;
    float ySpacing = yOffset / 3.0f;
    SizeF tickFontSize = g.MeasureString("A", TickFont);
    float tickSpacing = 2f;
    SizeF yTickSize = g.MeasureString(
        YLimMin.ToString(), TickFont);
    for (float yTick = YLimMin + YTickOffset;
        yTick <= YLimMax; yTick += YTick)
    {
        SizeF tempSize = g.MeasureString(
            yTick.ToString(), TickFont);
        if (yTickSize.Width < tempSize.Width)
        {
            yTickSize = tempSize;
        }
    }
    float leftMargin = xOffset + labelFontSize.Width +
            xSpacing + yTickSize.Width + tickSpacing;
    float rightMargin = xOffset;
    float topMargin = yOffset + titleFontSize.Height + ySpacing;
    float bottomMargin = yOffset + labelFontSize.Height +
            ySpacing + tickSpacing + tickFontSize.Height;

    // Define the plot panel size:
    int[] panelsize = new int[4];
    form1.PlotPanel.Left = ChartArea.X + (int)leftMargin;
    form1.PlotPanel.Top = ChartArea.Y + (int)topMargin;
    form1.PlotPanel.Width = ChartArea.Width -
        (int)leftMargin - 2 * (int)rightMargin;
    form1.PlotPanel.Height = ChartArea.Height -
        (int)topMargin - (int)bottomMargin;
    form1.PlotPanel.BackColor = plotBackColor;
}

private void AddLabels(Graphics g)
{
    float xOffset = ChartArea.Width / 30.0f;
    float yOffset = ChartArea.Height / 30.0f;
    SizeF labelFontSize = g.MeasureString("A", LabelFont);
    SizeF titleFontSize = g.MeasureString("A", TitleFont);

    // Add horizontal axis label:
    SolidBrush aBrush = new SolidBrush(LabelFontColor);
    SizeF stringSize = g.MeasureString(XLabel, LabelFont);
    g.DrawString(XLabel, LabelFont, aBrush,
        new Point(form1.PlotPanel.Left +
        form1.PlotPanel.Width / 2 -
        (int)stringSize.Width / 2, ChartArea.Bottom -
        (int)yOffset - (int)labelFontSize.Height));

    // Add y-axis label:
    StringFormat sFormat = new StringFormat();
    sFormat.Alignment = StringAlignment.Center;
```

```
            stringSize = g.MeasureString(YLabel, LabelFont);
            // Save the state of the current Graphics object
            GraphicsState gState = g.Save();
            g.TranslateTransform(ChartArea.X + xOffset, ChartArea.Y
                + yOffset + titleFontSize.Height
                + yOffset / 3 + form1.PlotPanel.Height / 2);
            g.RotateTransform(-90);
            g.DrawString(YLabel, LabelFont, aBrush, 0, 0, sFormat);
            // Restore it:
            g.Restore(gState);

            // Add title:
            aBrush = new SolidBrush(TitleFontColor);
            stringSize = g.MeasureString(Title, TitleFont);
            if (Title.ToUpper() != "NO TITLE")
            {
                g.DrawString(Title, TitleFont, aBrush,
                    new Point(form1.PlotPanel.Left +
                    form1.PlotPanel.Width / 2 -
                    (int)stringSize.Width / 2,
                    ChartArea.Top + (int)yOffset));
            }
            aBrush.Dispose();
        }
```

The `DataSeries` class is the same as the one used in the previous project *Example3_7*. However, in the `DataCollection` class, we need to change the public method `AddLines` to `AddBars`. This method is specific to the bar chart:

```
    public void AddBars(Graphics g, ChartStyle cs,
                        int numberOfDataSeries, int numberOfPoints)
    {
        // Draw bars:
        ArrayList temp = new ArrayList();
        float[] tempy = new float[numberOfPoints];
        int n = 0;
        foreach (DataSeries ds in DataSeriesList)
        {
            Pen aPen = new Pen(ds.BarStyle.BorderColor,
            ds.BarStyle.BorderThickness);
            SolidBrush aBrush = new SolidBrush(ds.BarStyle.FillColor);
            aPen.DashStyle = ds.BarStyle.BorderPattern;
            PointF[] pts = new PointF[4];
            PointF pt;
            float width;

            if (cs.BarType == ChartStyle.BarTypeEnum.Vertical)
            {
                if (numberOfDataSeries == 1)
                {
                    width = cs.XTick * ds.BarStyle.BarWidth;
                    for (int i = 0; i < ds.PointList.Count; i++)
                    {
                        pt = (PointF)ds.PointList[i];
```

```
            float x = pt.X - cs.XTick / 2;
            pts[0] = cs.Point2D(new PointF(x -
                     width / 2, 0));
            pts[1] = cs.Point2D(new PointF(x +
                     width / 2, 0));
            pts[2] = cs.Point2D(new PointF(x +
                     width / 2, pt.Y));
            pts[3] = cs.Point2D(new PointF(x -
                     width / 2, pt.Y));
            g.FillPolygon(aBrush, pts);
            g.DrawPolygon(aPen, pts);
        }
    }
    else if (numberOfDataSeries > 1)
    {
        width = 0.7f * cs.XTick;
        for (int i = 0; i < ds.PointList.Count; i++)
        {
            pt = (PointF)ds.PointList[i];
            float w1 = width / numberOfDataSeries;
            float w = ds.BarStyle.BarWidth * w1;
            float space = (w1 - w) / 2;
            float x = pt.X - cs.XTick / 2;
            pts[0] = cs.Point2D(new PointF(
                x - width / 2 + space + n * w1, 0));
            pts[1] = cs.Point2D(new PointF(
                x - width / 2 + space + n * w1 + w, 0));
            pts[2] = cs.Point2D(new PointF(
                x - width / 2 + space +
                n * w1 + w, pt.Y));
            pts[3] = cs.Point2D(new PointF(
                x - width / 2 + space + n * w1, pt.Y));
            g.FillPolygon(aBrush, pts);
            g.DrawPolygon(aPen, pts);
        }
    }
}
else if (cs.BarType ==
    ChartStyle.BarTypeEnum.VerticalOverlay
    && numberOfDataSeries >1)
{
    width = cs.XTick * ds.BarStyle.BarWidth;
    width = width / (float)Math.Pow(2,n);
    for (int i = 0; i < ds.PointList.Count; i++)
    {
        pt = (PointF)ds.PointList[i];
        float x = pt.X - cs.XTick / 2;
        pts[0] = cs.Point2D(new PointF(x -
                 width / 2, 0));
        pts[1] = cs.Point2D(new PointF(x +
                 width / 2, 0));
        pts[2] = cs.Point2D(new PointF(x +
                 width / 2, pt.Y));
        pts[3] = cs.Point2D(new PointF(x -
```

```
                            width / 2, pt.Y));
                g.FillPolygon(aBrush, pts);
                g.DrawPolygon(aPen, pts);
            }
        }
        else if (cs.BarType ==
                ChartStyle.BarTypeEnum.VerticalStack
                && numberOfDataSeries > 1)
        {
            width = cs.XTick * ds.BarStyle.BarWidth;
            for (int i = 0; i < ds.PointList.Count; i++)
            {
                pt = (PointF)ds.PointList[i];
                if (temp.Count > 0)
                {
                    tempy[i] = tempy[i] + ((PointF)temp[i]).Y;
                }
                float x = pt.X - cs.XTick / 2;
                pts[0] = cs.Point2D(new PointF(x -
                        width / 2, 0 + tempy[i]));
                pts[1] = cs.Point2D(new PointF(x +
                        width / 2, 0 + tempy[i]));
                pts[2] = cs.Point2D(new PointF(x +
                        width / 2, pt.Y + tempy[i]));
                pts[3] = cs.Point2D(new PointF(x -
                        width / 2, pt.Y + tempy[i]));
                g.FillPolygon(aBrush, pts);
                g.DrawPolygon(aPen, pts);
            }
            temp = ds.PointList;
        }

        else if (cs.BarType ==
                ChartStyle.BarTypeEnum.Horizontal)
        {
            if (numberOfDataSeries == 1)
            {
                width = cs.YTick * ds.BarStyle.BarWidth;
                for (int i = 0; i < ds.PointList.Count; i++)
                {
                    pt = (PointF)ds.PointList[i];
                    float y = pt.Y - cs.YTick / 2;
                    pts[0] = cs.Point2D(new PointF(0, y -
                            width / 2));
                    pts[1] = cs.Point2D(new PointF(0, y +
                            width / 2));
                    pts[2] = cs.Point2D(new PointF(pt.X,
                            y + width / 2));
                    pts[3] = cs.Point2D(new PointF(pt.X,
                            y - width / 2));
                    g.FillPolygon(aBrush, pts);
                    g.DrawPolygon(aPen, pts);
                }
            }
```

```
        else if (numberOfDataSeries > 1)
        {
            width = 0.7f * cs.YTick;
            for (int i = 0; i < ds.PointList.Count; i++)
            {
                pt = (PointF)ds.PointList[i];
                float w1 = width / numberOfDataSeries;
                float w = ds.BarStyle.BarWidth * w1;
                float space = (w1 - w) / 2;
                float y = pt.Y - cs.YTick / 2;
                pts[0] = cs.Point2D(new PointF(0,
                            y - width / 2 + space + n * w1));
                pts[1] = cs.Point2D(new PointF(0,
                            y - width / 2 + space + n * w1 + w));
                pts[2] = cs.Point2D(new PointF(pt.X,
                            y - width / 2 + space + n * w1 + w));
                pts[3] = cs.Point2D(new PointF(pt.X,
                            y - width / 2 + space + n * w1));
                g.FillPolygon(aBrush, pts);
                g.DrawPolygon(aPen, pts);
            }
        }
    }
    else if (cs.BarType ==
            ChartStyle.BarTypeEnum.HorizontalOverlay &&
            numberOfDataSeries > 1)
    {
        width = cs.YTick * ds.BarStyle.BarWidth;
        width = width / (float)Math.Pow(2, n);
        for (int i = 0; i < ds.PointList.Count; i++)
        {
            pt = (PointF)ds.PointList[i];
            float y = pt.Y - cs.YTick / 2;
            pts[0] = cs.Point2D(new PointF(0,
                        y - width / 2));
            pts[1] = cs.Point2D(new PointF(0,
                        y + width / 2));
            pts[2] = cs.Point2D(new PointF(pt.X,
                        y + width / 2));
            pts[3] = cs.Point2D(new PointF(pt.X,
                        y - width / 2));
            g.FillPolygon(aBrush, pts);
            g.DrawPolygon(aPen, pts);
        }
    }
    else if (cs.BarType ==
            ChartStyle.BarTypeEnum.HorizontalStack &&
                numberOfDataSeries > 1)
    {
        {
            width = cs.YTick * ds.BarStyle.BarWidth;
            for (int i = 0; i < ds.PointList.Count; i++)
            {
                pt = (PointF)ds.PointList[i];
```

```
                              if (temp.Count > 0)
                              {
                                  tempy[i] = tempy[i] + ((PointF)temp[i]).X;
                              }
                              float y = pt.Y - cs.YTick / 2;
                              pts[0] = cs.Point2D(new PointF(0 +
                                      tempy[i], y - width / 2));
                              pts[1] = cs.Point2D(new PointF(0 +
                                      tempy[i], y + width / 2));
                              pts[2] = cs.Point2D(new PointF(pt.X +
                                      tempy[i], y + width / 2));
                              pts[3] = cs.Point2D(new PointF(pt.X +
                                      tempy[i], y - width / 2));
                              g.FillPolygon(aBrush, pts);
                              g.DrawPolygon(aPen, pts);
                          }
                          temp = ds.PointList;
                      }
                  }
                  n++;
                  aPen.Dispose();
              }
          }
```

In this method we implement six different types of bar charts. The bar rectangle is defined by the point coordinates of its four corners, and is then created using the FillPolygon and DrawPolygon methods.

We now turn our attention to the Form1 class:

```
Using System;
using System.Drawing;
using System.Drawing.Drawing2D;
using System.Windows.Forms;

namespace Example4_1
{
    public partial class Form1 : Form
    {
        private ChartStyle cs;
        private DataCollection dc;
        private DataSeries ds;

        public Form1()
        {
            InitializeComponent();
            this.SetStyle(ControlStyles.ResizeRedraw, true);

            // Subscribing to a paint eventhandler to PlotPanel:
            PlotPanel.Paint +=
                new PaintEventHandler(PlotPanelPaint);

            cs = new ChartStyle(this);
            dc = new DataCollection();
```

```
        // Specify chart style parameters:
         ......
    }

    private void AddData(Graphics g)
    {
        // Add first data series:
         ......
    }

    private void PlotPanelPaint(object sender, PaintEventArgs e)
    {
        Graphics g = e.Graphics;
        AddData(g);
        cs.PlotPanelStyle(g);
        dc.AddBars(g, cs,
                dc.DataSeriesList.Count, ds.PointList.Count);
    }

    protected override void OnPaint(PaintEventArgs e)
    {
        Graphics g = e.Graphics;
        cs.ChartArea = this.ClientRectangle;
        cs.SetChartArea(g);
    }
   }
}
```

This class in this example is very simple. However, you must be careful here. The first thing you may notice is that we subscribe a paint even handler for the PlotPanel:

```
    PlotPanel.Paint += new PaintEventHandler(PlotPanelPaint);
```

This enables you to draw graphics objects on the PlotPanel using the PlotPanelPaint (which you can give any name) method. We also override Form1's OnPaint method. This method is used to draw graphics objects directly on Form1 (outside of the PlotPanel). These two paint methods are responsible for drawing in different regions by calling their methods. You can see that the PlotPanelPaint method calls AddData, PlotPanelStyle, and AddBars, all of which are related to drawing inside the PlotPanel. Additionally, we define the chart area by calling the SetChartArea method inside the OnPaint method in the Form1 class.

Bar Charts

In order to create a bar chart using this example program, you need to specify the chart style parameters and add data points to the project in the Form1 class. Here is the code snippet for creating a vertical bar chart:

```
Using System;
using System.Drawing;
using System.Drawing.Drawing2D;
using System.Windows.Forms;
```

```csharp
namespace Example4_1
{
    public partial class Form1 : Form
    {
        private ChartStyle cs;
        private DataCollection dc;
        private DataSeries ds;

        public Form1()
        {
            InitializeComponent();
            this.SetStyle(ControlStyles.ResizeRedraw, true);
            this.BackColor = Color.White;

            // Subscribing to a paint eventhandler to drawingPanel:
            PlotPanel.Paint +=
                new PaintEventHandler(PlotPanelPaint);

            cs = new ChartStyle(this);
            dc = new DataCollection();
            // Specify chart style parameters:
            cs.Title = "Bar Chart";
            cs.XLimMin = 0f;
            cs.XLimMax = 5f;
            cs.YLimMin = 0f;
            cs.YLimMax = 10f;
            cs.XTick = 1f;
            cs.YTick = 2f;
            cs.BarType = ChartStyle.BarTypeEnum.Vertical;
        }

        private void AddData(Graphics g)
        {
            float x, y;
            // Add data series:
            dc.DataSeriesList.Clear();
            ds = new DataSeries();
            ds.BarStyle.BorderColor = Color.Red;
            ds.BarStyle.FillColor = Color.Green;
            ds.BarStyle.BarWidth = 0.6f;
            for (int i = 0; i < 5; i++)
            {
                x = i + 1;
                y = 2.0f * x;
                ds.AddPoint(new PointF(x, y));
            }
            dc.Add(ds);
        }

        private void PlotPanelPaint(object sender, PaintEventArgs e)
        {
            Graphics g = e.Graphics;
            AddData(g);
            cs.PlotPanelStyle(g);
```

```
        dc.AddBars(g, cs, dc.DataSeriesList.Count,
            ds.PointList.Count);
    }

    protected override void OnPaint(PaintEventArgs e)
    {
        Graphics g = e.Graphics;
        cs.ChartArea = this.ClientRectangle;
        cs.SetChartArea(g);
    }
}
}
```

This code generates the output of Figure 4-1.

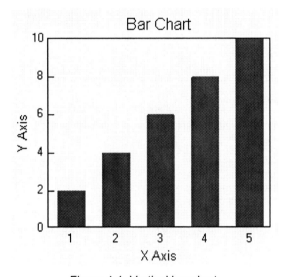

Figure 4-1 Vertical bar chart.

In this class, we set the BarType property to Vertical (this is also the default value). The other parameters defined in the constructor are standard properties for any chart. Inside the AddData method, we associate bar style properties with the data series. Here we set the bar width = 0.6 (the default value is 0.8). The value of the bar width must be in the region of [0, 1].

In some cases, some of your points may be missing data. You can create a bar chart by assigning a zero value for y at the missing data point. For example:

$$x = [1, 2, 3, 4, 5], \ y = [2, 0, 3, 8, 10]$$

This data set will create the result shown in Figure 4-2.

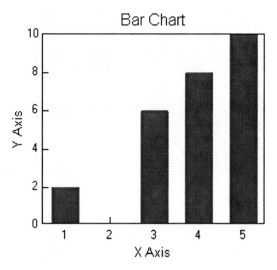

Figure 4-2 Vertical bar chart with a missing data at x = 2.

You can create a horizontal bar chart just as easily using the current program. Change some of the parameters in the above code listing of Form1.cs to the following:

```
cs.XLimMin = 0f;
cs.XLimMax = 10f;
cs.YLimMin = 0f;
cs.YLimMax = 5f;
cs.XTick = 2f;
cs.YTick = 1f;
cs.BarType = ChartStyle.BarTypeEnum.Horizontal;
```

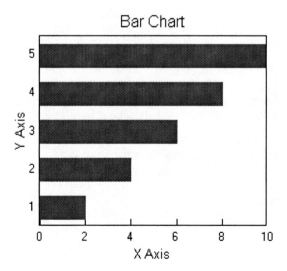

Figure 4-3 Horizontal bar chart.

Here we specify the `BarType` as `Horizontal` and switch the X and Y axis limits. There is no need to change anything inside the `AddData` method. Build and run the project. You should obtain the horizontal chart of Figure 4-3.

Group Bar Charts

When you have multiple sets of data with the same X values, you can create a group vertical bar chart using the current example program. The Y values are distributed along the X-axis, with each Y at a different X drawn at a different location. All of the Y values at the same X are clustered around the same location on the X-axis. In order to create such a bar chart, we use the following parameters in `Form1`'s constructor:

```
cs.XLimMin = 0f;
cs.XLimMax = 5f;
cs.YLimMin = 0f;
cs.YLimMax = 10f;
cs.XTick = 1f;
cs.YTick = 2f;
cs.BarType = ChartStyle.BarTypeEnum.Vertical;
```

And we change the `AddData` method to be following:

```
private void AddData(Graphics g)
{
    float x, y;
    // Add first data series:
    dc.DataSeriesList.Clear();
    ds = new DataSeries();
    ds.BarStyle.BorderColor = Color.Red;
    ds.BarStyle.FillColor = Color.Green;
    for (int i = 0; i < 5; i++)
    {
        x = i + 1;
        y = 2.0f * x;
        ds.AddPoint(new PointF(x, y));
    }
    dc.Add(ds);

    // Add second data series:
    ds = new DataSeries();
    ds.BarStyle.BorderColor = Color.Red;
    ds.BarStyle.FillColor = Color.Yellow;
    for (int i = 0; i < 5; i++)
    {
        x = i + 1;
        y = 1.5f * x;
        ds.AddPoint(new PointF(x, y));
    }
    dc.Add(ds);

    // Add third data series:
    ds = new DataSeries();
    ds.BarStyle.BorderColor = Color.Red;
```

```
ds.BarStyle.FillColor = Color.Blue;
for (int i = 0; i < 5; i++)
{
    x = i + 1;
    y = 1.0f * x;
    ds.AddPoint(new PointF(x, y));
}
dc.Add(ds);
}
```

We add three sets of data series to the project, all with the same set of X values. The default bar width = 0.8 is used. The fill colors are green, yellow, and blue, while the border color is red for all of the bars. These data sets produce the results shown in Figure 4-4.

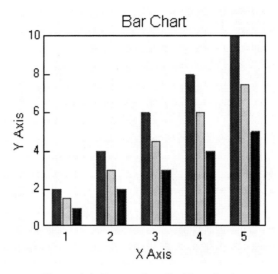

Figure 4-4 Grouped vertical bar chart.

Using the same data series, you can also generate a grouped horizontal bar chart. Just change the parameters in Form1's constructor to the following:

```
cs.XLimMin = 0f;
cs.XLimMax = 10f;
cs.YLimMin = 0f;
cs.YLimMax = 5f;
cs.XTick = 2f;
cs.YTick = 1f;
cs.BarType = ChartStyle.BarTypeEnum.Horizontal;
```

This produces the results of Figure 4-5.

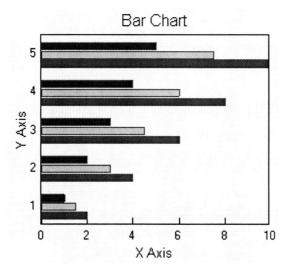

Figure 4-5 Grouped horizontal chart.

Overlay Bar Charts

It is also easy to create an overlay bar chart using the current example program. Use the same code for the AddData method as the previous sub-section, and change the parameters in Form1's constructor:

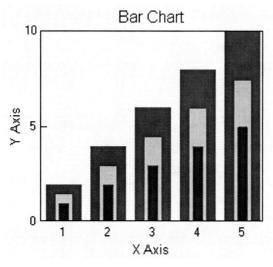

Figure 4-6 Overlaid vertical bar chart.

```
cs.XLimMin = 0f;
cs.XLimMax = 5f;
cs.YLimMin = 0f;
cs.YLimMax = 10f;
cs.XTick = 1f;
cs.YTick = 5f;
cs.BarType = ChartStyle.BarTypeEnum.VerticalOverlay;
```

This project will create the output of Figure 4-6.

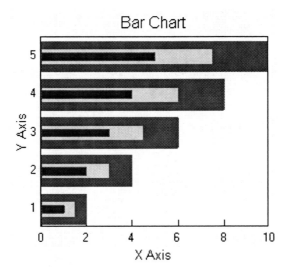

Figure 4-7 Overlaid horizontal bar chart.

To create a horizontal chart, change the parameters to:

```
cs.XLimMin = 0f;
cs.XLimMax = 10f;
cs.YLimMin = 0f;
cs.YLimMax = 5f;
cs.XTick = 2f;
cs.YTick = 1f;
cs.BarType = ChartStyle.BarTypeEnum.HorizontalOverlay;
```

This gives a horizontal overlay bar chart, as shown in Figure 4-7.

Stacked Bar Charts

Bar charts can show how different Y values at the same X point contribute to the sum of all of the Y values at the point. These types of bar charts are referred to as stacked bar charts.

Stacked bar graphs display one bar per X value. The bars are divided into several fragments according to the number of X values. For vertical stacked bar charts, the height of each bar equals the sum of all of the Y values at a given X value. Each fragment is equal to the value of its respective Y value.

In order to create a vertical stacked bar chart, change the parameters in `Form1`'s constructor:

```
cs.XLimMin = 0f;
cs.XLimMax = 5f;
cs.YLimMin = 0f;
cs.YLimMax = 25f;
cs.XTick = 1f;
cs.YTick = 5f;
cs.BarType = ChartStyle.BarTypeEnum.VerticalStack;
```

Here we set the `BarType` to `VerticalStack`. We also increase the Y axis's maximum limit to 25. This produces the results of Figure 4-8.

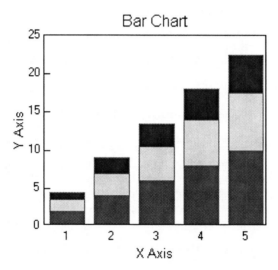

Figure 4-8 Vertical stacked bar chart.

For horizontal stacked bar charts, you need to change the parameters as follows:

```
cs.XLimMin = 0f;
cs.XLimMax = 25f;
cs.YLimMin = 0f;
cs.YLimMax = 5f;
cs.XTick = 5f;
cs.YTick = 1f;
cs.BarType = ChartStyle.BarTypeEnum.HorizontalStack;
```

Building and executing the project generate the output of Figure 4-9

Bar Charts with Color Map

You might notice from the previous sections that all of the bars in the same data series have the same color. With little effort, however, you can assign a desired color map to each bar. The typical approach is to associate bar colors with bar heights (the Y-values). The following steps describe one way to do this, first by using faceted shading and then using smooth (interpolated) shading.

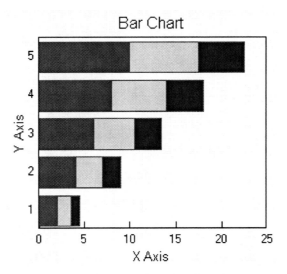

Figure 4-9 Horizontal stacked bar chart.

Here we illustrate how to create a bar chart with a color map using a vertical bar chart with a single set of data series. Let's start with a new C# Windows Application project, *Example4_2*. This project is based on the previous project, *Example4_1*. Add all of the class files of *Example4_1* to the current project and change their namespace to *Example4_2*. Also, add the ColorMap class of *Example1_8* to this project and change its namespace to *Example4_2*. Add three new field members and their corresponding properties to the DataSeries class:

```
private bool isColorMap = false;
private bool isSingleColorMap = false;
private int[,] cmap;

public int[,] CMap
{
    get { return cmap; }
    set { cmap = value; }
}

public bool IsColorMap
{
    get { return isColorMap; }
    set { isColorMap = value; }
}

public bool IsSingleColorMap
{
    get { return isSingleColorMap; }
    set { isSingleColorMap = value; }
}
```

Add a private `DrawColorMap` method to the `DataCollection` class:

```
private void DrawColorMap(Graphics g, PointF[] pts, int[,] cmap,
                         float ymin, float ymax, float y)
{
    int colorLength = cmap.GetLength(0);
    int cindex = (int)Math.Round((colorLength * (y - ymin) +
               (ymax - y)) / (ymax - ymin));
    if (cindex < 1)
        cindex = 1;
    if (cindex > colorLength)
        cindex = colorLength;
    Color color = Color.FromArgb(cmap[cindex - 1, 0],
        cmap[cindex - 1, 1], cmap[cindex - 1, 2],
        cmap[cindex - 1, 3]);
    SolidBrush aBrush = new SolidBrush(color);
    g.FillPolygon(aBrush, pts);
}
```

Modify the `AddBars` method in the `DataCollection` class for vertical bar chart with one `DataSeries`:

```
public void AddBars(Graphics g, ChartStyle cs,
        int numberOfDataSeries, int numberOfPoints)
{
.......
        if (cs.BarType == ChartStyle.BarTypeEnum.Vertical)
        {
            if (numberOfDataSeries == 1)
            {
                // Find the minumum and maximum y values:
                float ymin = 0;
                float ymax = 0;
                for (int i = 0; i < ds.PointList.Count; i++)
                {
                    pt = (PointF)ds.PointList[i];
                    ymin = Math.Min(ymin, pt.Y);
                    ymax = Math.Max(ymax, pt.Y);
                }

                width = cs.XTick * ds.BarStyle.BarWidth;
                for (int i = 0; i < ds.PointList.Count; i++)
                {
                    pt = (PointF)ds.PointList[i];
                    float x = pt.X - cs.XTick / 2;
                    pts[0] = cs.Point2D(new PointF(
                            x - width / 2, 0));
                    pts[1] = cs.Point2D(new PointF(
                            x + width / 2, 0));
                    pts[2] = cs.Point2D(new PointF(
                            x + width / 2, pt.Y));
                    pts[3] = cs.Point2D(new PointF(
                            x - width / 2, pt.Y));
                    if (ds.IsSingleColorMap)
                    {
```

```
                        DrawColorMap(g, pts, ds.CMap,
                                ymin, ymax, pt.Y);
                }
                else if (ds.IsColorMap)
                {
                    float dy = (ymax - ymin) / 100;
                    PointF[] points = new PointF[4];
                    for (int j = 0; j <= (int)Math.Round(100 *
                        (pt.Y - ymin) / (ymax - ymin)); j++)
                    {
                        points[0] = cs.Point2D(new PointF(
                            x - width / 2, (j - 1) * dy));
                        points[1] = cs.Point2D(new PointF(
                            x + width / 2, (j - 1) * dy));
                        points[2] = cs.Point2D(new PointF(
                            x + width / 2, j * dy));
                        points[3] = cs.Point2D(new PointF(
                            x - width / 2, j * dy));
                        DrawColorMap(g, points, ds.CMap,
                            ymin, ymax, j * dy);
                    }
                }
                else
                {
                    g.FillPolygon(aBrush, pts);
                }
                g.DrawPolygon(aPen, pts);
            }
        }
        else if (numberOfDataSeries > 1)
        {
            ......
        }
    ......
}
```

Here, we implement two kinds of color maps. One involves the bar's color assigning according to its y value; i.e., each bar has a different single color. This single color map for each bar is controlled by the bool parameter IsSingleColorMap. The other color map involves setting different colors for the vertices on the baseline and on the top, and then applying interpolated shading to change the ARGB values going up the bars. This color map is specified by the property IsColorMap.

In order to examine the effect of the color map, we need to modify the Form1 class as well. Here is the code listing of the Form1 class that creates a bar chart with a single color map:

```
using System;
using System.Drawing;
using System.Drawing.Drawing2D;
using System.Windows.Forms;

namespace Example4_2
{
    public partial class Form1 : Form
```

```
{
    private ChartStyle cs;
    private DataCollection dc;
    private DataSeries ds;
    private ColorMap cm;

    public Form1()
    {
        InitializeComponent();
        this.SetStyle(ControlStyles.ResizeRedraw, true);

        // Subscribing to a paint eventhandler to drawingPanel:
        PlotPanel.Paint +=
            new PaintEventHandler(PlotPanelPaint);

        cs = new ChartStyle(this);
        dc = new DataCollection();
        cm = new ColorMap(100, 180);
        // Specify chart style parameters:
        cs.Title = "Bar Chart";
        cs.XLimMin = 0f;
        cs.XLimMax = 5f;
        cs.YLimMin = 0f;
        cs.YLimMax = 10f;
        cs.XTick = 1f;
        cs.YTick = 2f;
        cs.BarType = ChartStyle.BarTypeEnum.Vertical;
    }

    private void AddData(Graphics g)
    {
        float x, y;
        // Add first data series:
        dc.DataSeriesList.Clear();
        ds = new DataSeries();
        ds.BarStyle.BorderColor = Color.Red;
        ds.IsSingleColorMap = true;
        ds.CMap = cm.Jet();
        for (int i = 0; i < 5; i++)
        {
            x = i + 1;
            y = 2.0f * x;
            ds.AddPoint(new PointF(x, y));
        }
        dc.Add(ds);
    }

    private void PlotPanelPaint(object sender, PaintEventArgs e)
    {
        Graphics g = e.Graphics;
        AddData(g);
        cs.PlotPanelStyle(g);
        dc.AddBars(g, cs, dc.DataSeriesList.Count,
                ds.PointList.Count);
```

```
        }

        protected override void OnPaint(PaintEventArgs e)
        {
            Graphics g = e.Graphics;
            cs.ChartArea = this.ClientRectangle;
            cs.SetChartArea(g);
        }
    }
}
```

Please note that in the AddData method, we specify two new parameters:

```
        ds.IsSingleColorMap = true;
        ds.CMap = cm.Jet();
```

The first parameter determines the color map type (single color), while the second parameter sets the color map matrix to "Jet" defined in the ColorMap class. By building and running this project, you should obtain the results of Figure 4-10.

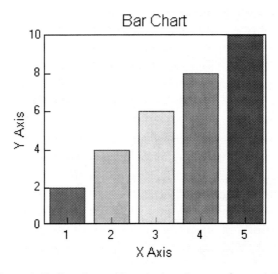

Figure 4-10 Bar chart with a single color map for each bar.

To make the chart more readable, you can apply a true color map for each bar. Just change the following two lines of the above code snippet to,

```
        ds.IsColorMap = true;
        ds.CMap = cm.Jet();
```

This produces the output of Figure 4-11. You can easily apply the same color maps to horizontal bar charts with little effort. I will leave this for you as practice.

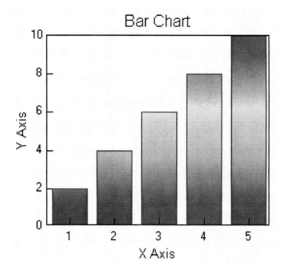

Figure 4-11 Bar chart with a true color map for each bar.

Creating Stair Step Charts

In this section, we will show you how to create a stair-step chart. Instead of creating lines which directly connect your data, you can choose to have your data plotted in such a way that emphasizes the discrete nature of the data. Namely, the stair-step charts draw horizontal lines at the level specified by the y data. This level will be held constant over the period between the values specified by the x data values. Stair-step charts are similar to bar charts excepting for the fact that vertical lines are not dropped down all the way to the zero value point on the y axis. This type of plot is useful for drawing time-history plots of digitally sampled data systems.

Implementation

Here we show you how to create a stair-step chart using C#. Let's start with a new C# Windows Application project and call it *Example4_3*, this project is based on the previous project, *Example3_4*, so you will need to add all of the class files from *Example3_4*, including the Form1 class, to the current project, and change the namespace of all of the files from *Example3_4* to *Example4_3*. In addition, add a new class called StairstepStyle to the project. The following is its code listing:

```
using System;
using System.Drawing;
using System.Drawing.Drawing2D;

namespace Example4_3
{
    public class StairstepStyle
    {
        private DashStyle linePattern = DashStyle.Solid;
        private Color lineColor = Color.Black;
```

```
                    private float LineThickness = 1.0f;

                    public StairstepStyle()
                    {
                    }

                    virtual public DashStyle Pattern
                    {
                        get { return linePattern; }
                        set { linePattern = value; }
                    }

                    public float Thickness
                    {
                        get { return LineThickness; }
                        set { LineThickness = value; }
                    }

                    virtual public Color LineColor
                    {
                        get { return lineColor; }
                        set { lineColor = value; }
                    }
                }
            }
```

This class is very similar to the LineStyle class. Add a new public method, AddStairSteps, to the DataCollection class:

```
    public void AddStairSteps(Graphics g, ChartStyle cs)
    {
        foreach (DataSeries ds in DataSeriesList)
        {
            Pen aPen = new Pen(ds.StairstepStyle.LineColor,
                    ds.StairstepStyle.Thickness);
            aPen.DashStyle = ds.StairstepStyle.Pattern;
            ArrayList aList = new ArrayList();
            PointF pt1 = new PointF();
            PointF pt2 = new PointF();

            // Create Stairstep data:
            for (int i = 0; i < ds.PointList.Count - 1; i++)
            {
                pt1 = (PointF)ds.PointList[i];
                pt2 = (PointF)ds.PointList[i + 1];
                aList.Add(pt1);
                aList.Add(new PointF(pt2.X, pt1.Y));
            }
            aList.Add(ds.PointList[ds.PointList.Count - 1]);
            // Draw stairstep chart:
            for (int i = 1; i < aList.Count; i++)
            {
                g.DrawLine(aPen, cs.Point2D((PointF)aList[i - 1]),
                            cs.Point2D((PointF)aList[i]));
            }
```

```
        aPen.Dispose();
    }
}
```

In the `DataSeries` class, add a field member and corresponding property:

```
private StairstepStyle stairstepStyle = new StairstepStyle();

public StairstepStyle StairstepStyle
{
    get { return stairstepStyle; }
    set { stairstepStyle = value; }
}
```

This enables you to access the properties of the `StairstepStyle` class from the `DataSeries` class and assign a stair-step style to each data series.

Testing Project

In order to test the stair-step chart project, you need to specify its style in the `Form1` class. The following code listing of `Form1` creates a simple Sine stair-step chart:

```
using System;
using System.Drawing;
using System.Drawing.Drawing2D;
using System.Collections;
using System.Windows.Forms;

namespace Example4_3
{
    public partial class Form1 : Form
    {
        private DataCollection dc;
        private ChartStyle cs;

        public Form1()
        {
            InitializeComponent();
            SetStyle(ControlStyles.ResizeRedraw, true);
            This.BackColor = Color.White;

            // Set Form1 size:
            this.Width = 350;
            this.Height = 350;
            dc = new DataCollection();
            cs = new ChartStyle(this);
            cs.XLimMin = 0f;
            cs.XLimMax = 8f;
            cs.YLimMin = -1.5f;
            cs.YLimMax = 1.5f;
            cs.XTick = 1.0f;
            cs.YTick = 0.5f;
            cs.XLabel = "This is X axis";
            cs.YLabel = "This is Y axis";
```

```
            cs.Title = "Sin(x)";
    }

    private void AddData(Graphics g)
    {
        dc.DataSeriesList.Clear();

        // Add Sine data points:
        DataSeries ds1 = new DataSeries();
        ds1.StairstepStyle.LineColor = Color.Red;

        for (int i = 0; i < 50; i++)
        {
            ds1.AddPoint(new PointF(0.4f * i,
                    (float)Math.Sin(0.4f * i)));
        }
        dc.Add(ds1);
    }

    protected override void OnPaint(PaintEventArgs e)
    {
        Graphics g = e.Graphics;
        cs.ChartArea = this.ClientRectangle;
        SetPlotArea(g);
        AddData(g);
        cs.AddChartStyle(g);
        dc.AddStairSteps(g, cs);
        g.Dispose();
    }

    private void SetPlotArea(Graphics g)
    {
        .....
    }
  }
}
```

Here we use a red pen to draw the stair-step chart by specifying the line style within the `AddData` method. Running this program generates the output of Figure 4-12.

You can overlap a stair-step chart with a line plot. This can be done by changing the `AddData` method:

```
private void AddData(Graphics g)
    {
        dc.DataSeriesList.Clear();
        // Add Sine data with 7 data point:
        DataSeries ds1 = new DataSeries();
        ds1.LineStyle.LineColor = Color.Black;
        ds1.LineStyle.Pattern = DashStyle.Dash;
        ds1.SymbolStyle.SymbolType =
                SymbolStyle.SymbolTypeEnum.Circle;
        ds1.StairstepStyle.LineColor = Color.Red;
```

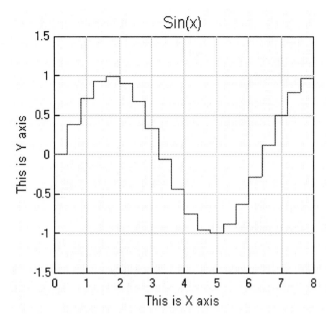

Figure 4-12 Stair-step chart of a sine function.

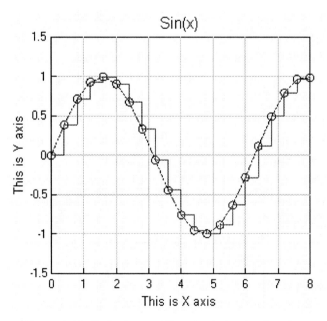

Figure 4-13 Stair-step and line chart of a sine function.

```
                        for (int i = 0; i < 50; i++)
                        {
                            ds1.AddPoint(new PointF(0.4f * i,
                                    (float)Math.Sin(0.4f * i)));
                        }
                        dc.Add(ds1);
                }
```

Here we specify both stair-step chart and line chart styles. Within the `OnPaint` method, we need to add the following code snippet:

```
            dc.AddLines(g, cs);
```

Rebuilding this project should obtain the results shown in Figure 4-13.

Creating Stem Charts

Stem charts provide another way to visualize discrete data sequences such as digitally sampled time series data. In this type of chart, vertical lines terminate with a marker symbol at each data value. In a 2D stem chart, these stem lines extend from the x axis.

Implementation

Start with a new C# Windows Application project, *Example4_4*. This project is also based on the previous project, *Example3_4*. Add all of the class files of *Example3_4* to the current project, and change their namespace from *Example3_4* to *Example4_4*. Add a new public method, `AddStems`, to the `DataCollection` class:

```
    public void AddStems(Graphics g, ChartStyle cs)
    {
        PointF pt = new PointF();
        PointF pt0 = new PointF();

        // Plot Stems:
        foreach (DataSeries ds in DataSeriesList)
        {
            Pen aPen = new Pen(ds.LineStyle.LineColor,
                    ds.LineStyle.Thickness);
            aPen.DashStyle = ds.LineStyle.Pattern;
            if (ds.LineStyle.PlotMethod ==
                        LineStyle.PlotLinesMethodEnum.Lines)
            {
                for (int i = 0; i < ds.PointList.Count; i++)
                {
                    pt = (PointF)ds.PointList[i];
                    pt0 = new PointF(pt.X, 0);
                    g.DrawLine(aPen, cs.Point2D(pt0), cs.Point2D(pt));
                }
            }
        }

        // Plot Symbols:
```

```
        foreach (DataSeries ds in DataSeriesList)
        {
            for (int i = 0; i < ds.PointList.Count; i++)
            {
                pt = (PointF)ds.PointList[i];
                if (pt.X >= cs.XLimMin && pt.X <= cs.XLimMax &&
                    pt.Y >= cs.YLimMin && pt.Y <= cs.YLimMax)
                {
                    ds.SymbolStyle.DrawSymbol(g,
                        cs.Point2D((PointF)ds.PointList[i]));
                }
            }
        }
    }
```

Testing Project

The `Form1` class is similar to that of the previous project, *Example4_3*, with this small modification of the `AddData` method:

```
private void AddData(Graphics g)
{
    dc.DataSeriesList.Clear();

    // Add Sine data:
    DataSeries ds1 = new DataSeries();
    ds1.LineStyle.LineColor = Color.Red;
    ds1.LineStyle.Pattern = DashStyle.Solid;
    ds1.LineStyle.PlotMethod = LineStyle.PlotLinesMethodEnum.Lines;
    ds1.SeriesName = "Sine";
    ds1.SymbolStyle.SymbolType = SymbolStyle.SymbolTypeEnum.Diamond;
    ds1.SymbolStyle.BorderColor = Color.Red;
    ds1.SymbolStyle.FillColor = Color.Yellow;
    ds1.SymbolStyle.BorderThickness = 1f;
    for (int i = 0; i < 50; i++)
    {
        ds1.AddPoint(new PointF(0.4f * i,
                (float)Math.Sin(0.4f * i)));
    }
    dc.Add(ds1);
}
```

This method is exactly the same as the one used in a standard line chart. The line and symbol styles specified are used to draw the stem chart. Finally, we need to call the public method `AddStems` from the `OnPaint` method:

```
protected override void OnPaint(PaintEventArgs e)
{
    Graphics g = e.Graphics;
    cs.ChartArea = this.ClientRectangle;
    SetPlotArea(g);
    AddData(g);
    cs.AddChartStyle(g);
    dc.AddStems(g, cs);
```

```
        g.Dispose();
    }
```

This project produces the output of Figure 4-14. The current program has the ability to create a stem chart that terminates at any marker symbol. In addition, these terminators can be filled or unfilled. You can also generate a stem chart with lines of various dash styles.

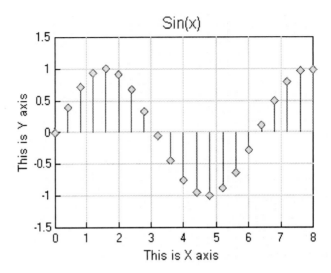

Figure 4-14 Stem chart of a sine function.

Creating Charts with Error Bars

Error bars show the confidence level of data or the deviation along a curve. Error bar charts plot the y data and draw an error bar at each Y data value. The error bar is the distance of the error function above and below the curve so that each bar is symmetric around the curve.

Implementation

Start a new C# Windows Application project and call it *Example4_5*. This project is based on the previous project, *Example4_4*. Add all of the class files of *Example4_4* to this project and change their namespace to *Example4_5*. Then, add a new class, ErrorbarStyle, to the project. The following is the code listing of this new class:

```
using System;
using System.Collections.Generic;
using System.Drawing;
using System.Drawing.Drawing2D;
using System.Text;

namespace Example4_5
{
    public class ErrorbarStyle
    {
```

```
private DashStyle linePattern = DashStyle.Solid;
private Color lineColor = Color.Black;
private float LineThickness = 1.0f;

public ErrorbarStyle()
{
}

virtual public DashStyle Pattern
{
    get { return linePattern; }
    set { linePattern = value; }
}

public float Thickness
{
    get { return LineThickness; }
    set { LineThickness = value; }
}

virtual public Color LineColor
{
    get { return lineColor; }
    set { lineColor = value; }
}
    }
}
```

This class is basically similar to the LineStyle class. Both the LineStyle and ErrorbarStyle classes allow you to specify the styles for the line and the error bar independently.

Inside the DataSeries method, add the following code snippet:

```
private ErrorbarStyle errorbarStyle;
private ArrayList errorList;

public ArrayList ErrorList
{
    get { return errorList; }
    set { errorList = value; }
}

public ErrorbarStyle ErrorbarStyle
{
    get { return errorbarStyle; }
    set { errorbarStyle = value; }
}

public void AddErrorData(PointF pt)
{
    errorList.Add(pt);
}
```

To this class, we add two field members and their corresponding properties. The `ErrorList` property holds the data of the error bars, and the `ErrorbarStyle` property allows you to specify the error bar style for each data series. The public method `AddErrorData` lets you add the data values of the error bars to the `ErrorList`.

Next, we need to add a public method, `AddErrorBars`, to the `DataCollection` class:

```csharp
public void AddErrorBars(Graphics g, ChartStyle cs)
{
    PointF pt = new PointF();
    PointF pt0 = new PointF();

    foreach (DataSeries ds in DataSeriesList)
    {
        Pen linePen = new Pen(ds.LineStyle.LineColor,
                ds.LineStyle.Thickness);
        linePen.DashStyle = ds.LineStyle.Pattern;
        Pen errorPen = new Pen(ds.ErrorbarStyle.LineColor,
                ds.ErrorbarStyle.Thickness);
        errorPen.DashStyle = ds.ErrorbarStyle.Pattern;
        float barLength = 0;

        // Draw lines:
        if (ds.LineStyle.PlotMethod ==
                LineStyle.PlotLinesMethodEnum.Lines)
        {
            for (int i = 1; i < ds.PointList.Count; i++)
            {
                pt0 = (PointF)ds.PointList[i - 1];
                pt = (PointF)ds.PointList[i];
                g.DrawLine(linePen, cs.Point2D(pt0), cs.Point2D(pt));
                barLength = (pt.X - pt0.X) / 4;
            }
        }

        // Draw error bars:
        for (int i = 0; i < ds.ErrorList.Count; i++)
        {
            PointF errorPoint = (PointF)ds.ErrorList[i];
            PointF linePoint = (PointF)ds.PointList[i];
            pt0 = new PointF(linePoint.X,
                    linePoint.Y - errorPoint.Y / 2);
            pt = new PointF(linePoint.X,
                    linePoint.Y + errorPoint.Y / 2);
            g.DrawLine(errorPen, cs.Point2D(pt0), cs.Point2D(pt));
            PointF pt1 = new PointF(pt0.X - barLength / 2, pt0.Y);
            PointF pt2 = new PointF(pt0.X + barLength / 2, pt0.Y);
            g.DrawLine(errorPen, cs.Point2D(pt1), cs.Point2D(pt2));
            pt1 = new PointF(pt.X - barLength / 2, pt.Y);
            pt2 = new PointF(pt.X + barLength / 2, pt.Y);
            g.DrawLine(errorPen, cs.Point2D(pt1), cs.Point2D(pt2));
        }
        linePen.Dispose();
        errorPen.Dispose();
```

```
        }
    }
```

In this method, we first draw lines with the data points from the `PointList`, and then draw error bars with the data values in the `ErrorList`.

Testing Project

To test this example project, you need to make a small modification to the `Form1` class. First, insert the following code snippet into the `Form1` constructor:

```
public Form1()
{
    InitializeComponent();
    SetStyle(ControlStyles.ResizeRedraw, true);
    This.BackColor = Color.White;

    // Set Form1 size:
    this.Width = 350;
    this.Height = 350;
    dc = new DataCollection();
    cs = new ChartStyle(this);
    cs.XLimMin = 0f;
    cs.XLimMax = 12f;
    cs.YLimMin = -1f;
    cs.YLimMax = 6f;
    cs.XTick = 2.0f;
    cs.YTick = 1.0f;
    cs.XLabel = "This is X axis";
    cs.YLabel = "This is Y axis";
    cs.Title = "Exp(x)";
}
```

Change the code of the `AddData` method to the following:

```
private void AddData(Graphics g)
{
    dc.DataSeriesList.Clear();

    // Add Sine data:
    DataSeries ds1 = new DataSeries();
    ds1.LineStyle.LineColor = Color.Red;
    ds1.LineStyle.Pattern = DashStyle.Solid;
    ds1.LineStyle.PlotMethod =
            LineStyle.PlotLinesMethodEnum.Lines;
    ds1.ErrorbarStyle.LineColor = Color.Blue;
    for (int i = 2; i < 22; i++)
    {
        ds1.AddPoint(new PointF(0.5f * i,
            10.0f * (float)Math.Exp(-0.5f * i)));
    }
    for (int i = 2; i < 22; i++)
    {
        ds1.AddErrorData(new PointF(0.5f * i,
```

```
                    3.0f / (0.5f * i)));
         }
         dc.Add(ds1);
     }
```

In this method, we assume that the error function is proportional to 1/x. However, you can specify any error function you like, such as the standard deviation, etc.

Add the following line of code to the `OnPaint` method:

```
dc.AddErrorBars(g, cs);
```

Run the application by pressing F5. You should obtain the results of Figure 4-15. The current program has the flexibility to allow you to specify the style of the data lines and the error bars separately.

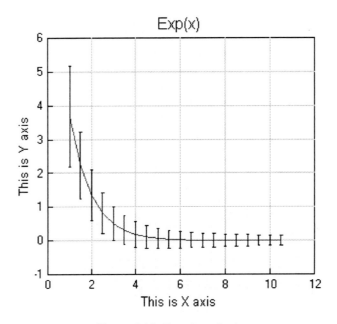

Figure 4-15 Error bar chart.

Creating Pie Charts

Creating a pie chart in C# is quite simple, since there is a `DrawPie` method already available in the Graphics class. This method accepts the start angle and sweep angle as arguments, so it is quite simple to use: just add up all of the values, calculate the portion for each one, and convert this value to a sweep angle for the corresponding pie slice.

Implementation

Start with a new C# Windows application project, *Example4_6*. Add the ColorMap class of the previous project *Example4_2* to the current project and change its namespace to *Example4_6*. Add the new classes of ChartStyle, DataSeries, and Legend to the project. The ChartStyle class is very simple in this case:

```
using System;
using System.Collections;
using System.Drawing;
using System.Drawing.Drawing2D;

namespace Example4_6
{
    public class ChartStyle
    {
        private Form1 form1;
        private int offset;

        public ChartStyle(Form1 fm1)
        {
            form1 = fm1;
        }

        public int Offset
        {
            get { return offset; }
            set { offset = value; }
        }

        public Rectangle SetPieArea()
        {
            Offset = form1.PlotPanel.Width / 10;
            int height =  form1.PlotPanel.Height - 2 * Offset;
            int width = height;
            Rectangle rect = new Rectangle(Offset,
                    Offset, width, height);
            return rect;
        }
    }
}
```

Here we want to draw the pie chart on a panel control, PlotPanel. The offset field and its corresponding property define the top and left margins of the pie chart, and also control the size of the pie chart. The public method SetPieArea returns the rectangle the pie chart occupies.

The following is the code listing of the DataSeries class:

```
using System;
using System.Collections;
using System.Drawing;

namespace Example4_6
```

```csharp
{
    public class DataSeries
    {
        private ArrayList dataList;
        private ArrayList labelList;
        private ArrayList explodeList;
        private int[,] cmap;
        private Color borderColor = Color.Black;
        private float borderThickness = 1.0f;

        public DataSeries()
        {
            dataList = new ArrayList();
            labelList = new ArrayList();
            explodeList = new ArrayList();
        }

        public int[,] CMap
        {
            get { return cmap; }
            set { cmap = value; }
        }

        public Color BorderColor
        {
            get { return borderColor; }
            set { borderColor = value; }
        }

        public float BorderThickness
        {
            get { return borderThickness; }
            set { borderThickness = value; }
        }

        public ArrayList DataList
        {
            get { return dataList; }
            set { dataList = value; }
        }

        public ArrayList LabelList
        {
            get { return labelList; }
            set { labelList = value; }
        }

        public ArrayList ExplodeList
        {
            get { return explodeList; }
            set { explodeList = value; }
        }

        public void AddData(float data)
```

```
            {
                dataList.Add(data);
                labelList.Add(data.ToString());
                explodeList.Add(0);
            }

            public void AddPie(Graphics g, ChartStyle cs)
            {
                SolidBrush aBrush = new SolidBrush(Color.Black);
                Pen aPen = new Pen(BorderColor);
                int nData = DataList.Count;
                float fSum = 0;
                for (int i = 0; i < nData; i++)
                {
                    fSum = fSum + (float)DataList[i];
                }
                float startAngle = 0;
                float sweepAngle = 0;
                Rectangle rect = cs.SetPieArea();

                for (int i = 0; i < nData; i++)
                {
                    Color fillColor = Color.FromArgb(CMap[i, 0],
                        CMap[i, 1], CMap[i, 2], CMap[i, 3]);
                    aBrush = new SolidBrush(fillColor);
                    int explode = (int)ExplodeList[i];

                    if (fSum < 1)
                    {
                        startAngle = startAngle + sweepAngle;
                        sweepAngle = 360 * (float)DataList[i];
                    }
                    else if (fSum >= 1)
                    {
                        startAngle = startAngle + sweepAngle;
                        sweepAngle = 360 * (float)DataList[i] / fSum;

                    }

                    int xshift = (int)(explode * Math.Cos((startAngle +
                        sweepAngle / 2) * Math.PI / 180));
                    int yshift = (int)(explode * Math.Sin((startAngle +
                        sweepAngle / 2) * Math.PI / 180));
                    Rectangle rect1 = new Rectangle(rect.X + xshift,
                        rect.Y + yshift, rect.Width, rect.Height);
                    g.FillPie(aBrush, rect1, startAngle, sweepAngle);
                    g.DrawPie(aPen, rect1, startAngle, sweepAngle);
                }
            }
        }
    }
```

In this class, we first define three `ArrayList` field members: `dataList`, `labelList`, and
`explodeList`. These hold the data used to create the pie chart, the labels for the data values

used in the legend, and the exploding data needed to highlight a particular pie slice by exploding the piece out from the rest of the pie, respectively. We also use the color map matrix, CMap, to specify the pie slices of the pie chart.

You can use the AddData method in this class to add data values to the dataList. At the same time, this method also adds the default data values to the labelList and explodeList. Both the labelList and explodeList can be overridden in the application.

The real action happens within the AddPie method. In this method, we first calculate the fSum, or the summation, of the data values. Each value in the dataList is normalized via 1/fSum to determine the area of each slice of the pie. If fSum ≥ 1, the values in the dataList directly specify the area of the pie slices. However, if fSum < 1, the current program draws only a partial pie, and the data values are not normalized by 1/fSum.

The Legend class is also slightly different than that used in the previous project. For completeness, here we present the code listing of the Legend class:

```
using System;
using System.Drawing;
using System.Drawing.Drawing2D;
using System.Collections;

namespace Example4_6
{
    public class Legend
    {
        private Form1 form1;
        private bool isLegendVisible;
        private Color textColor;
        private bool isBorderVisible;
        private Color legendBackColor;
        private Color legendBorderColor;
        private Font legendFont;

        public Legend(Form1 fm1)
        {
            form1 = fm1;
            textColor = Color.Black;
            isLegendVisible = false;
            isBorderVisible = true;
            legendBackColor = Color.White;
            legendBorderColor = Color.Black;
            legendFont = new Font("Arial", 8, FontStyle.Regular);
        }

        public Font LegendFont
        {
            get { return legendFont; }
            set { legendFont = value; }
        }

        public Color LegendBackColor
        {
```

```csharp
        get { return legendBackColor; }
        set { legendBackColor = value; }
    }

    public Color LegendBorderColor
    {
        get { return legendBorderColor; }
        set { legendBorderColor = value; }
    }

    public bool IsBorderVisible
    {
        get { return isBorderVisible; }
        set { isBorderVisible = value; }
    }

    public Color TextColor
    {
        get { return textColor; }
        set { textColor = value; }
    }

    public bool IsLegendVisible
    {
        get { return isLegendVisible; }
        set { isLegendVisible = value; }
    }

    public void AddLegend(Graphics g, DataSeries ds,
            ChartStyle cs)
    {
        if (ds.DataList.Count < 1)
        {
            return;
        }
        if (!IsLegendVisible)
        {
            return;
        }
        int numberOfDataValues = ds.DataList.Count;
        string[] legendLabels = new string[ds.LabelList.Count];
        for (int i = 0; i < ds.LabelList.Count;i++)
        {
            legendLabels[i] = (string)ds.LabelList[i];
        }

        // float offSet = 20;
        float xc = 0f;
        float yc = 0f;
        SizeF size = g.MeasureString(legendLabels[0], LegendFont);
        float legendWidth = size.Width;
        for (int i = 0; i < legendLabels.Length; i++)
        {
            size = g.MeasureString(legendLabels[i], LegendFont);
```

```
                float tempWidth = size.Width;
                if (legendWidth < tempWidth)
                    legendWidth = tempWidth;
        }
        legendWidth = legendWidth + 35.0f;
        float hWidth = legendWidth / 2;
        float legendHeight = 18.0f * numberOfDataValues;
        float hHeight = legendHeight / 2;

        Rectangle rect = cs.SetPieArea();
        xc = rect.X + rect.Width + cs.Offset + 20 + hWidth / 2;
        yc = rect.Y + rect.Height / 2;
        DrawLegend(g, xc, yc, hWidth, hHeight, ds, cs);
    }

    private void DrawLegend(Graphics g, float xCenter,
        float yCenter, float hWidth, float hHeight,
        DataSeries ds, ChartStyle cs)
    {
        float spacing = 8.0f;
        float textHeight = 8.0f;
        float htextHeight = textHeight / 2.0f;
        float lineLength = 12.0f;
        float hlineLength = lineLength / 2.0f;
        Rectangle legendRectangle;
        Pen aPen = new Pen(LegendBorderColor, 1f);
        SolidBrush aBrush = new SolidBrush(LegendBackColor);

        if (isLegendVisible)
        {
            legendRectangle = new Rectangle((int)xCenter -
                (int)hWidth, (int)yCenter - (int)hHeight,
                (int)(2.0f * hWidth), (int)(2.0f * hHeight));
            g.FillRectangle(aBrush, legendRectangle);
            if (IsBorderVisible)
            {
                g.DrawRectangle(aPen, legendRectangle);
            }

            for (int i = 0; i < ds.DataList.Count; i++)
            {
                float xSymbol = legendRectangle.X +
                    spacing + hlineLength;
                float xText = legendRectangle.X +
                    2 * spacing + lineLength;
                float yText = legendRectangle.Y + (i + 1) *
                    spacing + (2 * i + 1) * htextHeight;
                aPen = new Pen(ds.BorderColor,
                    ds.BorderThickness);
                Color fillColor = Color.FromArgb(ds.CMap[i, 0],
                    ds.CMap[i, 1], ds.CMap[i, 2], ds.CMap[i, 3]);
                aBrush = new SolidBrush(fillColor);

                // Draw symbols:
```

```
            float hsize = 5f;
            PointF[] pts = new PointF[4];
            pts[0] = new PointF(xSymbol - hsize,
                yText - hsize);
            pts[1] = new PointF(xSymbol + hsize,
                yText - hsize);
            pts[2] = new PointF(xSymbol + hsize,
                yText + hsize);
            pts[3] = new PointF(xSymbol - hsize,
                yText + hsize);
            g.FillPolygon(aBrush, pts);
            g.DrawPolygon(aPen, pts);

            // Draw text:
            StringFormat sFormat = new StringFormat();
            sFormat.Alignment = StringAlignment.Near;
            g.DrawString((string)ds.LabelList[i], LegendFont,
                new SolidBrush(TextColor),
                new PointF(xText, yText - 8), sFormat);
        }
    }
    aPen.Dispose();
    aBrush.Dispose();
}
    }
}
```

Here the Legend is always located on the right side of the pie chart.

Testing Project

We can easily test the pie chart project using the following code listing for the Form1 class:

```
using System;
using System.Drawing;
using System.Drawing.Drawing2D;
using System.Windows.Forms;

namespace Example4_6
{
    public partial class Form1 : Form
    {
        private ChartStyle cs;
        private DataSeries ds;
        private ColorMap cm;
        private Legend lg;

        public Form1()
        {
            InitializeComponent();
            this.SetStyle(ControlStyles.ResizeRedraw, true);
            this.BackColor = Color.White;

            // Subscribing to a paint eventhandler to drawingPanel:
```

```
            PlotPanel.Paint +=
                new PaintEventHandler(PlotPanelPaint);

            cs = new ChartStyle(this);
            ds = new DataSeries();
            lg = new Legend(this);
            lg.IsLegendVisible = true;
        }

        private void AddData()
        {
            float[] data = new float[5] { 30, 35, 15, 10, 8 };
            string[] labels = new string[5] { "Soc. Sec. Tax",
                "Income Tax", "Borrowing", "Corp. Tax", "Misc." };
            cm = new ColorMap(data.Length);
            ds.CMap = cm.Jet();
            ds.DataList.Clear();
            for (int i = 0; i < data.Length; i++)
            {
                ds.AddData(data[i]);
                ds.LabelList[i] = labels[i];
            }
        }

        private void PlotPanelPaint(object sender, PaintEventArgs e)
        {
            Graphics g = e.Graphics;
            AddData();
            ds.AddPie(g, cs);
            lg.AddLegend(g, ds, cs);
        }
    }
}
```

Please pay special attention to the AddData method, which shows you how to add data values to the DataList, how to create labels for each data value, and how to specify the color map for each pie slice.

Build and run this application by pressing F5. You should obtain the output of Figure 4-16.

The current project also gives you the option of highlighting a particular pie slice by exploding the piece out from the rest of the pie. To do this, you simply need to override the ExplodeList property. For example, if you want to highlight the pie slice for the Social Security Tax data, you can add the following code snippet after the for-loop in the AddData method:

```
            ds.ExplodeList[0] = 15;
```

Here we specify that the first element in the ExplodeList should be exploded out 15 pixels (the default value is always zero) from the center of the pie chart, since the Social Security Tax is the first element in the DataList. This produces the results of Figure 4-17.

As mentioned previously, the program draws a partial pie if the summation of the data values is less than 1. To demonstrate this effect, we replace the AddData method with the following code snippet:

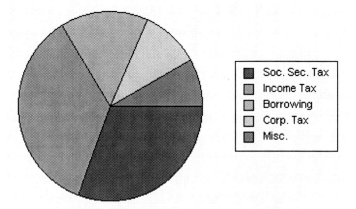

Figure 4-16 A pie chart of revenue data.

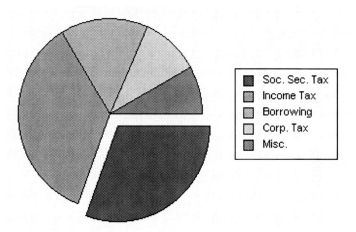

Figure 4-17 A pie chart with an exploded piece.

```
private void AddData()
{
    // Create a partial pie:
    float[] data = new float[3] { 0.3f, 0.1f, 0.25f};
    string[] labels = new string[3] { "0.3 -- 30%", "0.1 -- 10%",
        "0.25 -- 25%"};
    cm = new ColorMap(data.Length);
    ds.CMap = cm.Cool();
    ds.DataList.Clear();
    for (int i = 0; i < data.Length; i++)
    {
        ds.AddData(data[i]);
        ds.LabelList[i] = labels[i];
    }
}
```

This generates the results of Figure 4-18.

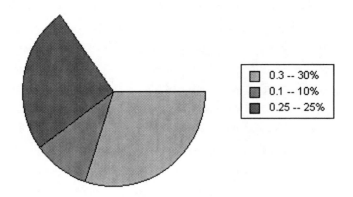

Figure 4-18 A partial pie chart.

Creating Area Charts

An area chart displays y data values as one or more curves and fills the area beneath each curve. When the DataCollection class has more than one data series, the curves are stacked, showing the relative contribution of each data series to the total height of the curve at each x value.

Implementation

The area chart is created by the FillPolygon method in the Graphics class. It is best to draw these polygon objects on a panel control, as in the previous project *Example4_2*. Now start with a new C# Windows Application project and call it *Example4_7*. Add the following classes from *Example4_2*: ChartStyle, ColorMap, DataCollection, and DataSeries, and change their namespace to *Example4_7*. Add the LineStyle class from *Example3_4* to the current project, and change its namespace to *Example4_7*. You can further simplify the DataSeries class, as shown by the following:

```
using System;
using System.Collections;
using System.Drawing;

namespace Example4_7
{
    public class DataSeries
    {
        private ArrayList pointList;
        private LineStyle lineStyle;
        private string seriesName = "";

        public DataSeries()
        {
```

```
            lineStyle = new LineStyle();
            pointList = new ArrayList();
        }

        public LineStyle LineStyle
        {
            get { return lineStyle; }
            set { lineStyle = value; }
        }

        public ArrayList PointList
        {
            get { return pointList; }
            set { pointList = value; }
        }

        public void AddPoint(PointF pt)
        {
            pointList.Add(pt);
        }

        public string SeriesName
        {
            get { return seriesName; }
            set { seriesName = value; }
        }
    }
}
```

Add two new field members and their corresponding properties to the DataCollection class:

```
        private int[,] cmap;
        private float areaAxis = 0;

        public float AreaAxis
        {
            get { return areaAxis; }
            set { areaAxis = value; }
        }

        public int[,] CMap
        {
            get { return cmap; }
            set { cmap = value; }
        }
```

The AreaAxis property defines the y axis at AreaAxis (the default axis is y = 0), at which the area will be filled. The CMap property is used to color the area.

Delete the public method AddBars from the DataCollection class and add a new public method, AddAreas, to the class. Here is the code listing of the AddAreas method:

```
public void AddAreas(Graphics g, ChartStyle cs,
        int nSeries, int nPoints)
{
```

```
float[] ySum = new float[nPoints];
PointF[] pts = new PointF[2 * nPoints];
PointF[] pt0 = new PointF[nPoints];
PointF[] pt1 = new PointF[nPoints];
for (int i = 0; i < nPoints; i++)
{
    ySum[i] = AreaAxis;
}

int n = 0;
foreach (DataSeries ds in DataSeriesList)
{
    Pen aPen = new Pen(ds.LineStyle.LineColor,
            ds.LineStyle.Thickness);
    aPen.DashStyle = ds.LineStyle.Pattern;
    Color fillColor = Color.FromArgb(CMap[n, 0], CMap[n, 1],
        CMap[n, 2], CMap[n, 3]);
    SolidBrush aBrush = new SolidBrush(fillColor);
    // Draw lines and areas:
    if (ds.LineStyle.PlotMethod ==
            LineStyle.PlotLinesMethodEnum.Lines)
    {
        for (int i = 0; i < nPoints; i++)
        {
            pt0[i] = new PointF(((PointF)ds.PointList[i]).X,
                        ySum[i]);
            ySum[i] = ySum[i] + ((PointF)ds.PointList[i]).Y;
            pt1[i] = new PointF(((PointF)ds.PointList[i]).X,
                        ySum[i]);
            pts[i] = cs.Point2D(pt0[i]);
            pts[2 * nPoints - 1 - i] = cs.Point2D(pt1[i]);
        }
        g.FillPolygon(aBrush, pts);
        g.DrawPolygon(Pens.Black, pts);
    }
    n++;
}
}
```

In this method, we process the data points inputted into the DataSeries and stack the y data values from all of the different DataSeries to show the relative contribution of each DataSeries to the total height of the curve at each x value. Finally, we draw the area by filling the polygon with the specified colormap colors.

Testing Project

The following code listing of the Form1 class will be used to test the area chart:

```
using System;
using System.Drawing;
using System.Drawing.Drawing2D;
using System.Windows.Forms;
```

```csharp
namespace Example4_7
{
    public partial class Form1 : Form
    {
        private DataCollection dc;
        private DataSeries ds;
        private ChartStyle cs;
        private ColorMap cm;

        public Form1()
        {
            InitializeComponent();
            this.SetStyle(ControlStyles.ResizeRedraw, true);

            // Subscribing to a paint eventhandler to drawingPanel:
            PlotPanel.Paint +=
                new PaintEventHandler(PlotPanelPaint);

            dc = new DataCollection();
            cs = new ChartStyle(this);
            cs.XLimMin = 0f;
            cs.XLimMax = 10f;
            cs.YLimMin = 0f;
            cs.YLimMax = 10f;
            cs.XTick = 2.0f;
            cs.YTick = 2.0f;
            cs.XLabel = "This is X axis";
            cs.YLabel = "This is Y axis";
            cs.Title = "Area Plot";
            cs.IsXGrid = true;
            cs.IsYGrid = true;
        }

        private void AddData()
        {
            dc.DataSeriesList.Clear();

            // Add Sine data:
            ds = new DataSeries();
            for (int i = 0; i < 21; i++)
            {
                ds.AddPoint(new PointF(0.5f * i,
                    2.0f + (float)Math.Sin(0.5f * i)));
            }
            dc.Add(ds);

            // Add Cosine data:
            ds = new DataSeries();
            for (int i = 0; i < 21; i++)
            {
                ds.AddPoint(new PointF(0.5f * i,
                    2.0f + (float)Math.Cos(0.5f * i)));
            }
            dc.Add(ds);
```

```
                    // Add another Sine data:
                    ds = new DataSeries();
                    for (int i = 0; i < 21; i++)
                    {
                        ds.AddPoint(new PointF(0.5f * i,
                            3.0f + (float)Math.Sin(0.5f * i)));
                    }
                    dc.Add(ds);

                    cm = new ColorMap(dc.DataSeriesList.Count, 150);
                    dc.CMap = cm.Summer();
                }

                private void PlotPanelPaint(object sender, PaintEventArgs e)
                {
                    Graphics g = e.Graphics;
                    g.SmoothingMode = SmoothingMode.AntiAlias;
                    AddData();
                    cs.PlotPanelStyle(g);
                    dc.AddAreas(g, cs, dc.DataSeriesList.Count,
                            ds.PointList.Count);
                }

                protected override void OnPaint(PaintEventArgs e)
                {
                    Graphics g = e.Graphics;
                    cs.ChartArea = this.ClientRectangle;
                    cs.SetChartArea(g);
                }
            }
        }
```

Within the AddData method, we add three sets of DataSeries to the project. At the end of this method, we create a color map with a color map length equal to the number of DataSeries and an alpha value = 150 (transparent color!). The Summer color map is used in this project.

Running this application produces the output of Figure 4-19.

Creating Polar Charts

So far, we have discussed various chart projects that make use of the Cartesian coordinate system. Now we want to show you how to plot data in polar coordinates (theta, r). Most polar charts, including commercial software packages, only plot positive r values; i.e., they plot absolute r values if r is both positive and negative. Here we will show you how to create a generalized polar chart using C#, in which r can contain the negative values. This new polar chart also allows you to specify the r range [rMin, rMax] and to draw multiple curves on a single polar chart.

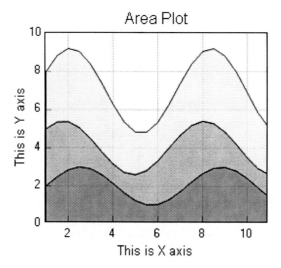

Figure 4-19 Area chart.

Implementation

Start with a new C# Windows Application project *Example4_8*. We will draw the polar chart on a panel control, as we did for the pie chart example. Add the following new classes to this project: `ChartStyle`, `DataSeries`, `DataCollection`, `LineStyle`, and `Legend`. The classes of `DataSeries`, `LineStyle`, and `Legend` are similar to those used in the previous projects, so we will not list their code here (you can look at the source code of *Example4_8* for details). However, the `ChartStyle` class needs to be modified. The following is the code listing of this class:

```
using System;
using System.Collections;
using System.Drawing;
using System.Drawing.Drawing2D;

namespace Example4_8
{
    public class ChartStyle
    {
        private Form1 form1;
        private int offset;
        private float angleStep = 30;
        private AngleDirectionEnum angleDirection =
            AngleDirectionEnum.CounterClockWise;
        private float rMin = 0;
        private float rMax = 1;
        private int nTicks = 4;
        private Font tickFont;
        private Color tickFontColor = Color.Black;
        private Color radiusColor = Color.Black;
        private float radiusThickness = 1f;
```

```csharp
private DashStyle radiusPattern = DashStyle.Dash;
private Color angleColor = Color.Black;
private float angleThickness = 1f;
private DashStyle anglePattern = DashStyle.Dash;

public ChartStyle(Form1 fm1)
{
    form1 = fm1;
    tickFont = form1.Font;
}

public AngleDirectionEnum AngleDirection
{
    get { return angleDirection; }
    set { angleDirection = value; }
}

public Color TickFontColor
{
    get { return tickFontColor; }
    set { tickFontColor = value; }
}

public Font TickFont
{
    get { return tickFont; }
    set { tickFont = value; }
}

public DashStyle AnglePattern
{
    get { return anglePattern; }
    set { anglePattern = value; }
}

public float AngleThickness
{
    get { return angleThickness; }
    set { angleThickness = value; }
}

public Color AngleColor
{
    get { return angleColor; }
    set { angleColor = value; }
}

public DashStyle RadiusPattern
{
    get { return radiusPattern; }
    set { radiusPattern = value; }
}

public float RadiusThickness
```

```
{
    get { return radiusThickness; }
    set { radiusThickness = value; }
}

public Color RadiusColor
{
    get { return radiusColor; }
    set { radiusColor = value; }
}

public int NTicks
{
    get { return nTicks; }
    set { nTicks = value; }
}

public float RMax
{
    get { return rMax; }
    set { rMax = value; }
}

public float RMin
{
    get { return rMin; }
    set { rMin = value; }
}

public float AngleStep
{
    get { return angleStep; }
    set { angleStep = value; }
}

public int Offset
{
    get { return offset; }
    set { offset = value; }
}

public enum AngleDirectionEnum
{
    CounterClockWise = 0,
    ClockWise = 1
}

public Rectangle SetPolarArea()
{
    Offset = form1.PlotPanel.Width / 10;
    int height = form1.PlotPanel.Height - 2 * Offset;
    int width = height;
    Rectangle rect = new Rectangle(Offset, Offset,
            width, height);
```

```
            return rect;
    }

    public void SetPolarAxes(Graphics g)
    {
        Pen aPen = new Pen(AngleColor, AngleThickness);
        SolidBrush aBrush = new SolidBrush(TickFontColor);
        StringFormat sFormat = new StringFormat();
        Rectangle rect = SetPolarArea();
        float xc = rect.X + rect.Width / 2;
        float yc = rect.Y + rect.Height / 2;

        // Draw circles:
        float dr = RNorm(RMax/NTicks) - RNorm(RMin/nTicks);
        aPen.DashStyle = AnglePattern;
        for (int i = 0; i < NTicks; i++)
        {
            RectangleF rect1 = new RectangleF(xc - (i + 1) * dr,
                yc - (i + 1) * dr, 2 * (i + 1) * dr,
                2 * (i + 1) * dr);
            g.DrawEllipse(aPen, rect1);
        }

        // Draw radii:
        aPen = new Pen(RadiusColor, RadiusThickness);
        aPen.DashStyle = RadiusPattern;
        for (int i = 0; i < (int)360 / AngleStep; i++)
        {
            float x = RNorm(RMax) * (float)Math.Cos(
                i * AngleStep * Math.PI / 180) + xc;
            float y = RNorm(RMax) * (float)Math.Sin(
                i * AngleStep * Math.PI / 180) + yc;
            g.DrawLine(aPen, xc, yc, x, y);
        }

        // Draw the radius labels:
        for (int i = 1; i <= nTicks; i++)
        {
            float rlabel = RMin + i * (RMax - RMin) / NTicks;
            sFormat.Alignment = StringAlignment.Near;
            g.DrawString(rlabel.ToString(), TickFont, aBrush,
                new PointF(xc, yc - i * dr + 5), sFormat);
        }

        // Draw the angle labels:
        SizeF tickFontSize = g.MeasureString("A", TickFont);
        float angleLabel = 0;
        for (int i = 0; i < (int)360 / AngleStep; i++)
        {
            if (AngleDirection == AngleDirectionEnum.ClockWise)
            {
                angleLabel = i*AngleStep;
            }
            else if (AngleDirection ==
```

```
                    AngleDirectionEnum.CounterClockWise)
            {
                angleLabel = 360 - i * AngleStep;
                if (i == 0)
                    angleLabel = 0;
            }
            sFormat.Alignment = StringAlignment.Center;
            float x = (RNorm(RMax) + 1.2f * tickFontSize.Width) *
                (float)Math.Cos(i * AngleStep * Math.PI /
                180) + xc;
            float y = (RNorm(RMax) + 1.2f * tickFontSize.Width) *
                (float)Math.Sin(i * AngleStep * Math.PI /
                180) + yc;
            g.DrawString(angleLabel.ToString(), TickFont, aBrush,
                new PointF(x, y - tickFontSize.Height / 2),
                sFormat);
        }
    }

    public float RNorm(float r)
    {
        float rNorm = new float();
        Rectangle rect = SetPolarArea();
        if (r < RMin || r > RMax)
        {
            r = Single.NaN;
        }
        rNorm = (r - RMin) * rect.Width / 2 / (RMax - RMin);
        return rNorm;
    }
  }
}
```

In this class, the `AngleStep` property controls the number of r grid lines, and the `AngleDirection` property allows you to draw the polar chart in a counter-clockwise (default) or clockwise manner. The other field members and their corresponding properties allow you to specify the r range, the grid line color, dash style, thickness, etc. In particular, you can specify the line styles of the r and `theta` gridlines separately to achieve a better visual effect.

The `SetPolarAxes` method in this class draws the r and theta gridlines, as well as the r and theta labels. Please pay special attention to the `RNorm` method, which transforms the r value in the world coordinate system to an r in the device coordinates system. A point in the polar coordinates is represented by `new PointF(theta, r)`. The theta has the same unit of degree in both the world and device coordinate systems, so we only need to perform the transformation on r.

We add a new public method, `AddPolar`, to the `DataCollection` class. The following is its code listing:

```
public void AddPolar(Graphics g, ChartStyle cs)
{
    Rectangle rect = cs.SetPolarArea();
    float xc = rect.X + rect.Width / 2;
```

```csharp
        float yc = rect.Y + rect.Height / 2;

        // Plot lines:
        foreach (DataSeries ds in DataSeriesList)
        {
            Pen aPen = new Pen(ds.LineStyle.LineColor,
                ds.LineStyle.Thickness);
            aPen.DashStyle = ds.LineStyle.Pattern;
            float r = ((PointF)ds.PointList[0]).Y;
            float theta = ((PointF)ds.PointList[0]).X;
            float x = cs.RNorm(r) * (float)Math.Cos(theta *
                Math.PI / 180) + xc;
            float y = cs.RNorm(r) * (float)Math.Sin(theta *
                Math.PI / 180) + yc;

            if (ds.LineStyle.IsVisible == true)
            {
                PointF ptStart = new PointF(x, y);
                PointF ptEnd = new PointF(x, y);
                for (int i = 1; i < ds.PointList.Count; i++)
                {
                    r = ((PointF)ds.PointList[i - 1]).Y;
                    theta = ((PointF)ds.PointList[i - 1]).X;
                    if (cs.AngleDirection ==
                        ChartStyle.AngleDirectionEnum.CounterClockWise)
                    {
                        theta = - theta;
                    }
                    x = cs.RNorm(r) * (float)Math.Cos(theta *
                        Math.PI / 180) + xc;
                    y = cs.RNorm(r) * (float)Math.Sin(theta *
                        Math.PI / 180) + yc;
                    ptStart = new PointF(x, y);
                    r = ((PointF)ds.PointList[i]).Y;
                    theta = ((PointF)ds.PointList[i]).X;
                    if (cs.AngleDirection ==
                        ChartStyle.AngleDirectionEnum.CounterClockWise)
                    {
                        theta = - theta;
                    }
                    x = cs.RNorm(r) * (float)Math.Cos(theta *
                        Math.PI / 180) + xc;
                    y = cs.RNorm(r) * (float)Math.Sin(theta *
                        Math.PI / 180) + yc;
                    ptEnd = new PointF(x, y);
                    g.DrawLine(aPen, ptStart, ptEnd);
                }
            }
            aPen.Dispose();
        }
    }
}
```

In this method, we first transform the polar points (r, theta) in the world coordinate system to the points (x, y) (the Cartesian coordinates) in the device system using the relationships:

```
x = cs.RNorm(r) * (float)Math.Cos(theta * Math.PI / 180) + xc;
y = cs.RNorm(r) * (float)Math.Sin(theta * Math.PI / 180) + yc;
```

The above equations indicate that the origin is located at (xc, yc), and the RNorm method transforms the polar points (r, theta) from the world to device coordinate system. In this method, the polar chart direction is controlled by setting the angle variable theta to be positive (clockwise) or negative (counter clockwise).

Testing Project

The polar chart can be tested using the following code for the Form1 class:

```
using System;
using System.Drawing;
using System.Drawing.Drawing2D;
using System.Windows.Forms;

namespace Example4_8
{
    public partial class Form1 : Form
    {
        private ChartStyle cs;
        private DataCollection dc;

        public Form1()
        {
            InitializeComponent();
            this.SetStyle(ControlStyles.ResizeRedraw, true);

            // Subscribing to a paint eventhandler to drawingPanel:
            PlotPanel.Paint +=
                new PaintEventHandler(PlotPanelPaint);

            dc = new DataCollection();
            cs = new ChartStyle(this);
            cs.RMax = 0.5f;
            cs.RMin = 0f;
            cs.NTicks = 4;
            cs.AngleStep = 30;
            cs.AngleDirection =
                ChartStyle.AngleDirectionEnum.CounterClockWise;
        }

        private void AddData()
        {
            dc.DataSeriesList.Clear();
            // Add data points to ds:
            DataSeries ds = new DataSeries();
            ds.LineStyle.LineColor = Color.Red;
            for (int i = 0; i < 360; i++)
            {
                float theta = 1.0f * i;
                float r = (float)Math.Abs(Math.Cos(
```

```
                        2*theta * Math.PI / 180) *
                        Math.Sin(2 * theta * Math.PI / 180));
                    ds.AddPoint(new PointF(theta, r));
                }
                dc.Add(ds);
            }
            private void PlotPanelPaint(object sender, PaintEventArgs e)
            {
                Graphics g = e.Graphics;
                g.SmoothingMode = SmoothingMode.AntiAlias;
                AddData();
                cs.SetPolarAxes(g);
                dc.AddPolar(g,cs);
            }
        }
    }
```

This application produces the output of Figure 4-20.

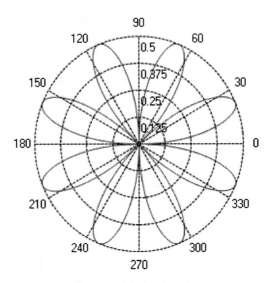

Figure 4-20 A polar plot.

You can also create multiple curves on a single polar chart with both positive and negative r values. To test these features, we draw two logarithm functions on the same polar chart. Change the AddData method accoding to the following code snippet:

```
        private void AddData()
        {
            dc.DataSeriesList.Clear();

            // Add log-sine data:
            DataSeries ds = new DataSeries();
            ds.LineStyle.LineColor = Color.Red;
            ds.SeriesName = "Sin(theta)";
            for (int i = 0; i < 360; i++)
```

```
    {
        float theta = 1.0f * i;
        float r = (float)Math.Log(1.001f +
                Math.Sin(2 * theta * Math.PI / 180));
        ds.AddPoint(new PointF(theta, r));
    }
    dc.Add(ds);

    // Add log-cosine data:
    ds = new DataSeries();
    ds.LineStyle.LineColor = Color.Green;
    ds.SeriesName = "Cos(theta)";
    for (int i = 0; i < 360; i++)
    {
        float theta = 1.0f * i;
        float r = (float)Math.Log(1.001f +
                Math.Cos(2 * theta * Math.PI / 180));
        ds.AddPoint(new PointF(theta, r));
    }
    dc.Add(ds);
}
```

Also change the r range to the following:

```
        cs.RMax = 1f;
        cs.RMin = -5f;
```

You can also add a legend to the polar chart. By running this project, you should obtain the results shown in Figure 4-21.

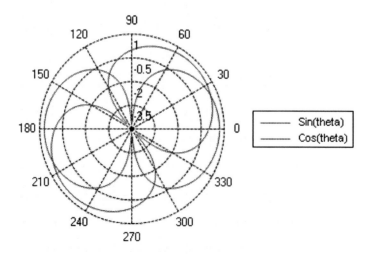

Figure 4-21 A polar plot with negative r values.

Creating Stock Charts

Stock charts usually show high, low, open, and close data, and play an important role in stock market research and analysis. These charts allow you to plot the change of a stock price over time, analyze the history of stock price changes, and predict the future price of a stock based on prior price history.

Here I will show you how to create a stock chart using C#.

Implementation

Start with a new C# Windows Application project, *Example4_9*. Add the following new classes to the project: ChartSTyle, LineStyle, DataSeries, DataCollection, and TextFileReader. The ChartStyle and LineStyle classes are similar to those used in previous projects. While TextFileReader class is a new class that allows you to import stock data into the application. Here is its code listing:

```
using System;
using System.Text;
using System.Collections.Specialized;
using System.Collections;
using System.Windows.Forms;
using System.IO;

namespace Example4_9
{
    class TextFileReader
    {
        public string[,] ReadTextFile(string fileName)
        {
            if (File.Exists(fileName))
            {
                string[,] sArray = ReadFile(fileName);
                return sArray;
            }
            else
            {
                return null;
            }
        }

        private string[,] ReadFile(string fileName)
        {
            try
            {
                StringCollection sc = new StringCollection();
                FileStream fs = new FileStream(fileName,
                        FileMode.Open, FileAccess.ReadWrite);
                StreamReader sr = new StreamReader(fs);

                // Read file into a string collection
                int noBytesRead = 0;
```

```
            string oneLine;
            while ((oneLine = sr.ReadLine()) != null)
            {
                noBytesRead += oneLine.Length;
                sc.Add(oneLine);
            }
            sr.Close();

            string[] sArray = new string[sc.Count];
            sc.CopyTo(sArray, 0);

            char[] cSplitter = { ' ', ',', ':', '\t' };
            string[] sArray1 = sArray[0].Split(cSplitter);
            string[,] sArray2 = new string[sArray1.Length,
                    sc.Count];

            for (int i = 0; i < sc.Count; i++)
            {
                sArray1 = sArray[i].Split(cSplitter);
                for (int j = 0; j < sArray1.Length; j++)
                {
                    sArray2[j, i] = sArray1[j];
                }
            }
            return sArray2;
        }
        catch (Exception e)
        {
            MessageBox.Show(e.Message, "Error Saving File.");
            return null;
        }
    }
  }
}
```

In this class, the public method ReadTextFile takes the file name string as an input variable and return a 2D string array. The stock text file should be formatted as shown in the same way as the following example, GE.txt, which is storing the stock price data for GE from 4-7-2006 to 5-5-2006:

```
5-May-06      34.94  35.22  34.87  35.16
4-May-06      34.5   34.94  34.48  34.8
3-May-06      34.22  34.67  34.19  34.4
2-May-06      34.39  34.59  34.1   34.48
1-May-06      34.64  34.72  34.32  34.39
28-Apr-06     34.49  34.78  34.35  34.59
27-Apr-06     33.9   34.68  33.89  34.43
26-Apr-06     34.07  34.44  33.88  34.13
25-Apr-06     34     34.06  33.8   33.97
24-Apr-06     33.81  34     33.8   33.93
21-Apr-06     34.25  34.32  33.68  33.97
20-Apr-06     33.8   34.18  33.63  34.12
19-Apr-06     33.95  33.97  33.5   33.89
18-Apr-06     33.52  33.97  33.21  33.87
```

```
17-Apr-06     33.76  33.76  33.07  33.29
13-Apr-06     34.19  34.36  33.61  33.89
12-Apr-06     34.3   34.53  34.17  34.46
11-Apr-06     33.92  34.07  33.63  34.05
10-Apr-06     34.06  34.08  33.8   33.92
```

In this file, the first column is the date; the second to fifth columns represent the open, high, low, and close prices of the stock, respectively. Please note that there is no header row in this text file. If you want the stock data file to have a header row or a different format, you must change the TextFileReader class correspondingly to take care of the file format change.

We also modify the DataSeries class to easily input stock data into the project:

```csharp
using System;
using System.Drawing;

namespace Example4_9
{
    public class DataSeries
    {
        private string[,] dataString;
        private LineStyle lineStyle;
        private string seriesName = "";

        public DataSeries()
        {
            lineStyle = new LineStyle();
        }

        public LineStyle LineStyle
        {
            get { return lineStyle; }
            set { lineStyle = value; }
        }

        public string[,] DataString
        {
            get { return dataString; }
            set { dataString = value; }
        }

        public string SeriesName
        {
            get { return seriesName; }
            set { seriesName = value; }
        }
    }
}
```

Here, the original array list, PointList, is replaced by a 2D string array, DataString. The following is the code listing of the DataCollection class:

```csharp
using System;
using System.Collections;
using System.Drawing;
```

```
namespace Example4_9
{
    public class DataCollection
    {
        private Form1 form1;
        private ArrayList dataSeriesList;
        private int dataSeriesIndex = 0;
        private StockChartTypeEnum stockChartType =
            StockChartTypeEnum.HiLoOpenClose;

        public DataCollection(Form1 fm1)
        {
            dataSeriesList = new ArrayList();
            form1 = fm1;
        }

        public StockChartTypeEnum StockChartType
        {
            get { return stockChartType; }
            set { stockChartType = value; }
        }

        public enum StockChartTypeEnum
        {
            HiLo = 0,
            HiLoOpenClose = 1,
            Candle = 2
        }

        public ArrayList DataSeriesList
        {
            get { return dataSeriesList; }
            set { dataSeriesList = value; }
        }
        public int DataSeriesIndex
        {
            get { return dataSeriesIndex; }
            set { dataSeriesIndex = value; }
        }

        public void Add(DataSeries ds)
        {
            dataSeriesList.Add(ds);
            if (ds.SeriesName == "")
            {
                ds.SeriesName = "DataSeries" +
                        dataSeriesList.Count.ToString();
            }
        }

        public void Insert(int dataSeriesIndex, DataSeries ds)
        {
            dataSeriesList.Insert(dataSeriesIndex, ds);
```

```csharp
        if (ds.SeriesName == "")
        {
            dataSeriesIndex = dataSeriesIndex + 1;
            ds.SeriesName = "DataSeries" +
                    dataSeriesIndex.ToString();
        }
    }

    public void Remove(string dataSeriesName)
    {
        if (dataSeriesList != null)
        {
            for (int i = 0; i < dataSeriesList.Count; i++)
            {
                DataSeries ds = (DataSeries)dataSeriesList[i];
                if (ds.SeriesName == dataSeriesName)
                {
                    dataSeriesList.RemoveAt(i);
                }
            }
        }
    }

    public void RemoveAll()
    {
        dataSeriesList.Clear();
    }

    public void AddStockChart(Graphics g, ChartStyle cs)
    {
        foreach (DataSeries ds in DataSeriesList)
        {
            Pen aPen = new Pen(ds.LineStyle.LineColor,
                    ds.LineStyle.Thickness);
            aPen.DashStyle = ds.LineStyle.Pattern;
            SolidBrush aBrush = new SolidBrush(
                    ds.LineStyle.LineColor);
            SolidBrush whiteBrush = new SolidBrush(Color.White);
            float barLength = form1.PlotPanel.Width /
                    (5*ds.DataString.GetLength(1));
            for (int i = 0; i < ds.DataString.GetLength(1); i++)
            {
                float[] stockdata = new float[4];
                for (int j = 0; j < stockdata.Length; j++)
                {
                    stockdata[j] = Convert.ToSingle(
                            ds.DataString[j+1,i]);
                }
                PointF ptHigh = cs.Point2D(new PointF(i,
                            stockdata[1]));
                PointF ptLow = cs.Point2D(new PointF(i,
                            stockdata[2]));
                PointF ptOpen = cs.Point2D(new PointF(i,
                            stockdata[0]));
```

```
PointF ptCLose = cs.Point2D(new PointF(i,
                  stockdata[3]));
PointF ptOpen1 = new PointF(ptOpen.X - barLength,
                  ptOpen.Y);
PointF ptClose1 = new PointF(ptCLose.X + barLength,
                  ptCLose.Y);
PointF ptOpen2 = new PointF(ptOpen.X + barLength,
                  ptOpen.Y);
PointF ptClose2 = new PointF(ptCLose.X - barLength,
                  ptCLose.Y);

// Draw Hi-Lo stock chart:
if (StockChartType == StockChartTypeEnum.HiLo)
{
    g.DrawLine(aPen, ptHigh, ptLow);
}

// Draw Hi-Li-Open-Close chart:
else if (StockChartType ==
        StockChartTypeEnum.HiLoOpenClose)
{
    g.DrawLine(aPen, ptHigh, ptLow);
    g.DrawLine(aPen,ptOpen, ptOpen1);
    g.DrawLine(aPen, ptCLose, ptClose1);
}

// Draw candle chart:
else if (stockChartType ==
        StockChartTypeEnum.Candle)
{
    PointF[] pts = new PointF[4];
    pts[0] = ptOpen1;
    pts[1] = ptOpen2;
    pts[2] = ptClose1;
    pts[3] = ptClose2;
    g.DrawLine(aPen, ptHigh, ptLow);
    if (stockdata[0] > stockdata[3])
    {
        g.FillPolygon(aBrush,pts);
    }
    else if (stockdata[0] < stockdata[3])
    {
        g.FillPolygon(whiteBrush, pts);
    }
    g.DrawPolygon(aPen, pts);
}
}
aPen.Dispose();
aBrush.Dispose();
whiteBrush.Dispose();
}
}
}
}
```

In this class, the StockChartType enumeration has been added, from which you can select a special chart from three stock chart types, HiLo, HiLoOpenClose, and Candle. The public method, AddStockChart, draws the stock data according to the specified stock chart type. Please pay special attention to the Candle chart type, in which we draw solid polygons when the close price is less than the open price and open polygons (filled with a white brush) otherwise.

Hi-Lo Chart

Now, it is time to test our stock chart project. First, we draw a Hi-Lo stock chart. The following code of Form1 achieves this goal:

```
using System;
using System.Drawing;
using System.Drawing.Drawing2D;
using System.Windows.Forms;

namespace Example4_9
{
    public partial class Form1 : Form
    {
        private ChartStyle cs;
        private DataCollection dc;

        public Form1()
        {
            InitializeComponent();
            this.SetStyle(ControlStyles.ResizeRedraw, true);

            // Subscribing to a paint eventhandler to drawingPanel:
            PlotPanel.Paint +=
                new PaintEventHandler(PlotPanelPaint);

            cs = new ChartStyle(this);
            dc = new DataCollection(this);
            // Specify chart style parameters:
            cs.Title = "Chart of GE Stock";
            cs.XTickOffset = 1;
            cs.XLimMin = -1f;
            cs.XLimMax = 20f;
            cs.YLimMin = 32f;
            cs.YLimMax = 36f;
            cs.XTick = 2f;
            cs.YTick = 0.5f;
            dc.StockChartType =
                    DataCollection.StockChartTypeEnum.HiLo;
        }

        private void AddData()
        {
            dc.DataSeriesList.Clear();
            TextFileReader tfr = new TextFileReader();
            DataSeries ds = new DataSeries();
```

```
    // Add GE stock data from a text data file:
    ds = new DataSeries();
    ds.DataString = tfr.ReadTextFile("GE.txt");
    ds.LineStyle.LineColor = Color.DarkBlue;
    dc.Add(ds);
}

private void PlotPanelPaint(object sender, PaintEventArgs e)
{
    Graphics g = e.Graphics;
    AddData();
    cs.PlotPanelStyle(g);
    dc.AddStockChart(g, cs);
}

protected override void OnPaint(PaintEventArgs e)
{
    Graphics g = e.Graphics;
    cs.ChartArea = this.ClientRectangle;
    cs.SetChartArea(g);
}
    }
}
```

Within the constructor, in addition to the standard definitions for a chart application, we add the following line of code:

```
dc.StockChartType = DataCollection.StockChartTypeEnum.HiLo;
```

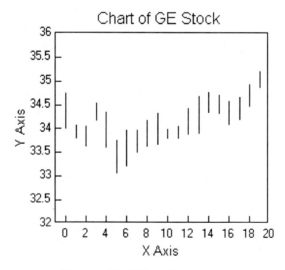

Figure 4-22 A Hi-Lo Stock chart.

This specifies the stock chart type to be a Hi-Lo plot. Inside the `AddData` method, we create a new instance of the `TextFileReader` and call its public method `ReadTextFile` to read the GE.txt file into the project:

```
ds.DataString = tfr.ReadTextFile("GE.txt");
```

In this application, we have added two text files, GE.txt and IBM.txt, to the following directory: Application directory\bin\debug. If your stock data file is stored in a different directory, you need to specify the file path as well.

Finally, we call the `AddStockChart` method of the `DataCollection` class from the `PlotPanelPaint` method.

Running this project by pressing the F5 key produces the results of Figure 4-22.

Hi-Lo-Open-Close Chart

A Hi-Lo-Open-Close stock chart can be created by replacing the `StockChartType` with the following line of code:

```
dc.StockChartType =
        DataCollection.StockChartTypeEnum.HiLoOpenClose;
```

This generates the output shown in Figure 4-23.

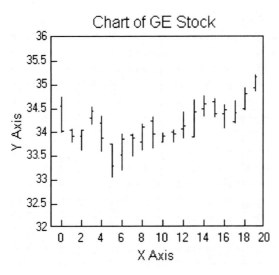

Figure 4-23 A Hi-Lo-Open-Close stock chart.

Candlestick Chart

Replacing the `StockChartType` with the following code snippet

```
dc.StockChartType = DataCollection.StockChartTypeEnum.Candle;
```

obtains the results of Figure 4-24.

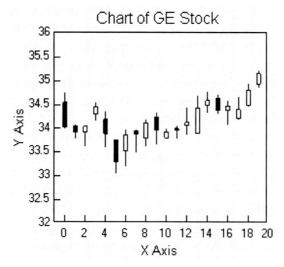

Figure 4-24 A candle stock chart.

5

3D Matrices and
Transformations

In the previous few chapters, we discussed 2D graphics, transformations, and a variety of 2D charts. In this chapter, we will explain the mathematical basics of 3D transformations, which are used to create 3D graphics objects on a 2D surface (the screen). Most 3D transformations are analogous to the 2D transformations described in Chapter 2. Using homogeneous coordinates and matrix representations similar to the ones used in 2D, we will show you how to perform basic transformations, including translation, scaling, reflection, and rotation, in 3D. We will also describe matrices that represent projections, allowing you to view 3D graphics objects on a 2D screen. As is the case with 2D, you can combine 3D basic transformation matrices to represent a complicated transformation with a single transformation matrix.

Unlike 2D, there is no built-in 3D matrix class defined in C# and GDI+. Even the simplest 3D point object must be defined first in order to be used in your applications. In this chapter, we will demonstrate how to create a variety of 3D transformation matrices and 3D graphics objects using examples. We will also discuss different 3D coordinate systems and show you how to implement them with C#.

Basics of Matrices and Transformations in 3D

Matrix representations play an important role in transformations and operations on graphics objects. A matrix is a multi-dimensional array. This section explains the basics of 3D matrices and transformations. General 3D transformations are quite complicated. As in the case of 2D, however, you can build more useful transformations with combinations of simple basic transformations: translation, scaling, rotation, and projection. The following sections describe these fundamental transformations. Once you understand how to use these basic 3D transformations, you can always compose them to create more general transformations.

3D Point and Matrix Operation in C#

As in the case of 2D, you can perform 3D matrix operations in a homogeneous coordinate system. Here, a point or vector is represented by a column matrix. In this notation, most 3D transformation matrices contain (0, 0, 0, 1) in their last row. You can use this special structure, as we did in 2D matrices defined in the C# matrix class, to speed up the matrix operations. This approach works for most transformation matrices, except for the perspective transformation described later in this chapter, which does not contain (0, 0, 0, 1) in its last row. This means that you cannot use this method when you deal with perspective transformations. Therefore, in this book, we will instead use a standard For-loop computation method to perform matrix operations. This standard For-loop method does not assume that transformation matrices contain (0, 0, 0, 1) in their last row.

Let's use an example to define a 3D point object and matrix with C#. Start with a new C# Windows Application project and name it *Example5_1*. Add a Label control, label1, to Form1. Add two new classes, Point3 and Matrix3, to the project. In the Point3 class, we define a 3D point in homogeneous coordinates and perform a basic transformation to the point using a public method Transform. The following is the code listing of the Point3 class:

```
using System;

namespace Example5_1
{
    public class Point3
    {
        public float X;
        public float Y;
        public float Z;
        public float W;

        public Point3()
        {
        }

        public Point3(float x, float y, float z, float w)
        {
            X = x;
            Y = y;
            Z = z;
            W = w;
        }
    }
```

```
            // Apply a transformation to a point:
            public void Transform(Matrix3 m)
            {
                float[] result = m.VectorMultiply(
                        new float[4] { X, Y, Z, W });
                X = result[0];
                Y = result[1];
                Z = result[2];
                W = result[3];
            }
        }
    }
```

The default W component of a 3D point in homogeneous coordinates is set to 1. The Matrix3 class contains the basic matrix operations, such as matrix multiplication. The following is its code listing:

```
using System;

namespace Example5_1
{
    class Matrix3
    {
        public float[,] M = new float[4, 4];

        public Matrix3()
        {
            Identity3();
        }

        public Matrix3(float m00, float m01, float m02, float m03,
                       float m10, float m11, float m12, float m13,
                       float m20, float m21, float m22, float m23,
                       float m30, float m31, float m32, float m33)
        {
            M[0, 0] = m00;
            M[0, 1] = m01;
            M[0, 2] = m02;
            M[0, 3] = m03;
            M[1, 0] = m10;
            M[1, 1] = m11;
            M[1, 2] = m12;
            M[1, 3] = m13;
            M[2, 0] = m20;
            M[2, 1] = m21;
            M[2, 2] = m22;
            M[2, 3] = m23;
            M[3, 0] = m30;
            M[3, 1] = m31;
            M[3, 2] = m32;
            M[3, 3] = m33;
        }

        // Define a Identity matrix:
```

```csharp
public void Identity3()
{
    for (int i = 0; i < 4; i++)
    {
        for (int j = 0; j < 4; j++)
        {
            if (i == j)
            {
                M[i, j] = 1;
            }
            else
            {
                M[i, j] = 0;
            }
        }
    }
}

/ Multiply two matrices together:
public static Matrix3 operator *(Matrix3 m1, Matrix3 m2)
{
    Matrix3 result = new Matrix3();
    for (int i = 0; i < 4; i++)
    {
        for (int j = 0; j < 4; j++)
        {
            float element = 0;
            for (int k = 0; k < 4; k++)
            {
                element += m1.M[i, k] * m2.M[k, j];
            }
            result.M[i, j] = element;
        }
    }
    return result;
}

// Apply a transformation to a vector (point):
public float[] VectorMultiply(float[] vector)
{
    float[] result = new float[4];
    for (int i = 0; i < 4; i++)
    {
        for (int j = 0; j < 4; j++)
        {
            result[i] += M[i, j] * vector[j];
        }
    }
    return result;
}
    }
}
```

These two classes in *Example5_1* can be used to perform basic transformation operations for a 3D point object. In the next few subsections, we will use these two classes to discuss basic 3D transformations.

Scaling

As in the case of 2D, to scale or stretch an object in the X direction, you need to multiply the X coordinates of each of the object's points by the scaling factor, s_x. Similarly, you can scale an object in the Y and Z directions. In the standard 3D Cartesian coordinate system, a scaling transformation can be represented in the form:

$$\begin{pmatrix} x_1 \\ y_1 \\ z_1 \end{pmatrix} = \begin{pmatrix} s_x & 0 & 0 \\ 0 & s_y & 0 \\ 0 & 0 & s_z \end{pmatrix} \begin{pmatrix} x \\ y \\ z \end{pmatrix} = \begin{pmatrix} s_x x \\ s_y y \\ s_z z \end{pmatrix} \tag{5.1}$$

The 3D scaling transformation can be generalized in the homogeneous coordinate system:

$$\begin{pmatrix} x_1 \\ y_1 \\ z_1 \\ 1 \end{pmatrix} = \begin{pmatrix} s_x & 0 & 0 & 0 \\ 0 & s_y & 0 & 0 \\ 0 & 0 & s_z & 0 \\ 0 & 0 & 0 & 1 \end{pmatrix} \begin{pmatrix} x \\ y \\ z \\ 1 \end{pmatrix} \tag{5.2}$$

For example, suppose that you have a 3D point (1, 2, 3, 1) in the homogeneous coordinates, and you want to apply a scaling matrix to the point. This scaling matrix shrinks x and y uniformly by a factor of two, and stretches Z by a factor of three-halves. This scaling operation can easily be computed using Equation (5.2):

$$\begin{pmatrix} x_1 \\ y_1 \\ z_1 \\ 1 \end{pmatrix} = \begin{pmatrix} 0.5 & 0 & 0 & 0 \\ 0 & 0.5 & 0 & 0 \\ 0 & 0 & 1.5 & 0 \\ 0 & 0 & 0 & 1 \end{pmatrix} \begin{pmatrix} 1 \\ 2 \\ 3 \\ 1 \end{pmatrix} = \begin{pmatrix} 0.5 \\ 1 \\ 4.5 \\ 1 \end{pmatrix} \tag{5.3}$$

We can also calculate this using the C# application project *Example5_1*. First, we add a static method Scale3 to the Matrix3 class:

```
// Create a scaling matrix:
public static Matrix3 Scale3(float sx, float sy, float sz)
{
    Matrix3 result = new Matrix3();
    result.M[0, 0] = sx;
    result.M[1, 1] = sy;
    result.M[2, 2] = sz;
    return result;
}
```

The following code listing of the Form1 class in *Example5_1* performs the scaling transformation:

```
using System;
```

```
using System.Drawing;
using System.Windows.Forms;

namespace Example5_1
{
    public partial class Form1 : Form
    {
        public Form1()
        {
            InitializeComponent();
        }
        private void Form1_Load(object sender, EventArgs e)
        {
            // Create the original point Point3 :
            Point3 pt = new Point3();
            pt.X = 1;
            pt.Y = 2;
            pt.Z = 3;

            // Perform transformation:
            ScaleTransform(pt);

            // Display result in label1 control:
            label1.Text = pt.X.ToString() + ",  " + pt.Y.ToString() +
                        ",  " + pt.Z.ToString() + ",  " + pt.W.ToString();

        }

        private void ScaleTransform(Point3 pt)
        {
            // Create a scaling matrix:
            Matrix3 m1 = Matrix3.Scale3(0.5f, 0.5f, 1.5f);

            // Perform the scaling operation:
            pt.Transform(m1);
        }
    }
}
```

Here, we first create the original point (1, 2, 3, 1) (note that the default W component is 1!), then create the scaling matrix by calling the static method Scale3 in the Matrix3 class. Finally, we perform a scaling operation by applying the scaling matrix to the original point. The results after the transformation are stored in the original point object. Running this application will produce the results displayed in Figure 5-1:

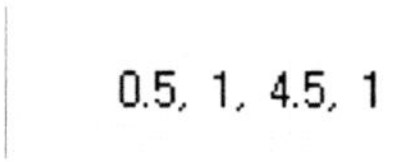

0.5, 1, 4.5, 1

Figure 5-1 A 3D point after scaling.

The above results are consistent with Equation (5.3), as expected. You can also perform two successive scaling transformations. For example, the first scaling matrix is the same as m1, while the second scaling matrix has scaling factors of sx = 1, sy = 0.5, and sz = 0.3. The following code snippet performs the scaling operation:

```
private void ScaleTransform(Point3 pt)
{
    // Create a scaling matrix:
    Matrix3 m1 = Matrix3.Scale3(0.5f, 0.5f, 1.5f);

    // Create another scaling matrix:
    Matrix3 m2 = Matrix3.Scale3(1f, 0.5f, 0.3f);

    // Perform the scaling operation:
    pt.Transform(m1 * m2);
}
```

Here we calculate the two successive scaling transformations using a matrix multiplication:

```
    pt.Transform(m1 * m2);
```

This matrix multiplication has been defined as a static method in the Matrix3 class. If you run the project now, you should obtain the results shown in Figure 5-2, which can be easily confirmed by direct matrix multiplication.

0.5, 0.5, 1.35, 1

Figure 5-2 A 3D point after two successive scaling operations.

Reflection

In the case of 2D objects, reflection across the X or Y axis is simple: you simply scale it with a negative scaling factor. In 3D, however, you must reflect an object across a plane instead of a line. Reflecting an object across the X-Y, X-Z, and Y-Z planes is easy. Simply scale the points using -1 as one of the scale factors. For example, to reflect an object across the X-Y planes, use a scaling transformation matrix with sx = 1, sy = 1, and sz = -1.

You can easily use the C# program *Example6_1* to perform these simple reflections by adding a ReflectTransform method to the Form1 class:

```
private void ReflectTransform(Point3 pt)
{
    // Create the reflection matrix across the X-Y plane and
    // perform reflection transformation:
    Matrix3 m = Matrix3.Scale3(1,1,-1);
    pt.Transform(m);

    // Create the reflection matrix across the X-Z plane and
    // perform reflection transformation:
    m = Matrix3.Scale3(1, -1, 1);
    pt.Transform(m);

    // Create the reflection matrix across the Y-Z plane and
    // perform reflection transformation:
    m = Matrix3.Scale3(-1, 1, 1);
```

```
        pt.Transform(m);
    }
```

Then call this method from `Form1_Load`.

Translation

A 2D translation matrix is easily generalized to the 3D case. To translate a point by a distance of dx in the X direction, dy in the Y direction, and dz in the Z direction, you simply multiply the point by a transform matrix in homogeneous coordinates:

$$
\begin{pmatrix} x_1 \\ y_1 \\ z_1 \\ 1 \end{pmatrix} = \begin{pmatrix} 1 & 0 & 0 & dx \\ 0 & 1 & 0 & dy \\ 0 & 0 & 1 & dz \\ 0 & 0 & 0 & 1 \end{pmatrix} \begin{pmatrix} x \\ y \\ z \\ 1 \end{pmatrix} = \begin{pmatrix} x + dy \\ y + dy \\ z + dz \\ 1 \end{pmatrix} \tag{5.4}
$$

The results of $x_1 = x + dx$, $y_1 = y + dy$, and $z_1 = z + dz$ are indeed the correct translation of a point $(x, y, z, 1)$.

The translation can also be performed using *Example5_1*. First add a static method, `Translate3`, to the `Matrix3` class:

```
public static Matrix3 Translate3(float dx, float dy, float dz)
{
    Matrix3 result = new Matrix3();
    result.M[0, 3] = dx;
    result.M[1, 3] = dy;
    result.M[2, 3] = dz;
    return result;
}
```

Then add a method `TranslateTransform` to the `Form1` class:

```
private void TranslateTransform(Point3 pt)
{
    // Create a translation matrix:
    Matrix3 m1 = Matrix3.Translate3(2, 2.5f, 3);
    pt.Transform(m1);
}
```

In this method, we translate the original point (1, 2, 3, 1) by 2 in the X direction, 2.5 in the Y direction, and 3 in the Z direction. Running the project creates a new point (3, 4.5, 6, 1) after the translation. You can also examine the point after two successive translations by changing the `TranslateTransform` method to the following code snippet:

```
private void TranslateTransform(Point3 pt)
{
    // Create a translation matrix:
    Matrix3 m1 = Matrix3.Translate3(2, 2.5f, 3);

    // Create another translation matrix:
    Matrix3 m2 = Matrix3.Translate3(-3, -2, -1);
```

```
        // Perform the translation operation:
        pt.Transform(m1 * m2);
}
```

After these two successive translations, you obtain a new point (0, 2.5, 5, 1).

Rotation

Rotating an object around an arbitrary axis in 3D is much more complicated than doing so in 2D. However, rotating an object around the X, Y, or Z axis is still quite simple. For example, to rotate a point around the Z axis, you can simply ignore the Z coordinate of the point and handle the rotation as if it were taking place in 2D. This is due to the fact that its Z coordinate remains unchanged when you rotate the point around the Z axis. We can easily write down this rotation matrix in homogeneous coordinates:

$$\begin{pmatrix} \cos\theta & -\sin\theta & 0 & 0 \\ \sin\theta & \cos\theta & 0 & 0 \\ 0 & 0 & 1 & 0 \\ 0 & 0 & 0 & 1 \end{pmatrix} \tag{5.5}$$

Similarly, we can represent rotation matrices around the Y and X directions:

$$\begin{pmatrix} \cos\theta & 0 & \sin\theta & 0 \\ 0 & 1 & 0 & 0 \\ -\sin\theta & 0 & \cos\theta & 0 \\ 0 & 0 & 0 & 1 \end{pmatrix} \tag{5.6}$$

$$\begin{pmatrix} 1 & 0 & 0 & 0 \\ 0 & \cos\theta & -\sin\theta & 0 \\ 0 & \sin\theta & \cos\theta & 0 \\ 0 & 0 & 0 & 1 \end{pmatrix} \tag{5.7}$$

Using these informations, you can create a rotation transformation matrix in the `Matrix3` class:

```
// Create a rotation matrix around the x axis:
public static Matrix3 Rotate3X(float theta)
{
    theta = theta * (float)Math.PI / 180.0f;
    float sn = (float)Math.Sin(theta);
    float cn = (float)Math.Cos(theta);

    Matrix3 result = new Matrix3();

    result.M[1, 1] = cn;
    result.M[1, 2] = -sn;
    result.M[2, 1] = sn;
    result.M[2, 2] = cn;
    return result;
```

```
        }

        // Create a rotation matrix around the y axis:
        public static Matrix3 Rotate3Y(float theta)
        {
            theta = theta * (float)Math.PI / 180.0f;
            float sn = (float)Math.Sin(theta);
            float cn = (float)Math.Cos(theta);

            Matrix3 result = new Matrix3();

            result.M[0, 0] = cn;
            result.M[0, 2] = sn;
            result.M[2, 0] = -sn;
            result.M[2, 2] = cn;
            return result;
        }

        // Create a rotation matrix around the z axis:
        public static Matrix3 Rotate3Z(float theta)
        {
            theta = theta * (float)Math.PI / 180.0f;
            float sn = (float)Math.Sin(theta);
            float cn = (float)Math.Cos(theta);

            Matrix3 result = new Matrix3();

            result.M[0, 0] = cn;
            result.M[0, 1] = -sn;
            result.M[1, 0] = sn;
            result.M[1, 1] = cn;
            return result;
        }
```

These rotation matrices can be examined by adding a `RotateTransForm` method to the `Form1` class:

```
    private void RotateTransform(Point3 pt)
    {
        // Create a rotation matrix around the z axis by 45 degrees:
        Matrix3 m1 = Matrix3.Rotate3Z(45);

        // Perform the rotation operation:
        pt.Transform(m1);
    }
```

Running the application generates the new point (-0.707, 2.121, 3, 1), which can easily be confirmed using a direct matrix (see Equation (5.5)) multiplication approach. You can also perform two successive rotations on the original point:

```
    private void RotateTransform(Point3 pt)
    {
        // Create a rotation matrix around the z axis by 20 degrees:
        Matrix3 m1 = Matrix3.Rotate3Z(20);
```

```
        // Create another rotation matrix around the
        // z axis by 25 degrees:
        Matrix3 m2 = Matrix3.Rotate3Z(25);

        // Perform the rotation operation:
        pt.Transform(m1 * m2);
    }
```

In this method, we first rotate the original point around the Z axis by 20 degrees, then rotate it around the same axis by 25 degrees. Running this application produces the same results as the above, i.e., the net result is equivalent to rotating around the Z axis by a total 45 degrees.

Projections

Because our computer screen is two dimensional, it cannot directly display 3D objects. In order to view 3D objects on a 2D screen, you have to project the objects from 3D to 2D.

The most common types of projections are called planar geometric projections. These are a distinct class of projections that maintain straight lines when mapping an object onto a viewing surface. In a planar geometric projection, a ray or projector is passed from a center of projection through the points being projected onto a planar viewing surface, called the view plane. Figure 5-3 shows the projection of a square object onto the view plane.

Planar geometric projections can be grouped into two categories, parallel and perspective, which are described in the following subsections.

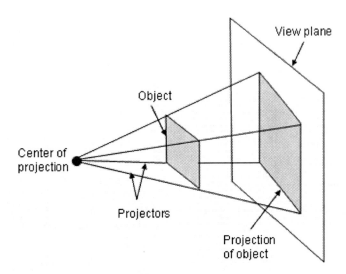

Figure 5-3 Projecting a square object from 3D to 2D view plane.

Parallel Projections

In a parallel projection, the center of projection is located at an infinite distance from the view plane. By placing the center of projection at an infinite distance from the view plane, projectors become parallel to the view plane. For a parallel projection, instead of specifying a center of projection, you need to specify a direction of projection. Figure 5-4 shows a parallel projection of a square object onto the view plane.

There are several useful parallel projections that fall into two subcategories: orthographic and oblique. In an orthographic projection, the projectors are perpendicular to the view plane; while in an oblique projection, they are not.

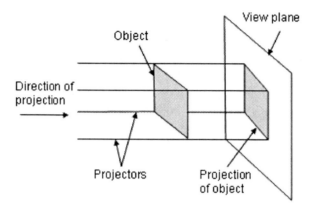

Figure 5-4 A parallel projection of a square object.

Orthographic Projections

Orthographic projections are one of two projection types derived by subdivision of the parallel projection subclass. In addition to being parallel, projectors in an orthographic projection are also perpendicular to the view plane. They are often used in architectural and mechanical drawings. Orthographic projections are further categorized as either multi-view or axonometric projections, which are described below.

Multi-View Projections

A multi-view projection shows a single face of a 3D object. Common choices for viewing an object in 2D include *front*, *side*, and *top* view. Figure 5-5 shows a house object as well as its front, side, and top views.

These projections are very simple. To project a point, simply ignore the point's unneeded third coordinate. In top view, the normal of the view plane is parallel with the positive Y axis in a right-handed system, as shown in Figure 5-5. To project the top view of a 3D object, the Y coordinates are discarded and the X and Z coordinates for each point are mapped to the view plane. By repositioning the normal of the view plane to the positive Z axis and selecting the X, and Y coordinates for each point, a front view is projected to the view plane. Likewise, a side view is realized when the normal of the view plane is directed along the positive X axis, while the Y and Z coordinates of a 3D object are projected to the view plane. These projections are often used in engineering and architectural drawings. While they do not show the 3D aspects of an object, multi-view projections are useful because the angles and dimensions of the object are maintained.

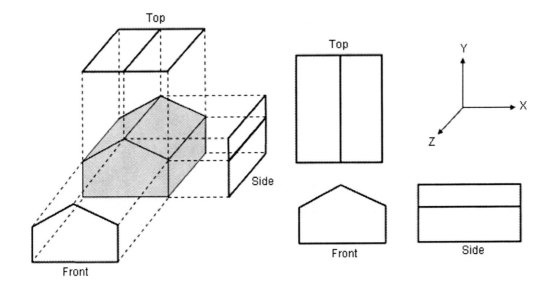

Figure 5-5 Front, side, and top views of orthographic projections.

Now, we can write down the transformation matrices for front, side, and top view. To create a front view, ignore the z coordinate. This means

$$\begin{pmatrix} x_1 \\ y_1 \\ z_1 \\ 1 \end{pmatrix} = \begin{pmatrix} 1 & 0 & 0 & 0 \\ 0 & 1 & 0 & 0 \\ 0 & 0 & 0 & 0 \\ 0 & 0 & 0 & 1 \end{pmatrix} \begin{pmatrix} x \\ y \\ z \\ 1 \end{pmatrix} = \begin{pmatrix} x \\ y \\ 0 \\ 1 \end{pmatrix} \tag{5.8}$$

To create a side view, you simply ignore the X coordinate. You may also want to map the Y and Z coordinates onto the X and Y coordinates to make it easier to display on a computer screen. In this case, the new coordinates should be given by $x_1 = -z$ and $y_1 = y$. Therefore, the transformation matrix for side view is as follows:

$$\begin{pmatrix} x_1 \\ y_1 \\ z_1 \\ 1 \end{pmatrix} = \begin{pmatrix} 0 & 0 & -1 & 0 \\ 0 & 1 & 0 & 0 \\ 0 & 0 & 0 & 0 \\ 0 & 0 & 0 & 1 \end{pmatrix} \begin{pmatrix} x \\ y \\ z \\ 1 \end{pmatrix} = \begin{pmatrix} -z \\ y \\ 0 \\ 1 \end{pmatrix} \tag{5.9}$$

Similarly, to create a top view, you should ignore the Y coordinate. To map points onto the X-Y plane, you should use the relation: $x_1 = x$, and $y_1 = -z$, which results in the following transformation matrix:

$$\begin{pmatrix} x_1 \\ y_1 \\ z_1 \\ 1 \end{pmatrix} = \begin{pmatrix} 1 & 0 & 0 & 0 \\ 0 & 0 & -1 & 0 \\ 0 & 0 & 0 & 0 \\ 0 & 0 & 0 & 1 \end{pmatrix} \begin{pmatrix} x \\ y \\ z \\ 1 \end{pmatrix} = \begin{pmatrix} x \\ -z \\ 0 \\ 1 \end{pmatrix}$$
(5.10)

You can now add these transformation matrices for front, side, and top views to the `Matrix3` class of *Example5_1*:

```
// Front view projection matrix:
public static Matrix3 FrontView()
{
    Matrix3 result = new Matrix3();
    result.M[2, 2] = 0;
    return result;
}

// Side view projection matrix:
public static Matrix3 SideView()
{
    Matrix3 result = new Matrix3();
    result.M[0, 0] = 0;
    result.M[2, 2] = 0;
    result.M[0, 2] = -1;
    return result;
}

// Top view projection matrix:
public static Matrix3 TopView()
{
    Matrix3 result = new Matrix3();
    result.M[1, 1] = 0;
    result.M[2, 2] = 0;
    result.M[1, 2] = -1;
    return result;
}
```

Axonometric Projections

Multi-view projections preserve distances and angles, in other words, you can measure distances and angles directly from the projection of an object. However, it is often difficult to understand the 3D structure of an object by examining only its multi-view projections. Reproducing a house object like the one in Figure 5-5 from these multi-view projections takes experience and good spatial intuition.

To make the 3D nature of an object more apparent, you can use projections that are not parallel to the X, Y, or Z axis. This type of projection is called an axonometric orthographic projection. Unlike multi-view projections, axonometric projections allow you to place the normal of the view plane in any direction so that three adjacent faces of a "cube-like" object are visible. To avoid duplication of the views displayed by multi-view projections, the normal of the view-plane for an axonometric view is usually not placed parallel to a major axis. The increased versatility in the direction of the normal of the view plane positions the view plane so that it intersects at least two of the major axes. Lines of a 3D object that are parallel in the world coordinate system are likewise projected to the view plane as parallel lines. In addition, the length of a line, or line preservation, is maintained for lines parallel to the view plane. Other receding lines maintain only their proportion and are foreshortened equally with lines along the same axes.

Let's try to construct a transformation matrix for an axonometric projection. Suppose that we first rotate over an angle β around the Y axis, and then over an angle α around the X axis. This corresponds to the product of two rotation matrices:

$$
\begin{pmatrix}
1 & 0 & 0 & 0 \\
0 & \cos\alpha & -\sin\alpha & 0 \\
0 & \sin\alpha & \cos\alpha & 0 \\
0 & 0 & 0 & 1
\end{pmatrix}
\begin{pmatrix}
\cos\beta & 1 & \sin\beta & 0 \\
0 & 1 & 0 & 0 \\
-\sin\beta & 0 & \cos\beta & 0 \\
0 & 0 & 0 & 1
\end{pmatrix}
$$

$$
=
\begin{pmatrix}
\cos\beta & 0 & \sin\beta & 0 \\
\sin\alpha\sin\beta & \cos\alpha & -\sin\alpha\cos\beta & 0 \\
-\cos\alpha\sin\beta & \sin\alpha & \cos\alpha\cos\beta & 0 \\
0 & 0 & 0 & 1
\end{pmatrix}
$$

In the above matrix, the first column is the result of applying the two rotations to the unit vector along the X axis: $e_1 = (1; 0; 0; 1)$; the second column contains the image of $e_2 = (0; 1; 0; 1)$ along the Y axis; and the third column contains the image of $e_3 = (0; 0; 1; 1)$ along the Z axis.

If we project along the Z axis (side view), the third row of the above matrix has to be replaced by zeros; i.e., the projected point $(x_1, y_1, z_1, 1)$ becomes:

$$
\begin{pmatrix} x_1 \\ y_1 \\ z_1 \\ 1 \end{pmatrix}
=
\begin{pmatrix}
\cos\beta & 0 & \sin\beta & 0 \\
\sin\alpha\sin\beta & \cos\alpha & -\sin\alpha\cos\beta & 0 \\
0 & 0 & 0 & 0 \\
0 & 0 & 0 & 1
\end{pmatrix}
\begin{pmatrix} x \\ y \\ z \\ 1 \end{pmatrix}
\tag{5.11}
$$

By varying the angles α and β, various axonometric projections can be created. Note an important property of the above projection matrix. Let's call the columns of the matrix **a1**, **a2** and **a3**. Then

$$
|a1|^2 + |a2|^2 + |a3|^2 = 2
\tag{5.12}
$$

Axonometric projections can be further divided into three types that depend upon the number of major axes that are foreshortened equally. These axonometric views are defined as isometric, dimetric, or trimetric projections.

Isometric Projections:

An isometric projection is a commonly used type of axonometric projection. In this projection, all three of the major axes are foreshortened equally since the normal of the view plane makes equal angles with all three coordinate axes. To satisfy this condition, we must have $|a1| = |a2| = |a3|$. Using equation (5.12), we obtain:

$$| a1 | = | a2 | = | a3 | = \sqrt{2/3}$$

From the second column of the projection matrix in Equation (5.11), we deduce $\cos \alpha = \pm\sqrt{2/3}$ (and $\sin \alpha = \pm1/\sqrt{3}$). The first and the third columns lead to the following equations:

$$\cos^2 \beta + \sin^2 \beta / 3 = 2/3$$
$$\sin^2 \beta + \cos^2 \beta / 3 = 2/3$$

This means that $\cos \beta = \sin \beta = \pm1/\sqrt{2}$. From all the possible solutions, we can take the ones with $\sin \beta = -1/\sqrt{2}$ and $\cos \beta = 1/\sqrt{2}$ (corresponding to β = - 45 degrees), $\cos \alpha = \sqrt{2/3}$, and $\sin \alpha = 1/\sqrt{3}$ (corresponding to α = 35.26 degrees). The projection matrix in Equation (5.11) becomes

$$\begin{pmatrix} 1/\sqrt{2} & 0 & -1/\sqrt{2} & 0 \\ -1/\sqrt{6} & \sqrt{2/3} & -1/\sqrt{6} & 0 \\ 0 & 0 & 0 & 0 \\ 0 & 0 & 0 & 1 \end{pmatrix}$$

We can then obtain the coordinates of the three unit vectors e_1, $e2$, and e_3 in the view plane (the 2D screen corresponding to the X-Y plane) using the above projection matrix:

$$e1 \rightarrow (1/\sqrt{2}, -1/\sqrt{6}) \approx (0.71, -0.41)$$
$$e2 \rightarrow (0, \sqrt{2/3}) \approx (0, 0.82)$$
$$e3 \rightarrow (-1/\sqrt{2}, -1/\sqrt{6}) \approx (-0.71, -0.41)$$

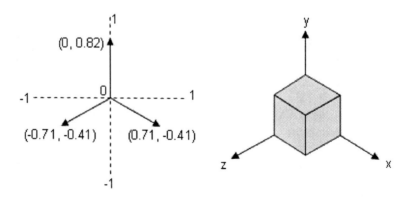

Figure 5-6 Isometric projections of the unit vectors of the coordinate axes
(left) and a cube object (right).

The above projected coordinates for the unit vectors determine the positions of the X, Y, and Z coordinate axes in the view plane (the screen). Figure 5-6 shows the isometric projections of three unit vectors of the coordinate axes and a cube object. Isometric projections scale lines equally along each axis, which is often useful since lines along the coordinate axes can be measured and converted using the same scale.

Dimetric Projections:

Dimetric projections differ from isometric projections in the direction of the normal of the view plane. In this case, (**a1, a2, a3**) are set so that they make equal angles with two of the coordinate axes. For example, a valid setting for a dimetric projection might be: $|a1| : |a2| : |a3| = 2 : 2 : 1$. If we set $|a1| = |a2| = \sqrt{8/9}$, then from Equation (5.12) we have $|a3| = \sqrt{2/9}$. The projection matrix in Equation (5.11) reduces to the following formulae:

$$\cos^2 \beta + \sin^2 \alpha \sin^2 \beta = 8/9$$
$$\cos^2 \alpha = 8/9$$
$$\sin^2 \beta + \sin^2 \alpha \cos^2 \beta = 2/9$$

A possible solution ($\alpha = 19.47$ and $\beta = -20.7$ degrees) gives the following projection matrix:

$$\begin{pmatrix} \sqrt{7/8} & 0 & -1/\sqrt{8} & 0 \\ -1/\sqrt{72} & \sqrt{8/9} & -\sqrt{7/72} & 0 \\ 0 & 0 & 0 & 0 \\ 0 & 0 & 0 & 1 \end{pmatrix}$$

Then, the three unit vectors e_1, e_2, and e_3 after this projection transformation become

$$e1 \rightarrow (\sqrt{7/8}, -1/\sqrt{72}) \approx (0.935, -0.118)$$
$$e2 \rightarrow (0, \sqrt{8/9}) \approx (0, 0.943)$$
$$e3 \rightarrow (-1/\sqrt{8}, -\sqrt{7/72}) \approx (-0.354, -0.312)$$

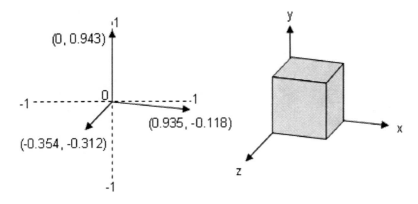

Figure 5-7 Dimetric projections of the unit vectors along the coordinate axes (left) and a cube object (right).

In this case, only lines drawn along the two equally foreshortened axes (i.e., the X and Y axes) are scaled by the same factor.

Figure 5-7 shows dimetric projections of three unit vectors along the coordinate axes and a cube object. When the normal of the view plane is set so that the view plane is parallel to a major axis, line measurements are maintained in the projection for lines that are parallel to the chosen axis.

Trimetric Projections:

In trimetric projections, the normal of the view plane makes different angles with each coordinate axis since no two components have the same value. As with a dimetric view, a trimetric view displays different orientations by placing differing amounts of emphasis on the faces. Trimetric projections have a potential disadvantage measuring lines along the axes is difficult because of the difference in scaling factors. For example, $|a1| = \sqrt{4/10}$, $|a2| = \sqrt{7/10}$, and $|a3| = \sqrt{9/10}$ is a possible trimetric projection because this selection satisfies Equation (5.12). We can then obtain the projection matrix with this trimetric projection (corresponding to $\alpha = 33.21$ and $\beta = -67.79$ degrees):

$$\begin{pmatrix} \sqrt{1/7} & 0 & -\sqrt{6/7} & 0 \\ -\sqrt{18/70} & \sqrt{7/10} & -\sqrt{3/70} & 0 \\ 0 & 0 & 0 & 0 \\ 0 & 0 & 0 & 1 \end{pmatrix}$$

Three unit vectors along the coordinate axes in the view plane can be obtained after this trimetric projection:

$$e1 \rightarrow (\sqrt{1/7}, -\sqrt{18/70}\,) \approx (0.378, -0.507)$$
$$e2 \rightarrow (0, \sqrt{8/9}) \approx (0, 0.837)$$
$$e3 \rightarrow (-\sqrt{6/7}, -\sqrt{3/70}) \approx (-0.926, -0.207)$$

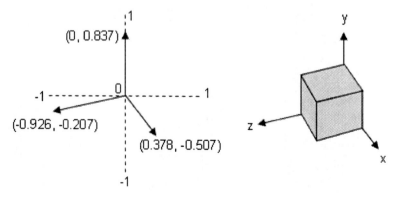

Figure 5-8 Trimetric projections of the unit vectors along the coordinate axes and a cube object.

Figure 5-8 shows trimetric projections of unit vectors of the coordinate axes and a cube object. You can see how the unequal-foreshortening characteristic of these projections affects line measurements along different axes. While disadvantageous in maintaining measurements, a trimetric projection, with the correct orientation, can offer a realistic and natural view of an object.

Orthographic Projections in C#

Using the projection matrices discussed in the last two subsections, we can write a C# program to visually demonstrate orthographic projections. Start with a new C# Windows Application project, *Example5_2*. Add classes, Matrix3 and Point3, from the previous project *Example5_1* to the current project and change their namespace to *Example5_2*. Add a new class, DrawHouse, to the project, which will draw a house object on the view plane. Add a public static method, Axonometric, to the Matrix3 class:

```
// Axonometric projection matrix:
public static Matrix3 Axonometric(float alpha, float beta)
{
    Matrix3 result = new Matrix3();

    float sna = (float)Math.Sin(alpha * Math.PI / 180);
    float cna = (float)Math.Cos(alpha * Math.PI / 180);
    float snb = (float)Math.Sin(beta * Math.PI / 180);
    float cnb = (float)Math.Cos(beta * Math.PI / 180);

    result.M[0, 0] = cnb;
    result.M[0, 2] = snb;
    result.M[1, 0] = sna * snb;
    result.M[1, 1] = cna;
    result.M[1, 2] = -sna * cnb;
    result.M[2, 2] = 0;

    return result;
}
```

This method creates a transformation matrix for an axonometric projection based on Equation (5.11).

The following is the code listing of the DrawHouse class:

```
using System;
using System.Drawing;

namespace Example5_2
{
    public class DrawHouse
    {
        private Form1 form1;
        private float a = 10;

        public DrawHouse(Form1 fm1)
        {
```

```
        form1 = fm1;
    }

    public DrawHouse(Form1 fm1, float a1)
    {
        form1 = fm1;
        a = a1;
    }

    public Point3[] HouseCoordinates()
    {
        Point3[] pts = new Point3[10];
        pts[0] = new Point3(0, 0, 0, 1);
        pts[1] = new Point3(a, 0, 0, 1);
        pts[2] = new Point3(a, a, 0, 1);
        pts[3] = new Point3(a / 2, 5 * a / 4, 0, 1);
        pts[4] = new Point3(0, a, 0, 1);
        pts[5] = new Point3(0, a, a, 1);
        pts[6] = new Point3(a / 2, 5 * a / 4, a, 1);
        pts[7] = new Point3(a, a, a, 1);
        pts[8] = new Point3(a, 0, a, 1);
        pts[9] = new Point3(0, 0, a, 1);
        return pts;
    }

    public void DrawFrontView(Graphics g)
    {
        // Project points to front view:
        Point3[] pts = HouseCoordinates();
        Matrix3 m = Matrix3.FrontView();

        for (int i = 0; i < pts.Length; i++)
        {
            pts[i].Transform(m);
        }

        PointF[] pta = new PointF[5];
        pta[0] = Point2D(new PointF(pts[5].X, pts[5].Y));
        pta[1] = Point2D(new PointF(pts[6].X, pts[6].Y));
        pta[2] = Point2D(new PointF(pts[7].X, pts[7].Y));
        pta[3] = Point2D(new PointF(pts[8].X, pts[8].Y));
        pta[4] = Point2D(new PointF(pts[9].X, pts[9].Y));

        g.FillPolygon(Brushes.LightGray, pta);
        g.DrawPolygon(Pens.Black, pta);
    }

    public void DrawSideView(Graphics g)
    {
        // Project points to front view:
        Point3[] pts = HouseCoordinates();
        Matrix3 m = Matrix3.SideView();

        for (int i = 0; i < pts.Length; i++)
```

```
    {
        pts[i].Transform(m);
    }

    PointF[] pta = new PointF[6];
    pta[0] = Point2D(new PointF(pts[1].X, pts[1].Y));
    pta[1] = Point2D(new PointF(pts[2].X, pts[2].Y));
    pta[2] = Point2D(new PointF(pts[3].X, pts[3].Y));
    pta[3] = Point2D(new PointF(pts[6].X, pts[6].Y));
    pta[4] = Point2D(new PointF(pts[7].X, pts[7].Y));
    pta[5] = Point2D(new PointF(pts[8].X, pts[8].Y));

    g.FillPolygon(Brushes.LightGray, pta);
    g.DrawPolygon(Pens.Black, pta);
    g.DrawLine(Pens.Black, pta[1], pta[4]);
}

public void DrawTopView(Graphics g)
{
    // Project points to front view:
    Point3[] pts = HouseCoordinates();
    Matrix3 m = Matrix3.TopView();

    for (int i = 0; i < pts.Length; i++)
    {
        pts[i].Transform(m);
    }

    PointF[] pta = new PointF[6];
    pta[0] = Point2D(new PointF(pts[2].X, pts[2].Y));
    pta[1] = Point2D(new PointF(pts[3].X, pts[3].Y));
    pta[2] = Point2D(new PointF(pts[4].X, pts[4].Y));
    pta[3] = Point2D(new PointF(pts[5].X, pts[5].Y));
    pta[4] = Point2D(new PointF(pts[6].X, pts[6].Y));
    pta[5] = Point2D(new PointF(pts[7].X, pts[7].Y));

    g.FillPolygon(Brushes.LightGray, pta);
    g.DrawPolygon(Pens.Black, pta);
    g.DrawLine(Pens.Black, pta[1], pta[4]);
}

public void DrawIsometricView(Graphics g)
{
    // Project points to front view:
    Point3[] pts = HouseCoordinates();
    Matrix3 m = Matrix3.Axonometric(35.26f,-45);

    for (int i = 0; i < pts.Length; i++)
    {
        pts[i].Transform(m);
    }

    PointF[] pta = new PointF[6];
    pta[0] = Point2D(new PointF(pts[2].X, pts[2].Y));
```

```
        pta[1] = Point2D(new PointF(pts[3].X, pts[3].Y));
        pta[2] = Point2D(new PointF(pts[4].X, pts[4].Y));
        pta[3] = Point2D(new PointF(pts[5].X, pts[5].Y));
        pta[4] = Point2D(new PointF(pts[6].X, pts[6].Y));
        pta[5] = Point2D(new PointF(pts[7].X, pts[7].Y));
        g.FillPolygon(Brushes.LightGray, pta);
        g.DrawPolygon(Pens.Black, pta);
        g.DrawLine(Pens.Black, pta[1], pta[4]);

        pta = new PointF[5];
        pta[0] = Point2D(new PointF(pts[5].X, pts[5].Y));
        pta[1] = Point2D(new PointF(pts[6].X, pts[6].Y));
        pta[2] = Point2D(new PointF(pts[7].X, pts[7].Y));
        pta[3] = Point2D(new PointF(pts[8].X, pts[8].Y));
        pta[4] = Point2D(new PointF(pts[9].X, pts[9].Y));
        g.FillPolygon(Brushes.LightGray, pta);
        g.DrawPolygon(Pens.Black, pta);

        pta = new PointF[4];
        pta[0] = Point2D(new PointF(pts[1].X, pts[1].Y));
        pta[1] = Point2D(new PointF(pts[2].X, pts[2].Y));
        pta[2] = Point2D(new PointF(pts[7].X, pts[7].Y));
        pta[3] = Point2D(new PointF(pts[8].X, pts[8].Y));
        g.FillPolygon(Brushes.LightGray, pta);
        g.DrawPolygon(Pens.Black, pta);
    }

    public void DrawDimetricView(Graphics g)
    {
        // Project points to front view:
        Point3[] pts = HouseCoordinates();
        Matrix3 m = Matrix3.Axonometric(19.47f, -20.7f);

        for (int i = 0; i < pts.Length; i++)
        {
            pts[i].Transform(m);
        }

        PointF[] pta = new PointF[6];
        pta[0] = Point2D(new PointF(pts[2].X, pts[2].Y));
        pta[1] = Point2D(new PointF(pts[3].X, pts[3].Y));
        pta[2] = Point2D(new PointF(pts[4].X, pts[4].Y));
        pta[3] = Point2D(new PointF(pts[5].X, pts[5].Y));
        pta[4] = Point2D(new PointF(pts[6].X, pts[6].Y));
        pta[5] = Point2D(new PointF(pts[7].X, pts[7].Y));
        g.FillPolygon(Brushes.LightGray, pta);
        g.DrawPolygon(Pens.Black, pta);
        g.DrawLine(Pens.Black, pta[1], pta[4]);

        pta = new PointF[5];
        pta[0] = Point2D(new PointF(pts[5].X, pts[5].Y));
        pta[1] = Point2D(new PointF(pts[6].X, pts[6].Y));
        pta[2] = Point2D(new PointF(pts[7].X, pts[7].Y));
        pta[3] = Point2D(new PointF(pts[8].X, pts[8].Y));
```

```
        pta[4] = Point2D(new PointF(pts[9].X, pts[9].Y));
        g.FillPolygon(Brushes.LightGray, pta);
        g.DrawPolygon(Pens.Black, pta);

        pta = new PointF[4];
        pta[0] = Point2D(new PointF(pts[1].X, pts[1].Y));
        pta[1] = Point2D(new PointF(pts[2].X, pts[2].Y));
        pta[2] = Point2D(new PointF(pts[7].X, pts[7].Y));
        pta[3] = Point2D(new PointF(pts[8].X, pts[8].Y));
        g.FillPolygon(Brushes.LightGray, pta);
        g.DrawPolygon(Pens.Black, pta);
}

public void DrawTrimetricView(Graphics g)
{
        // Project points to front view:
        Point3[] pts = HouseCoordinates();
        Matrix3 m = Matrix3.Axonometric(33.21f, -67.79f);

        for (int i = 0; i < pts.Length; i++)
        {
            pts[i].Transform(m);
        }

        PointF[] pta = new PointF[6];
        pta[0] = Point2D(new PointF(pts[2].X, pts[2].Y));
        pta[1] = Point2D(new PointF(pts[3].X, pts[3].Y));
        pta[2] = Point2D(new PointF(pts[4].X, pts[4].Y));
        pta[3] = Point2D(new PointF(pts[5].X, pts[5].Y));
        pta[4] = Point2D(new PointF(pts[6].X, pts[6].Y));
        pta[5] = Point2D(new PointF(pts[7].X, pts[7].Y));
        g.FillPolygon(Brushes.LightGray, pta);
        g.DrawPolygon(Pens.Black, pta);
        g.DrawLine(Pens.Black, pta[1], pta[4]);

        pta = new PointF[5];
        pta[0] = Point2D(new PointF(pts[5].X, pts[5].Y));
        pta[1] = Point2D(new PointF(pts[6].X, pts[6].Y));
        pta[2] = Point2D(new PointF(pts[7].X, pts[7].Y));
        pta[3] = Point2D(new PointF(pts[8].X, pts[8].Y));
        pta[4] = Point2D(new PointF(pts[9].X, pts[9].Y));
        g.FillPolygon(Brushes.LightGray, pta);
        g.DrawPolygon(Pens.Black, pta);

        pta = new PointF[4];
        pta[0] = Point2D(new PointF(pts[1].X, pts[1].Y));
        pta[1] = Point2D(new PointF(pts[2].X, pts[2].Y));
        pta[2] = Point2D(new PointF(pts[7].X, pts[7].Y));
        pta[3] = Point2D(new PointF(pts[8].X, pts[8].Y));
        g.FillPolygon(Brushes.LightGray, pta);
        g.DrawPolygon(Pens.Black, pta);
}

public void DrawAxonometricView(Graphics g,
```

```
                    float alpha, float beta)
    {
        // Project points to front view:
        Point3[] pts = HouseCoordinates();
        Matrix3 m = Matrix3.Axonometric(alpha, beta);

        for (int i = 0; i < pts.Length; i++)
        {
            pts[i].Transform(m);
        }

        PointF[] pta = new PointF[4];
        pta[0] = Point2D(new PointF(pts[3].X, pts[3].Y));
        pta[1] = Point2D(new PointF(pts[4].X, pts[4].Y));
        pta[2] = Point2D(new PointF(pts[5].X, pts[5].Y));
        pta[3] = Point2D(new PointF(pts[6].X, pts[6].Y));
        g.FillPolygon(Brushes.LightGray, pta);
        g.DrawPolygon(Pens.Black, pta);

        pta = new PointF[4];
        pta[0] = Point2D(new PointF(pts[2].X, pts[2].Y));
        pta[1] = Point2D(new PointF(pts[3].X, pts[3].Y));
        pta[2] = Point2D(new PointF(pts[6].X, pts[6].Y));
        pta[3] = Point2D(new PointF(pts[7].X, pts[7].Y));
        g.FillPolygon(Brushes.LightGray, pta);
        g.DrawPolygon(Pens.Black, pta);

        pta = new PointF[5];
        pta[0] = Point2D(new PointF(pts[5].X, pts[5].Y));
        pta[1] = Point2D(new PointF(pts[6].X, pts[6].Y));
        pta[2] = Point2D(new PointF(pts[7].X, pts[7].Y));
        pta[3] = Point2D(new PointF(pts[8].X, pts[8].Y));
        pta[4] = Point2D(new PointF(pts[9].X, pts[9].Y));
        g.FillPolygon(Brushes.LightGray, pta);
        g.DrawPolygon(Pens.Black, pta);

        pta = new PointF[4];
        pta[0] = Point2D(new PointF(pts[1].X, pts[1].Y));
        pta[1] = Point2D(new PointF(pts[2].X, pts[2].Y));
        pta[2] = Point2D(new PointF(pts[7].X, pts[7].Y));
        pta[3] = Point2D(new PointF(pts[8].X, pts[8].Y));
        g.FillPolygon(Brushes.LightGray, pta);
        g.DrawPolygon(Pens.Black, pta);
    }

    private PointF Point2D(PointF pt)
    {
        PointF aPoint = new PointF();
        aPoint.X = form1.panel1.Width / 2 + pt.X;
        aPoint.Y = form1.panel1.Height / 2 - pt.Y;
        return aPoint;
    }
  }
}
```

In this class, we first define two field members, one for the Form1 object and the other for the side length of the house object. The Form1 object defined in this class is necessary because we need to access the panel1 control of the Form1 class from the Point2D method. The side length field member and its corresponding property allow you to specify a specific side length for the house object.

Then, we create point coordinates for the house object. This house object contains a cube and a triangular top. You can set its size by specifying the side length of the cube. Next, we draw various projection views of the house object. Please note that all of the points are passed through a coordinate transformation using the Point2D method before drawing the house. The Point2D method moves the origin of the coordinate system to the center of panel1 and redefines the Y axis in a conventional manner (i.e., from bottom to top).

You might wonder why we use a different point array to draw the house object for each different projection view. The answer is that here, we use a try-and-error approach to draw polygon surfaces visible on your computer screen. You can also draw the 3D house object using advanced surface hidden algorithms, such as the Hi-Lo or Z-order technique that allows you to automatically select which surfaces of the house object will be displayed on top of your computer screen. We will use the Z-order method to draw 3D surface charts in the following chapter.

The following Form1 class can be used to test the application:

```
using System;
using System.Drawing;
using System.Windows.Forms;

namespace Example5_2
{
    public partial class Form1 : Form
    {
        public Form1()
        {
            InitializeComponent();
            this.SetStyle(ControlStyles.ResizeRedraw, true);
            this.BackColor = Color.White;

            // Subscribing to a paint eventhandler to drawingPanel:
            panel1.Paint +=
                new PaintEventHandler(panel1Paint);
        }

        private void panel1Paint(object sender, PaintEventArgs e)
        {
            Graphics g = e.Graphics;
            float a = panel1.Width / 3;
            DrawHouse dh = new DrawHouse(this, a);

            if (rbFront.Checked)
                dh.DrawFrontView(g);

            else if (rbSide.Checked)
                dh.DrawSideView(g);
```

```
            else if (rbTop.Checked)
                dh.DrawTopView(g);

            else if (rbIsometric.Checked)
                dh.DrawIsometricView(g);

            else if (rbDimetric.Checked)
                dh.DrawDimetricView(g);

            else if (rbTrimetric.Checked)
                dh.DrawTrimetricView(g);

            else if (rbAxonometric.Checked)
            {
                float alpha = Convert.ToSingle(tbAlpha.Text);
                if (alpha < 0)
                    alpha = -alpha;
                float beta = Convert.ToSingle(tbBeta.Text);
                if (beta > 0)
                    beta = -beta;
                dh.DrawAxonometricView(g, alpha, beta);
            }         }

        private void btnApply_Click(object sender, EventArgs e)
        {
            panel1.Invalidate();
        }
    }
}
```

In this class, we draw the house object on the `panel1` control using the `panel1Paint` method. Within the `panel1Paint` method, we define the side length of the house object in terms of the width of the `panel1` control so that the house object will be resized proportionally when `panel1` is resized. Then, we pass this side length parameter to the object of the `DrawHouse` class using the statement:

```
            DrawHouse dh = new DrawHouse(this, a);
```

Finally, we draw a variety of projection views of the house object on the screen by calling different drawing methods from the `DrawHouse` class.

This application creates the output of Figure 5-9. From this project, you can draw different projection views by selecting the corresponding radio buttons and clicking the `Apply` button. In particular, you can also examine general axonometric projections by specifying angles of α and β. You might note that only the surfaces of the house object that are visible get drawn on the screen, as expected.

It can be seen from this example that in order to draw a 3D object on a 2D computer screen (the view plane), you need first to perform a projection transformation on 3D points of the object. The X and Y components of projected points provide coordinates in the 2D view plane. After corresponding coordinate transformation from the world to device system, you draw the projected object on the 2D screen using this projected information.

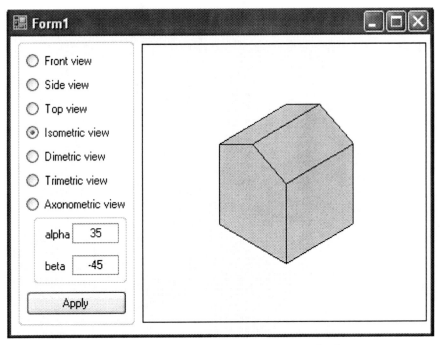

Figure 5-9 Demonstration of orthographic projections.

Oblique Projections

Oblique projections represent the second category of parallel projections. Oblique views are useful because they combine the advantageous qualities of both multi-view and axonometric projections. Like axonometric projections, this type of projection emphasizes the 3D features of an object. At the same time, like multi-view projections, oblique views display the exact shape of one face. Oblique view use parallel projectors, but the angle between projectors and the view plane is no longer orthogonal. Because of these properties, more than one face of the object is visible in an oblique projection. Figure 5-10 shows the difference between orthographic and oblique projections.

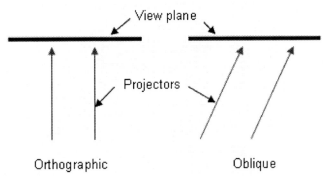

Figure 5-10 Orthographic and oblique projections.

Now let's try to construct a transformation matrix for an oblique projection. As shown in Figure 5-11, there are two angles that need to be considered: the one that the projector makes with the projection plane (α) and the one in the projection plane (θ).

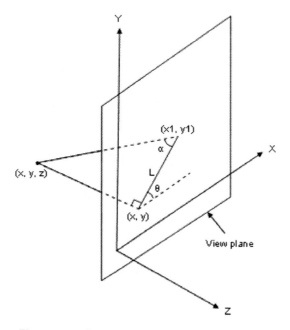

Figure 5-11 Oblique projection of a point (x, y, z).

The equations for the projected point are given below. The x and y components of the projected point are computed in relation to the angle in the projection plane (θ). The coefficient L, the length of the projected line, is computed from the angle (α) that the projector makes with the plane.

$$x_1 = x + L\cos\theta$$
$$y_1 = y + L\sin\theta$$
$$L = -z / \tan\alpha$$

The transformation matrix for oblique projections is given by the following:

$$\begin{pmatrix} 1 & 0 & -\cos\theta/\tan\alpha & 0 \\ 0 & 1 & -\sin\theta/\tan\alpha & 0 \\ 0 & 0 & 0 & 0 \\ 0 & 0 & 0 & 1 \end{pmatrix} \tag{5.13}$$

Notice that this transformation matrix represents an orthographic projection with L = 0. Oblique projections are further divided into either **cavalier** or **cabinet** projections.

Cavalier Projections

Cavalier projections are a very useful type of oblique projection. In this case, the projectors meet the view plane at a 45-degree angle (i.e. α = 45 degrees). With this type of projection, a line perpendicular to the view plane is transformed into a line that has a same length as the original line. This means that you can measure lengths using the same scale along all three coordinate axes. In this projection, the angle θ is typically set to 30 or 45 degrees.

Cabinet Projections

On the other hand, when α = 63.4 degrees, the projection is called a cabinet projection. When projected at this angle, lines that are perpendicular to the view plane are displayed as one-half of their actual length. Because of the reduction of length for lines perpendicular to the view plane, cabinet projections appear more realistic than cavalier projections.

Oblique Projections in C#

Using the transformation matrix given previously, we can write a C# application program to visually demonstrate oblique projections. Start with a new C# Windows Application project and name it *Example5_3*. Add the Matrix3, Point3, and DrawHouse classes from the previous project *Example5_2* to the current project, and change their namespace to *Example5_3*.

Add a public static method, Oblique, to the Matrix3 class:

```
// Oblique projection matrix:
public static Matrix3 Oblique(float alpha, float theta)
{
    Matrix3 result = new Matrix3();

    float ta = (float)Math.Tan(alpha * Math.PI / 180);
    float snt = (float)Math.Sin(theta * Math.PI / 180);
    float cnt = (float)Math.Cos(theta * Math.PI / 180);
    result.M[0, 2] = -cnt / ta;
    result.M[1, 2] = -snt / ta;
    result.M[2, 2] = 0;
    return result;
}
```

The static method Oblique represents a general oblique projection transformation with arbitrary angles of α and β. You can derive either a cavalier or a cabinet projection from this matrix by specifying proper angles of α and β.

Then, add following methods to the DrawHouse class:

```
public void DrawCavalierView(Graphics g, float theta)
{
    // Project points to front view:
    Point3[] pts = HouseCoordinates();
    Matrix3 m = Matrix3.Oblique(45, theta);

    for (int i = 0; i < pts.Length; i++)
    {
```

```
                pts[i].Transform(m);
        }

        PointF[] pta = new PointF[4];
        pta[0] = Point2D(new PointF(pts[3].X, pts[3].Y));
        pta[1] = Point2D(new PointF(pts[4].X, pts[4].Y));
        pta[2] = Point2D(new PointF(pts[5].X, pts[5].Y));
        pta[3] = Point2D(new PointF(pts[6].X, pts[6].Y));
        g.FillPolygon(Brushes.LightGray, pta);
        g.DrawPolygon(Pens.Black, pta);

        pta = new PointF[4];
        pta[0] = Point2D(new PointF(pts[2].X, pts[2].Y));
        pta[1] = Point2D(new PointF(pts[3].X, pts[3].Y));
        pta[2] = Point2D(new PointF(pts[6].X, pts[6].Y));
        pta[3] = Point2D(new PointF(pts[7].X, pts[7].Y));
        g.FillPolygon(Brushes.LightGray, pta);
        g.DrawPolygon(Pens.Black, pta);

        pta = new PointF[5];
        pta[0] = Point2D(new PointF(pts[5].X, pts[5].Y));
        pta[1] = Point2D(new PointF(pts[6].X, pts[6].Y));
        pta[2] = Point2D(new PointF(pts[7].X, pts[7].Y));
        pta[3] = Point2D(new PointF(pts[8].X, pts[8].Y));
        pta[4] = Point2D(new PointF(pts[9].X, pts[9].Y));
        g.FillPolygon(Brushes.LightGray, pta);
        g.DrawPolygon(Pens.Black, pta);

        pta = new PointF[4];
        pta[0] = Point2D(new PointF(pts[1].X, pts[1].Y));
        pta[1] = Point2D(new PointF(pts[2].X, pts[2].Y));
        pta[2] = Point2D(new PointF(pts[7].X, pts[7].Y));
        pta[3] = Point2D(new PointF(pts[8].X, pts[8].Y));
        g.FillPolygon(Brushes.LightGray, pta);
        g.DrawPolygon(Pens.Black, pta);
    }

    public void DrawCabinetView(Graphics g, float theta)
    {
        // Project points to front view:
        Point3[] pts = HouseCoordinates();
        Matrix3 m = Matrix3.Oblique(63.4f, theta);

        for (int i = 0; i < pts.Length; i++)
        {
            pts[i].Transform(m);
        }

        PointF[] pta = new PointF[4];
        pta[0] = Point2D(new PointF(pts[3].X, pts[3].Y));
        pta[1] = Point2D(new PointF(pts[4].X, pts[4].Y));
        pta[2] = Point2D(new PointF(pts[5].X, pts[5].Y));
        pta[3] = Point2D(new PointF(pts[6].X, pts[6].Y));
        g.FillPolygon(Brushes.LightGray, pta);
```

```
            g.DrawPolygon(Pens.Black, pta);

            pta = new PointF[4];
            pta[0] = Point2D(new PointF(pts[2].X, pts[2].Y));
            pta[1] = Point2D(new PointF(pts[3].X, pts[3].Y));
            pta[2] = Point2D(new PointF(pts[6].X, pts[6].Y));
            pta[3] = Point2D(new PointF(pts[7].X, pts[7].Y));
            g.FillPolygon(Brushes.LightGray, pta);
            g.DrawPolygon(Pens.Black, pta);

            pta = new PointF[5];
            pta[0] = Point2D(new PointF(pts[5].X, pts[5].Y));
            pta[1] = Point2D(new PointF(pts[6].X, pts[6].Y));
            pta[2] = Point2D(new PointF(pts[7].X, pts[7].Y));
            pta[3] = Point2D(new PointF(pts[8].X, pts[8].Y));
            pta[4] = Point2D(new PointF(pts[9].X, pts[9].Y));
            g.FillPolygon(Brushes.LightGray, pta);
            g.DrawPolygon(Pens.Black, pta);

            pta = new PointF[4];
            pta[0] = Point2D(new PointF(pts[1].X, pts[1].Y));
            pta[1] = Point2D(new PointF(pts[2].X, pts[2].Y));
            pta[2] = Point2D(new PointF(pts[7].X, pts[7].Y));
            pta[3] = Point2D(new PointF(pts[8].X, pts[8].Y));
            g.FillPolygon(Brushes.LightGray, pta);
            g.DrawPolygon(Pens.Black, pta);
        }

        public void DrawObliqueView(Graphics g,
                float alpha, float theta)
        {
            // Project points to front view:
            Point3[] pts = HouseCoordinates();
            Matrix3 m = Matrix3.Oblique(alpha, theta);

            for (int i = 0; i < pts.Length; i++)
            {
                pts[i].Transform(m);
            }

            PointF[] pta = new PointF[4];
            pta[0] = Point2D(new PointF(pts[3].X, pts[3].Y));
            pta[1] = Point2D(new PointF(pts[4].X, pts[4].Y));
            pta[2] = Point2D(new PointF(pts[5].X, pts[5].Y));
            pta[3] = Point2D(new PointF(pts[6].X, pts[6].Y));
            g.FillPolygon(Brushes.LightGray, pta);
            g.DrawPolygon(Pens.Black, pta);

            pta = new PointF[4];
            pta[0] = Point2D(new PointF(pts[2].X, pts[2].Y));
            pta[1] = Point2D(new PointF(pts[3].X, pts[3].Y));
            pta[2] = Point2D(new PointF(pts[6].X, pts[6].Y));
            pta[3] = Point2D(new PointF(pts[7].X, pts[7].Y));
            g.FillPolygon(Brushes.LightGray, pta);
```

```
            g.DrawPolygon(Pens.Black, pta);

            pta = new PointF[5];
            pta[0] = Point2D(new PointF(pts[5].X, pts[5].Y));
            pta[1] = Point2D(new PointF(pts[6].X, pts[6].Y));
            pta[2] = Point2D(new PointF(pts[7].X, pts[7].Y));
            pta[3] = Point2D(new PointF(pts[8].X, pts[8].Y));
            pta[4] = Point2D(new PointF(pts[9].X, pts[9].Y));
            g.FillPolygon(Brushes.LightGray, pta);
            g.DrawPolygon(Pens.Black, pta);

            pta = new PointF[4];
            pta[0] = Point2D(new PointF(pts[1].X, pts[1].Y));
            pta[1] = Point2D(new PointF(pts[2].X, pts[2].Y));
            pta[2] = Point2D(new PointF(pts[7].X, pts[7].Y));
            pta[3] = Point2D(new PointF(pts[8].X, pts[8].Y));
            g.FillPolygon(Brushes.LightGray, pta);
            g.DrawPolygon(Pens.Black, pta);
        }
```

These three methods are similar to those in the previous project, *Example5_2*. We use these methods to draw various oblique projection views of the house object, including cavalier, cabinet, and general oblique views. We first perform a projection transformation on a point array that describes the house object by calling the static method `Oblique` from `Matrix3` class. Then, these points are passed through a coordinate transformation using the `Point2D` method before drawing the house. The `Point2D` method moves the origin of the coordinate system to the center of `panel1` and redefines the Y axis in a conventional manner (i.e., from bottom to top).

Finally, the following `Form1` class is implemented, which can be used to test the project:

```
using System;
using System.Drawing;
using System.Windows.Forms;

namespace Example5_3
{
    public partial class Form1 : Form
    {
        public Form1()
        {
            InitializeComponent();
            this.SetStyle(ControlStyles.ResizeRedraw, true);

            // Subscribing to a paint eventhandler to drawingPanel:
            panel1.Paint +=
                new PaintEventHandler(panel1Paint);
        }

        private void panel1Paint(object sender, PaintEventArgs e)
        {
            Graphics g = e.Graphics;
            float a = panel1.Width / 3;
            DrawHouse dh = new DrawHouse(this, a);
            float theta = Convert.ToSingle(tbTheta.Text);
```

```
            if (rbCavalier.Checked)
            {
                dh.DrawCavalierView(g, theta);
            }

            else if (rbCabinet.Checked)
            {
                dh.DrawCabinetView(g, theta);
            }

            else if (rbOblique.Checked)
            {
                float alpha = Convert.ToSingle(tbAlpha.Text);
                dh.DrawObliqueView(g, alpha, theta);
            }
        }

        private void btnApply_Click(object sender, EventArgs e)
        {
            panel1.Invalidate();
        }

        private void rbCavalier_CheckedChanged(object sender,
                EventArgs e)
        {
            tbAlpha.Enabled = false;
        }

        private void rbCabinet_CheckedChanged(object sender,
                EventArgs e)
        {
            tbAlpha.Enabled = false;
        }

        private void rbOblique_CheckedChanged(object sender,
                EventArgs e)
        {
            tbAlpha.Enabled = true;
        }
    }
}
```

This generates the output shown in Figure 5-12. You can examine Cavalier, Cabinet, and general Oblique projections by clicking their corresponding radio buttons and entering proper angle values into the text boxes. Please note that the textbox for the angle α is disabled when you are clicking on the Cavalier or Cabinet radio button, because the angle α is fixed in these two cases ($\alpha = 45$ degrees for a Cavalier view and 63.4 degrees for a Cabinet view). However, you can still change the angle β for both cases. When you select the general Oblique view, the textbox for the angle α is enabled so you can specify both α and β angles in this case.

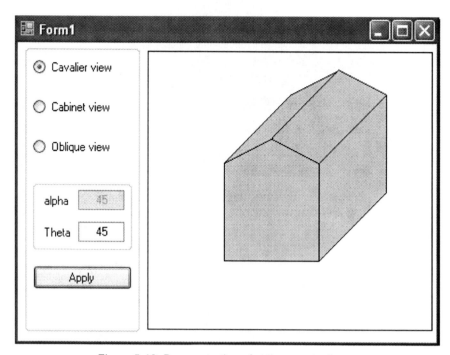

Figure 5-12 Demonstration of oblique projections.

Perspective Projections

In a perspective projection, objects of equal size at different distances from the view plane will be projected at different sizes, nearer objects will appear closer. The projectors pass from a center of projection through each point in the object to the view plane.

Figure 5-13 shows perspective projections of two square objects. The square that is further from the center of projection is projected into a smaller image on the view plane. In comparison to parallel projections, perspective projections often provide a more natural and realistic view of a 3D object. By comparing the view plane of a perspective projection with the view seen from lens of a camera, the underlying principle of perspective projection can easily be understood. Like the view from a camera, lines in a perspective projection not parallel to the view plane converge at a distant point (called a vanishing point) in the background. When the eye or camera is positioned is close to the object, perspective foreshortening occurs, with distant objects appearing smaller in the view plane than closer objects of the same size, as shown in Figure 5-13.

Perspective projections can be classified by the number of vanishing points they contain. There are three types of perspective projections: one-point, two-point, and three-point projections. Each type differs in the orientation of the view plane and the number of vanishing points.

One-Point Perspective Projections

In one-point perspective, lines of a 3D object along a coordinate axis converge at a single vanishing point while lines parallel to the other axes remain horizontal or vertical in the view plane. To create a one-point perspective view, the view plane is set parallel to one of the principal planes in the world coordinate system. Figure 5-14 shows a one-point perspective view of a cube. In this projection, the view plane is positioned in front of the cube and parallel to the X-Y plane.

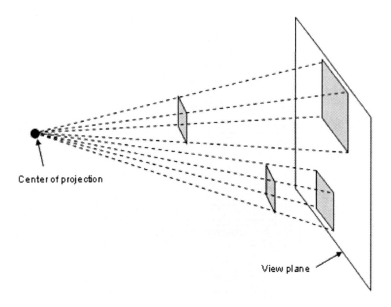

Figure 5-13 Perspective projections: objects farther from the center of projection appear smaller than closer objects.

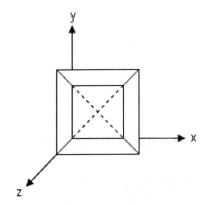

Figure 5-14 One-point perspective projection.

Two-Point Perspective Projections

Two-point perspective projects an object to the view plane so that lines parallel to two of the major axes converge at two separate vanishing points. To create a two-point perspective, the view plane is set parallel to a coordinate axis rather than a plane. to satisfy this condition, the normal of the view plane should be set perpendicular to one of the major world coordinate system axes.

Figure 5-15 shows a two-point perspective view of a cube. In this figure, lines parallel to the x-axis converge to a vanishing point while lines parallel to the z-axis converge at another vanishing point. Two-point perspective views often provide additional realism in comparison to other projection types; for this reason, they are commonly used in architectural, engineering, and industrial designs.

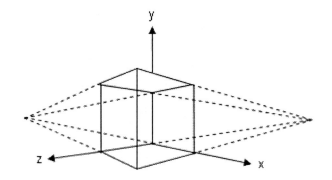

Figure 5-15 Two-point perspective projection.

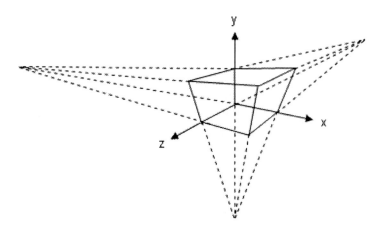

Figure 5-16 Three-point perspective projection.

Three-Point Perspective Projections

 A three-point perspective projection has three vanishing points. In this case, the view plane is not parallel to any of the major axes. To position the view plane, each component of the view plane's normal is set to a non-zero value so that the view plane intersects three major axes. Vanishing points are often used by artists for highlighting features or increasing dramatic effects. Figure 5-16 shows a three-point perspective projection of a cube.

Perspective Projection Matrix

Constructing a general perspective projection matrix is quite complicated. Here, we only discuss a simple case of perspective projection. This simple perspective view projects onto the X-Y plane when the center of projection lies on the Z axis. Figure 5-17 shows a point P = (x, y, z) being projected onto the point P1 = (x1, y1, z1) in the X-Y plane. The center of projection is located at (0, 0, d), where d is the distance along the Z axis. On the right of Figure 5-17 is a side view of the projection showing the Y and Z axes. The point A is the center of projection, and the point B is the point on the Z axis with the same Z coordinates as the point P.

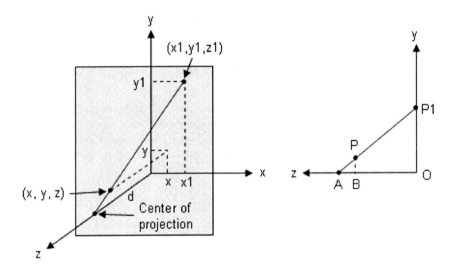

Figure 5-17 Perspective projection of a point P = (x, y, z).

From this figure, we note that AO = d, OP1 = y1, BP = y, and AB = d-z. Solving for y1, we get y1 = d*y/(d-z). This gives to the Y coordinate of the projected point P1. By examining a similar top view that shows the X and Z axes, we can find that x1 = d*x/(d-z). For the projected point on the X-Y plane, z1 should equal 0. From this information, we can construct a transformation matrix for this perspective projection:

$$
\begin{pmatrix} x1 \\ y1 \\ z1 \\ w1 \end{pmatrix} = \begin{pmatrix} 1 & 0 & 0 & 0 \\ 0 & 1 & 0 & 0 \\ 0 & 0 & 0 & 0 \\ 0 & 0 & -1/d & 1 \end{pmatrix} \begin{pmatrix} x \\ y \\ z \\ 1 \end{pmatrix} = \begin{pmatrix} x \\ y \\ 0 \\ 1-z/d \end{pmatrix} \tag{5.14}
$$

Remember that the w-component of a point in the homogeneous coordinates represents a scaling factor. Normalizing the projected point P1 by w1, we have

$$\begin{pmatrix} x1/w1 \\ y1/w1 \\ z1/w1 \\ 1 \end{pmatrix} = \begin{pmatrix} x/(1-z/d) \\ y/(1-z/d) \\ 0 \\ 1 \end{pmatrix}$$

This agrees with the information deduced from Figure 5-17.

Perspective Projection in C#

Using the transformation matrix for perspective projections created in the previous section, you can write a C# application project to test perspective transformations. Start with a new C# Windows Application project and name it *Example5_4*. Add the Matrix3, Point3, and DrawHouse classes from the previous project, *Example5_3*, to this project and change their namespace to *Example5_4*.

Usually, when you apply a perspective transformation to a point, you destroy its Z component information. In this case, you cannot compare the point's Z coordinate to see if it lies behind or in front of the center of projection. In order to preserve the Z coordinate information, you need to modify the perspective transformation matrix from Equation (5.14) to the following:

$$\begin{pmatrix} 1 & 0 & 0 & 0 \\ 0 & 1 & 0 & 0 \\ 0 & 0 & 1 & 0 \\ 0 & 0 & -1/d & 1 \end{pmatrix} \tag{5.15}$$

Here, we change the third row from (0, 0, 0, 0) to (0, 0, 1, 0) so that the Z component is not lost. Using (5.15), we add the perspective matrix to the Matrix3 class:

```
// Perspective projection matrix:
public static Matrix3 Perspective(float d)
{
    Matrix3 result = new Matrix3();
    result.M[3, 2] = -1 / d;
    return result;
}
```

When you multiply a point with this modified perspective matrix, you need to normalize the X, Y, and Z components by the W component. This step would mess up the Z coordinate information. To preserve the Z-component information, we normalize only the X and Y components of the point. So, add a new method TransformNormalize to the Point3 class:

```
public void TransformNormalize(Matrix3 m)
{
    float[] result = m.VectorMultiply(new float[4] { X, Y, Z, W });
    X = result[0] / result[3];
    Y = result[1] / result[3];
    Z = result[2];
    W = 1;
}
```

This method is specifically applied to perspective projections. Here the X and Y components of a point after a perspective projection are normalized by its W component; while the Z component is unchanged.

Add a public method `DrawPerspectiveView` to the `DrawHouse` class:

```
public void DrawPerspectiveView(Graphics g, float d)
{
    Point3[] pts = HouseCoordinates();

    // Translate the center of the house to the origin:
    Matrix3 m = Matrix3.Translate3(-pts[1].X / 2,
        -pts[1].X / 2, pts[1].X / 2);

    for (int i = 0; i < pts.Length; i++)
    {
        pts[i].Transform(m);
    }

    // Perform perspective transformation:
    m = Matrix3.Perspective(d);
    for (int i = 0; i < pts.Length; i++)
    {
        pts[i].TransformNormalize(m);
    }

    PointF[] pta = new PointF[5];
    pta[0] = Point2D(new PointF(pts[5].X, pts[5].Y));
    pta[1] = Point2D(new PointF(pts[6].X, pts[6].Y));
    pta[2] = Point2D(new PointF(pts[7].X, pts[7].Y));
    pta[3] = Point2D(new PointF(pts[8].X, pts[8].Y));
    pta[4] = Point2D(new PointF(pts[9].X, pts[9].Y));
    g.FillPolygon(Brushes.LightGray, pta);
    g.DrawPolygon(Pens.Black, pta);

    pta = new PointF[4];
    pta[0] = Point2D(new PointF(pts[0].X, pts[0].Y));
    pta[1] = Point2D(new PointF(pts[4].X, pts[4].Y));
    pta[2] = Point2D(new PointF(pts[5].X, pts[5].Y));
    pta[3] = Point2D(new PointF(pts[9].X, pts[9].Y));
    g.FillPolygon(Brushes.LightGray, pta);
    g.DrawPolygon(Pens.Black, pta);

    pta = new PointF[4];
    pta[0] = Point2D(new PointF(pts[0].X, pts[0].Y));
    pta[1] = Point2D(new PointF(pts[1].X, pts[1].Y));
    pta[2] = Point2D(new PointF(pts[8].X, pts[8].Y));
    pta[3] = Point2D(new PointF(pts[9].X, pts[9].Y));
    g.FillPolygon(Brushes.LightGray, pta);
    g.DrawPolygon(Pens.Black, pta);

    pta = new PointF[4];
    pta[0] = Point2D(new PointF(pts[1].X, pts[1].Y));
    pta[1] = Point2D(new PointF(pts[2].X, pts[2].Y));
```

```
            pta[2] = Point2D(new PointF(pts[7].X, pts[7].Y));
            pta[3] = Point2D(new PointF(pts[8].X, pts[8].Y));
            g.FillPolygon(Brushes.LightGray, pta);
            g.DrawPolygon(Pens.Black, pta);

            pta = new PointF[4];
            pta[0] = Point2D(new PointF(pts[2].X, pts[2].Y));
            pta[1] = Point2D(new PointF(pts[3].X, pts[3].Y));
            pta[2] = Point2D(new PointF(pts[6].X, pts[6].Y));
            pta[3] = Point2D(new PointF(pts[7].X, pts[7].Y));
            g.FillPolygon(Brushes.LightGray, pta);
            g.DrawPolygon(Pens.Black, pta);

            pta = new PointF[4];
            pta[0] = Point2D(new PointF(pts[3].X, pts[3].Y));
            pta[1] = Point2D(new PointF(pts[4].X, pts[4].Y));
            pta[2] = Point2D(new PointF(pts[5].X, pts[5].Y));
            pta[3] = Point2D(new PointF(pts[6].X, pts[6].Y));
            g.FillPolygon(Brushes.LightGray, pta);
            g.DrawPolygon(Pens.Black, pta);

            pta = new PointF[5];
            pta[0] = Point2D(new PointF(pts[0].X, pts[0].Y));
            pta[1] = Point2D(new PointF(pts[1].X, pts[1].Y));
            pta[2] = Point2D(new PointF(pts[2].X, pts[2].Y));
            pta[3] = Point2D(new PointF(pts[3].X, pts[3].Y));
            pta[4] = Point2D(new PointF(pts[4].X, pts[4].Y));
            g.FillPolygon(Brushes.LightGray, pta);
            g.DrawPolygon(Pens.Black, pta);
        }
```

In this method, we first translate the center of the house project to the origin of the world coordinate system to get a better perspective view. Then, we make a perspective transformation by calling the `Point3.TransformNormalize` method using the modified perspective transformation matrix.

You can use the following `Form1` class to test the application:

```
using System;
using System.Drawing;
using System.Windows.Forms;

namespace Example5_4
{
    public partial class Form1 : Form
    {
        public Form1()
        {
            InitializeComponent();
            this.SetStyle(ControlStyles.ResizeRedraw, true);
            this.BackColor = Color.White;

            // Subscribing to a paint eventhandler to drawingPanel:
            panel1.Paint +=
                new PaintEventHandler(panel1Paint);
```

```
        }

        private void panel1Paint(object sender, PaintEventArgs e)
        {
            Graphics g = e.Graphics;
             float a = panel1.Height / 4;
            DrawHouse dh = new DrawHouse(this, a);
            float d = Convert.ToSingle(tbDistance.Text);
            dh.DrawPerspectiveView(g, d * a);
        }

        private void btnApply_Click(object sender, EventArgs e)
        {
            panel1.Invalidate();
        }
    }
}
```

This produces the result shown in Figure 5-18. Here, you can specify the distance d (in units of a, the side length of the house object) between the center of projection and the view plane. In Figure 5-18, the perspective view of the house is obtained by setting d = 3a. If this distance d is set to a very large value, such as d = 500a, you should expect the perspective view to become a side view because the projectors become almost parallel. This is confirmed in Figure 5-19.

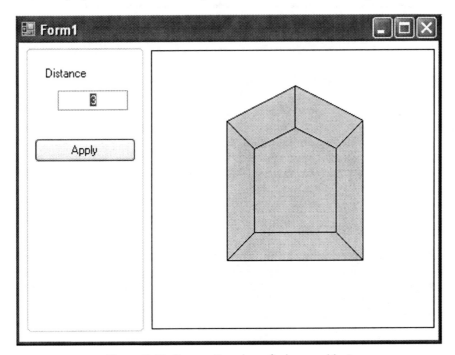

Figure 5-18 Perspective view of a house object.

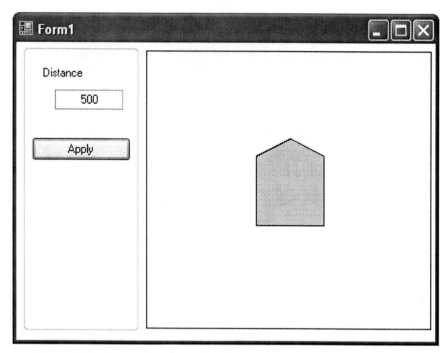

Figure 5-19 Perspective view of the house object at a very large distance
(d = 500a) between the center of projection and the view plane.

Special Coordinate Systems in 3D

Normally, the Cartesian coordinate system is used in transformations and projections. In this case, you simply specify a point using X, Y, and Z coordinates. In practice, other coordinate systems can also be applied, and are sometimes more convenient than the Cartesian coordinate system. In this section, we will discuss some special coordinate systems in 3D space, including the cylindrical, spherical, and Euler angles coordinate systems, as well as the azimuth and elevation view.

Cylindrical Coordinates

In the cylindrical coordinate system, a point is specified by three parameters, r, θ, and y, which are a bit different from the conventional definition of the system using r, θ, and z. The notation we use here is only for convenience because the computer screen can always be described using the X-Y plane. r is the distance of a projected point on the X-Z plane from the origin, and θ is the azimuthal angle. Figure 5-20 shows a point in the cylindrical coordinate system. From this figure we have:

$$x = r \cos \theta$$
$$z = -r \sin \theta$$
$$y = y$$

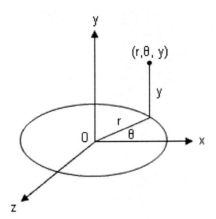

Figure 5-20 Cylindrical coordinate system.

You can also find reverse relations:

$$r = \sqrt{x^2 + z^2}$$
$$\theta = \tan^{-1}(-z/x)$$
$$y = y$$

Using the cylindrical coordinate system, you can easily create cylindrical objects. The following example C# project creates a cylinder object using parallel isometric projection. Start with a new C# project, *Example5_5*. Add the `Matrix3` and `Point3` classes from the previous project *Example5_4* to this project, and change their namespace to *Example5_5*. Add a new, class `DrawCylinder`, to the project. Add the following method to the `Matrix3` class:

```
public Point3 Cylindrical(float r, float theta, float y)
{
    Point3 pt = new Point3();

    float sn = (float)Math.Sin(theta * Math.PI / 180);
    float cn = (float)Math.Cos(theta * Math.PI / 180);

    pt.X = r * cn;
    pt.Y = y;
    pt.Z = -r * sn;
    pt.W = 1;
    return pt;
}
```

This method transforms a point in the cylindrical coordinate system to a point in the Cartesian coordinates system.

The following is the code listing of the `DrawCylinder` class:

```
using System;
using System.Drawing;

namespace Example5_5
```

```csharp
{
    public class DrawCylinder
    {
        private Form1 form1;
        private float r = 10;
        private float h = 10;

        public DrawCylinder(Form1 fm1)
        {
            form1 = fm1;
        }

        public DrawCylinder(Form1 fm1, float r1, float h1)
        {
            form1 = fm1;
            r = r1;
            h = h1;
        }

        public Point3[] CircleCoordinates(float y)
        {
            Point3[] pts = new Point3[30];
            Matrix3 m = new Matrix3();

            for (int i = 0; i < pts.Length; i++)
            {
                pts[i] = m.Cylindrical(r, i*360/(pts.Length-1), y);
            }
            return pts;
        }


        public void DrawIsometricView(Graphics g)
        {
            Point3[] ptsBottom = CircleCoordinates(-h / 2);
            PointF[] ptaBottom = new PointF[ptsBottom.Length];
            Point3[] ptsTop = CircleCoordinates(h / 2);
            PointF[] ptaTop = new PointF[ptsTop.Length];
            Matrix3 m = Matrix3.Axonometric(35.26f, -45);

            for (int i = 0; i < ptsBottom.Length; i++)
            {
                ptsBottom[i].Transform(m);
                ptaBottom[i] = Point2D(new PointF(ptsBottom[i].X,
                        ptsBottom[i].Y));
                ptsTop[i].Transform(m);
                ptaTop[i] = Point2D(new PointF(ptsTop[i].X,
                        ptsTop[i].Y));
            }

            PointF[] ptf = new PointF[4];
            for (int i = 1; i < ptsTop.Length; i++)
            {
                ptf[0] = ptaBottom[i - 1];
```

```
                    ptf[1] = ptaTop[i - 1];
                    ptf[2] = ptaTop[i];
                    ptf[3] = ptaBottom[i];
                    if (i < 5 || i > ptsTop.Length - 12)
                    {
                        g.FillPolygon(Brushes.White, ptf);
                        g.DrawPolygon(Pens.Black, ptf);
                    }
                }

                g.FillPolygon(Brushes.White, ptaTop);
                g.DrawPolygon(Pens.Black, ptaTop);
            }

            private PointF Point2D(PointF pt)
            {
                PointF aPoint = new PointF();
                aPoint.X = form1.panel1.Width / 2 + pt.X;
                aPoint.Y = form1.panel1.Height / 2 - pt.Y;
                return aPoint;
            }
        }
    }
```

In this class, we first create a circle by specifying its points in the cylindrical coordinates, and then convert these points to Cartesian coordinates by calling the `Matrix3.Cylindrical` method. Finally, we draw the cylinder object using isometric projection. This project can be tested using the following `Form1` class:

```
using System;
using System.Drawing;
using System.Windows.Forms;

namespace Example5_5
{
    public partial class Form1 : Form
    {
        public Form1()
        {
            InitializeComponent();
            this.SetStyle(ControlStyles.ResizeRedraw, true);
            this.BackColor = Color.White;

            // Subscribing to a paint eventhandler to drawingPanel:
            panel1.Paint +=
                new PaintEventHandler(panel1Paint);
        }

        private void panel1Paint(object sender, PaintEventArgs e)
        {
            Graphics g = e.Graphics;
            float a = panel1.Height / 4;
            DrawCylinder dc = new DrawCylinder(this, a, 2 * a);
            dc.DrawIsometricView(g);
```

```
            }
        }
    }
```

Here we draw the cylinder by calling the `DrawIsometricView` method from the `DrawCylinder` class with input parameters of radius and height for the cylinder. This application produces the output of Figure 5-21.

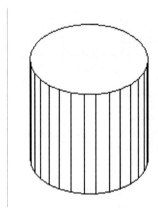

Figure 5-21 A cylinder object created using cylindrical coordinates.

Spherical Coordinates

In the spherical coordinate system, a point is specified by r, θ, and φ. Here r is the distance from the point to the origin, θ is the polar angle, and φ is the azimuthal angle in the X-Z plane from the X axis. In this notation, we also alternate the conventional Y and Z axes so that the computer screen is described by the X-Y plane. Figure 5-22 shows a point in this spherical coordinate system.

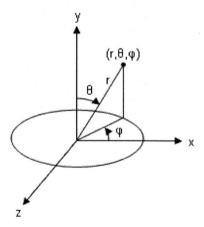

Figure 5-22 Spherical coordinate system.

From this figure, we can obtain the following relationships:

$$x = r \sin \theta \cos \varphi$$
$$y = r \cos \theta$$
$$z = -r \sin \theta \sin \varphi$$

The spherical coordinates (r, θ, φ) are related to the Cartesian coordinates by:

$$r = \sqrt{x^2 + y^2 + z^2}$$
$$\theta = \cos^{-1}\left(y / \sqrt{x^2 + y^2 + z^2}\right)$$
$$\varphi = \tan^{-1}(-z / x)$$

Sometimes it is more convenient to create sphere-like objects in terms of the spherical coordinate system. The following example application program will create two spheres. Start with a new C# Windows Application project, *Example5_6*. Add the Matrix3 and Point3 classes of the previous project to the current one, and change their namespace to *Example5_6*. Add a new class, DrawSphere, to the project.

Now we need to add a Spherical method to the Matrix3 class:

```
public Point3 Spherical(float r, float theta, float phi)
{
    Point3 pt = new Point3();

    float snt = (float)Math.Sin(theta * Math.PI / 180);
    float cnt = (float)Math.Cos(theta * Math.PI / 180);
    float snp = (float)Math.Sin(phi * Math.PI / 180);
    float cnp = (float)Math.Cos(phi * Math.PI / 180);

    pt.X = r * snt * cnp;
    pt.Y = r * cnt;
    pt.Z = -r * snt * snp;
    pt.W = 1;
    return pt;
}
```

This method transforms a point in the spherical coordinate system to a point in the Cartesian coordinates system.

The following is the code listing of the DrawSphere class:

```
using System;
using System.Drawing;

namespace Example5_6
{
    public class DrawSphere
    {
        private Form1 form1;
        private float r = 10;
        private float xc = 0;
```

```csharp
private float yc = 0;
private float zc = 0;

public DrawSphere(Form1 fm1)
{
    form1 = fm1;
}

public DrawSphere(Form1 fm1, float r1, float xc1,
    float yc1, float zc1)
{
    form1 = fm1;
    r = r1;
    xc = xc1;
    yc = yc1;
    zc = zc1;
}

public Point3[,] SphereCoordinates()
{
    Point3[,] pts = new Point3[30, 20];
    Matrix3 m = new Matrix3();
    Matrix3 mt = Matrix3.Translate3(xc, yc, zc);

    for (int i = 0; i < pts.GetLength(0); i++)
    {
        for (int j = 0; j < pts.GetLength(1); j++)
        {
            pts[i, j] = m.Spherical(r,
                i * 180 / (pts.GetLength(0) - 1),
                j * 360 / (pts.GetLength(1) - 1));
            pts[i, j].Transform(mt);
        }
    }
    return pts;
}

public void DrawIsometricView(Graphics g)
{
    Matrix3 m = Matrix3.Axonometric(35.26f, -45);
    Point3[,] pts = SphereCoordinates();
    PointF[,] pta = new PointF[pts.GetLength(0),
            pts.GetLength(1)];

    for (int i = 0; i < pts.GetLength(0); i++)
    {
        for (int j = 0; j < pts.GetLength(1); j++)
        {
            pts[i, j].Transform(m);
            pta[i, j] = Point2D(new PointF(pts[i, j].X,
                        pts[i, j].Y));
        }
    }
```

```
                PointF[] ptf = new PointF[4];
                for (int i = 1; i < pts.GetLength(0); i++)
                {
                    for (int j = 1; j < pts.GetLength(1); j++)
                    {
                        ptf[0] = pta[i - 1, j - 1];
                        ptf[1] = pta[i, j - 1];
                        ptf[2] = pta[i, j];
                        ptf[3] = pta[i - 1, j];
                        g.FillPolygon(Brushes.White, ptf);
                        g.DrawPolygon(Pens.Black, ptf);
                    }
                }
            }

            private PointF Point2D(PointF pt)
            {
                PointF aPoint = new PointF();
                aPoint.X = form1.panel1.Width / 2 + pt.X;
                aPoint.Y = form1.panel1.Height / 2 - pt.Y;
                return aPoint;
            }
        }
    }
```

In this class, you can specify the radius and positions (the center location) of a sphere. The SphereCoordinates method creates the points on a sphere surface by specifying their longitude and latitude. The DrawIsometricView draws the sphere using the isometric projection.

This application can be tested using the following Form1 class:

```
using System;
using System.Drawing;
using System.Drawing.Drawing2D;
using System.Windows.Forms;

namespace Example5_6
{
    public partial class Form1 : Form
    {
        public Form1()
        {
            InitializeComponent();
            this.SetStyle(ControlStyles.ResizeRedraw, true);

            // Subscribing to a paint eventhandler to drawingPanel:
            panel1.Paint +=
                new PaintEventHandler(panel1Paint);
        }

        private void panel1Paint(object sender, PaintEventArgs e)
        {
            Graphics g = e.Graphics;
            g.SmoothingMode = SmoothingMode.AntiAlias;
```

```
float a = panel1.Height / 3;
DrawSphere ds = new DrawSphere(this, a, 0, 0, -a / 2);
ds.DrawIsometricView(g);
ds = new DrawSphere(this, 2 * a / 3, -a/2, -a/2, a / 2);
ds.DrawIsometricView(g);
        }
    }
}
```

Here we create two spheres with different radii and positions. By building and running this project, you should obtain the results shown in Figure 5-23.

Figure 5-23 Spheres created in a spherical coordinate system.

Euler Angles

The Euler angles (α, β, γ) are used to describe the rotations or orientations of orthogonal coordinate systems. They relate two orthogonal coordinate systems that have the same origin. The transition from one system to another is achieved by a series of 2D rotations. The rotation is performed about the coordinate axes generated by the previous rotation. The convention used here is that α is the rotation about the Y axis of the initial coordinate system. A rotation β is performed about the X' axis of this newly generated coordinate system, followed by a rotation by γ about the new Y1 axis, as shown in Figure 5-24.

The transformation matrix of the Euler angles can be constructed by three 2D rotation matrices. The first rotation involves the Euler angle α. The rotation matrix to describe this 2D rotation operation is given by

$$R_y(\alpha) = \begin{pmatrix} \cos\alpha & 0 & \sin\alpha & 0 \\ 0 & 1 & 0 & 0 \\ -\sin\alpha & 0 & \cos\alpha & 0 \\ 0 & 0 & 0 & 1 \end{pmatrix}$$

The second rotation involves the Euler angle β. The system is rotated by β about the X axis of the new coordinate system. The rotation matrix to describe this operation is given by

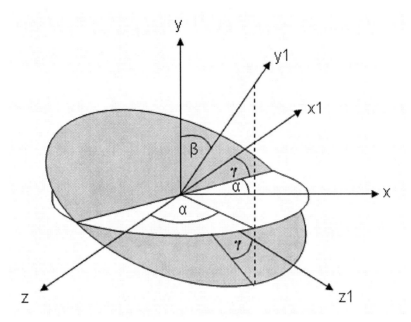

Figure 5-24 Euler angle system.

$$R_x(\beta) = \begin{pmatrix} 1 & 0 & 0 & 0 \\ 0 & \cos\beta & \sin\beta & 0 \\ 0 & -\sin\beta & \cos\beta & 0 \\ 0 & 0 & 0 & 1 \end{pmatrix}$$

The last rotation involves the Euler angle γ. The system is rotated about the Y1 axis through an angle γ to generate the final coordinate system (x1, y1, z1). The rotation matrix to describe this operation is given by

$$R_y(\gamma) = \begin{pmatrix} \cos\gamma & 0 & \sin\gamma & 0 \\ 0 & 1 & 0 & 0 \\ -\sin\gamma & 0 & \cos\gamma & 0 \\ 0 & 0 & 0 & 1 \end{pmatrix}$$

The total effect of these three 2D rotations is given by the transformation matrix:

$$R_y(\gamma)R_x(\beta)R_y(\alpha) =$$

$$\begin{pmatrix} \cos\alpha\cos\gamma - \sin\alpha\sin\beta\sin\gamma & -\sin\beta\sin\gamma & \sin\alpha\cos\gamma - \cos\alpha\cos\beta\sin\gamma & 0 \\ -\sin\alpha\sin\beta & \cos\beta & \cos\alpha\sin\beta & 0 \\ -\cos\alpha\sin\gamma - \sin\alpha\cos\beta\cos\gamma & -\sin\beta\cos\gamma & \cos\alpha\cos\beta\cos\gamma - \sin\alpha\sin\beta & 0 \\ 0 & 0 & 0 & 1 \end{pmatrix}$$

You can use this transformation matrix to rotate a point about any axis by specifying three Euler angles. In real-world applications, you can add a static method to the `Matrix3` class:

```
public static Matrix3 Euler(float alpha, float beta, float gamma)
{
    Matrix3 result = new Matrix3();

    alpha = alpha * (float)Math.PI / 180.0f;
    float sna = (float)Math.Sin(alpha);
    float cna = (float)Math.Cos(alpha);
    beta = beta * (float)Math.PI / 180.0f;
    float snb = (float)Math.Sin(beta);
    float cnb = (float)Math.Cos(beta);
    gamma = gamma * (float)Math.PI / 180.0f;
    float sng = (float)Math.Sin(gamma);
    float cng = (float)Math.Cos(gamma);

    result.M[0, 0] = cna * cng - sna * snb * sng;
    result.M[0, 1] = -snb * sng;
    result.M[0, 2] = sna * cng - cna * cnb * sng;
    result.M[1, 0] = -sna * snb;
    result.M[1, 1] = cnb;
    result.M[1, 2] = cna * snb;
    result.M[2, 0] = -cna * sng - sna * cnb * cng;
    result.M[2, 1] = -snb * cng;
    result.M[2, 2] = cna * cnb * cng - sna * snb;
    return result;
}
```

Then you can use this as a standard matrix transformation in your applications.

Azimuth and Elevation View

The azimuth and elevation view is often used in controlling the orientation of 3D charts and graphics objects displayed in the coordinate axes. Specifying the viewpoint in terms of azimuth and elevation is conceptually simple. The 3D charts that will be represented in the following chapter will use this azimuth and elevation view to display various 3D plots on a 2D computer screen. There are some limitations in this view setting, however. Azimuth and elevation view does not allow you to specify the actual position of the viewpoint, just its direction, and the Z axis is always pointing up. It does not allow you to zoom in and out on the scene or perform arbitrary rotations and translations. Even with these limitations, this view setting is good enough for most 3D chart and graphics applications.

In this view setting, the conventional Cartesian coordinate system is used. The azimuth angle is a polar angle in the X-Y plane, with positive angles indicating a counterclockwise rotation of the viewpoint. Elevation is the angle above (positive angle) or below (negative angle) the X-Y plane, as shown in Figure 5-25.

The transformation matrix of this view system can be constructed by considering two successive 2D rotations. First we rotate the original coordinate system by an angle $-\varphi$ about the Z axis, then rotate the newly generated coordinate system by $\theta - \pi/2$ about the X axis. Using Equations (5.5) and (5.7), we can obtain the combined effect of these two 2D rotations:

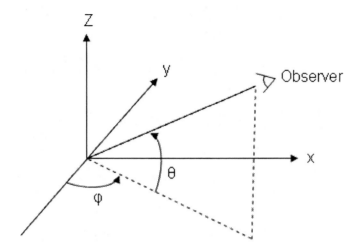

Figure 5-25 Azimuth and elevation view system.

$$R_x(\theta - \pi/2) \cdot R_z(-\varphi) = \begin{pmatrix} \cos\varphi & \sin\varphi & 0 & 0 \\ -\sin\theta\sin\varphi & \sin\theta\cos\varphi & \cos\theta & 0 \\ \cos\theta\sin\varphi & -\cos\theta\cos\varphi & \sin\theta & 0 \\ 0 & 0 & 0 & 1 \end{pmatrix} \qquad (5.16)$$

You can test how a cube object is rotated by elevation and azimuth angles in an example C# project. To this end, we start with a new C# project, *Example5_7*. Add the Matrix3 and Point3 classes from the previous project *Example5_6*, and change their namespace to *Example5_7*. Add a new class, DrawCube, to the project.

Implement a public static method, AzimuthElevation, and add it to the Matrix3 class:

```
public static Matrix3 AzimuthElevation(float elevation,
    float azimuth, float oneOverd)
{
    Matrix3 result = new Matrix3();
    Matrix3 rotate = new Matrix3();

    // make sure elevation in the range of [-90, 90]:
    if (elevation > 90)
        elevation = 90;
    else if (elevation < -90)
        elevation = -90;

    // Make sure azimuth in the range of [-180, 180]:
    if (azimuth > 180)
        azimuth = 180;
```

```
        else if (azimuth < -180)
            azimuth = -180;

        elevation = elevation * (float)Math.PI / 180.0f;
        float sne = (float)Math.Sin(elevation);
        float cne = (float)Math.Cos(elevation);
        azimuth = azimuth * (float)Math.PI / 180.0f;
        float sna = (float)Math.Sin(azimuth);
        float cna = (float)Math.Cos(azimuth);

        rotate.M[0, 0] = cna;
        rotate.M[0, 1] = sna;
        rotate.M[0, 2] = 0;
        rotate.M[1, 0] = -sne * sna;
        rotate.M[1, 1] = sne * cna;
        rotate.M[1, 2] = cne;
        rotate.M[2, 0] = cne * sna;
        rotate.M[2, 1] = -cne * cna;
        rotate.M[2, 2] = sne;

        if (oneOverd <= 0)
            result = rotate;
        else if (oneOverd > 0)
        {
            Matrix3 perspective = Matrix3.Perspective(1/oneOverd);
            result = perspective * rotate;
        }
        return result;
    }
}
```

This method takes elevation and azimuth angles, as well as focal length, as input parameters. Here the input parameter oneOverd is defined as oneOverd = 1/d, where d is the distance between the center of projection and the origin. This means that we get a perspective projection when oneOverd > 0 and a parallel projection when oneOverd = 0 (corresponding to d = infinity). You can see from the above code snippet that when oneOverd > 0, the transformation is performed by a rotation, followed by a perspective projection. In this case, you can examine how the cube object is displayed on your computer screen under perspective projections from different view angles.

The following is the code listing of the DrawCube class:

```
using System;
using System.Drawing;
using System.Windows.Forms;

namespace Example5_7
{
    public class DrawCube
    {
        private Form1 form1;
        private float side = 10;
        private float elevation = 30;
        private float azimuth = -37.5f;
        private float oneOverd = 0;
```

```
public DrawCube(Form1 fm1)
{
    form1 = fm1;
}

public DrawCube(Form1 fm1, float side1)
{
    form1 = fm1;
    side = side1;
}

public DrawCube(Form1 fm1, float side1, float elevation1,
        float azimuth1, float oneOverd1)
{
    form1 = fm1;
    side = side1;
    elevation = elevation1;
    azimuth = azimuth1;
    oneOverd = oneOverd1;
}

public Point3[] CubeCoordinates()
{
    Point3[] pts = new Point3[11];

    // Create the cube:
    pts[0] = new Point3(side, -side, -side, 1);
    pts[1] = new Point3(side, side, -side, 1);
    pts[2] = new Point3(-side, side, -side, 1);
    pts[3] = new Point3(-side, -side, -side, 1);
    pts[4] = new Point3(-side, -side, side, 1);
    pts[5] = new Point3(side, -side, side, 1);
    pts[6] = new Point3(side, side, side, 1);
    pts[7] = new Point3(-side, side, side, 1);

    // Create coordinate axes:
    pts[8] = new Point3(2*side, -side, -side, 1);
    pts[9] = new Point3(-side, 2*side, -side, 1);
    pts[10] = new Point3(-side, -side, 2*side, 1);
    return pts;
}

public void AddCube(Graphics g)
{
    Matrix3 m = Matrix3.AzimuthElevation(elevation,
                azimuth, oneOverd);
    Point3[] pts = CubeCoordinates();
    PointF[] pta = new PointF[4];

    for (int i = 0; i < pts.Length; i++)
    {
        pts[i].TransformNormalize(m);
    }
```

```
int[] i0, i1;
i0 = new int[4] { 1, 2, 7, 6 };
i1 = new int[4] { 2, 3, 4, 7 };
if (elevation >= 0)
{
    if (azimuth >= -180 && azimuth < -90)
    {
        i0 = new int[4] { 1, 2, 7, 6 };
        i1 = new int[4] { 2, 3, 4, 7 };
    }
    else if (azimuth >= -90 && azimuth < 0)
    {
        i0 = new int[4] { 3, 4, 5, 0 };
        i1 = new int[4] { 2, 3, 4, 7 };
    }
    else if (azimuth >= 0 && azimuth < 90)
    {
        i0 = new int[4] { 3, 4, 5, 0 };
        i1 = new int[4] { 0, 1, 6, 5 };
    }
    else if (azimuth >= 90 && azimuth <= 180)
    {
        i0 = new int[4] { 1, 2, 7, 6 };
        i1 = new int[4] { 0, 1, 6, 5 };
    }
}

else if (elevation < 0)
{
    if (azimuth >= -180 && azimuth < -90)
    {
        i0 = new int[4] { 0, 1, 6, 5 };
        i1 = new int[4] { 0, 3, 4, 5 };
    }
    else if (azimuth >= -90 && azimuth < 0)
    {
        i0 = new int[4] { 1, 2, 7, 6 };
        i1 = new int[4] { 0, 1, 6, 5 };
    }
    else if (azimuth >= 0 && azimuth < 90)
    {
        i0 = new int[4] { 2, 3, 4, 7 };
        i1 = new int[4] { 1, 2, 7, 6 };
    }
    else if (azimuth >= 90 && azimuth <= 180)
    {
        i0 = new int[4] { 2, 3, 4, 7 };
        i1 = new int[4] { 0, 3, 4, 5 };
    }

}

// Create the cube:
```

```
            pta[0] = Point2D(new PointF(pts[i0[0]].X, pts[i0[0]].Y));
            pta[1] = Point2D(new PointF(pts[i0[1]].X, pts[i0[1]].Y));
            pta[2] = Point2D(new PointF(pts[i0[2]].X, pts[i0[2]].Y));
            pta[3] = Point2D(new PointF(pts[i0[3]].X, pts[i0[3]].Y));
            g.FillPolygon(Brushes.LightCoral, pta);
            g.DrawPolygon(Pens.Black, pta);

            pta[0] = Point2D(new PointF(pts[i1[0]].X, pts[i1[0]].Y));
            pta[1] = Point2D(new PointF(pts[i1[1]].X, pts[i1[1]].Y));
            pta[2] = Point2D(new PointF(pts[i1[2]].X, pts[i1[2]].Y));
            pta[3] = Point2D(new PointF(pts[i1[3]].X, pts[i1[3]].Y));
            g.FillPolygon(Brushes.LightGreen, pta);
            g.DrawPolygon(Pens.Black, pta);

            pta[0] = Point2D(new PointF(pts[4].X, pts[4].Y));
            pta[1] = Point2D(new PointF(pts[5].X, pts[5].Y));
            pta[2] = Point2D(new PointF(pts[6].X, pts[6].Y));
            pta[3] = Point2D(new PointF(pts[7].X, pts[7].Y));
            g.FillPolygon(Brushes.LightGray, pta);
            g.DrawPolygon(Pens.Black, pta);

            // Create coordinate axes:
            pta = new PointF[2];
            pta[0] = Point2D(new PointF(pts[3].X, pts[3].Y));
            pta[1] = Point2D(new PointF(pts[8].X, pts[8].Y));
            g.DrawLine(Pens.Red, pta[0], pta[1]);
            pta[1] = Point2D(new PointF(pts[9].X, pts[9].Y));
            g.DrawLine(Pens.Green, pta[0], pta[1]);
            pta[1] = Point2D(new PointF(pts[10].X, pts[10].Y));
            g.DrawLine(Pens.Blue, pta[0], pta[1]);
        }

        private PointF Point2D(PointF pt)
        {
            PointF aPoint = new PointF();
            aPoint.X = form1.panel1.Width / 2 + pt.X;
            aPoint.Y = form1.panel1.Height / 2 - pt.Y;
            return aPoint;
        }
    }
}
```

In this class, we draw a cube object and the coordinate axes with the origin located at one corner of the cube. Within the DrawCube method, we carefully select three faces of the cube to be drawn on the screen according to changes of the elevation and azimuth angles.

Finally, you can use the following Form1 class to test the project:

```
using System;
using System.Drawing;
using System.Drawing.Drawing2D;
using System.Windows.Forms;

namespace Example5_7
{
```

```
public partial class Form1 : Form
{
    public Form1()
    {
        InitializeComponent();
        this.SetStyle(ControlStyles.ResizeRedraw, true);

        // Subscribing to a paint eventhandler to drawingPanel:
        panel1.Paint +=
            new PaintEventHandler(panel1Paint);
    }

    private void panel1Paint(object sender, PaintEventArgs e)
    {
        Graphics g = e.Graphics;
        g.SmoothingMode = SmoothingMode.AntiAlias;
        float a = panel1.Height / 6;
        float elevation = Convert.ToSingle(tbElevation.Text);
        float azimuth = Convert.ToSingle(tbAzimuth.Text);
        float oneOverd = Convert.ToSingle(tbOneOverd.Text);
        DrawCube ds = new DrawCube(this, a,
                elevation, azimuth, oneOverd / (2 * a));
        ds.AddCube(g);

    }

    private void btnApply_Click(object sender, EventArgs e)
    {
        panel1.Invalidate();
    }
}
}
```

Here, the `oneOverd` parameter is normalized by the side-length of the cube. The proper range of this parameter is [0, 1]. `oneOverd` = 0 and 1 correspond to the center of projection at infinity and the right on the face of the cube, respectively. Figure 5-26 shows the output of this project, in which the view of the cube corresponds to an orthogonal projection with the elevation angle = 30 and the azimuth angle = -30 degrees.

You can rotate the cube by entering different elevation and azimuth angles. In particular, you can see the change of the cube's view under a perspective projection. Figure 5-27 shows a perspective view of the cube with the elevation angle = 30 degrees, azimuth angle = 45 degrees, and 1/d = 0.5 (corresponding to d = 2 times the side length of the cube).

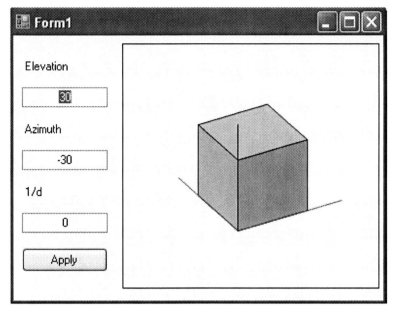

Figure 5-26 Azimuth and elevation view of a cube object.

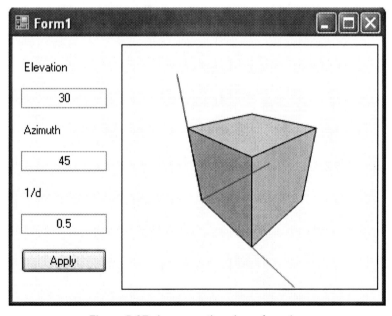

Figure 5-27 A perspective view of a cube.

6

3D Charts

In the previous chapter, we covered the 3D matrices, transformations, and coordinate systems that form the foundation for creating 3D graphics objects. In this chapter, we will use these matrix representations and transformations to discuss fundamental 3D charts. We will starts with a description of the coordinate system that is used in 3D charts. We will show you how to create 3D coordinate axes, tick marks, axis labels, and grid lines. The 3D coordinate system used in 3D charts is the most fundamental part in creating 3D chart applications, because it involves almost all of the matrix operations and transformations used in creating 3D charts.

The chapter then shows you how to create various 3D chart applications that include 3D line charts, 3D mesh and surface charts, contour charts, 3D bar charts, 4D slice charts, and 3D combination charts. In creating these 3D charts, we will use a few specialized techniques to manipulate the data displayed on your computer screen.

The example C# application programs in this chapter provide basic solutions for your 3D chart applications. The example project *Example6_1* implements the basic framework used in 3D charts, including the coordinate system, labels, and gridlines. *Example6_2* shows you how easy it is to create a 3D line chart based on *Example6_1*. Finally, the project *Example6_3* is a complete package of 3D charts that contains 3D line, mesh, surface, contour, 3D bar charts, and others. Based on these example projects, with or without modifications, you can easily create your own professional and sophisticated 3D charts in your C# applications.

3D Chart Basics

The coordinate system we are going to use in our 3D chart applications is an orthogonal coordinate system, which is the standard approach for 3D charting. This means we do not use perspective projection transformations in 3D chart applications. The elevation and azimuth transformation will be used to manipulate the view of our 3D charts on a 2D computer screen. We begin by discussing the basic `Point3`, `Matrix3`, and `ChartStyle` classes used in 3D charts.

Point3 and Matrix3 Classes

In the previous chapter, we always used the `Point3` class to discuss transformations on a 3D point. This class is very general and can be used in any 3D graphics application. Here we want to modify this class by incorporating some specific features of 3D charts. The following is the code listing of this modified class:

```
public class Point3
{
    public float X;
    public float Y;
    public float Z;
    public float W = 1f;

    public Point3()
    {
    }

    public Point3(float x, float y, float z, float w)
    {
        X = x;
        Y = y;
        Z = z;
        W = w;
    }

    public void Transform(Matrix3 m)
    {
        float[] result = m.VectorMultiply(new float[4] { X, Y, Z, W });
        X = result[0];
        Y = result[1];
        Z = result[2];
        W = result[3];
    }

    public void Transform(Matrix3 m, Form1 form1, ChartStyle cs)
    {
        // Normalize the point:
        float x1 = (X - cs.XMin) / (cs.XMax-cs.XMin) - 0.5f;
        float y1 = (Y - cs.YMin) / (cs.YMax - cs.YMin) - 0.5f;
        float z1 = (Z - cs.ZMin) / (cs.ZMax - cs.ZMin) - 0.5f;

        // Perform transformation on the point using matrix m:
```

```
float[] result = m.VectorMultiply(new float[4] { x1, y1, z1, W });
X = result[0];
Y = result[1];

// Coordinate transformation from World to Device system:
float xShift = 1.05f;
float xScale = 1;
float yShift = 1.05f;
float yScale = 0.9f;
if (cs.Title == "No Title")
{
    yShift = 0.95f;
    yScale = 1f;
}
if (cs.IsColorBar)
{
    xShift = 0.95f;
    xScale = 0.9f;
}
X = (xShift + xScale * X) * form1.PlotPanel.Width / 2;
Y = (yShift - yScale * Y) * form1.PlotPanel.Height / 2;
        }
    }
```

To this class, we add an overloaded `Transform` method:

```
public void Transform(Matrix3 m, Form1 form1, ChartStyle cs)
```

It takes three input parameters: the transformation matrix, the `Form1` class used to display the chart, and the object of the `ChartStyle` class. In this method, we first normalize the X, Y, and Z data ranges into a unit cube, so that the transformations that are performed on the point within this unit cube are independent from the real data ranges. Then we transform the normalized point using the transformation matrix m. Finally, we carry out the coordinate transformation on the point from the world to device coordinate system that was originally accomplished in the `ChartStyle` class in the previous chapters. It can be seen that this overloaded method performs all of the necessary transformations on a point to be displayed on a 2D screen, which will greatly simplify the programming procedure for 3D chart applications.

You might notice that in this overloaded method, only the X and Y components of the point undertake the transformations, while the Z and W components retain their original values. This can be seen from the code snippet:

```
// Perform transformation on the point using matrix m:
float[] result = m.VectorMultiply(new float[4] { x1, y1, z1, W });
X = result[0];
Y = result[1];
```

Here, the float array `result` stores the coordinate information after the transformation, and the X and Y coordinates take the corresponding transformed coordinate components from the `result` array. However, the Z and W components don't take new values from the `result` array, and retain their original information. Otherwise, after orthogonal transformations, the Z component could end up a combination of the original X, Y, and Z, which destroys the original Z coordinate information, meaning that you cannot use the Z component to compare the points' Z values. In 3D charts, we do need the original Z coordinate information, for instance, in performing color maps for a 3D chart. Since we modify the points' `Transform` method, and the way transformations are applied to the points, we preserve the original Z component information.

Correspondingly, we also add another overloaded method, `AzimuthElevation`, to the `Matrix3` class:

```
public static Matrix3 AzimuthElevation(float elevation, float azimuth)
{
    Matrix3 result = new Matrix3();

    // make sure elevation in the range of [-90, 90]:
    if (elevation > 90)
        elevation = 90;
    else if (elevation < -90)
        elevation = -90;

    // Make sure azimuth in the range of [-180, 180]:
    if (azimuth > 180)
        azimuth = 180;
    else if (azimuth < -180)
        azimuth = -180;

    elevation = elevation * (float)Math.PI / 180.0f;
    float sne = (float)Math.Sin(elevation);
    float cne = (float)Math.Cos(elevation);
    azimuth = azimuth * (float)Math.PI / 180.0f;
    float sna = (float)Math.Sin(azimuth);
    float cna = (float)Math.Cos(azimuth);

    result.M[0, 0] = cna;
    result.M[0, 1] = sna;
    result.M[0, 2] = 0;
    result.M[1, 0] = -sne * sna;
    result.M[1, 1] = sne * cna;
    result.M[1, 2] = cne;
    result.M[2, 0] = cne * sna;
    result.M[2, 1] = -cne * cna;
    result.M[2, 2] = sne;
    return result;
}
```

This overloaded method is just a simplified version of the original method that was used in the previous chapter. Here we remove the perspective projection from the method, and keep only the orthogonal transformation that will be used in our 3D chart applications.

Chart Style in 3D

The `ChartStyle` class in 3D charts is similar to that in 2D case. The following code snippet shows its member fields and their corresponding public properties:

```
public class ChartStyle
{
```

```
private Form1 form1;
private float xMax = 5f;
private float xMin = -5f;
private float yMax = 3f;
private float yMin = -3f;
private float zMax = 6f;
private float zMin = -6f;
private float xTick = 1f;
private float yTick = 1f;
private float zTick = 3f;
private Font tickFont = new Font("Arial Narrow",8,
    FontStyle.Regular);
private Color tickColor = Color.Black;
private string title = "My 3D Chart";
private Font titleFont = new Font("Arial Narrow", 14,
    FontStyle.Regular);
private Color titleColor = Color.Black;
private string xLabel = "X Axis";
private string yLabel = "Y Axis";
private string zLabel = "Z Axis";
private Font labelFont = new Font("Arial Narrow", 10,
    FontStyle.Regular);
private Color labelColor = Color.Black;
private float elevation = 30;
private float azimuth = -37.5f;
private bool isXGrid = true;
private bool isYGrid = true;
private bool isZGrid = true;
LineStyle gridStyle;
LineStyle axisStyle;
private bool isColorBar = false;

public ChartStyle(Form1 fm1)
{
    form1 = fm1;
    gridStyle = new LineStyle();
    axisStyle = new LineStyle();
}

public bool IsColorBar
{
    get { return isColorBar; }
    set { isColorBar = value; }
}

public LineStyle AxisStyle
{
    get { return axisStyle; }
    set { axisStyle = value; }
}

public LineStyle GridStyle
{
    get { return gridStyle; }
```

```
        set { gridStyle = value; }
    }

    public Font LabelFont
    {
        get { return labelFont; }
        set { labelFont = value; }
    }

    public Color LabelColor
    {
        get { return labelColor; }
        set { labelColor = value; }
    }

    public Font TileFont
    {
        get { return titleFont; }
        set { titleFont = value; }
    }

    public Color TitleColor
    {
        get { return titleColor; }
        set { titleColor = value; }
    }

    public Font TickFont
    {
        get { return tickFont; }
        set { tickFont = value; }
    }

    public Color TickColor
    {
        get { return tickColor; }
        set { tickColor = value; }
    }

    public bool IsXGrid
    {
        get { return isXGrid; }
        set { isXGrid = value; }
    }

    public bool IsYGrid
    {
        get { return isYGrid; }
        set { isYGrid = value; }
    }

    public bool IsZGrid
    {
        get { return isZGrid; }
```

```csharp
        set { isZGrid = value; }
    }

    public string Title
    {
        get { return title; }
        set { title = value; }
    }

    public string XLabel
    {
        get { return xLabel; }
        set { xLabel = value; }
    }

    public string YLabel
    {
        get { return yLabel; }
        set { yLabel = value; }
    }

    public string ZLabel
    {
        get { return zLabel; }
        set { zLabel = value; }
    }

    public float Elevation
    {
        get { return elevation; }
        set { elevation = value; }
    }

    public float Azimuth
    {
        get { return azimuth; }
        set { azimuth = value; }
    }

    public float XMax
    {
        get { return xMax; }
        set { xMax = value; }
    }

    public float XMin
    {
        get { return xMin; }
        set { xMin = value; }
    }

    public float YMax
    {
        get { return yMax; }
```

```
            set { yMax = value; }
        }

        public float YMin
        {
            get { return yMin; }
            set { yMin = value; }
        }

        public float ZMax
        {
            get { return zMax; }
            set { zMax = value; }
        }

        public float ZMin
        {
            get { return zMin; }
            set { zMin = value; }
        }

        public float XTick
        {
            get { return xTick; }
            set { xTick = value; }
        }

        public float YTick
        {
            get { return yTick; }
            set { yTick = value; }
        }

        public float ZTick
        {
            get { return zTick; }
            set { zTick = value; }
        }
    }
```

You can specify and change the chart style for a 3D chart using the above properties. If you need more features to control the appearance of a 3D chart, you can easily add your own member fields and corresponding properties to this class.

The other basic classes in 3D charts include the `LineStyle` (exactly the same as it is in the case of 2D), `DataSeries`, etc. which will be discussed in the following example projects. The `DataCollection` class is not needed in 3D charts because most 3D charts plot only one set of data.

Coordinate Axes

Creating 3D coordinate axes on a 2D screen is more involving than it is in the coordinates of 2D. First we need to create the coordinates of the chart box, as shown in Figure 6-1. In 3D charts, all data should be plotted within the chart box defined by [xMin, xMax, yMin, yMax, zMin, zMax] in the world coordinate system. The coordinate axes are defined by the bold lines in Figure 6-1. The Z axis is the vertical bold line that can be independent of the elevation and azimuth angles. On the other hand, the X and Y axes cannot be predefined. Which edge of the chart box represents the X or Y axis depends on both the elevation and azimuth angles.

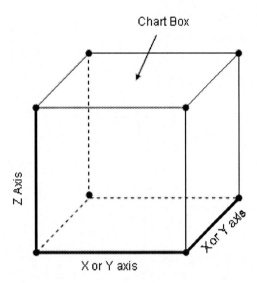

Figure 6-1 Chart box and coordinate axes.

In order to create such a coordinate system in C#, we first need to create the eight-point coordinates of the chart box. Then we select four points from these eight points to define three coordinate axes. The following code snippet is the method CoordinatesOfChartBox in the ChartStyle class:

```
private Point3[] CoordinatesOfChartBox()
{
    // Create coordinate of the axes:
    Point3[] pta = new Point3[8];
    pta[0] = new Point3(XMax, YMin, ZMin, 1);
    pta[1] = new Point3(XMin, YMin, ZMin, 1);
    pta[2] = new Point3(XMin, YMax, ZMin, 1);
    pta[3] = new Point3(XMin, YMax, ZMax, 1);
    pta[4] = new Point3(XMin, YMin, ZMax, 1);
    pta[5] = new Point3(XMax, YMin, ZMax, 1);
    pta[6] = new Point3(XMax, YMax, ZMax, 1);
    pta[7] = new Point3(XMax, YMax, ZMin, 1);

    Point3[] pts = new Point3[4];
    int[] npts = new int[4] { 0, 1, 2, 3 };

    if (elevation >= 0)
    {
```

```
        if (azimuth >= -180 && azimuth < -90)
            npts = new int[4] { 1, 2, 7, 6 };
        else if (azimuth >= -90 && azimuth < 0)
            npts = new int[4] { 0, 1, 2, 3 };
        else if (azimuth >= 0 && azimuth < 90)
            npts = new int[4] { 7, 0, 1, 4 };
        else if (azimuth >= 90 && azimuth <= 180)
            npts = new int[4] { 2, 7, 0, 5 };
    }
    else if (elevation < 0)
    {
        if (azimuth >= -180 && azimuth < -90)
            npts = new int[4] { 1, 0, 7, 6 };
        else if (azimuth >= -90 && azimuth < 0)
            npts = new int[4] { 0, 7, 2, 3 };
        else if (azimuth >= 0 && azimuth < 90)
            npts = new int[4] { 7, 2, 1, 4 };
        else if (azimuth >= 90 && azimuth <= 180)
            npts = new int[4] { 2, 1, 0, 5 };
    }

    for (int i = 0; i < 4; i++)
        pts[i] = pta[npts[i]];
    return pts;
}
```

In this method, we select a different four-point array according to the changes of the azimuth and elevation angles using a try-and-error approach. Calling this method creates a point array of four points that determines the X, Y, and Z axes for arbitrary elevation and azimuth angles. Now we can create the coordinate axes using the following code:

```
private void AddAxes(Graphics g)
{
    Matrix3 m = Matrix3.AzimuthElevation(Elevation, Azimuth);
    Point3[] pts = CoordinatesOfChartBox();
    Pen aPen = new Pen(AxisStyle.LineColor, AxisStyle.Thickness);
    aPen.DashStyle = AxisStyle.Pattern;

    for (int i = 0; i < pts.Length; i++)
    {
        pts[i].Transform(m, form1, this);
    }

    g.DrawLine(aPen, pts[0].X, pts[0].Y, pts[1].X, pts[1].Y);
    g.DrawLine(aPen, pts[1].X, pts[1].Y, pts[2].X, pts[2].Y);
    g.DrawLine(aPen, pts[2].X, pts[2].Y, pts[3].X, pts[3].Y);
    aPen.Dispose();
}
```

In this method, we first get the coordinates of the three coordinate axes by calling the CoordinatesOfChartBox method. Then we perform the transformation on these four points by calling Transform method using the elevation and azimuth matrix. As mentioned previously, the Transform method actually performs three transformations: normalization, elevation and azimuth transformation (corresponding to the orthogonal projection), and coordinate transformation from the world to device system. Finally, we use the X and Y components of the transformed points to draw the coordinate axes. Although the AddAxes method creates three coordinate axes, we still do not know which axis is the X or Y axis yet. The program will tell you automatically when you place labels on the coordinate axes.

The following AddTicks method in the ChartStyle class creates tick marks on the coordinate axes:

```
private void AddTicks(Graphics g)
{
    Matrix3 m = Matrix3.AzimuthElevation(Elevation, Azimuth);
    Point3[] pta = new Point3[2];
    Point3[] pts = CoordinatesOfChartBox();
    Pen aPen = new Pen(AxisStyle.LineColor, AxisStyle.Thickness);
    aPen.DashStyle = AxisStyle.Pattern;

    // Add x ticks:
    float offset = (YMax - YMin) / 30.0f;
    float ticklength = offset;

    for (float x = XMin; x <= XMax; x = x + XTick)
    {
        if (elevation >= 0)
        {
            if (azimuth >= -90 && azimuth < 90)
                ticklength = -offset;
        }
        else if (elevation < 0)
        {
            if ((azimuth >= -180 && azimuth < -90) ||
                azimuth >= 90 && azimuth <= 180)
                ticklength = -(YMax - YMin) / 30;
        }
        pta[0] = new Point3(x, pts[1].Y + ticklength,
                    pts[1].Z, pts[1].W);
        pta[1] = new Point3(x, pts[1].Y, pts[1].Z, pts[1].W);
        for (int i = 0; i < pta.Length; i++)
        {
            pta[i].Transform(m, form1, this);
        }
        g.DrawLine(aPen, pta[0].X, pta[0].Y, pta[1].X, pta[1].Y);
    }

    // Add y ticks:
    offset = (XMax - XMin) / 30.0f;
    ticklength = offset;
    for (float y = YMin; y <= YMax; y = y + YTick)
    {
        pts = CoordinatesOfChartBox();
        if (elevation >= 0)
        {
            if (azimuth >= -180 && azimuth < 0)
                ticklength = -offset;
        }
```

```
        else if (elevation < 0)
        {
            if (azimuth >= 0 && azimuth < 180)
                ticklength = -offset;
        }
        pta[0] = new Point3(pts[1].X + ticklength, y,
                    pts[1].Z, pts[1].W);
        pta[1] = new Point3(pts[1].X, y, pts[1].Z, pts[1].W);
        for (int i = 0; i < pta.Length; i++)
        {
            pta[i].Transform(m, form1, this);
        }
        g.DrawLine(aPen, pta[0].X, pta[0].Y, pta[1].X, pta[1].Y);
    }

    // Add z ticks:
    float xoffset = (XMax - XMin) / 45.0f;
    float yoffset = (YMax - YMin) / 20.0f;
    float xticklength = xoffset;
    float yticklength = yoffset;
    for (float z = ZMin; z <= ZMax; z = z + ZTick)
    {
        if (elevation >= 0)
        {
            if (azimuth >= -180 && azimuth < -90)
            {
                xticklength = 0;
                yticklength = yoffset;
            }
            else if (azimuth >= -90 && azimuth < 0)
            {
                xticklength = xoffset;
                yticklength = 0;
            }
            else if (azimuth >= 0 && azimuth < 90)
            {
                xticklength = 0;
                yticklength = -yoffset;
            }
            else if (azimuth >= 90 && azimuth <= 180)
            {
                xticklength = -xoffset;
                yticklength = 0;
            }
        }
        else if (elevation <0)
        {
            if (azimuth >= -180 && azimuth < -90)
            {
                yticklength = 0;
                xticklength = xoffset;
            }
            else if (azimuth >= -90 && azimuth < 0)
            {
```

```
                    yticklength = -yoffset;
                    xticklength = 0;
                }
                else if (azimuth >= 0 && azimuth < 90)
                {
                    yticklength = 0;
                    xticklength = -xoffset;
                }
                else if (azimuth >= 90 && azimuth <= 180)
                {
                    yticklength = yoffset;
                    xticklength = 0;
                }
            }

            pta[0] = new Point3(pts[2].X, pts[2].Y, z, pts[2].W);
            pta[1] = new Point3(pts[2].X + yticklength ,
                        pts[2].Y + xticklength, z, pts[2].W);
            for (int i = 0; i < pta.Length; i++)
            {
                pta[i].Transform(m, form1, this);
            }
            g.DrawLine(aPen, pta[0].X, pta[0].Y, pta[1].X, pta[1].Y);
        }
        aPen.Dispose();
    }
```

In this method, we define the length of the ticks in terms of the axis limit instead of a fixed length
in the device coordinate system. This can keep the ticks resized proportionally when the chart is
resized. Please note how we place the tick markers in the right positions on the coordinate axes
when the elevation and azimuth angles are changed.

Gridlines

As in 2D charts, gridlines in 3D charts can help you to get a better view of the data ranges. In the
case of 3D, we want to place gridlines on three faces that must be the behind your data curves or
surfaces. These three faces (or planes) must be properly selected according to the variation of the
elevation and azimuth angles. The following AddGrids method in the ChartStyle class
creates gridlines on the right faces:

```
private void AddGrids(Graphics g)
{
    Matrix3 m = Matrix3.AzimuthElevation(Elevation, Azimuth);
    Point3[] pta = new Point3[3];
    Point3[] pts = CoordinatesOfChartBox();
    Pen aPen = new Pen(GridStyle.LineColor, GridStyle.Thickness);
    aPen.DashStyle = GridStyle.Pattern;

    // Draw x gridlines:
    if (IsXGrid)
    {
        for (float x = XMin; x <= XMax; x = x + XTick)
        {
```

```csharp
        pts = CoordinatesOfChartBox();
        pta[0] = new Point3(x, pts[1].Y, pts[1].Z, pts[1].W);
        if (elevation >= 0)
        {
            if ((azimuth >= -180 && azimuth < -90) ||
                (azimuth >= 0 && azimuth < 90))
            {
                pta[1] = new Point3(x, pts[0].Y,
                            pts[1].Z, pts[1].W);
                pta[2] = new Point3(x, pts[0].Y,
                            pts[3].Z, pts[1].W);
            }
            else
            {
                pta[1] = new Point3(x, pts[2].Y,
                            pts[1].Z, pts[1].W);
                pta[2] = new Point3(x, pts[2].Y,
                            pts[3].Z, pts[1].W);
            }
        }
        else if (elevation < 0)
        {
            if ((azimuth >= -180 && azimuth < -90) ||
                (azimuth >= 0 && azimuth < 90))
            {
                pta[1] = new Point3(x, pts[2].Y,
                            pts[1].Z, pts[1].W);
                pta[2] = new Point3(x, pts[2].Y,
                            pts[3].Z, pts[1].W);
            }
            else
            {
                pta[1] = new Point3(x, pts[0].Y,
                            pts[1].Z, pts[1].W);
                pta[2] = new Point3(x, pts[0].Y,
                            pts[3].Z, pts[1].W);
            }
        }
        for (int i = 0; i < pta.Length; i++)
        {
            pta[i].Transform(m, form1, this);
        }
        g.DrawLine(aPen, pta[0].X,pta[0].Y,pta[1].X,pta[1].Y);
        g.DrawLine(aPen, pta[1].X,pta[1].Y,pta[2].X,pta[2].Y);
    }

// Draw y gridlines:
if (IsYGrid)
{
    for (float y = YMin; y <= YMax; y = y + YTick)
    {
        pts = CoordinatesOfChartBox();
        pta[0] = new Point3(pts[1].X, y, pts[1].Z, pts[1].W);
        if (elevation >= 0)
```

```
        {
            if ((azimuth >= -180 && azimuth < -90) ||
                (azimuth >= 0 && azimuth < 90))
            {
                pta[1] = new Point3(pts[2].X, y,
                    pts[1].Z, pts[1].W);
                pta[2] = new Point3(pts[2].X, y,
                    pts[3].Z, pts[1].W);
            }
            else
            {
                pta[1] = new Point3(pts[0].X, y,
                    pts[1].Z, pts[1].W);
                pta[2] = new Point3(pts[0].X, y,
                    pts[3].Z, pts[1].W);
            }
        }
        if (elevation < 0)
        {
            if ((azimuth >= -180 && azimuth < -90) ||
                (azimuth >= 0 && azimuth < 90))
            {
                pta[1] = new Point3(pts[0].X, y,
                    pts[1].Z, pts[1].W);
                pta[2] = new Point3(pts[0].X, y,
                    pts[3].Z, pts[1].W);

            }
            else
            {
                pta[1] = new Point3(pts[2].X, y,
                    pts[1].Z, pts[1].W);
                pta[2] = new Point3(pts[2].X, y,
                    pts[3].Z, pts[1].W);
            }
        }
        for (int i = 0; i < pta.Length; i++)
        {
            pta[i].Transform(m, form1, this);
        }
                g.DrawLine(aPen, pta[0].X, pta[0].Y,
                    pta[1].X, pta[1].Y);
                g.DrawLine(aPen, pta[1].X, pta[1].Y,
                    pta[2].X, pta[2].Y);
        }
    }

// Draw Z gridlines:
if (IsZGrid)
{
    for (float z = ZMin; z <= ZMax; z = z + ZTick)
    {
        pts = CoordinatesOfChartBox();
        pta[0] = new Point3(pts[2].X, pts[2].Y, z, pts[2].W);
```

```
                    if (elevation >= 0)
                    {
                        if ((azimuth >= -180 && azimuth < -90) ||
                            (azimuth >= 0 && azimuth < 90))
                        {
                            pta[1] = new Point3(pts[2].X,
                                    pts[0].Y, z, pts[1].W);
                            pta[2] = new Point3(pts[0].X,
                                    pts[0].Y, z, pts[1].W);
                        }
                        else
                        {
                            pta[1] = new Point3(pts[0].X,
                                    pts[2].Y, z, pts[1].W);
                            pta[2] = new Point3(pts[0].X,
                                    pts[1].Y, z, pts[1].W);
                        }
                    }
                    if (elevation < 0)
                    {
                        if ((azimuth >= -180 && azimuth < -90) ||
                            (azimuth >= 0 && azimuth < 90))
                        {
                            pta[1] = new Point3(pts[0].X,
                                    pts[2].Y, z, pts[1].W);
                            pta[2] = new Point3(pts[0].X,
                                        pts[0].Y, z, pts[1].W);
                        }
                        else
                        {
                            pta[1] = new Point3(pts[2].X,
                                    pts[0].Y, z, pts[1].W);
                            pta[2] = new Point3(pts[0].X,
                                    pts[0].Y, z, pts[1].W);
                        }
                    }
                    for (int i = 0; i < pta.Length; i++)
                    {
                        pta[i].Transform(m, form1, this);
                    }
                    g.DrawLine(aPen, pta[0].X, pta[0].Y,
                            pta[1].X, pta[1].Y);
                    g.DrawLine(aPen, pta[1].X, pta[1].Y,
                            pta[2].X, pta[2].Y);
                }
            }
        }
```

Labels

3D labels include three parts: he title, tick labels, and labels for the coordinate axes. Creating a title label in 3D is similar to doing so in 2D. However, the tick labels and axis labels in 3D charts are much more complicated than those in 2D charts. First we need to position these labels in the right position by considering the variation of the elevation and azimuth angles. Then, we need to rotate them to be parallel to the coordinate axes when the elevation and azimuth angles are changed. Finally, we want these labels to be properly spaced from the coordinate axes.

The following AddLabels method in the ChartStyle class creates labels in a 3D chart:

```
private void AddLabels(Graphics g)
{
    Matrix3 m = Matrix3.AzimuthElevation(Elevation, Azimuth);
    Point3 pt = new Point3();
    Point3[] pts = CoordinatesOfChartBox();
    SolidBrush aBrush = new SolidBrush(LabelColor);
    StringFormat sf = new StringFormat();
    sf.Alignment = StringAlignment.Center;

    // Add x tick labels:
    float offset = (YMax - YMin) / 20;
    float labelSpace = offset;
    for (float x = XMin + XTick; x < XMax; x = x + XTick)
    {
        if (elevation >= 0)
        {
            if (azimuth >= -90 && azimuth < 90)
                labelSpace = -offset;
        }
        else if (elevation < 0)
        {
            if ((azimuth >= -180 && azimuth < -90) ||
                azimuth >= 90 && azimuth <= 180)
                labelSpace = -offset;
        }
        pt = new Point3(x, pts[1].Y + labelSpace, pts[1].Z, pts[1].W);
        pt.Transform(m, form1, this);
        g.DrawString(x.ToString(), TickFont, aBrush,
            new PointF(pt.X, pt.Y), sf);
    }

    // Add y tick labels:
    offset = (XMax - XMin) / 20;
    labelSpace = offset;
    for (float y = YMin + yTick; y < YMax; y = y + YTick)
    {
        pts = CoordinatesOfChartBox();
        if (elevation >= 0)
        {
            if (azimuth >= -180 && azimuth < 0)
                labelSpace = -offset;
        }
        else if (elevation < 0)
        {
            if (azimuth >= 0 && azimuth < 180)
                labelSpace = -offset;
        }
        pt = new Point3(pts[1].X + labelSpace, y, pts[1].Z, pts[1].W);
```

```
        pt.Transform(m, form1, this);
        g.DrawString(y.ToString(), TickFont, aBrush,
            new PointF(pt.X, pt.Y), sf);

    }


// Add z tick labels:
float xoffset = (XMax - XMin) / 30.0f;
float yoffset = (YMax - YMin) / 15.0f;
float xlabelSpace = xoffset;
float ylabelSpace = yoffset;
SizeF s = g.MeasureString("A", TickFont);
for (float z = ZMin; z <= ZMax; z = z + ZTick)
{
    sf.Alignment = StringAlignment.Far;
    pts = CoordinatesOfChartBox();
    if (elevation >= 0)
    {
        if (azimuth >= -180 && azimuth < -90)
        {
            xlabelSpace = 0;
            ylabelSpace = yoffset;
        }
        else if (azimuth >= -90 && azimuth < 0)
        {
            xlabelSpace = xoffset;
            ylabelSpace = 0;
        }
        else if (azimuth >= 0 && azimuth < 90)
        {
            xlabelSpace = 0;
            ylabelSpace = -yoffset;
        }
        else if (azimuth >= 90 && azimuth <= 180)
        {
            xlabelSpace = -xoffset;
            ylabelSpace = 0;
        }
    }
    else if (elevation < 0)
    {
        if (azimuth >= -180 && azimuth < -90)
        {
            ylabelSpace = 0;
            xlabelSpace = xoffset;
        }
        else if (azimuth >= -90 && azimuth < 0)
        {
            ylabelSpace = -yoffset;
            xlabelSpace = 0;
        }
        else if (azimuth >= 0 && azimuth < 90)
        {
            ylabelSpace = 0;
```

```
                    xlabelSpace = -xoffset;
            }
            else if (azimuth >= 90 && azimuth <= 180)
            {
                ylabelSpace = yoffset;
                xlabelSpace = 0;
            }
        }
    }

    pt = new Point3(pts[2].X + ylabelSpace,
        pts[2].Y + xlabelSpace, z, pts[2].W);
    pt.Transform(m, form1, this);
    g.DrawString(z.ToString(), TickFont, aBrush,
        new PointF(pt.X - labelSpace, pt.Y - s.Height / 2), sf);
}

// Add Title:
sf.Alignment = StringAlignment.Center;
aBrush = new SolidBrush(TitleColor);
if (Title != "No Title")
{
    g.DrawString(Title, titleFont, aBrush,
        new PointF(form1.PlotPanel.Width / 2,
        form1.Height / 30), sf);
}
aBrush.Dispose();

// Add x axis label:
offset = (YMax - YMin) / 3;
labelSpace = offset;
sf.Alignment = StringAlignment.Center;
aBrush = new SolidBrush(LabelColor);
float offset1 = (XMax - XMin) / 10;
float xc = offset1;
if (elevation >= 0)
{
    if (azimuth >= -90 && azimuth < 90)
        labelSpace = -offset;
    if (azimuth >= 0 && azimuth <= 180)
        xc = -offset1;
}
else if (elevation < 0)
{
    if ((azimuth >= -180 && azimuth < -90) ||
        azimuth >= 90 && azimuth <= 180)
        labelSpace = -offset;
    if (Azimuth >= -180 && azimuth <= 0)
        xc = -offset1;
}
Point3[] pta = new Point3[2];
pta[0] = new Point3(XMin, pts[1].Y + labelSpace,
        pts[1].Z, pts[1].W);
pta[1] = new Point3((XMin + XMax) / 2 - xc,
        pts[1].Y + labelSpace, pts[1].Z, pts[1].W);
```

```csharp
pta[0].Transform(m, form1, this);
pta[1].Transform(m, form1, this);
float theta = (float)Math.Atan((pta[1].Y - pta[0].Y) /
        (pta[1].X - pta[0].X));
theta = theta * 180 / (float)Math.PI;
GraphicsState gs = g.Save();
g.TranslateTransform(pta[1].X, pta[1].Y);
g.RotateTransform(theta);
g.DrawString(XLabel, LabelFont, aBrush,
    new PointF(0, 0), sf);
g.Restore(gs);

// Add y axis label:
offset = (XMax - XMin) / 3;
offset1 = (YMax - YMin) / 5;
labelSpace = offset;
float yc = YTick;
if (elevation >= 0)
{
    if (azimuth >= -180 && azimuth < 0)
        labelSpace = -offset;
    if (azimuth >= -90 && azimuth <= 90)
        yc = -offset1;
}
else if (elevation < 0)
{
    yc = -offset1;
    if (azimuth >= 0 && azimuth < 180)
        labelSpace = -offset;
    if (azimuth >= -90 && azimuth <= 90)
        yc = offset1;
}
pta[0] = new Point3(pts[1].X + labelSpace,
        YMin, pts[1].Z, pts[1].W);
pta[1] = new Point3(pts[1].X + labelSpace,
        (YMin + YMax)/2 + yc, pts[1].Z, pts[1].W);
pta[0].Transform(m, form1, this);
pta[1].Transform(m, form1, this);
theta = (float)Math.Atan((pta[1].Y - pta[0].Y) /
        (pta[1].X - pta[0].X));
theta = theta * 180 / (float)Math.PI;
gs = g.Save();
g.TranslateTransform(pta[1].X, pta[1].Y);
g.RotateTransform(theta);
g.DrawString(YLabel, LabelFont, aBrush,
    new PointF(0, 0), sf);
g.Restore(gs);

// Add z axis labels:
float zticklength = 10;
labelSpace = -1.3f * offset;
offset1 = (ZMax - ZMin) / 8;
float zc = -offset1;
for (float z = ZMin; z < ZMax; z = z + ZTick)
```

```
    {
        SizeF size = g.MeasureString(z.ToString(), TickFont);
        if (zticklength < size.Width)
            zticklength = size.Width;
    }
    float zlength = -zticklength;
    if (elevation >= 0)
    {
        if (azimuth >= -180 && azimuth < -90)
        {
            zlength = -zticklength;
            labelSpace = -1.3f * offset;
            zc = -offset1;
        }
        else if (azimuth >= -90 && azimuth < 0)
        {
            zlength = zticklength;
            labelSpace = 2 * offset / 3;
            zc = offset1;
        }
        else if (azimuth >= 0 && azimuth < 90)
        {
            zlength = zticklength;
            labelSpace = 2 * offset / 3;
            zc = -offset1;
        }
        else if (azimuth >= 90 && azimuth <= 180)
        {
            zlength = -zticklength;
            labelSpace = -1.3f * offset;
            zc = offset1;
        }
    }
    else if (elevation < 0)
    {
        if (azimuth >= -180 && azimuth < -90)
        {
            zlength = -zticklength;
            labelSpace = -1.3f * offset;
            zc = offset1;
        }
        else if (azimuth >= -90 && azimuth < 0)
        {
            zlength = zticklength;
            labelSpace = 2 * offset / 3;
            zc = -offset1;
        }
        else if (azimuth >= 0 && azimuth < 90)
        {
            zlength = zticklength;
            labelSpace = 2 * offset / 3;
            zc = offset1;
        }
        else if (azimuth >= 90 && azimuth <= 180)
```

```
            {
                zlength = -zticklength;
                labelSpace = -1.3f * offset;
                zc = -offset1;
            }
        }
        pta[0] = new Point3(pts[2].X - labelSpace, pts[2].Y,
            (ZMin + ZMax) / 2 + zc, pts[2].W);
        pta[0].Transform(m, form1, this);
        gs = g.Save();
        g.TranslateTransform(pta[0].X - zlength, pta[0].Y);
        g.RotateTransform(270);
        g.DrawString(ZLabel, LabelFont, aBrush,
            new PointF(0, 0), sf);
        g.Restore(gs);
}
```

Testing Project

Now, we can put all of the basic classes we have created together into a new C# project, *Example6_1*. This project contains the following classes: Point3, Matrix3, LineStyle (from the previous projects, such as *Example3_6*), and ChartStyle. Add a public method, AddChartStyle, to the ChartStyle class:

```
        public void AddChartStyle(Graphics g)
        {
            AddTicks(g);
            AddGrids(g);
            AddAxes(g);
            AddLabels(g);
        }
```

The following Form1 class can be used to test the basic features of a 3D coordinate system:

```
using System;
using System.Drawing;
using System.Drawing.Drawing2D;
using System.Windows.Forms;

namespace Example6_1
{
    public partial class Form1 : Form
    {
        ChartStyle cs;

        public Form1()
        {
            InitializeComponent();
            this.SetStyle(ControlStyles.AllPaintingInWmPaint |
                ControlStyles.UserPaint |
                ControlStyles.DoubleBuffer,true);
            this.SetStyle(ControlStyles.ResizeRedraw, true);
```

```
        // Subscribing to a paint eventhandler to drawingPanel:
        PlotPanel.Paint +=
            new PaintEventHandler(PlotPanelPaint);

        // Specify chart style parameters:
        cs = new ChartStyle(this);
        cs.GridStyle.LineColor = Color.LightGray;
        cs.GridStyle.Pattern = DashStyle.Dash;
        cs.AxisStyle.LineColor = Color.Blue;
        cs.AxisStyle.Thickness = 2;
        cs.YTick = 1f;
    }

    private void PlotPanelPaint(object sender, PaintEventArgs e)
    {
        Graphics g = e.Graphics;
        g.SmoothingMode = SmoothingMode.AntiAlias;
        cs.Elevation = trkElevation.Value;
        cs.Azimuth = trkAzimuth.Value;
        cs.AddChartStyle(g);
    }

    private void trkElevation_Scroll(object sender, EventArgs e)
    {
        tbElevation.Text = trkElevation.Value.ToString();
        PlotPanel.Invalidate();
    }

    private void trkAzimuth_Scroll(object sender, EventArgs e)
    {
        tbAzimuth.Text = trkAzimuth.Value.ToString();
        PlotPanel.Invalidate();
    }

    private void tbElevation_KeyUp(object sender, KeyEventArgs e)
    {
        int value;
        bool result = Int32.TryParse(tbElevation.Text, out value);
        if (result)
        {
            if (value <= -90)
                value = -90;
            else if (value >= 90)
                value = 90;
            trkElevation.Value = value;
        }
        PlotPanel.Invalidate();
    }
    private void tbAzimuth_KeyUp(object sender, KeyEventArgs e)
    {
        int value;
        bool result = Int32.TryParse(tbAzimuth.Text, out value);
        if (result)
```

```
{
```

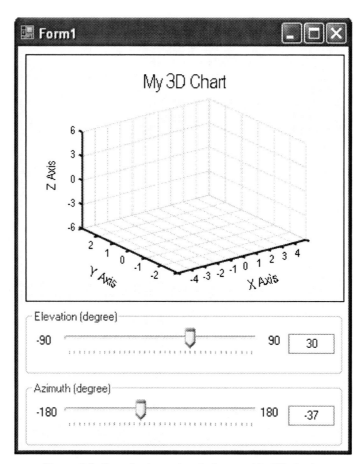

Figure 6-2 Coordinate system to be used in 3D charts.

```
        if (value <= -180)
            value = -180;
        else if (value >= 180)
            value = 180;
        trkAzimuth.Value = value;
    }
    PlotPanel.Invalidate();
  }
 }
}
```

In this class, there are two track-bars that can be used to continuously change the elevation and azimuth angles. We also put two textboxes in Form1 to display the values of the corresponding track-bars. You can also directly enter the elevation and azimuth angles into the textboxes.

This project produces the output of Figure 6-2. You can see how the coordinate axes, gridlines, and labels respond to the changes of the elevation and azimuth angles.

3D Line Charts

In the previous section, we implemented the basic coordinate system for 3D charts in C#, which seems very involved. However, once you have finished this framework, you can use it without any modification for a variety of 3D chart applications. Here, I will show you how easy it is to create a 3D line chart based on this basic framework of *Example6_1*. The 3D line chart displays a 3D plot of a set of data points. It is similar to a 2D line chart, except that an additional component, Z, is used to provide data for the third dimension.

Implementation

Start with a new C# Windows Application project, *Example6_2*. Import all of the classes of the previous project *Example6_1*, including the Form1 class, to the current project, and change their namespace to *Example6_2*. Add a DataSeries class to the current project. The DataSeries used here is very similar to the one used in 2D charts, except that the PointList in this class must hold 3D points. The following is its code listing:

```
using System;
using System.Collections;
using System.Drawing;

namespace Example6_2
{
    public class DataSeries
    {
        private ArrayList pointList;
        private LineStyle lineStyle;

        public DataSeries()
        {
            lineStyle = new LineStyle();
            pointList = new ArrayList();
        }

        public LineStyle LineStyle
        {
            get { return lineStyle; }
            set { lineStyle = value; }
        }

        public ArrayList PointList
        {
            get { return pointList; }
            set { pointList = value; }
        }

        public void AddPoint(Point3 pt)
```

```
            {
                PointList.Add(pt);
            }
        }
    }
```

Unlike 2D charts, here we do not need a `DataCollection` class because we only allow one set of data points to be drawn in a 3D chart. Drawing multiple sets of data points in a 3D chart becomes more confusing than it does in the case of 2D. If you do want to have this capability, you can easily add it to your applications using the `DataCollection` class in the same manner as you do in the 2D charts. To simplify our discussion, we will only consider 3D charts with one set of data points.

Add another new class, `DrawChart`, to the project. We want to implement all chart-drawing related code in this class, and keep the other basic classes unchanged.

```csharp
using System;
using System.Drawing;

namespace Example6_2
{
    public class DrawChart
    {
        Form1 form1;
        public DrawChart(Form1 fm1)
        {
            form1 = fm1;
        }

        public void AddLine(Graphics g, DataSeries ds, ChartStyle cs)
        {
            Pen aPen = new Pen(ds.LineStyle.LineColor,
                    ds.LineStyle.Thickness);
            aPen.DashStyle = ds.LineStyle.Pattern;

            Matrix3 m = Matrix3.AzimuthElevation(
                    cs.Elevation, cs.Azimuth);
            Point3[] pts = new Point3[ds.PointList.Count];

            for (int i = 0; i < pts.Length; i++)
            {
                pts[i] = (Point3)ds.PointList[i];
                pts[i].Transform(m, form1, cs);
            }

            // Draw line:
            if (ds.LineStyle.IsVisible == true)
            {
                for (int i = 1; i < pts.Length; i++)
                {
                    g.DrawLine(aPen, pts[i - 1].X,
                            pts[i - 1].Y, pts[i].X, pts[i].Y);
                }
                aPen.Dispose();
```

```
            }
         }
      }
   }
}
```

In this class, we first perform the transformations on the 3D data points by calling the Point3.Transform method using the AzimuthElevation orthogonal projection matrix. Then we draw the line chart using the X and Y components of the projected 3D data points.

All the other classes from the previous *Example6_1* remain unchanged.

Testing Project

You can test the 3D line chart using the following Form1 class, in which we need to specify the data range, add the data points, and call the AddLine method to draw the chart. Here is the code listing of the Form1 class:

```
using System;
using System.Drawing;
using System.Drawing.Drawing2D;
using System.Windows.Forms;

namespace Example6_2
{
    public partial class Form1 : Form
    {
        ChartStyle cs;
        DataSeries ds;
        DrawChart dc;

        public Form1()
        {
            InitializeComponent();
            this.SetStyle(ControlStyles.AllPaintingInWmPaint |
                ControlStyles.UserPaint |
                ControlStyles.DoubleBuffer,true);
            this.SetStyle(ControlStyles.ResizeRedraw, true);
            this.BackColor = Color.White;

            // Subscribing to a paint eventhandler to drawingPanel:
            PlotPanel.Paint +=
                new PaintEventHandler(PlotPanelPaint);

            // Specify parameters for the chart:
            cs = new ChartStyle(this);
            ds = new DataSeries();
            dc = new DrawChart(this);
            cs.GridStyle.LineColor = Color.LightGray;
            cs.GridStyle.Pattern = DashStyle.Dash;
            cs.XMin = -1f;
            cs.XMax = 1f;
            cs.YMin = -1f;
            cs.YMax = 1f;
```

```
        cs.ZMin = 0;
        cs.ZMax = 30;
        cs.XTick = 0.5f;
        cs.YTick = 0.5f;
        cs.ZTick = 5;
    }

    private void AddData()
    {
        ds.PointList.Clear();
        ds.LineStyle.LineColor = Color.Red;

        for (int i = 0; i < 300; i++)
        {
            float t = 0.1f * i;
            float x = (float)Math.Exp(-t / 30) *
                    (float)Math.Cos(t);
            float y = (float)Math.Exp(-t / 30) *
                    (float)Math.Sin(t);
            float z = t;
            ds.AddPoint(new Point3(x, y, z, 1));
        }
    }

    private void PlotPanelPaint(object sender, PaintEventArgs e)
    {
        Graphics g = e.Graphics;
        g.SmoothingMode = SmoothingMode.AntiAlias;
        cs.Elevation = trkElevation.Value;
        cs.Azimuth = trkAzimuth.Value;
        cs.AddChartStyle(g);
        AddData();
        dc.AddLine(g, ds, cs);
    }

    private void trkElevation_Scroll(object sender, EventArgs e)
    {
        tbElevation.Text = trkElevation.Value.ToString();
        PlotPanel.Invalidate();
    }

    private void trkAzimuth_Scroll(object sender, EventArgs e)
    {
        tbAzimuth.Text = trkAzimuth.Value.ToString();
        PlotPanel.Invalidate();
    }

    private void tbElevation_KeyUp(object sender, KeyEventArgs e)
    {
        int value;
        bool result = Int32.TryParse(tbElevation.Text, out value);
        if (result)
        {
            if (value <= -90)
```

```
                        value = -90;
                else if (value >= 90)
                    value = 90;
                trkElevation.Value = value;
        }
        PlotPanel.Invalidate();
}
private void tbAzimuth_KeyUp(object sender, KeyEventArgs e)
{
        int value;
        bool result = Int32.TryParse(tbAzimuth.Text, out value);
        if (result)
        {
            if (value <= -180)
                value = -180;
            else if (value >= 180)
                value = 180;
```

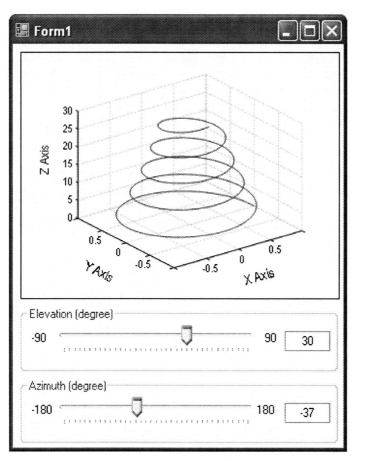

Figure 6-3 A 3D line chart.

```
                    trkAzimuth.Value = value;
                }
                PlotPanel.Invalidate();
            }
        }
    }
}
```

Please note how we add the 3D data points to the `PointList` in the `AddData` method. This project generates the result of Figure 6-3. As in the case of 2D, here you can specify the line color, dash type, and width. You can also look at the line chart from a different viewport by changing the elevation and azimuth angles.

3D Chart Package

Since all of the different 3D charts share the same framework, instead of creating a separate program for each type of 3D chart, here we will implement a complete 3D charting package that integrates various types of 3D charts together. Using this package as a basis, you can easily create your own professional 3D chart applications.

This package uses several classes from the previous projects, including `ChartStyle`, `LineStyle`, `ColorMap`, `Matrix3`, and `DataSeries`. The `LineStyle`, `ColorMap`, and `Matrix3` classes are the same as those in the previous projects, while the others need to be modified to reflect 3D features. In the following subsections, we will show you how to modify these classes, and also discuss the new classes added to this 3D package.

Chart Style

The 3D chart style is exactly the same as the `ChartStyle` class used in the previous project, *Example6_2*. But for 2D plots projecte from 3D charts, such as contour and color map plots on the X-Y plane, that are to be implemented into this package, we also need to add a 2D chart style that is similar to the `ChartStyle` class used in 2D charts discussed in Chapters 3 and 4. Here we add a class, `ChartStyle2D`, to the project:

```
using System;
using System.Collections;
using System.Drawing;
using System.Drawing.Drawing2D;
using System.Text;

namespace Example6_3
{
    public class ChartStyle2D
    {
        private Form1 form1;
        private Rectangle chartArea;
        private Color chartBackColor;
        private Color chartBorderColor;
        private Color plotBackColor = Color.White;
        private Color plotBorderColor = Color.Black;
```

```
public ChartStyle2D(Form1 fm1)
{
    form1 = fm1;
    Rectangle rect = form1.ClientRectangle;
    chartArea = new Rectangle(rect.X, rect.Y,
            rect.Width, 3 * rect.Height / 5);
    chartBackColor = fm1.BackColor;
    chartBorderColor = fm1.BackColor;
}

public Color ChartBackColor
{
    get { return chartBackColor; }
    set { chartBackColor = value; }
}

public Color ChartBorderColor
{
    get { return chartBorderColor; }
    set { chartBorderColor = value; }
}

public Rectangle ChartArea
{
    get { return chartArea; }
    set { chartArea = value; }
}

public void AddChartStyle2D(Graphics g, ChartStyle cs3d)
{
    Pen aPen = new Pen(Color.Black, 1f);

    SizeF tickFontSize = g.MeasureString("A", cs3d.TickFont);
    // Create vertical gridlines:
    float fX, fY;
    if (cs3d.IsYGrid == true)
    {
        aPen = new Pen(cs3d.GridStyle.LineColor, 1f);
        aPen.DashStyle = cs3d.GridStyle.Pattern;
        for (fX = cs3d.XMin + cs3d.XTick; fX < cs3d.XMax;
            fX += cs3d.XTick)
        {
            g.DrawLine(aPen, Point2D(new PointF(fX,
                        cs3d.YMin), cs3d),
                Point2D(new PointF(fX, cs3d.YMax), cs3d));
        }
    }

    // Create horizontal gridlines:
    if (cs3d.IsXGrid == true)
    {
        aPen = new Pen(cs3d.GridStyle.LineColor, 1f);
        aPen.DashStyle = cs3d.GridStyle.Pattern;
        for (fY = cs3d.YMin + cs3d.YTick; fY < cs3d.YMax;
```

```
                            fY += cs3d.YTick)
                {
                    g.DrawLine(aPen, Point2D(new PointF(
                        cs3d.XMin, fY),cs3d),
                        Point2D(new PointF(cs3d.XMax, fY),cs3d));
                }
            }

            // Create the x-axis tick marks:
            for (fX = cs3d.XMin; fX <= cs3d.XMax; fX += cs3d.XTick)
            {
                PointF yAxisPoint = Point2D(new PointF(fX,
                    cs3d.YMin), cs3d);
                g.DrawLine(Pens.Black, yAxisPoint, new PointF(
                    yAxisPoint.X, yAxisPoint.Y - 5f));
            }

            // Create the y-axis tick marks:
            for (fY = cs3d.YMin; fY <= cs3d.YMax; fY += cs3d.YTick)
            {
                PointF xAxisPoint = Point2D(new PointF(cs3d.XMin,
                    fY), cs3d);
                g.DrawLine(Pens.Black, xAxisPoint,
                    new PointF(xAxisPoint.X + 5f, xAxisPoint.Y));
            }

            aPen.Dispose();
        }

        private void AddLabels(Graphics g, ChartStyle cs3d)
        {
            float xOffset = ChartArea.Width / 30.0f;
            float yOffset = ChartArea.Height / 30.0f;
            SizeF labelFontSize = g.MeasureString("A",
                    cs3d.LabelFont);
            SizeF titleFontSize = g.MeasureString("A",
                    cs3d.TitleFont);
            SizeF tickFontSize = g.MeasureString("A",
                    cs3d.TickFont);

            SolidBrush aBrush = new SolidBrush(cs3d.TickColor);
            StringFormat sFormat = new StringFormat();

            // Create the x-axis tick marks:
            aBrush = new SolidBrush(cs3d.TickColor);
            for (float fX = cs3d.XMin; fX <= cs3d.XMax;
                    fX += cs3d.XTick)
            {
                PointF yAxisPoint = Point2D(new PointF(fX,
                        cs3d.YMin), cs3d);
                sFormat.Alignment = StringAlignment.Far;
                SizeF sizeXTick = g.MeasureString(fX.ToString(),
                        cs3d.TickFont);
                g.DrawString(fX.ToString(), cs3d.TickFont, aBrush,
```

```
            new PointF(yAxisPoint.X +
            sizeXTick.Width / 2 + form1.PlotPanel.Left,
        yAxisPoint.Y + 4f + form1.PlotPanel.Top),
            sFormat);
}

// Create the y-axis tick marks:
for (float fY = cs3d.YMin; fY <= cs3d.YMax; fY +=
    cs3d.YTick)
{
    PointF xAxisPoint = Point2D(new PointF(cs3d.XMin,
        fY), cs3d);
    sFormat.Alignment = StringAlignment.Far;
    g.DrawString(fY.ToString(), cs3d.TickFont, aBrush,
        new PointF(xAxisPoint.X - 3f +
        form1.PlotPanel.Left,
        xAxisPoint.Y - tickFontSize.Height / 2 +
        form1.PlotPanel.Top), sFormat);
}

// Add horizontal axis label:
aBrush = new SolidBrush(cs3d.LabelColor);
SizeF stringSize = g.MeasureString(cs3d.XLabel,
    cs3d.LabelFont);
g.DrawString(cs3d.XLabel, cs3d.LabelFont, aBrush,
    new Point(form1.PlotPanel.Left +
    form1.PlotPanel.Width / 2 -
    (int)stringSize.Width / 2, ChartArea.Bottom -
    (int)yOffset - (int)labelFontSize.Height));

// Add y-axis label:
sFormat.Alignment = StringAlignment.Center;
stringSize = g.MeasureString(cs3d.YLabel, cs3d.LabelFont);
// Save the state of the current Graphics object
GraphicsState gState = g.Save();
g.TranslateTransform(xOffset, yOffset +
    titleFontSize.Height + yOffset / 3 +
    form1.PlotPanel.Height / 2);
g.RotateTransform(-90);
g.DrawString(cs3d.YLabel, cs3d.LabelFont,
    aBrush, 0, 0, sFormat);
// Restore it:
g.Restore(gState);

// Add title:
aBrush = new SolidBrush(cs3d.TitleColor);
stringSize = g.MeasureString(cs3d.Title, cs3d.TitleFont);
if (cs3d.Title.ToUpper() != "NO TITLE")
{
    g.DrawString(cs3d.Title, cs3d.TitleFont, aBrush,
        new Point(form1.PlotPanel.Left +
        form1.PlotPanel.Width / 2 -
        (int)stringSize.Width / 2, ChartArea.Top +
        (int)yOffset));
```

```
        }
        aBrush.Dispose();
    }

    public void SetPlotArea(Graphics g, ChartStyle cs3d)
    {
        // Draw chart area:
        SolidBrush aBrush = new SolidBrush(ChartBackColor);
        Pen aPen = new Pen(ChartBorderColor, 2);
        g.FillRectangle(aBrush, ChartArea);
        g.DrawRectangle(aPen, ChartArea);

        // Set PlotArea:
        float xOffset = ChartArea.Width / 30.0f;
        float yOffset = ChartArea.Height / 30.0f;
        SizeF labelFontSize = g.MeasureString("A",
                cs3d.LabelFont);
        SizeF titleFontSize = g.MeasureString("A",
                cs3d.TitleFont);
        if (cs3d.Title.ToUpper() == "NO TITLE")
        {
            titleFontSize.Width = 8f;
            titleFontSize.Height = 8f;
        }
        float xSpacing = xOffset / 3.0f;
        float ySpacing = yOffset / 3.0f;
        SizeF tickFontSize = g.MeasureString("A", cs3d.TickFont);
        float tickSpacing = 2f;
        SizeF yTickSize = g.MeasureString(
                cs3d.YMin.ToString(), cs3d.TickFont);
        for (float yTick = cs3d.YMin; yTick <= cs3d.YMax;
                yTick += cs3d.YTick)
        {
            SizeF tempSize = g.MeasureString(yTick.ToString(),
                    cs3d.TickFont);
            if (yTickSize.Width < tempSize.Width)
            {
                yTickSize = tempSize;
            }
        }
        float leftMargin = xOffset + labelFontSize.Width +
                xSpacing + yTickSize.Width + tickSpacing;
        float rightMargin = 2 * xOffset;
        float topMargin = yOffset +
                titleFontSize.Height + ySpacing;
        float bottomMargin = yOffset + labelFontSize.Height +
                ySpacing + tickSpacing + tickFontSize.Height;

        // Define the plot area:
        int plotX = ChartArea.X + (int)leftMargin;
        int plotY = ChartArea.Y + (int)topMargin;
        int plotWidth = ChartArea.Width - (int)leftMargin -
                (int)rightMargin;
        int plotHeight = ChartArea.Height - (int)topMargin -
```

```
                        (int)bottomMargin;
            form1.PlotPanel.Left = plotX;
            form1.PlotPanel.Top = plotY;
            if (cs3d.IsColorBar)
                form1.PlotPanel.Width = 25 * plotWidth / 30;
            else
                form1.PlotPanel.Width = plotWidth;
            form1.PlotPanel.Height = plotHeight;
            AddLabels(g, cs3d);
        }

        public PointF Point2D(PointF pt, ChartStyle cs3d)
        {
            PointF aPoint = new PointF();
            if (pt.X < cs3d.XMin || pt.X > cs3d.XMax ||
                pt.Y < cs3d.YMin || pt.Y > cs3d.YMax)
            {
                pt.X = Single.NaN;
                pt.Y = Single.NaN;
            }
            aPoint.X = (pt.X - cs3d.XMin) *
                form1.PlotPanel.Width / (cs3d.XMax - cs3d.XMin);
            aPoint.Y = form1.PlotPanel.Height - (pt.Y - cs3d.YMin) *
                form1.PlotPanel.Height / (cs3d.YMax - cs3d.YMin);
            return aPoint;
        }
    }
}
```

Most of this class is similar to that used in Chapters 3 and 4, except for a minor modification: the size of the plot area now depends on whether the chart has a color bar.

Point4 Class

In discussing 3D graphics objects, we defined the Point3 class. However, if you want to display a data set that is defined on the 3D grids, you need to define a 4D point to represent a value defined on the position of the X, Y, and Z. This is called the volume visualization technique. The volume data sets are characterized by multidimensional arrays of scalar or vector data. This data is typically defined on lattice structures representing values sampled in 3D space. There are two basic types of volume data: scalar and vector. Scalar volume data contains a single value for each 3D grid point, while vector volume data contains two or three values for each point, defining the components of a vector.

In this package, we consider only scalar volume data, and show you how to create a slice plane to view this scalar volume data. You can easily create the vector volume data simply by extending the Point4 class. You can use the Point4 class to create scalar volume data. Here is the code listing of this class:

```
using System;

namespace Example6_3
{
    public class Point4
```

```
        {
            public Point3 point3 = new Point3();
            public float V = 0;

            public Point4()
            {

            }

            public Point4(Point3 pt3, float v)
            {
                point3 = pt3;
                V = v;
            }
        }
    }
```

This class is very simple: the first component is the Point3 object that contains the X, Y, Z, and W components defined in 3D homogeneous coordinate system, and the second component is the value defined at the position of Point3.

Data Series

The DataSeries class is extended to include an array list, PointList, to hold the data points for a 3D line plot, a 2D point array of Point3[,], PointArray, to hold the data for standard 3D mesh and surface charts; and a 3D point array of Point4[, ,], Point4Array, to hold the volume data for slice charts. In addition, we add a few methods to compute the minimum and maximum of a data set. Here is the code listing for this class:

```
using System;
using System.Collections;
using System.Drawing;

namespace Example6_3
{
    public class DataSeries
    {
        private ArrayList pointList;
        private LineStyle lineStyle;
        private BarStyle barStyle;
        private float xdataMin = -5;
        private float ydataMin = -5;
        private float zzdataMin = -5;
        private float xSpacing = 1;
        private float ySpacing = 1;
        private float zSpacing = 1;
        private int xNumber = 10;
        private int yNumber = 10;
        private int zNumber = 10;
        private Point3[,] pointArray;
        private Point4[, ,] point4Array;

        public DataSeries()
```

```
{
    lineStyle = new LineStyle();
    barStyle = new BarStyle();
    pointList = new ArrayList();
}

public Point4[, ,] Point4Array
{
    get { return point4Array; }
    set { point4Array = value; }
}

public Point3[,] PointArray
{
    get { return pointArray; }
    set { pointArray = value; }
}

public int XNumber
{
    get { return xNumber; }
    set { xNumber = value; }
}

public int YNumber
{
    get { return yNumber; }
    set { yNumber = value; }
}

public int ZNumber
{
    get { return zNumber; }
    set { zNumber = value; }
}

public float XSpacing
{
    get { return xSpacing; }
    set { xSpacing = value; }
}

public float YSpacing
{
    get { return ySpacing; }
    set { ySpacing = value; }
}

public float ZSpacing
{
    get { return zSpacing; }
    set { zSpacing = value; }
}
```

```csharp
public float XDataMin
{
    get { return xdataMin; }
    set { xdataMin = value; }
}

public float YDataMin
{
    get { return ydataMin; }
    set { ydataMin = value; }
}

public float ZZDataMin
{
    get { return zzdataMin; }
    set { zzdataMin = value; }
}

public LineStyle LineStyle
{
    get { return lineStyle; }
    set { lineStyle = value; }
}

public BarStyle BarStyle
{
    get { return barStyle; }
    set { barStyle = value; }
}

public ArrayList PointList
{
    get { return pointList; }
    set { pointList = value; }
}

public void AddPoint(Point3 pt)
{
    PointList.Add(pt);
}

public float ZDataMin()
{
    float zmin = 0;
    for (int i = 0; i < PointArray.GetLength(0); i++)
    {
        for (int j = 0; j < PointArray.GetLength(1); j++)
        {
            zmin = Math.Min(zmin, PointArray[i, j].Z);
        }
    }
    return zmin;
}
```

```
public float ZDataMax()
{
    float zmax = 0;
    for (int i = 0; i < PointArray.GetLength(0); i++)
    {
        for (int j = 0; j < PointArray.GetLength(1); j++)
        {
            zmax = Math.Max(zmax, PointArray[i, j].Z);
        }
    }
    return zmax;
}

public float VDataMin()
{
    float vmin = 0;
    for (int i = 0; i < Point4Array.GetLength(0); i++)
    {
        for (int j = 0; j < Point4Array.GetLength(1); j++)
        {
            for (int k = 0; k < Point4Array.GetLength(2); k++)
            {
                vmin = Math.Min(vmin, Point4Array[i, j, k].V);
            }
        }
    }
    return vmin;
}

public float VDataMax()
{
    float vmax = 0;
    for (int i = 0; i < Point4Array.GetLength(0); i++)
    {
        for (int j = 0; j < Point4Array.GetLength(1); j++)
        {
            for (int k = 0; k < Point4Array.GetLength(2); k++)
            {
                vmax = Math.Max(vmax, Point4Array[i, j, k].V);
            }
        }
    }
    return vmax;
}
    }
}
```

Chart Functions

For convenience when testing the 3D package, we create several data sets from different functions and put them together into the ChartFunctions class:

```
using System;
```

```
namespace Example6_3
{
    public class ChartFunctions
    {
        public ChartFunctions()
        {
        }

        public void Line3D(DataSeries ds, ChartStyle cs)
        {
            cs.XMin = -1f;
            cs.XMax = 1f;
            cs.YMin = -1f;
            cs.YMax = 1f;
            cs.ZMin = 0;
            cs.ZMax = 30;
            cs.XTick = 0.5f;
            cs.YTick = 0.5f;
            cs.ZTick = 5;

            ds.XDataMin = cs.XMin;
            ds.YDataMin = cs.YMin;
            ds.XSpacing = 0.3f;
            ds.YSpacing = 0.3f;
            ds.XNumber = Convert.ToInt16((cs.XMax - cs.XMin) /
                    ds.XSpacing) + 1;
            ds.YNumber = Convert.ToInt16((cs.YMax - cs.YMin) /
                    ds.YSpacing) + 1;
            ds.PointList.Clear();

            for (int i = 0; i < 300; i++)
            {
                float t = 0.1f * i;
                float x = (float)Math.Exp(-t / 30) *
                    (float)Math.Cos(t);
                float y = (float)Math.Exp(-t / 30) *
                    (float)Math.Sin(t);
                float z = t;
                ds.AddPoint(new Point3(x, y, z, 1));
            }
        }

        public void Peak3D(DataSeries ds, ChartStyle cs)
        {
            cs.XMin = -3;
            cs.XMax = 3;
            cs.YMin = -3;
            cs.YMax = 3;
            cs.ZMin = -8;
            cs.ZMax = 8;
            cs.XTick = 1;
            cs.YTick = 1;
            cs.ZTick = 4;
```

```
        ds.XDataMin = cs.XMin;
        ds.YDataMin = cs.YMin;
        ds.XSpacing = 0.5f;
        ds.YSpacing = 0.5f;
        ds.XNumber = Convert.ToInt16((cs.XMax - cs.XMin) /
                ds.XSpacing) + 1;
        ds.YNumber = Convert.ToInt16((cs.YMax - cs.YMin) /
                ds.YSpacing) + 1;

        Point3[,] pts = new Point3[ds.XNumber, ds.YNumber];
        for (int i = 0; i < ds.XNumber; i++)
        {
            for (int j = 0; j < ds.YNumber; j++)
            {
                float x = ds.XDataMin + i * ds.XSpacing;
                float y = ds.YDataMin + j * ds.YSpacing;
                double zz = 3 * Math.Pow((1 - x), 2) *
                    Math.Exp(-x * x - (y + 1) * (y + 1)) - 10 *
                    (0.2 * x - Math.Pow(x, 3) - Math.Pow(y, 5)) *
                    Math.Exp(-x * x - y * y) - 1 / 3 *
                    Math.Exp(-(x + 1) * (x + 1) - y * y);
                float z = (float)zz;
                pts[i, j] = new Point3(x, y, z, 1);
            }
        }
        ds.PointArray = pts;
    }

    public void SinROverR3D(DataSeries ds, ChartStyle cs)
    {
        cs.XMin = -8;
        cs.XMax = 8;
        cs.YMin = -8;
        cs.YMax = 8;
        cs.ZMin = -0.5f;
        cs.ZMax = 1;
        cs.XTick = 4;
        cs.YTick = 4;
        cs.ZTick = 0.5f;

        ds.XDataMin = cs.XMin;
        ds.YDataMin = cs.YMin;
        ds.XSpacing = 1f;
        ds.YSpacing = 1f;
        ds.XNumber = Convert.ToInt16((cs.XMax - cs.XMin) /
                ds.XSpacing) + 1;
        ds.YNumber = Convert.ToInt16((cs.YMax - cs.YMin) /
                ds.YSpacing) + 1;

        Point3[,] pts = new Point3[ds.XNumber, ds.YNumber];
        for (int i = 0; i < ds.XNumber; i++)
        {
            for (int j = 0; j < ds.YNumber; j++)
```

```
            {
                float x = ds.XDataMin + i * ds.XSpacing;
                float y = ds.YDataMin + j * ds.YSpacing;
                float r = (float)Math.Sqrt(x * x + y * y) +
                    0.000001f;
                float z = (float)Math.Sin(r) / r;
                pts[i, j] = new Point3(x, y, z, 1);
            }
        }
    ds.PointArray = pts;
}

public void Exp4D(DataSeries ds, ChartStyle cs)
{
    cs.XMin = -2;
    cs.XMax = 2;
    cs.YMin = -2;
    cs.YMax = 2;
    cs.ZMin = -2;
    cs.ZMax = 2;
    cs.XTick = 1;
    cs.YTick = 1;
    cs.ZTick = 1;

    ds.XDataMin = cs.XMin;
    ds.YDataMin = cs.YMin;
    ds.ZZDataMin = cs.ZMin;
    ds.XSpacing = 0.1f;
    ds.YSpacing = 0.1f;
    ds.ZSpacing = 0.1f;
    ds.XNumber = Convert.ToInt16((cs.XMax - cs.XMin) /
            ds.XSpacing) + 1;
    ds.YNumber = Convert.ToInt16((cs.YMax - cs.YMin) /
            ds.YSpacing) + 1;
    ds.ZNumber = Convert.ToInt16((cs.ZMax - cs.ZMin) /
            ds.ZSpacing) + 1;

    Point4[, ,] pts = new Point4[ds.XNumber, ds.YNumber,
            ds.ZNumber];
    for (int i = 0; i < ds.XNumber; i++)
    {
        for (int j = 0; j < ds.YNumber; j++)
        {
            for (int k = 0; k < ds.ZNumber; k++)
            {
                float x = ds.XDataMin + i * ds.XSpacing;
                float y = ds.YDataMin + j * ds.YSpacing;
                float z = cs.ZMin + k * ds.ZSpacing;
                float v = z * (float)Math.Exp(-x * x -
                    y * y - z * z);
                pts[i, j, k] = new Point4(new Point3(
                    x, y, z, 1), v);
            }
        }
```

```
            }
            ds.Point4Array = pts;
        }
    }
}
```

The `Line3D` method creates data for drawing 3D line charts. Both the `Peak3D` and `SinROverR3D` methods create data for testing mesh, surface, and contour charts. Finally, the `Exp4D` method is used to create scalar volume data for testing slice charts.

DrawChart Class

As shown in the previous project, *Example6_2*, we implement all chart-drawing related codes in the `DrawChart` class. Here is the code fragment of this class:

```
using System;
using System.Drawing;

namespace Example6_3
{
    public class DrawChart
    {
        private Form1 form1;
        private ChartTypeEnum chartType;
        private int[,] cmap;
        private bool isColorMap = true;
        private bool isHiddenLine = false;
        private bool isInterp = false;
        private int numberInterp = 2;
        private int numberContours = 10;
        private SliceEnum xyzSlice = SliceEnum.XSlice;
        private float sliceLocation = 0;
        private bool isBarSingleColor = true;

        public DrawChart(Form1 fm1)
        {
            form1 = fm1;
        }

        public float SliceLocation
        {
            get { return sliceLocation; }
            set { sliceLocation = value; }
        }

        public bool IsBarSingleColor
        {
            get { return isBarSingleColor; }
            set { isBarSingleColor = value; }
        }

        public int NumberContours
        {
```

```csharp
        get { return numberContours; }
        set { numberContours = value; }
    }

    public int NumberInterp
    {
        get { return numberInterp; }
        set { numberInterp = value; }
    }

    public bool IsInterp
    {
        get { return isInterp; }
        set { isInterp = value; }
    }

    public bool IsColorMap
    {
        get { return isColorMap; }
        set { isColorMap = value; }
    }

    public bool IsHiddenLine
    {
        get { return isHiddenLine; }
        set { isHiddenLine = value; }
    }

    public int[,] CMap
    {
        get { return cmap; }
        set { cmap = value; }
    }

    public ChartTypeEnum ChartType
    {
        get { return chartType; }
        set { chartType = value; }
    }

    public SliceEnum XYZSlice
    {
        get { return xyzSlice; }
        set { xyzSlice = value; }
    }

    public enum SliceEnum
    {
        XSlice,
        YSlice,
        ZSlice
    }

    public enum ChartTypeEnum
```

```
{
    Line,
    Mesh,
    MeshZ,
    Waterfall,
    Surface,
    XYColor,
    Contour,
    FillContour,
    MeshContour,
    SurfaceContour,
    Slice,
    Bar3D,
}

public void AddChart(Graphics g, DataSeries ds,
        ChartStyle cs, ChartStyle2D cs2d)
{
    switch (ChartType)
    {
        case ChartTypeEnum.Line:
            AddLine(g, ds, cs);
            break;
        case ChartTypeEnum.Mesh:
            AddMesh(g, ds, cs);
            AddColorBar(g, ds, cs, cs2d);
            break;
        case ChartTypeEnum.MeshZ:
            AddMeshZ(g, ds, cs);
            AddColorBar(g, ds, cs, cs2d);
            break;
        case ChartTypeEnum.Waterfall:
            AddWaterFall(g, ds, cs);
            AddColorBar(g, ds, cs, cs2d);
            break;
        case ChartTypeEnum.Surface:
            AddSurface(g, ds, cs, cs2d);
            AddColorBar(g, ds, cs, cs2d);
            break;
        case ChartTypeEnum.XYColor:
            AddXYColor(g, ds, cs, cs2d);
            break;
        case ChartTypeEnum.Contour:
            AddContour(g, ds, cs, cs2d);
            break;
        case ChartTypeEnum.FillContour:
            AddXYColor(g, ds, cs, cs2d);
            AddContour(g, ds, cs, cs2d);
            break;
        case ChartTypeEnum.MeshContour:
            AddContour3D(g, ds, cs, cs2d);
            AddMesh(g, ds, cs);
            AddColorBar(g, ds, cs, cs2d);
            break;
```

```
                case ChartTypeEnum.SurfaceContour:
                    AddXYColor3D(g, ds, cs, cs2d);
                    AddContour3D(g, ds, cs, cs2d);
                    AddSurface(g, ds, cs, cs2d);
                    AddColorBar(g, ds, cs, cs2d);
                    break;
                case ChartTypeEnum.Slice:
                    AddSlice(g, ds, cs, cs2d);
                    AddColorBar(g, ds, cs, cs2d);
                    break;
                case ChartTypeEnum.Bar3D:
                    AddBar3D(g, ds, cs, cs2d);
                    AddColorBar(g,ds,cs,cs2d);
                    break;
            }
        }

        public void AddColorBar(Graphics g, DataSeries ds,
                ChartStyle cs, ChartStyle2D cs2d)
        {
            if (cs.IsColorBar && IsColorMap)
            {
                Pen aPen = new Pen(Color.Black, 1);
                SolidBrush aBrush = new SolidBrush(cs.TickColor);
                StringFormat sFormat = new StringFormat();
                sFormat.Alignment = StringAlignment.Near;
                SizeF size = g.MeasureString("A", cs.TickFont);

                int x, y, width, height;
                Point3[] pts = new Point3[64];
                PointF[] pta = new PointF[4];
                float zmin, zmax;
                if (ChartType == ChartTypeEnum.Slice)
                {
                    zmin = ds.VDataMin();
                    zmax = ds.VDataMax();
                }
                else
                {
                    zmin = ds.ZDataMin();
                    zmax = ds.ZDataMax();
                }
                float dz = (zmax - zmin) / 63;
                if (ChartType == ChartTypeEnum.Contour ||
                    ChartType == ChartTypeEnum.FillContour ||
                    ChartType == ChartTypeEnum.XYColor)
                {
                    x = 5 * cs2d.ChartArea.Width / 6;
                    y = form1.PlotPanel.Top;
                    width = cs2d.ChartArea.Width / 25;
                    height = form1.PlotPanel.Height;
                    // Add color bar:
                    for (int i = 0; i < 64; i++)
                    {
```

```
                pts[i] = new Point3(x, y, zmin + i * dz, 1);
        }
        for (int i = 0; i < 63; i++)
        {
            Color color = AddColor(cs, pts[i],
                zmin, zmax);
            aBrush = new SolidBrush(color);
            float y1 = y + height - (pts[i].Z - zmin) *
                height / (zmax - zmin);
            float y2 = y + height - (pts[i + 1].Z -
                zmin) * height / (zmax - zmin);
            pta[0] = new PointF(x, y2);
            pta[1] = new PointF(x + width, y2);
            pta[2] = new PointF(x + width, y1);
            pta[3] = new PointF(x, y1);
            g.FillPolygon(aBrush, pta);
        }
        g.DrawRectangle(aPen, x, y, width, height);

        // Add ticks and labels to the color bar:
        float ticklength = 0.1f * width;
        for (float z = zmin; z <= zmax; z = z +
            (zmax - zmin) / 6)
        {
            float yy = y + height - (z - zmin) *
                height / (zmax - zmin);
            g.DrawLine(aPen, x, yy, x + ticklength, yy);
            g.DrawLine(aPen, x + width, yy, x +
                width - ticklength, yy);
            g.DrawString((Math.Round(z, 2)).ToString(),
                cs.TickFont, aBrush, new PointF(x + width
                + 5, yy - size.Height / 2), sFormat);
        }
    }
}
else
{
    x = 5 * form1.PlotPanel.Width / 6;
    y = form1.PlotPanel.Height / 10;
    width = form1.PlotPanel.Width / 25;
    height = 8 * form1.PlotPanel.Height / 10;

    // Add color bar:
    for (int i = 0; i < 64; i++)
    {
        pts[i] = new Point3(x, y, zmin + i * dz, 1);
    }
    for (int i = 0; i < 63; i++)
    {
        Color color = AddColor(cs, pts[i],
            zmin, zmax);
        aBrush = new SolidBrush(color);
        float y1 = y + height - (pts[i].Z - zmin) *
            height / (zmax - zmin);
        float y2 = y + height - (pts[i + 1].Z -
```

```
                              zmin) * height / (zmax - zmin);
                pta[0] = new PointF(x, y2);
                pta[1] = new PointF(x + width, y2);
                pta[2] = new PointF(x + width, y1);
                pta[3] = new PointF(x, y1);
                g.FillPolygon(aBrush, pta);
            }
            g.DrawRectangle(aPen, x, y, width, height);

            // Add ticks and labels to the color bar:
            float ticklength = 0.1f * width;
            for (float z = zmin; z <= zmax; z = z +
                    (zmax - zmin) / 6)
            {
                float yy = y + height - (z - zmin) *
                        height / (zmax - zmin);
                g.DrawLine(aPen, x, yy, x + ticklength, yy);
                g.DrawLine(aPen, x + width, yy, x + width -
                        ticklength, yy);
                g.DrawString((Math.Round(z, 2)).ToString(),
                        cs.TickFont, aBrush, new PointF(x +
                        width + 5, yy - size.Height / 2),
                        sFormat);
            }
        }
    }
}


        private Color AddColor(ChartStyle cs, Point3 pt,
            float zmin, float zmax)
        {
            int colorLength = CMap.GetLength(0);
            int cindex = (int)Math.Round((colorLength *
                    (pt.Z - zmin) + (zmax - pt.Z)) /
                    (zmax - zmin));
            if (cindex < 1)
                cindex = 1;
            if (cindex > colorLength)
                cindex = colorLength;
            Color color = Color.FromArgb(CMap[cindex - 1, 0],
                CMap[cindex - 1, 1], CMap[cindex - 1, 2],
                CMap[cindex - 1, 3]);
            return color;
        }
        .....
        .....
    }
}
```

In this class, the field members and their corresponding public properties are used to control the appearance of various 3D charts. You can create a specific 3D chart by selecting the ChartType from the enumeration of ChartTypeEnum. You can see that there are 12 different chart types to select from in this enumeration. You can add more chart types to this enumeration and create their corresponding 3D charts in the same manner as we do here.

The `AddColor` method is used to create the color map for a specified 3D chart type. In this method, the color map is associated with the Z value. The `AddColorBar` method creates a color bar at the right side of a 3D chart. This color bar, much like the legend in a 2D chart, indicates the data values for different colors in the color map.

In the following few sections, I wil present detailed information on creating various 3D chats.

Surface Charts

Mathematically, a surface chart draws a Z function on a surface for each X and Y coordinate in a region of interest. In this book, we discuss only simple types of surface charts. This means that for each X and Y value, a simple surface can have at most one Z value. Complicated surfaces that can have multiple Z values for each pair of X and Y values are beyond the scope of this book.

We now define a surface by the z-coordinates of points above a rectangular grid in the X-Y plane. The surface chart is formed by joining adjacent points with straight lines. Surface plots are useful for visualizing 2D data arrays (matrices) that are too large to display in numerical form, and for graphing functions of two variables.

In this section, I will show you how to create different forms of surface charts. Mesh charts are special cases of surface charts. They are basically wire-frame surfaces that draw only the lines connecting the defining points. On the other hand, surface plots display both the connecting lines and the faces of the surface in color. I implement these specific methods in C# to create various surface charts, as listed in the following table:

Method	Used to Create
Mesh	Mesh chart with or without hidden lines
MeshZ	Mesh chart with curtain (reference plane)
WaterFall	Simile to MeshZ, but without lines from the Y data
Surface	Surface chart with or without color map
XYColor	Flat surface chart on the X-Y plane (Z value is proportional only to color)

The simplest way to store surface data is in a 2D array. For each point (X, Y) in the region defined for the surface, the (X, Y) entry in the array gives the Z coordinate of the corresponding point on the surface. To make managing the surface easier, we can create a data structure specifically for surface charts in the `DataSeries` class. This class should contain variables to describe the data it holds, including the minimum X and Y data values, the spacing between the rows of data in the X and Y directions, and the number of data points in the X and Y directions. The following is the code listing of the `DataSeries` class to be used in surface charts:

```
using System;
using System.Collections;
using System.Drawing;
```

```csharp
namespace Example6_3
{
    public class DataSeries
    {
        private ArrayList pointList;
        private LineStyle lineStyle;
        private float xdataMin = -5;
        private float ydataMin = -5;
        private float xSpacing = 1;
        private float ySpacing = 1;
        private int xNumber = 10;
        private int yNumber = 10;
        private Point3[,] pointArray;

        public DataSeries()
        {
            lineStyle = new LineStyle();
            pointList = new ArrayList();
        }

        public Point3[,] PointArray
        {
            get { return pointArray; }
            set { pointArray = value; }
        }

        public float XNumber
        {
            get { return xNumber; }
            set { xNumber = value; }
        }

        public float YNumber
        {
            get { return yNumber; }
            set { yNumber = value; }
        }

        public float XSpacing
        {
            get { return xSpacing; }
            set { xSpacing = value; }
        }

        public float YSpacing
        {
            get { return ySpacing; }
            set { ySpacing = value; }
        }

        public float XDataMin
        {
            get { return xdataMin; }
            set { xdataMin = value; }
```

```
        }

        public float YDataMin
        {
            get { return ydataMin; }
            set { ydataMin = value; }
        }

        public LineStyle LineStyle
        {
            get { return lineStyle; }
            set { lineStyle = value; }
        }

        public ArrayList PointList
        {
            get { return pointList; }
            set { pointList = value; }
        }

        public void AddPoint(Point3 pt)
        {
            PointList.Add(pt);
        }
    }
}
```

In this class, the `PointList` holds the data for 3D line charts, while the 2D `PointArray` stores the data for surface charts.

Mesh Charts

Add the `AddMesh` method to the `DrawChart` class. Mesh charts can be created using this `AddMesh` method. The following is its code listing:

```
private void AddMesh(Graphics g, DataSeries ds, ChartStyle cs)
{
    Pen aPen = new Pen(ds.LineStyle.LineColor,
        ds.LineStyle.Thickness);
    aPen.DashStyle = ds.LineStyle.Pattern;
    SolidBrush aBrush = new SolidBrush(Color.White);
    Matrix3 m = Matrix3.AzimuthElevation(cs.Elevation, cs.Azimuth);
    PointF[] pta = new PointF[4];
    Point3[,] pts = ds.PointArray;

    // Find the minumum and maximum z values:
    float zmin = ds.ZDataMin();
    float zmax = ds.ZDataMax();

    // Perform transformations on points:
    for (int i = 0; i < pts.GetLength(0); i++)
    {
```

```
            for (int j = 0; j < pts.GetLength(1); j++)
            {
                pts[i, j].Transform(m, form1, cs);
            }
        }

        // Draw mesh:
        for (int i = 0; i < pts.GetLength(0) - 1; i++)
        {
            for (int j = 0; j < pts.GetLength(1) - 1; j++)
            {
                int ii = i;
                if (cs.Azimuth >= -180 && cs.Azimuth < 0)
                {
                    ii = pts.GetLength(0) - 2 - i;
                }
                pta[0] = new PointF(pts[ii, j].X, pts[ii, j].Y);
                pta[1] = new PointF(pts[ii, j + 1].X, pts[ii, j + 1].Y);
                pta[2] = new PointF(pts[ii + 1, j + 1].X, pts[ii + 1,
                        j + 1].Y);
                pta[3] = new PointF(pts[ii + 1, j].X, pts[ii + 1, j].Y);
                if (!IsHiddenLine)
                {
                    g.FillPolygon(aBrush, pta);
                }
                if (IsColorMap)
                {
                    Color color = AddColor(cs, pts[ii, j], zmin, zmax);
                    aPen = new Pen(color, ds.LineStyle.Thickness);
                    aPen.DashStyle = ds.LineStyle.Pattern;
                }
                g.DrawPolygon(aPen, pta);
            }
        }
        aPen.Dispose();
        aBrush.Dispose();
    }
```

You can select the Mesh chart type using the following code snippet:

```
        dc.ChartType = DrawChart.ChartTypeEnum.Mesh;
```

Using this method, you can create a 3D mesh chart with or without hidden lines. You can also produce a mesh chart with a single color or with a complete scaled color map. We use the Z-Order algorithm to remove hidden lines in a mesh plot. The Z-Order algorithm draws polygons from back to front. When drawn in this order, a polygon can obscure only the polygon that has been drawn before it. When it fills the polygon with a white color (or the background color of the plot area), it covers up any lines that it should obscure. Pay special attention that when the elevation and azimuth angles change, we change the order of drawing the polygons, making sure that the program always draws the polygons from back to front.

The mesh chart can be tested using the following code snippet of the Form1 class:

```
using System;
using System.Drawing;
```

```
using System.Drawing.Drawing2D;
using System.Windows.Forms;

namespace Example6_3
{
    public partial class Form1 : Form
    {
        ChartStyle cs;
        ChartStyle2D cs2d;
        DataSeries ds;
        DrawChart dc;
        ChartFunctions cf;
        ColorMap cm;

        public Form1()
        {
            InitializeComponent();
            this.SetStyle(ControlStyles.AllPaintingInWmPaint |
                ControlStyles.UserPaint |
                ControlStyles.DoubleBuffer,true);
            this.SetStyle(ControlStyles.ResizeRedraw, true);

            // Subscribing to a paint eventhandler to drawingPanel:
            PlotPanel.Paint +=
                new PaintEventHandler(PlotPanelPaint);
            cs = new ChartStyle(this);
            cs2d = new ChartStyle2D(this);
            ds = new DataSeries();
            dc = new DrawChart(this);
            cf = new ChartFunctions();
            cm = new ColorMap();

            cs.GridStyle.LineColor = Color.LightGray;
            cs.GridStyle.Pattern = DashStyle.Dash;
            cs.Title = "No Title";

            dc.ChartType = DrawChart.ChartTypeEnum.Mesh;
            dc.IsColorMap = false;
            dc.IsHiddenLine = true;
            dc.CMap = cm.Jet();
        }

        protected override void OnPaint(PaintEventArgs e)
        {
            Graphics g = e.Graphics;

            if (dc.ChartType == DrawChart.ChartTypeEnum.XYColor||
                dc.ChartType == DrawChart.ChartTypeEnum.Contour ||
                dc.ChartType == DrawChart.ChartTypeEnum.FillContour)
            {
                Rectangle rect = this.ClientRectangle;
                cs2d.ChartArea = new Rectangle(rect.X, rect.Y,
                    rect.Width, 19 * rect.Height / 30);
                cf.Peak3D(ds, cs);
```

```
                cs2d.SetPlotArea(g, cs);
                dc.AddColorBar(g, ds, cs, cs2d);
            }
        }

        private void PlotPanelPaint(object sender, PaintEventArgs e)
        {
            Graphics g = e.Graphics;
            g.SmoothingMode = SmoothingMode.AntiAlias;

            if (dc.ChartType == DrawChart.ChartTypeEnum.XYColor||
                dc.ChartType == DrawChart.ChartTypeEnum.Contour||
                dc.ChartType == DrawChart.ChartTypeEnum.FillContour)
            {
                cs2d.AddChartStyle2D(g, cs);
                dc.AddChart(g, ds, cs, cs2d);
            }
            else
            {
                cs.Elevation = trkElevation.Value;
                cs.Azimuth = trkAzimuth.Value;
                cf.Peak3D(ds, cs);
                cs.AddChartStyle(g);
                dc.AddChart(g, ds, cs, cs2d);
            }
        }
        ... ...
    }
}
```

By building and running this project, you will create a mesh chart with hidden lines, as shown in Figure 6-4.

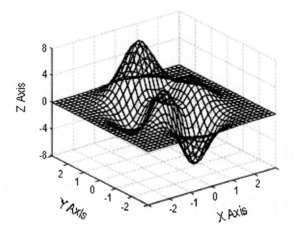

Figure 6-4 Mesh plot with hidden lines.

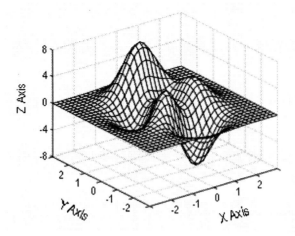

Figure 6-5 Mesh plot without hidden lines.

You can just as easily create a mesh chart without hidden lines by changing one line of code:

```
dc.IsHiddenLine = false;
```

The `bool` parameter `IsHiddenLine` is set to false, meaning that you do not want to show the hidden lines in your mesh plot. This produces the results of Figure 6-5.

You can also create a color mapped mesh chart with a color bar using the following code snippet:

```
cs.IsColorBar = true;
dc.IsColorMap = true;
```

This tells the program to draw the mesh plot with a color bar using a color mapped pen. The result is shown in Figure 6-6.

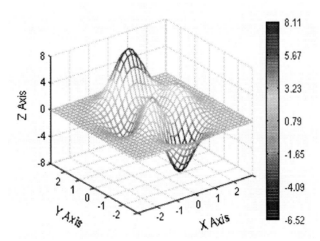

Figure 6-6 Color mapped mesh chart with color bar.

The data structures in the DataSeries class allow you to manage many types of simple surfaces.

Curtain Charts

The chart type, MeshZ, creates a curtain plot from a reference plane around the mesh chart. The curtain is drawn by dropping lines down from the edge of the surface to the plane parallel to the X-Y plane, at a height equal to the lowest point in the surface.

The curtain chart can be created using the AddMeshZ method in the DrawChart class:

```
private void AddMeshZ(Graphics g, DataSeries ds, ChartStyle cs)
{
    Pen aPen = new Pen(ds.LineStyle.LineColor,
        ds.LineStyle.Thickness);
    aPen.DashStyle = ds.LineStyle.Pattern;
    SolidBrush aBrush = new SolidBrush(Color.White);
    Matrix3 m = Matrix3.AzimuthElevation(cs.Elevation, cs.Azimuth);
    PointF[] pta = new PointF[4];
    Point3[,] pts = ds.PointArray;
    Point3[,] pts1 = new Point3[pts.GetLength(0), pts.GetLength(1)];
    Color color;

    // Find the minumum and maximum z values:
    float zmin = ds.ZDataMin();
    float zmax = ds.ZDataMax();

    for (int i = 0; i < pts.GetLength(0); i++)
    {
        for (int j = 0; j < pts.GetLength(1); j++)
        {
            // Make a deep copy the points array:
            pts1[i, j] = new Point3(pts[i, j].X, pts[i, j].Y,
                    pts[i, j].Z, 1);
            // Perform transformations on points:
            pts[i, j].Transform(m, form1, cs);
        }
    }

    // Draw mesh using Z-order method:
    for (int i = 0; i < pts.GetLength(0) - 1; i++)
    {
        for (int j = 0; j < pts.GetLength(1) - 1; j++)
        {
            int ii = i;
            if (cs.Azimuth >= -180 && cs.Azimuth < 0)
            {
                ii = pts.GetLength(0) - 2 - i;
            }
            pta[0] = new PointF(pts[ii, j].X, pts[ii, j].Y);
            pta[1] = new PointF(pts[ii, j + 1].X, pts[ii, j + 1].Y);
            pta[2] = new PointF(pts[ii + 1, j + 1].X,
                    pts[ii + 1, j + 1].Y);
```

```
            pta[3] = new PointF(pts[ii + 1, j].X, pts[ii + 1, j].Y);
            g.FillPolygon(aBrush, pta)
            if (IsColorMap)
            {
                color = AddColor(cs, pts[ii, j], zmin, zmax);
                aPen = new Pen(color, ds.LineStyle.Thickness);
                aPen.DashStyle = ds.LineStyle.Pattern;
            }
            g.DrawPolygon(aPen, pta);
        }
}

// Draw curtain lines:
Point3[] pt3 = new Point3[4];
for (int i = 0; i < pts1.GetLength(0); i++)
{
    int jj = pts1.GetLength(0) - 1;
    if (cs.Elevation >= 0)
    {
        if (cs.Azimuth >= -90 && cs.Azimuth <= 90)
            jj = 0;
    }
    else if (cs.Elevation < 0)
    {
        jj = 0;
        if (cs.Azimuth >= -90 && cs.Azimuth <= 90)
            jj = pts1.GetLength(0) - 1;
    }

    if (i < pts1.GetLength(0) - 1)
    {
        pt3[0] = new Point3(pts1[i, jj].X, pts1[i, jj].Y,
                ts1[i, jj].Z, 1);
        pt3[1] = new Point3(pts1[i + 1, jj].X,
                pts1[i + 1, jj].Y, pts1[i + 1, jj].Z, 1);
        pt3[2] = new Point3(pts1[i + 1, jj].X,
                pts1[i + 1, jj].Y, cs.ZMin, 1);
        pt3[3] = new Point3(pts1[i, jj].X,
                pts1[i, jj].Y, cs.ZMin, 1);
        for (int k = 0; k < 4; k++)
            pt3[k].Transform(m, form1, cs);
        pta[0] = new PointF(pt3[0].X, pt3[0].Y);
        pta[1] = new PointF(pt3[1].X, pt3[1].Y);
        pta[2] = new PointF(pt3[2].X, pt3[2].Y);
        pta[3] = new PointF(pt3[3].X, pt3[3].Y);
        g.FillPolygon(aBrush, pta);
        if (IsColorMap)
        {
            color = AddColor(cs, pt3[0], zmin, zmax);
            aPen = new Pen(color, ds.LineStyle.Thickness);
            aPen.DashStyle = ds.LineStyle.Pattern;
        }
        g.DrawPolygon(aPen, pta);
    }
```

```
        }
        for (int j = 0; j < pts1.GetLength(1); j++)
        {
            int ii = 0;
            if (cs.Elevation >= 0)
            {
                if (cs.Azimuth >= 0 && cs.Azimuth <= 180)
                    ii = pts1.GetLength(1) - 1;
            }
            else if (cs.Elevation < 0)
            {
                if (cs.Azimuth >= -180 && cs.Azimuth <= 0)
                    ii = pts1.GetLength(1) - 1;
            }
            if (j < pts1.GetLength(1) - 1)
            {
                pt3[0] = new Point3(pts1[ii, j].X, pts1[ii, j].Y,
                        pts1[ii, j].Z, 1);
                pt3[1] = new Point3(pts1[ii, j + 1].X,
                        pts1[ii, j + 1].Y, pts1[ii, j + 1].Z, 1);
                pt3[2] = new Point3(pts1[ii, j + 1].X,
                        pts1[ii, j + 1].Y, cs.ZMin, 1);
                pt3[3] = new Point3(pts1[ii, j].X,
                        pts1[ii, j].Y, cs.ZMin, 1);
                for (int k = 0; k < 4; k++)
                    pt3[k].Transform(m, form1, cs);
                pta[0] = new PointF(pt3[0].X, pt3[0].Y);
                pta[1] = new PointF(pt3[1].X, pt3[1].Y);
                pta[2] = new PointF(pt3[2].X, pt3[2].Y);
                pta[3] = new PointF(pt3[3].X, pt3[3].Y);
                g.FillPolygon(aBrush, pta);
                if (IsColorMap)
                {
                    color = AddColor(cs, pt3[0], zmin, zmax);
                    aPen = new Pen(color, ds.LineStyle.Thickness);
                    aPen.DashStyle = ds.LineStyle.Pattern;
                }
                g.DrawPolygon(aPen, pta);
            }
        }
    }
    aPen.Dispose();
    aBrush.Dispose();
}
```

In this method, we first create a mesh plot, then add the curtain to it. The curtain lines must be drawn on the corresponding surface when changing both the elevation and azimuth angles.

The curtain chart can be tested using the same code of the `Form1` class, except for a change in the following line:

```
dc.ChartType = DrawChart.ChartTypeEnum.MeshZ;
```

You can also change the chart function to `SinROverR3D` and the color map matrix to `Cool`:

```
dc.CMap = cm.Cool();
```

```
                cf.SinROverR3D(ds, cs);
```

This produces the output of Figure 6-7.

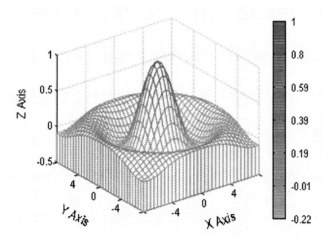

Figure 6-7 Curtain mesh chart.

Water Fall Charts

A waterfall chart draws a mesh plot similar to the curtain chart, but does not generate vertical lines from the X component of the data. This produces a "waterfall" effect.

The waterfall chart can be created using the AddWaterfall method in the DrawChart class:

```
private void AddWaterfall(Graphics g, DataSeries ds, ChartStyle cs)
{
    Pen aPen = new Pen(ds.LineStyle.LineColor,
        ds.LineStyle.Thickness);
    aPen.DashStyle = ds.LineStyle.Pattern;
    SolidBrush aBrush = new SolidBrush(Color.White);

    Matrix3 m = Matrix3.AzimuthElevation(cs.Elevation, cs.Azimuth);
    Point3[,] pts = ds.PointArray;
    Point3[] pt3 = new Point3[pts.GetLength(0) + 2];
    PointF[] pta = new PointF[pts.GetLength(0) + 2];
    Color color;

    // Find the minumum and maximum z values:
    float zmin = ds.ZDataMin();
    float zmax = ds.ZDataMax();

    for (int j = 0; j < pts.GetLength(1); j++)
    {
        int jj = j;
        if (cs.Elevation >= 0)
        {
            if (cs.Azimuth >= -90 && cs.Azimuth < 90)
```

```
            {
                jj = pts.GetLength(1) - 1 - j;
            }
        }
        else if (cs.Elevation < 0)
        {
            jj = pts.GetLength(1) - 1 - j;
            if (cs.Azimuth >= -90 && cs.Azimuth < 90)
            {
                jj = j;
            }
        }
        for (int i = 0; i < pts.GetLength(0); i++)
        {
            pt3[i + 1] = pts[i, jj];
            if (i == 0)
            {
                pt3[0] = new Point3(pt3[i + 1].X,
                        pt3[i + 1].Y, cs.ZMin, 1);
            }
            if (i == pts.GetLength(0) - 1)
            {
                pt3[pts.GetLength(0) + 1] = new Point3(pt3[i + 1].X,
                    pt3[i + 1].Y, cs.ZMin, 1);
            }
        }
        for (int i = 0; i < pt3.Length; i++)
        {
            pt3[i].Transform(m, form1, cs);
            pta[i] = new PointF(pt3[i].X, pt3[i].Y);
        }
        g.FillPolygon(aBrush, pta);
        for (int i = 1; i < pt3.Length; i++)
        {
            if (IsColorMap)
            {
                color = AddColor(cs, pt3[i], zmin, zmax);
                aPen = new Pen(color, ds.LineStyle.Thickness);
                aPen.DashStyle = ds.LineStyle.Pattern;
            }
            g.DrawLine(aPen, pta[i - 1], pta[i]);
        }
    }
    aPen.Dispose();
    aBrush.Dispose();
}
```

In this method, we first create the mesh plot, then add the vertical lines from the Y component of the data, producing the waterfall effect. The vertical lines must be drawn on the corresponding surface when elevation and azimuth angles change.

The waterfall chart can be tested using the same code of the Form1 class, except for a change in the following line:

```
dc.ChartType = DrawChart.ChartTypeEnum.Waterfall;
```

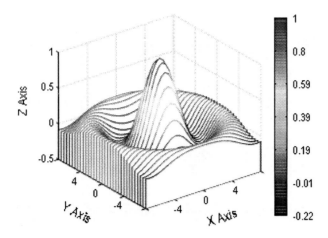

Figure 6-8 Waterfall chart.

This generates the output result of Figure 6-8.

Surface Charts

Surface charts are similar to the mesh charts in that both display data as a shaded surface. The difference between the surface and mesh charts is that the surface chart creates colored quadrilaterals and black mesh lines, whereas a mesh plot only creates black or colored mesh lines.

The surface chart can be created using the `AddSurface` method in the `DrawChart` class:

```
private void AddSurface(Graphics g, DataSeries ds,
        ChartStyle cs, ChartStyle2D cs2d)
{
    Pen aPen = new Pen(ds.LineStyle.LineColor,
            ds.LineStyle.Thickness);
    aPen.DashStyle = ds.LineStyle.Pattern;
    SolidBrush aBrush = new SolidBrush(Color.White);

    Matrix3 m = Matrix3.AzimuthElevation(cs.Elevation, cs.Azimuth);
    PointF[] pta = new PointF[4];
    Point3[,] pts = ds.PointArray;
    Point3[,] pts1 = new Point3[pts.GetLength(0), pts.GetLength(1)];

    // Find the minumum and maximum z values:
    float zmin = ds.ZDataMin();
    float zmax = ds.ZDataMax();

    // Perform transformation on points:
    for (int i = 0; i < pts.GetLength(0); i++)
    {
        for (int j = 0; j < pts.GetLength(1); j++)
        {
            // Make a deep copy the points array:
```

```
            pts1[i, j] = new Point3(pts[i, j].X,
                    pts[i, j].Y, pts[i, j].Z, 1);
            // Perform transformation on points:
            pts[i, j].Transform(m, form1, cs);
        }
    }
}

// Draw surface:
if (!IsInterp)
{
    for (int i = 0; i < pts.GetLength(0) - 1; i++)
    {
        for (int j = 0; j < pts.GetLength(1) - 1; j++)
        {
            int ii = i;
            if (cs.Azimuth >= -180 && cs.Azimuth < 0)
            {
                ii = pts.GetLength(0) - 2 - i;
            }
            pta[0] = new PointF(pts[ii, j].X, pts[ii, j].Y);
            pta[1] = new PointF(pts[ii, j + 1].X,
                    pts[ii, j + 1].Y);
            pta[2] = new PointF(pts[ii + 1, j + 1].X,
                    pts[ii + 1, j + 1].Y);
            pta[3] = new PointF(pts[ii + 1, j].X, pts[ii + 1, j].Y);
            Color color = AddColor(cs, pts[ii, j], zmin, zmax);
            aBrush = new SolidBrush(color);
            g.FillPolygon(aBrush, pta);
            if (ds.LineStyle.IsVisible)
            {
                g.DrawPolygon(aPen, pta);
            }
        }
    }
}

// Draw refined surface:
else if (IsInterp)
{
    for (int i = 0; i < pts.GetLength(0) - 1; i++)
    {
        for (int j = 0; j < pts.GetLength(1) - 1; j++)
        {
            int ii = i;
            if (cs.Azimuth >= -180 && cs.Azimuth < 0)
            {
                ii = pts.GetLength(0) - 2 - i;
            }
            Point3[] points = new Point3[4];
            points[0] = pts1[ii, j];
            points[1] = pts1[ii, j + 1];
            points[2] = pts1[ii + 1, j + 1];
            points[3] = pts1[ii + 1, j];
```

```
            Interp(g, cs, cs2d, m, points, zmin, zmax, 1);

            pta[0] = new PointF(pts[ii, j].X, pts[ii, j].Y);
            pta[1] = new PointF(pts[ii, j + 1].X,
                    pts[ii, j + 1].Y);
            pta[2] = new PointF(pts[ii + 1, j + 1].X,
                    pts[ii + 1, j + 1].Y);
            pta[3] = new PointF(pts[ii + 1, j].X,
                    pts[ii + 1, j].Y);
            if (ds.LineStyle.IsVisible)
            {
                g.DrawPolygon(aPen, pta);
            }
          }
        }
      }
    }
```

In this method, we draw surface charts using two different approaches: one is similar to the approach used to create mesh charts, while the other applies interpolated shading to the surface plot by calling the following `Interp` method:

```
    private void Interp(Graphics g, ChartStyle cs, ChartStyle2D cs2d,
        Matrix3 m, Point3[] pta, float zmin, float zmax, int flag)
    {
        SolidBrush aBrush = new SolidBrush(Color.Black);
        PointF[] points = new PointF[4];
        int npoints = NumberInterp;
        Point3[,] pts = new Point3[npoints + 1, npoints + 1];
        Point3[,] pts1 = new Point3[npoints + 1, npoints + 1];
        float x0 = pta[0].X;
        float y0 = pta[0].Y;
        float x1 = pta[2].X;
        float y1 = pta[2].Y;
        float dx = (x1 - x0) / npoints;
        float dy = (y1 - y0) / npoints;
        float C00 = pta[0].Z;
        float C10 = pta[3].Z;
        float C11 = pta[2].Z;
        float C01 = pta[1].Z;
        float x, y, C;
        Color color;

        if(flag == 1)   // For Surface chart:
        {
            for (int i = 0; i <= npoints; i++)
            {
                x = x0 + i * dx;
                for (int j = 0; j <= npoints; j++)
                {
                    y = y0 + j * dy;
                    C = (y1 - y) * ((x1 - x) * C00 +
                        (x - x0) * C10) / (x1 - x0) / (y1 - y0) +
                        (y - y0) * ((x1 - x) * C01 +
                        (x - x0) * C11) / (x1 - x0) / (y1 - y0);
```

```
                pts[i, j] = new Point3(x, y, C, 1);
                pts[i, j].Transform(m, form1, cs);
            }
        }

        for (int i = 0; i < npoints; i++)
        {
            for (int j = 0; j < npoints; j++)
            {
                color = AddColor(cs, pts[i, j], zmin, zmax);
                aBrush = new SolidBrush(color);
                points[0] = new PointF(pts[i, j].X, pts[i, j].Y);
                points[1] = new PointF(pts[i + 1, j].X,
                        pts[i + 1, j].Y);
                points[2] = new PointF(pts[i + 1, j + 1].X,
                        pts[i + 1, j + 1].Y);
                points[3] = new PointF(pts[i, j + 1].X,
                        pts[i, j + 1].Y);
                g.FillPolygon(aBrush, points);
                aBrush.Dispose();
            }
        }
    }
    else if (flag == 2)   // For XYColor chart:
    {
        for (int i = 0; i <= npoints; i++)
        {
            x = x0 + i * dx;
            for (int j = 0; j <= npoints; j++)
            {
                y = y0 + j * dy;
                C = (y1 - y) * ((x1 - x) * C00 +
                    (x - x0) * C10) / (x1 - x0) / (y1 - y0) +
                    (y - y0) * ((x1 - x) * C01 +
                    (x - x0) * C11) / (x1 - x0) / (y1 - y0);
                pts[i, j] = new Point3(x, y, C, 1);
            }
        }

        for (int i = 0; i < npoints; i++)
        {
            for (int j = 0; j < npoints; j++)
            {
                color = AddColor(cs, pts[i, j], zmin, zmax);
                aBrush = new SolidBrush(color);
                points[0] = cs2d.Point2D(new PointF(pts[i, j].X,
                        pts[i, j].Y), cs);
                points[1] = cs2d.Point2D(new PointF(pts[i + 1, j].X,
                        pts[i + 1, j].Y), cs);
                points[2] = cs2d.Point2D(new PointF(pts[i + 1,
                        j + 1].X, pts[i + 1, j + 1].Y), cs);
                points[3] = cs2d.Point2D(new PointF(
                        pts[i, j + 1].X, pts[i, j + 1].Y), cs);
                g.FillPolygon(aBrush, points);
```

```
                    aBrush.Dispose();
                }
            }
        }
        else if(flag == 3)   // For XYColor3D chart:
        {
            for (int i = 0; i <= npoints; i++)
            {
                x = x0 + i * dx;
                for (int j = 0; j <= npoints; j++)
                {
                    y = y0 + j * dy;
                    C = (y1 - y) * ((x1 - x) * C00 +
                        (x - x0) * C10) / (x1 - x0) / (y1 - y0) +
                        (y - y0) * ((x1 - x) * C01 +
                        (x - x0) * C11) / (x1 - x0) / (y1 - y0);
                    pts1[i, j] = new Point3(x, y, C, 1);
                    pts[i, j] = new Point3(x, y, cs.ZMin, 1);
                    pts[i, j].Transform(m, form1, cs);
                }
            }

            for (int i = 0; i < npoints; i++)
            {
                for (int j = 0; j < npoints; j++)
                {
                    color = AddColor(cs, pts1[i, j], zmin, zmax);
                    aBrush = new SolidBrush(color);
                    points[0] = new PointF(pts[i, j].X, pts[i, j].Y);
                    points[1] = new PointF(pts[i + 1, j].X,
                            pts[i + 1, j].Y);
                    points[2] = new PointF(pts[i + 1, j + 1].X,
                            pts[i + 1, j + 1].Y);
                    points[3] = new PointF(pts[i, j + 1].X, pts[i, j + 1].Y);
                    g.FillPolygon(aBrush, points);
                    aBrush.Dispose();
                }
            }
        }
    }
```

This interpolation method forces the color within each polygon of a surface chart to vary bi-linearly, producing the effect of a smooth color variation across the surface. You can control the fineness of the interpolated surface by changing the `NumberInterp` property.

The surface chart can be tested using the same code of the `Form1` class, except for a change in the following line:

```
    dc.ChartType = DrawChart.ChartTypeEnum.Surface;
```

You can also change the chart function to `Peak3D` and the color map matrix to `Jet`:

```
    dc.CMap = cm.Jet();
    cf.Peak3D(ds, cs);
```

This produces the output of Figure 6-9.

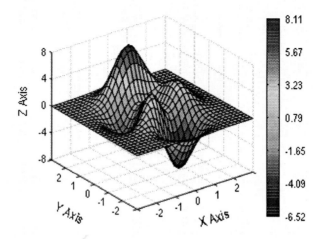

Figure 6-9 A standard surface chart.

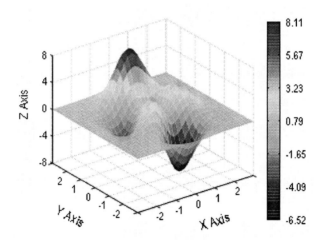

Figure 6-10 A surface chart without mesh lines.

You can also create a shaded surface chart without mesh lines by adding the following line of code:

```
ds.LineStyle.IsVisible = false;
```

This produces the results shown in Figure 6-10, in which the mesh lines are no longer visible. It can be seen from this figure that the color map is still coarse, and the single color is clearly seen for each polygon on the surface. You can obtain a surface chart with a much better color map by applying interpolated shading with the following code snippet:

```
dc.IsInterp = true;
dc.NumberInterp = 5;
```

This creates the output of Figure 6-11, which has a much smoother color across the whole surface.

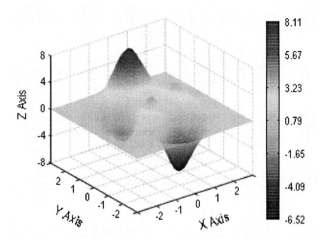

Figure 6-11 A surface chart with interpolated shading.

Color Charts on X-Y Plane

The X-Y color chart can be considered as a projected surface chart on the X-Y plane. In fact, it is a rectangle mesh grid in the X-Y plane with colors determined by the data values on the grid points. In this subsection, we create an X-Y color chart using each set of four adjacent points to define a polygon. Each polygon has a single colored shading. As in surface charts, the X-Y color chart can also have interpolated shading, in which each polygon is colored by bilinear interpolation of the colors at its four vertices using all of the elements of the data values. The minimum and maximum elements of the data values at the grid points are assigned the first and last colors in the color map. Colors for the remaining elements in the data values are determined by linear mapping from the value to the color map element.

The X-Y color chart is created by the AddXYColor method in the DrawChart class:

```
private void AddXYColor(Graphics g, DataSeries ds,
        ChartStyle cs, ChartStyle2D cs2d)
{
    Pen aPen = new Pen(ds.LineStyle.LineColor, ds.LineStyle.Thickness);
    aPen.DashStyle = ds.LineStyle.Pattern;
    SolidBrush aBrush = new SolidBrush(Color.White);
    PointF[] pta = new PointF[4];
    Point3[,] pts = ds.PointArray;
    Matrix3 m = new Matrix3();

    // Find the minumum and maximum z values:
    float zmin = ds.ZDataMin();
    float zmax = ds.ZDataMax();

    // Draw surface on the XY plane:
    if (!IsInterp)
    {
```

```csharp
        for (int i = 0; i < pts.GetLength(0) - 1; i++)
        {
            for (int j = 0; j < pts.GetLength(1) - 1; j++)
            {
                pta[0] = cs2d.Point2D(new PointF(pts[i, j].X,
                        pts[i, j].Y), cs);
                pta[1] = cs2d.Point2D(new PointF(pts[i, j + 1].X,
                        pts[i, j + 1].Y), cs);
                pta[2] = cs2d.Point2D(new PointF(pts[i + 1, j + 1].X,
                        pts[i + 1, j + 1].Y), cs);
                pta[3] = cs2d.Point2D(new PointF(pts[i + 1, j].X,
                        pts[i + 1, j].Y), cs);
                Color color = AddColor(cs, pts[i, j], zmin, zmax);
                aBrush = new SolidBrush(color);
                g.FillPolygon(aBrush, pta);
                if (ds.LineStyle.IsVisible)
                {
                    g.DrawPolygon(aPen, pta);
                }
            }
        }
    }

    // Draw refined surface:
    else if (IsInterp)
    {
        for (int i = 0; i < pts.GetLength(0) - 1; i++)
        {
            for (int j = 0; j < pts.GetLength(1) - 1; j++)
            {
                Point3[] points = new Point3[4];
                points[0] = pts[i, j];
                points[1] = pts[i, j + 1];
                points[2] = pts[i + 1, j + 1];
                points[3] = pts[i + 1, j];

                Interp(g, cs, cs2d, m, points, zmin, zmax, 2);

                pta[0] = cs2d.Point2D(new PointF(pts[i, j].X,
                        pts[i, j].Y),cs);
                pta[1] = cs2d.Point2D(new PointF(pts[i, j + 1].X,
                        pts[i, j + 1].Y),cs);
                pta[2] = cs2d.Point2D(new PointF(pts[i + 1, j + 1].X,
                        pts[i + 1, j + 1].Y), cs);
                pta[3] = cs2d.Point2D(new PointF(pts[i + 1, j].X,
                        pts[i + 1, j].Y), cs);

                if (ds.LineStyle.IsVisible)
                {
                    g.DrawPolygon(aPen, pta);
                }
            }
        }
    }
```

}

The X-Y color chart can be tested using the same code of the `Form1` class as the surface chart, except for a change in the following lines:

```
cs2d.ChartBackColor = Color.White;
cs2d.ChartBorderColor = Color.Black;
ds.LineStyle.IsVisible = true;
dc.ChartType = DrawChart.ChartTypeEnum.XYColor;
```

This creates Figure 6-12. Notice that the appearance of the X-Y color charts is controlled by the 2D chart style.

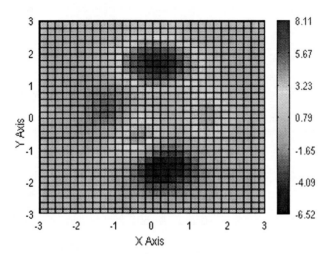

Figure 6-12 An X-Y color chart with mesh lines.

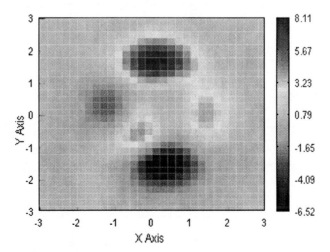

Figure 6-13 An X-Y color chart without mesh lines.

You can remove the mesh lines from this X-Y color chart by changing the `LineStyle.IsVisible` property:

```
ds.LineStyle.IsVisible = false;
```

This produces the illustration shown in Figure 6-13. It can be seen from this figure that the single color is clearly seen for each polygon on an X-Y color chart. You can obtain an X-Y color chart with a much better color map by applying interpolated shading with the following code snippet:

```
dc.IsInterp = true;
dc.NumberInterp = 5;
```

This produces the interpolated X-Y color chart shown in Figure 6-14.

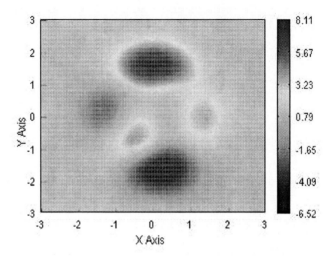

Figure 6-14 An X-Y color chart with an interpolated color shading.

Contour Charts

Contour charts help visualizing 3D surfaces on a 2D computer screen. In this case, data values are plotted as a function of mesh grid points in the X-Y plane. To do contouring in a C# application, you need to describe the data surface and the contour levels you want to draw. Given this information, the program must call the algorithm that calculates the line segments that make up a contour curve, then plot these line segments on your computer screen.

In order to satisfy the above description, here we use an algorithm that is relatively simple to implement, very reliable, and does not require sophisticated programming techniques or a high level of mathematics to understand how it works.

Algorithm

Suppose that 3D surface data is stored in a 2D array to form a rectangular grid in the X-Y plane. We consider four grid points at a time; namely the rectangle cell (i, j), (i+1, j), (i, j+1), and (i+1, j+1). This rectangular grid cell is further divided into two triangular grid cells, as shown in Figure 6-15. The contouring is drawn by systematically examining each triangular grid cell. Intersection points, if any, between each edge of the cell and a given contour level curve are computed using bilinear interpolation. Line segments are plotted between intersection points of a contour level curve, with each of the two edges belonging to the cell. Note that if any edges belonging to a triangular cell are intersected by a given level curve, then exactly two edges are intersected.

It can be seen from Figure 6-15 that there are three cases for each triangular grid cell in which certain types of contouring line segments are drawn depending on the contouring level with respect to the data values at the grid points of a triangle cell. Thus, by examining all of the left and right triangular cells and adding all of the possible contouring line segments together, we can obtain a contour chart for any function defined on a rectangular grid in the X-Y plane.

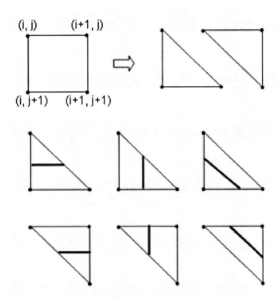

Figure 6-15 A rectangle grid cell is further divided into two triangular grid cells. Each triangular grid cell has three possible cases that draw different contouring line segments.

Implementation

Using the algorithm discussed in the previous section, we can easily create contour charts in C#. We add the AddContour method to the DrawChart class:

```
private void AddContour(Graphics g, DataSeries ds, ChartStyle cs,
            ChartStyle2D cs2d)
{
    Pen aPen = new Pen(ds.LineStyle.LineColor,
            ds.LineStyle.Thickness);
    aPen.DashStyle = ds.LineStyle.Pattern;
    SolidBrush aBrush = new SolidBrush(Color.White);
    PointF[] pta = new PointF[2];
```

```
Point3[,] pts = ds.PointArray;
Matrix3 m = new Matrix3();

// Find the minumum and maximum z values:
float zmin = ds.ZDataMin();
float zmax = ds.ZDataMax();
float[] zlevels = new float[numberContours];
for (int i = 0; i < numberContours; i++)
{
    zlevels[i] = zmin + i * (zmax - zmin) / (numberContours - 1);
}

int i0, i1, i2, j0, j1, j2;
float zratio = 1;
// Draw contour on the XY plane:
for (int i = 0; i < pts.GetLength(0) - 1; i++)
{
    for (int j = 0; j < pts.GetLength(1) - 1; j++)
    {
        if (IsColorMap && ChartType != ChartTypeEnum.FillContour)
        {
            Color color = AddColor(cs, pts[i, j], zmin, zmax);
            aPen = new Pen(color, ds.LineStyle.Thickness);
            aPen.DashStyle = ds.LineStyle.Pattern;
        }
        for (int k = 0; k < numberContours; k++)
        {
            // Left triangle:
            i0 = i;
            j0 = j;
            i1 = i;
            j1 = j + 1;
            i2 = i + 1;
            j2 = j + 1;
            if ((zlevels[k] >= pts[i0, j0].Z && zlevels[k] <
                    pts[i1, j1].Z || zlevels[k] < pts[i0, j0].Z
                    && zlevels[k] >= pts[i1, j1].Z) &&
                    (zlevels[k] >= pts[i1, j1].Z && zlevels[k] <
                    pts[i2, j2].Z || zlevels[k] < pts[i1, j1].Z
                    && zlevels[k] >= pts[i2, j2].Z))
            {
                zratio = (zlevels[k] - pts[i0, j0].Z) /
                    (pts[i1, j1].Z - pts[i0, j0].Z);
                pta[0] = cs2d.Point2D(new PointF(pts[i0, j0].X,
                    (1 - zratio) * pts[i0, j0].Y + zratio *
                    pts[i1, j1].Y), cs);
                zratio = (zlevels[k] - pts[i1, j1].Z) /
                    (pts[i2, j2].Z - pts[i1, j1].Z);
                pta[1] = cs2d.Point2D(new PointF((1- zratio) *
                    pts[i1, j1].X + zratio * pts[i2, j2].X,
                    pts[i1, j1].Y), cs);
                g.DrawLine(aPen, pta[0], pta[1]);
            }
            else if ((zlevels[k] >= pts[i0, j0].Z && zlevels[k]
```

```
                 < pts[i2, j2].Z || zlevels[k] < pts[i0, j0].Z
                 && zlevels[k] >= pts[i2, j2].Z) &&
                 (zlevels[k] >= pts[i1, j1].Z && zlevels[k] <
                 pts[i2, j2].Z || zlevels[k] < pts[i1, j1].Z
                 && zlevels[k] >= pts[i2, j2].Z))
        {
            zratio = (zlevels[k] - pts[i0, j0].Z) /
                 (pts[i2, j2].Z - pts[i0, j0].Z);
            pta[0] = cs2d.Point2D(new PointF((1-zratio) *
                 pts[i0, j0].X + zratio * pts[i2, j2].X,
                 (1-zratio) * pts[i0, j0].Y + zratio *
                 pts[i2, j2].Y), cs);
            zratio = (zlevels[k] - pts[i1, j1].Z) /
                 (pts[i2, j2].Z - pts[i1, j1].Z);
            pta[1] = cs2d.Point2D(new PointF((1-zratio) *
                 pts[i1, j1].X + zratio * pts[i2, j2].X,
                 pts[i1, j1].Y), cs);
            g.DrawLine(aPen, pta[0], pta[1]);
        }
        else if ((zlevels[k] >= pts[i0, j0].Z && zlevels[k]
            < pts[i1, j1].Z || zlevels[k] < pts[i0, j0].Z
            && zlevels[k] >= pts[i1, j1].Z) &&
            (zlevels[k] >= pts[i0, j0].Z && zlevels[k] <
            pts[i2, j2].Z || zlevels[k] < pts[i0, j0].Z &&
            zlevels[k] >= pts[i2, j2].Z))
        {
            zratio = (zlevels[k] - pts[i0, j0].Z) /
                 (pts[i1, j1].Z - pts[i0, j0].Z);
            pta[0] = cs2d.Point2D(new PointF(pts[i0, j0].X,
                 (1-zratio)* pts[i0, j0].Y  + zratio *
                 pts[i1, j1].Y), cs);
            zratio = (zlevels[k] - pts[i0, j0].Z) /
                 (pts[i2, j2].Z - pts[i0, j0].Z);
            pta[1] = cs2d.Point2D(new PointF(pts[i0, j0].X *
                 (1-zratio) + pts[i2, j2].X * zratio,
                 pts[i0, j0].Y * (1-zratio) +
                 pts[i2,j2].Y *zratio), cs);
            g.DrawLine(aPen, pta[0], pta[1]);
        }


        // right triangle:
        i0 = i;
        j0 = j;
        i1 = i+1;
        j1 = j;
        i2 = i + 1;
        j2 = j + 1;
        if ((zlevels[k] >= pts[i0, j0].Z && zlevels[k] <
                 pts[i1, j1].Z || zlevels[k] < pts[i0, j0].Z
                 && zlevels[k] >= pts[i1, j1].Z) &&
                 (zlevels[k] >= pts[i1, j1].Z && zlevels[k]
                 < pts[i2, j2].Z || zlevels[k] < pts[i1, j1].Z
                 && zlevels[k] >= pts[i2, j2].Z))
        {
```

```
            zratio = (zlevels[k] - pts[i0, j0].Z) /
                (pts[i1, j1].Z - pts[i0, j0].Z);
            pta[0] = cs2d.Point2D(new PointF(pts[i0, j0].X *
                (1 - zratio) + pts[i1, j1].X * zratio,
                pts[i0, j0].Y), cs);
            zratio = (zlevels[k] - pts[i1, j1].Z) /
                (pts[i2, j2].Z - pts[i1, j1].Z);
            pta[1] = cs2d.Point2D(new PointF(pts[i1, j1].X,
                pts[i1, j1].Y * (1 - zratio) + pts[i2, j2].Y
                * zratio), cs);
            g.DrawLine(aPen, pta[0], pta[1]);
        }
        else if ((zlevels[k] >= pts[i0, j0].Z && zlevels[k]
                < pts[i2, j2].Z || zlevels[k] < pts[i0, j0].Z
                && zlevels[k] >= pts[i2, j2].Z) &&
                (zlevels[k] >= pts[i1, j1].Z && zlevels[k] <
                pts[i2, j2].Z || zlevels[k] < pts[i1, j1].Z
                && zlevels[k] >= pts[i2, j2].Z))
        {
            zratio = (zlevels[k] - pts[i0, j0].Z) /
                (pts[i2, j2].Z - pts[i0, j0].Z);
            pta[0] = cs2d.Point2D(new PointF(pts[i0, j0].X *
                (1-zratio) + pts[i2, j2].X *zratio,
                pts[i0, j0].Y *(1-zratio) +
                pts[i2, j2].Y *zratio), cs);
            zratio = (zlevels[k] - pts[i1, j1].Z) /
                (pts[i2, j2].Z - pts[i1, j1].Z);
            pta[1] = cs2d.Point2D(new PointF(pts[i1, j1].X,
                pts[i1, j1].Y *(1-zratio) +
                pts[i2, j2].Y *zratio), cs);
            g.DrawLine(aPen, pta[0], pta[1]);
        }
        else if ((zlevels[k] >= pts[i0, j0].Z && zlevels[k]
                < pts[i1, j1].Z || zlevels[k] < pts[i0, j0].Z
                && zlevels[k] >= pts[i1, j1].Z) &&
                (zlevels[k] >= pts[i0, j0].Z && zlevels[k] <
                pts[i2, j2].Z || zlevels[k] < pts[i0, j0].Z
                && zlevels[k] >= pts[i2, j2].Z))
        {
            zratio = (zlevels[k] - pts[i0, j0].Z) /
                (pts[i1, j1].Z - pts[i0, j0].Z);
            pta[0] = cs2d.Point2D(new PointF(pts[i0, j0].X *
                (1-zratio) + pts[i1,j1].X * zratio,
                pts[i0, j0].Y), cs);
            zratio = (zlevels[k] - pts[i0, j0].Z) /
                (pts[i2, j2].Z - pts[i0, j0].Z);
            pta[1] = cs2d.Point2D(new PointF(pts[i0, j0].X *
                (1-zratio) + pts[i2, j2].X *zratio,
                pts[i0, j0].Y * (1-zratio) +
                pts[i2, j2].Y *zratio), cs);
            g.DrawLine(aPen, pta[0], pta[1]);
        }
    }
}
```

```
        }
    }
```

In this method, there are several parameters that can be used to control the appearance of a contour chart. The most important parameter is the `NumberContours` property that determines how many contour lines to be drawn. You can also specify the `IsColorMap` property to determine what kind of pen will be used to draw the contour lines. If this property is set to be false, a single colored pen (the color specified by the `LineStyle` property) is used to draw the contour. On the other hand, if this property is set to be true, a color mapped pen is used, depending on the values of the contour levels.

Testing Contour Charts

Contour charts can be tested by using the following code snippet of the `Form1` class:

```csharp
using System;
using System.Drawing;
using System.Drawing.Drawing2D;
using System.Windows.Forms;

namespace Example6_3
{
    public partial class Form1 : Form
    {
        ChartStyle cs;
        ChartStyle2D cs2d;
        DataSeries ds;
        DrawChart dc;
        ChartFunctions cf;
        ColorMap cm;

        public Form1()
        {
            InitializeComponent();
            this.SetStyle(ControlStyles.AllPaintingInWmPaint |
                ControlStyles.UserPaint |
                ControlStyles.DoubleBuffer,true);
            this.SetStyle(ControlStyles.ResizeRedraw, true);

            // Subscribing to a paint eventhandler to drawingPanel:
            PlotPanel.Paint +=
                new PaintEventHandler(PlotPanelPaint);
            cs = new ChartStyle(this);
            cs2d = new ChartStyle2D(this);
            ds = new DataSeries();
            dc = new DrawChart(this);
            cf = new ChartFunctions();
            cm = new ColorMap();

            cs.GridStyle.LineColor = Color.LightGray;
            cs.GridStyle.Pattern = DashStyle.Dash;
            cs.Title = "No Title";
            cs.IsColorBar = false;
```

```
            cs2d.ChartBackColor = Color.White;
            cs2d.ChartBorderColor = Color.Black;

            ds.LineStyle.IsVisible = false;

            dc.ChartType = DrawChart.ChartTypeEnum.Contour;
            dc.IsColorMap = false;
            dc.NumberContours = 15;
        }

        protected override void OnPaint(PaintEventArgs e)
        {
            Graphics g = e.Graphics;

            if (dc.ChartType == DrawChart.ChartTypeEnum.XYColor||
                dc.ChartType == DrawChart.ChartTypeEnum.Contour ||
                dc.ChartType == DrawChart.ChartTypeEnum.FillContour)
            {
                Rectangle rect = this.ClientRectangle;
                cs2d.ChartArea = new Rectangle(rect.X, rect.Y,
                    rect.Width, 19 * rect.Height / 30);
                cf.Peak3D(ds, cs);
                cs2d.SetPlotArea(g, cs);
                dc.AddColorBar(g, ds, cs, cs2d);
            }
        }

        private void PlotPanelPaint(object sender, PaintEventArgs e)
        {
            Graphics g = e.Graphics;

            g.SmoothingMode = SmoothingMode.AntiAlias;

            if (dc.ChartType == DrawChart.ChartTypeEnum.XYColor||
                dc.ChartType == DrawChart.ChartTypeEnum.Contour||
                dc.ChartType == DrawChart.ChartTypeEnum.FillContour)
            {
                cs2d.AddChartStyle2D(g, cs);
                dc.AddChart(g, ds, cs, cs2d);
            }
            else
            {
                cs.Elevation = trkElevation.Value;
                cs.Azimuth = trkAzimuth.Value;
                cf.Peak3D(ds, cs);
                cs.AddChartStyle(g);
                dc.AddChart(g, ds, cs, cs2d);
            }
        }
    }
}
```

This produces Figure 6-16, which has single colored contour lines.

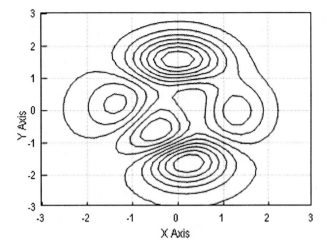

Figure 6-16 Contour chart.

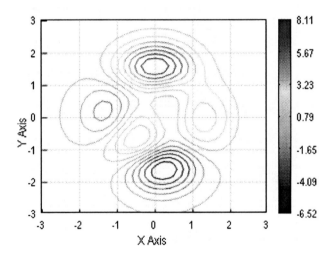

Figure 6-17 Color mapped contour chart.

You can also easily create a contour chart with color-mapped contouring lines by adding the following code snippet:

```
cs.IsColorBar = true;
dc.IsColorMap = true;
dc.CMap = cm.Jet();
```

This generates Figure 6-17.

Filled Contour Charts

You can also create a filled contour chart by combining the contour chart and the X-Y color chart together, as implemented in the AddChart method of the DrawChart class:

```
case ChartTypeEnum.FillContour:
    AddXYColor(g, ds, cs, cs2d);
    AddContour(g, ds, cs, cs2d);
    break;
```

Here we first draw the X-Y color chart and then the contour. This can be tested by using the same code for Form1 as we did for the contour chart, except for the changes in the following code snippet:

```
dc.ChartType = DrawChart.ChartTypeEnum.FillContour;
dc.IsInterp = true;
dc.NumberInterp = 5;
```

Here we set the chart type to FillContour, and use the interpolated color shading to draw the X-Y color chart. Running this project, you obtain the output of Figure 6-18.

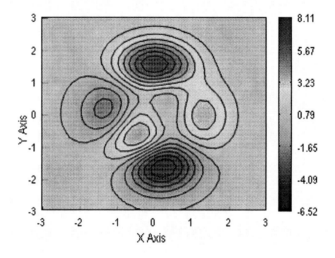

Figure 6-18 A filled contour chart.

Combination Charts

Combination charts are a useful way to exploit the informative properties of various types of graphics charting methods. In this section, we will show you only three examples of typical combination charts: mesh-contour, surface-contour, and surface-filled contour plots. By using a similar approach, you can easily create your own combination plots.

Notice that when discussing contour and the X-Y color charts in previous sections, we draw these charts directly on the 2D computer screen. However, in order to combine a contour or X-Y color chart with a 3D mesh or surface chart, we must modify the original 2D contour and X-Y color chart to be consistent with the 3D coordinate system used in the mesh and surface chart.

X-Y Charts in 3D

In creating original 2D X-Y charts, we transform the world to device coordinates by directly using the X and Y components of the data points and neglecting the Z component. In order to add the 3D feature to X-Y charts, you must perform an orthogonal projection transformation on the X and Y components of the data points at a constant Z value (the projection plane where the X-Y color chart is drawn) using the transformation matrix defined in the Matrix3 class. The AddXYColor3D method in the DrawChart class is implemented in this manner:

```
private void AddXYColor3D(Graphics g, DataSeries ds,
        ChartStyle cs, ChartStyle2D cs2d)
{
    Pen aPen = new Pen(ds.LineStyle.LineColor,
            ds.LineStyle.Thickness);
    aPen.DashStyle = ds.LineStyle.Pattern;
    SolidBrush aBrush = new SolidBrush(Color.White);

    PointF[] pta = new PointF[4];
    Point3[,] pts = ds.PointArray;
    Point3[,] pts1 = new Point3[pts.GetLength(0), pts.GetLength(1)];
    Point3[,] pts2 = new Point3[pts.GetLength(0), pts.GetLength(1)];
    Matrix3 m = Matrix3.AzimuthElevation(cs.Elevation, cs.Azimuth);

    // Find the minumum and maximum z values:
    float zmin = ds.ZDataMin();
    float zmax = ds.ZDataMax();

    // Perform transformation on points:
    for (int i = 0; i < pts.GetLength(0); i++)
    {
        for (int j = 0; j < pts.GetLength(1); j++)
        {
            // Make a deep copy the points array:
            pts1[i, j] = new Point3(pts[i, j].X,
                    pts[i, j].Y, cs.ZMin, 1);
            pts2[i, j] = new Point3(pts[i, j].X,
                    pts[i, j].Y, cs.ZMin, 1);
            pts1[i, j].Transform(m, form1, cs);
        }
    }

    // Draw surface on the XY plane:
    if (!IsInterp)
    {
        for (int i = 0; i < pts.GetLength(0) - 1; i++)
        {
            for (int j = 0; j < pts.GetLength(1) - 1; j++)
            {
                pta[0] = new PointF(pts1[i, j].X, pts1[i, j].Y);
```

```
                    pta[1] = new PointF(pts1[i, j + 1].X,
                            pts1[i, j + 1].Y);
                    pta[2] = new PointF(pts1[i + 1, j + 1].X,
                            pts1[i + 1, j + 1].Y);
                    pta[3] = new PointF(pts1[i + 1, j].X,
                            pts1[i + 1, j].Y);
                    Color color = AddColor(cs, pts[i, j], zmin, zmax);
                    aBrush = new SolidBrush(color);
                    g.FillPolygon(aBrush, pta);
                    if (ds.LineStyle.IsVisible)
                    {
                        g.DrawPolygon(aPen, pta);
                    }
                }
            }
        }

        // Draw refined surface:
        else if (IsInterp)
        {
            for (int i = 0; i < pts1.GetLength(0) - 1; i++)
            {
                for (int j = 0; j < pts1.GetLength(1) - 1; j++)
                {
                    Point3[] points = new Point3[4];
                    points[0] = pts[i, j];
                    points[1] = pts[i, j + 1];
                    points[2] = pts[i + 1, j + 1];
                    points[3] = pts[i + 1, j];
                    Interp(g, cs, cs2d, m, points, zmin, zmax, 3);
                }
            }
        }
    }
```

You can see that the transformation is indeed performed on the data points at a constant Z = cs.ZMin using the elevation-azimuth transformation matrix. This indicates that we will draw the X-Y color chart on the Z = cs.ZMin plane.

Contour Charts in 3D

Similarly, in order to combine the contour chart with the 3D mesh and surface charts, you must create a contour chart that is consistent with the 3D coordinate system. The following code listing is for the AddContour3D method in the DrawChart class:

```
    private void AddContour3D(Graphics g, DataSeries ds,
            ChartStyle cs, ChartStyle2D cs2d)
    {
        Pen aPen = new Pen(ds.LineStyle.LineColor, ds.LineStyle.Thickness);
        aPen.DashStyle = ds.LineStyle.Pattern;
        Point3[] pta = new Point3[2];
        Point3[,] pts = ds.PointArray;
        Matrix3 m = Matrix3.AzimuthElevation(cs.Elevation, cs.Azimuth);
```

```
// Find the minumum and maximum z values:
float zmin = ds.ZDataMin();
float zmax = ds.ZDataMax();
float[] zlevels = new float[numberContours];
for (int i = 0; i < numberContours; i++)
{
    zlevels[i] = zmin + i * (zmax - zmin) / (numberContours - 1);
}

int i0, i1, i2, j0, j1, j2;
float zratio = 1;
// Draw contour on the XY plane:
for (int i = 0; i < pts.GetLength(0) - 1; i++)
{
    for (int j = 0; j < pts.GetLength(1) - 1; j++)
    {
        for (int k = 0; k < numberContours; k++)
        {
            // Left triangle:
            i0 = i;
            j0 = j;
            i1 = i;
            j1 = j + 1;
            i2 = i + 1;
            j2 = j + 1;
            if ((zlevels[k] >= pts[i0, j0].Z && zlevels[k] <
                    pts[i1, j1].Z || zlevels[k] < pts[i0, j0].Z
                    && zlevels[k] >= pts[i1, j1].Z) &&
                    (zlevels[k] >= pts[i1, j1].Z && zlevels[k]
                    < pts[i2, j2].Z || zlevels[k] < pts[i1, j1].Z
                    && zlevels[k] >= pts[i2, j2].Z))
            {
                zratio = (zlevels[k] - pts[i0, j0].Z) /
                    (pts[i1, j1].Z - pts[i0, j0].Z);
                pta[0] = new Point3(pts[i0, j0].X, (1 - zratio) *
                    pts[i0, j0].Y + zratio * pts[i1, j1].Y,
                    cs.ZMin, 1);
                zratio = (zlevels[k] - pts[i1, j1].Z) /
                    (pts[i2, j2].Z - pts[i1, j1].Z);
                pta[1] = new Point3((1 - zratio) *
                    pts[i1, j1].X + zratio * pts[i2, j2].X,
                    pts[i1, j1].Y, cs.ZMin, 1);
                pta[0].Transform(m, form1, cs);
                pta[1].Transform(m, form1, cs);
                g.DrawLine(aPen, pta[0].X, pta[0].Y, pta[1].X,
                    pta[1].Y);
            }
            else if ((zlevels[k] >= pts[i0, j0].Z && zlevels[k]
                    < pts[i2, j2].Z || zlevels[k] < pts[i0, j0].Z
                    && zlevels[k] >= pts[i2, j2].Z) &&
                    (zlevels[k] >= pts[i1, j1].Z && zlevels[k]
                    < pts[i2, j2].Z || zlevels[k] < pts[i1, j1].Z
                    && zlevels[k] >= pts[i2, j2].Z))
```

```
        {
            zratio = (zlevels[k] - pts[i0, j0].Z) /
                (pts[i2, j2].Z - pts[i0, j0].Z);
            pta[0] = new Point3((1 - zratio) *
                pts[i0, j0].X + zratio * pts[i2, j2].X,
                (1 - zratio) * pts[i0, j0].Y +
                zratio * pts[i2, j2].Y, cs.ZMin, 1);
            zratio = (zlevels[k] - pts[i1, j1].Z) /
                (pts[i2, j2].Z - pts[i1, j1].Z);
            pta[1] = new Point3((1 - zratio) *
                pts[i1, j1].X + zratio * pts[i2, j2].X,
                pts[i1, j1].Y, cs.ZMin, 1);
            pta[0].Transform(m, form1, cs);
            pta[1].Transform(m, form1, cs);
            g.DrawLine(aPen, pta[0].X, pta[0].Y, pta[1].X,
                pta[1].Y);
        }
        else if ((zlevels[k] >= pts[i0, j0].Z && zlevels[k]
                < pts[i1, j1].Z || zlevels[k] < pts[i0, j0].Z
                && zlevels[k] >= pts[i1, j1].Z) &&
                (zlevels[k] >= pts[i0, j0].Z && zlevels[k]
                < pts[i2, j2].Z || zlevels[k] < pts[i0, j0].Z
                && zlevels[k] >= pts[i2, j2].Z))
        {
            zratio = (zlevels[k] - pts[i0, j0].Z) /
                (pts[i1, j1].Z - pts[i0, j0].Z);
            pta[0] = new Point3(pts[i0, j0].X, (1 - zratio) *
                pts[i0, j0].Y + zratio * pts[i1, j1].Y,
                cs.ZMin, 1);
            zratio = (zlevels[k] - pts[i0, j0].Z) /
                (pts[i2, j2].Z - pts[i0, j0].Z);
            pta[1] = new Point3(pts[i0, j0].X *
                    (1 - zratio) + pts[i2, j2].X * zratio,
                    pts[i0, j0].Y * (1 - zratio) +
                    pts[i2, j2].Y * zratio, cs.ZMin, 1);
            pta[0].Transform(m, form1, cs);
            pta[1].Transform(m, form1, cs);
            g.DrawLine(aPen, pta[0].X, pta[0].Y, pta[1].X,
                    pta[1].Y);
        }


        // right triangle:
        i0 = i;
        j0 = j;
        i1 = i + 1;
        j1 = j;
        i2 = i + 1;
        j2 = j + 1;
        if ((zlevels[k] >= pts[i0, j0].Z && zlevels[k] <
                pts[i1, j1].Z || zlevels[k] < pts[i0, j0].Z
                && zlevels[k] >= pts[i1, j1].Z) &&
                (zlevels[k] >= pts[i1, j1].Z && zlevels[k]
                < pts[i2, j2].Z || zlevels[k] < pts[i1, j1].Z
                && zlevels[k] >= pts[i2, j2].Z))
```

```
        {
            zratio = (zlevels[k] - pts[i0, j0].Z) /
                (pts[i1, j1].Z - pts[i0, j0].Z);
            pta[0] = new Point3(pts[i0, j0].X *
                (1 - zratio) + pts[i1, j1].X * zratio,
                pts[i0, j0].Y, cs.ZMin, 1);
            zratio = (zlevels[k] - pts[i1, j1].Z) /
                (pts[i2, j2].Z - pts[i1, j1].Z);
            pta[1] = new Point3(pts[i1, j1].X, pts[i1, j1].Y *
                (1 - zratio) + pts[i2, j2].Y * zratio,
                cs.ZMin, 1);
            pta[0].Transform(m, form1, cs);
            pta[1].Transform(m, form1, cs);
            g.DrawLine(aPen, pta[0].X, pta[0].Y, pta[1].X,
                pta[1].Y);
        }
        else if ((zlevels[k] >= pts[i0, j0].Z && zlevels[k]
                < pts[i2, j2].Z || zlevels[k] < pts[i0, j0].Z
                && zlevels[k] >= pts[i2, j2].Z) &&
                (zlevels[k] >= pts[i1, j1].Z && zlevels[k] <
                pts[i2, j2].Z || zlevels[k] < pts[i1, j1].Z
                && zlevels[k] >= pts[i2, j2].Z))
        {
            zratio = (zlevels[k] - pts[i0, j0].Z) /
                (pts[i2, j2].Z - pts[i0, j0].Z);
            pta[0] = new Point3(pts[i0, j0].X *
                (1 - zratio) + pts[i2, j2].X * zratio,
                pts[i0, j0].Y * (1 - zratio) +
                pts[i2, j2].Y * zratio, cs.ZMin, 1);
            zratio = (zlevels[k] - pts[i1, j1].Z) /
                (pts[i2, j2].Z - pts[i1, j1].Z);
            pta[1] = new Point3(pts[i1, j1].X,
                pts[i1, j1].Y * (1 - zratio) +
                pts[i2, j2].Y * zratio, cs.ZMin, 1);
            pta[0].Transform(m, form1, cs);
            pta[1].Transform(m, form1, cs);
            g.DrawLine(aPen, pta[0].X, pta[0].Y, pta[1].X, pta[1].Y);
        }
        else if ((zlevels[k] >= pts[i0, j0].Z && zlevels[k]
                < pts[i1, j1].Z || zlevels[k] < pts[i0, j0].Z
                && zlevels[k] >= pts[i1, j1].Z) &&
                (zlevels[k] >= pts[i0, j0].Z && zlevels[k] <
                pts[i2, j2].Z || zlevels[k] < pts[i0, j0].Z
                && zlevels[k] >= pts[i2, j2].Z))
        {
            zratio = (zlevels[k] - pts[i0, j0].Z) /
                (pts[i1, j1].Z - pts[i0, j0].Z);
            pta[0] = new Point3(pts[i0, j0].X *
                (1 - zratio) + pts[i1, j1].X * zratio,
                pts[i0, j0].Y, cs.ZMin, 1);
            zratio = (zlevels[k] - pts[i0, j0].Z) /
                (pts[i2, j2].Z - pts[i0, j0].Z);
            pta[1] = new Point3(pts[i0, j0].X *
                (1 - zratio) + pts[i2, j2].X * zratio,
```

```
                                pts[i0, j0].Y * (1 - zratio) +
                                pts[i2, j2].Y * zratio, cs.ZMin, 1);
                            pta[0].Transform(m, form1, cs);
                            pta[1].Transform(m, form1, cs);
                            g.DrawLine(aPen, pta[0].X, pta[0].Y, pta[1].X,
                                pta[1].Y);
                    }
                }
            }
        }
        aPen.Dispose();
    }
```

In this method, we draw the contour on the Z = cs.Zmin plane.

Mesh-Contour Charts

It is easy to create a mesh-contour combination chart by successively using the AddContour3D and AddMesh methods. Within the AddChart method in the DrawChart class, add the following code snippet:

```
case ChartTypeEnum.MeshContour:
    AddContour3D(g, ds, cs, cs2d);
    AddMesh(g, ds, cs);
    AddColorBar(g, ds, cs, cs2d);
    break;
```

You can test this project by setting the chart type to a mesh-contour chart in the Form1 class:

```
dc.ChartType = DrawChart.ChartTypeEnum.MeshContour;
```

This produces Figure 6-19.

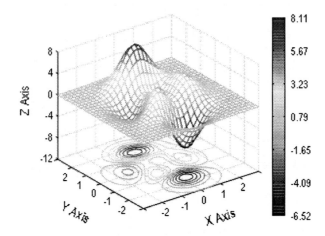

Figure 6-19 A mesh-contour chart.

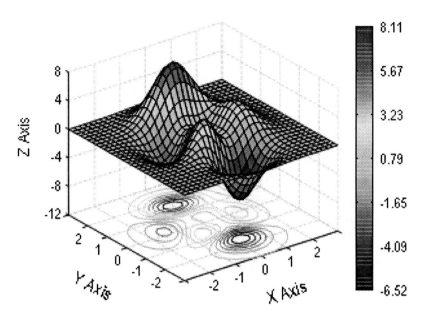

Figure 6-20 A surface-contour chart.

Surface-Contour Charts

Similarly, you can easily create surface-contour charts. Within the `AddChart` method in the `DrawChart` class, add the following lines:

```
case ChartTypeEnum.SurfaceContour:
    AddContour3D(g, ds, cs, cs2d);
    AddSurface(g, ds, cs, cs2d);
    AddColorBar(g, ds, cs, cs2d);
    break;
```

In the `Form1` class, set the chart type to Surface-Contour:

```
dc.ChartType = DrawChart.ChartTypeEnum.SurfaceContour;
```

This creates the result shown in Figure 6-20.

Surface-Filled-Contour Charts

The surface-filled contour chart is created by combining the surface chart with the X-Y color and contour charts. Within the `AddChart` method in the `DrawChart` class, add the following code snippet:

```
case ChartTypeEnum.SurfaceFillContour:
    AddXYColor3D(g, ds, cs, cs2d);
    AddContour3D(g, ds, cs, cs2d);
    AddSurface(g, ds, cs, cs2d);
    AddColorBar(g, ds, cs, cs2d);
```

```
                break;
```

In the `Form1` class, set the chart type to surface-filled contour:

```
dc.ChartType = DrawChart.ChartTypeEnum.SurfaceFillContour;
```

This creates the result shown in Figure 6-21.

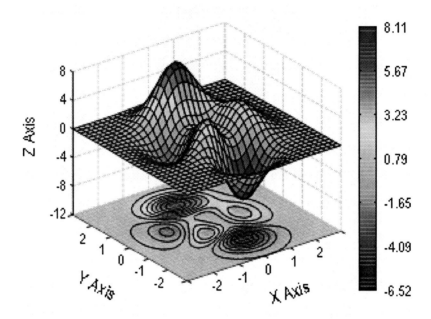

Figure 6-21 A surface-filled contour chart.

3D Bar Charts

Using the same data series as we did in the mesh and surface charts, we can also create 3D bar charts. A 3D bar can be constructed in 3D space, as shown in Figure 6-22.

Suppose there is a data point (x, y, z) in 3D space. We can define a 3D bar around this point by specifying 3 parameters: zorigin, xlength, and ylength. The parameter zorigin defines the Z = zorigin plane from which the 3D bar is filled, while the parameters xlength and ylength set the size of the 3D bar in the X and Y direction. These length parameters are measured as a percentage of the total amount of space available. In this book, we set these parameters to be in the range [0.1, 0.5]. If setting xlength = ylength = 0.5, you will obtain the so-called histogram bar chart, namely, each bar fills the space up to its adjoining bars.

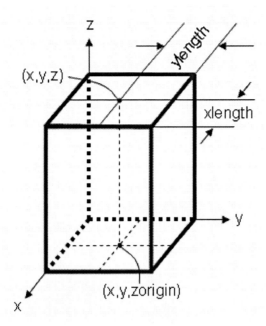

Figure 6-22 A 3D bar defined in 3D space.

Implementation

First we need to add a `BarStyle` class to our C# project *Example6_3*:

```
using System;
using System.Drawing;
namespace Example6_3
{
    public class BarStyle
    {
        private float xLength = 0.5f;
        private float yLength = 0.5f;
        private float zOrigin = 0;
        private bool isBarSingleColor = true;


        public BarStyle()
        {

        }

        public bool IsBarSingleColor
        {
            get { return isBarSingleColor; }
            set { isBarSingleColor = value; }
        }
```

```
        public float ZOrigin
        {
            get { return zOrigin; }
            set { zOrigin = value; }
        }

        public float YLength
        {
            get { return yLength; }
            set { yLength = value; }
        }

        public float XLength
        {
            get { return xLength; }
            set { xLength = value; }
        }
    }
}
```

This class is very simple. We define the field members and their corresponding properties that allow you to control the appearance and size of 3D bars in 3D space. The `bool` property `IsBarSingleColor` lets you specify whether the bars are drawn with a single color or color map. Next, we need to create an `AddBar3D` method in the `DrawChart` class:

```
private void AddBar3D(Graphics g, DataSeries ds,
        ChartStyle cs, ChartStyle2D cs2d)
{
    Matrix3 m = Matrix3.AzimuthElevation(cs.Elevation, cs.Azimuth);
    PointF[] pt = new PointF[4];
    Point3[,] pts = ds.PointArray;

    // Find the minumum and maximum z values:
    float zmin = ds.ZDataMin();
    float zmax = ds.ZDataMax();

    // Check parameters:
    float xlength = ds.BarStyle.XLength;
    if (xlength <= 0)
        xlength = 0.1f * ds.XSpacing;
    else if (xlength > 0.5f)
        xlength = 0.5f * ds.XSpacing;
    else
        xlength = ds.BarStyle.XLength * ds.XSpacing;
    float ylength = ds.BarStyle.YLength;
    if (ylength <= 0)
        ylength = 0.1f * ds.YSpacing;
    else if (ylength > 0.5f)
        ylength = 0.5f * ds.YSpacing;
    else
        ylength = ds.BarStyle.YLength * ds.YSpacing;
    float zorigin = ds.BarStyle.ZOrigin;

    // Draw 3D bars:
```

```
for (int i = 0; i < pts.GetLength(0) - 1; i++)
{
    for (int j = 0; j < pts.GetLength(1) - 1; j++)
    {
        int ii = i;
        int jj = j;
        if (cs.Azimuth >= -180 && cs.Azimuth < -90)
        {
            ii = pts.GetLength(0) - 2 - i;
            jj = j;
        }
        else if (cs.Azimuth >= -90 && cs.Azimuth < 0)
        {
            ii = pts.GetLength(0) - 2 - i;
            jj = pts.GetLength(1) - 2 - j;
        }
        else if (cs.Azimuth >= 0 && cs.Azimuth < 90)
        {
            ii = i;
            jj = pts.GetLength(1) - 2 - j;
        }
        else if (cs.Azimuth >= 90 && cs.Azimuth <= 180)
        {
            ii = i;
            jj = j;
        }
        DrawBar(g, ds, cs, m, pts[ii, jj], xlength, ylength,
          zorigin, zmax, zmin);
    }
}
}
```

In this method, we first examine whether the parameters provided by users are in the right ranges. Then, we examine the order of drawing the bars according to the variations of the elevation and azimuth angles, making sure that we always draw the bars in back-to-front (the Z-Order approach). As mentioned previously, when drawn in this order, a bar can obscure only the bars that have been drawn before it. When the program draws a bar, it fills it so that it covers up any bars that it should obscure. Finally, this method calls another method, DrawBar, that performs the actual bar-drawing task:

```
private void DrawBar(Graphics g, DataSeries ds, ChartStyle cs,
        Matrix3 m, Point3 pt, float xlength, float ylength,
        float zorign, float zmax, float zmin)
{
    Pen aPen = new Pen(ds.LineStyle.LineColor, ds.LineStyle.Thickness);
    aPen.DashStyle = ds.LineStyle.Pattern;
    Color color = AddColor(cs, pt, zmin, zmax);
    SolidBrush aBrush = new SolidBrush(color);
    Point3[] pts = new Point3[8];
    Point3[] pts1 = new Point3[8];
    Point3[] pt3 = new Point3[4];
    PointF[] pta = new PointF[4];
    pts[0] = new Point3(pt.X - xlength, pt.Y - ylength, zorign, 1);
    pts[1] = new Point3(pt.X - xlength, pt.Y + ylength, zorign, 1);
```

```
pts[2] = new Point3(pt.X + xlength, pt.Y + ylength, zorign, 1);
pts[3] = new Point3(pt.X + xlength, pt.Y - ylength, zorign, 1);
pts[4] = new Point3(pt.X + xlength, pt.Y - ylength, pt.Z, 1);
pts[5] = new Point3(pt.X + xlength, pt.Y + ylength, pt.Z, 1);
pts[6] = new Point3(pt.X - xlength, pt.Y + ylength, pt.Z, 1);
pts[7] = new Point3(pt.X - xlength, pt.Y - ylength, pt.Z, 1);

for (int i = 0; i < pts.Length; i++)
{
    pts1[i] = new Point3(pts[i].X, pts[i].Y, pts[i].Z, 1);
    pts[i].Transform(m, form1, cs);
}

int[] nconfigs = new int[8];
if (IsBarSingleColor)
{
    pta[0] = new PointF(pts[4].X, pts[4].Y);
    pta[1] = new PointF(pts[5].X, pts[5].Y);
    pta[2] = new PointF(pts[6].X, pts[6].Y);
    pta[3] = new PointF(pts[7].X, pts[7].Y);
    g.FillPolygon(aBrush, pta);
    g.DrawPolygon(aPen, pta);
    pta[0] = new PointF(pts[0].X, pts[0].Y);
    pta[1] = new PointF(pts[1].X, pts[1].Y);
    pta[2] = new PointF(pts[2].X, pts[2].Y);
    pta[3] = new PointF(pts[3].X, pts[3].Y);
    g.FillPolygon(aBrush, pta);
    g.DrawPolygon(aPen, pta);

    if (cs.Azimuth >= -180 && cs.Azimuth < -90)
    {
        nconfigs = new int[8] { 1, 2, 5, 6, 1, 0, 7, 6 };
    }
    else if (cs.Azimuth >= -90 && cs.Azimuth < 0)
    {
        nconfigs = new int[8] { 1, 0, 7, 6, 0, 3, 4, 7 };
    }
    else if (cs.Azimuth >= 0 && cs.Azimuth < 90)
    {
        nconfigs = new int[8] { 0, 3, 4, 7, 2, 3, 4, 5 };
    }
    else if (cs.Azimuth >= 90 && cs.Azimuth < 180)
    {
        nconfigs = new int[8] { 2, 3, 4, 5, 1, 2, 5, 6 };
    }
    pta[0] = new PointF(pts[nconfigs[0]].X, pts[nconfigs[0]].Y);
    pta[1] = new PointF(pts[nconfigs[1]].X, pts[nconfigs[1]].Y);
    pta[2] = new PointF(pts[nconfigs[2]].X, pts[nconfigs[2]].Y);
    pta[3] = new PointF(pts[nconfigs[3]].X, pts[nconfigs[3]].Y);
    g.FillPolygon(aBrush, pta);
    g.DrawPolygon(aPen, pta);
    pta[0] = new PointF(pts[nconfigs[4]].X, pts[nconfigs[4]].Y);
    pta[1] = new PointF(pts[nconfigs[5]].X, pts[nconfigs[5]].Y);
    pta[2] = new PointF(pts[nconfigs[6]].X, pts[nconfigs[6]].Y);
```

```
        pta[3] = new PointF(pts[nconfigs[7]].X, pts[nconfigs[7]].Y);
        g.FillPolygon(aBrush, pta);
        g.DrawPolygon(aPen, pta);
}
else if (!IsBarSingleColor && IsColorMap)
{
        pta[0] = new PointF(pts[4].X, pts[4].Y);
        pta[1] = new PointF(pts[5].X, pts[5].Y);
        pta[2] = new PointF(pts[6].X, pts[6].Y);
        pta[3] = new PointF(pts[7].X, pts[7].Y);
        g.FillPolygon(aBrush, pta);
        g.DrawPolygon(aPen, pta);
        pta[0] = new PointF(pts[0].X, pts[0].Y);
        pta[1] = new PointF(pts[1].X, pts[1].Y);
        pta[2] = new PointF(pts[2].X, pts[2].Y);
        pta[3] = new PointF(pts[3].X, pts[3].Y);
        color = AddColor(cs, pts[0], zmin, zmax);
        aBrush = new SolidBrush(color);
        g.FillPolygon(aBrush, pta);
        g.DrawPolygon(aPen, pta);

        float dz = (zmax - zmin) / 63;
        if (pt.Z < zorign)
            dz = -dz;
        int nz = (int)((pt.Z - zorign) / dz) + 1;
        if (nz < 1)
            nz = 1;
        float z = zorign;

        if (cs.Azimuth >= -180 && cs.Azimuth < -90)
        {
            nconfigs = new int[4] { 1, 2, 1, 0 };
        }
        else if (cs.Azimuth >= -90 && cs.Azimuth < 0)
        {
            nconfigs = new int[4] { 1, 0, 0, 3 };
        }
        else if (cs.Azimuth >= 0 && cs.Azimuth < 90)
        {
            nconfigs = new int[4] { 0, 3, 2, 3 };
        }
        else if (cs.Azimuth >= 90 && cs.Azimuth <= 180)
        {
            nconfigs = new int[4] { 2, 3, 1, 2 };
        }
        for (int i = 0; i < nz; i++)
        {
            z = zorign + i * dz;
            pt3[0] = new Point3(pts1[nconfigs[0]].X,
                    pts1[nconfigs[0]].Y, z, 1);
            pt3[1] = new Point3(pts1[nconfigs[1]].X,
                    pts1[nconfigs[1]].Y, z, 1);
            pt3[2] = new Point3(pts1[nconfigs[1]].X,
                    pts1[nconfigs[1]].Y, z + dz, 1);
```

```csharp
        pt3[3] = new Point3(pts1[nconfigs[0]].X,
               pts1[nconfigs[0]].Y, z + dz, 1);
        for (int j = 0; j < pt3.Length; j++)
        {
            pt3[j].Transform(m, form1, cs);
        }
        pta[0] = new PointF(pt3[0].X, pt3[0].Y);
        pta[1] = new PointF(pt3[1].X, pt3[1].Y);
        pta[2] = new PointF(pt3[2].X, pt3[2].Y);
        pta[3] = new PointF(pt3[3].X, pt3[3].Y);
        color = AddColor(cs, pt3[0], zmin, zmax);
        aBrush = new SolidBrush(color);
        g.FillPolygon(aBrush, pta);
    }
    pt3[0] = new Point3(pts1[nconfigs[0]].X,
           pts1[nconfigs[0]].Y, zorign, 1);
    pt3[1] = new Point3(pts1[nconfigs[1]].X,
           pts1[nconfigs[1]].Y, zorign, 1);
    pt3[2] = new Point3(pts1[nconfigs[1]].X,
           pts1[nconfigs[1]].Y, pt.Z, 1);
    pt3[3] = new Point3(pts1[nconfigs[0]].X,
           pts1[nconfigs[0]].Y, pt.Z, 1);
    for (int j = 0; j < pt3.Length; j++)
    {
        pt3[j].Transform(m, form1, cs);
    }
    pta[0] = new PointF(pt3[0].X, pt3[0].Y);
    pta[1] = new PointF(pt3[1].X, pt3[1].Y);
    pta[2] = new PointF(pt3[2].X, pt3[2].Y);
    pta[3] = new PointF(pt3[3].X, pt3[3].Y);
    g.DrawPolygon(aPen, pta);
    for (int i = 0; i < nz; i++)
    {
        z = zorign + i * dz;
        pt3[0] = new Point3(pts1[nconfigs[2]].X,
               pts1[nconfigs[2]].Y, z, 1);
        pt3[1] = new Point3(pts1[nconfigs[3]].X,
               pts1[nconfigs[3]].Y, z, 1);
        pt3[2] = new Point3(pts1[nconfigs[3]].X,
               pts1[nconfigs[3]].Y, z + dz, 1);
        pt3[3] = new Point3(pts1[nconfigs[2]].X,
               pts1[nconfigs[2]].Y, z + dz, 1);
        for (int j = 0; j < pt3.Length; j++)
        {
            pt3[j].Transform(m, form1, cs);
        }
        pta[0] = new PointF(pt3[0].X, pt3[0].Y);
        pta[1] = new PointF(pt3[1].X, pt3[1].Y);
        pta[2] = new PointF(pt3[2].X, pt3[2].Y);
        pta[3] = new PointF(pt3[3].X, pt3[3].Y);
        color = AddColor(cs, pt3[0], zmin, zmax);
        aBrush = new SolidBrush(color);
        g.FillPolygon(aBrush, pta);
    }
```

```
        pt3[0] = new Point3(pts1[nconfigs[2]].X,
              pts1[nconfigs[2]].Y, zorign, 1);
        pt3[1] = new Point3(pts1[nconfigs[3]].X,
              pts1[nconfigs[3]].Y, zorign, 1);
        pt3[2] = new Point3(pts1[nconfigs[3]].X,
              pts1[nconfigs[3]].Y, pt.Z, 1);
        pt3[3] = new Point3(pts1[nconfigs[2]].X,
              pts1[nconfigs[2]].Y, pt.Z, 1);
        for (int j = 0; j < pt3.Length; j++)
        {
            pt3[j].Transform(m, form1, cs);
        }
        pta[0] = new PointF(pt3[0].X, pt3[0].Y);
        pta[1] = new PointF(pt3[1].X, pt3[1].Y);
        pta[2] = new PointF(pt3[2].X, pt3[2].Y);
        pta[3] = new PointF(pt3[3].X, pt3[3].Y);
        g.DrawPolygon(aPen, pta);
    }
    aPen.Dispose();
    aBrush.Dispose();
}
```

In this method, we first create eight vertices of a 3D bar using a single data point, xlength, ylength, and zorigin parameters. We then perform an orthogonal projection transformation on these vertices using the azimuth-elevation matrix. Next, we consider two cases separately: drawing bars with a single color or a color map. For each case, we examine which faces should be drawn, depending on the elevation and azimuth angles. In the case of a single color, the color of a bar is determined by the Z value of the input point, while in the case of a color map, each bar is color mapped linearly from the Z value of its input point to the zorigin.

We also need to add the following code fragment to the AddChart method in the DrawChart class:

```
case ChartTypeEnum.Bar3D:
    AddBar3D(g, ds, cs, cs2d);
    AddColorBar(g,ds,cs,cs2d);
    break;
```

Testing 3D Bar Charts

The following code snippet of the Form1 class can be used to test the 3D bar chart:

```
ds.BarStyle.XLength = 0.3f;
ds.BarStyle.YLength = 0.3f;
ds.BarStyle.IsBarSingleColor = true;
ds.BarStyle.ZOrigin = cs.ZMin;
dc.ChartType = DrawChart.ChartTypeEnum.Bar3D;
```

Here we set the Xlength = Ylength = 0.3, and ZOrigin = cs.ZMin. We draw the bars with a single color because we set the parameter IsBarSingleColor to true. This produces the output of Figure 6-23.

```
If you set the property IsBarSingleColor to false:
```

Figure 6-23 A single colored 3D bar chart.

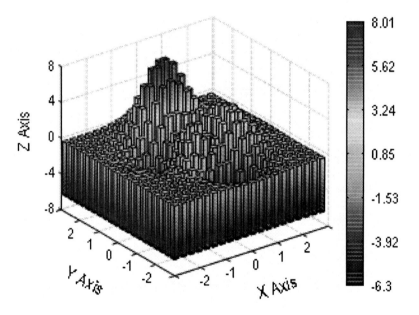

Figure 6-24 A color mapped 3D bar chart.

```
ds.BarStyle.IsBarSingleColor = false;
```

you will obtain a color mapped 3D bar chart, as shown in Figure 6-24.

You can also change the ZOrigin property. Figure 6-25 is created by setting the ZOrigin property to zero:

```
ds.BarStyle.ZOrigin = 0;
```

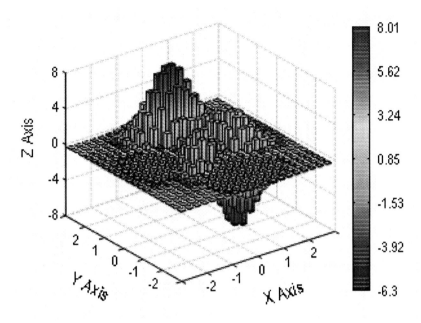

Figure 6-25 A color mapped 3D bar chart with ZOrigin = 0.

Slice Charts

In some cases, 3D surface charts or contour plots might not be a sufficient representation for visualizing your data sets. For example, if you want to determine the heat transfer or density characteristics of a solid object, you probably need a slice chart. A slice chart allows you to plot slices of the volume data on projection planes.

In discussing the Point4 class previously, we defined a 4D point to represent a value defined on the position of the X, Y, and Z. Using the Point4 class, we can easily create volume data. For a slice chart application, we only need scalar volume data that contains single values for each 3D grid point.

Now, we will look at how to create a slice plane to view this scalar volume data.

Implementation

For simplicity, here we only consider three slices: xslice, yslice, and zslice. The xslice, yslice, or zslice is created on the X, Y, or Z = constant plane in 3D coordinate space, respectively. We need to add some field members and their corresponding properties to the DrawChart class to manage the slice chart:

```
private SliceEnum xyzSlice = SliceEnum.XSlice;
private float sliceLocation = 0;
```

```
        public float SliceLocation
        {
            get { return sliceLocation; }
            set { sliceLocation = value; }
        }

        public SliceEnum XYZSlice
        {
            get { return xyzSlice; }
            set { xyzSlice = value; }
        }

        public enum SliceEnum
        {
            XSlice,
            YSlice,
            ZSlice
        }
```

We define the XYZSlice property using the SliceEnum enumeration, which allows you to select which slice you want to create. Another property, SliceLocation, specifies the position where the slice will be created. Then, we need to add the AddSlice method to the DrawChart class:

```
    private void AddSlice(Graphics g, DataSeries ds, ChartStyle cs,
            ChartStyle2D cs2d)
    {
        Pen aPen = new Pen(ds.LineStyle.LineColor, ds.LineStyle.Thickness);
        aPen.DashStyle = ds.LineStyle.Pattern;
        SolidBrush aBrush = new SolidBrush(Color.Black);
        Point4[, ,] pts = ds.Point4Array;
        PointF[] pta = new PointF[4];
        Matrix3 m = Matrix3.AzimuthElevation(cs.Elevation, cs.Azimuth);

        // Find the minumum and maximum v values:
        float vmin = ds.VDataMin();
        float vmax = ds.VDataMax();

        // Perform transformation on points:
        for (int i = 0; i < pts.GetLength(0); i++)
        {
            for (int j = 0; j < pts.GetLength(1); j++)
            {
                for (int k = 0; k < pts.GetLength(2); k++)
                {
                    pts[i, j, k].point3.Transform(m, form1, cs);
                    pts[i, j, k].point3.Z = pts[i, j, k].V;
                }
            }
        }

        // Select slice:
        if (XYZSlice == SliceEnum.XSlice)
```

```
{
    // Examine the imputer parameters:
    if (SliceLocation < cs.XMin)
        SliceLocation = cs.XMin;
    if (SliceLocation > cs.XMax)
        SliceLocation = cs.XMax;

    int nfix = (int)((SliceLocation - ds.XDataMin) /
        ds.XSpacing) + 1;
    for (int j = 0; j < pts.GetLength(1)-1; j++)
    {
        for (int k = 0; k < pts.GetLength(2) - 1; k++)
        {
            pta[0] = new PointF(pts[nfix, j, k].point3.X,
                    pts[nfix, j, k].point3.Y);
            pta[1] = new PointF(pts[nfix, j+1, k].point3.X,
                    pts[nfix, j+1, k].point3.Y);
            pta[2] = new PointF(pts[nfix, j+1, k+1].point3.X,
                    pts[nfix, j+1, k+1].point3.Y);
            pta[3] = new PointF(pts[nfix, j, k+1].point3.X,
                    pts[nfix, j, k+1].point3.Y);
            Color color = AddColor(cs, pts[nfix, j, k].point3,
                    vmin, vmax);
            aBrush = new SolidBrush(color);
            g.FillPolygon(aBrush, pta);
            if (ds.LineStyle.IsVisible)
            {
                g.DrawPolygon(aPen, pta);
            }
        }
    }
}
else if (XYZSlice == SliceEnum.YSlice)
{
    if (SliceLocation < cs.YMin)
        SliceLocation = cs.YMin;
    if (SliceLocation > cs.YMax)
        SliceLocation = cs.YMax;
    int nfix = (int)((SliceLocation - ds.YDataMin) /
        ds.YSpacing) + 1;
    for (int i = 0; i < pts.GetLength(0) - 1; i++)
    {
        for (int k = 0; k < pts.GetLength(2) - 1; k++)
        {
            pta[0] = new PointF(pts[i, nfix, k].point3.X,
                    pts[i, nfix, k].point3.Y);
            pta[1] = new PointF(pts[i + 1, nfix, k].point3.X,

                    pts[i + 1, nfix, k].point3.Y);
            pta[2] = new PointF(pts[i + 1, nfix, k + 1].point3.X,
                    pts[i + 1, nfix, k + 1].point3.Y);
            pta[3] = new PointF(pts[i, nfix, k + 1].point3.X,
                    pts[i, nfix, k + 1].point3.Y);
            Color color = AddColor(cs, pts[i,nfix, k].point3,
```

```
                                vmin, vmax);

                    aBrush = new SolidBrush(color);
                    g.FillPolygon(aBrush, pta);
                    if (ds.LineStyle.IsVisible)
                    {
                        g.DrawPolygon(aPen, pta);
                    }
                }
            }
        }
        else if (XYZSlice == SliceEnum.ZSlice)
        {
            if (SliceLocation < cs.ZMin)
                SliceLocation = cs.ZMin;
            if (SliceLocation > cs.ZMax)
                SliceLocation = cs.ZMax;
            int nfix = (int)((SliceLocation - ds.ZZDataMin) /
                    ds.ZSpacing) + 1;
            for (int i = 0; i < pts.GetLength(0) - 1; i++)
            {
                for (int j = 0; j < pts.GetLength(1) - 1; j++)
                {
                    pta[0] = new PointF(pts[i, j,nfix].point3.X,
                            pts[i,j, nfix].point3.Y);
                    pta[1] = new PointF(pts[i + 1, j,nfix].point3.X,
                            pts[i + 1,j, nfix].point3.Y);
                    pta[2] = new PointF(pts[i + 1, j+1,nfix].point3.X,
                            pts[i + 1,j+1, nfix].point3.Y);
                    pta[3] = new PointF(pts[i, j+1,nfix].point3.X,
                            pts[i, j+1,nfix].point3.Y);
                    Color color = AddColor(cs, pts[i, j,nfix].point3,
                            vmin, vmax);
                    aBrush = new SolidBrush(color);
                    g.FillPolygon(aBrush, pta);
                    if (ds.LineStyle.IsVisible)
                    {
                        g.DrawPolygon(aPen, pta);
                    }
                }
            }
        }
        aPen.Dispose();
        aBrush.Dispose();
    }
```

In this method, we implement the XSlice, YSlice, and ZSlice separately. For each case, we first examine the SliceLocation property to see if it is within the valid parameter range. Then we draw the polygons using the Z-Order approach.

Testing Slice Charts

In order to test your slice charts, you need to add the following code fragment to the Form1 class:

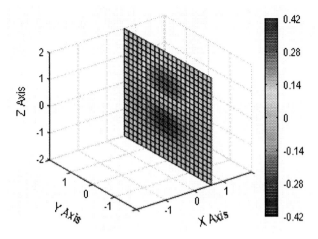

Figure 6-26 A slice chart at X = 0.5 plane.

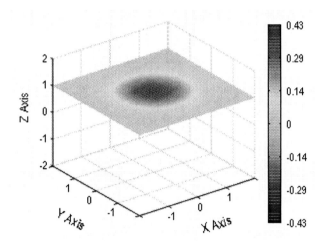

Figure 6-27 A slice chart at Z = 1 plane without gridlines.

```
dc.ChartType = DrawChart.ChartTypeEnum.Slice;
dc.CMap = cm.Jet();
dc.XYZSlice = DrawChart.SliceEnum.XSlice;
dc.SliceLocation = 0.5f;
```

You also need to change the chart function within both the OnPaint and PlotPanelPaint methods:

```
cf.Exp4D(ds, cs);
```

This produces the XSlice chart shown in Figure 6-26.

You can also create a slice chart without gridlines using the following code snippet:

```
ds.LineStyle.IsVisible = false;
```

```
dc.XYZSlice = DrawChart.SliceEnum.ZSlice;
dc.SliceLocation = 1;
```

This generates a ZSlice chart at Z = 1 plane without drawing gridlines, as shown in Figure 6-27.

7

Charts and User Controls

In the previous chapters, we directly implemented the source code for all of the classes in our graphics and chart programs. For simple applications, this approach works well. However, if you want to reuse the same code in multiple-form applications, you should avoid using this method. The .NET framework and C# provide a powerful means, the user control, to solve this problem.

The custom user controls in a Windows form are just like the simple buttons or text boxes already provided with .NET. Typically, the controls you design are to be used in multiple forms or modularize your code. These custom controls can reduce the amount of code you have to type, as well as make it easier for you to change the implementation. There is no reason to duplicate code in your applications because this leaves a lot of room for bugs, which makes it a good programming practice to create functionality specific to the user control in the control's source code, which can reduce code duplication and modularize your code.

Custom user controls are a key theme in .NET development. They can greatly enhance your programming style by improving encapsulation, simplifying a programming model, and making the user interface more pluggable. Of course, custom controls can also have other benefits, including the ability to transform a generic window into a state-of-the-art modern interface.

In this chapter, I will show you how to put the chart and graphics applications we developed previously into a custom user control, and how to use such a control in C# applications. This chapter begins by explaining the basics of the custom user controls in a C# Windows application, including how to provide design-time support to the controls. Then, the chapter describes the detailed procedure in creating custom user controls for 2D and 3D chart applications, and demonstrates how to use these controls in your real-world C# applications using examples.

User Control Basics

The C# developers often make a distinction between the different types of controls provided by C# and .NET. The user control is the simplest type of control, and inherits from the System.Windows.Forms.UserControl class. This kind of control is a collection of Windows Forms controls encapsulated in a common container. The user control holds all of the inherent functionality associated with each of the contained Windows Forms controls and enables you to selectively expose and bind their properties. It also provides a great deal of default keyboard handling functionality without extra development effort on the programmer's part.

Another type of control is called the inherited control, which is inherited directly from any existing Windows Forms control. With this control, you can retain all of the inherent functionality of a Windows Forms control, then extend that functionality by adding custom properties, methods, or other features. Basically, you choose an existing .NET control that is closest to what you want to provide. Then, you derive a custom class that overrides or adds your own properties and methods.

The other way to create a custom control is to create one from scratch by inheriting from the base class, System.Windows.Forms.Control. This basic class provides all of the basic functionality required by controls, including mouse and keyboard handling events, but no associated control-specific functionality or graphical interface. Creating such a custom control by inheriting from the Control class requires much more effort than inheriting from the UserControl class or an existing Windows Forms control. Because a great deal of implementation is left up to you, your control can have greater flexibility than a user control or inherited control, and you can tailor your control to suit your exact needs.

In this chapter, we create user controls for graphics and chart applications that are inherited from the UserControl class.

Design Time Support

As mentioned previously, user controls are reusable components that encapsulate user interface functionality and are used in client-side Windows-based applications. Windows Forms provides the basic framework for developing your own custom user controls.

The design time support architecture allows you to develop customized design-time extensions which you can use to configure the properties of your user controls. You may often encounter the situation where, while developing a custom user control, you need to provide the user interface for modifying its properties at design time.

C# and .NET provide interfaces used to implement customized design time support. There are three approaches to perform this task: UITypeEditor, TypeConverter, and Designer.

UITypeEditor allows you to provide a custom user interface for editing the value of a property of the user control. It also allows you to display a visual representation of the current value in the properties window. For example, the Dock, Anchor, and ForeColor properties of the C# controls provide a user interface for supplying and setting their values. These are called Property Editors. Figure 7-1 shows the ForeColor property, which provides the user with an interface-based property editing mechanism, accessed by a dropdown arrow in the property browser. You can use the UITypeEditor class to create such interfaces for the properties of your custom user controls. Property Editors are generally displayed in the drop-down area inside the properties window itself. You can also make them appear as modal windows.

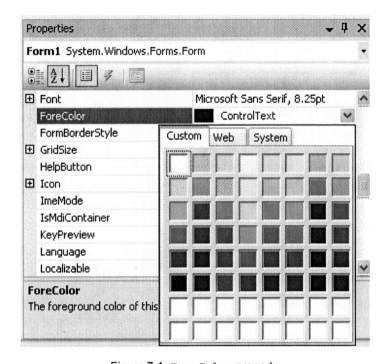

Figure 7-1 ForeColor property.

TypeConverter can be used to convert your values between data types. It also provides logic for the configuration of a property in the property browser. You might notice in the property browser that some properties, such as Font, Size, etc., return objects instead of scalar values, and that these properties are displayed in the property browser with a "+" sign. Figure 7-2 shows the Font property with the "+" sign. If user controls contain any properties that return objects (Font, Point, Location, Size) then they will inherit the same kind of behavior. However, if your custom controls contain any property that returns a custom object, you need to create a custom TypeConverter class to perform this task. In this chapter, I will show you how to implement chart user controls using a custom TypeConverter.

⊟ Font		Microsoft Sans Serif, 8.25pt	⊡
	Name	ab Microsoft Sans Serif	
	Size	8.25	
	Unit	Point	
	Bold	False	
	GdiCharSet	0	
	GdiVerticalFont	False	
	Italic	False	
	Strikeout	False	
	Underline	False	

Figure 7-2 Font Property.

Finally, you can also use Designers to provide design-time support. C# and .NET Framework provide interfaces, classes, and attributes for design-time support. The IDesigner interface allows you to create designer classes that provide logic that can adjust the appearance or behavior of a type at design time. The IDesigner interface has a read-only Verbs property which allows you to create custom menu commands and hyperlinks. This property returns a DesignerVerbCollection containing the DesignerVerb objects for generating menu commands. The ControlDesigner class allows you to create custom designers which can be sited on the form.

Event Handling

Because the basic .NET controls are contained within your user control, events are not fired for the contained applications. In this regard, the user control is treated like any other control and must implement its own properties and events.

For example, if a button is embedded in a Windows Form, in order to receive a button click notification, you simply hook up an event handler to the button's Click event. However, if a button is embedded in a user control, how do you add an event handler to this button? Adding a notification handler to that user control's Click event will notify your event handler only if that control is clicked. In fact, there is little need to be notified when the mouse is clicked over a user control.

Event handlers are normally assigned across one level of the control hierarchy, from the Form directly to a button or from a user control directly to a button. To assign an event handler from a Form to a button that is embedded in a user control is not straightforward. One way to accomplish this is to expose the button from the user control to the Form. But this is an awkward thing to do if the button is nested many layers deep. Another way is to use a delegate to override the Click event in the user control and redirect the captured Click event.

When an object generates an event, it must send the event out. The way that events are dispatched is through the use of delegates. For instance, if a button is embedded in a user control and the user control is placed into a form, the button's Click event is ultimately processed by the form's event handlers. Therefore, the routing needs to be built into the user control.

User Control for 2D Charts

In this section, we will show you how to create a custom user control for a 2D chart application. Specifically, we want to convert the 2D chart project *Example3_6* from Chapter 3 into a 2D chart user control. In this control, we expect that most of the properties in the ChartStyle class should appear in the property browser and can be changed from this browser at the design time. In addition, we want to modularize the properties in the ChartStyle class into several groups according to their functionalities so that the properties in the property browser become more organized.

By following the procedure of creating the 2D chart control described in this chapter, yo can easily develop an advanced 2D chart control that incorporates more features and more chart types. For example, you can integrate a variety of specific 2D charts discussed in Chapter 4 into your 2D chart control.

Creating User Control

In order to create the Chart2DLib control library and the Chart2D control, follow the following steps:

- On the **File** menu, point to **New** and select **Project** to open the **New Project** dialog box.

- Select the **Windows Control Library** project template from the list of C# Projects and type Chart2DLib in the Name box.

- In the Solution Explorer, right-click **UserControl1** and select **View Code** from the shortcut menu. Locate the Class statement public class UserControl1 and change UserControl1 to Chart2D to change the name of the component.

- Locate the constructor public UserControl1() and change UserControl1 to Chart2D.

- In the Solution Explorer, click UserControl1, and in the property window, change the **FileName** property to Chart2D.cs.

- Add the classes, ChartStyle, DataCollection, DataSeries, Legend, LineStyle, and SymbolStyle from project *Example3_6* to the current project and change their namespace to Chart2DLib.

Next, you need to convert the classes from *Example3_6* into classes compatible with the user control.

Using TypeConverter

Here, we want to modularize the ChartStyle class by dividing it into a few different classes, including ChartArea, XAxis, YAxis, Y2Axis, XYLabel, Title2D, and Grid. All of these classes are placed into a single file: ChartStyle.cs.

The use of TypeConverter can be illustrated using the XAxis class, which contains three public properties. This class allows you to enter the XLimMin, XLimMax, and XTick. We want the property browser to expose this data in a single property instead of exposing it in four different properties, as shown in Figure 7-3.

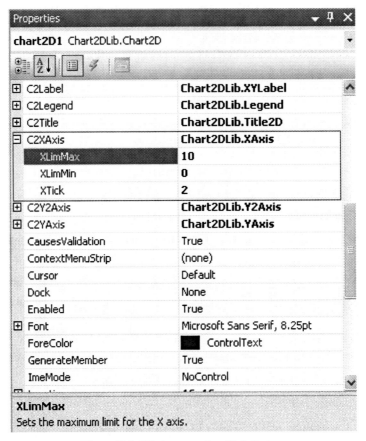

Figure 7-3 XAxis property with "+" sign.

The first step in doing so is to create the XAxis class, which wraps all of the properties related to the X axis together. You need to decorate this class with the TypeConverter attribute:

```
[TypeConverter(typeof(XAxisConverter))]
public class XAxis
{
    private float xLimMin = 0f;
    private float xLimMax = 10f;
    private float xTick = 2f;
    private Chart2D chart2d;

    public XAxis(Chart2D ct2d)
    {
        chart2d = ct2d;
    }

    [Description("Sets the maximum limit for the X axis."),
```

```
                        Category("Appearance")]
            public float XLimMax
            {
                get { return xLimMax; }
                set
                {
                    xLimMax = value;
                    chart2d.Invalidate();
                }
            }

            [Description("Sets the minimum limit for the X axis."),
            Category("Appearance")]
            public float XLimMin
            {
                get { return xLimMin; }
                set
                {
                    xLimMin = value;
                    chart2d.Invalidate();
                }
            }

            [Description("Sets the ticks for the X axis."),
            Category("Appearance")]
            public float XTick
            {
                get { return xTick; }
                set
                {
                    xTick = value;
                    chart2d.Invalidate();
                }
            }
        }
```

The `TypeConverter` attribute tells the form designer that the `XAxisConverter` is associated with the `XAxis` class.

In the second step we need to create the `XAxisConverter` class, which is derived from the `System.ComponentModel.TypeConverter` class, and override two methods. They are the `GetPropertiesSupported()` and `GetProperties()` methods:

```
        public class XAxisConverter : TypeConverter
        {
            // Display the "+" symbol near the property name:
            public override bool GetPropertiesSupported(
                ITypeDescriptorContext context)
            {
                return true;
            }

            public override PropertyDescriptorCollection
                GetProperties(ITypeDescriptorContext context,
```

```
                    object value, Attribute[] attributes)
        {
            return TypeDescriptor.GetProperties(typeof(XAxis));
        }
    }
```

The `GetPropertiesSupported()` method returns whether or not the object supports properties. The form designer uses this value to display a "+" symbol at XAxis property. The `GetProperties()` method returns the `PropertiesDescriptorCollection` object that describes the items that appear when the "+" symbol is clicked. Please note that the `typeof(XAxis)` is used as the input parameter of the `GetProperties()` method, indicating that the text strings in the Property Browser are converted to XAxis objects by the `TypeConverter`.

The final step is to set the `DesignerSerializationVisibility` attribute of the XAxis to `Content` in the `Chart2D` class:

```
    public partial class Chart2D : UserControl
    {
        private XAxis xa;
        ... ...

        public Chart2D()
        {
            InitializeComponent();
            this.SetStyle(ControlStyles.ResizeRedraw, true);
            xa = new XAxis(this);
            ... ...
        }

        [DesignerSerializationVisibility(
                DesignerSerializationVisibility.Content)]
        public XAxis C2XAxis
        {
            get { return this.xa; }
            set
            {
                if (value != null)
                {
                    this.xa = value;
                }
            }
        }
        ... ...
    }
```

The `DesignerSerializationVisibility` attribute specifies the type of persistence used when serializing a property on a control at design time. Setting this value to `content` tells C# and the .NET framework to serialize the contents of the C2XAis property. Here C2 (which stands for Chart 2D) is placed in front of the XAxis class name to group all of the properties related to Chart2D together in the Property Browser.

You can convert all of the properties in the ChartStyle class into formats compatible with the user control in the same way we did for the XAxis class.

ChartStyle Class

For your reference, here we list the code of the ChartStyle class after the conversion:

```
using System;
using System.Drawing;
using System.Drawing.Drawing2D;
using System.ComponentModel;

namespace Chart2DLib
{
    public class ChartStyle
    {
        private Chart2D chart2d;
        private Rectangle chartArea;
        private Rectangle plotArea;

        public ChartStyle(Chart2D ct2d)
        {
            chart2d = ct2d;
            chartArea = chart2d.ClientRectangle;
            PlotArea = chartArea;
        }

        [Description("Sets the size for the chart area."),
        Category("Appearance")]
        public Rectangle ChartArea
        {
            get { return chartArea; }
            set { chartArea = value; }
        }

        [Description("Sets size for the plot area."),
        Category("Appearance")]
        public Rectangle PlotArea
        {
            get { return plotArea; }
            set { plotArea = value; }
        }

        public void AddChartStyle(Graphics g, ChartArea ca, XAxis xa,
            YAxis ya, Y2Axis y2a, Grid gd, XYLabel lb, Title2D tl)
        {
            // Draw TotalChartArea, ChartArea, and PlotArea:
            SetPlotArea(g, xa, ya, y2a, gd, lb, tl);
            Pen aPen = new Pen(ca.ChartBorderColor, 1f);
            SolidBrush aBrush = new SolidBrush(ca.ChartBackColor);
            g.FillRectangle(aBrush, ChartArea);
            g.DrawRectangle(aPen, ChartArea);
            aPen = new Pen(ca.PlotBorderColor, 1f);
```

```
aBrush = new SolidBrush(ca.PlotBackColor);
g.FillRectangle(aBrush, PlotArea);
g.DrawRectangle(aPen, PlotArea);

SizeF tickFontSize = g.MeasureString("A", lb.TickFont);
// Create vertical gridlines:
float fX, fY;
if (gd.IsYGrid == true)
{
    aPen = new Pen(gd.GridColor, 1f);
    aPen.DashStyle = gd.GridPattern;
    for (fX = xa.XLimMin + xa.XTick; fX < xa.XLimMax;
        fX += xa.XTick)
    {
        g.DrawLine(aPen, Point2D(new PointF(fX,
            ya.YLimMin), xa, ya), Point2D(new PointF(fX,
            ya.YLimMax), xa, ya));
    }

    // Create horizontal gridlines:
    if (gd.IsXGrid == true)
    {
        aPen = new Pen(gd.GridColor, 1f);
        aPen.DashStyle = gd.GridPattern;
        for (fY = ya.YLimMin + ya.YTick; fY < ya.YLimMax;
            fY += ya.YTick)
        {
            g.DrawLine(aPen, Point2D(new PointF(
                xa.XLimMin, fY), xa, ya), Point2D(new
                PointF(xa.XLimMax, fY), xa, ya));
        }
    }
}

// Create the x-axis tick marks:
aBrush = new SolidBrush(lb.TickFontColor);
for (fX = xa.XLimMin; fX <= xa.XLimMax; fX +=
        xa.XTick)
{
    PointF yAxisPoint = Point2D(new PointF(fX,
        ya.YLimMin), xa, ya);
    g.DrawLine(Pens.Black, yAxisPoint, new PointF(
        yAxisPoint.X, yAxisPoint.Y - 5f));
    StringFormat sFormat = new StringFormat();
    sFormat.Alignment = StringAlignment.Far;
    SizeF sizeXTick = g.MeasureString(fX.ToString(),
        lb.TickFont);
    g.DrawString(fX.ToString(), lb.TickFont, aBrush,
        new PointF(yAxisPoint.X + sizeXTick.Width / 2,
        yAxisPoint.Y + 4f), sFormat);
}

// Create the y-axis tick marks:
for (fY = ya.YLimMin; fY <= ya.YLimMax; fY +=
        ya.YTick)
```

```
            {
                PointF xAxisPoint = Point2D(new PointF(
                    xa.XLimMin, fY), xa, ya);
                g.DrawLine(Pens.Black, xAxisPoint,
                    new PointF(xAxisPoint.X + 5f, xAxisPoint.Y));
                StringFormat sFormat = new StringFormat();
                sFormat.Alignment = StringAlignment.Far;
                g.DrawString(fY.ToString(), lb.TickFont, aBrush,
                    new PointF(xAxisPoint.X - 3f, xAxisPoint.Y -
                    tickFontSize.Height / 2), sFormat);
            }

            // Create the y2-axis tick marks:
            if (y2a.IsY2Axis)
            {
                for (fY = y2a.Y2LimMin; fY <= y2a.Y2LimMax;
                    fY += y2a.Y2Tick)
                {
                    PointF x2AxisPoint = Point2DY2(new
                        PointF(xa.XLimMax, fY), xa, y2a);
                    g.DrawLine(Pens.Black, x2AxisPoint,
                        new PointF(x2AxisPoint.X - 5f,
                        x2AxisPoint.Y));
                    StringFormat sFormat = new StringFormat();
                    sFormat.Alignment = StringAlignment.Near;
                    g.DrawString(fY.ToString(), lb.TickFont,
                        aBrush, new PointF(x2AxisPoint.X + 3f,
                        x2AxisPoint.Y - tickFontSize.Height / 2),
                        sFormat);
                }
            }
            aPen.Dispose();
            aBrush.Dispose();
            AddLabels(g, xa, ya, y2a, gd, lb, tl);
        }
    }

    private void SetPlotArea(Graphics g, XAxis xa, YAxis ya,
        Y2Axis y2a, Grid gd, XYLabel lb, Title2D tl)
    {
        // Set PlotArea:
        float xOffset = ChartArea.Width / 30.0f;
        float yOffset = ChartArea.Height / 30.0f;
        SizeF labelFontSize = g.MeasureString("A", lb.LabelFont);
        SizeF titleFontSize = g.MeasureString("A", tl.TitleFont);
        if (tl.Title.ToUpper() == "NO TITLE")
        {
            titleFontSize.Width = 8f;
            titleFontSize.Height = 8f;
        }
        float xSpacing = xOffset / 3.0f;
        float ySpacing = yOffset / 3.0f;
        SizeF tickFontSize = g.MeasureString("A", lb.TickFont);
        float tickSpacing = 2f;
```

```
SizeF yTickSize = g.MeasureString(ya.YLimMin.ToString(),
        lb.TickFont);
for (float yTick = ya.YLimMin; yTick <= ya.YLimMax;
        yTick += ya.YTick)
{
    SizeF tempSize = g.MeasureString(yTick.ToString(),
            lb.TickFont);
    if (yTickSize.Width < tempSize.Width)
    {
        yTickSize = tempSize;
    }
}
float leftMargin = xOffset + labelFontSize.Width +
            xSpacing + yTickSize.Width + tickSpacing;
float rightMargin = xOffset;
float topMargin = yOffset + titleFontSize.Height +
        ySpacing;
float bottomMargin = yOffset + labelFontSize.Height +
            ySpacing + tickSpacing + tickFontSize.Height;

if (!y2a.IsY2Axis)
{
    // Define the plot area with one Y axis:
    int plotX = ChartArea.X + (int)leftMargin;
    int plotY = ChartArea.Y + (int)topMargin;
    int plotWidth = ChartArea.Width - (int)leftMargin -
            2 * (int)rightMargin;
    int plotHeight = ChartArea.Height -
            (int)topMargin - (int)bottomMargin;
    PlotArea = new Rectangle(plotX, plotY,
            plotWidth, plotHeight);
}
else
{
    // Define the plot area with Y and Y2 axes:
    SizeF y2TickSize = g.MeasureString(
            y2a.Y2LimMin.ToString(), lb.TickFont);
    for (float y2Tick = y2a.Y2LimMin; y2Tick <=
            y2a.Y2LimMax; y2Tick += y2a.Y2Tick)
    {
        SizeF tempSize2 = g.MeasureString(
            y2Tick.ToString(), lb.TickFont);
        if (y2TickSize.Width < tempSize2.Width)
        {
            y2TickSize = tempSize2;
        }
    }

    rightMargin = xOffset + labelFontSize.Width +
            xSpacing + y2TickSize.Width + tickSpacing;
    int plotX = ChartArea.X + (int)leftMargin;
    int plotY = ChartArea.Y + (int)topMargin;
    int plotWidth = ChartArea.Width -
            (int)leftMargin - (int)rightMargin;
```

```
            int plotHeight = ChartArea.Height -
                    (int)topMargin - (int)bottomMargin;
            PlotArea = new Rectangle(plotX, plotY, plotWidth,
                    plotHeight);
        }
    }

    private void AddLabels(Graphics g, XAxis xa, YAxis ya,
        Y2Axis y2a, Grid gd, XYLabel lb, Title2D tl)
    {
        float xOffset = ChartArea.Width / 30.0f;
        float yOffset = ChartArea.Height / 30.0f;
        SizeF labelFontSize = g.MeasureString("A", lb.LabelFont);
        SizeF titleFontSize = g.MeasureString("A", tl.TitleFont);

        // Add horizontal axis label:
        SolidBrush aBrush = new SolidBrush(lb.LabelFontColor);
        SizeF stringSize = g.MeasureString(lb.XLabel,
            lb.LabelFont);
        g.DrawString(lb.XLabel, lb.LabelFont, aBrush,
            new Point(PlotArea.Left + PlotArea.Width / 2 -
            (int)stringSize.Width / 2, ChartArea.Bottom -
            (int)yOffset - (int)labelFontSize.Height));

        // Add y-axis label:
        StringFormat sFormat = new StringFormat();
        sFormat.Alignment = StringAlignment.Center;
        stringSize = g.MeasureString(lb.YLabel, lb.LabelFont);
        // Save the state of the current Graphics object
        GraphicsState gState = g.Save();
        g.TranslateTransform(ChartArea.X + xOffset, ChartArea.Y
            + yOffset + titleFontSize.Height
            + yOffset / 3 + PlotArea.Height / 2);
        g.RotateTransform(-90);
        g.DrawString(lb.YLabel, lb.LabelFont, aBrush, 0, 0,
            sFormat);
        // Restore it:
        g.Restore(gState);

        // Add y2-axis label:
        if (y2a.IsY2Axis)
        {
            stringSize = g.MeasureString(lb.Y2Label,
                lb.LabelFont);
            // Save the state of the current Graphics object
            GraphicsState gState2 = g.Save();
            g.TranslateTransform(ChartArea.X + ChartArea.Width -
                xOffset - labelFontSize.Width,
                ChartArea.Y + yOffset + titleFontSize.Height
                + yOffset / 3 + PlotArea.Height / 2);
            g.RotateTransform(-90);
            g.DrawString(lb.Y2Label, lb.LabelFont, aBrush, 0, 0,
                sFormat);
            // Restore it:
```

```csharp
                g.Restore(gState2);
            }

            // Add title:
            aBrush = new SolidBrush(tl.TitleFontColor);
            stringSize = g.MeasureString(tl.Title, tl.TitleFont);
            if (tl.Title.ToUpper() != "NO TITLE")
            {
                g.DrawString(tl.Title, tl.TitleFont, aBrush,
                    new Point(PlotArea.Left + PlotArea.Width / 2 -
                    (int)stringSize.Width / 2, ChartArea.Top +
                    (int)yOffset));
            }
            aBrush.Dispose();
        }

        public PointF Point2DY2(PointF pt, XAxis xa, Y2Axis y2a)
        {
            PointF aPoint = new PointF();
            if (pt.X < xa.XLimMin || pt.X > xa.XLimMax ||
                pt.Y < y2a.Y2LimMin || pt.Y > y2a.Y2LimMax)
            {
                pt.X = Single.NaN;
                pt.Y = Single.NaN;
            }
            aPoint.X = PlotArea.X + (pt.X - xa.XLimMin) *
                PlotArea.Width / (xa.XLimMax - xa.XLimMin);
            aPoint.Y = PlotArea.Bottom - (pt.Y - y2a.Y2LimMin) *
                PlotArea.Height / (y2a.Y2LimMax - y2a.Y2LimMin);
            return aPoint;
        }

        public PointF Point2D(PointF pt, XAxis xa, YAxis ya)
        {
            PointF aPoint = new PointF();
            if (pt.X < xa.XLimMin || pt.X > xa.XLimMax ||
                pt.Y < ya.YLimMin || pt.Y > ya.YLimMax)
            {
                pt.X = Single.NaN;
                pt.Y = Single.NaN;
            }
            aPoint.X = PlotArea.X + (pt.X - xa.XLimMin) *
                PlotArea.Width / (xa.XLimMax - xa.XLimMin);
            aPoint.Y = PlotArea.Bottom - (pt.Y - ya.YLimMin) *
                PlotArea.Height / (ya.YLimMax - ya.YLimMin);
            return aPoint;
        }
    }

[TypeConverter(typeof(ChartAreaConverter))]
public class ChartArea
{
    private Chart2D chart2d;
    private Color chartBackColor;
```

```csharp
private Color chartBorderColor;
private Color plotBackColor = Color.White;
private Color plotBorderColor = Color.Black;

public ChartArea(Chart2D ct2d)
{
    chart2d = ct2d;
    chartBackColor = chart2d.BackColor;
    chartBorderColor = chart2d.BackColor;
}

[Description("The background color of the chart area."),
Category("Appearance")]
public Color ChartBackColor
{
    get { return chartBackColor; }
    set
    {
        chartBackColor = value;
        chart2d.Invalidate();
    }
}

[Description("The border color of the chart area."),
Category("Appearance")]
public Color ChartBorderColor
{
    get { return chartBorderColor; }
    set
    {
        chartBorderColor = value;
        chart2d.Invalidate();
    }
}

[Description("The background color of the plot area."),
Category("Appearance")]
public Color PlotBackColor
{
    get { return plotBackColor; }
    set
    {
        plotBackColor = value;
        chart2d.Invalidate();
    }
}

[Description("The border color of the plot area."),
Category("Appearance")]
public Color PlotBorderColor
{
    get { return plotBorderColor; }
    set
    {
```

```
                plotBorderColor = value;
                chart2d.Invalidate();
            }
        }
    }

    public class ChartAreaConverter : TypeConverter
    {
        // allows us to display the + symbol near the property name
        public override bool GetPropertiesSupported(
                ITypeDescriptorContext context)
        {
            return true;
        }

        public override PropertyDescriptorCollection
                GetProperties(ITypeDescriptorContext context,
                object value, Attribute[] attributes)
        {
            return TypeDescriptor.GetProperties(typeof(ChartArea));
        }
    }

    [TypeConverter(typeof(XAxisConverter))]
    public class XAxis
    {
        private float xLimMin = 0f;
        private float xLimMax = 10f;
        private float xTick = 2f;
        private Chart2D chart2d;

        public XAxis(Chart2D ct2d)
        {
            chart2d = ct2d;
        }

        [Description("Sets the maximum limit for the X axis."),
        Category("Appearance")]
        public float XLimMax
        {
            get { return xLimMax; }
            set
            {
                xLimMax = value;
                chart2d.Invalidate();
            }
        }

        [Description("Sets the minimum limit for the X axis."),
        Category("Appearance")]
        public float XLimMin
        {
            get { return xLimMin; }
            set
```

```
            {
                xLimMin = value;
                chart2d.Invalidate();
            }
        }

        [Description("Sets the ticks for the X axis."),
        Category("Appearance")]
        public float XTick
        {
            get { return xTick; }
            set
            {
                xTick = value;
                chart2d.Invalidate();
            }
        }
    }

    public class XAxisConverter : TypeConverter
    {
        public XAxisConverter()
        {

        }

        // allows us to display the + symbol near the property name
        public override bool GetPropertiesSupported(
                ITypeDescriptorContext context)
        {
            return true;
        }

        public override PropertyDescriptorCollection
                GetProperties(ITypeDescriptorContext context,
                object value, Attribute[] attributes)
        {
            return TypeDescriptor.GetProperties(typeof(XAxis));
        }
    }

    [TypeConverter(typeof(YAxisConverter))]
    public class YAxis
    {
        private float yLimMin = 0f;
        private float yLimMax = 10f;
        private float yTick = 2f;
        private Chart2D chart2d;

        public YAxis(Chart2D ct2d)
        {
            chart2d = ct2d;
        }
```

```csharp
        [Description("Sets the maximum limit for the Y axis."),
        Category("Appearance")]
        public float YLimMax
        {
            get { return yLimMax; }
            set
            {
                yLimMax = value;
                chart2d.Invalidate();
            }
        }

        [Description("Sets the minimum limit for the Y axis."),
        Category("Appearance")]
        public float YLimMin
        {
            get { return yLimMin; }
            set
            {
                yLimMin = value;
                chart2d.Invalidate();
            }
        }

        [Description("Sets the ticks for the Y axis."),
        Category("Appearance")]
        public float YTick
        {
            get { return yTick; }
            set
            {
                yTick = value;
                chart2d.Invalidate();
            }
        }
    }

    public class YAxisConverter : TypeConverter
    {
        public YAxisConverter()
        {

        }

        // allows us to display the + symbol near the property name
        public override bool GetPropertiesSupported(
                ITypeDescriptorContext context)
        {
            return true;
        }

        public override PropertyDescriptorCollection
                GetProperties(ITypeDescriptorContext context,
                object value, Attribute[] attributes)
```

```
        {
            return TypeDescriptor.GetProperties(typeof(YAxis));
        }
}

[TypeConverter(typeof(Y2AxisConverter))]
public class Y2Axis
{
    private float y2LimMin = 0f;
    private float y2LimMax = 100f;
    private float y2Tick = 20f;
    private bool isY2Axis = false;
    private Chart2D chart2d;

    public Y2Axis(Chart2D ct2d)
    {
        chart2d = ct2d;
    }

    [Description("Indicates whether the chart has the Y2 axis."),
    Category("Appearance")]
    public bool IsY2Axis
    {
        get { return isY2Axis; }
        set
        {
            isY2Axis = value;
            chart2d.Invalidate();
        }
    }

    [Description("Sets the maximum limit for the Y2 axis."),
    Category("Appearance")]
    public float Y2LimMax
    {
        get { return y2LimMax; }
        set
        {
            y2LimMax = value;
            chart2d.Invalidate();
        }
    }

    [Description("Sets the minimum limit for the Y2 axis."),
    Category("Appearance")]
    public float Y2LimMin
    {
        get { return y2LimMin; }
        set
        {
            y2LimMin = value;
            chart2d.Invalidate();
        }
    }
```

```csharp
    [Description("Sets the ticks for the Y2 axis."),
    Category("Appearance")]
    public float Y2Tick
    {
        get { return y2Tick; }
        set
        {
            y2Tick = value;
            chart2d.Invalidate();
        }
    }
}

public class Y2AxisConverter : TypeConverter
{
    public Y2AxisConverter()
    {

    }

    // allows us to display the + symbol near the property name
    public override bool GetPropertiesSupported(
        ITypeDescriptorContext context)
    {
        return true;
    }

    public override PropertyDescriptorCollection
        GetProperties(ITypeDescriptorContext context,
        object value, Attribute[] attributes)
    {
        return TypeDescriptor.GetProperties(typeof(Y2Axis));
    }
}

[TypeConverter(typeof(GridConverter))]
public class Grid
{
    private DashStyle gridPattern = DashStyle.Solid;
    private Color gridColor = Color.LightGray;
    private float gridLineThickness = 1.0f;
    private bool isXGrid = true;
    private bool isYGrid = true;
    private Chart2D chart2d;

    public Grid(Chart2D ct2d)
    {
        chart2d = ct2d;
    }

    [Description("Indicates whether the X grid is shown."),
    Category("Appearance")]
    public bool IsXGrid
```

```csharp
{
    get { return isXGrid; }
    set
    {
        isXGrid = value;
        chart2d.Invalidate();
    }
}

[Description("Indicates whether the Y grid is shown."),
Category("Appearance")]
public bool IsYGrid
{
    get { return isYGrid; }
    set
    {
        isYGrid = value;
        chart2d.Invalidate();
    }
}

[Description("Sets the line pattern for the grid lines."),
Category("Appearance")]
virtual public DashStyle GridPattern
{
    get { return gridPattern; }
    set
    {
        gridPattern = value;
        chart2d.Invalidate();
    }
}

[Description("Sets the thickness for the grid lines."),
Category("Appearance")]
public float GridThickness
{
    get { return gridLineThickness; }
    set
    {
        gridLineThickness = value;
        chart2d.Invalidate();
    }
}

[Description("The color used to display the grid lines."),
Category("Appearance")]
virtual public Color GridColor
{
    get { return gridColor; }
    set
    {
        gridColor = value;
        chart2d.Invalidate();
```

```
            }
        }
    }

    public class GridConverter : TypeConverter
    {
        public GridConverter()
        {

        }

        // allows us to display the + symbol near the property name
        public override bool GetPropertiesSupported(
                ITypeDescriptorContext context)
        {
            return true;
        }

        public override PropertyDescriptorCollection
                GetProperties(ITypeDescriptorContext context,
                object value, Attribute[] attributes)
        {
            return TypeDescriptor.GetProperties(typeof(Grid));
        }
    }

    [TypeConverter(typeof(XYLabelConverter))]
    public class XYLabel
    {
        private string xLabel = "X Axis";
        private string yLabel = "Y Axis";
        private string y2Label = "Y2 Axis";
        private Font labelFont = new Font("Arial", 10, FontStyle.Regular);
        private Color labelFontColor = Color.Black;
        private Font tickFont;
        private Color tickFontColor = Color.Black;


        private Chart2D chart2d;

        public XYLabel(Chart2D ct2d)
        {
            chart2d = ct2d;
            tickFont = ct2d.Font;
        }

        [Description("Creates a label for the X axis."),
        Category("Appearance")]
        public string XLabel
        {
            get { return xLabel; }
            set
            {
                xLabel = value;
```

```
            chart2d.Invalidate();
        }
    }

    [Description("Creates a label for the Y axis."),
    Category("Appearance")]
    public string YLabel
    {
        get { return yLabel; }
        set
        {
            yLabel = value;
            chart2d.Invalidate();
        }
    }


    [Description("Creates a label for the Y2 axis."),
    Category("Appearance")]
    public string Y2Label
    {
        get { return y2Label; }
        set
        {
            y2Label = value;
            chart2d.Invalidate();
        }
    }

    [Description("The font used to display the axis labels."),
        Category("Appearance")]
    public Font LabelFont
    {
        get { return labelFont; }
        set
        {
            labelFont = value;
            chart2d.Invalidate();
        }
    }

    [Description("Sets the color of the axis labels."),
    Category("Appearance")]
    public Color LabelFontColor
    {
        get { return labelFontColor; }
        set
        {
            labelFontColor = value;
            chart2d.Invalidate();
        }
    }

    [Description("The font used to display the tick labels."),
```

```
            Category("Appearance")]
        public Font TickFont
        {
            get { return tickFont; }
            set
            {
                tickFont = value;
                chart2d.Invalidate();
            }
        }

        [Description("Sets the color of the tick labels."),
        Category("Appearance")]
        public Color TickFontColor
        {
            get { return tickFontColor; }
            set
            {
                tickFontColor = value;
                chart2d.Invalidate();
            }
        }
    }

    public class XYLabelConverter : TypeConverter
    {
        public override bool GetPropertiesSupported(
            ITypeDescriptorContext context)
        {
            return true;
        }

        public override PropertyDescriptorCollection
            GetProperties(ITypeDescriptorContext context,
            object value, Attribute[] attributes)
        {
            return TypeDescriptor.GetProperties(typeof(XYLabel));
        }
    }

    [TypeConverter(typeof(Title2DConverter))]
    public class Title2D
    {
        private string title = "Title";
        private Font titleFont = new Font("Arial", 12, FontStyle.Regular);
        private Color titleFontColor = Color.Black;
        private Chart2D chart2d;

        public Title2D(Chart2D ct2d)
        {
            chart2d = ct2d;
        }

        [Description("Creates a title for the chart."),
```

```csharp
        Category("Appearance")]
        public string Title
        {
            get { return title; }
            set
            {
                title = value;
                chart2d.Invalidate();
            }
        }

        [Description("The font used to display the title."),
        Category("Appearance")]
        public Font TitleFont
        {
            get { return titleFont; }
            set
            {
                titleFont = value;
                chart2d.Invalidate();
            }
        }

        [Description("Sets the color of the tile."),
        Category("Appearance")]
        public Color TitleFontColor
        {
            get { return titleFontColor; }
            set
            {
                titleFontColor = value;
                chart2d.Invalidate();
            }
        }
    }

    public class Title2DConverter : TypeConverter
    {
        public override bool GetPropertiesSupported(
            ITypeDescriptorContext context)
        {
            return true;
        }

        public override PropertyDescriptorCollection
            GetProperties(ITypeDescriptorContext context,
            object value, Attribute[] attributes)
        {
            return TypeDescriptor.GetProperties(typeof(Title2D));
        }
    }
}
```

In this class, we add two attributes to each property: `Category` and `Description`. The `Category("Appearance")` attribute shows whether the property is visible in the containing application. This description attribute allows the property browser to provide a brief description of the property when users click on it. There are only two properties left in the `ChartStyle` class: `ChartArea` and `PlotArea`. In most cases, their default values should be used, so we don't want to expose them in the property browser. However, if you do want to change them in some situations, you can do so via code. That is why we don't use the `TypeConverter` for the `ChartStyle` class.

Note that we also make corresponding modifications to the methods in `ChartStyle` class due to the changes we made to the class.

Legend Class

Similarly, we need to decorate the `Legend` class with the `TypeConverter` attribute because we want its properties to be exposed in the property browser:

```
using System;
using System.Drawing;
using System.Drawing.Drawing2D;
using System.Collections;
using System.ComponentModel;

namespace Chart2DLib
{
    [TypeConverter(typeof(LegendConverter))]
    public class Legend
    {
        private bool isLegendVisible;
        private Color textColor;
        private LegendPositionEnum legendPosition;
        private bool isBorderVisible;
        private Color legendBackColor;
        private Color legendBorderColor;
        private Font legendFont;
        private Chart2D chart2d;

        public Legend(Chart2D ct2d)
        {
            chart2d = ct2d;
            legendPosition = LegendPositionEnum.NorthEast;
            textColor = Color.Black;
            isLegendVisible = false;
            isBorderVisible = true;
            legendBackColor = Color.White;
            legendBorderColor = Color.Black;
            legendFont = new Font("Arial", 8, FontStyle.Regular);
        }

        [Description("Font used to display the legend text."),
        Category("Appearance")]
        public Font LegendFont
```

```csharp
{
    get { return legendFont; }
    set
    {
        legendFont = value;
        chart2d.Invalidate();
    }
}

[Description("Background color of the legend box."),
Category("Appearance")]
public Color LegendBackColor
{
    get { return legendBackColor; }
    set
    {
        legendBackColor = value;
        chart2d.Invalidate();
    }
}

[Description("The color of the legend box border."),
Category("Appearance")]
public Color LegendBorderColor
{
    get { return legendBorderColor; }
    set
    {
        legendBorderColor = value;
        chart2d.Invalidate();
    }
}

[Description("Indicates whether the legend border should be shown."),
Category("Appearance")]
public bool IsBorderVisible
{
    get { return isBorderVisible; }
    set
    {
        isBorderVisible = value;
        chart2d.Invalidate();
    }
}

[Description("Specifies the legend position in the chart ."),
Category("Appearance")]
public LegendPositionEnum LegendPosition
{
    get { return legendPosition; }
    set
    {
        legendPosition = value;
        chart2d.Invalidate();
```

```
        }
    }

    [Description("Color of the legend text."),
    Category("Appearance")]
    public Color TextColor
    {
        get { return textColor; }
        set
        {
            textColor = value;
            chart2d.Invalidate();
        }
    }

    [Description("Indicates whether the legend is shown in the chart."),
    Category("Appearance")]
    public bool IsLegendVisible
    {
        get { return isLegendVisible; }
        set
        {
            isLegendVisible = value;
            chart2d.Invalidate();
        }
    }

    public enum LegendPositionEnum
    {
        North,
        NorthWest,
        West,
        SouthWest,
        South,
        SouthEast,
        East,
        NorthEast
    }

    public void AddLegend(Graphics g, DataCollection dc,
            ChartStyle cs)
    {
        .....
    }

    private void DrawLegend(Graphics g, float xCenter,
        float yCenter, float hWidth, float hHeight,
        DataCollection dc, ChartStyle cs)
    {
        .....
    }
}

public class LegendConverter : TypeConverter
```

```
    {
        public override bool GetPropertiesSupported(
              ITypeDescriptorContext context)
        {
            return true;
        }

        public override PropertyDescriptorCollection
              GetProperties(ITypeDescriptorContext context,
              object value, Attribute[] attributes)
        {
            return TypeDescriptor.GetProperties(typeof(Legend));
        }
    }
}
```

Note that the LegendConverter class is added to the Legend.cs. Thus, you can set all property values for the Legend from the property browser, including the legend text font and color, the legend box background color, and the position of the legend in the chart.

Chart2D Class

The Chart2D class hooks all of the classes together and performs the chart drawing. Additionally, it is also responsible for which classes' properties should and should not be exposed in the property browser. The following is its code listing:

```
using System;
using System.Drawing;
using System.Drawing.Drawing2D;
using System.ComponentModel;
using System.Windows.Forms;

namespace Chart2DLib
{
    public partial class Chart2D : UserControl
    {
        private ChartStyle cs;
        private ChartArea ca;
        private DataCollection dc;
        private DataSeries ds;
        private Legend lg;
        private XAxis xa;
        private YAxis ya;
        private Y2Axis y2a;
        private Grid gd;
        private XYLabel lb;
        private Title2D tl;
        private SymbolStyle ss;

        public Chart2D()
        {
            InitializeComponent();
            this.SetStyle(ControlStyles.ResizeRedraw, true);
```

```
        cs = new ChartStyle(this);
        ca = new ChartArea(this);
        dc = new DataCollection();
        ds = new DataSeries();
        lg = new Legend(this);
        xa = new XAxis(this);
        ya = new YAxis(this);
        y2a = new Y2Axis(this);
        gd = new Grid(this);
        lb = new XYLabel(this);
        tl = new Title2D(this);
        ss = new SymbolStyle();
    }

    protected override void OnPaint(PaintEventArgs e)
    {
        Graphics g = e.Graphics;
        cs.ChartArea = this.ClientRectangle;
        cs.AddChartStyle(g, ca, xa, ya, y2a, gd, lb, tl);
        dc.AddLines(g, cs, xa, ya, y2a);
        lg.AddLegend(g, dc, cs);
        g.Dispose();
    }

    [BrowsableAttribute(false)]
    public ChartStyle C2ChartStyle
    {
        get { return this.cs; }
        set { this.cs = value; }
    }

    [DesignerSerializationVisibility(
     DesignerSerializationVisibility.Content)]
    public ChartArea C2ChartArea
    {
        get { return this.ca; }
        set
        {
            if (value != null)
            {
                this.ca = value;
            }
        }
    }

    [DesignerSerializationVisibility(
     DesignerSerializationVisibility.Content)]
    public XAxis C2XAxis
    {
        get { return this.xa; }
        set
        {
            if (value != null)
```

```
            {
                this.xa = value;
            }
        }
    }

    [DesignerSerializationVisibility(
     DesignerSerializationVisibility.Content)]
    public YAxis C2YAxis
    {
        get { return this.ya; }
        set
        {
            if (value != null)
            {
                this.ya = value;
            }
        }
    }

    [DesignerSerializationVisibility(
     DesignerSerializationVisibility.Content)]
    public Y2Axis C2Y2Axis
    {
        get { return this.y2a; }
        set
        {
            if (value != null)
            {
                this.y2a = value;
            }
        }
    }

    [DesignerSerializationVisibility(
     DesignerSerializationVisibility.Content)]
    public Grid C2Grid
    {
        get { return this.gd; }
        set
        {
            if (value != null)
            {
                this.gd = value;
            }
        }
    }

    [DesignerSerializationVisibility(
     DesignerSerializationVisibility.Content)]
    public XYLabel C2Label
    {
        get { return this.lb; }
        set
```

```
            {
                if (value != null)
                {
                    this.lb = value;
                }
            }
        }

        [DesignerSerializationVisibility(
         DesignerSerializationVisibility.Content)]
        public Title2D C2Title
        {
            get { return this.tl; }
            set
            {
                if (value != null)
                {
                    this.tl = value;
                }
            }
        }

        [BrowsableAttribute(false)]
        public DataCollection C2DataCollection
        {
            get { return this.dc; }
            set { this.dc = value; }
        }

        [DesignerSerializationVisibility(
         DesignerSerializationVisibility.Content)]
        public Legend C2Legend
        {
            get { return this.lg; }
            set
            {
                if (value != null)
                {
                    this.lg = value;
                }
            }
        }
    }
}
```

Note that we set the BrowsableAttribute of ChartStyle and DataCollection to false, indicating that the properties of the ChartStyle and DataCollection classes should not be exposed in the property browser. In order to change their properties, you must do so through code.

Testing User Control

Using the Chart2D user control in a Windows form is trivial. It's just like adding any other built-in control like a `Button` or a `TextBox`. First, create a new C# Windows Application project named: `Example7_1`. Make sure the Toolbox is visible (select **Toolbox** in the **View** menu if necessary). Right-click the Toolbox to open its context menu. If you want the Chart2D control to appear in its own tab in the Toolbox, right-click in the gray Toolbox area, select **Add Tab** from the context menu, and type in the tab name, such as "Chart".

Right-click the Chart tab or one of the existing tabs and select **Choose Items** from the context menu. The **Choose Toolbox Items** dialog box will open.

In the **Choose Toolbox Items** dialog box, go to the **.NET Framework Components** tab. Sort the list by Namespace (click the *Namespace* column header), as shown in Figure 7-4.

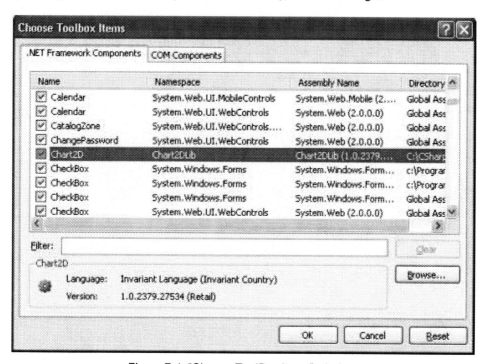

Figure 7-4 "Choose ToolBox Items" window.

Select the **Browse** button and find the Chart2D user control DLL file named `Chart2DLib.dll`, which should be located at ~\Examples\Chart2DLib\bin\Debug directory, and open it. The Chart2D user control is highlighted in blue. Click the OK button, and the Chart2D control is now added to the `ToolBox`, as shown in Figure 7-5.

Double-click the Chart2D control from the Toolbox to add it to `Form1`, as shown in Figure 7-6.

There is a Chart2D user control named chart2D1 in `Form1`. Various properties of this control can be viewed from the property browser, as shown in Figure 7-7.

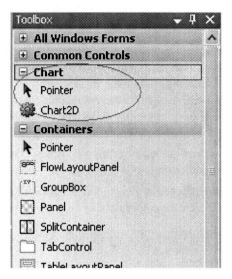

Figure 7-5 Chart2D user control in the ToolBox.

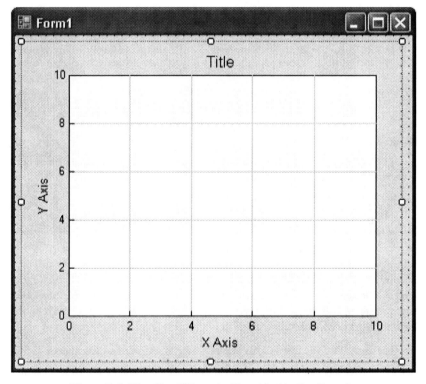

Figure 7-6 The Chart2D control is added to the Form1.

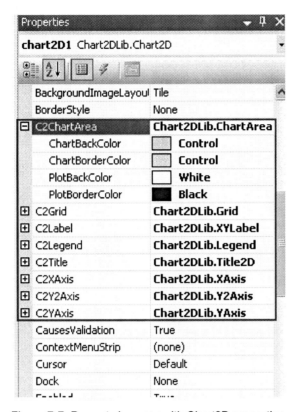

Figure 7-7 Property browser with Chart2D properties.

In order to create a 2D chart using the chart2D1 control, you need to add the following code to the Form1.cs class:

```
using System;
using System.Drawing;
using System.Drawing.Drawing2D;
using System.Windows.Forms;
using Chart2DLib;

namespace Example7_1
{
    public partial class Form1 : Form
    {
        private DataSeries ds;

        public Form1()
        {
            InitializeComponent();
            chart2D1.Dock = DockStyle.Fill;
            chart2D1.C2ChartArea.ChartBackColor = Color.White;
```

```csharp
        ds = new DataSeries();
        chart2D1.C2Legend.IsLegendVisible = true;
        AddData();
    }

    private void AddData()
    {
        // Override ChartStyle properties:
        chart2D1.C2XAxis.XLimMin = 0f;
        chart2D1.C2XAxis.XLimMax = 6f;
        chart2D1.C2YAxis.YLimMin = -1.5f;
        chart2D1.C2YAxis.YLimMax = 1.5f;
        chart2D1.C2XAxis.XTick = 1.0f;
        chart2D1.C2YAxis.YTick = 0.5f;
        chart2D1.C2Label.XLabel = "This is X axis";
        chart2D1.C2Label.YLabel = "This is Y axis";
        chart2D1.C2Title.Title = "Sine and Cosine Chart";

        chart2D1.C2DataCollection.DataSeriesList.Clear();
        // Add Sine data with 7 data points:
        ds = new DataSeries();
        ds.LineStyle.LineColor = Color.Red;
        ds.LineStyle.Thickness = 2f;
        ds.LineStyle.Pattern = DashStyle.Dash;
        ds.LineStyle.PlotMethod =
            LineStyle.PlotLinesMethodEnum.Lines;
        ds.SeriesName = "Sine";
        ds.SymbolStyle.SymbolType =
            SymbolStyle.SymbolTypeEnum.Diamond;
        ds.SymbolStyle.BorderColor = Color.Red;
        ds.SymbolStyle.FillColor = Color.Yellow;
        ds.SymbolStyle.BorderThickness = 1f;
        for (int i = 0; i < 7; i++)
        {
            ds.AddPoint(new PointF(i / 1.0f,
                (float)Math.Sin(i / 1.0f)));
        }
        chart2D1.C2DataCollection.Add(ds);

        // Add Cosine data with 7 data points:
        ds = new DataSeries();
        ds.LineStyle.LineColor = Color.Blue;
        ds.LineStyle.Thickness = 1f;
        ds.LineStyle.Pattern = DashStyle.Solid;
        ds.LineStyle.PlotMethod =
            LineStyle.PlotLinesMethodEnum.Splines;
        ds.SeriesName = "Cosine";
        ds.SymbolStyle.SymbolType =
            SymbolStyle.SymbolTypeEnum.Triangle;
        ds.SymbolStyle.BorderColor = Color.Blue;
        for (int i = 0; i < 7; i++)
        {
            ds.AddPoint(new PointF(i / 1.0f,
                (float)Math.Cos(i / 1.0f)));
```

```
            }
            chart2D1.C2DataCollection.Add(ds);
        }
    }
}
```

Note that at the top of the program, we add a line at the end of the using clauses:

```
using Chart2DLib;
```

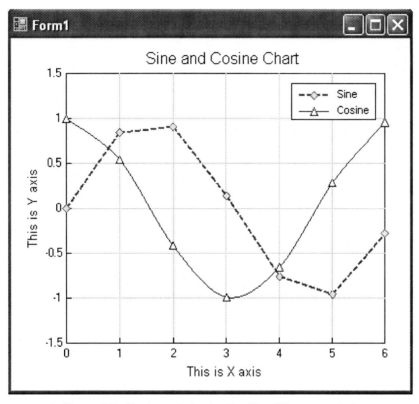

Figure 7-8 Chart created using the Chart2D user control.

This way, we save a lot of typing, since we do not need to fully qualify each item before using it. Here we set the chart2D1 properties using code. You can also change its properties directly from the property browser.

You might note that we set the chart2D1's dock property to Fill, and its ChartArea background color to White using a simple code snippet:

```
            chart2D1.Dock = DockStyle.Fill;
            chart2D1.C2ChartArea.ChartBackColor = Color.White;
```

You can access and set all of the properties of the chart2D1 control in the same manner.

The rest of this code listing is similar to the `Form1.cs` code listing of `Example3_4` in Chapter 3. Building and executing this project, you should obtain the results of Figure 7-8, which is exactly the same as Figure 3-8 in Chapter 3.

With the `Chart2D` control, you can easily create multiple charts in a single Form. Let's start a new C# Windows Application project, *Example7_2*. Add a 2x2 `TableLayoutPanel` control to `Form1`. Add a `Chart2D` control to each of the four cells of the `TableLayoutPanel` control, as shown in Figure 7-9. Add the following code listing to `Form1` class:

```
using System;
using System.Drawing;
using System.Drawing.Drawing2D;
using System.Windows.Forms;
using Chart2DLib;

namespace Example7_2
{
    public partial class Form1 : Form
    {
        private DataSeries ds;

        public Form1()
        {
            InitializeComponent();
            tableLayoutPanel1.Dock = DockStyle.Fill;
            chart2D1.Dock = DockStyle.Fill;
            chart2D2.Dock = DockStyle.Fill;
            chart2D3.Dock = DockStyle.Fill;
            chart2D4.Dock = DockStyle.Fill;
            ds = new DataSeries();
            chart2D4.C2Legend.IsLegendVisible = true;
            AddData();
        }

        private void AddData()
        {
            float x, y, x2, y2;

            // Create sub-chart 1 (0, 0):

            // Parameters for sub-chart 1 (0, 0):
            chart2D1.C2Label.TickFont = new Font("Arial", 7,
                    FontStyle.Regular);
            chart2D1.C2Label.TickFont = new Font("Arial", 7,
                    FontStyle.Regular);
            chart2D1.C2Title.TitleFont = new Font("Arial", 10,
                    FontStyle.Regular);
            chart2D1.C2XAxis.XLimMin = 0f;
            chart2D1.C2XAxis.XLimMax = 7f;
            chart2D1.C2YAxis.YLimMin = -1.5f;
            chart2D1.C2YAxis.YLimMax = 1.5f;
            chart2D1.C2XAxis.XTick = 1.0f;
            chart2D1.C2YAxis.YTick = 0.5f;
            chart2D1.C2Title.Title = "Sin(x)";
```

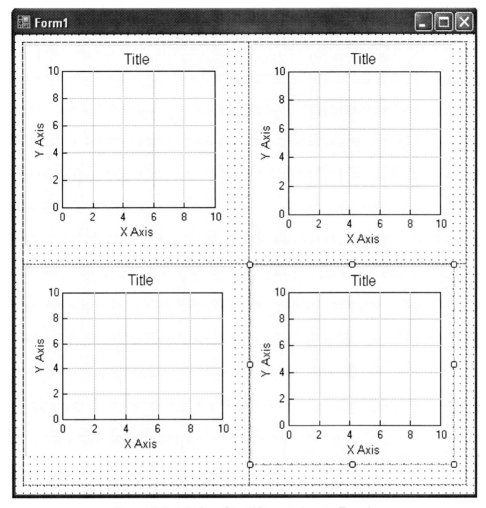

Figure 7-9 Add four Chart2D controls onto Form1.

```
// Add Sin(x) data to sub-chart 1:
chart2D1.C2DataCollection.DataSeriesList.Clear();
ds = new DataSeries();
ds.LineStyle.LineColor = Color.Red;
ds.LineStyle.Thickness = 2f;
ds.LineStyle.Pattern = DashStyle.Dash;
for (int i = 0; i < 50; i++)
{
    x = i / 5.0f;
    y = (float)Math.Sin(x);
    ds.AddPoint(new PointF(x, y));
}
chart2D1.C2DataCollection.Add(ds);
```

```csharp
// Create sub-chart 2 (0, 1):

// Parameters for sub-chart 2 (0, 1):
chart2D2.C2Label.TickFont = new Font("Arial", 7,
        FontStyle.Regular);
chart2D2.C2Title.TitleFont = new Font("Arial", 10,
        FontStyle.Regular);
chart2D2.C2XAxis.XLimMin = 0f;
chart2D2.C2XAxis.XLimMax = 7f;
chart2D2.C2YAxis.YLimMin = -1.5f;
chart2D2.C2YAxis.YLimMax = 1.5f;
chart2D2.C2XAxis.XTick = 1.0f;
chart2D2.C2YAxis.YTick = 0.5f;
chart2D2.C2Title.Title = "Cos(x)";

// Add Cos(x) data sub-chart 2:
chart2D2.C2DataCollection.DataSeriesList.Clear();
ds = new DataSeries();
ds.LineStyle.LineColor = Color.Blue;
ds.LineStyle.Thickness = 1f;
ds.SymbolStyle.SymbolType =
 SymbolStyle.SymbolTypeEnum.OpenDiamond;
for (int i = 0; i < 50; i++)
{
    x = i / 5.0f;
    y = (float)Math.Cos(x);
    ds.AddPoint(new PointF(x, y));
}
chart2D2.C2DataCollection.Add(ds);

// Create sub-chart 3 (1, 0):

// Parameters for sub-chart 3 (1, 0):
chart2D3.C2Label.TickFont = new Font("Arial", 7,
        FontStyle.Regular);
chart2D3.C2Title.TitleFont = new Font("Arial", 10,
        FontStyle.Regular);
chart2D3.C2XAxis.XLimMin = 0f;
chart2D3.C2XAxis.XLimMax = 7f;
chart2D3.C2YAxis.YLimMin = -0.5f;
chart2D3.C2YAxis.YLimMax = 1.5f;
chart2D3.C2XAxis.XTick = 1.0f;
chart2D3.C2YAxis.YTick = 0.5f;
chart2D3.C2Title.Title = "Sin(x)^2";

// Add Sin(x)^2 data to sub-chart 3:
chart2D3.C2DataCollection.DataSeriesList.Clear();
ds = new DataSeries();
ds.LineStyle.IsVisible = false;
ds.SymbolStyle.SymbolType =
        SymbolStyle.SymbolTypeEnum.Dot;
ds.SymbolStyle.FillColor = Color.Yellow;
ds.SymbolStyle.BorderColor = Color.DarkCyan;
for (int i = 0; i < 50; i++)
```

```
{
    x = i / 5.0f;
    y = (float)Math.Sin(x);
    ds.AddPoint(new PointF(x, y * y));
}
chart2D3.C2DataCollection.Add(ds);

// Create sub-chart 4 (1, 1):

// Parameters for sub-chart 4 (1, 1):
chart2D4.C2Y2Axis.IsY2Axis = true;
chart2D4.C2Grid.IsXGrid = false;
chart2D4.C2Grid.IsYGrid = false;
chart2D4.C2Label.TickFont = new Font("Arial", 7,
        FontStyle.Regular);
chart2D4.C2Title.TitleFont = new Font("Arial", 10,
        FontStyle.Regular);
chart2D4.C2XAxis.XLimMin = 0f;
chart2D4.C2XAxis.XLimMax = 30f;
chart2D4.C2YAxis.YLimMin = -20f;
chart2D4.C2YAxis.YLimMax = 20f;
chart2D4.C2XAxis.XTick = 5.0f;
chart2D4.C2YAxis.YTick = 5f;
chart2D4.C2Y2Axis.Y2LimMin = 100f;
chart2D4.C2Y2Axis.Y2LimMax = 700f;
chart2D4.C2Y2Axis.Y2Tick = 100f;
chart2D4.C2Label.XLabel = "X Axis";
chart2D4.C2Label.YLabel = "Y Axis";
chart2D4.C2Label.Y2Label = "Y2 Axis";
chart2D4.C2Title.Title = "With Y2 Axis";
chart2D4.C2Legend.IsLegendVisible = true;
chart2D4.C2Legend.LegendPosition =
        Legend.LegendPositionEnum.SouthEast;

// Add y1 and y2 data to sub-chart 4:
chart2D4.C2DataCollection.DataSeriesList.Clear();
// Add y1 data:
ds = new DataSeries();
ds.LineStyle.LineColor = Color.Red;
ds.LineStyle.Thickness = 2f;
ds.LineStyle.Pattern = DashStyle.Dash;
ds.SeriesName = "x1*cos(x1)";
for (int i = 0; i < 20; i++)
{
    float x1 = 1.0f * i;
    float y1 = x1 * (float)Math.Cos(x1);
    ds.AddPoint(new PointF(x1, y1));
}
chart2D4.C2DataCollection.Add(ds);
// Add y2 data:
ds = new DataSeries();
ds.LineStyle.LineColor = Color.Blue;
ds.LineStyle.Thickness = 2f;
ds.SeriesName = "100 + 20*x2";
```

```
                ds.IsY2Data = true;
                for (int i = 5; i < 30; i++)
                {
                    x2 = 1.0f * i;
                    y2 = 100.0f + 20.0f * x2;
                    ds.AddPoint(new PointF(x2, y2));
                }
                chart2D4.C2DataCollection.Add(ds);
            }
        }
    }
```

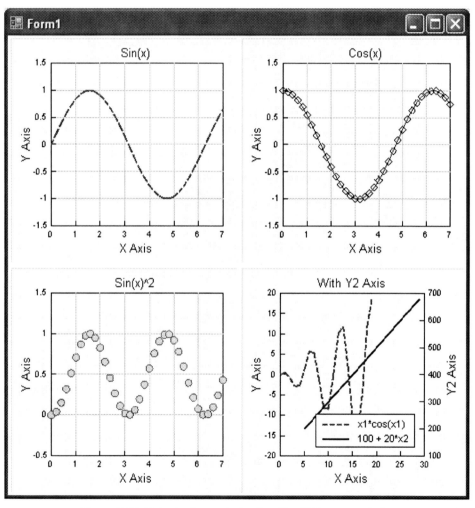

Figure 7-10 Sub-charts created using Chart2D user controls.

This class implements a 2x2 sub-charts, similar to the project *Example3_6* in Chapter 3. It can be seen that like any other built-in control, you can place as many Chart2D controls as you need in a single Form. C# and .NET assign the default names for each Chart2D control as chart2D1, chart2D2, etc.

This project produces the output of Figure 7-10, which is the same as Figure 3-12 in Chapter 3.

User Control for 3D Charts

In this section, we will create a custom user control for 3D chart applications. Specifically, we want to convert the 3D chart project *Example6_3* in Chapter 6 into a 3D chart user control. In this control, we expect that most of the properties in the ChartStyle class should appear in the property browser, and can be accessed and changed from this browser at design time. In addition, we want to modularize the properties in the ChartStyle class into several groups according to their functionalities so that the properties in the property browser become more organized.

Creating User Control

The procedure for creating the user control for 3D charts is the same as it is in case of 2D charts. You can create the Chart3DLib control library and the Chart3D control by the following steps:

- In the **File** menu, point to **New** and select **Project** to open the **New Project** dialog box.

- Select the **Windows Control Library** project template from the list of C# Projects and type Chart3DLib in the Name box.

- In the Solution Explorer, right-click **UserControl1** and select **View Code** from the shortcut menu. Locate the Class statement public class UserControl1 and change UserControl1 to Chart3D to change the name of the component.

- Locate the constructor public UserControl1() and change UserControl1 to Chart3D.

- In the Solution Explorer, click UserControl1. In the property window, change the **FileName** property to Chart3D.cs.

- Add the BarStyle, ChartStyle, ChartStyle2D, ColorMap, DataSeries, DrawChart, LineStyle, Matrix3, Point3, and Point4, classes from *Example6_3* to the current project and change their namespace to Chart3DLib.

Next, we need to convert the classes from *Example6_3* into classes compatible with the user control.

ChartStyle Class

For the Chart3D user control, the chart area is set to be the client rectangle of the Chart3D form, instead of the size of the PlotPanel as it was in *Example6_3*. This means that the panel control is not needed in creating the `Chart3D` control. Correspondingly, several related classes, including `ChartStyle`, `ChartStyle2D`, `DrawChart`, and `Point3`, need to be modified.

First, we want to modularize original `ChartStyle` class and convert it into a format compatible with the user control using the `TypeConverter`:

```
using System;
using System.Drawing;
using System.Drawing.Drawing2D;
using System.ComponentModel;

namespace Chart3DLib
{
    public class ChartStyle
    {
        private Chart3D chart3d;
        private bool isColorBar = false;

        public ChartStyle(Chart3D ct3d)
        {
            chart3d = ct3d;
        }

        public bool IsColorBar
        {
            get { return isColorBar; }
            set { isColorBar = value; }
        }

        private Point3[] CoordinatesOfChartBox(Axes ax, ViewAngle va)
        {
            // Create coordinate of the axes:
            Point3[] pta = new Point3[8];
            pta[0] = new Point3(ax.XMax, ax.YMin, ax.ZMin, 1);
            pta[1] = new Point3(ax.XMin, ax.YMin, ax.ZMin, 1);
            pta[2] = new Point3(ax.XMin, ax.YMax, ax.ZMin, 1);
            pta[3] = new Point3(ax.XMin, ax.YMax, ax.ZMax, 1);
            pta[4] = new Point3(ax.XMin, ax.YMin, ax.ZMax, 1);
            pta[5] = new Point3(ax.XMax, ax.YMin, ax.ZMax, 1);
            pta[6] = new Point3(ax.XMax, ax.YMax, ax.ZMax, 1);
            pta[7] = new Point3(ax.XMax, ax.YMax, ax.ZMin, 1);

            Point3[] pts = new Point3[4];
            int[] npts = new int[4] { 0, 1, 2, 3 };
            if (va.Elevation >= 0)
            {
                if (va.Azimuth >= -180 && va.Azimuth < -90)
                {
                    npts = new int[4] { 1, 2, 7, 6 };
                }
                else if (va.Azimuth >= -90 && va.Azimuth < 0)
                {
                    npts = new int[4] { 0, 1, 2, 3 };
                }
```

```
            else if (va.Azimuth >= 0 && va.Azimuth < 90)
            {
                npts = new int[4] { 7, 0, 1, 4 };
            }
            else if (va.Azimuth >= 90 && va.Azimuth <= 180)
            {
                npts = new int[4] { 2, 7, 0, 5 };
            }
        }
        else if (va.Elevation < 0)
        {
            if (va.Azimuth >= -180 && va.Azimuth < -90)
            {
                npts = new int[4] { 1, 0, 7, 6 };
            }
            else if (va.Azimuth >= -90 && va.Azimuth < 0)
            {
                npts = new int[4] { 0, 7, 2, 3 };
            }
            else if (va.Azimuth >= 0 && va.Azimuth < 90)
            {
                npts = new int[4] { 7, 2, 1, 4 };
            }
            else if (va.Azimuth >= 90 && va.Azimuth <= 180)
            {
                npts = new int[4] { 2, 1, 0, 5 };
            }

        }

        for (int i = 0; i < 4; i++)
        {
            pts[i] = pta[npts[i]];
        }
        return pts;
    }

    public void AddChartStyle(Graphics g, Axes ax,
            ViewAngle va, Grid gd, ChartLabels cl)
    {
        AddTicks(g, ax, va, cl);
        AddGrids(g, ax, va, gd, cl);
        AddAxes(g, ax, va, cl);
        AddLabels(g, ax, va, cl);
    }

    private void AddAxes(Graphics g, Axes ax,
            ViewAngle va, ChartLabels cl)
    {
        Matrix3 m = Matrix3.AzimuthElevation(va.Elevation,
                va.Azimuth);
        Point3[] pts = CoordinatesOfChartBox(ax, va);
        Pen aPen = new Pen(ax.AxisStyle.LineColor,
                ax.AxisStyle.Thickness);
```

```
        aPen.DashStyle = ax.AxisStyle.Pattern;
        for (int i = 0; i < pts.Length; i++)
        {
            pts[i].Transform(m, chart3d, ax, this, cl);
        }
        g.DrawLine(aPen, pts[0].X, pts[0].Y, pts[1].X, pts[1].Y);
        g.DrawLine(aPen, pts[1].X, pts[1].Y, pts[2].X, pts[2].Y);
        g.DrawLine(aPen, pts[2].X, pts[2].Y, pts[3].X, pts[3].Y);
        aPen.Dispose();
    }

    private void AddTicks(Graphics g, Axes ax, ViewAngle va,
            ChartLabels cl)
    {
        Matrix3 m = Matrix3.AzimuthElevation(va.Elevation,
                va.Azimuth);
        Point3[] pta = new Point3[2];
        Point3[] pts = CoordinatesOfChartBox(ax, va); ;
        Pen aPen = new Pen(ax.AxisStyle.LineColor,
                ax.AxisStyle.Thickness);
        aPen.DashStyle = ax.AxisStyle.Pattern;

        // Add x ticks:
        float offset = (ax.YMax - ax.YMin) / 30.0f;
        float ticklength = offset;
        for (float x = ax.XMin; x <= ax.XMax; x = x + ax.XTick)
        {
            if (va.Elevation >= 0)
            {
                if (va.Azimuth >= -90 && va.Azimuth < 90)
                    ticklength = -offset;
            }
            else if (va.Elevation < 0)
            {
                if ((va.Azimuth >= -180 && va.Azimuth < -90) ||
                    va.Azimuth >= 90 && va.Azimuth <= 180)
                    ticklength = -(ax.YMax - ax.YMin) / 30;
            }
            pta[0] = new Point3(x, pts[1].Y + ticklength,
                    pts[1].Z, pts[1].W);
            pta[1] = new Point3(x, pts[1].Y, pts[1].Z, pts[1].W);
            for (int i = 0; i < pta.Length; i++)
            {
                pta[i].Transform(m, chart3d, ax, this, cl);
            }
            g.DrawLine(aPen, pta[0].X, pta[0].Y,
                    pta[1].X, pta[1].Y);
        }

        // Add y ticks:
        offset = (ax.XMax - ax.XMin) / 30.0f;
        ticklength = offset;
        for (float y = ax.YMin; y <= ax.YMax; y = y + ax.YTick)
        {
```

```
        pts = CoordinatesOfChartBox(ax, va); ;
        if (va.Elevation >= 0)
        {
            if (va.Azimuth >= -180 && va.Azimuth < 0)
                ticklength = -offset;
        }
        else if (va.Elevation < 0)
        {
            if (va.Azimuth >= 0 && va.Azimuth < 180)
                ticklength = -offset;
        }
        pta[0] = new Point3(pts[1].X + ticklength, y,
                pts[1].Z, pts[1].W);
        pta[1] = new Point3(pts[1].X, y, pts[1].Z, pts[1].W);
        for (int i = 0; i < pta.Length; i++)
        {
            pta[i].Transform(m, chart3d, ax, this, cl);
        }
        g.DrawLine(aPen, pta[0].X, pta[0].Y,
                pta[1].X, pta[1].Y);
}

float xoffset = (ax.XMax - ax.XMin) / 45.0f;
float yoffset = (ax.YMax - ax.YMin) / 20.0f;
float xticklength = xoffset;
float yticklength = yoffset;
for (float z = ax.ZMin; z <= ax.ZMax; z = z + ax.ZTick)
{
    if (va.Elevation >= 0)
    {
        if (va.Azimuth >= -180 && va.Azimuth < -90)
        {
            xticklength = 0;
            yticklength = yoffset;
        }
        else if (va.Azimuth >= -90 && va.Azimuth < 0)
        {
            xticklength = xoffset;
            yticklength = 0;
        }
        else if (va.Azimuth >= 0 && va.Azimuth < 90)
        {
            xticklength = 0;
            yticklength = -yoffset;
        }
        else if (va.Azimuth >= 90 && va.Azimuth <= 180)
        {
            xticklength = -xoffset;
            yticklength = 0;
        }
    }
    else if (va.Elevation < 0)
    {
        if (va.Azimuth >= -180 && va.Azimuth < -90)
```

```
            {
                yticklength = 0;
                xticklength = xoffset;
            }
            else if (va.Azimuth >= -90 && va.Azimuth < 0)
            {
                yticklength = -yoffset;
                xticklength = 0;
            }
            else if (va.Azimuth >= 0 && va.Azimuth < 90)
            {
                yticklength = 0;
                xticklength = -xoffset;
            }
            else if (va.Azimuth >= 90 && va.Azimuth <= 180)
            {
                yticklength = yoffset;
                xticklength = 0;
            }
        }
        pta[0] = new Point3(pts[2].X, pts[2].Y, z, pts[2].W);
        pta[1] = new Point3(pts[2].X + yticklength,
            pts[2].Y + xticklength, z, pts[2].W);
        for (int i = 0; i < pta.Length; i++)
        {
            pta[i].Transform(m, chart3d, ax, this, cl);
        }
        g.DrawLine(aPen, pta[0].X, pta[0].Y,
                pta[1].X, pta[1].Y);
    }
    aPen.Dispose();
}

private void AddGrids(Graphics g, Axes ax,
        ViewAngle va, Grid gd, ChartLabels cl)
{
    Matrix3 m = Matrix3.AzimuthElevation(va.Elevation,
            va.Azimuth);
    Point3[] pta = new Point3[3];
    Point3[] pts = CoordinatesOfChartBox(ax, va);
    Pen aPen = new Pen(gd.GridStyle.LineColor,
            gd.GridStyle.Thickness);
    aPen.DashStyle = gd.GridStyle.Pattern;

    // Draw x gridlines:
    if (gd.IsXGrid)
    {
        for (float x = ax.XMin; x <= ax.XMax;
                x = x + ax.XTick)
        {
            pts = CoordinatesOfChartBox(ax, va);
            pta[0] = new Point3(x, pts[1].Y,
                pts[1].Z, pts[1].W);
            if (va.Elevation >= 0)
```

```
        {
            if ((va.Azimuth >= -180 &&
                 va.Azimuth < -90) ||
                (va.Azimuth >= 0 && va.Azimuth < 90))
            {
                pta[1] = new Point3(x, pts[0].Y,
                        pts[1].Z, pts[1].W);
                pta[2] = new Point3(x, pts[0].Y,
                        pts[3].Z, pts[1].W);
            }
            else
            {
                pta[1] = new Point3(x, pts[2].Y,
                        pts[1].Z, pts[1].W);
                pta[2] = new Point3(x, pts[2].Y,
                        pts[3].Z, pts[1].W);

            }
        }
        else if (va.Elevation < 0)
        {
            if ((va.Azimuth >= -180 && va.Azimuth < -90)
                 || (va.Azimuth >= 0 && va.Azimuth < 90))
            {
                pta[1] = new Point3(x, pts[2].Y,
                        pts[1].Z, pts[1].W);
                pta[2] = new Point3(x, pts[2].Y,
                        pts[3].Z, pts[1].W);

            }
            else
            {
                pta[1] = new Point3(x, pts[0].Y,
                        pts[1].Z, pts[1].W);
                pta[2] = new Point3(x, pts[0].Y,
                        pts[3].Z, pts[1].W);
            }
        }
        for (int i = 0; i < pta.Length; i++)
        {
            pta[i].Transform(m, chart3d, ax, this, cl);
        }
        g.DrawLine(aPen, pta[0].X, pta[0].Y,
                pta[1].X, pta[1].Y);
        g.DrawLine(aPen, pta[1].X, pta[1].Y,
                pta[2].X, pta[2].Y);
    }
}
// Draw y gridlines:
if (gd.IsYGrid)
{
    for (float y = ax.YMin; y <= ax.YMax;
            y = y + ax.YTick)
    {
```

```
pts = CoordinatesOfChartBox(ax, va);
pta[0] = new Point3(pts[1].X, y,
        pts[1].Z, pts[1].W);
if (va.Elevation >= 0)
{
    if ((va.Azimuth >= -180 && va.Azimuth < -90)
        || (va.Azimuth >= 0 && va.Azimuth < 90))
    {
        pta[1] = new Point3(pts[2].X, y,
                pts[1].Z, pts[1].W);
        pta[2] = new Point3(pts[2].X, y,
                pts[3].Z, pts[1].W);
    }
    else
    {
        pta[1] = new Point3(pts[0].X, y,
                pts[1].Z, pts[1].W);
        pta[2] = new Point3(pts[0].X, y,
                pts[3].Z, pts[1].W);
    }
}
if (va.Elevation < 0)
{
    if ((va.Azimuth >= -180 && va.Azimuth < -90)
        || (va.Azimuth >= 0 && va.Azimuth < 90))
    {
        pta[1] = new Point3(pts[0].X, y,
                pts[1].Z, pts[1].W);
        pta[2] = new Point3(pts[0].X, y,
                pts[3].Z, pts[1].W);
    }
    else
    {
        pta[1] = new Point3(pts[2].X, y,
                pts[1].Z, pts[1].W);
        pta[2] = new Point3(pts[2].X, y,
                pts[3].Z, pts[1].W);
    }
}
for (int i = 0; i < pta.Length; i++)
{
    pta[i].Transform(m, chart3d, ax, this, cl);
}
g.DrawLine(aPen, pta[0].X, pta[0].Y,
        pta[1].X, pta[1].Y);
g.DrawLine(aPen, pta[1].X, pta[1].Y,
        pta[2].X, pta[2].Y);
    }
}

// Draw Z gridlines:
if (gd.IsZGrid)
{
    for (float z = ax.ZMin; z <= ax.ZMax;
```

```
                            z = z + ax.ZTick)
{
    pts = CoordinatesOfChartBox(ax, va);
    pta[0] = new Point3(pts[2].X, pts[2].Y,
            z, pts[2].W);
    if (va.Elevation >= 0)
    {
        if ((va.Azimuth >= -180 && va.Azimuth < -90)
            || (va.Azimuth >= 0 && va.Azimuth < 90))
        {
            pta[1] = new Point3(pts[2].X, pts[0].Y,
                    z, pts[1].W);
            pta[2] = new Point3(pts[0].X, pts[0].Y,
                    z, pts[1].W);
        }
        else
        {
            pta[1] = new Point3(pts[0].X, pts[2].Y,
                    z, pts[1].W);
            pta[2] = new Point3(pts[0].X, pts[1].Y,
                    z, pts[1].W);
        }
    }
    if (va.Elevation < 0)
    {
        if ((va.Azimuth >= -180 && va.Azimuth < -90)
            || (va.Azimuth >= 0 && va.Azimuth < 90))
        {
            pta[1] = new Point3(pts[0].X, pts[2].Y,
                    z, pts[1].W);
            pta[2] = new Point3(pts[0].X, pts[0].Y,
                    z, pts[1].W);

        }
        else
        {
            pta[1] = new Point3(pts[2].X, pts[0].Y,
                    z, pts[1].W);
            pta[2] = new Point3(pts[0].X, pts[0].Y,
                    z, pts[1].W);
        }
    }
    for (int i = 0; i < pta.Length; i++)
    {
        pta[i].Transform(m, chart3d, ax, this, cl);
    }
    g.DrawLine(aPen, pta[0].X, pta[0].Y,
            pta[1].X, pta[1].Y);
    g.DrawLine(aPen, pta[1].X, pta[1].Y,
            pta[2].X, pta[2].Y);
}
}

}
```

```csharp
private void AddLabels(Graphics g, Axes ax,
        ViewAngle va, ChartLabels cl)
{
    Matrix3 m = Matrix3.AzimuthElevation(va.Elevation,
            va.Azimuth);
    Point3 pt = new Point3();
    Point3[] pts = CoordinatesOfChartBox(ax, va);
    SolidBrush aBrush = new SolidBrush(cl.LabelFontColor);
    StringFormat sf = new StringFormat();
    sf.Alignment = StringAlignment.Center;

    // Add x tick labels:
    float offset = (ax.YMax - ax.YMin) / 20;
    float labelSpace = offset;
    for (float x = ax.XMin + ax.XTick; x < ax.XMax;
            x = x + ax.XTick)
    {
        if (va.Elevation >= 0)
        {
            if (va.Azimuth >= -90 && va.Azimuth < 90)
                labelSpace = -offset;
        }
        else if (va.Elevation < 0)
        {
            if ((va.Azimuth >= -180 && va.Azimuth < -90)
                || va.Azimuth >= 90 && va.Azimuth <= 180)
                labelSpace = -offset;
        }
        pt = new Point3(x, pts[1].Y + labelSpace,
                pts[1].Z, pts[1].W);
        pt.Transform(m, chart3d, ax, this, cl);
        g.DrawString(x.ToString(), cl.TickFont, aBrush,
            new PointF(pt.X, pt.Y), sf);
    }

    // Add y tick labels:
    offset = (ax.XMax - ax.XMin) / 20;
    labelSpace = offset;
    for (float y = ax.YMin + ax.YTick; y < ax.YMax;
            y = y + ax.YTick)
    {
        pts = CoordinatesOfChartBox(ax, va);
        if (va.Elevation >= 0)
        {
            if (va.Azimuth >= -180 && va.Azimuth < 0)
                labelSpace = -offset;
        }
        else if (va.Elevation < 0)
        {
            if (va.Azimuth >= 0 && va.Azimuth < 180)
                labelSpace = -offset;
        }
        pt = new Point3(pts[1].X + labelSpace, y,
```

```
                pts[1].Z, pts[1].W);
        pt.Transform(m, chart3d, ax, this, cl);
        g.DrawString(y.ToString(), cl.TickFont, aBrush,
            new PointF(pt.X, pt.Y), sf);

}

// Add z tick labels:
float xoffset = (ax.XMax - ax.XMin) / 30.0f;
float yoffset = (ax.YMax - ax.YMin) / 15.0f;
float xlabelSpace = xoffset;
float ylabelSpace = yoffset;
SizeF s = g.MeasureString("A", cl.TickFont);
for (float z = ax.ZMin; z <= ax.ZMax; z = z + ax.ZTick)
{
    sf.Alignment = StringAlignment.Far;
    pts = CoordinatesOfChartBox(ax, va);
    if (va.Elevation >= 0)
    {
        if (va.Azimuth >= -180 && va.Azimuth < -90)
        {
            xlabelSpace = 0;
            ylabelSpace = yoffset;
        }
        else if (va.Azimuth >= -90 && va.Azimuth < 0)
        {
            xlabelSpace = xoffset;
            ylabelSpace = 0;
        }
        else if (va.Azimuth >= 0 && va.Azimuth < 90)
        {
            xlabelSpace = 0;
            ylabelSpace = -yoffset;
        }
        else if (va.Azimuth >= 90 && va.Azimuth <= 180)
        {
            xlabelSpace = -xoffset;
            ylabelSpace = 0;
        }
    }
    else if (va.Elevation < 0)
    {
        if (va.Azimuth >= -180 && va.Azimuth < -90)
        {
            ylabelSpace = 0;
            xlabelSpace = xoffset;
        }
        else if (va.Azimuth >= -90 && va.Azimuth < 0)
        {
            ylabelSpace = -yoffset;
            xlabelSpace = 0;
        }
        else if (va.Azimuth >= 0 && va.Azimuth < 90)
        {
```

```
                    ylabelSpace = 0;
                    xlabelSpace = -xoffset;
                }
                else if (va.Azimuth >= 90 && va.Azimuth <= 180)
                {
                    ylabelSpace = yoffset;
                    xlabelSpace = 0;
                }
            }
        }

        pt = new Point3(pts[2].X + ylabelSpace,
            pts[2].Y + xlabelSpace, z, pts[2].W);
        pt.Transform(m, chart3d, ax, this, cl);
        g.DrawString(z.ToString(), cl.TickFont, aBrush,
            new PointF(pt.X - labelSpace, pt.Y -
            s.Height / 2), sf);
    }

    // Add Title:
    sf.Alignment = StringAlignment.Center;
    aBrush = new SolidBrush(cl.TitleColor);
    if (cl.Title != "No Title")
    {
        g.DrawString(cl.Title, cl.TitleFont, aBrush,
            new PointF(chart3d.Width / 2,
            chart3d.Height / 30), sf);
    }
    aBrush.Dispose();

    // Add x axis label:
    offset = (ax.YMax - ax.YMin) / 3;
    labelSpace = offset;
    sf.Alignment = StringAlignment.Center;
    aBrush = new SolidBrush(cl.LabelFontColor);
    float offset1 = (ax.XMax - ax.XMin) / 10;
    float xc = offset1;
    if (va.Elevation >= 0)
    {
        if (va.Azimuth >= -90 && va.Azimuth < 90)
            labelSpace = -offset;
        if (va.Azimuth >= 0 && va.Azimuth <= 180)
            xc = -offset1;
    }
    else if (va.Elevation < 0)
    {
        if ((va.Azimuth >= -180 && va.Azimuth < -90) ||
            va.Azimuth >= 90 && va.Azimuth <= 180)
            labelSpace = -offset;
        if (va.Azimuth >= -180 && va.Azimuth <= 0)
            xc = -offset1;
    }
    Point3[] pta = new Point3[2];
    pta[0] = new Point3(ax.XMin, pts[1].Y + labelSpace,
                pts[1].Z, pts[1].W);
```

```
pta[1] = new Point3((ax.XMin + ax.XMax) / 2 - xc,
            pts[1].Y + labelSpace,
      pts[1].Z, pts[1].W);
pta[0].Transform(m, chart3d, ax, this, cl);
pta[1].Transform(m, chart3d, ax, this, cl);
float theta = (float)Math.Atan((pta[1].Y - pta[0].Y) /
        (pta[1].X - pta[0].X));
theta = theta * 180 / (float)Math.PI;
GraphicsState gs = g.Save();
g.TranslateTransform(pta[1].X, pta[1].Y);
g.RotateTransform(theta);
g.DrawString(cl.XLabel, cl.LabelFont, aBrush,
    new PointF(0, 0), sf);
g.Restore(gs);

// Add y axis label:
offset = (ax.XMax - ax.XMin) / 3;
offset1 = (ax.YMax - ax.YMin) / 5;
labelSpace = offset;
float yc = ax.YTick;
if (va.Elevation >= 0)
{
    if (va.Azimuth >= -180 && va.Azimuth < 0)
        labelSpace = -offset;
    if (va.Azimuth >= -90 && va.Azimuth <= 90)
        yc = -offset1;
}
else if (va.Elevation < 0)
{
    yc = -offset1;
    if (va.Azimuth >= 0 && va.Azimuth < 180)
        labelSpace = -offset;
    if (va.Azimuth >= -90 && va.Azimuth <= 90)
        yc = offset1;
}
pta[0] = new Point3(pts[1].X + labelSpace,
        ax.YMin, pts[1].Z, pts[1].W);
pta[1] = new Point3(pts[1].X + labelSpace, (ax.YMin +
    ax.YMax) / 2 + yc, pts[1].Z, pts[1].W);
pta[0].Transform(m, chart3d, ax, this, cl);
pta[1].Transform(m, chart3d, ax, this, cl);
theta = (float)Math.Atan((pta[1].Y - pta[0].Y) /
        (pta[1].X - pta[0].X));
theta = theta * 180 / (float)Math.PI;
gs = g.Save();
g.TranslateTransform(pta[1].X, pta[1].Y);
g.RotateTransform(theta);
g.DrawString(cl.YLabel, cl.LabelFont, aBrush,
    new PointF(0, 0), sf);
g.Restore(gs);

// Add z axis labels:
float zticklength = 10;
labelSpace = -1.3f * offset;
```

```
offset1 = (ax.ZMax - ax.ZMin) / 8;
float zc = -offset1;
for (float z = ax.ZMin; z < ax.ZMax; z = z + ax.ZTick)
{
    SizeF size = g.MeasureString(z.ToString(),
            cl.TickFont);
    if (zticklength < size.Width)
        zticklength = size.Width;
}
float zlength = -zticklength;
if (va.Elevation >= 0)
{
    if (va.Azimuth >= -180 && va.Azimuth < -90)
    {
        zlength = -zticklength;
        labelSpace = -1.3f * offset;
        zc = -offset1;
    }
    else if (va.Azimuth >= -90 && va.Azimuth < 0)
    {
        zlength = zticklength;
        labelSpace = 2 * offset / 3;
        zc = offset1;
    }
    else if (va.Azimuth >= 0 && va.Azimuth < 90)
    {
        zlength = zticklength;
        labelSpace = 2 * offset / 3;
        zc = -offset1;
    }
    else if (va.Azimuth >= 90 && va.Azimuth <= 180)
    {
        zlength = -zticklength;
        labelSpace = -1.3f * offset;
        zc = offset1;
    }
}
else if (va.Elevation < 0)
{
    if (va.Azimuth >= -180 && va.Azimuth < -90)
    {
        zlength = -zticklength;
        labelSpace = -1.3f * offset;
        zc = offset1;
    }
    else if (va.Azimuth >= -90 && va.Azimuth < 0)
    {
        zlength = zticklength;
        labelSpace = 2 * offset / 3;
        zc = -offset1;
    }
    else if (va.Azimuth >= 0 && va.Azimuth < 90)
    {
        zlength = zticklength;
```

```
                    labelSpace = 2 * offset / 3;
                    zc = offset1;
                }
                else if (va.Azimuth >= 90 && va.Azimuth <= 180)
                {
                    zlength = -zticklength;
                    labelSpace = -1.3f * offset;
                    zc = -offset1;
                }
            }
            pta[0] = new Point3(pts[2].X - labelSpace, pts[2].Y,
                (ax.ZMin + ax.ZMax) / 2 + zc, pts[2].W);
            pta[0].Transform(m, chart3d, ax, this, cl);
            gs = g.Save();
            g.TranslateTransform(pta[0].X - zlength, pta[0].Y);
            g.RotateTransform(270);
            g.DrawString(cl.ZLabel, cl.LabelFont, aBrush,
                new PointF(0, 0), sf);
            g.Restore(gs);
        }
    }
}

[TypeConverter(typeof(AxesConverter))]
public class Axes
{
    LineStyle axisStyle;
    private float xMax = 5f;
    private float xMin = -5f;
    private float yMax = 3f;
    private float yMin = -3f;
    private float zMax = 6f;
    private float zMin = -6f;
    private float xTick = 1f;
    private float yTick = 1f;
    private float zTick = 3f;
    private Chart3D chart3d;

    public Axes(Chart3D ct3d)
    {
        chart3d = ct3d;
        axisStyle = new LineStyle();
    }


    [Description("Sets line style for the axes."),
    Category("Appearance")]
    public LineStyle AxisStyle
    {
        get { return axisStyle; }
        set
        {
            axisStyle = value;
            chart3d.Invalidate();
        }
```

```
}

[Description("Sets the minimum limit for the X axis."),
Category("Appearance")]
public float XMin
{
    get { return xMin; }
    set
    {
        xMin = value;
        chart3d.Invalidate();
    }
}

[Description("Sets the maximum limit for the X axis."),
Category("Appearance")]
public float XMax
{
    get { return xMax; }
    set
    {
        xMax = value;
        chart3d.Invalidate();
    }
}

[Description("Sets the ticks for the X axis."),
Category("Appearance")]
public float XTick
{
    get { return xTick; }
    set
    {
        xTick = value;
        chart3d.Invalidate();
    }
}

[Description("Sets the minimum limit for the Y axis."),
Category("Appearance")]
public float YMin
{
    get { return yMin; }
    set
    {
        yMin = value;
        chart3d.Invalidate();
    }
}

[Description("Sets the maximum limit for the Y axis."),
Category("Appearance")]
public float YMax
{
```

```
        get { return yMax; }
        set
        {
            yMax = value;
            chart3d.Invalidate();
        }
    }

    [Description("Sets the ticks for the Y axis."),
    Category("Appearance")]
    public float YTick
    {
        get { return yTick; }
        set
        {
            yTick = value;
            chart3d.Invalidate();
        }
    }

    [Description("Sets the minimum limit for the Z axis."),
    Category("Appearance")]
    public float ZMin
    {
        get { return zMin; }
        set
        {
            zMin = value;
            chart3d.Invalidate();
        }
    }

    [Description("Sets the maximum limit for the Z axis."),
    Category("Appearance")]
    public float ZMax
    {
        get { return zMax; }
        set
        {
            zMax = value;
            chart3d.Invalidate();
        }
    }

    [Description("Sets the ticks for the Z axis."),
    Category("Appearance")]
    public float ZTick
    {
        get { return zTick; }
        set
        {
            zTick = value;
            chart3d.Invalidate();
        }
```

```csharp
        }
    }

    public class AxesConverter : TypeConverter
    {
        // Display the "+" symbol near the property name
        public override bool GetPropertiesSupported(
            ITypeDescriptorContext context)
        {
            return true;
        }

        public override PropertyDescriptorCollection
            GetProperties(ITypeDescriptorContext context,
            object value, Attribute[] attributes)
        {
            return TypeDescriptor.GetProperties(typeof(Axes));
        }
    }

    [TypeConverter(typeof(ChartLabelsConverter))]
    public class ChartLabels
    {
        private string xLabel = "X Axis";
        private string yLabel = "Y Axis";
        private string zLabel = "Z Axis";
        private Font labelFont = new Font("Arial", 10,
                    FontStyle.Regular);
        private Color labelFontColor = Color.Black;
        private Font tickFont;
        private Color tickFontColor = Color.Black;
        private string title = "My 3D Chart";
        private Font titleFont = new Font("Arial Narrow",
                    14, FontStyle.Regular);
        private Color titleColor = Color.Black;
        private Chart3D chart3d;

        public ChartLabels(Chart3D ct3d)
        {
            chart3d = ct3d;
            tickFont = ct3d.Font;
        }

        [Description("Creates a label for the X axis."),
        Category("Appearance")]
        public string XLabel
        {
            get { return xLabel; }
            set
            {
                xLabel = value;
                chart3d.Invalidate();
            }
        }
```

```csharp
[Description("Creates a label for the Y axis."),
Category("Appearance")]
public string YLabel
{
    get { return yLabel; }
    set
    {
        yLabel = value;
        chart3d.Invalidate();
    }
}


[Description("Creates a label for the Z axis."),
Category("Appearance")]
public string ZLabel
{
    get { return zLabel; }
    set
    {
        zLabel = value;
        chart3d.Invalidate();
    }
}

[Description("The font used to display the axis labels."),
Category("Appearance")]
public Font LabelFont
{
    get { return labelFont; }
    set
    {
        labelFont = value;
        chart3d.Invalidate();
    }
}

[Description("Sets the color of the axis labels."),
Category("Appearance")]
public Color LabelFontColor
{
    get { return labelFontColor; }
    set
    {
        labelFontColor = value;
        chart3d.Invalidate();
    }
}

[Description("The font used to display the tick labels."),
Category("Appearance")]
public Font TickFont
{
```

```
            get { return tickFont; }
            set
            {
                tickFont = value;
                chart3d.Invalidate();
            }
        }

        [Description("Sets the color of the tick labels."),
        Category("Appearance")]
        public Color TickFontColor
        {
            get { return tickFontColor; }
            set
            {
                tickFontColor = value;
                chart3d.Invalidate();
            }
        }

        [Description("Sets title for the chart."),
        Category("Appearance")]
        public string Title
        {
            get { return title; }
            set
            {
                title = value;
                chart3d.Invalidate();
            }
        }

        [Description("The font used to display the title."),
        Category("Appearance")]
        public Font TitleFont
        {
            get { return titleFont; }
            set
            {
                titleFont = value;
                chart3d.Invalidate();
            }
        }

        [Description("Sets the color of the title."),
        Category("Appearance")]
        public Color TitleColor
        {
            get { return titleColor; }
            set
            {
                titleColor = value;
                chart3d.Invalidate();
            }
```

```
        }
}

public class ChartLabelsConverter : TypeConverter
{
    public override bool GetPropertiesSupported(
        ITypeDescriptorContext context)
    {
        return true;
    }

    public override PropertyDescriptorCollection
        GetProperties(ITypeDescriptorContext context,
        object value, Attribute[] attributes)
    {
        return TypeDescriptor.GetProperties(typeof(ChartLabels));
    }
}

[TypeConverter(typeof(GridConverter))]
public class Grid
{
    LineStyle gridStyle;
    private bool isXGrid = true;
    private bool isYGrid = true;
    private bool isZGrid = true;
    private Chart3D chart3d;

    public Grid(Chart3D ct3d)
    {
        chart3d = ct3d;
        gridStyle = new LineStyle();
    }

    [Description("Indicates whether the X grid is shown."),
    Category("Appearance")]
    public bool IsXGrid
    {
        get { return isXGrid; }
        set
        {
            isXGrid = value;
            chart3d.Invalidate();
        }
    }

    [Description("Indicates whether the Y grid is shown."),
    Category("Appearance")]
    public bool IsYGrid
    {
        get { return isYGrid; }
        set
        {
            isYGrid = value;
```

```csharp
                chart3d.Invalidate();
            }
        }

        [Description("Indicates whether the Z grid is shown."),
             Category("Appearance")]
        public bool IsZGrid
        {
            get { return isZGrid; }
            set
            {
                isZGrid = value;
                chart3d.Invalidate();
            }
        }

        [Description("Sets the line pattern for the
         grid line style."), Category("Appearance")]
        public LineStyle GridStyle
        {
            get { return gridStyle; }
            set
            {
                gridStyle = value;
                chart3d.Invalidate();
            }
        }
    }

    public class GridConverter : TypeConverter
    {
        public override bool GetPropertiesSupported(
            ITypeDescriptorContext context)
        {
            return true;
        }

        public override PropertyDescriptorCollection
            GetProperties(ITypeDescriptorContext context,
            object value, Attribute[] attributes)
        {
            return TypeDescriptor.GetProperties(typeof(Grid));
        }
    }

    [TypeConverter(typeof(ViewAngleConverter))]
    public class ViewAngle
    {
        private float elevation = 30;
        private float azimuth = -37.5f;
        private Chart3D chart3d;

        public ViewAngle(Chart3D ct3d)
        {
```

```
                    chart3d = ct3d;
                }

                [Description("Sets the elevation angle."),
                Category("Appearance")]
                public float Elevation
                {
                    get { return elevation; }
                    set
                    {
                        elevation = value;
                        chart3d.Invalidate();
                    }
                }

                [Description("Sets the azimuth angle."),
                Category("Appearance")]
                public float Azimuth
                {
                    get { return azimuth; }
                    set
                    {
                        azimuth = value;
                        chart3d.Invalidate();
                    }
                }
            }

            public class ViewAngleConverter : TypeConverter
            {
                public override bool GetPropertiesSupported(
                    ITypeDescriptorContext context)
                {
                    return true;
                }

                public override PropertyDescriptorCollection
                    GetProperties(ITypeDescriptorContext context,
                    object value, Attribute[] attributes)
                {
                    return TypeDescriptor.GetProperties(typeof(ViewAngle));
                }
            }
        }
    }
```

Note that we have divided the original ChartStyle class into several classes, including the newly created ChartStyle, Axes, Grid, ChartLabels, and ViewAngle classes, as well as their corresponding TypeConverter classes. There is only one property, IsColorBar, left in the ChartStyle class.

The properties such as ChartArea, Plot Area and their corresponding background colors are all contained in the ChartStyle2D class. In this Chart3D control, we do not want to expose these properties in the property browser. These properties can be changed only through code.

The properties of the other classes, including `DrawChart`, `LineStyle`, `BarStyle`, `ColorMap`, etc., are not exposed in the property browser, so that these classes do not need to be modified using `TyperConverter`. Their properties can only be changed through code.

Chart3D Class

The `Chart3D` class hooks all of the classes together and performs the chart drawing within its `OnPaint` method. Additionally, it is responsible for which classes' properties should be exposed in the property browser. The following is its code listing:

```
using System;
using System.ComponentModel;
using System.Drawing;
using System.Drawing.Drawing2D;
using System.Windows.Forms;

namespace Chart3DLib
{
    public partial class Chart3D : UserControl
    {
        private ChartStyle cs;
        private ChartStyle2D cs2d;
        private DrawChart dc;
        private DataSeries ds;
        private Axes ax;
        private ViewAngle va;
        private Grid gd;
        private ChartLabels cl;
        private ColorMap cm;

        public Chart3D()
        {
            InitializeComponent();
            this.SetStyle(ControlStyles.ResizeRedraw, true);
            cs = new ChartStyle(this);
            cs2d = new ChartStyle2D(this);
            dc = new DrawChart(this);
            ds = new DataSeries();
            ax = new Axes(this);
            va = new ViewAngle(this);
            gd = new Grid(this);
            cl = new ChartLabels(this);
            gd.GridStyle.LineColor = Color.LightGray;
            this.BackColor = Color.White;
            cm = new COlorMap();
            dc.CMap = cm.Jet();
        }

        protected override void OnPaint(PaintEventArgs e)
        {
            Graphics g = e.Graphics;
            g.SmoothingMode = SmoothingMode.AntiAlias;
```

```csharp
        cs2d.ChartArea = this.ClientRectangle;

    if (dc.ChartType == DrawChart.ChartTypeEnum.XYColor ||
        dc.ChartType == DrawChart.ChartTypeEnum.Contour ||
        dc.ChartType == DrawChart.ChartTypeEnum.FillContour)
    {
        cs2d.AddChartStyle2D(g, cs, ax, gd, cl);
        dc.AddColorBar(g, ds, cs, cs2d, ax, va, cl);
        dc.AddChart(g, ds, cs, cs2d, ax, va, cl);
    }
    else
    {
        cs.AddChartStyle(g, ax, va, gd, cl);
        dc.AddChart(g, ds, cs, cs2d, ax, va, cl);
    }
    g.Dispose();
}

[BrowsableAttribute(false)]
public DrawChart C3DrawChart
{
    get { return this.dc; }
    set { this.dc = value; }
}

[BrowsableAttribute(false)]
public ChartStyle C3ChartStyle
{
    get { return this.cs; }
    set {
        if (value != null)
        {
            this.cs = value;
        }
    }
}

[BrowsableAttribute(false)]
public ChartStyle2D C3ChartStyle2D
{
    get { return this.cs2d; }
    set { this.cs2d = value; }
}

[BrowsableAttribute(false)]
public DataSeries C3DataSeries
{
    get { return this.ds; }
    set { this.ds = value; }
}

[DesignerSerializationVisibility(
DesignerSerializationVisibility.Content)]
public Axes C3Axes
```

```csharp
    {
        get { return this.ax; }
        set
        {
            if (value != null)
            {
                this.ax = value;
            }
        }
    }

    [DesignerSerializationVisibility(
    DesignerSerializationVisibility.Content)]
    public ViewAngle C3ViewAngle
    {
        get { return this.va; }
        set
        {
            if (value != null)
            {
                this.va = value;
            }
        }
    }

    [DesignerSerializationVisibility(
    DesignerSerializationVisibility.Content)]
    public ChartLabels C3Labels
    {
        get { return this.cl; }
        set
        {
            if (value != null)
            {
                this.cl = value;
            }
        }
    }

    [DesignerSerializationVisibility(
    DesignerSerializationVisibility.Content)]
    public Grid C3Grid
    {
        get { return this.gd; }
        set
        {
            if (value != null)
            {
                this.gd = value;
            }
        }
    }
    }
}
```

In this class, we set the browsable attributes of `ChartStyle`, `ChartStyle2D`, `DrawChart`, and `DataSeries` to be false, indicating that the properties of these classes are not shown in the property browser. On the other hand, the `DesignerSerializationVisibility` attribute for the other classes is set to content, telling C# and the .NET framework that it should serialize the contents of the properties of these classes. Here C3 (stands for Chart 3D) is placed in front of the property name to group all of the properties related to `Chart3D` together in the property browser.

Testing User Control

Using the `Chart3D` user control in a Windows Form is similar to using the `Chart2D` user control. Following the same procedure you used in the 2D case, you can add the `Chart3D` user control to the Toolbox. Then you can use it just like any other built-in control, such as a `Button` or a `TextBox`. In the following subsections, we will demonstrate how to create various 3D charts using the `Chart3D` user control.

3D Line Charts

Start with a new C# Windows Application project named *Example7_3*. Add a `Chart3D` user control to `Form1`. A 3D line chart can easily be created using the `Chart3D` user control and the following code listing of the `Form1` class:

```
using System;
using System.ComponentModel;
using System.Drawing;
using System.Drawing.Drawing2D;
using System.Windows.Forms;
using Chart3DLib;

namespace Example7_3
{
    public partial class Form1 : Form
    {
        public Form1()
        {
            InitializeComponent();
            this.SetStyle(ControlStyles.ResizeRedraw, true);
            chart3D1.Dock = DockStyle.Fill;
            chart3D1.C3DrawChart.ChartType =
                    DrawChart.ChartTypeEnum.Line;
            chart3D1.C3Labels.Title = "No Title";
            chart3D1.C3DrawChart.IsColorMap = false;
        }
        protected override void OnPaint(PaintEventArgs e)
        {
            AddData();
        }
    private void AddData()
        {
```

```
chart3D1.C3Axes.XMin = -1;
chart3D1.C3Axes.XMax = 1;
chart3D1.C3Axes.YMin = -1;
chart3D1.C3Axes.YMax = 1;
chart3D1.C3Axes.ZMin = 0;
chart3D1.C3Axes.ZMax = 30;
chart3D1.C3Axes.XTick = 0.5f;
chart3D1.C3Axes.YTick = 0.5f;
chart3D1.C3Axes.ZTick = 5;

chart3D1.C3DataSeries.PointList.Clear();
chart3D1.C3DataSeries.LineStyle.LineColor = Color.Red;
for (int i = 0; i < 300; i++)
{
    float t = 0.1f * i;
    float x = (float)Math.Exp(-t / 30) *
        (float)Math.Cos(t);
    float y = (float)Math.Exp(-t / 30) *
        (float)Math.Sin(t);
    float z = t;
    chart3D1.C3DataSeries.AddPoint(new
            Point3(x, y, z, 1));
}
        }
    }
}
```

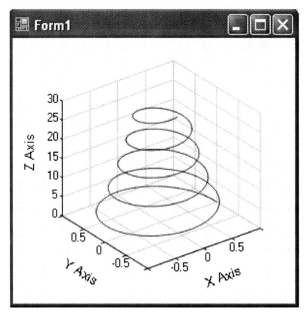

Figure 7-11 3D line chart created using the Chart3D user control.

Here the `ChartType` property is set to `Line` with the following code snippet:

```
chart3D1.C3DrawChart.ChartType = DrawChart.ChartTypeEnum.Line;
```

And the `IsColorMap` property is set to `false` (the default value is `true`) because we want to draw the 3D line with a single color:

```
chart3D1.C3DrawChart.IsColorMap = false;
```

Also note that we place the `AddData` method inside the `OnPaint` method to obtain a consistent resize effect.

This project produces the output of Figure 7-11.

Surface Charts

Various mesh and surface charts can be created using the `Chart3D` user control. Start with a new C# Windows Application project, *Example7_4*. Add a `Chart3D` control to `Form1` and implement the following code in the `Form1` class:

```
using System;
using System.ComponentModel;
using System.Drawing;
using System.Drawing.Drawing2D;
using System.Windows.Forms;
using Chart3DLib;

namespace Example7_4
{
    public partial class Form1 : Form
    {
        public Form1()
        {
            InitializeComponent();
            this.SetStyle(ControlStyles.ResizeRedraw, true);
            chart3D1.C3DrawChart.ChartType =
                    DrawChart.ChartTypeEnum.Surface;
            chart3D1.C3ChartStyle.IsColorBar = true;
            chart3D1.Dock = DockStyle.Fill;
        }

        protected override void OnPaint(PaintEventArgs e)
        {
            AddData();
        }

        private void AddData()
        {
            chart3D1.C3Axes.XMin = -3;
            chart3D1.C3Axes.XMax = 3;
            chart3D1.C3Axes.YMin = -3;
            chart3D1.C3Axes.YMax = 3;
            chart3D1.C3Axes.ZMin = -8;
            chart3D1.C3Axes.ZMax = 8;
```

```
chart3D1.C3Axes.XTick = 1;
chart3D1.C3Axes.YTick = 1;
chart3D1.C3Axes.ZTick = 4;

chart3D1.C3DataSeries.XDataMin = chart3D1.C3Axes.XMin;
chart3D1.C3DataSeries.YDataMin = chart3D1.C3Axes.YMin;
chart3D1.C3DataSeries.XSpacing = 0.3f;
chart3D1.C3DataSeries.YSpacing = 0.3f;
chart3D1.C3DataSeries.XNumber = Convert.ToInt16(
    (chart3D1.C3Axes.XMax - chart3D1.C3Axes.XMin) /
    chart3D1.C3DataSeries.XSpacing) + 1;
chart3D1.C3DataSeries.YNumber = Convert.ToInt16(
    (chart3D1.C3Axes.YMax - chart3D1.C3Axes.YMin) /
    chart3D1.C3DataSeries.YSpacing) + 1;

Point3[,] pts = new Point3[chart3D1.C3DataSeries.XNumber,
    chart3D1.C3DataSeries.YNumber];
for (int i = 0; i < chart3D1.C3DataSeries.XNumber; i++)
{
    for (int j = 0; j < chart3D1.C3DataSeries.YNumber;
            j++)
    {
        float x = chart3D1.C3DataSeries.XDataMin +
            i * chart3D1.C3DataSeries.XSpacing;
        float y = chart3D1.C3DataSeries.YDataMin +
            j * chart3D1.C3DataSeries.YSpacing;
        double zz = 3 * Math.Pow((1 - x), 2) *
            Math.Exp(-x * x - (y + 1) * (y + 1)) - 10 *
            (0.2 * x - Math.Pow(x, 3) - Math.Pow(y, 5)) *
            Math.Exp(-x * x - y * y) - 1 / 3 *
            Math.Exp(-(x + 1) * (x + 1) - y * y);
        float z = (float)zz;
        pts[i, j] = new Point3(x, y, z, 1);
    }
}
chart3D1.C3DataSeries.PointArray = pts;
        }
    }
}
```

This generates the results of Figure 7-12.

If you change the ChartType to Mesh with the code snippet:

```
chart3D1.C3DrawChart.ChartType = DrawChart.ChartTypeEnum.Mesh;
```

you get the mesh chart shown in Figure 7-13.

Similarly, you can easily create curtain, waterfall, and XYColor charts by specifying the corresponding ChartType property.

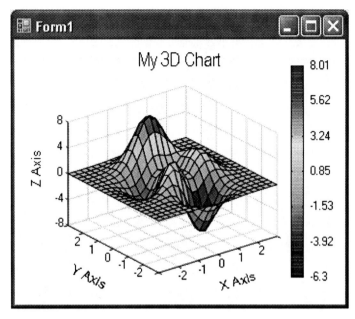

Figure 7-12 Surface chart created using Chart3D user control.

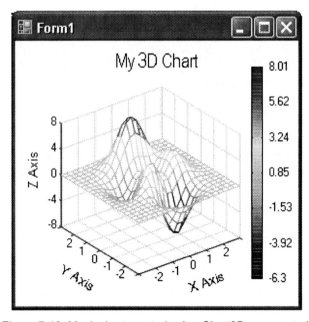

Figure 7-13 Mesh chart created using Chart3D user control.

Contour Charts

Using the same data set as we did for the surface charts, we can easily create contour charts. Inside the Form1 constructor, change the ChartType to FillContour and set the LineStyle.IsVisible property to false:

```
chart3D1.C3DrawChart.ChartType = DrawChart.ChartTypeEnum.FillContour;
chart3D1.C3DataSeries.LineStyle.IsVisible = false;
```

Inside the AddData method, change the XSpacing and YSpacing properties to the following:

```
chart3D1.C3DataSeries.XSpacing = 0.1f;
chart3D1.C3DataSeries.YSpacing = 0.1f;
```

This allows you to create smoother contour curves. Building and running this project, you obtain the filled-contour chart shown in Figure 7-14.

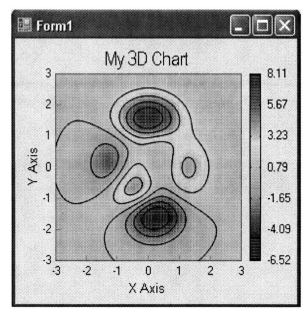

Figure 7-14 Filled contour chart created using Chart3D user control.

Combination Charts

In the Form1 constructor, change the ChartType to SurfaceFillContour:

```
chart3D1.C3DrawChart.ChartType =
        DrawChart.ChartTypeEnum.SurfaceFillContour;
chart3D1.C3DataSeries.LineStyle.IsVisible = true;
```

Inside the AddData method, change the following properties:

```
chart3D1.C3Axes.ZMin = -12;
chart3D1.C3DataSeries.XSpacing = 0.2f;
chart3D1.C3DataSeries.YSpacing = 0.2f;
```

This creates a combination chart of a surface chart with a filled contour chart, as shown in Figure 7-15.

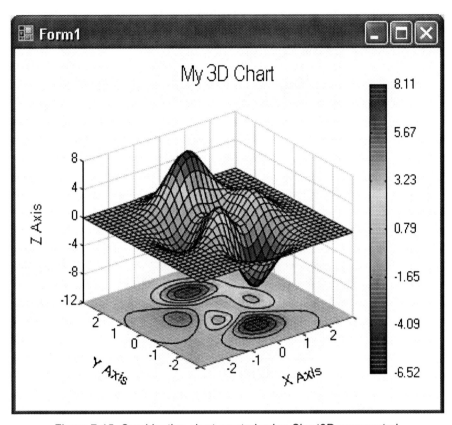

Figure 7-15 Combination chart created using Chart3D user control.

3D Bar Charts

We can easily create 3D bar charts using the same data set as we did for surface charts. Change the Form1 constructor according to the following code listing:

```
public Form1()
{
    InitializeComponent();
    this.SetStyle(ControlStyles.ResizeRedraw, true);
    chart3D1.C3DrawChart.ChartType = DrawChart.ChartTypeEnum.Bar3D;
    chart3D1.C3ChartStyle.IsColorBar = true;
    chart3D1.Dock = DockStyle.Fill;
    chart3D1.C3DataSeries.BarStyle.XLength = 0.3f;
    chart3D1.C3DataSeries.BarStyle.YLength = 0.3f;
    chart3D1.C3DataSeries.BarStyle.IsBarSingleColor = false;
    chart3D1.C3DataSeries.BarStyle.ZOrigin = -8;
}
```

Change the following properties within the AddData method:

```
chart3D1.C3Axes.ZMin = -8;
chart3D1.C3DataSeries.XSpacing = 0.5f;
chart3D1.C3DataSeries.YSpacing = 0.5f;
```

This project generates the output of Figure 7-16.

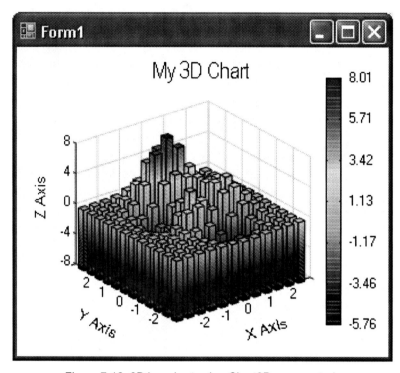

Figure 7-16 3D bar chart using Chart3D user control.

Slice Charts

Create a new C# Windows Application project and call it *Example7_5*. Add a Chart3D user control to Form1 and implement the following code in the Form1 class:

```
using System;
using System.ComponentModel;
using System.Drawing;
using System.Drawing.Drawing2D;
using System.Windows.Forms;
using Chart3DLib;

namespace Example7_5
{
    public partial class Form1 : Form
    {
        public Form1()
```

```
{
    InitializeComponent();
    this.SetStyle(ControlStyles.ResizeRedraw, true);
    chart3D1.C3DrawChart.ChartType =
        DrawChart.ChartTypeEnum.Slice;
    chart3D1.C3DrawChart.XYZSlice =
        DrawChart.SliceEnum.XSlice;
    chart3D1.C3DrawChart.SliceLocation = 0.5f;
    chart3D1.C3ChartStyle.IsColorBar = true;
    chart3D1.Dock = DockStyle.Fill;
}

protected override void OnPaint(PaintEventArgs e)
{
    AddData();
}

private void AddData()
{
    chart3D1.C3Axes.XMin = -2;
    chart3D1.C3Axes.XMax = 2;
    chart3D1.C3Axes.YMin = -2;
    chart3D1.C3Axes.YMax = 2;
    chart3D1.C3Axes.ZMin = -2;
    chart3D1.C3Axes.ZMax = 2;
    chart3D1.C3Axes.XTick = 1;
    chart3D1.C3Axes.YTick = 1;
    chart3D1.C3Axes.ZTick = 1;

    chart3D1.C3DataSeries.XDataMin = chart3D1.C3Axes.XMin;
    chart3D1.C3DataSeries.YDataMin = chart3D1.C3Axes.YMin;
    chart3D1.C3DataSeries.ZZDataMin = chart3D1.C3Axes.ZMin;
    chart3D1.C3DataSeries.XSpacing = 0.2f;
    chart3D1.C3DataSeries.YSpacing = 0.2f;
    chart3D1.C3DataSeries.ZSpacing = 0.2f;
    chart3D1.C3DataSeries.XNumber =
        Convert.ToInt16((chart3D1.C3Axes.XMax -
        chart3D1.C3Axes.XMin) /
        chart3D1.C3DataSeries.XSpacing) + 1;
    chart3D1.C3DataSeries.YNumber =
        Convert.ToInt16((chart3D1.C3Axes.YMax -
        chart3D1.C3Axes.YMin) /
        chart3D1.C3DataSeries.YSpacing) + 1;
    chart3D1.C3DataSeries.ZNumber =
        Convert.ToInt16((chart3D1.C3Axes.ZMax -
        chart3D1.C3Axes.ZMin) /
        chart3D1.C3DataSeries.ZSpacing) + 1;

    Point4[, ,] pts = new
        Point4[chart3D1.C3DataSeries.XNumber,
        chart3D1.C3DataSeries.YNumber,
        chart3D1.C3DataSeries.ZNumber];
    for (int i = 0; i < chart3D1.C3DataSeries.XNumber; i++)
    {
```

```
                for (int j = 0; j <
                    chart3D1.C3DataSeries.YNumber; j++)
                {
                    for (int k = 0; k <
                        chart3D1.C3DataSeries.ZNumber; k++)
                    {
                        float x = chart3D1.C3DataSeries.XDataMin +
                            i * chart3D1.C3DataSeries.XSpacing;
                        float y = chart3D1.C3DataSeries.YDataMin +
                            j * chart3D1.C3DataSeries.YSpacing;
                        float z = chart3D1.C3Axes.ZMin +
                            k * chart3D1.C3DataSeries.ZSpacing;
                        float v = z * (float)Math.Exp(-x * x -
                            y * y - z * z);
                        pts[i, j, k] = new Point4(new
                            Point3(x, y, z, 1), v);
                    }
                }
            }
            chart3D1.C3DataSeries.Point4Array = pts;
        }
    }
}
```

This produces the XSlice chart shown in Figure 7-17.

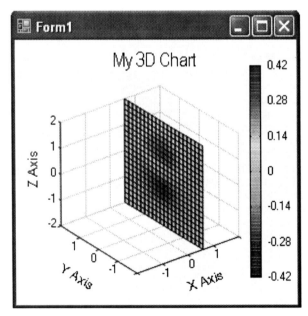

Figure 7-17 A slice chart at x = 0.5 plane created using the Chart3D user control.

8

DataGridView and Chart User Controls

The DataGridView control is a powerful, flexible, and easy to use control for presenting tabular data. With this control, you can display and edit tabular data from different types of data sources. The DataGridView control is highly configurable and extendible, and provides many properties, methods, and events to customize its appearance and behavior. Introduced with .NET 2.0, the DataGridView control replaces and adds functionality to the DataGrid control provided in prior versions of the .NET framework. Although the DataGrid class is retained for backward compatibility, the DataGridView control is the preferred mechanism for displaying tabular data as of the .NET 2.0 release. This control can be used in bound mode, where it displays data from any .NET data source, including ADO.NET, or in unbound mode, where the grid itself manages the data.

In this chapter, we start off with a discussion on the basics of the DataGridView. We then explore the possibility of combining the DataGridView with the Chart2D and Chart3D controls developed in the previous chapter to create spreadsheet-like chart applications. You will learn how to implement the spreadsheet-like interface that is common to many chart applications, such as Microsoft Excel charts. In this interface, the charting data is displayed in the

`DataGridView` control; the displayed data in the `DataGridView` is plotted using chart user controls, and direct interaction is allowed between the `DataGridView` and the Chart controls.

To illustrate the combination of the `DataGridView` and Chart Controls (i.e. Chart2D and Chat3D user controls), this chapter will create spreadsheet-like chart applications. This new application, as it will appear later in this chapter, is shown in Figure 8-1. You can see from this figure that data is displayed in the `DataGridView` control, and that the same set of data is plotted in the Chart2D control.

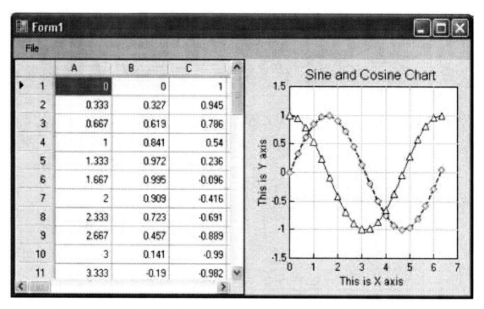

Figure 8-1 A combination of the DataGridView and Chart2D controls.

DataGridView Basics

A `DataGridView` control is just a grid in which tabular data is displayed. It allows various collections of data to be displayed and manipulated by users. As shown in Figure 8-1, the `DataGridView` control displays data as a set of rows and columns. The grid in general represents a specific collection of data, and in this case represents the charting data object. Each row, in turn, represents a specific item in the overall collection, and each column represents a specific field that can be assigned to each item. In chart applications, the first column represents the X data, the second column represents the Y data, and the third column represents another Y data field.

The `DataGridView` class is one of the most complicated classes in the Windows Forms namespace. It has more members and is more flexible and customizable than most realize. Many of its members are concentrated on displaying, manipulating, and managing cells, columns, and rows. For example, there are methods to begin, end, commit, and cancel edits to a specific cell, and a related set of events for processing these actions. There is also an `EditMode` property that defines what action initiates editing a cell.

Despite its rich features, the DataGridView control has a simple structure. As shown in Figure 8-1, in its most elemental form, it consists of column headers (labeled with "X", "Y1", and "Y2"), row headers (labeled with "1", "2", "3", etc.), and cells. You can easily add column and row collections to the DataGridView control, which allow the application to access the grid by indexing a row or column.

The cell is the basic unit of presentation within the DataGridView, and is highly customizable in appearance and behavior through the properties and events exposed by the grid. The header cells for the rows and columns can be used to maintain the context of the data presented in the grid. The grid can also have different modes or functions, such as sorting, editing, adding new rows, and selecting. It can contain cells of many different types and can even mix different cell types in the same column if the grid is not data bound.

Unbound Mode

In order to display tabular data that does not originate from a database, you can use the DataGridView in unbound mode. For example, you may want to show the contents of a two-dimensional array of strings. The DataGridView class provides an easy and highly customizable way to display data without binding to a data source.

To populate a DataGridView in unbound mode, you need to create all the columns in the grid programmatically. An unbound column is a column that is not bound to a data. The rows of the grid can be created using the Rows.Add method.

The DataGridView control gives you explicit control over whether users can edit, delete, or add rows. After the DataGridView is populated with data, you can interact directly with the data presented in the grid in a number of ways. By default, those interactions include editing the contents of the cells in a row, selecting a row and deleting it, or adding a new row using an empty row that is presented as the last row in the grid.

If you do not want any of these interactions, all you need to do is set the AllowUserToAddRows or AllowUserToDeleteRows properties to false, or set the ReadOnly property to true for adding, deleting, or editing, respectively. Each of these properties also raises corresponding property-changed events whenever their values are set. When you support adding, editing, or deletions, you may need to handle certain additional events to accept new values for unbound rows.

Let's look at a simple example that shows how to populate a DataGridView control and manage the addition and deletion of rows in unbound mode. By default, the user can add new rows. Start off with a new C# Windows Application project and call it *Example8_1*. Add a DataGridView and two button controls from Toolbox to Form1. Set the "Text" properties of the two buttons to "Add Row" and "Delete Row". The following is the code listing of the Form1 class:

```
using System;
using System.Drawing;
using System.Windows.Forms;

namespace Example8_1
{
```

```
public partial class Form1 : Form
{
    public Form1()
    {
        InitializeComponent();
        DataGridViewSetup();
        DataGridViewPopulate();
    }

    private void DataGridViewSetup()
    {
        dataGridView1.ColumnCount = 3;
        dataGridView1.ColumnHeadersDefaultCellStyle.BackColor =
            Color.Navy;
        dataGridView1.ColumnHeadersDefaultCellStyle.ForeColor =
            Color.White;
        dataGridView1.AutoSizeRowsMode =
            DataGridViewAutoSizeRowsMode.
            DisplayedCellsExceptHeaders;
        dataGridView1.ColumnHeadersBorderStyle =
            DataGridViewHeaderBorderStyle.Single;
        dataGridView1.CellBorderStyle =
            DataGridViewCellBorderStyle.Single;
        dataGridView1.GridColor = Color.Black;
        dataGridView1.RowHeadersVisible = true;
        dataGridView1.RowHeadersWidth = 50;
        dataGridView1.ColumnHeadersDefaultCellStyle.Alignment =
            DataGridViewContentAlignment.MiddleCenter;
        dataGridView1.RowHeadersDefaultCellStyle.Alignment =
            DataGridViewContentAlignment.MiddleRight;

        dataGridView1.Columns[0].Name = "X Data";
        dataGridView1.Columns[1].Name = "Y1 Data";
        dataGridView1.Columns[2].Name = "Y2 Data";

        dataGridView1.SelectionMode =
            DataGridViewSelectionMode.FullRowSelect;
        dataGridView1.MultiSelect = false;
    }

    private void DataGridViewPopulate()
    {
        int nRows = 20;
        for (int i = 0; i < dataGridView1.ColumnCount; i++)
        {
            dataGridView1.Columns[i].Width = 80;
            dataGridView1.Columns[i].DefaultCellStyle.Alignment =
                DataGridViewContentAlignment.MiddleLeft;
            for (int j = 0; j < nRows; j++)
            {
                if (i == 0)
                {
                    dataGridView1.Rows.Add();
                    dataGridView1.Rows[j].HeaderCell.Value =
```

```
                        (j + 1).ToString();
            }

            float x = (float)Math.Round(j / 3.0, 3);
            float y1 = (float)Math.Round(Math.Sin(x), 3);
            float y2 = (float)Math.Round(Math.Cos(x), 3);

            float value = 0;
            if (i == 0)
                value = x;
            else if (i == 1)
                value = y1;
            else if (i == 2)
                value = y2;
            dataGridView1[i, j].Value = value.ToString();
        }
    }
}

private void btnAddRow_Click(object sender, EventArgs e)
{
    dataGridView1.Rows.Add();
}

private void btnDetaleRow_Click(object sender, EventArgs e)
{
    if (dataGridView1.SelectedRows.Count > 0 &&
        dataGridView1.SelectedRows[0].Index !=
        dataGridView1.Rows.Count - 1)
    {
        dataGridView1.Rows.RemoveAt(
            dataGridView1.SelectedRows[0].Index);
    }
}
}
}
```

In this class, we implement a DataGridViewSetup method to set up the DataGridView columns and properties.

This method first sets the number of columns to be displayed using the ColumnCount property. The default style for the column headers is set by setting the BackColor and Forecolor properties of the DataGridViewCellStyle returned by the ColumnHeadersDefaultCellStyle property. Then the layout, appearance properties, and column names are set. When this method executes, the DataGridView control is ready to be populated.

Next, we create a DataGridViewPopulate method to add data to the DataGridView control. We first add rows by calling the Rows.Add method. Then, we directly assign the value to the cell using the code snippet:

```
dataGridView1[i, j].Value = value.ToString();
```

With the utility methods in place, you can now attach event handlers. When the Add Row Buttons' Click event is raised, a new, empty row is added to the DataGridView. When the Delete Row button's Click event is raised, the selected row is deleted, unless it is the row for new records, which enables the user to add new rows. This row for new records is always the last row in the DataGridView control.

Building and running this project, you should obtain the output of Figure 8-2.

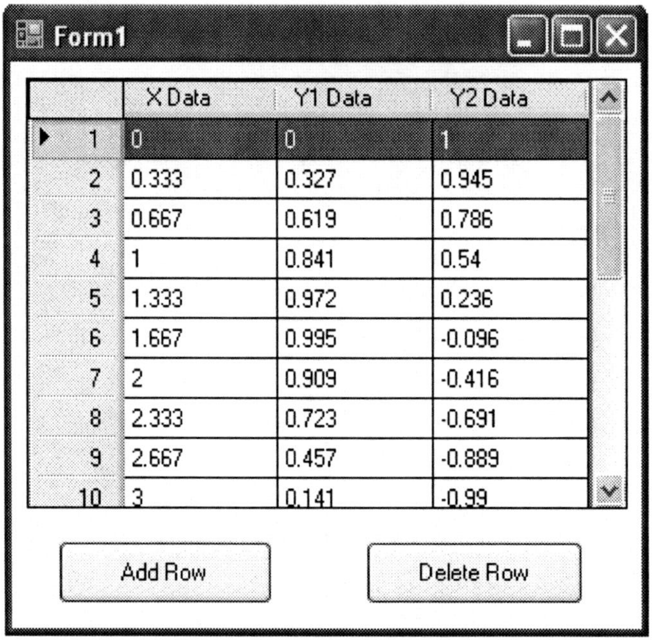

Figure 8-2 DataGridView control in unbound mode.

Data Binding

The DataGridView control supports the standard Windows Forms data binding model, meaning that it can bind to various data sources. Binding data to the DataGridView control is straightforward, and in many cases as simple as setting its DataSource property. When you bind to a data source that contains multiple lists or tables, set the DataMember property to a string that specifies the list or table to be bound to.

In practice, in order to bind data to a DataGridView, you first need to obtain a collection of data, typically through databases or data files. You then set the data binding properties of the DataGridView to bind to the data collection. Typically, you bind the DataGridView to an intermediate BindingSource component and bind this intermediate BindingSource component to another data source or populate it with business objects. The BindingSource component is the preferred data source because it can bind to a wide variety of data sources and can resolve many data binding issues automatically.

When binding to data, the `DataGridView` creates columns based on the properties of the data items, and generates rows for each data item found in the data collection. If the data binding is set up statically using the designer, the types and properties of the columns in the grid are set during design time. If the data binding is performed dynamically, the `AutoGenerateColumns` property is set to `true` by default, indicating that the column types will be determined based upon the type of the bound data items. Sometimes you may want to create and populate a grid programmatically, particularly when working with a grid that contains only unbound data.

In this book, we will deal with two kinds of data files: text and XML files. The delimited text file is still one of the most frequently used file formats even though the process of handling this kind of data can be a pain sometimes. XML is now used everywhere to create cross-platform interoperable file formats. It is also the central part of C# and the .NET Framework because XML eases the process of sharing data between components.

In this section, we will implement several converters that can load text or XML files into a `DataSet`. The `DataSet` will then be displayed in a `DataGridView`. Datasets are objects that contain data tables where you can temporarily store the data you use in your application. It is a good programming practice to use the `dataset` to hold your data if your application requires working with data, because it provides your application with a local in-memory cache of the data you are working with. The `dataset` maintains information about changes to its data so that updates can be tracked. The `DataSet` corresponds to the traditional ADO `RecordSet`. The structure of a `DataSet` is similar to that of a relational database: it exposes a hierarchical object model of tables, rows, columns, constraints, and relationships. You can create a `DataSet` from XML files and write XML file directly to the `DataSet`.

Now, start off with a new C# Windows Application project, *Example8_2*. Add four new classes, `Text2DataSet`, `XML2DataSet`, `DataSet2Text`, and `DataSet2XML`, to the current project. These classes convert text and XML files into a `DataSet`, and vice versa. They can be used as utility tools for handling the text and XML files. First, let's examine the XML2DataSet class:

```
using System;
using System.IO;
using System.Data;
using System.Windows.Forms;

namespace Example8_2
{
    class XML2DataSet
    {
        public static DataSet Convert2DataSet()
        {
            DataSet ds = new DataSet();
            OpenFileDialog openFileDialog1 = new OpenFileDialog();
            openFileDialog1.Filter = "XML files (*.xml)|*.xml|
                All files (*.*)|*.*";
            openFileDialog1.FilterIndex = 1;
            openFileDialog1.RestoreDirectory = true;

            if (openFileDialog1.ShowDialog() == DialogResult.OK)
            {
```

```
                ds.ReadXml(openFileDialog1.FileName);
            }
            else
            {
                MessageBox.Show("No XML file is read!");
                Return null;
            }
            return ds;
        }
    }
}
```

This class implements a static method `Convert2DataSet` that allows you to select the XML files from an `OpenFileDialog`. Then the default `ReadXml` of the `DataSet` class is used to load the XML file into the `DataSet`.

The `Text2DataSet` class is more involved and the following is its code listing:

```
using System;
using System.IO;
using System.Data;
using System.Windows.Forms;

namespace Example8_2
{
    public class Text2DataSet
    {
        public static DataSet Convert2DataSet(string tableName)
        {
            DataSet ds = new DataSet();
            OpenFileDialog openFileDialog1 = new OpenFileDialog();
            openFileDialog1.Filter = "Text files (*.txt)|*.txt|
                All files (*.*)|*.*";
            openFileDialog1.FilterIndex = 1;
            openFileDialog1.RestoreDirectory = true;

            if (openFileDialog1.ShowDialog() == DialogResult.OK)
            {
                StreamReader sr = new StreamReader(
                        openFileDialog1.FileName);
                char[] cSplitter = { ' ', ',', ':', '\t' };

                // Split the first line into the columns
                string[] columns = sr.ReadLine().Split(cSplitter);
                ds.Tables.Add(tableName);

                foreach (string col in columns)
                {
                    ds.Tables[tableName].Columns.Add(col);
                }

                //Read the rest of the data in the file.
                string AllData = sr.ReadToEnd();
                string[] rows = AllData.Split("\r".ToCharArray());
```

```
                    // Add data to the DataSet
                    foreach (string row in rows)
                    {
                          string[] items = row.Split(cSplitter);
                          ds.Tables[tableName].Rows.Add(items);
                    }
               }
               else
               {
                    MessageBox.Show("No text file is read!");
                    Return null;
               }
               return ds;
          }
     }
}
```

This class allows you to select the delimited text file (with the delimiters of space, comma, colon, and tab) from an `OpenFileDialog` and read it into a `DataSet`'s Tables. Here the `StreamReader`, derived from the abstract `TextReader` class, is used to read to and from a stream. The next step is to use the `ReadLine` method in the `StreamReader` to read the header line in. Then, the `ReadToEnd` method is applied to read the rest of the stream into one single string. Finally, the data string is added to the data table of the `DataSet`.

In order to use this converter, the text data file should be in a specific format. Namely, the first line of the text file is assumed to be the header text. A sample text file with Tab delimiters is given here:

X	Y1	Y2
0	0	1
0.333	0.327	0.945
0.667	0.619	0.786
1	0.841	0.54
1.333	0.972	0.236
1.667	0.995	-0.096
2	0.909	-0.416
2.333	0.723	-0.691
2.667	0.457	-0.889
3	0.141	-0.99
3.333	-0.19	-0.982
3.667	-0.502	-0.865
4	-0.757	-0.654
4.333	-0.929	-0.37
4.667	-0.999	-0.045
5	-0.959	0.284
5.333	-0.814	0.582
5.667	-0.578	0.816
6	-0.279	0.96
6.333	0.05	0.999

The first column represents the X data, and the second and third columns represent Y1 = Sin(X) and Y2 = Cos(X), respectively. This text file, named Text01.txt, is included in the current project for your reference.

The following is the code listing of the `DataSet2XML` class:

```csharp
using System;
using System.Text;
using System.IO;
using System.Data;
using System.Windows.Forms;

namespace Example8_2
{
    class DataSet2XML
    {
        public static void Convert2XML(DataSet ds)
        {
            SaveFileDialog saveFileDialog1 = new SaveFileDialog();
            saveFileDialog1.Filter = "XML files (*.xml)|*.xml|
                All files (*.*)|*.*";
            saveFileDialog1.FilterIndex = 1;
            saveFileDialog1.RestoreDirectory = true;

            if (saveFileDialog1.ShowDialog() == DialogResult.OK)
            {
                StreamWriter sw = new StreamWriter(
                    saveFileDialog1.FileName);
                ds.WriteXml(sw);
            }
        }
    }
}
```

This class allows you to save the `DataSet` into an XML file using the default method `WriteXml` of the `DataSet` class.

This following is the code listing of the `DataSet2Text` class:

```csharp
using System;
using System.Text;
using System.IO;
using System.Collections;
using System.Windows.Forms;

namespace Example8_2
{
    class DataSet2Text
    {
        public static void Convert2Text(DataGridView dgv)
        {
            SaveFileDialog saveFileDialog1 = new SaveFileDialog();

            saveFileDialog1.Filter = "Text files (*.txt)|*.txt|
                All files (*.*)|*.*";
            saveFileDialog1.FilterIndex = 1;
            saveFileDialog1.RestoreDirectory = true;

            if (saveFileDialog1.ShowDialog() == DialogResult.OK)
```

```
            {
                try
                {
                    StreamWriter sr = new StreamWriter(
                        saveFileDialog1.FileName);
                    string textLine = dgv.Columns[0].HeaderText;
                    for (int i = 1; i < dgv.ColumnCount; i++)
                    {
                        textLine = textLine + "\t" +
                            dgv.Columns[i].HeaderText;
                    }
                    sr.WriteLine(textLine);
                    for (int j = 0; j < dgv.RowCount; j++)
                    {
                        string value = dgv[0, j].Value as string;
                        if (value != null)
                        {
                            textLine = dgv[0, j].Value.ToString();
                            for (int i = 1; i < dgv.ColumnCount; i++)
                            {
                                string value1 = dgv[i, j].Value as
                                        string;
                                if (value1 != null)
                                {
                                    textLine = textLine + "\t" +
                                        dgv[i, j].Value.ToString();
                                }
                            }
                            sr.WriteLine(textLine);
                        }
                    }
                    sr.Close();
                }
                catch (Exception e)
                {
                    MessageBox.Show(e.Message, "Error saving file.");
                }
            }
        }
    }
}
```

In this class, instead of using the intermediate `DataSet`, we directly save the `DataGridView`'s content into a text file that includes the column headers.

With these conversion classes, you can easily create a C# application that populates a `DataGridView` using a `DataSet`. To demonstrate this, we will create a user interface for this project. From the Toolbox, drag the following controls onto `Form1`:

- A `SplitContainer` control that holds a `DataGridView` in its left panel and a multi-line `TextBox` control in its right panel.

- A `DataGridView` control that displays the contents of the data.

- A `TextBox` control that displays the XML Schema or the XML file.

- Six Button controls: one button reads the text file into the dataset and displays it in the DataGridView. Another button reads the XML file into the dataset and displays it in the DataGridView. The third button extracts the XML file from the dataset and displays it in the TextBox. The forth button extracts the schema from the dataset and displays it in the TextBox. The fifth button saves a text file directly from the DataGridView's content, and the last button save the XML file from the dataset.

Next, set the following properties:

Control	Property	Setting
splitContainer1	Anchor	Left, Top, Right, Bottom
dataGridView1	Dock	Fill
textBox1	Dock	Fill
	Multiline	True
	Scrollbars	Vertical
button1	Name	btnReadText
	Text	Read Text
button2	Name	btnReadXML
	Text	Read XML
button3	Name	btnShowXML
	Text	Show XML
button4	Name	btnShowSchema
	Text	Show Schema
button5	Name	btnSaveText
	Text	Save Text
button6	Name	btnSaveXML
	Text	Save XML

The following is the code listing of the Form1 class:

```csharp
using System;
using System.ComponentModel;
using System.Data;
using System.IO;
using System.Drawing;
using System.Text;
using System.Windows.Forms;

namespace Example8_2
{
    public partial class Form1 : Form
    {
        private DataSet dataSet1;
```

```csharp
public Form1()
{
    InitializeComponent();
    dataSet1 = new DataSet();
    dataGridView1.ColumnHeadersDefaultCellStyle.Alignment =
        DataGridViewContentAlignment.MiddleCenter;
    dataGridView1.RowHeadersDefaultCellStyle.Alignment =
        DataGridViewContentAlignment.MiddleRight;
    dataGridView1.RowHeadersWidth = 50;
}

private void btnReadXML_Click(object sender, EventArgs e)
{
    dataSet1 = XML2DataSet.Convert2DataSet();
    dataGridView1.DataSource = dataSet1;
    dataGridView1.DataMember = "MyDataSet";

    for (int i = 0; i < dataGridView1.ColumnCount; i++)
    {
        dataGridView1.Columns[i].Width = 70;
        dataGridView1.Columns[i].DefaultCellStyle.Alignment =
            DataGridViewContentAlignment.MiddleRight;
    }

    for (int i = 0; i < dataGridView1.Rows.Count - 1; i++)
    {
        dataGridView1.Rows[i].HeaderCell.Value =
                (i + 1).ToString();
    }
}

private void btnReadText_Click(object sender, EventArgs e)
{
    dataSet1 = Text2DataSet.Convert2DataSet("MyDataSet");
    dataGridView1.DataSource = dataSet1;
    dataGridView1.DataMember = "MyDataSet";

    for (int i = 0; i < dataGridView1.ColumnCount; i++)
    {
        dataGridView1.Columns[i].Width = 70;
        dataGridView1.Columns[i].DefaultCellStyle.Alignment =
            DataGridViewContentAlignment.MiddleRight;
    }

    for (int i = 0; i < dataGridView1.Rows.Count - 1; i++)
    {
        dataGridView1.Rows[i].HeaderCell.Value =
                (i + 1).ToString();
    }
}

private void btnShowSchema_Click(object sender, EventArgs e)
{
    System.IO.StringWriter swXML =
```

```
                    new System.IO.StringWriter();
            dataSet1.WriteXmlSchema(swXML);
            textBox1.Text = swXML.ToString();
        }

        private void btnShowXML_Click(object sender, EventArgs e)
        {
            StringWriter sw = new StringWriter();
            dataSet1.WriteXml(sw);
            textBox1.Text = sw.ToString();
        }

        private void btnSaveText_Click(object sender, EventArgs e)
        {
            if (dataGridView1.RowCount > 0)
            {
                DataSet2Text.Convert2Text(dataGridView1);
            }
            else
            {
                MessageBox.Show("DataGridView is empty." +
                    " Please populate it first.");
            }
        }

        private void btnSaveXML_Click(object sender, EventArgs e)
        {
            if (textBox1.Text.Trim() != "")
            {
                DataSet2XML.Convert2XML(dataSet1);
            }
            else
            {
                MessageBox.Show("There is no Xml file to save." +
                        " Please convert data to Xml file first.");
            }
        }
    }
}
```

In this class, we first create a new DataSet instance, dataSet1, that will be used to hold the text or XML data. Inside Form1's constructor, we also specify some properties of the dataGridView1 that control its appearance.

Next, we create various event handlers for reading text or XML data, displaying the XML and its schema in textBox1, and saving text or XML files. The Read Text button reads the text file into dataSet1 by calling the Convert2DataSet method of the Text2DataSet class and sets properties on the dataGridView1 control that bind it to dataSet1. Similarly, the Read XML button loads the XML file into dataSet1 by calling the Convert2DataSet method of the XML2DataSet class and sets properties on the dataGridView1 control that bind it to dataSet1.

The Show XML (or Show Schema) button creates a `StringWriter` object that is filled with the XML data (or schema) and displayed in the `textBox1`. The Save Text button saves `dataGridView1`'s content into a text file by calling the `Convert2Text` method of the `DataSet2Text` class. Finally, the Save XML button saves `dataSet1` into an XML file by calling the `Convert2XML` method of the `DataSet2XML` class.

You can test the project by pressing the F5 key. Click the Read Text file button and select the sample text file `Text01.txt`, which is included with the example in the directory ~\Examples\Example8_2\Example8_2\Text01.txt. The `dataGridView1` displays the contents of the text file. If you click the Show XML button now, textBox1 will display the XML file. You can also click the Show Schema button, and textBox1 will display the XML schema for the XML file, as shown in Figure 8-3.

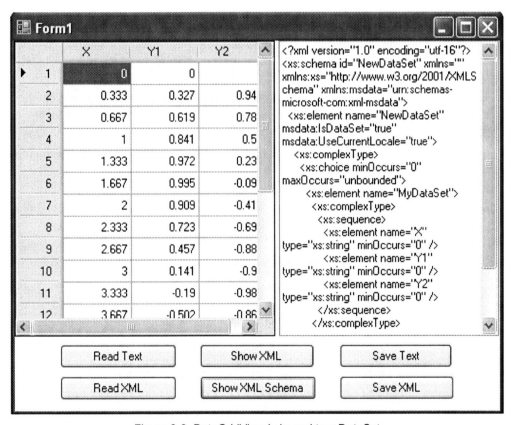

Figure 8-3 DataGridView is bound to a DataSet.

You can also click the Save XML button to save the dataset into an XML file. If you click on the Read XML button to open the XML file you just saved, the `dataGridView1` will display the XML data.

Inside the `dataGridView1` control, you can change the cell contents and add or delete rows. All the changes you made in the `dataGridView1` are updated automatically in the `dataSet1` that is bound to the `dataGridView1.DataSource`. Thus, the changes in the `dataGridView1` will be reflected automatically in the saved Text or XML file.

DataGridView and Chart2D Control

While the `DataGridView` class contains numerous members, it is possible to create a very simple grid with only a few lines of code, as shown previously. In this section, we will create a combination application of a `DataGridView` and a `Chart2D` control, and enhance it over the course of the chapter.

Creating DataGridView Application

The following steps lay out the user interface for the current project:

- Create a new C# Windows Application project and call it *Example8_3*.

- Drag a `MenuStrip` control from the Toolbox onto `Form1`.

- Add a `SplitContainer` control holding a `DataGridView` in its left panel and a `Chart2D` control in its right panel to `Form1`. Set the Dock property to `Fill` from the property browser.

- Add a `DataGridView` control to the left panel and set its `Dock` property to `Fill` from the property browser.

- Add a `Chart2D` control to the right panel and set its `Dock` property to `Fill` from the property browser. Before you can add the `Chart2D` control to you application, you need to add this control to the ToolBox first, using the method described in the previous chapter.

- Add the `Text2DataSet`, `XML2DataSet`, `DataSet2Text`, and `DataSet2XML` classes from the previous project *Example8_2* to the current project, and change their namespace to *Example8_3*.

- Implement the following code in the `Form1` class:

```
using System;
using System.ComponentModel;
using System.Data;
using System.Drawing;
using System.Drawing.Drawing2D;
using System.Windows.Forms;
using Chart2DLib;

namespace Example8_3
{
    public partial class Form1 : Form
    {
        private DataSeries ds;
        private DataSet dataSet1;

        public Form1()
        {
```

```
        InitializeComponent();
        ds = new DataSeries();
        dataSet1 = new DataSet();
        dataGridView1.ColumnHeadersDefaultCellStyle.Alignment =
            DataGridViewContentAlignment.MiddleCenter;
        dataGridView1.RowHeadersDefaultCellStyle.Alignment =
            DataGridViewContentAlignment.MiddleRight;
        dataGridView1.RowHeadersWidth = 50;

        // Override ChartStyle properties:
        chart2D1.C2XAxis.XLimMin = 0f;
        chart2D1.C2XAxis.XLimMax = 7f;
        chart2D1.C2YAxis.YLimMin = -1.5f;
        chart2D1.C2YAxis.YLimMax = 1.5f;
        chart2D1.C2XAxis.XTick = 1.0f;
        chart2D1.C2YAxis.YTick = 0.5f;
        chart2D1.C2Label.XLabel = "This is X axis";
        chart2D1.C2Label.YLabel = "This is Y axis";
        chart2D1.C2Title.Title = "Sine and Cosine Chart";
    }

    protected override void OnPaint(PaintEventArgs e)
    {
        if (dataGridView1.RowCount > 0)
        {
            AddData();
        }
    }

    private void AddData()
    {
        chart2D1.C2DataCollection.DataSeriesList.Clear();
        // Add first data series:
        ds = new DataSeries();
        ds.LineStyle.LineColor = Color.Red;
        ds.LineStyle.Thickness = 2f;
        ds.LineStyle.Pattern = DashStyle.Dash;
        ds.LineStyle.PlotMethod =
            LineStyle.PlotLinesMethodEnum.Lines;
        ds.SeriesName = "Sine";
        ds.SymbolStyle.SymbolType =
            SymbolStyle.SymbolTypeEnum.Diamond;
        ds.SymbolStyle.BorderColor = Color.Red;
        ds.SymbolStyle.FillColor = Color.Yellow;
        ds.SymbolStyle.BorderThickness = 1f;
        for (int i = 0; i < dataGridView1.RowCount; i++)
        {
            string value1 = dataGridView1[0, i].Value as string;
            string value2 = dataGridView1[1, i].Value as string;
            if (value1 != null && value2 != null)
            {

                float x = Convert.ToSingle(
                    (string)dataGridView1[0, i].Value);
```

```
            float y = Convert.ToSingle(
                (string)dataGridView1[1, i].Value);
            ds.AddPoint(new PointF(x, y));
        }
    }
    chart2D1.C2DataCollection.Add(ds);

    // Add second data series:
    ds = new DataSeries();
    ds.LineStyle.LineColor = Color.Blue;
    ds.LineStyle.Thickness = 1f;
    ds.LineStyle.Pattern = DashStyle.Solid;
    ds.LineStyle.PlotMethod =
        LineStyle.PlotLinesMethodEnum.Splines;
    ds.SeriesName = "Cosine";
    ds.SymbolStyle.SymbolType =
        SymbolStyle.SymbolTypeEnum.Triangle;
    ds.SymbolStyle.BorderColor = Color.Blue;
    for (int i = 0; i < dataGridView1.RowCount; i++)
    {
        string value1 = dataGridView1[0, i].Value as string;
        string value2 = dataGridView1[2, i].Value as string;
        if (value1 != null && value2 != null)
        {

            float x = Convert.ToSingle(
                (string)dataGridView1[0, i].Value);
            float y = Convert.ToSingle(
                (string)dataGridView1[2, i].Value);
            ds.AddPoint(new PointF(x, y));
        }
    }
    chart2D1.C2DataCollection.Add(ds);
}


private void openTextFileToolStripMenuItem_Click(object
    sender, EventArgs e)
{
    dataSet1 = Text2DataSet.Convert2DataSet("MyDataSet");
    dataGridView1.DataSource = dataSet1;
    dataGridView1.DataMember = "MyDataSet";

    for (int i = 0; i < dataGridView1.ColumnCount; i++)
    {
        dataGridView1.Columns[i].Width = 70;
        dataGridView1.Columns[i].DefaultCellStyle.Alignment =
            DataGridViewContentAlignment.MiddleRight;
    }

    for (int i = 0; i < dataGridView1.Rows.Count - 1; i++)
    {
        dataGridView1.Rows[i].HeaderCell.Value =
            (i + 1).ToString();
```

```
            }
        }

        private void openXMLFileToolStripMenuItem_Click(object
                sender, EventArgs e)
        {
            dataSet1 = XML2DataSet.Convert2DataSet();
            dataGridView1.DataSource = dataSet1;
            dataGridView1.DataMember = "MyDataSet";

            for (int i = 0; i < dataGridView1.ColumnCount; i++)
            {
                dataGridView1.Columns[i].Width = 70;
                dataGridView1.Columns[i].DefaultCellStyle.Alignment =
                    DataGridViewContentAlignment.MiddleRight;
            }

            for (int i = 0; i < dataGridView1.Rows.Count - 1; i++)
            {
                dataGridView1.Rows[i].HeaderCell.Value =
                    (i + 1).ToString();
            }
        }

        private void saveTextFileToolStripMenuItem_Click(object
            sender, EventArgs e)
        {
            if (dataGridView1.RowCount > 0)
            {
                DataSet2Text.Convert2Text(dataGridView1);
            }
        }

        private void saveXMLFileToolStripMenuItem_Click(object
            sender, EventArgs e)
        {
            if (dataGridView1.RowCount > 0)
            {
                DataSet2XML.Convert2XML(dataSet1);
            }
        }

        private void dataGridView1_CellValueChanged(object
            sender, DataGridViewCellEventArgs e)
        {
            this.Invalidate();
        }
    }
}
```

In this class, we first initialize the dataGridView1 and chart2D1 controls in Form1's constructor. Then we implement the AddData method, which will be called by the OnPain method. In the AddData method, we create two sets of data series using the data displayed in the dataGridView1 control. For each set of data series, the line style and symbol style are specified. For practical applications, you will need to change the `AddData` method corresponding to the data contained in the `dataGridView1`. For example, if the `dataGridView1` contain data for three curves, you need to add one more data series to the `chart2D1` control.

Next we implement the standard menu click event handlers for Open Text, Open XML, Save Text, and Save XML, which are similar to the commands in the project *Example8_2* where corresponding Button controls were used. Finally, we create a `CellValueChanged` event for the `dataGridView1` that will fire when the value of a cell changes. The code snippet

```
this.Invalidate();
```

ensures that the chart gets redrawn when the cell value changes. Press F5 to run the application. Click the Open Text File menu and select the text file Text01.txt, which is included in the previous project *Example8_2*. This produces the output of Figure 8-4.

If you change the value of the cells or add or delete rows in the `dataGridView1`, the 2D chart will reflect the changes immediately.

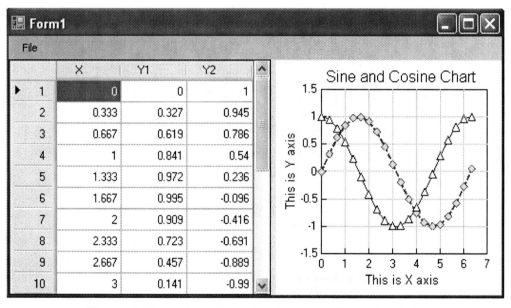

Figure 8-4 Combination of `DataGridView` and Chart2D controls.

Runtime Support

In the previous chapter, we implemented design-time support in the property browser for custom user controls. The properties of the `Chart2D` user control can easily be set at design-time from the property browser. However, these properties have to be specified by code when the user control is being used in an application, such as in the previous example. It would be better to provide a richer editing experience by having the user interact directly with the properties of the user controls at runtime. The .NET framework `PropertyGrid` control can bridge this gap and display and set properties at runtime for any object or type.

To demonstrate the application of the PropertyGrid, we start off with a new C# Windows Application project, *Example8_4*, which is based on the previous example project. Copy all of the classes, including the Form1 class, from *Example8_3* to the current project and change their corresponding namespace to *Example8_4*. Open Form1.Designer.cs and change the following code snippet

```
private Chart2DLib.Chart2D chart2D1;
```

to

```
public Chart2DLib.Chart2D chart2D1;
```

This changes the chart2D1 control from private to public, indicating that the control can be accessed from other classes.

Add two new classes, ChartStyle and DataGridViewStyle, to the current project. The former contains properties for the chart2D1 control, while the later contains properties for the dataGridView1 control. All of the properties in these two classes are to be displayed in the PropertyGrid. The following is the code listing for the ChartStyle class:

```
using System;
using System.Drawing;
using System.Drawing.Drawing2D;
using System.ComponentModel;
using Chart2DLib;

namespace Example8_4
{
    public class ChartStyle
    {
        private Color chartBackColor = Color.White;
        private Color plotBackColor = Color.White;
        private bool isLegendVisible = false;
        private float xLimMin = 0f;
        private float xLimMax = 10f;
        private float xTick = 2f;
        private float yLimMin = 0f;
        private float yLimMax = 10f;
        private float yTick = 2f;
        private DashStyle gridPattern = DashStyle.Solid;
        private Color gridColor = Color.LightGray;
        private float gridLineThickness = 1.0f;
        private bool isXGrid = true;
        private bool isYGrid = true;
        private string xLabel = "X Axis";
        private string yLabel = "Y Axis";
        private string title = "My 2D Chart";

        public ChartStyle()
        {
        }

        [Description("The background color of the chart area."),
        Category("Chart Style")]
```

```csharp
public Color ChartBackColor
{
    get { return chartBackColor; }
    set { chartBackColor = value; }
}

[Description("The background color of the plot area."),
Category("Chart Style")]
public Color PlotBackColor
{
    get { return plotBackColor; }
    set { plotBackColor = value; }
}

[Description("Indicates whether the legend should be shown."),
Category("Chart Style"), DefaultValue(false)]
public bool IsLegendVisible
{
    get { return isLegendVisible; }
    set { isLegendVisible = value; }
}

[Description("Sets the maximum limit for the X axis."),
 Category("Axes"), DefaultValue(10)]
public float XLimMax
{
    get { return xLimMax; }
    set { xLimMax = value; }
}

[Description("Sets the maximum limit for the X axis."),
Category("Axes"), DefaultValue(0)]
public float XLimMin
{
    get { return xLimMin; }
    set { xLimMin = value; }
}

[Description("Sets the ticks for the X axis."),
Category("Axes"), DefaultValue(2)]
public float XTick
{
    get { return xTick; }
    set { xTick = value; }
}

[Description("Sets the maximum limit for the Y axis."),
 Category("Axes"), DefaultValue(10)]
public float YLimMax
{
    get { return yLimMax; }
    set { yLimMax = value; }
}
```

```
[Description("Sets the maximum limit for the Y axis."),
Category("Axes"), DefaultValue(0)]
public float YLimMin
{
    get { return yLimMin; }
    set { yLimMin = value; }
}

[Description("Sets the ticks for the X axis."),
Category("Axes"), DefaultValue(2)]
public float YTick
{
    get { return yTick; }
    set { yTick = value; }
}

[Description("Indicates whether the X grid is shown."),
Category("Grid"), DefaultValue(true)]
public bool IsXGrid
{
    get { return isXGrid; }
    set { isXGrid = value; }
}

[Description("Indicates whether the Y grid is shown."),
Category("Grid"), DefaultValue(true)]
public bool IsYGrid
{
    get { return isYGrid; }
    set { isYGrid = value; }
}

[Description("Sets the line pattern for the grid lines."),
Category("Grid")]
virtual public DashStyle GridPattern
{
    get { return gridPattern; }
    set { gridPattern = value; }
}

[Description("Sets the thickness for the grid lines."),
Category("Grid"), DefaultValue(1)]
public float GridThickness
{
    get { return gridLineThickness; }
    set { gridLineThickness = value; }
}

[Description("The color used to display the grid lines."),
Category("Grid")]
virtual public Color GridColor
{
    get { return gridColor; }
    set { gridColor = value; }
```

```
        }

        [Description("Creates a label for the X axis."),
        Category("Title and Labels"), DefaultValue("X Axis")]
        public string XLabel
        {
            get { return xLabel; }
            set { xLabel = value; }
        }

        [Description("Creates a label for the Y axis."),
        Category("Title and Labels"), DefaultValue("Y Axis")]
        public string YLabel
        {
            get { return yLabel; }
            set { yLabel = value; }
        }

        [Description("Creates a title for the chart."),
        Category("Title and Labels"), DefaultValue("My 2D Chart")]
        public string Title
        {
            get { return title; }
            set { title = value; }
        }
    }
}
```

This class includes the basic properties for the Chart2D control , which can be changed by the
user at the runtime. You can add or delete properties from this class according to your application
requirements.

The following code is for the DataGridViewStyle class:

```
using System;
using System.ComponentModel;
using System.Drawing;

namespace Example8_4
{
    public class DataGridViewStyle
    {
        private Color firstColumnColor = Color.White;
        private Color secondColumnColor = Color.White;
        private Color thirdColumnColor = Color.White;


        [Description("Sets the background color of the first column."),
        Category("Background Color")]
        public Color FirstColumnColor
        {
            get { return firstColumnColor; }
            set { firstColumnColor = value; }
        }
```

```
        [Description("Sets the background color of the second column."),
        Category("Background Color")]
        public Color SecondColumnColor
        {
            get { return secondColumnColor; }
            set { secondColumnColor = value; }
        }

        [Description("Sets the background color of the third column."),
        Category("Background Color")]
        public Color ThirdColumnColor
        {
            get { return thirdColumnColor; }
            set { thirdColumnColor = value; }
        }
    }
}
```

In this class, we simply add some column color properties as examples to show you how to make the DataGridView's properties appear in the PropertyGrid control at runtime. You can easily add more properties to this class according to your application requirements.

Next, add a new Window Form named SetProperties to the current project and set its Text property to Runtime Properties Editor.

In order to add a PropertyGrid control to the Form SetProperties, we need to add the PropertyGrid to the toolbox since it is not included by default. From the Tools menu, select Choose Toolbox Items.... In the dialog box, select the Framework Components tab, then PropertyGrid.

Now drag the PropertyGrid control onto the SetProperties form and add two button controls. Set one button's name to btnOK and its Text property to OK. Set the other button's name to btnClose and its Text property to Close. The following is the code listing of the SetProperties class:

```
using System;
using System.ComponentModel;
using System.Data;
using System.Drawing;
using System.Windows.Forms;

namespace Example8_4
{
    public partial class SettProperties : Form
    {
        private Form1 form1;
        private ChartStyle cs;
        private DataGridViewStyle dgvs;
        private string sProperty;

        public SetProperties(Form1 fm1, ChartStyle chartStyle,
            string sproperty)
        {
            InitializeComponent();
```

```
        form1 = fm1;
        sProperty = sproperty;
        cs = chartStyle;
        cs.ChartBackColor = form1.BackColor;
        propertyGrid1.SelectedObject = cs;
    }

    public SetProperties(Form1 fm1, DataGridViewStyle
            dataGridViewStyle, string sproperty)
    {
        InitializeComponent();
        form1 = fm1;
        sProperty = sproperty;
        dgvs = dataGridViewStyle;
        propertyGrid1.SelectedObject = dgvs;
    }

    private void btnOK_Click(object sender, EventArgs e)
    {
        if (sProperty == "ChartStyle")
        {
            Chart2DSettings();
        }
        else if (sProperty == "DataGridViewStyle")
        {
            DataGridViewSettings();
        }
    }

    private void Chart2DSettings()
    {
        form1.chart2D1.C2Legend.IsLegendVisible =
                cs.IsLegendVisible;
        form1.chart2D1.C2ChartArea.ChartBackColor =
                cs.ChartBackColor;
        form1.chart2D1.C2ChartArea.PlotBackColor =
                cs.PlotBackColor;
        form1.chart2D1.C2XAxis.XLimMax = cs.XLimMax;
        form1.chart2D1.C2XAxis.XLimMin = cs.XLimMin;
        form1.chart2D1.C2XAxis.XTick = cs.XTick;
        form1.chart2D1.C2YAxis.YLimMax = cs.YLimMax;
        form1.chart2D1.C2YAxis.YLimMin = cs.YLimMin;
        form1.chart2D1.C2YAxis.YTick = cs.YTick;
        form1.chart2D1.C2Grid.GridColor = cs.GridColor;
        form1.chart2D1.C2Grid.GridPattern = cs.GridPattern;
        form1.chart2D1.C2Grid.GridThickness = cs.GridThickness;
        form1.chart2D1.C2Grid.IsXGrid = cs.IsXGrid;
        form1.chart2D1.C2Grid.IsYGrid = cs.IsYGrid;
        form1.chart2D1.C2Title.Title = cs.Title;
        form1.chart2D1.C2Label.XLabel = cs.XLabel;
        form1.chart2D1.C2Label.YLabel = cs.YLabel;
    }

    private void DataGridViewSettings()
```

```
        {
            if (form1.dataGridView1.ColumnCount > 2)
            {
                form1.dataGridView1.Columns[0].DefaultCellStyle.
                    BackColor = dgvs.FirstColumnColor;
                form1.dataGridView1.Columns[1].DefaultCellStyle.
                    BackColor = dgvs.SecondColumnColor;
                form1.dataGridView1.Columns[2].DefaultCellStyle.
                    BackColor = dgvs.ThirdColumnColor;
            }
        }

        private void btnClose_Click(object sender, EventArgs e)
        {
            this.Close();
        }
    }
}
```

There are two overloaded constructors in this class: one is for the Chart2D control and the other for the DataGridView control. In order to get the PropertyGrid running, we need to assign instances of the ChartStyle and DataGridViewStyle classes to the PropertyGrid. This is done using the SelectObject property of the PropertyGrid:

```
            propertyGrid1.SelectedObject = cs;
            propertyGrid1.SelectedObject = dgvs;
```

This way, the PropertyGrid can automatically figure out all of the fields of the ChartStyle or DataGridViewStyle through reflection and display the property name along with the property value on each line of the PropertyGrid. Another useful feature of the PropertyGrid is that it can create special editing controls on each line that correspond to the value type of that line.

The Form1 class is basically the same as that in the previous project, with a few modifications. We add a Property Setting menu that includes Chart Style and DataGridView Style. The click event handlers for these two items will open the corresponding PropertyGrid window. Here is the new code added to the Form1 class:

```
namespace Example8_4
{
    public partial class Form1 : Form
    {
        ... ...
        private ChartStyle cs;
        private DataGridViewStyle dgvs;

        public Form1()
        {
            InitializeComponent();
            ... ...
            cs = new ChartStyle();
            dgvs = new DataGridViewStyle();
        }
        ... ...
```

```
private void chartStyleToolStripMenuItem1_Click(
      object sender, EventArgs e)
{
    SetProperties sp = new SettProperties(this,
          cs, "ChartStyle");
    sp.ShowDialog();
}
```

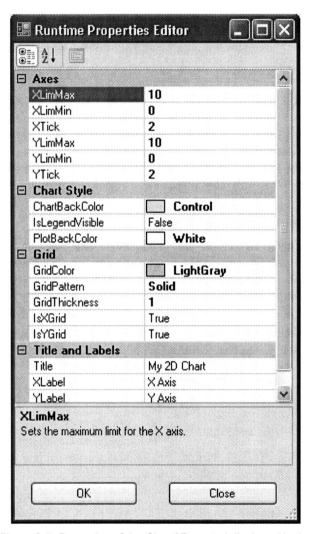

Figure 8-5 Properties of the Chart2D control displayed in the
PropertyGrid.

```
            private void dataGridViewStyleToolStripMenuItem_Click(
                object sender, EventArgs e)
        {
            SetProperties sp = new SettProperties(this, dgvs,
                "DataGridViewStyle");
            sp.ShowDialog();
        }
    }
}
```

Press F5 to run the application. Open the text file Text01.txt from the previous project, Example8_2. This produces output similar to Figure 8-4. Now click the Property Setting menu and select Chart Style item to open the PropertyGrid window, as shown in Figure 8-5. From this window, you can set properties for the Chart2D control at runtime. After changing the values of the properties, you can click OK button to make the changes effective.

Similarly, you can select the DataGridView Style from the Property Setting menu to open the PropertyGrid window, which allows you to set properties for the DataGridView control at runtime, as shown in Figure 8-6. If you change the properties of the dataGridView1 control from this window and click the OK button, the change will take effect immediately.

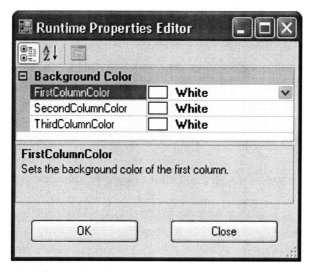

Figure 8-6 Properties of the dataGridView1 control displayed in the PropertyGrid.

DataGridView and Chart3D Control

In the same manner as we did for 2D charts, you can combine the DataGridView with a Chart3D control. However, the 3D case is much more complicated than the 2D case. In this section, we will only consider standard 3D surface data files with formats defined so that for each X and Y value, there is a corresponding Z value, as shown in the following table:

NA	X1	X2	X3	...
Y1	Z(X1,Y1)	Z(X2,Y1)	Z(X3,Y1)	...
Y2	Z(X1,Y2)	Z(X2,Y2)	Z(X3,Y2)	...
Y3	Z(X1,Y3)	Z(X2,Y3)	Z(X3,Y3)	...
...	...	...	...	...

We will not discuss data formats for 3D lines and 4D slice charts. You can easily create C# applications containing these special charts and `DataGridView` controls, following the same procedure discussed here.

Creating Text Data File

In this subsection, we will show you how to create a 3D data file using a C# application. In practice, you can create such a data file using any other program, including Microsoft Excel and special CAD tools. The following steps lay out the user interface for the current project:

- Create a new C# Windows Application project and call it *Example8_5*.

- Drag a `MenuStrip` control from the Toolbox onto `Form1`.

- Right click the `MenuStrip` control, select Insert, and choose the `ComboBox`.

- Add a `SplitContainer` control, which will hold a `DataGridView` in its left panel and a `Chart3D` control in its right panel, to `Form1`. Set its Dock property to `Fill` from the property browser.

- Add a `DataGridView` control to the left panel and set its `Dock` property to `Fill` from the property browser.

- Add a `Chart3D` control to the right panel and set its `Dock` property to `Fill` from the property browser.

- Add the class `DataSet2Text` from the previous project *Example8_2* to the current project, and change its namespace to *Example8_5*. Modify it according to the following code to reflect the 3D features:

```
using System;
using System.Collections.Generic;
using System.Text;
using System.IO;
using System.Collections.Specialized;
using System.Collections;
using System.Windows.Forms;

namespace Example8_5
{
    class DataSet2Text
    {
```

```csharp
public static void Convert2Text(DataGridView dgv)
{
    SaveFileDialog saveFileDialog1 = new SaveFileDialog();
    saveFileDialog1.Filter =
        "Text files (*.txt)|*.txt|All files (*.*)|*.*";
    saveFileDialog1.FilterIndex = 1;
    saveFileDialog1.RestoreDirectory = true;

    if (saveFileDialog1.ShowDialog() == DialogResult.OK)
    {
        try
        {
            StreamWriter sr = new StreamWriter(
                saveFileDialog1.FileName);
            string textLine;
            for (int j = 0; j < dgv.RowCount - 1; j++)
            {
                string value = dgv[0, j].Value as string;
                if (value != null)
                {
                    textLine = dgv[0, j].Value.ToString();
                    for (int i = 1; i < dgv.ColumnCount; i++)
                    {
                        string value1 = dgv[i, j].Value
                                as string;
                        if (value1 != null)
                        {
                            textLine = textLine + "\t" +
                                dgv[i, j].Value.ToString();
                        }
                    }
                    sr.WriteLine(textLine);
                }
            }
            sr.Close();
        }
        catch (Exception e)
        {
            MessageBox.Show(e.Message, "Error saving file.");
        }
    }
}
```

- Finally, implement the following code in the `Form1` class:

```csharp
using System;
using System.ComponentModel;
using System.Drawing;
using System.Drawing.Drawing2D;
using System.Data;
using System.Windows.Forms;
using Chart3DLib;
```

```
namespace Example8_5
{
    public partial class Form1 : Form
    {
        private DataSeries ds;
        private DataSet dataSet1;

        public Form1()
        {
            InitializeComponent();
            this.SetStyle(ControlStyles.ResizeRedraw, true);
            ComboboxSetup();
            ds = new DataSeries();
            dataSet1 = new DataSet();
            dataGridView1.ColumnHeadersDefaultCellStyle.Alignment =
                DataGridViewContentAlignment.MiddleCenter;
            dataGridView1.RowHeadersDefaultCellStyle.Alignment =
                DataGridViewContentAlignment.MiddleRight;
            dataGridView1.RowHeadersWidth = 70;
        }

        private void ComboboxSetup()
        {
            toolStripComboBox1.Items.Add("Mesh");
            toolStripComboBox1.Items.Add("MeshZ");
            toolStripComboBox1.Items.Add("Waterfall");
            toolStripComboBox1.Items.Add("Surface");
            toolStripComboBox1.Items.Add("XYColor");
            toolStripComboBox1.Items.Add("Contour");
            toolStripComboBox1.Items.Add("Filled Contour");
            toolStripComboBox1.Items.Add("Mesh + Contour");
            toolStripComboBox1.Items.Add("Surface + Contour");
            toolStripComboBox1.Items.Add("Surface + Contour");
            toolStripComboBox1.Items.Add("Surface + Filled Contour");
            toolStripComboBox1.Items.Add("Bar3D");
            toolStripComboBox1.SelectedItem = "Surface";
        }

        private void ChartTypeSetup()
        {
            string chartType = toolStripComboBox1.
                SelectedItem.ToString();
            switch (chartType)
            {
                case "Mesh":
                    chart3D1.C3DrawChart.ChartType =
                        DrawChart.ChartTypeEnum.Mesh;
                    break;
                case "MeshZ":
                    chart3D1.C3DrawChart.ChartType =
                        DrawChart.ChartTypeEnum.MeshZ;
                    break;
                case "Waterfall":
```

```
                        chart3D1.C3DrawChart.ChartType =
                            DrawChart.ChartTypeEnum.Waterfall;
                        break;
                case "Surface":
                        chart3D1.C3DrawChart.ChartType =
                            DrawChart.ChartTypeEnum.Surface;
                        break;
                case "XYColor":
                        chart3D1.C3DrawChart.ChartType =
                            DrawChart.ChartTypeEnum.XYColor;
                        break;
                case "Contour":
                        chart3D1.C3DrawChart.ChartType =
                            DrawChart.ChartTypeEnum.Contour;
                        break;
                case "Filled Contour":
                        chart3D1.C3DrawChart.ChartType =
                            DrawChart.ChartTypeEnum.FillContour;
                        break;
                case "Mesh + Contour":
                        chart3D1.C3DrawChart.ChartType =
                            DrawChart.ChartTypeEnum.MeshContour;
                        break;
                case "Surface + Contour":
                        chart3D1.C3DrawChart.ChartType =
                            DrawChart.ChartTypeEnum.SurfaceContour;
                        break;
                case "Surface + Filled Contour":
                        chart3D1.C3DrawChart.ChartType =
                            DrawChart.ChartTypeEnum.SurfaceFillContour;
                        break;
                case "Bar3D":
                        chart3D1.C3DrawChart.ChartType =
                            DrawChart.ChartTypeEnum.Bar3D;
                        break;
        }
}

protected override void OnPaint(PaintEventArgs e)
{
    AddData();
    if (dataGridView1.RowCount == 0)
    {
        PopulateDadaGridView();
    }
    if (dataGridView1.RowCount > 0)
    {
        ChartTypeSetup();
    }
}

private void PopulateDadaGridView()
{
    Point3[,] zdata = chart3D1.C3DataSeries.PointArray;
```

```csharp
        int nx = zdata.GetLength(0);
        int ny = zdata.GetLength(1);
        float[] xdata = new float[nx];
        float[] ydata = new float[ny];
        for (int i = 0; i < nx; i++)
        {
            xdata[i] = chart3D1.C3DataSeries.XDataMin +
                i * chart3D1.C3DataSeries.XSpacing;
        }
        for (int j = 0; j < ny; j++)
        {
            ydata[j] = chart3D1.C3DataSeries.YDataMin +
                j * chart3D1.C3DataSeries.YSpacing;
        }
        dataGridView1.ColumnCount = nx + 1;
        for (int i = 0; i < dataGridView1.ColumnCount; i++)
        {
            dataGridView1.RowHeadersDefaultCellStyle.Alignment =
                DataGridViewContentAlignment.MiddleRight;
            dataGridView1.Columns[i].Width = 80;
            dataGridView1.Columns[i].DefaultCellStyle.Alignment =
                DataGridViewContentAlignment.MiddleRight;

            for (int j = 0; j < ny + 1; j++)
            {
                if (i == 0)
                {
                    dataGridView1.Rows.Add();
                    dataGridView1[0, 0].Value = "NA";
                    if (j > 0)
                    {
                        dataGridView1.Rows[j].HeaderCell.Value =
                            "Y" + j.ToString();
                        dataGridView1[0, j].Value =
                            ydata[j - 1].ToString();
                    }
                }
                if (i > 0)
                {
                    dataGridView1.Columns[i].Name =
                        "X" + i.ToString();
                    dataGridView1[i, 0].Value =
                        xdata[i - 1].ToString();
                }
                if (i > 0 && j > 0)
                {
                    dataGridView1[i, j].Value =
                        zdata[i - 1, j - 1].Z.ToString();
                }
            }
        }
    }

    private void AddData()
```

```
{
    chart3D1.C3Axes.XMin = -3;
    chart3D1.C3Axes.XMax = 3;
    chart3D1.C3Axes.YMin = -3;
    chart3D1.C3Axes.YMax = 3;
    chart3D1.C3Axes.ZMin = -8;
    chart3D1.C3Axes.ZMax = 8;
    chart3D1.C3Axes.XTick = 1;
    chart3D1.C3Axes.YTick = 1;
    chart3D1.C3Axes.ZTick = 4;

    chart3D1.C3DataSeries.XDataMin = chart3D1.C3Axes.XMin;
    chart3D1.C3DataSeries.YDataMin = chart3D1.C3Axes.YMin;
    chart3D1.C3DataSeries.XSpacing = 0.3f;
    chart3D1.C3DataSeries.YSpacing = 0.3f;
    chart3D1.C3DataSeries.XNumber = Convert.ToInt16(
        (chart3D1.C3Axes.XMax - chart3D1.C3Axes.XMin) /
        chart3D1.C3DataSeries.XSpacing) + 1;
    chart3D1.C3DataSeries.YNumber = Convert.ToInt16(
        (chart3D1.C3Axes.YMax - chart3D1.C3Axes.YMin) /
        chart3D1.C3DataSeries.YSpacing) + 1;

    Point3[,] pts = new Point3[chart3D1.C3DataSeries.XNumber,
        chart3D1.C3DataSeries.YNumber];
    for (int i = 0; i < chart3D1.C3DataSeries.XNumber; i++)
    {
        for (int j = 0; j < chart3D1.C3DataSeries.YNumber;
            j++)
        {
            float x = chart3D1.C3DataSeries.XDataMin +
                i * chart3D1.C3DataSeries.XSpacing;
            float y = chart3D1.C3DataSeries.YDataMin +
                j * chart3D1.C3DataSeries.YSpacing;
            double zz = 3 * Math.Pow((1 - x), 2) *
            Math.Exp(-x * x - (y + 1) * (y + 1)) - 10 *
            (0.2 * x - Math.Pow(x, 3) - Math.Pow(y, 5)) *
            Math.Exp(-x * x - y * y) - 1 / 3 *
            Math.Exp(-(x + 1) * (x + 1) - y * y);
            float z = (float)zz;
            pts[i, j] = new Point3(x, y, z, 1);
        }
    }
    chart3D1.C3DataSeries.PointArray = pts;
}

private void toolStripComboBox1_SelectedIndexChanged(
    object sender, EventArgs e)
{
    this.Invalidate();
}

private void saveTextFileToolStripMenuItem_Click(
    object sender, EventArgs e)
{
```

```
            if (dataGridView1.RowCount > 0)
            {
                DataSet2Text.Convert2Text(dataGridView1);
            }
        }
    }
}
```

In this project, we create a 3D data file for a peak function. You can easily create a text data file for any other function using the current application.

This project generates the output of Figure 8-7.

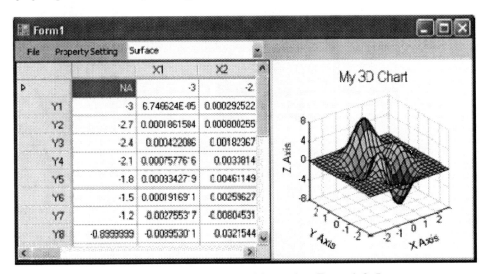

Figure 8-7 Output window of the project Example8_5.

Now click the File menu, select "Save Text File", and enter the file name "data3d.txt". The data is saved in the following format shown in Figure 8-8.

NA	-3	-2.7	-2.4	-2.1	-1.8	-1.5	-1.2	-0.8999999	-0
-3	6.746624E-05			0.0002925229			0.001004677	0.002640	
-2.7	0.0001861584			0.0008002551			0.002701343	0.006841	
-2.4	0.000422086	0.001823675	0.006161598	0.01547654		0.024730			
-2.1	0.0007577616			0.00338148	0.01183304		0.03109406	0.	
-1.8	0.0009342719			0.004611494	0.01783587		0.05274227	0.	
-1.5	0.0001916911			0.002596272	0.01556833		0.06236493	0.	
-1.2	-0.002755317			-0.008045319			-0.01320627	0.010420	
-0.8999999	-0.008953011			-0.03215449	-0.08714014		-0.16304		
-0.5999999	-0.01774956	-0.0676195		-0.2019487	-0.457725		-0		
-0.2999999	-0.0261498	-0.1022233		-0.3174155	-0.7677316		-1		
1.192093E-07		-0.03040099	-0.1203089		-0.3802821	-0.94572			
0.3000001	-0.02868027	-0.1141899		-0.3640592	-0.9172148		-1		
0.6000001	-0.02220554	-0.0885926		-0.2832044	-0.7160659		-1		
0.9000002	-0.01400913	-0.05555602	-0.175822		-0.4366523	-0			
1.2	-0.006944744			-0.02670277	-0.08018281	-0.1801798		-0	
1.5	-0.002434747			-0.008251747			-0.018887	-0.01530	
1.8	-0.0003603667			-5.505608E-05			0.00689434	0.048002	
2.1	0.0002170223			0.001801472	0.01053931		0.047303	0.	
2.4	0.0002070417			0.001300712	0.006582536		0.02711574	0.	
2.7	9.860261E-05			0.000578951	0.002798358		0.01116786	0.	
3	3.298877E-05			0.0001885039			0.0008930928	0.	

Figure 8-8 Text data file of data3d.txt.

Creating DataGridView Application

Start off with a new C# Windows Application project and call it *Example8_6*. Add all of the classes from the previous project *Example8_5*, as well as `DataSet2XML`, `Text2DataSet`, and `XML2DataSet` classes from *Example8_2*, to the current project and change their namespace to *Example8_6*.

Change the `Form1` class using the following code snippet:

```
using System;
using System.ComponentModel;
using System.Drawing;
using System.Drawing.Drawing2D;
using System.Data;
using System.Windows.Forms;
using Chart3DLib;

namespace Example8_6
{
    public partial class Form1 : Form
    {
        private DataSeries ds;
        private DataSet dataSet1;

        public Form1()
```

```
{
    InitializeComponent();
    this.SetStyle(ControlStyles.ResizeRedraw, true);
    ComboboxSetup();
    ds = new DataSeries();
    dataSet1 = new DataSet();
    dataGridView1.ColumnHeadersDefaultCellStyle.Alignment =
        DataGridViewContentAlignment.MiddleCenter;
    dataGridView1.RowHeadersDefaultCellStyle.Alignment =
        DataGridViewContentAlignment.MiddleRight;
    dataGridView1.RowHeadersWidth = 70;
}

private void ComboboxSetup()
{
    toolStripComboBox1.Items.Add("Mesh");
    toolStripComboBox1.Items.Add("MeshZ");
    toolStripComboBox1.Items.Add("Waterfall");
    toolStripComboBox1.Items.Add("Surface");
    toolStripComboBox1.Items.Add("XYColor");
    toolStripComboBox1.Items.Add("Contour");
    toolStripComboBox1.Items.Add("Filled Contour");
    toolStripComboBox1.Items.Add("Mesh + Contour");
    toolStripComboBox1.Items.Add("Surface + Contour");
    toolStripComboBox1.Items.Add("Surface + Contour");
    toolStripComboBox1.Items.Add("Surface + Filled Contour");
    toolStripComboBox1.Items.Add("Bar3D");
    toolStripComboBox1.SelectedItem = "Surface";
}

private void ChartTypeSetup()
{
    string chartType =
            toolStripComboBox1.SelectedItem.ToString();
    switch (chartType)
    {
        case "Mesh":
            chart3D1.C3DrawChart.ChartType =
                DrawChart.ChartTypeEnum.Mesh;
            break;
        case "MeshZ":
            chart3D1.C3DrawChart.ChartType =
                DrawChart.ChartTypeEnum.MeshZ;
            break;
        case "Waterfall":
            chart3D1.C3DrawChart.ChartType =
                DrawChart.ChartTypeEnum.Waterfall;
            break;
        case "Surface":
            chart3D1.C3DrawChart.ChartType =
                DrawChart.ChartTypeEnum.Surface;
            break;
        case "XYColor":
            chart3D1.C3DrawChart.ChartType =
```

```
                    DrawChart.ChartTypeEnum.XYColor;
                break;
            case "Contour":
                chart3D1.C3DrawChart.ChartType =
                    DrawChart.ChartTypeEnum.Contour;
                break;
            case "Filled Contour":
                chart3D1.C3DrawChart.ChartType =
                    DrawChart.ChartTypeEnum.FillContour;
                break;
            case "Mesh + Contour":
                chart3D1.C3DrawChart.ChartType =
                    DrawChart.ChartTypeEnum.MeshContour;
                break;
            case "Surface + Contour":
                chart3D1.C3DrawChart.ChartType =
                    DrawChart.ChartTypeEnum.SurfaceContour;
                break;
            case "Surface + Filled Contour":
                chart3D1.C3DrawChart.ChartType =
                    DrawChart.ChartTypeEnum.SurfaceFillContour;
                break;
            case "Bar3D":
                chart3D1.C3DrawChart.ChartType =
                    DrawChart.ChartTypeEnum.Bar3D;
                break;
        }
    }

    protected override void OnPaint(PaintEventArgs e)
    {
        if (dataGridView1.RowCount > 0)
        {
            AddData();
            ChartTypeSetup();
        }
    }

    private void AddData()
    {
        chart3D1.C3Axes.XMin = -3;
        chart3D1.C3Axes.XMax = 3;
        chart3D1.C3Axes.YMin = -3;
        chart3D1.C3Axes.YMax = 3;
        chart3D1.C3Axes.ZMin = -8;
        chart3D1.C3Axes.ZMax = 8;
        chart3D1.C3Axes.XTick = 1;
        chart3D1.C3Axes.YTick = 1;
        chart3D1.C3Axes.ZTick = 4;

        Point3[,] pts = new Point3[
                dataGridView1.Columns.Count - 1,
                dataGridView1.RowCount - 3];
        float x, y, z;
```

```
    for (int i = 1; i < dataGridView1.ColumnCount; i++)
    {
        x = Convert.ToSingle((
                string)dataGridView1[i, 0].Value);
        for (int j = 1; j < dataGridView1.RowCount - 2; j++)
        {
            y = Convert.ToSingle((
                string)dataGridView1[0, j].Value);
            z = Convert.ToSingle((
                string)dataGridView1[i, j].Value);
            pts[i - 1, j - 1] = new Point3(x, y, z, 1);
        }
    }
    chart3D1.C3DataSeries.PointArray = pts;
    chart3D1.C3DataSeries.XDataMin = pts[0, 0].X;
    chart3D1.C3DataSeries.YDataMin = pts[0, 0].Y;
    chart3D1.C3DataSeries.XSpacing =
            pts[1, 0].X - pts[0, 0].X;
    chart3D1.C3DataSeries.YSpacing =
            pts[0, 1].Y - pts[0, 0].Y;
    chart3D1.C3DataSeries.XNumber = pts.GetLength(0);
    chart3D1.C3DataSeries.YNumber = pts.GetLength(1);
}

private void toolStripComboBox1_SelectedIndexChanged(
        object sender, EventArgs e)
{
    this.Invalidate();
}

private void saveTextFileToolStripMenuItem_Click(
    object sender, EventArgs e)
{
    if (dataGridView1.RowCount > 0)
    {
        DataSet2Text.Convert2Text(dataGridView1);
    }
}

private void openTextFileToolStripMenuItem_Click(
    object sender, EventArgs e)
{
    dataSet1 = Text2DataSet.Convert2DataSet("MyDataSet");
    dataGridView1.DataSource = dataSet1;
    dataGridView1.DataMember = "MyDataSet";

    for (int i = 0; i < dataGridView1.ColumnCount; i++)
    {
        dataGridView1.Columns[i].Width = 70;
        dataGridView1.Columns[i].DefaultCellStyle.Alignment =
            DataGridViewContentAlignment.MiddleRight;
    }

    for (int i = 1; i < dataGridView1.RowCount - 2; i++)
```

```
            {
                dataGridView1.Rows[i].HeaderCell.Value =
                     "Y" + i.ToString();
            }
            this.Invalidate();
        }

        private void openXMLFileToolStripMenuItem_Click(
            object sender, EventArgs e)
        {
            dataSet1 = XML2DataSet.Convert2DataSet();
            dataGridView1.DataSource = dataSet1;
            dataGridView1.DataMember = "MyDataSet";

            for (int i = 0; i < dataGridView1.ColumnCount; i++)
            {
                dataGridView1.Columns[i].Width = 70;
                dataGridView1.Columns[i].DefaultCellStyle.Alignment =
                    DataGridViewContentAlignment.MiddleRight;
            }

            for (int i = 0; i < dataGridView1.Rows.Count - 1; i++)
            {
                dataGridView1.Rows[i].HeaderCell.Value =
                (i + 1).ToString();
            }
            this.Invalidate();
        }

        private void saveXMLFileToolStripMenuItem_Click(
            object sender, EventArgs e)
        {
            if (dataGridView1.RowCount > 0)
            {
                DataSet2XML.Convert2XML(dataSet1);
            }
        }
    }
}
```

In this class, the text data file, text3d.txt, created in the previous project is read into the dataGridView1 control with an Open Text File menu click. Then, the AddData method adds data from the dataGridView1 to the Chart3D control.

Next we implement standard menu click event handlers for Open Text, Open XML, Save Text, and Save XML, which are similar to those in the previous project *Example8_2*. Finally, we create a CellValueChanged event for the dataGridView1 that fires when the value of a cell changes. The code snippet:

```
this.Invalidate();
```

ensures that the chart gets redrawn when the cell value changes. Press F5 to run the application. Click the Open Text File menu and select the text file data3d.txt created in the previous example. Select Surface + Filled Contour from the ComboBox. This produces output of Figure 8-9.

Instead of importing a text data file, you can also read an XML file, such as xml3d.xml, which
was created in the previous example, into the dataGridView1 control.

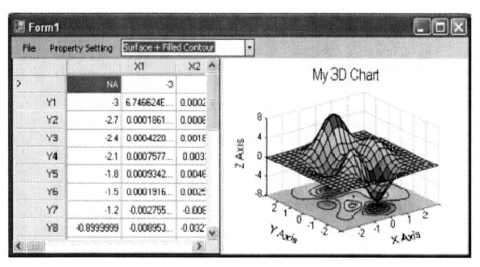

Figure 8-9 Combination of DataGridView and Chart3D controls.

Runtime Support

In this section, we will create runtime support for the DataGridView and Chart3D controls.
This runtime support provides a rich editing experience by allowing the user to interact directly
with the properties of the user controls at runtime. As in the case of 2D applications, we will use
the PropertyGrid control to display and set properties at runtime for any object.

To demonstrate the application of the PropertyGrid in a 3D charting application, we start off
with a new C# Windows Application project, *Example8_7*, based on the previous project. Copy all
of the classes, including Form1.cs, from *Example8_6* to the current project and change their
corresponding namespace to *Example8_7*. Open Form1.Designer.cs, and change the
following code snippet

```
        private Chart3DLib.Chart3D chart3D1;
```

to

```
        public Chart3DLib.Chart3D chart3D1;
```

This changes the chart3D1 control from private to public, indicating that the control can be
accessed from other classes.

Add three new classes, ChartStyle, Axes, and Grid, to the current project. These classes
contain different types of properties for the chart3D1 control. All of the properties in these three
classes will be displayed in the PropertyGrid. The following is the code listing for the
ChartStyle class:

```
using System;
using System.Drawing;
```

```csharp
using System.Drawing.Drawing2D;
using System.ComponentModel;
using Chart3DLib;

namespace Example8_7
{
    public class ChartStyle
    {
        private bool isColorBar = false;
        private string xLabel = "X Axis";
        private string yLabel = "Y Axis";
        private string zLabel = "Z Axis";
        private Font labelFont = new Font("Arial", 10,
                FontStyle.Regular);
        private Color labelFontColor = Color.Black;
        private string title = "My 3D Chart";
        private Font titleFont = new Font("Arial Narrow",
                14, FontStyle.Regular);
        private Color titleColor = Color.Black;

        public ChartStyle()
        {
        }

        [Description("Whether or not the chart has a color bar."),
        Category("Color Bar")]
        public bool IsColorBar
        {
            get { return isColorBar; }
            set { isColorBar = value; }
        }

        [Description("The label for the X axis ."),
        Category("Axis Labels")]
        public string XLabel
        {
            get { return xLabel; }
            set { xLabel = value; }
        }

        [Description("The label for the Y axis ."),
        Category("Axis Labels")]
        public string YLabel
        {
            get { return yLabel; }
            set { yLabel = value; }
        }

        [Description("The label for the Z axis ."),
        Category("Axis Labels")]
        public string ZLabel
        {
            get { return zLabel; }
            set { zLabel = value; }
```

```
        }

        [Description("The font for the axis labels ."),
        Category("Axis Labels")]
        public Font LabelFont
        {
            get { return labelFont; }
            set { labelFont = value; }
        }

        [Description("The color for axis labels ."),
        Category("Axis Labels")]
        public Color LabelFontColor
        {
            get { return labelFontColor; }
            set { labelFontColor = value; }
        }

        [Description("The chart title ."),
        Category("Title")]
        public string Title
        {
            get { return title; }
            set { title = value; }
        }

        [Description("The font for the title."),
        Category("Title")]
        public Font TitleFont
        {
            get { return titleFont; }
            set { titleFont = value; }
        }

        [Description("The color for the title ."),
        Category("Title")]
        public Color TitleColor
        {
            get { return titleColor; }
            set { titleColor = value; }
        }
    }
}
```

This class includes basic chart style properties for the Chart3D control which can be changed by the user at the runtime. These properties can be used to control the appearance of the color bar, labels, and title of a 3D chart. You can add or delete properties from this class according to your application requirements.

The following code is for the AxisLimits class:

```
using System;
using System.Drawing;
using System.Drawing.Drawing2D;
using System.ComponentModel;
```

```csharp
using Chart3DLib;

namespace Example8_7
{
    public class AxisLimits
    {
        private float xMax = 5f;
        private float xMin = -5f;
        private float yMax = 3f;
        private float yMin = -3f;
        private float zMax = 6f;
        private float zMin = -6f;
        private float xTick = 1f;
        private float yTick = 1f;
        private float zTick = 3f;
        private Chart3D chart3d;

        public AxisLimits()
        {
        }

        [Description("Sets the maximum limit for the X axis."),
                Category("Axes"), DefaultValue(5)]
        public float XMax
        {
            get { return xMax; }
            set { xMax = value; }
        }

        [Description("Sets the maximum limit for the X axis."),
        Category("Axes"), DefaultValue(-5)]
        public float XMin
        {
            get { return xMin; }
            set { xMin = value; }
        }

        [Description("Sets the maximum limit for the Y axis."),
        Category("Axes"), DefaultValue(5)]
        public float YMax
        {
            get { return yMax; }
            set { yMax = value; }
        }

        [Description("Sets the maximum limit for the Y axis."),
        Category("Axes"), DefaultValue(-5)]
        public float YMin
        {
            get { return yMin; }
            set { yMin = value; }
        }

        [Description("Sets the maximum limit for the Z axis."),
```

```
            Category("Axes"), DefaultValue(6)]
        public float ZMax
        {
            get { return zMax; }
            set { zMax = value; }
        }

        [Description("Sets the maximum limit for the Z axis."),
        Category("Axes"), DefaultValue(-6)]
        public float ZMin
        {
            get { return zMin; }
            set { zMin = value; }
        }

        [Description("Sets the X ticks."),
        Category("Axes"), DefaultValue(1)]
        public float XTick
        {
            get { return xTick; }
            set { xTick = value; }
        }

        [Description("Sets the Y tick."),
        Category("Axes"), DefaultValue(1)]
        public float YTick
        {
            get { return yTick; }
            set { yTick = value; }
        }

        [Description("Sets the Z ticks."),
        Category("Axes"), DefaultValue(3)]
        public float ZTick
        {
            get { return zTick; }
            set { zTick = value; }
        }
    }
}
```

This class allows users to change the axis properties of the 3D chart at runtime, such as the axis limits and ticks for the X, Y, and Z axes. The following code is for the *GridStyle* class:

```
using System;
using System.Drawing;
using System.Drawing.Drawing2D;
using System.ComponentModel;
using Chart3DLib;

namespace Example8_7
{
    public class GridStyle
    {
        private bool isXGrid = true;
```

```
        private bool isYGrid = true;
        private bool isZGrid = true;

        public GridStyle()
        {
        }

        [Description("Whether the chart has the X grid."),
        Category("Grid")]
        public bool IsXGrid
        {
            get { return isXGrid; }
            set { isXGrid = value; }
        }

        [Description("Whether the chart has the Y grid."),
        Category("Grid")]
        public bool IsYGrid
        {
            get { return isYGrid; }
            set { isYGrid = value; }
        }

        [Description("Whether the chart has the Z grid."),
        Category("Grid")]
        public bool IsZGrid
        {
            get { return isZGrid; }
            set { isZGrid = value; }
        }
    }
}
```

You can display or hide the gridlines for the individual coordinate axes of a 3D chart by setting the *GridStyle* properties at runtime using this class.

Next, add a new Window Form named SetProperties to the current project and set its Text property to Runtime Properties Editor.

In order to add a PropertyGrid control to the SetProperties Form, we need to add the PropertyGrid to the toolbox because it is not included by default. From the Tools menu, select Choose Toolbox Items…. In the dialog box, select the Framework Components tab, then PropertyGrid.

Now drag the PropertyGrid control onto the SetProperties form and add two button controls. Set one button's name to btnOK and its Text property to OK. Set the other button's name to btnClose and its Text property to Close. The following is the code listing of the SetProperties class:

```
using System;
using System.ComponentModel;
using System.Data;
using System.Drawing;
using System.Windows.Forms;
```

```
namespace Example8_7
{
    public partial class SetProperties : Form
    {
        private Form1 form1;
        private ChartStyle cs;
        private AxisLimits al;
        private GridStyle gs;
        private string sProperty;

        public SetProperties(Form1 fm1, ChartStyle chartStyle, string sproperty)
        {
            InitializeComponent();
            form1 = fm1;
            sProperty = sproperty;
            cs = chartStyle;
            propertyGrid1.SelectedObject = cs;
        }

        public SetProperties(Form1 fm1, AxisLimits axisLimits, string sproperty)
        {
            InitializeComponent();
            form1 = fm1;
            sProperty = sproperty;
            al = axisLimits;
            propertyGrid1.SelectedObject = al;
        }

        public SetProperties(Form1 fm1, GridStyle gridStyle, string sproperty)
        {
            InitializeComponent();
            form1 = fm1;
            sProperty = sproperty;
            gs = gridStyle;
            propertyGrid1.SelectedObject = gs;
        }

        private void btnOK_Click(object sender, EventArgs e)
        {
            if (sProperty == "ChartStyle")
            {
                Chart3DSettings();
            }
            else if (sProperty == "AxisLimits")
            {
                AxisLimitSettings();
            }
            else if (sProperty == "GridStyle")
            {
                GridSettings();
            }
            form1.Invalidate();
        }
```

```
        private void Chart3DSettings()
        {
            form1.chart3D1.C3ChartStyle.IsColorBar = cs.IsColorBar;
            form1.chart3D1.C3Labels.XLabel = cs.XLabel;
            form1.chart3D1.C3Labels.YLabel = cs.YLabel;
            form1.chart3D1.C3Labels.ZLabel = cs.ZLabel;
            form1.chart3D1.C3Labels.LabelFont = cs.LabelFont;
            form1.chart3D1.C3Labels.LabelFontColor = cs.LabelFontColor;
            form1.chart3D1.C3Labels.Title = cs.Title;
            form1.chart3D1.C3Labels.TitleFont = cs.TitleFont;
            form1.chart3D1.C3Labels.TitleColor = cs.TitleColor;
        }

        private void AxisLimitSettings()
        {
            form1.chart3D1.C3Axes.XMax = al.XMax;
            form1.chart3D1.C3Axes.XMin = al.XMin;
            form1.chart3D1.C3Axes.YMax = al.YMax;
            form1.chart3D1.C3Axes.YMin = al.YMin;
            form1.chart3D1.C3Axes.ZMax = al.ZMax;
            form1.chart3D1.C3Axes.ZMin = al.ZMin;
            form1.chart3D1.C3Axes.XTick = al.XTick;
            form1.chart3D1.C3Axes.YTick = al.YTick;
            form1.chart3D1.C3Axes.ZTick = al.ZTick;
        }

        private void GridSettings()
        {
            form1.chart3D1.C3Grid.IsXGrid = gs.IsXGrid;
            form1.chart3D1.C3Grid.IsYGrid = gs.IsYGrid;
            form1.chart3D1.C3Grid.IsZGrid = gs.IsZGrid;
        }

        private void btnClose_Click(object sender, EventArgs e)
        {
            this.Close();
        }
    }
}
```

There are three overloaded constructors in this class, which are used to assign instances of the *ChartStyle*, *AxisLimits*, and *GridStyle* classes to the PropertyGrid. This is done using the SelectObject property of the PropertyGrid:

```
            propertyGrid1.SelectedObject = cs;
            propertyGrid1.SelectedObject = al;
            propertyGrid1.SelectedObject = gs;
```

This way, the PropertyGrid can automatically figure out all of the fields of the *ChartStyle*, *AxisLimits*, or *GridStyle* through reflection, and display the property name along with the property value on each line of the PropertyGrid.

The `Form1` class is basically the same as it was in the previous example, with a few modifications. We add a Property Setting menu that includes the Chart Style, Axes, and Grid. The click event handlers for these three items will open the `PropertyGrid` window. Here is the code listing of the `Form1` class:

```csharp
using System;
using System.ComponentModel;
using System.Data;
using System.Drawing;
using System.Windows.Forms;

namespace Example8_7
{
    public partial class SetProperties : Form
    {
        private Form1 form1;
        private ChartStyle cs;
        private AxisLimits al;
        private GridStyle gs;
        private string sProperty;

        public SetProperties(Form1 fm1, ChartStyle chartStyle, string sproperty)
        {
            InitializeComponent();
            form1 = fm1;
            sProperty = sproperty;
            cs = chartStyle;
            propertyGrid1.SelectedObject = cs;
        }

        public SetProperties(Form1 fm1, AxisLimits axisLimits, string sproperty)
        {
            InitializeComponent();
            form1 = fm1;
            sProperty = sproperty;
            al = axisLimits;
            propertyGrid1.SelectedObject = al;
        }

        public SetProperties(Form1 fm1, GridStyle gridStyle, string sproperty)
        {
            InitializeComponent();
            form1 = fm1;
            sProperty = sproperty;
            gs = gridStyle;
            propertyGrid1.SelectedObject = gs;
        }

        private void btnOK_Click(object sender, EventArgs e)
        {
            if (sProperty == "ChartStyle")
            {
                Chart3DSettings();
            }
```

```
            else if (sProperty == "AxisLimits")
            {
                AxisLimitSettings();
            }
            else if (sProperty == "GridStyle")
            {
                GridSettings();
            }
            form1.Invalidate();
        }

        private void Chart3DSettings()
        {
            form1.chart3D1.C3ChartStyle.IsColorBar = cs.IsColorBar;
            form1.chart3D1.C3Labels.XLabel = cs.XLabel;
            form1.chart3D1.C3Labels.YLabel = cs.YLabel;
            form1.chart3D1.C3Labels.ZLabel = cs.ZLabel;
            form1.chart3D1.C3Labels.LabelFont = cs.LabelFont;
            form1.chart3D1.C3Labels.LabelFontColor = cs.LabelFontColor;
            form1.chart3D1.C3Labels.Title = cs.Title;
            form1.chart3D1.C3Labels.TitleFont = cs.TitleFont;
            form1.chart3D1.C3Labels.TitleColor = cs.TitleColor;
        }

        private void AxisLimitSettings()
        {
            form1.chart3D1.C3Axes.XMax = al.XMax;
            form1.chart3D1.C3Axes.XMin = al.XMin;
            form1.chart3D1.C3Axes.YMax = al.YMax;
            form1.chart3D1.C3Axes.YMin = al.YMin;
            form1.chart3D1.C3Axes.ZMax = al.ZMax;
            form1.chart3D1.C3Axes.ZMin = al.ZMin;
            form1.chart3D1.C3Axes.XTick = al.XTick;
            form1.chart3D1.C3Axes.YTick = al.YTick;
            form1.chart3D1.C3Axes.ZTick = al.ZTick;
        }

        private void GridSettings()
        {
            form1.chart3D1.C3Grid.IsXGrid = gs.IsXGrid;
            form1.chart3D1.C3Grid.IsYGrid = gs.IsYGrid;
            form1.chart3D1.C3Grid.IsZGrid = gs.IsZGrid;
        }
        private void btnClose_Click(object sender, EventArgs e)
        {
            this.Close();
        }
    }
}
```

Figure 8-10 Chart style Properties of Chart3D control displayed in
PropertyGrid.

Press F5 to run and test the application. Open the text file text3d.txt created in the previous project
Example8_5. This produces output similar to Figure 8-9. Now click the Property Setting menu,
and select Chart Style item to open the `PropertyGrid` window, as shown in Figure 8-10. From
this window, you can set the chart style properties for the Chart3D control at runtime. After
changing the values of the properties, you click the OK button to make the changes take effect.
For instance, setting the `IsColorBar` property to true will generate a 3D chart with a color bar,
as shown in Figure 8-11.

Similarly, you can select `Axes` or `Grid` from the Property Setting menu to open the
corresponding `PropertyGrid` window, which allows you to set the properties of the axis limits
or the grid line style for the 3D chart control at runtime.

Here we introduced an approach to create runtime support for a 3D chart control and intentionally
separate the chart style, axis limits, and grid style properties into three different `PropertyGrid`
windows. In practical applications, you may want to arrange these properties differently according
to the requirements of your applications. You can easily create your own professional C# chart
applications with sophisticated runtime support using the methods explained in this chapter.

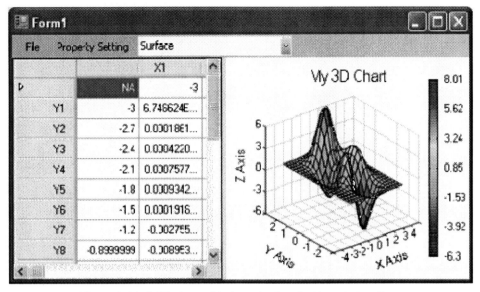

Figure 8-11 A 3D chart with the color bar that is set at runtime.

9

Excel Charts in C# Applications

In the previous chapters, we have shown how to create various graphics and charts, as well as corresponding user controls, in C# applications. However, if you still believe it is too time-consuming to create C# chart and graphics programs from scratch, then finding development shortcuts can save valuable time. One way to achieve this goal is to take advantage of existing products as opposed to developing everything from scratch. Microsoft Excel is one product you should consider because it offers a wide selection of standard graphics and chart types, each with several subtypes. Using Excel's built-in chart features directly in C# applications is a practical development shortcut.

Microsoft Visual Studio .NET makes it possible for you to create rich Microsoft Excel-based applications based on the C# framework. You can take advantage of all of the functionality provided by Excel's large object models in C# applications. In this chapter, we will represent the chart types in Excel, and show you how to select and modify the built in chart-types and create the stand-alone and embedded Excel charts in a C# project. We will also provide a variety of examples that demonstrate how to create various Excel charts you can directly modify to fit your real-world C# applications.

Excel and C# Interoperability

In order for Excel to be used in C# applications, you have to resolve the issue of interoperation between C# and Excel. Excel application can be regarded as a COM server, so the basis of interoperation between C# and Excel applications is COM Interop. The .NET framework provides good support for interaction with COM components. To use Excel COM components in a C# project, you simply need to add this COM component to reference. This can be done by right clicking the project in the Solution Explorer and selecting Add Reference. Click the COM tab and select the appropriate type of Object library depending on the version of the Microsoft Office you are using:

- Office 97: Microsoft Excel 8.0 Object Library
- Office 2000: Microsoft Excel 9.0 Object Library
- Office XP: Microsoft Excel 10.0 Object Library
- Office 2003: Microsoft Excel 11.0 Object Library

After this step, you should find that references have been added for the Office Core and Excel as well.

Next, we will use a simple example to demonstrate how to involve Excel in a C# application. In this example, we will create a Windows Form application with two buttons on `Form1`. One button is used to start Excel, and the other to quit Excel and close `Form1`. Clicking the Start Excel button will launch Excel, add a new workbook to the collection of workbooks, get Active Sheet, and put data into Excel cells.

Let's start off with a new C# Windows application project called *Example9_1*. Put two Button controls on `Form1` and set their Text properties to Start Excel and Close. In the Solution Explorer, right-click and select Add Reference. Click the COM tab. For the Office XP that I am using, I will select the Microsoft Excel 10.0 Object Library from the list.

Add a using statement for Excel:

```
using Excel;
```

Add a private property field for the Excel Application:

```
Private Excel.Application;
```

And instantiate the Excel Application inside `Form1`'s constructor:

```
xla = new Excel.Application();
```

In the Start Excel button Click handler, make the Excel Application object `xla` visible. Add a workbook to the collection of workbooks and get the active worksheet:

```
Workbook wb = xla.Workbooks.Add(xlsheettype.xlworksheet);
Worksheet ws = (Worksheet)wb.ActiveSheet;
```

Specify the cell Range A2, B2, and C2 and set their values to some arbitrary data:

```
Range rg = (Range)ws.Cells[2, 1];
rg.Value2 = "CellA2";
rg = (Range)ws.Cells[2, 2];
rg.Value2 = "CellB2";
```

```
rg = (Range)ws.Cells[2, 3];
rg.Value2 = "CellC2";
```

In the Close button Click handler, add the following code snippet:

```
xla.DisplayAlerts = false;
if (xla != null)
  {
    xla.Quit();
    xla = null;
  }
  this.Close();
```

When you quit Excel, you will get the usual prompt about saving your changes, which might be hidden behind the main Excel window. In order to avoid receiving this message box, we have inserted the following code snippet in the Close button handler:

```
xla.DisplayAlerts = false;
```

For your reference, we present the complete code listing of the Form1 class here:

```
using System;
using System.Windows.Forms;
using Excel;

namespace Example9_1
{
    public partial class Form1 : Form
    {
        private Excel.Application xla;

        public Form1()
        {
            InitializeComponent();
            xla = new Excel.Application();
        }

        private void btnStartExcel_Click(object sender, EventArgs e)
        {
            xla.Visible = true;
            Workbook wb = xla.Workbooks.Add(XlSheetType.xlWorksheet);
            Worksheet ws = (Worksheet)xla.ActiveSheet;
            Range rg = (Range)ws.Cells[2, 1];
            rg.Value2 = "Cell2A";
            rg = (Range)ws.Cells[2, 2];
            rg.Value2 = "Cell2B";
            rg = (Range)ws.Cells[2, 3];
            rg.Value2 = "Cell2C";
        }

        private void btnClose_Click(object sender, EventArgs e)
        {
            xla.DisplayAlerts = false;
            if (xla != null)
            {
                xla.Quit();
```

```
                    xla = null;
                }
                this.Close();
            }
        }
    }
```

Press F5 to build and run the project. Click the Start Excel button to bring up the Excel application, as shown in Figure 9-1.

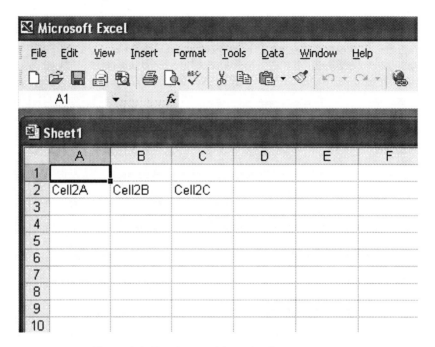

Figure 9-1 Excel started from the C# application.

Simple Excel Charts in C# Applications

Microsoft Excel has many types of charts, including bar charts, line charts, pie charts, 3D charts, and so on. It supports almost all the basic chart types and even some esoteric chart types, such as radar charts and stock charts. In this section, we will discuss the simple Excel chart types and show you how to use these chart types in a C# application.

Excel Chart Object Model

When you try to create Excel charts in a C# application, you need to work with standard Excel worksheets, because Excel charts are implicitly tied to the worksheets. One or more cells on worksheets are used as the chart's data source. Therefore, you need to be familiar with Excel objects as well as their related chart objects, which include the following:

- *Application*: represents the entire Excel application.

- *Workbook*: a single Excel workbook that may contain one or more worksheets.

- *Worksheet*: an individual Excel worksheet.

- *Range*: a range of cells within a worksheet.

- *Chart*: a single Excel chart. Its `ChartType` property specifies the type of chart to be created.

- *Charts*: a collection of Excel Sheet objects (the parent of both the Chart and Worksheet objects) containing references to each of the charts contained in the active workbook. In addition, it contains an Add method for adding a new chart to the workbook.

The Excel Chart object can have either of two different parent objects. The parent object of an Excel chart on a Chart sheet is the Workbook object that contains the Chart sheet. The object hierarchy is

```
Workbook
     Chart
```

This Excel Chart model can be accessed using the following C# code snippet:

```
Excel.Application xla = new Excel.Application();
Workbook wb = xla.Workbooks.Add(XlSheetType.xlWorksheet);
Chart xlChart = wb.Charts.Add();
```

Here, we first create a new Excel application, add a Workbook to the collection of Workbooks, then add Chart to the collections of Charts in the Workbook.

The parent object of an embedded chart is a `ChartObject` object. The parent of a `ChartObject` object is a `Worksheet`. The object hierarchy for an embedded chart is:

```
Workbook
     Worksheet
          ChartObject
               Chart
```

In this case, the corresponding C# code becomes:

```
Excel.Application xla = new Excel.Application();
Workbooks wb = xla.Workbooks.Add(XlSheetType.xlWorksheet);
Worksheet ws = (Worksheet)xla.ActiveSheet;
ChartObjects chartObjs = (ChartObjects)ws.ChartObjects(missing);
ChartObject chartObj = chartObjs.Add();
```

Here, we first create a new Excel application, add a workbook to the collection of workbooks, and get the active worksheet. Then, we create a collection of `ChartObjects` in the Worksheet, and add the `ChartObject` to the collection of `ChartObjects`.

An Excel `Chart` object can contain other objects too. Following is a partial object hierarchy for a `Chart` object:

```
Chart
     ChartArea
     PlotArea
     ChartTitle
     Legend
     Axes
     SeriesCollection
```

These `Chart` objects can be accessed from a C# application. For example, the `ChartArea` object can be accessed through `chart.ChartArea` (for embedded Excel charts, use `chartObject.Chart.ChartArea`), and so on.

These `Chart` objects, in turn, can contain other objects. Assume that you want to use C# code to set the chart title of an Excel chart. The following code snippet does the job:

```
chart.ChartTitle.Text = "Excel Chart in C#";
```

Creating Stand-Alone Excel Charts

An Excel chart can either be an embedded chart (contained in a chart object) or a separate chart sheet (stand-alone chart).

In this subsection, we will use an example to show how to create a simple stand-alone Excel 2D XY chart in a C# application. In this example, we will create a Windows Form application with two buttons on the `Form1`. One button is used to plot the Excel chart, while the other is used to quit Excel and close `Form1`.

Let's start off with a new C# Windows application project called *Example9_2*. Place two Button controls on the `Form1` and set their Text properties to Plot and Close. In the Solution Explorer, right-click and select Add Reference. Click the COM tab and select the corresponding Microsoft Excel Object Library from the list.

Add a using statement for Excel:

```
using Excel;
```

Create an Excel Application property field:

```
Private Excel.Application xla;
```

Initialize `xla` inside `Form1`'s constructor:

```
Xla = new Excel.Application();
```

In the Plot button Click handler, add the following code snippet:

```
private void btnPlot_Click(object sender, EventArgs e)
{
    xla.Visible = true;
    Workbook wb = xla.Workbooks.Add(XlSheetType.xlWorksheet);
    Worksheet ws = (Worksheet)xla.ActiveSheet;

    // Create a stand-alone Excel chart:
    Chart xlChart = (Chart)wb.Charts.Add(Type.Missing, ws,
        Type.Missing, Type.Missing);

    int nRows = 25;
    int nColumns = 3;
    string upperLeftCell = "A1";
    int endRowNumber = System.Int32.Parse(upperLeftCell.Substring(1))
        + nRows - 1;
    char endColumnLetter = System.Convert.ToChar(
        Convert.ToInt32(upperLeftCell[0]) + nColumns - 1);
```

```
        string upperRightCell = System.String.Format("{0}{1}",
            endColumnLetter, System.Int32.Parse(upperLeftCell.Substring(1)));
        string lowerRightCell = System.String.Format("{0}{1}",
            endColumnLetter, endRowNumber);
        Range rg = ws.get_Range(upperLeftCell,lowerRightCell);
        rg.Value2 = AddData(nRows,nColumns);
        xlChart.ChartType = XlChartType.xlXYScatterLines;
        xlChart.SetSourceData(rg,XlRowCol.xlColumns);
}

private double[,] AddData(int nRows, int nColumns)
{
        double[,] dataArray = new double[nRows, nColumns];
        for (int i = 0; i < nRows; i++)
        {
            double x = i / 3.0;
            dataArray[i, 0] = x;
            dataArray[i, 1] = Math.Sin(x);
            dataArray[i, 2] = Math.Cos(x);
        }
        return dataArray;
}
```

In this Plot button handler event, we first make the Excel Application object xla visible, then create the Workbook and Worksheet that are used to hold the chart. Next, we create a new Excel chart on the Worksheet ws by calling the Add method of the Charts collection:

```
Chart xlChart = (Chart)wb.Charts.Add(Type.Missing, ws,
        Type.Missing, Type.Missing);
```

In the above code snippet, Type.Missing is used. This is because the above Excel method requires multiple optional parameters that describe the behavior of the Excel chart you are creating. In C#, you can only pass the Type.Missing value for parameters that accept reference types. However, for value-type parameters, you need to determine the actual default value and pass that value instead.

The following code is used to populate the Excel worksheet with a 2D data array that is generated by the AddData method. We specify the number of Rows and Columns of the data, as well as which cell is in the upper left. We then determine the corresponding bottom right cell using this information.

Next, we use parameters of the upperLeftCell and bottomRightCell to set the Cell Range of the data and assign the data array to this Cell Range, as shown in the code snippet:

```
Range rg = ws.get_Range(upperLeftCell,lowerRightCell);
rg.Value2 = AddData(nRows,nColumns);
```

Finally, we set the chart type and the data source:

```
xlChart.ChartType = XlChartType.xlXYScatterLines;
xlChart.SetSourceData(rg,XlRowCol.xlColumns);
```

If you press F5 to run the program, you will obtain an Excel worksheet that holds the plotted data, and a separate (stand-alone) Excel chart, as shown in Figure 9-2.

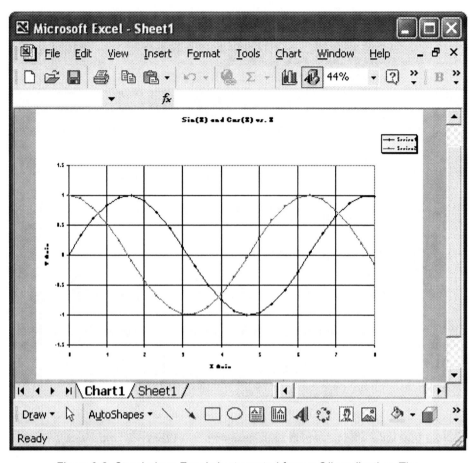

Figure 9-2 Stand-alone Excel chart created from a C# application. The
chart is separated from the sheet1 that holds the plot data.

After creating an Excel chart, you can easily customize it. The following code snippet is used to
customize the Axes property:

```
// Customize axes:
Axis xAxis = (Axis)xlChart.Axes(XlAxisType.xlCategory,
    XlAxisGroup.xlPrimary);
xAxis.HasMajorGridlines = true;
xAxis.MaximumScale = 8;
xAxis.HasTitle = true;
xAxis.AxisTitle.Text = "X Axis";

Axis yAxis = (Axis)xlChart.Axes(XlAxisType.xlValue, XlAxisGroup.xlPrimary);
yAxis.HasMajorGridlines = true;
yAxis.CrossesAt = -1.5;
yAxis.HasTitle = true;
yAxis.AxisTitle.Text = "Y Axis";
```

Please note that the X and Y axes are specified by XlAxisType.xlCategory and XlAxisType.xlValue respectively. We turn on the major grid lines and assign axis labels for both axes. We also shift the X axis from the default location (crosses at Y = 0) to the minimum Y value of -1.5 with the code snippet:

```
yAxis.CrossesAt = -1.5;
```

It is also easy to add a title to your chart:

```
// Add title:
xlChart.HasTitle = true;
xlChart.ChartTitle.Text = "Sin(X) and Cos(X) vs. X";
```

The following code listing is used to customize the legend:

```
// Customize legend:
xlChart.HasLegend = true;
xlChart.Legend.Position = XlLegendPosition.xlLegendPositionCorner;
xlChart.Legend.Shadow = true;
xlChart.Legend.Interior.ColorIndex = 20;
```

There are many other chart properties that can easily be modified for Excel charts. We will leave the rest for you to practice using the current C# project Example9_2 as a basis.

Creating Embedded Excel Charts

As the name implies, embedded Excel charts are created as part of the worksheet instead of a separate chart. In this section, we will present an example that uses the Chart Wizard to generate an embedded Excel chart in a C# application.

Start off with a new C# project called *Example9_3*. Add the existing Form1 class from the previous example to the current application and change its namespace to *Example9_3*. Add the Microsoft Excel Object Library to the reference.

Creating an embedded Excel chart in a C# application is very simple. Just change the code snippet within the Plot button click handler of the previous project

```
// Create a stand-alone Excel chart:
Chart xlChart = (Chart)wb.Charts.Add(Type.Missing, ws,
    Type.Missing, Type.Missing);
```

to the following

```
// Now create the chart.
ChartObjects chartObjs = (ChartObjects)ws.ChartObjects(Type.Missing);
ChartObject chartObj = chartObjs.Add(20, 20, 400, 300);
Chart xlChart = chartObj.Chart;
```

Here, we add a chart object chartObj to the collection of ChartObjects, in which we define the location and size of the chart in the active worksheet. This project produces the results of Figure 9-3.

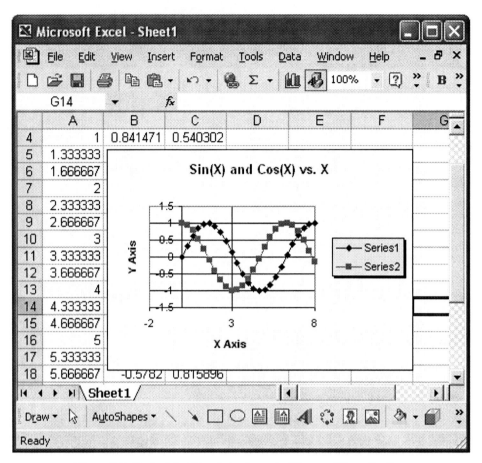

Figure 9-3 Embedded Excel chart created from a C# application.

More Excel Charts

In the previous section, we showed you how to create stand-alone and embedded Excel XY scatter line charts in a C# application. In fact, the Excel chart object model contains many more chart types, including area charts, bar charts, column charts, line charts, pie charts, doughnut charts, radar charts, surface charts, bubble charts, stock charts, and so on. Each chart type, in turn, contains a different number of subtypes.

When you use the Excel Chart Wizard to create a chart, the first step is to select the type of chart. The Chart Wizard dialog box contains two tabs: Standard Types and Custom Types. Selecting an item from the Chart type list box displays a number of subtypes for the chart type. These rich Excel chart types can also be accessed from a C# application. In the following subsections, we will explore some commonly used Excel charts and show you how to create them in a C# application.

Column and Bar Charts

Excel column (also called vertical) bar charts are one of the most common chart types. A column chart displays each data point as a vertical column with the bar height corresponding to the value. The value scale is shown on the vertical axis. You can specify any number of data series, and the corresponding data points from each series can be stacked on top of each other. Usually, each data series is plotted in a different color or pattern. A horizontal bar chart is basically a column chart that is rotated 90 degrees clockwise.

Let's start off with a new C# Windows application called *Example9_4*. Add the Microsoft Excel Object Library to the reference and implement the following code listing to the Form1 class:

```csharp
using System;
using System.Windows.Forms;
using Excel;

namespace Example9_4
{
    public partial class Form1 : Form
    {
        private Excel.Application xla;

        public Form1()
        {
            InitializeComponent();
            xla = new Excel.Application();
        }

        private void btnPlot_Click(object sender, EventArgs e)
        {
            xla.Visible = true;
            Workbook wb = xla.Workbooks.Add(XlSheetType.xlWorksheet);
            Worksheet ws = (Worksheet)xla.ActiveSheet;

            // Now create the chart.
            ChartObjects chartObjs =
                    (ChartObjects)ws.ChartObjects(Type.Missing);
            ChartObject chartObj = chartObjs.Add(100, 20, 300, 200);
            Chart xlChart = chartObj.Chart;

            int nRows = 6;
            int nColumns = 3;
            string upperLeftCell = "A2";
            int endRowNumber =
                System.Int32.Parse(upperLeftCell.Substring(1))
                + nRows - 1;
            char endColumnLetter = System.Convert.ToChar(
                Convert.ToInt32(upperLeftCell[0]) + nColumns - 1);
            string upperRightCell = System.String.Format("{0}{1}",
                endColumnLetter,
                System.Int32.Parse(upperLeftCell.Substring(1)));
            string lowerRightCell = System.String.Format("{0}{1}",
                endColumnLetter, endRowNumber);
            Range rg = ws.get_Range(upperLeftCell, lowerRightCell);
```

```csharp
        rg.Value2 = AddData(nRows,nColumns);

        ws.Cells[1, 1] = "Year";
        ws.Cells[1, 2] = "Revenue";
        ws.Cells[1, 3] = "Profit";
        Range rgn = ws.get_Range("A1", "C7");

        xlChart.ChartWizard(rgn.CurrentRegion, Constants.xlColumn,
            Type.Missing, Type.Missing, 1, 1,
            true, "Revenue & Profit",
            Type.Missing, Type.Missing, Type.Missing);

        Axis xAxis = (Axis)xlChart.Axes(XlAxisType.xlCategory,
            XlAxisGroup.xlPrimary);
        xAxis.HasTitle = true;
        xAxis.AxisTitle.Text = "Year";

        Axis yAxis = (Axis)xlChart.Axes(XlAxisType.xlValue,
            XlAxisGroup.xlPrimary);
        yAxis.HasTitle = true;
        yAxis.AxisTitle.Text = "Dollars (M)";
    }

private double[,] AddData(int nRows, int nColumns)
{
    double[,] dataArray = new double[nRows, nColumns];
    dataArray[0, 0] = 2001;
    dataArray[1, 0] = 2002;
    dataArray[2, 0] = 2003;
    dataArray[3, 0] = 2004;
    dataArray[4, 0] = 2005;
    dataArray[5, 0] = 2006;
    dataArray[0, 1] = 5;
    dataArray[1, 1] = 11;
    dataArray[2, 1] = 7;
    dataArray[3, 1] = 14;
    dataArray[4, 1] = 16;
    dataArray[5, 1] = 18;
    dataArray[0, 2] = 1.8;
    dataArray[1, 2] = 4.2;
    dataArray[2, 2] = 2.7;
    dataArray[3, 2] = 6.5;
    dataArray[4, 2] = 7.1;
    dataArray[5, 2] = 7.8;
    return dataArray;
}

private void btnClose_Click(object sender, EventArgs e)
{
    xla.DisplayAlerts = false;
    if (xla != null)
    {
        xla.Quit();
        xla = null;
```

```
        }
        this.Close();
      }
    }
  }
```

The above code is very similar to the code used in the previous project, *Example9_3*. Here we create data that represents a company's annual revenue and profit. In creating the Excel column chart, we use the `ChartWizard`:

```
xlChart.ChartWizard(rgn.CurrentRegion, Constants.xlColumn,
    Type.Missing, Type.Missing, 1, 1,
    true, "Revenue & Profit",
    Type.Missing, Type.Missing, Type.Missing);
```

The ChartWizard method is defined as the following:

```
public void ChartWizard (
    [OptionalAttribute] Object Source,
    [OptionalAttribute] Object Gallery,
    [OptionalAttribute] Object Format,
    [OptionalAttribute] Object PlotBy,
    [OptionalAttribute] Object CategoryLabels,
    [OptionalAttribute] Object SeriesLabels,
    [OptionalAttribute] Object HasLegend,
    [OptionalAttribute] Object Title,
    [OptionalAttribute] Object CategoryTitle,
    [OptionalAttribute] Object ValueTitle,
    [OptionalAttribute] Object ExtraTitle
)
```

You can use this method to modify the properties of Excel charts and format the charts without setting all of the individual properties. Here, we specify five parameters of this method. First we defined the source that contains the data range for the Excel chart. We also specified the Gallery that represents the chart type. The `CategoryLabels` and `SeriesLabels` specify the number of rows or columns that are used as labels. The first row and the first column are used as labels for the series and category, respectively. Finally, we defined the chart title with the Title parameter.

The output of this project is shown in Figure 9-4.

A horizontal bar chart can be generated using the same code except for a change in the chart type:

```
xlChart.ChartWizard(rgn.CurrentRegion, Constants.xlBar,
    Type.Missing, Type.Missing, 1, 1,
    true, "Revenue & Profit",
    Type.Missing, Type.Missing, Type.Missing);
```

Here the chart type has been changed from `xlColumn` to `xlBar`. Now if you run the project, you will get a horizontal bar chart.

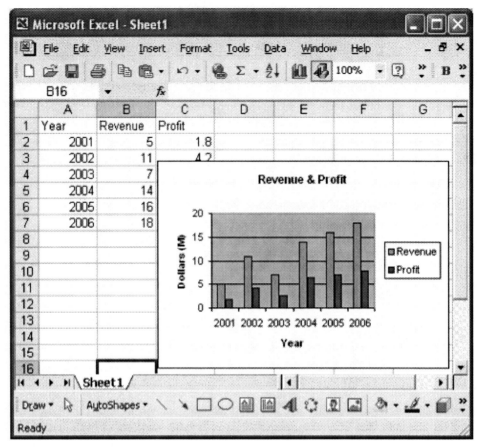

Figure 9-4 The Excel column chart compares a company's revenue and profit.

Pie Charts

Pie charts are useful when you want to represent relative proportions or contributions to a whole. Please note that a pie chart can use only one data series, and that the data values used in the pie chart must all be positive. Pie charts are most effective with a small number of data points.

We will use an example to show how to create an Excel pie chart in a C# application. This application is similar to the previous project. Start off with a new C# Windows Form project called *Example9_5* and add the Excel reference to the project. The following is the code listing of the Form1 class:

```
using System;
using System.Windows.Forms;
using Excel;

namespace Example9_5
{
```

```csharp
public partial class Form1 : Form
{
    private Excel.Application xla;

    public Form1()
    {
        InitializeComponent();
        xla = new Excel.Application();
    }

    private object missing = Missing.Value;

    private void btnPlot_Click(object sender, EventArgs e)
    {
        xla.Visible = true;
        Workbook wb = xla.Workbooks.Add(XlSheetType.xlWorksheet);
        Worksheet ws = (Worksheet)xla.ActiveSheet;

        // Now create the chart.
        ChartObjects chartObjs =
                (ChartObjects)ws.ChartObjects(Type.Missing);
        ChartObject chartObj = chartObjs.Add(100, 20, 300, 200);
        Chart xlChart = chartObj.Chart;

        ws.Cells[1, 1] = "Soc. Sec. Tax";
        ws.Cells[2, 1] = "Income Tax";
        ws.Cells[3, 1] = "Brorrowing";
        ws.Cells[4, 1] = "Corp. Tax";
        ws.Cells[5, 1] = "Misc.";
        ws.Cells[1, 2] = 30;
        ws.Cells[2, 2] = 36;
        ws.Cells[3, 2] = 19;
        ws.Cells[4, 2] = 5;
        ws.Cells[5, 2] = 10;
        Range rg = ws.get_Range("A1", "B5");

        xlChart.ChartType = XlChartType.xlPie;
        xlChart.SetSourceData(rg, Type.Missing);
    }

    private void btnClose_Click(object sender, EventArgs e)
    {
        xla.DisplayAlerts = false;
        if (xla != null)
        {
            xla.Quit();
            xla = null;
        }
        this.Close();
    }
}
}
```

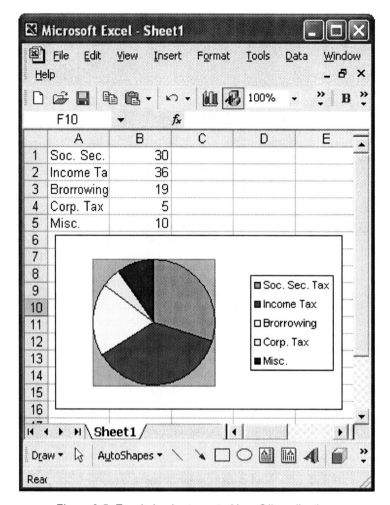

Figure 9-5 Excel pie chart created in a C# application.

Here, we create two columns of data that reside in the range A1:B5 of the Excel worksheet, and set this to the source data. Then we specify the chart type as an Excel pie chart:

```
xlChart.ChartType = XlChartType.xlPie;
xlChart.SetSourceData(rg,Type.Missing);
```

There are several subtypes of the pie charts that you can use in your application:

- xlPie: creates a standard pie chart.

- xl3DPie: creates a pie chart with the appearance of perspective.

- xlPieOfPie: creates a pie chart with one slice broken into another pie chart.

- xlPieExploded: creates a pie chart with one or more slices exploded.

- xl3DPieExploded: creates a pie chart with the appearance of perspective, with one or more slices exploded.

- xlBarOfPie: creates a pie chart with one slice broken into a column.

You can create different type of pie charts easily using the current application by specifying the corresponding chart type.

Running the current project creates the standard Excel pie chart, as shown in Figure 9-5.

Area Charts

Area charts can be regarded as line charts in which the area below the line is colored. An area chart allows the user to generate a filled area plot from data in the Excel worksheet. There are six subtypes of area charts:

- xlArea: creates a standard area chart.

- xlAreaStacked: createsan area chart with stacked data series.

- xlAreaStacked100: creates an area chart represented as percentage.

- xl3DArea: creates a 3D area chart.

- xl3DAreaStacked: creates a 3D area chart with stacked data series.

- xl3DAreaStacked100: creates a 3D area chart expressed as percentage.

Based on *Example9_5*, we can create a stacked area chart by changing the Form1 class with the following code:

```
using System;
using System.Windows.Forms;
using Excel;

namespace Example9_5
{
    public partial class Form1 : Form
    {
        private Excel.Application xla;

        public Form1()
        {
            InitializeComponent();
            xla = new Excel.Application();
        }

        private object missing = Missing.Value;

        private void btnPlot_Click(object sender, EventArgs e)
        {
            xla.Visible = true;
            Workbook wb = xla.Workbooks.Add(XlSheetType.xlWorksheet);
            Worksheet ws = (Worksheet)xla.ActiveSheet;

            // Now create the chart.
            ChartObjects chartObjs =
                    (ChartObjects)ws.ChartObjects(Type.Missing);
            ChartObject chartObj = chartObjs.Add(100, 20, 300, 200);
```

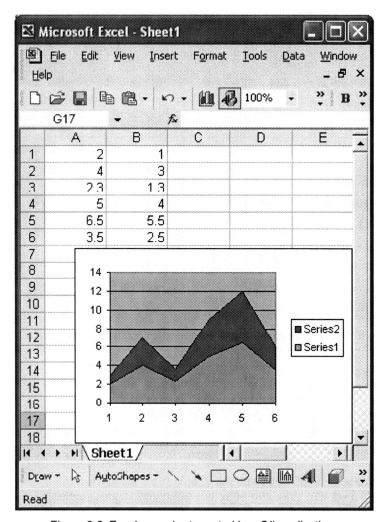

Figure 9-6 Excel area chart created in a C# application.

```
Chart xlChart = chartObj.Chart;

        ws.Cells[1, 1] = 2;
        ws.Cells[2, 1] = 4;
        ws.Cells[3, 1] = 2.3;
        ws.Cells[4, 1] = 5;
        ws.Cells[5, 1] = 6.5;
        ws.Cells[6, 1] = 3.5;
        ws.Cells[1, 2] = 1;
        ws.Cells[2, 2] = 3;
        ws.Cells[3, 2] = 1.3;
        ws.Cells[4, 2] = 4;
        ws.Cells[5, 2] = 5.5;
        ws.Cells[6, 2] = 2.5;
```

```
            Range rg = ws.get_Range("A1", "B6");

            xlChart.ChartType = XlChartType.xlAreaStacked;
            xlChart.SetSourceData(rg, Type.Missing);

        }

        private void btnClose_Click(object sender, EventArgs e)
        {
            xla.DisplayAlerts = false;
            if (xla != null)
            {
                xla.Quit();
                xla = null;
            }
            this.Close();
        }
    }
}
```

This project produces Figure 9-6.

Doughnut Charts

A doughnut chart is similar to a pie chart, with two exceptions: it has a hole in the middle and can have more than one series of data. Excel has two subtypes of doughnut charts: one is the standard doughnut chart (xlDoughnut), and the other is the exploded doughnut chart (xlDoughnutExploded) with all slices exploded. We can use the previous project, *Example9_5*, and the same data to create a doughnut chart by changing one line of the code snippet. Namely, just change

```
    xlChart.ChartType = XlChartType.xlAreaStacked;
```

to

```
    xlChart.ChartType = XlChartType.xlDoughnut;
```

Running the project generates the output of Figure 9-7.

Radar Charts

An Excel radar chart has a separate axis for each category, and axes extend outward from the center of the chart. The data values used in creating a radar chart must be positive. The value of each data point is plotted on the corresponding axis.

Again, we can use the previous project, *Example9_5*, and the same data to create a radar chart by replacing the corresponding code snippet with the following:

```
    xlChart.ChartType = XlChartType.xlRadarFilled;
    xlChart.SetSourceData(rg, Type.Missing);
```

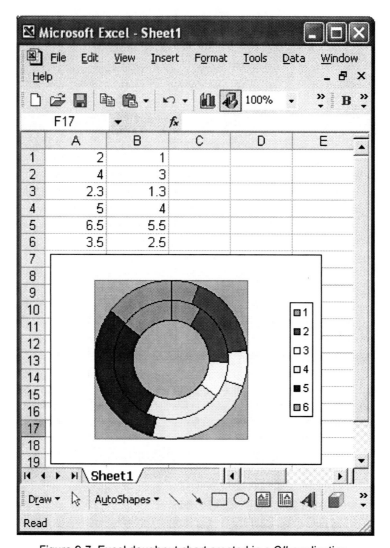

Figure 9-7 Excel doughnut chart created in a C# application.

```
xlChart.PlotArea.Interior.ColorIndex = 2;
xlChart.PlotArea.Border.ColorIndex = 2;
```

This project produces the output shown in Figure 9-8.

This radar chart displays two data series across six categories. There are three subtypes of the radar charts: standard radar charts (xlRadar), radar charts with data markers (xlRadarMarkers), and filled radar charts (xlRadarFilled).

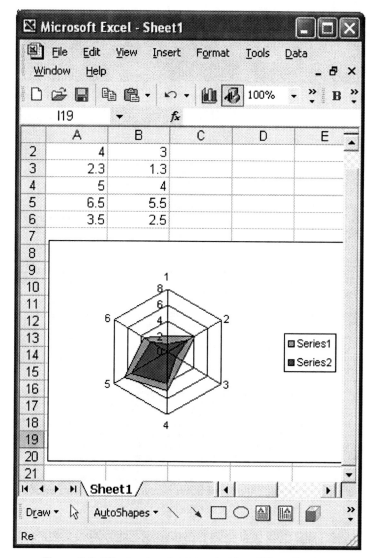

Figure 9-8 Filled radar chart created in a C# application.

Stock Charts

Stock charts are used to display stock market information. Excel supports four different subtypes of stock charts:

- `xlStockHLC`: displays a stock's high, low, and closing prices.
- `xlStockOHLC`: displays a stock's opening, high, low, and closing prices.
- `xlStockVHLC`: displays a stock's volume and its high, low, and closing prices.
- `xlStockVOHLC`: displays a stock's volume and its opening, high, low, and closing prices.

The example project *Example9_6* shows the IBM stock's opening, high, low, and closing prices. Here is the code listing of the `Form1` class:

```
using System;
using System.Windows.Forms;
using System.Reflection;
using System.IO;
using Excel;

namespace Example9_6
{
    public partial class Form1 : Form
    {
        private Excel.Application xla;
        private object missing = Missing.Value;

        public Form1()
        {
            InitializeComponent();
            xla = new Excel.Application();
        }

        private void btnPlot_Click(object sender, EventArgs e)
        {
            xla.Visible = true;

            // Load IBM stock data to Excel worksheet:
            string filePath =
                    Directory.GetCurrentDirectory().ToString();
            string fileName = filePath + "\\IBM.txt";
            xla.Workbooks.OpenText(fileName, missing, 1, missing,
                XlTextQualifier.xlTextQualifierNone, missing, missing,
                missing, true, missing, missing, missing, missing,
                missing, missing, missing, missing, missing);

            // Now create the stock chart.
            Worksheet ws = (Worksheet)xla.ActiveSheet;
            ChartObjects chartObjs =
                    (ChartObjects)ws.ChartObjects(Type.Missing);
            ChartObject chartObj = chartObjs.Add(100, 20, 300, 300);
            Chart xlChart = chartObj.Chart;

            Range rg = ws.get_Range("A1", "E20");
            xlChart.SetSourceData(rg, XlRowCol.xlColumns);
            xlChart.ChartType = XlChartType.xlStockOHLC;

            // Customize axes:
            Axis xAxis = (Axis)xlChart.Axes(XlAxisType.xlCategory,
                XlAxisGroup.xlPrimary);
            xAxis.HasMajorGridlines = true;
            xAxis.HasTitle = true;
            xAxis.AxisTitle.Text = "Time";

            Axis yAxis = (Axis)xlChart.Axes(XlAxisType.xlValue,
```

```
                    XlAxisGroup.xlPrimary);
            yAxis.HasMajorGridlines = true;
            yAxis.CrossesAt = -1.5;
            yAxis.HasTitle = true;
            yAxis.AxisTitle.Text = "Stock Price ($)";

            // Add title:
            xlChart.HasTitle = true;
            xlChart.ChartTitle.Text = "IBM Stock Price";

            // Change default background color:
            xlChart.PlotArea.Interior.ColorIndex = 2;

            // Remove legend:
            xlChart.HasLegend = false;
        }

        private void btnClose_Click(object sender, EventArgs e)
        {
            xla.DisplayAlerts = false;
            if (xla != null)
            {
                xla.Quit();
                xla = null;
            }
            this.Close();
        }
    }
}
```

In this class, we first programmatically open the stock text file that is stored in the application directory (~\Examples\Example9_6\Example9_6\bin\Debug\IMB.txt) using the following code snippet:

```
xla.Workbooks.OpenText(fileName, missing, 1, missing,
    XlTextQualifier.xlTextQualifierNone, missing, missing,
    missing, true, missing, missing, missing, missing,
    missing, missing, missing, missing, missing);
```

The OpenText method is a very useful method that loads and parses the text file to Excel as a new workbook with a single sheet. Its syntax is defined by:

```
void OpenText(
    [In] string Filename,
    [In, Optional] object Origin,
    [In, Optional] object StartRow,
    [In, Optional] object DataType,
    [In, Optional] XlTextQualifier TextQualifier,
    [In, Optional] object ConsecutiveDelimiter,
    [In, Optional] object Tab,
    [In, Optional] object Semicolon,
    [In, Optional] object Comma,
    [In, Optional] object Space,
    [In, Optional] object Other,
    [In, Optional] object OtherChar,
```

```
        [In, Optional] object FieldInfo,
        [In, Optional] object TextVisualLayout,
        [In, Optional] object DecimalSeparator,
        [In, Optional] object ThousandsSeparator,
        [In, Optional] object TrailingMinusNumbers,
        [In, Optional] object Local
    );
```

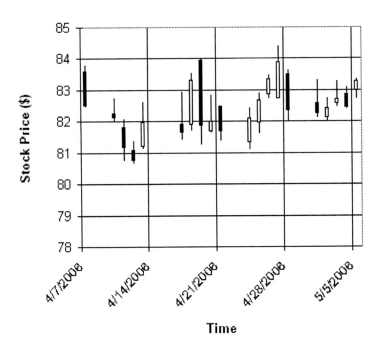

Figure 9-9 Excel stock chart created in a C# application.

In this method, there are many parameters that can be specified, including delimiters. Most of these parameters are optional objects that can be set to default values using the Type.Missing word. However, you have to specify the fifth parameter, XlTextQualifier, specifically because it cannot be set to Type.Missing word since it is not an object.

We can then use the text data imported to the Excel sheet to create the stock chart. The output of the current application is shown in Figure 9-9.

Surface Charts

Excel surface charts display multiple-series data on a surface using the category axis, value axis, and a third axis that displays the series name. Surface charts are used to show the optimum combination of category and series data.

Let's use an example project, *Example9_7*, to see how we create an Excel surface chart in a C# application. The code listing of the `Form1` class is listed here for your reference:

```csharp
using System;
using System.Windows.Forms;
using Excel;

namespace Example9_7
{
    public partial class Form1 : Form
    {
        private Excel.Application xla;

        public Form1()
        {
            InitializeComponent();
            xla = new Excel.Application();
        }

        private void btnPlot_Click(object sender, EventArgs e)
        {
            xla.Visible = true;
            Workbook wb = xla.Workbooks.Add(XlSheetType.xlWorksheet);
            Worksheet ws = (Worksheet)xla.ActiveSheet;

            // Now create the chart.
            ChartObjects chartObjs =
                    (ChartObjects)ws.ChartObjects(Type.Missing);
            ChartObject chartObj = chartObjs.Add(100, 20, 300, 300);
            Chart xlChart = chartObj.Chart;

            int nRows = 25;
            int nColumns = 25;
            string upperLeftCell = "B3";
            int endRowNumber =
                    System.Int32.Parse(upperLeftCell.Substring(1))
                    + nRows - 1;
            char endColumnLetter = System.Convert.ToChar(
                    Convert.ToInt32(upperLeftCell[0]) + nColumns - 1);
            string upperRightCell = System.String.Format("{0}{1}",
                    endColumnLetter,
                    System.Int32.Parse(upperLeftCell.Substring(1)));
            string lowerRightCell = System.String.Format("{0}{1}",
                endColumnLetter, endRowNumber);

            // Send single dimensional array to Excel:
            Range rg1 = ws.get_Range("B2", "Z2");
            double[] xarray = new double[nColumns];
            ws.Cells[1, 1] = "Data for surface chart";
            for (int i = 0; i < xarray.Length; i++)
            {
                xarray[i] = -3.0f + i * 0.25f;
                ws.Cells[i + 3, 1] = xarray[i];
                ws.Cells[2, 2 + i] = xarray[i];
```

```
    }

    Range rg = ws.get_Range(upperLeftCell, lowerRightCell);
    rg.Value2 = AddData(nRows,nColumns);

    Range chartRange = ws.get_Range("A2", lowerRightCell);
    xlChart.SetSourceData(chartRange, missing);
    xlChart.ChartType = XlChartType.xlSurface;

    // Customize axes:
    Axis xAxis = (Axis)xlChart.Axes(XlAxisType.xlCategory,
        XlAxisGroup.xlPrimary);
    xAxis.HasTitle = true;
    xAxis.AxisTitle.Text = "X Axis";

    Axis yAxis = (Axis)xlChart.Axes(XlAxisType.xlSeriesAxis,
        XlAxisGroup.xlPrimary);
    yAxis.HasTitle = true;
    yAxis.AxisTitle.Text = "Y Axis";

    Axis zAxis = (Axis)xlChart.Axes(XlAxisType.xlValue,
        XlAxisGroup.xlPrimary);
    zAxis.HasTitle = true;
    zAxis.AxisTitle.Text = "Z Axis";

    // Add title:
    xlChart.HasTitle = true;
    xlChart.ChartTitle.Text = "Peak Function";

    // Remove legend:
    xlChart.HasLegend = false;
}

private double[,] AddData(int nRows, int nColumns)
{
    double[,] dataArray = new double[nRows, nColumns];
    double[] xarray = new double[nColumns];
    for (int i = 0; i < xarray.Length; i++)
    {
        xarray[i] = -3.0f + i * 0.25f;
    }
    double[] yarray = xarray;

    for (int i = 0; i < dataArray.GetLength(0); i++)
    {
        for (int j = 0; j < dataArray.GetLength(1); j++)
        {
            dataArray[i, j] = 3 * Math.Pow((1 - xarray[i]), 2)
                * Math.Exp(-xarray[i] * xarray[i] -
                (yarray[j] + 1) * (yarray[j] + 1)) -
                10 * (0.2 * xarray[i] - Math.Pow(xarray[i], 3)
                - Math.Pow(yarray[j], 5)) *
                Math.Exp(-xarray[i] * xarray[i] - yarray[j] *
                yarray[j]) - 1 / 3 * Math.Exp(-(xarray[i]
```

```
                               + 1) * (xarray[i] + 1) -
                       yarray[j] * yarray[j]);
               }
           }
           return dataArray;
       }

       private void btnClose_Click(object sender, EventArgs e)
       {
           xla.DisplayAlerts = false;
           if (xla != null)
           {
               xla.Quit();
               xla = null;
           }
           this.Close();
       }
   }
}
```

In this class, we first create data using a 1D and 2D array and assign them to the Excel worksheet. This data must be structured in a certain format. The categories (used as the X axis) are in the first column. The second row represents the series names (used as the Y axis). Finally, the data values are formed by a 2D data array.

As long as the data is assigned to the Excel worksheet, you can create a surface chart by selecting the surface chart type:

```
xlChart.ChartType = XlChartType.xlSurface;
```

The rest of the code in the `Form1` class is used to customize the axes, add axis labels and a title, and remove the legend from the chart.

This project produces the output of Figure 9-10. It can be seen that the chart is created by ranges of data values, which is evident by the fact that the colors vary with the values along the vertical (the Z) axis. The number of colors on the surface chart is based on the major unit of the Z axis.

The Excel surface chart has four subtypes:

- `xlSurface`: displays a standard surface chart.
- `xlSurfaceWireFrame`: displays a surface chart without colors.
- `xlSurfaceTopView`: displaysthe a surface chart viewed from above.
- `xlSurfaceTopViewWireFrame`: displays a surface chart without colors, viewed from above.

You can select a different subtype of surface chart from the above four options according to your application requirements.

I should point out here that Excel surface charts have some limits: they are not true X-Y-Z charts. X and Y are not treated as numeric data, and must consist of regularly defined, evenly spaced categories. Exactly one Z value is needed for each X-Y pair. Excel surface charts are drawn by connecting Z values at X-Y nodes with straight lines and planar sections. A saddle point is not accurately drawn if it occurs between the X-Y nodes. Color-filled surface charts in Excel do not allow transparency, meaning that you can not visualize the hidden parts of the surface.

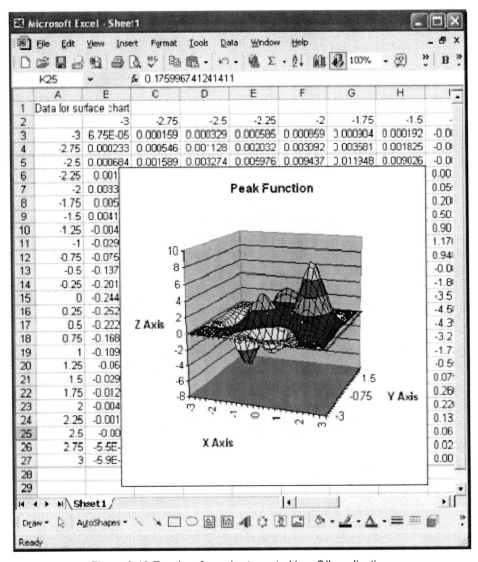

Figure 9-10 Excel surface chart created in a C# application.

Color Map

When creating Excel surface charts in the previous subsection, we used the default color map. In some situations, you may want to use a customized color map for your Excel charts, which can be achieved by using the Excel color indices. Excel displays 56 color indices at any given time. You can use the following C# code snippet to extract Excel 56 default color indices:

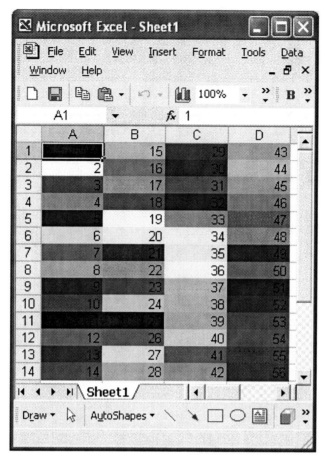

Figure 9-11 Default Excel colors with color indices.

```
for (int i = 0; i < 14; i++)
{
    string cellString = "A" + (i + 1).ToString();
    ws.get_Range(cellString, cellString).Interior.ColorIndex = i + 1;
    ws.get_Range(cellString, cellString).Value2 = i + 1;
    cellString = "B" + (i + 1).ToString();
    ws.get_Range(cellString,
        cellString).Interior.ColorIndex = 14 + i + 1;
    ws.get_Range(cellString, cellString).Value2 = 14 + i + 1;
    cellString = "C" + (i + 1).ToString();
    ws.get_Range(cellString,
        cellString).Interior.ColorIndex = 2 * 14 + i + 1;
    ws.get_Range(cellString, cellString).Value2 = 2 * 14 + i + 1;
    cellString = "D" + (i + 1).ToString();
    ws.get_Range(cellString,
        cellString).Interior.ColorIndex = 3 * 14 + i + 1;
    ws.get_Range(cellString, cellString).Value2 = 3 * 14 + i + 1;
}
```

This generates Excel's 56 default colors with corresponding color indices, as shown in Figure 9-11.

After understanding the definition of the Excel color indices, we can easily create a customized color map. Let's use an example to demonstrate how to create such a customized Excel color map and apply it to a surface chart.

This example is based on the previous project, *Example9_7*. Start off with new C# Windows application called *Example9_8*. Add the Excel Object Library to the reference. Add the Form1 class of *Example9_7* to the current application, and change the corresponding namespace to *Example9_8*. Add a new class named ColorMap to the project. In the ColorMap class, define a color map using Excel color indices with the following code:

```
using System;

namespace Example9_8
{
    public class ColorMap
    {
        public static int[] colorMap()
        {
            int[] colorArray = new int[16];
            colorArray[0] = 5;
            colorArray[1] = 8;
            colorArray[2] = 4;
            colorArray[3] = 6;
            colorArray[4] = 44;
            colorArray[5] = 46;
            colorArray[6] = 3;
            colorArray[7] = 29;
            colorArray[8] = 4;
            colorArray[9] = 6;
            colorArray[10] = 36;
            colorArray[11] = 40;
            colorArray[12] = 44;
            colorArray[13] = 45;
            colorArray[14] = 46;
            colorArray[15] = 53;

            return colorArray;
        }
    }
}
```

In this class, we define a static integer array that holds the Excel color indices. You can define your own color map array in the same manner. The problem now is how to assign this color map to the Excel charts. The trick is to use the Excel's LegendEntry objects. In the Plot button click event handler, add the axis scale parameters to the Z axis:

```
Axis zAxis = (Axis)xlChart.Axes(XlAxisType.xlValue,
    XlAxisGroup.xlPrimary);
zAxis.HasTitle = true;
zAxis.AxisTitle.Text = "Z Axis";
zAxis.MinimumScale = -8;
```

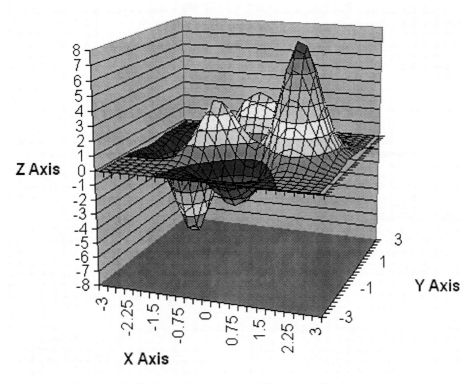

Figure 9-12 Surface chart colored with a customized color map.

```
zAxis.MaximumScale = 8;
zAxis.MajorUnit = 1;
```

Then, add the following code snippet to assign the color map to the `LegendEntry`:

```
xlChart.HasLegend = true;
int[] cm = ColorMap.colorMap();
int numberOfLegendEntries = Convert.ToInt16((zAxis.MaximumScale
    - zAxis.MinimumScale) / zAxis.MajorUnit);
for (int i = 1; i <= numberOfLegendEntries; i++)
{
    LegendEntry legendEntry =
        (LegendEntry)xlChart.Legend.LegendEntries(i);
    legendEntry.LegendKey.Interior.ColorIndex = cm[i - 1];
}

// Remove the legend, and reset the size of the plot area:
xlChart.HasLegend = false;
xlChart.PlotArea.Width = 300;
xlChart.PlotArea.Height = 300;
```

Here, we first use the Z axis scale and major unit to calculate the number of legend entries, which determines the number of colors used in the color map. Then we assign the color from the color map to the `LegendKey` of each `LegendEntry` of the Excel chart. Finally, we remove the legend from the chart and reset the size of the chart's `PlotArea`.

This application produces the output of Figure 9-12. It is evident that the new customized color map is used in the Excel surface chart.

Integrating Excel Charts into Windows Forms

In the previous sections, we demonstrated how to create both stand-alone and embedded Excel charts in C# applications. This is very useful and powerful. However, you might notice that your Excel application is separated from your C# Windows Form. Namely, the Excel charts and C# project are two separate applications. In some cases, you may want to integrate the Excel application and Excel charts into your C# application and handle the Excel objects just like the usual custom controls.

There are two approaches to achieve this integration. One approach is based on the Windows Win32 API, and the other method is using the `WebBrowser` control. Here, we will discuss the second approach that uses `WebBrowser` control as a host for the Excel applications and Excel charts.

Stand-Alone Excel Charts on Windows Forms

We will use an example to demonstrate how to create a stand-alone Excel chart directly on a Windows Form. This example is based on the previous application, *Example9_7*, which plots a surface chart for a peak function

Let's start off with a new C# Windows application project called *Example9_9*. Add the `Form1` class from *Example9_7* and change its corresponding namespace to `Example9_9`. In addition to two Button controls, add a `WebBrowser` control to `Form1`. Add the corresponding Excel Object Library to the reference.

In the Plot button click event handler, set `xla`'s visible property to `false` by replacing the code snippet

```
xla.Visible = true;
```

with

```
xla.Visible = false;
```

Add the following code at the end of the Plot button click event handler:

```
xla.DisplayAlerts = false;

// Save the Excel chart to a gif file:
string filePath = Directory.GetCurrentDirectory().ToString();
string pctFile = filePath + "\\" + "example9_9.gif";
xlChart.Export(pctFile, Type.Missing, Type.Missing);

// Quit the background (not visible) Excel application.
xla.UserControl = false;
xla.Quit();
```

```
// Open the Excel chart file with webBrowser:
webBrowser1.Navigate(pctFile);
```

In this code, we first turn off the usual prompt message box about saving the Excel chart, since this message box might be hidden behind the main Excel window. Then, we save the Excel chart to your application directory as a gif file using the following code snippet:

```
xlChart.Export(pctFile, Type.Missing, Type.Missing);
```

We kill the background Excel application because it is still running regardless of its `Visible` property. Finally, we open the saved Excel picture file with the `webBrowser`:

```
webBrowser1.Navigate(pctFile);
```

In this way, the Excel chart is integrated to the Windows Form.

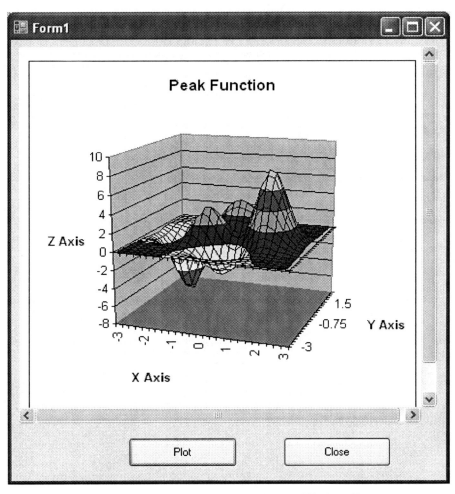

Figure 9-13 Excel chart is integrated onto a Windows Form.

Pressing F5 to run this project generates the output of Figure 9-13. It can be seen that scroll bars automatically appear in the `webBrowser` when the Excel chart is bigger than the size of the `webBrowser` control.

Embedding Excel Charts on Windows Forms

In the previous subsection, we showed you how to create stand-alone Excel charts in a Windows Form. This approach allows you to develop integrated C# applications using Excel chart functionality. However, this method has one disadvantage: it does not support any interaction between the Excel application and the created charts. In order to overcome this difficulty, we will integrate both the Excel application and Excel charts into a C# Windows Form, which allows you to interact with and modify the charts through Excel.

This can be done by saving the Excel workbook that contains both the data and the charts into an Excel file (with a *.xls* extension). Then we use the `webBrowser` to open the saved Excel file. We can use the previous project, *Example9_9*, to illustrate how to perform the corresponding procedure. In the Plot button click event handler, we need to change the file name. Replace

```
string pctFile = filePath + "\\" + "example9_9.gif";
```

with

```
string xlFile = filePath + "\\" + "example9_9.xls";
```

Next, you need to save the Excel workbook instead of the Excel chart by replacing

```
xlChart.Export(pctFile, Type.Missing, Type.Missing);
```

with

```
wb.SaveAs(xlFile, Excel.XlFileFormat.xlWorkbookNormal, Type.Missing,
    Type.Missing, Type.Missing, Type.Missing,
    Excel.XlSaveAsAccessMode.xlShared,
    Type.Missing, Type.Missing, Type.Missing,
    Type.Missing, Type.Missing);
```

Finally, you need to open the Excel file instead of the gif picture file with the `webBrowser`. Replace

```
webBrowser1.Navigate(pctFile);
```

with

```
webBrowser1.Navigate(xlFile);
```

The output of this project becomes Figure 9-14. Now, if you change the data in the Excel cells, the chart will immediately reflect the change.

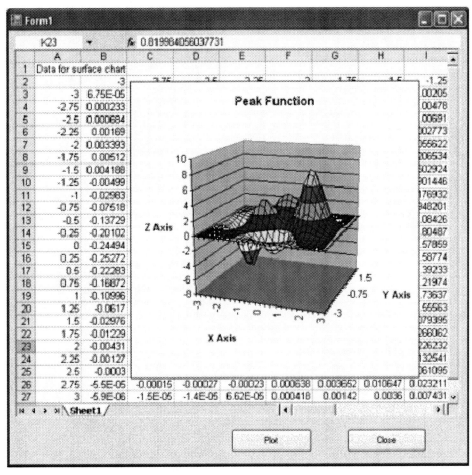

	K23	▼		0.819964056037731					
	A	B	C	D	E	F	G	H	I
1	Data for surface chart								
2		3	2.75	2.5	2.25	2	1.75	1.5	-1.25
3	-3	6.75E-05							.00205
4	-2.75	0.000233							.00478
5	-2.5	0.000684							.00691
6	-2.25	0.00169							.002773
7	-2	0.003393							.055622
8	-1.75	0.00512							.006534
9	-1.5	0.004188							.002924
10	-1.25	-0.00499							.001446
11	-1	-0.02963							.176932
12	-0.75	-0.07518							.048201
13	-0.5	-0.13729							.08426
14	-0.25	-0.20102							.80487
15	0	-0.24494							.57859
16	0.25	-0.25272							.58774
17	0.5	-0.22283							.39233
18	0.75	-0.16872							.21974
19	1	-0.10996							.73637
20	1.25	-0.0617							.55563
21	1.5	-0.02976							.079395
22	1.75	-0.01229							.066062
23	2	-0.00431							.226232
24	2.25	-0.00127							.132541
25	2.5	-0.0003							.061096
26	2.75	-5.5E-05	-0.00015	-0.00027	-0.00023	0.000638	0.003652	0.010647	0.023211
27	3	-5.9E-06	-1.5E-05	-1.4E-05	6.62E-05	0.000418	0.00142	0.0036	0.007431

Figure 9-14 Excel application is integrated onto a Windows Form

Index

Printed in the United States
154211LV00003B/25/A

9 780979 372506